THE BOMBERS
AND
THE BOMBED

Also by Richard Overy

The Twilight Years: The Paradox of Britain Between the Wars

1939: Countdown to War

Interrogations: The Nazi Elite in Allied Hands, 1945

Russia's War: A History of the Soviet Effort, 1941–1945

The Penguin Historical Atlas of the Third Reich

The Dictators: Hitler's Germany, Stalin's Russia

The Battle of Britain: The Myth and the Reality

Why the Allies Won

Richard Overy

THE BOMBERS
AND
THE BOMBED

Allied Air War over Europe, 1940–1945

VIKING

VIKING
Published by the Penguin Group
Penguin Group (USA) LLC
375 Hudson Street
New York, New York 10014

USA | Canada | UK | Ireland | Australia | New Zealand | India | South Africa | China
penguin.com
A Penguin Random House Company

Published by Viking Penguin, a member of Penguin Group (USA) LLC, 2014

First published in Great Britain as *The Bombing War: Europe 1939–1945* by Allen Lane, an imprint of Penguin Books Ltd.

Epigraph on page vii from *Collected Poems* by John Betjeman. Copyright 1955, 1958, 1962, 1964, 1968, 1970, 1979, 1981, 1982, 2001 the Estate of John Betjeman. Reprinted by permission of John Murray (Publishers).

Excerpts from *England's Hour* by Vera Brittain. Reprinted by permission of Mark Bostridge and T. J. Brittain-Catlin, literary executors of the estate of Vera Brittain, 1970.

Illustrations are courtesy of the RAF Museum, Hendon (insert pp. 1 top and bottom, 3 top), the Imperial War Museum, London (2 top and bottom, 3 bottom, 5 top, 7 top and bottom, 9 top and bottom, 11, 15 bottom, 16 top), Library of Congress, Washington, D.C. (4 top and bottom, 5 bottom, 6 top and bottom, 8 top and bottom), Hamburg Staatsarchiv (10 top and bottom, 12 top), Stadtarchiv Kassel (13 top), Archivio di Stato di Brescia (13 middle), Archivio Storico della Città di Torino (14 top), Archivio di Stato di Genova (14 bottom left), Archivio Fondazione Micheletti, Brescia (14 bottom right), Santuario Basilica della Consolata, Turin (15 top), Archivio di Stato di Napoli (16 bottom). I am grateful to all the archives involved for kind permission to reproduce these images.

LIBRARY OF CONGRESS CATALOGING-IN-PUBLICATION DATA
Overy, R. J.
The bombers and the bombed : Allied air war over Europe, 1940–1945 / Richard Overy.
pages cm
Includes bibliographical references and index.
ISBN 978-0-670-02515-2
1. World War, 1939–1945—Aerial operations, Allied. 2. World War, 1939–1945—Europe—Aerial operations, Allied. 3. World War, 1939–1945—Aerial operations, Allied—Moral and ethical aspects. 4. Bombing, Aerial—Europe—History—20th century. 5. Bombing, Aerial—Social aspects—Europe—History—20th century. 6. Civil defense—Social aspects—Europe—History—20th century. 7. Bombing, Aerial—Germany—History—20th century. 8. Bombing, Aerial—Europe—Public opinion. 9. Public opinion—Europe. 10. World War, 1939–1945—Europe.
I. Title. II. Title: Allied air war over Europe 1940–1945.
D785.O92 2013
940.54'4—dc23
2013018405

Printed in the United States of America
1 3 5 7 9 10 8 6 4 2

Set in Baskerville MT Std
Designed by Francesca Belanger

Oh bountiful Gods of the air! Oh Science and Progress!
You great big wonderful world! Oh what have you done?

—John Betjeman, "1940"

CONTENTS

PREFACE

Between 1939 and 1945 hundreds of European cities and hundreds more small townships and villages were subjected to aerial bombing. During the course of the conflict a staggering estimate of around 600,000 European civilians were killed by bomb attack and well over a million more were seriously injured, in some cases physically or mentally disabled for life. The landscape of much of Europe was temporarily transformed into a vision of ruin as complete as the dismal relics of the once triumphant Roman Empire. To anyone wandering through the devastated urban wastelands immediately after the end of the war, the most obvious question to ask was: How could this ever have been agreed to? Then a second thought: How would Europe ever recover?

These are not the questions usually asked about the bombing war. That bombing would be an integral part of future war had been taken for granted by most Europeans and Americans in the late 1930s after watching Japan's war in China and air operations in the Spanish Civil War; it would have seemed almost inconceivable that states should willingly forgo the most obvious instrument of total war. Technology shapes the nature of all wars, but the Second World War more than most. Once the bombing weapon had been unleashed, its potential was unpredictable. The ruins of Europe in 1945 were mute testament to the remorseless power of bombing and the inevitability of escalation. Yet the remarkable thing is that European cities did indeed recover in the decade that followed and became the flourishing centers of the consumer boom released by the postwar economic miracle. To anyone walking along the boulevards and shopping precincts of modern cities in Germany, Italy, or Britain, it now seems inconceivable that only seventy years ago they were the unwitting objects of violent aerial assault. In

Europe only the fate of Belgrade at the hands of NATO air forces in 1999 is a reminder that bombing has continued to be viewed as a strategy of choice by the Western world.

Most of the history written about the bombing offensives in Europe focuses on two different questions: What were the strategic effects of bombing, and was it moral? The two have been linked more often in recent accounts, on the assumption that something that is strategically unjustifiable must also be ethically dubious, and vice versa. These arguments have generated as much heat as light, but the striking thing is that they have generally relied on a shallow base of evidence, still culled in the most part from the official histories and postwar surveys of the bombing war, and focused almost entirely on the bombing of Germany and Britain. There have been some excellent recent studies of the bombing war that have gone beyond the standard narrative (though still confined to Allied bombing of Germany), but in most general accounts of the air campaigns established myths and misrepresentations abound, while the philosophical effort to wrestle with the issue of its legality or morality has produced an outcome that is increasingly distanced from historical reality.

The purpose of the present study is to provide the first full narrative history of the bombing war as it was conducted by the Allied powers— Britain, the British Commonwealth, and the United States—against targets across continental Europe. There is no shortage of books on aspects of the campaign, or on the operations of either the RAF or the U.S. Army Air Forces against Germany, but a general history covering all aspects of the Allied bombing war, including the response of the societies that were bombed and the lessons learned from German practice in the Blitz on Britain, is still lacking. Three things distinguish this book from the conventional histories of bombing. First, it covers the whole of Europe. Between 1940 and 1945 almost all continental European countries (including neutrals) were bombed by the Allies, either deliberately or by accident. The broad field of battle was dictated by the nature of the German New Order, carved out between 1938 and 1941, which turned most of continental Europe into an involuntary war zone. The bombing of France and Italy (which in each case resulted in casualties the equal of the Blitz on Britain) is scarcely known in the existing historiography of the war, though an excellent recent study by Claudia Baldoli and Andrew Knapp has finally advertised it properly. The bombing of Scandinavia, Belgium, the Netherlands, Romania, Bulgaria, and eastern Europe by the Western Allies is almost invisible in accounts of the conflict. This wider geographical range raises important questions about what British and American commanders were seeking to achieve.

Second, bombing has all too often been treated as if it could be abstracted in some way from what else was going on. Bombing, as the account here will show, was always only one part of a broad strategic picture, and a much smaller part than air force leaders liked to think. Even when bombing was chosen as an option, it was often by default, always subject to the wider political and military priorities of the wartime leadership and influenced by the politics of interservice rivalry that could limit what ambitious airmen wanted to achieve. Whatever claims might be made for airpower in the Second World War, they need to be put into perspective. Bombing in Europe was never a war-winning strategy, and the other services knew it.

Third, most accounts of bombing deal either with those doing the bombing or with the societies being bombed. *The Bombers and the Bombed* is a title chosen deliberately to give weight to both sides of the history. Though links between these narratives are sometimes made, the operational history is all too often seen as distinct from the political, social, and cultural consequences for the victim communities: a battle history rather than a history of societies at war. The following account looks at bombing from both perspectives—what bombing campaigns were designed to achieve, and what impact they had in reality on the populations that were bombed, both enemy peoples and those waiting for their liberation from German rule. Armed with this double narrative, the issues of effectiveness and ethical ambiguity can be assessed afresh.

No doubt this is an ambitious project, both in geographical scope and in narrative range. Not everything can be given the coverage it deserves. This is not a book about the postwar memory of bombing, on which there is now a growing literature that is both original and conceptually mature. Nor does it deal with the reconstruction of Europe in the decade after the end of the war in more than an oblique way. Here once again there is a rich and expanding history, fueled by other disciplines interested in issues of urban geography and community rebuilding. This is a history limited to the air war in Europe as it was fought between 1940 and 1945. The object has been to research areas where there is little available in the existing literature, or to revisit established narratives to see whether the archive record really supports them. I have been fortunate in gaining access to new sources from the former Soviet archives. These include German Air Force (Luftwaffe) documents covering the period of the Allied air offensive, and in particular the Air Force Operations Staff. These can be found in the Central Archive of the Ministry of Defense of the Russian Federation (TsAMO), Podolsk. I am very grateful to Dr. Matthias Uhl of the German Historical Institute in Moscow for obtaining access to these sources, which make it possible to reconstruct neglected aspects of the bombing war. I have also been fortunate in finding a large collection of original Italian files from the Ministero dell'Aeronautica (Air Ministry) in the Imperial War Museum archive at Duxford, which cover both Italian antiaircraft defenses and the bombing of Italy from the island of Malta. I would like to record my thanks to Stephen Walton for making these records freely available to me.

My second purpose has been to reexamine the established narratives on the bombing war, chiefly British and American, by looking again at archive sources in both countries. For a long time the official histories have shaped the way the story has been told. Although the British history by Charles Webster and Noble Frankland published in 1961 is among the very best of the British official histories of the war (later dismissed by Air Chief Marshal Sir Arthur Harris as "that schoolboy's essay"), the four volumes reflected the official record in the National Archives and focused narrowly on the bombing of Germany rather than Europe. The American seven-volume official history by Wesley Craven and James Cate also follows closely the operational history of the U.S. Army Air Forces, of which the bombing campaign was only a part. Since this work was written in the 1950s, the sources used reflected the official record, now deposited in National Archives II at College Park, Maryland, and the Air Force Historical Research Agency, in Maxwell,

Alabama. However, much of the history of the bombing campaign and the politics that surrounded it can only be fully understood by looking at private papers of individuals and institutions, or at areas of the official record not directly linked to bombing operations or that were originally closed to public scrutiny because they raised awkward questions. The extensive preparations for gas and biological warfare, for example, could not easily be talked about in the 1950s (and many of the records remained closed for far longer than the statutory minimum), nor could intelligence, whose secrets have gradually been unearthed over the past thirty years.

On the experience of being bombed there is less of an official voice. For most European societies there is no official history (though the volumes on the home front produced by the semiofficial Military History Research Office [Militärgeschichtliches Forschungsamt] in Potsdam serve the same purpose very successfully), but there is a plethora of local studies on bombed cities in every state that was subjected to raids. These studies supply an invaluable source on local conditions, popular responses, civil defense performance, and casualties; without them it would have been impossible to reconstruct the history of the bombed societies in France, Italy, the Low Countries, and Germany. Where possible these studies have been supplemented by national records deposited in Berlin, Freiburg im Breisgau, Rome, Paris, and Malta.

It is necessary to say something about the use of statistics throughout the book. Many wartime statistics are known to be deficient for one reason or another, not least those that have survived from the popular beliefs of the wartime period about levels of casualty. I have relied in the text on figures for the dead and injured from what is available in the archive record, though with the usual caveats about reliability and completeness. I have tried as scrupulously as possible to allow for reasonable margins of error, but there are nevertheless wide differences between the statistical picture presented here and many of the standard figures, particularly for Germany. In most cases figures of bomb casualties have had to be scaled down. This is not intended in any way to diminish the stark reality that hundreds of thousands of Europeans died or were seriously injured under the bombs. The search for more historically plausible statistics does not make the killing of civilians from the air any more or less legitimate; it simply registers a more reliable narrative account of what happened.

In a book of this scale it has been difficult to do full justice to the human element, either for those doing the bombing or for those being bombed. This is, nonetheless, a very human story, rooted in the wider narrative of twentieth-century violence. Throughout these pages there are individuals whose experiences have been chosen to illuminate an issue that touched thousands more, whether aircrew fighting the elements and the enemy at great physical and psychological cost, or the communities below them who became the victims of a technology that was never accurate enough to limit the wide destruction of civilian lives and the urban environment. It is one of the terrible paradoxes of total war that both the bomber crews and the bombed could be traumatized by their experience. Looking at the bombing war from the distance of seventy years, this paradox will, I hope, strengthen the resolve of the developed world never to repeat it.

Richard Overy
London, July 2013

ACKNOWLEDGMENTS

This book owes much to the generosity of the Arts and Humanities Research Council (AHRC) and to the Leverhulme Trust, the first for funding a major research project on "Bombing, States and Peoples in Western Europe" in the years 2007–10, which I helped to direct at the University of Exeter, the second for funding a year of research leave in 2010–11 to allow me to complete most of the archive research and begin writing. I would also like to thank the University of Exeter for allowing me a number of semesters of leave to work on the bombing project. I owe a particular debt to the support and help given by the team on the AHRC project—Claudia Baldoli, Vanessa Chambers, Lindsey Dodd, Stephan Glienke, Andy Knapp, and Marc Wiggam—and I hope they find that the end product has been worth all our many brainstorming sessions. I would also like to thank Claire Keyte for all her unstinting assistance in helping us manage the AHRC project and its aftermath.

Over the course of the preparation and writing of this book I have relied on the help, advice, and criticism of a great many people. I owe a particular debt to those who have helped me find archive material or have translated what I couldn't read. The Bulgarian account of the bombing of Bulgaria was made accessible to me thanks to the help of Professor Dobrinka Parusheva in Sofia and Vladislava Ibberson, who did the translation. Material on the bombing of Rotterdam and other Dutch cities was supplied by Major Joris van Esch during his time at the U.S. Military Academy. Pieter Serrien was generous in providing information on the bombing of Belgium. As ever, I am indebted to the assistance given in the many archives I have visited, with the exception of the U.S. National Archives at College Park, Maryland, which astonishingly still remains a researcher's nightmare.

Many other people have contributed in one way or another in helping to get this book finished and providing material, information, or advice: in particular Martin Alexander, Monika Baar, Maria Bucur, Nicholas Chapman, Sebastian Cox, Jeremy Crang, Lara Feigal, Juliet Gardiner, Jim Goodchild, Hein Klemann, Sergei Kudryashov, Nicola Labanca, James Mark, Phillips O'Brien, Anna Reid, Matthias Reiss, Laura Rowe, Nick Terry, Martin Thomas, Richard Toye, and Matthias Uhl. I would also like to offer a general thanks to all my students at Exeter who have taken my course on the history of bombing over the last five years and made the teaching so enjoyable. They have often made me think about issues differently or reassess things I took for granted. I hope they will see some of that intellectual conversation reproduced here. For any remaining errors I have only myself to blame.

To my agent, Gill Coleridge, and her assistant, Cara Jones, my grateful thanks for their enthusiastic support. I am indebted as ever to the Penguin teams on both sides of the Atlantic—Wendy Wolf, Melanie Tortoroli, Roland Ottewell, and Bruce Giffords in New York, and Simon Winder, Richard Duguid, Penelope Vogler, Richard Mason, and Marina Kemp in London. They have all helped in one way or another to turn the raw manuscript into a polished book.

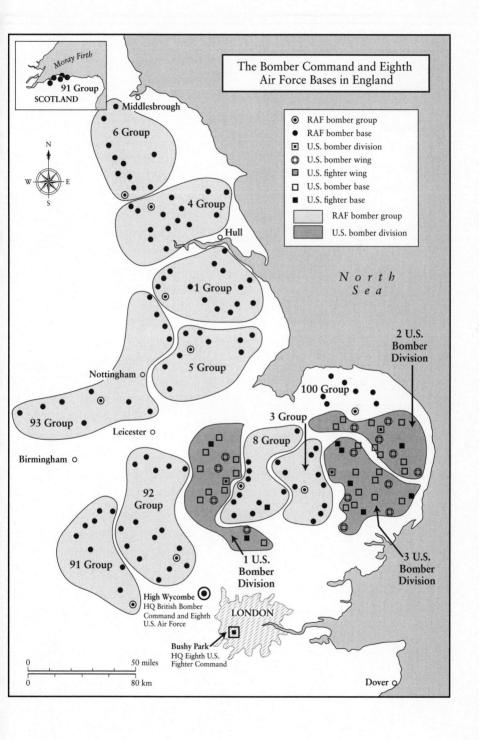

The Bomber Command and Eighth
Air Force Bases in England

⊙ RAF bomber group
● RAF bomber base
⊡ U.S. bomber division
◍ U.S. bomber wing
▣ U.S. fighter wing
□ U.S. bomber base
■ U.S. fighter base

RAF bomber group
U.S. bomber division

Moray Firth
91 Group
SCOTLAND

Middlesbrough
6 Group

N
W E
S

4 Group

Hull

North
Sea

1 Group

2 U.S.
Bomber
Division

Nottingham

5 Group

100 Group

3 Group

93 Group

Leicester

8 Group

Birmingham

92
Group

1 U.S.
Bomber
Division

3 U.S.
Bomber
Division

91 Group

High Wycombe ⊙
HQ British Bomber
Command and Eighth
U.S. Air Force

LONDON

Bushy Park
HQ Eighth U.S.
Fighter Command

0   50 miles
0   80 km

Dover

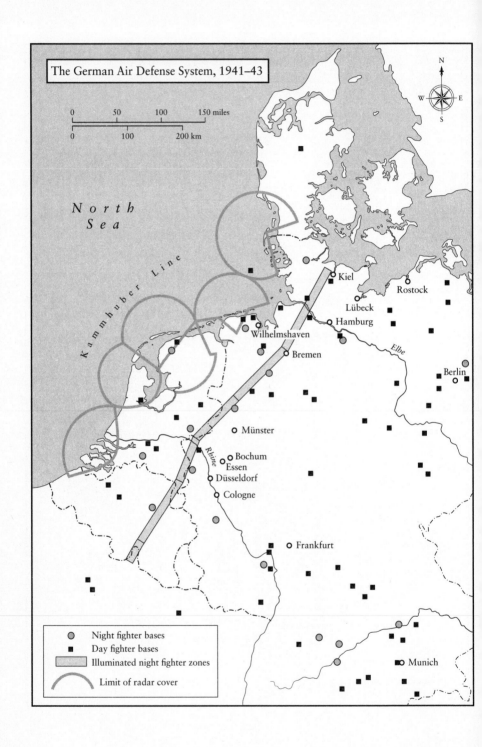

The German Air Defense System, 1941–43

0   50   100   150 miles

0   100   200 km

North Sea

Kammhuber Line

Kiel

Rostock

Lübeck

Hamburg

Wilhelmshaven

Elbe

Bremen

Berlin

Münster

Rhine

Bochum
Essen
Düsseldorf

Cologne

Frankfurt

Munich

○ Night fighter bases
■ Day fighter bases
▨ Illuminated night fighter zones
◠ Limit of radar cover

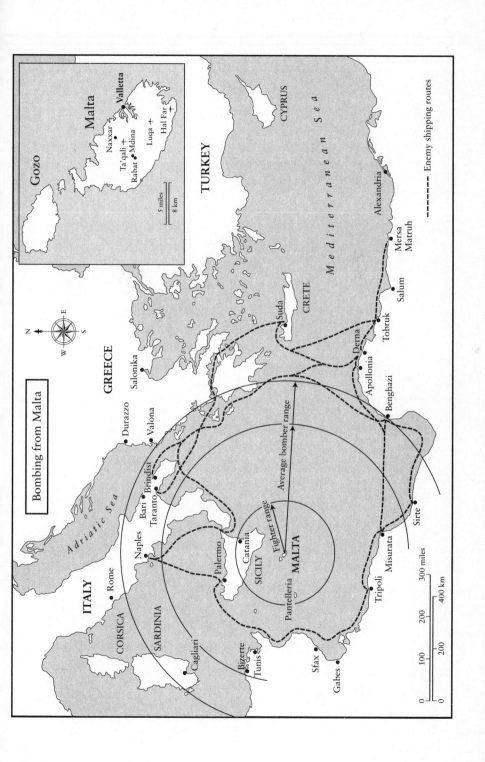

Bombing from Malta

Malta

Gozo

Naxxar
Ta'qali +
Rabat • Mdina
Luqa +
Hal Far +
Valletta

5 miles
8 km

ITALY

Rome •

CORSICA

SARDINIA

Cagliari •

Bizerte •
Tunis •

Naples •

Palermo •

Catania •
SICILY

Pantelleria •
MALTA
Fighter range

Average bomber range

GREECE

Salonika •

Durazzo •
Valona •

Bari •
Brindisi •
Taranto •

Adriatic Sea

TURKEY

Suda •
CRETE

Derna •
Apollonia •
Benghazi •

Tobruk •

Salum •

Mersa
Matruh •

Alexandria •

Mediterranean Sea

CYPRUS

Sfax •
Gabes •

Tripoli •
Misurata •

Sirte •

------ Enemy shipping routes

N
W   E
S

0   100   200   300 miles
0   200   400 km

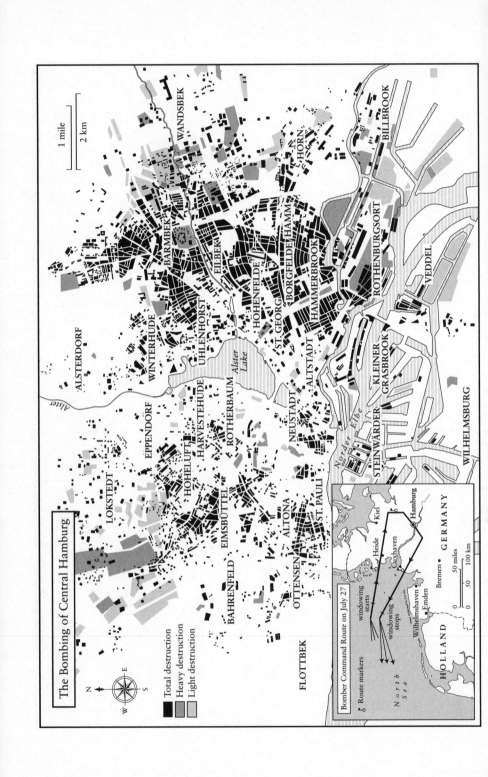

The Bombing of Central Hamburg

1 mile
2 km

N
E
W
S

Total destruction
Heavy destruction
Light destruction

ALSTERDORF
LOKSTEDT
EPPENDORF
WINTERHUDE
HOHELUFT
HARVESTEHUDE
EIMSBÜTTEL
ROTHERBAUM
Alster Lake
UHLENHORST
BARMBEK
WANDSBEK
EILBEK
HOHENFELDE
BORGFELDE
HAMM
HORN
ST. GEORG
ALTSTADT
NEUSTADT
HAMMERBROOK
ROTHENBURGSORT
BILLBROOK
VEDDEL
BILLWERDER
KLEINER GRASBROOK
STEINWÄRDER
Norder Elbe
Elbe
Alster
WILHELMSBURG
BAHRENFELD
ALTONA
OTTENSEN
ST. PAULI
FLOTTBEK

Bomber Command Route on July 27
♪ Route markers

North Sea

HOLLAND

GERMANY

Heide
Kiel
Cuxhaven
Hamburg
Bremen
Wilhelmshaven
Emden

windowing starts
windowing stops

0   50   100 km
0   50 miles

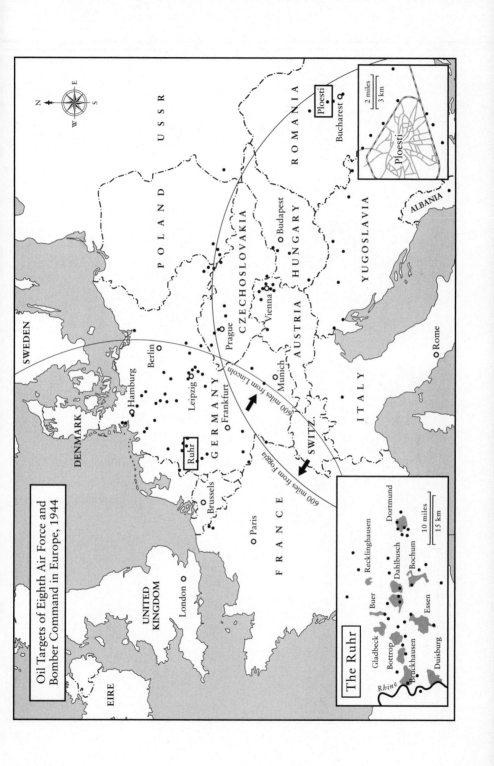

Oil Targets of Eighth Air Force and Bomber Command in Europe, 1944

The Ruhr

2 miles / 3 km

Ploesti

Bucharest

10 miles / 15 km

Rhine

Recklinghausen · Dortmund · Buer · Dahlbusch · Bochum · Gladbeck · Bottrop · Essen · Bruckhausen · Duisburg

Ruhr · Hamburg · Berlin · Leipzig · Frankfurt · Munich · Prague · Vienna · Budapest · Brussels · Paris · London · Rome

600 miles from Lincoln
600 miles from Foggia

EIRE · UNITED KINGDOM · DENMARK · SWEDEN · POLAND · U S S R · GERMANY · CZECHOSLOVAKIA · AUSTRIA · HUNGARY · ROMANIA · YUGOSLAVIA · ALBANIA · FRANCE · SWITZ. · ITALY

N · E · W · S

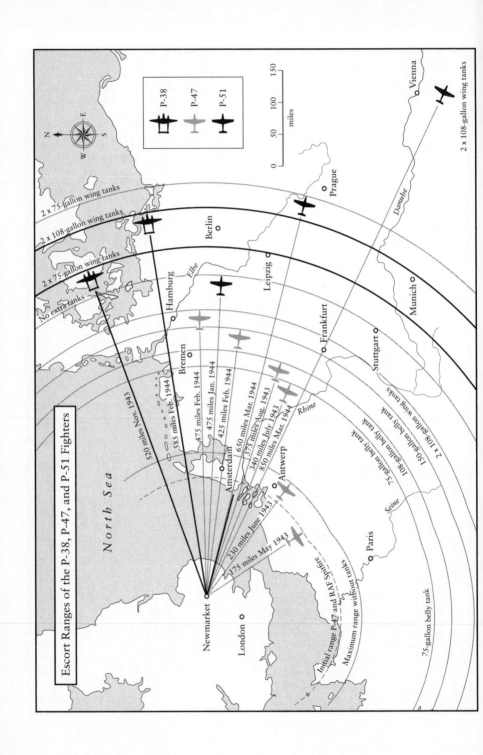

Escort Ranges of the P-38, P-47, and P-51 Fighters

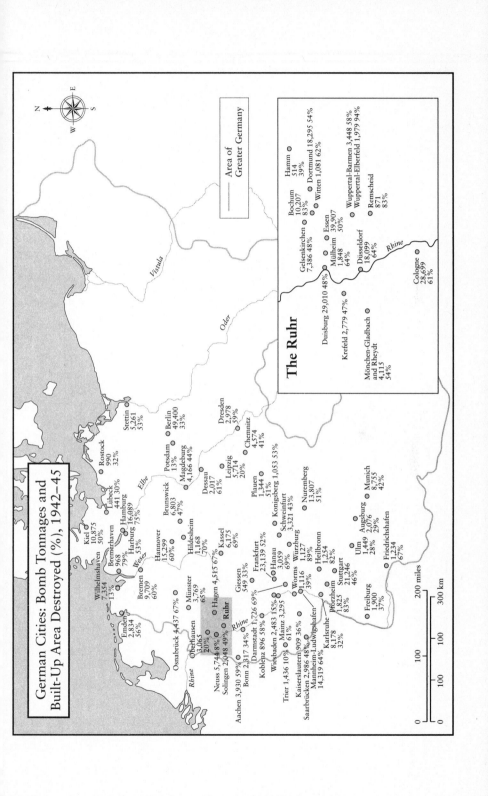

German Cities: Bomb Tonnages and
Built-Up Area Destroyed (%), 1942–45

Area of
Greater Germany

The Ruhr

Hamm 514 39%
Dortmund 18,295 54%
Witten 1,081 62%
Wuppertal-Barmen 3,448 58%
Wuppertal-Elberfeld 1,979 94%
Bochum 10,207 83%
Remscheid 871 83%
Gelsenkirchen 7,386 48%
Essen 39,907 50%
Mülheim 1,848 64%
Düsseldorf 18,099 64%
Duisburg 29,010 48%
Krefeld 2,779 47%
Cologne 28,699 61%
Mönchen-Gladbach and Rheydt 4,115 54%

Stettin 5,261 53%
Rostock 990 32%
Berlin 49,400 33%
Dresden 2,978 59%
Kiel 10,875 50%
Lübeck 441 30%
Hamburg 16,089 75%
Harburg 53%
Potsdam 13%
Magdeburg 4,166 44%
Chemnitz 4,574 41%
Bremerhaven 968 79%
Brunswick 6,803 47%
Dessau 2,017 61%
Leipzig 5,714 20%
Plauen 1,344 51%
Wilhelmshaven 7,354 13%
Bremen 9,709 60%
Hannover 15,299 60%
Hildesheim 1,168 70%
Kassel 6,175 69%
Königsberg 1,053 53%
Nuremberg 13,807 51%
Emden 2,834 56%
Osnabrück 4,437 67%
Münster 3,769 65%
Hagen 4,515 67%
Giessen 549 33%
Frankfurt 23,139 52%
Schweinfurt 3,321 43%
Würzburg 1,127 89%
Munich 8,755 42%
Oberhausen 3,065 20%
Solingen 2,048 49%
Hanau 3,059 69%
Heilbronn 1,254 82%
Augsburg 2,076 29%
Neuss 5,744 8%
Ruhr
Darmstadt 1,726 69%
Worms 11,116 39%
Ulm 1,449 28%
Aachen 3,930 59%
Koblenz 896 58%
Wiesbaden 2,483 15%
Mainz 3,295 61%
Pforzheim 1,825 83%
Stuttgart 21,246 46%
Freiburg 1,900 37%
Friedrichshafen 1,234 67%
Bonn 2,317 34%
Trier 1,436 10%
Kaiserslautern 909 36%
Saarbrücken 2,986 48%
Mannheim-Ludwigshafen 14,319 64%
Karlsruhe 8,178 32%

Rhine
Weser
Elbe
Oder
Vistula
Rhine

0 100 200 miles
0 100 200 300 km

ABBREVIATIONS USED IN THE TEXT

AI   Airborne Interception (British night-fighter radar)
AWPD   Air War Plans Division
BBC   British Broadcasting Corporation
BBSU   British Bombing Survey Unit
BMW   Bayerische Motorenwerke
CBO   Combined Bomber Offensive
CCS   Combined Chiefs of Staff
COSI   Comité Ouvrier de Secours Immédiat (Committee for Workers'
            Emergency Assistance)
DICAT   Difesa Contraerea Territoriale
Do   Dornier
Fw   Focke-Wulf
GHQ   General Headquarters (U.S.)
He   Heinkel
JIC   Joint Intelligence Committee (UK)
JIGSAW   Joint Inter-Service Group for Study of All-Out Warfare
Ju   Junkers
KLV   Kinderlandverschickung
LMF   lack of moral fiber
MAAF   Mediterranean Allied Air Forces
Me   Messerschmitt
MEW   Ministry of Economic Warfare
NFPA   National Fire Protection Association
NSV   Nationalsozialistische Volkswohlfahrt (National Socialist People's
            Welfare)
OSS   Office of Strategic Services
OTU   Operational Training Unit
PWB   Psychological Warfare Branch (U.S.)
PWE   Political Warfare Executive
RAF   Royal Air Force
RM   reichsmark
SA   Sturmabteilung (literally "storm section")
SAP   Securité Aérienne Publique (Public Air Protection)

SD   Sicherheitsdienst (Security Service—German secret home intelligence)
SHAEF   Supreme Headquarters Allied Expeditionary Force
SIPEG   Service Interministériel de Protection contre les Événements de Guerre (Interministerial Protection Service Against the Events of War)
SNCF   Societé Nationale des Chemins de Fer Français (French National Society for Railways)
SS   Schutzstaffel (literally "protection squad")
T4   Tiergarten-4 (cover name for German euthanasia program)
UNPA   Unione Nazionale Protezione Antiaerea (National Union for Anti-air Protection)
USAAF   United States Army Air Forces
USSBS   United States Strategic Bombing Survey

THE BOMBERS
AND
THE BOMBED

Prologue

Bombing Bulgaria

The modern aerial bomb, with its distinctive elongated shape, stabilizing fins, and nose-fitted detonator, is a Bulgarian invention. In the Balkan War of 1912, waged by Bulgaria, Greece, Serbia, and Montenegro (the Balkan League) against Turkey, a Bulgarian army captain, Simeon Petrov, adapted and enlarged a number of grenades for use from an airplane. They were dropped on a Turkish railway station on October 16, 1912, from an Albatros F.2 biplane piloted by Radul Milkov. Petrov afterward modified the design by adding a stabilizing tail and a fuse designed to detonate on impact, and the six-kilogram bomb became the standard Bulgarian issue until 1918. The plans of the so-called Chataldzha bomb were later passed on to Germany, Bulgaria's ally during the First World War. The design, or something like it, soon became standard issue in all the world's first air forces.

Petrov's invention came back to haunt Bulgaria during the Second World War. On November 14, 1943, a force of ninety-one American B-25 Mitchell bombers escorted by forty-nine P-38 Lightning fighters attacked the marshaling yards in the Bulgarian capital, Sofia. The bombing was spread over a wide area, including three villages. The raid destroyed some of the rail system, the Vrajedna airfield, and a further 187 buildings, resulting in around 150 casualties. A second attack ten days later by B-24 Liberator bombers was less successful. There was poor weather across southern Bulgaria, and only seventeen of the force reached what they hoped was Sofia and bombed through cloud, hitting another seven villages around the capital.[1] The attacks were enough to spread panic through the city. In the absence of effective air defenses or civil defense measures, thousands fled to the surrounding area. The Royal Bulgarian Air Force, though equipped with sixteen Messerschmitt

Me109G fighters supplied by Bulgaria's ally Germany, could do little against raids that, though not entirely unexpected, came as a complete surprise when they happened.[2]

The raid in November 1943 was not the first attack on a Bulgarian target during the war, though it was the heaviest and most destructive so far. Bulgaria became a target only because of the decision taken in March 1941 by the Bulgarian government, after much hesitation, to tie the country to Germany by signing the Tripartite Pact, which had been made among the principal Axis powers, Germany, Italy, and Japan, the previous September.[3] When in the spring of 1941 German forces were based in Bulgaria to attack Greece and Yugoslavia, the RAF sent a force of six Wellington bombers to bomb the Sofia rail links in order to hamper the concentration of German troops. A British night raid on April 13 made a lucky hit on an ammunition train, causing major fires and widespread destruction. Further small raids occurred on July 23 and August 11, 1941, which the Bulgarian government blamed on the Soviet air force. Although Bulgaria did not actively participate in the Axis invasion of the Soviet Union on June 22, 1941, it gave supplies to Germany and allowed German ships to use the major ports of Varna and Burgas. On September 13, 1942, a further small Soviet raid hit Burgas, where German ships laden with oil-drilling equipment were awaiting the signal to cross the Black Sea to supply German engineers with the materials they would need to restart production once the Caucasus oilfields had been captured. The Soviet Union was not at war with Bulgaria and denied the intrusions in 1941 and 1942, for which it was almost certainly responsible, but the attacks were of such small scale that the Bulgarian government did not insist on reparations.[4]

The handful of pinprick attacks in 1941 and 1942 were enough to make Bulgaria anxious about what might happen if the Allies ever did decide to bomb its cities heavily. Bulgaria's position in the Second World War was an ambiguous one. The tsar, Boris III, did not want his country to be actively engaged in fighting a war after the heavy territorial and financial losses Bulgaria had sustained in the peace settlement of 1919 as punishment for joining with Germany and Austria-Hungary in the First World War. Only with great reluctance and under German pressure did the prime minister, Bogdan Filov, declare war on Britain and the United States on December 13, 1941. Aware of Bulgaria's vulnerability, the government and the tsar wanted to avoid an actual state of belligerence with the Western powers, just as the country had refused to declare war on the Soviet Union. Bulgaria's small armed forces therefore undertook no operations against the Allies; instead they were used by the Germans as occupation troops in Macedonia and Thrace, territories given to Bulgaria after the German defeat of Yugoslavia and Greece in 1941. By 1943 it was evident to the Bulgarian government and people that they had once again backed the wrong side. Much of the population was anti-German and some of it pro-Soviet. In 1942 a left-wing Fatherland Front had been formed, demanding an end to the war and the severing of links with Germany. Partisan movements in the occupied territories and in Bulgaria itself became more active during 1943, and in August of that year they launched a major recruitment drive. The partisans were chiefly communist and campaigned not only for an end to the war but for a new social order and closer ties with the Soviet Union. In May 1943 and again in October, Filov authorized contacts with the Western Allies to see whether there was a possibility of reaching an agreement. He was told that only unconditional surrender and the evacuation of the occupied territories could be accepted.[5]

It is against this background that sense can be made of the Allied decision to launch a series of heavy air attacks on Bulgarian cities. Knowing that Bulgaria was facing a mounting crisis, caught between its German ally and the growing threat of a likely Soviet victory, Allied leaders were encouraged to use bombing as a political tool in the hope that it might produce a quick dividend by forcing Bulgaria out of the war. The idea that bombing was capable of a sudden decisive blow by demoralizing a population and causing a government crisis had been at the heart of much interwar thinking about the use of airpower. It was the logic of the most famous statement of this principle, made in 1921 by the Italian general Giulio Douhet in his classic study *The Command of the Air* (*Il dominio dell'aria*). The principle was also a central element in the view of airpower held by the British prime minister, Winston Churchill, who had previously applied it to both Germany and Italy. It was not by chance that in a meeting with the British chiefs of staff on October 19, 1943, it was Churchill who would suggest that in his view the Bulgarians were a "peccant people to whom a sharp lesson should be administered." Their fault was to have sided once again with the Germans despite, Churchill claimed, his efforts to get them to see sense. Bombing was designed to undo the cord that bound Bulgaria to her German patron.

The sharp lesson was to be a heavy bombing attack on Sofia. Churchill justified the operation on political grounds: "Experience shows," he told the meeting, "that the effect of bombing a country where there were antagonistic elements was not to unite those elements, but rather to increase the anger of the anti-war party."[6] Others present, including Air Chief Marshal Sir Charles Portal, chief of the air staff, and the chief of the imperial general staff, General Alan Brooke, were less keen and insisted that leaflets should be dropped along with the bombs explaining that the Allies wanted Bulgaria to withdraw its occupation troops and surrender (in the end leaflets were dropped with the curious headline "This is not about Allied terror, but about Bulgarian insanity").[7] But the idea of a "sharp lesson" quickly circulated. The American military chiefs thought that Sofia was so low a military priority that an attack was scarcely justified, but they were impressed by the possible "great psychological effect."[8] Both the British and American ambassadors in Ankara urged an attack so as to interrupt Turkish-German commercial rail traffic.[9] On October 24 the Anglo-American Combined Chiefs of Staff directed General Dwight D. Eisenhower, supreme commander in the Mediterranean, to give such a lesson as soon as this was operationally practical.[10] The Turkish government approved, hopeful perhaps despite neutrality to profit from Bulgaria's discomfiture in any postwar settlement. Churchill wanted Stalin's say-so as well, because Bulgaria was clearly in the Soviet sphere of interest, and on October 29 the British foreign minister, Anthony Eden, who was in Moscow for negotiations, was able to report back Stalin's comment that Sofia should certainly be bombed, as it was nothing more than "a province of Germany."[11]

The Bulgarian government had expected bombing for some time. While the regime struggled to come to terms with internal dissent, the

Soviet presence in the east, and Allied demands for unconditional surrender, it also sought ways to appease the Germans in case they decided
to occupy Bulgaria. In the course of 1943 the deportation of Jews from
the occupied areas of Thrace was completed, and despite the hostility of
the tsar, the German authorities in Sofia persuaded the Bulgarian government to deport native Bulgarian Jews as well. It was agreed that they
would first be transferred to twenty small towns in the hinterland around
Sofia, and in May 1943 some 16,000 Jews were taken at short notice
from the capital and parceled out among eight provinces. The Filov government linked the Jewish policy with bombing. When the Swiss ambassador asked Filov on humanitarian grounds to stop sending Thracian
Jews to Auschwitz, Filov retorted that talk of humanity was miscon-
ceived when the Allies were busy obliterating the cities of Europe from
the air. Moreover, when he failed to take up a British offer in February
1943 to transport 4,500 Jewish children from Bulgaria to Palestine, he
feared that Sofia might be bombed in retaliation.[12] Once the Jews of
Sofia had been deported to the provinces, anxiety revived again in Bulgaria that the Allies would now no longer hesitate to bomb for fear of
killing Jews. In the end the Jews of Bulgaria escaped not only deportation to Auschwitz but also the bombing, which left much of Sofia's Jewish quarter in ruins.

It was not the Jewish question that invited Allied bombing in November 1943, though many Bulgarians assumed that it was. The first
raids seemed to presage an onslaught of aerial punishment, and the
population of the capital gave way to a temporary panic. Yet the first
two attacks in November were followed by two desultory operations the
next month and nothing more. Some 209 inhabitants in Sofia had been
killed and 247 buildings damaged. The "sharp lesson" was not sharp
enough for the Allies, because it did little to encourage Bulgaria to seek
a political solution, while the military value of the attacks was at best
limited, hampered by poor bombing accuracy and gloomy Balkan
weather. On Christmas Day 1943, Churchill wrote to Eden that the
"heaviest possible air attacks" were now planned for Sofia in the hope
that this might result in more productive "political reactions."[13] On January 4, 1944, a large force of 108 B-17 Flying Fortresses was dispatched

to Sofia, but with poor visibility the attack was aborted after a few bombs were dropped on a bridge. Finally, on January 10, 1944, the first heavy attack was mounted by 141 B-17s, supported during the night of January 10–11 by a force of some forty-four RAF Wellington bombers. This attack was devastating for the Bulgarian capital: there were 750 dead and 710 seriously injured, with widespread damage to residential housing and public buildings. The air-raid sirens failed to sound because of a power cut. This time the population panicked entirely, creating a mass exodus. By January 16, 300,000 people had left the capital. The government abandoned the administrative district and moved out to nearby townships. It took more than two weeks to restore services in the capital, while much of the population abandoned it permanently in fear of a repeat attack. On January 23 the German ambassador telegraphed back to Berlin that the bombing had changed completely the "psychological-political situation," exposing the incompetence of the authorities and raising the danger of Bulgarian defection.[14] The government ordered church bells to be pealed as an air-raid warning, in case of further power cuts.[15]

The second major raid, of January 10, did pay political dividends. While Filov tried unsuccessfully to persuade a visiting German general, Walter Warlimont, deputy for operations on Hitler's staff, to mount a revenge attack on neutral Istanbul—the consequences of which might well have been even more disastrous for Bulgaria—most Bulgarian leaders had come to realize that the German connection had to be severed as soon as possible and a deal struck with the Allies.[16] The bishop of Sofia used the occasion of the funeral for the victims of the bombing to launch an attack on the government for tying Bulgaria to Germany and failing to save the people from war. That month an effort was made to get the Soviet Union to intercede with the Western Allies to stop the bombing, but instead Moscow increased its pressure on Bulgaria to abandon its support for the Axis.[17] In February the first informal contacts were made with the Allies through a Bulgarian intermediary in Istanbul to see whether terms could be agreed upon for an armistice. Although hope for negotiation had been the principal reason for starting the bombing, the Allied reaction to the first Bulgarian approach following the raids was mixed. Roosevelt wrote to Churchill on February 9 suggesting that the bombing should now be suspended if the Bulgarians wanted to talk, a view shared by British diplomats in the Middle Eastern headquarters in Cairo.[18] Churchill scrawled "why?" in the margin of the letter. He was opposed to ending the bombing despite a recent report from the British Joint Intelligence Committee (JIC), which observed that the first bombing in November 1943 had achieved no "decisive political result." He had already authorized the bombing of the Bulgarian ports of Burgas and Varna, which were added to the list of priority targets, subject to political considerations.[19] In January 1944 the British War Cabinet, in the event of a German gas attack, considered the possibility of retaliatory gas bomb attacks against Germany and its allies, and included Bulgaria on the list.[20] On February 12, Churchill replied to Roosevelt that in his view the bombing had had "exactly the effect we hoped for" and urged him to accept the argument that bombing should continue until the Bulgarians began full and formal negotiations: "If the medicine has done good, let them have more of it."[21] Roosevelt immediately wired back his full agreement: "Let the good work go on."[22]

Some of the evidence coming out of Bulgaria seemed to support Churchill's stance. Intelligence reports arrived detailing the rapid expansion of both the communist partisan movement and the Fatherland Front. The partisans contacted the Allies through a British liaison officer stationed in Bulgaria, encouraging them to keep up the bombing in order to provoke the collapse of the pro-German regime and help expand support for the resistance. The partisans sent details about the central administrative area in Sofia, bordered by the recently renamed Adolfi Hitler Boulevard, which they said was ripe for attack; at the same time, partisan leaders asked the Allies not to bomb the working-class districts of Sofia, from which most of their recruits were drawn. By March the partisans were finally organized by the Bulgarian communists into the National Liberation Revolutionary Army.[23] As a result of the evidence on the ground, the Western Allies, with Stalin's continued though secret support (the Soviet Union did not want Bulgarians to think they had actively abetted the bombing), accepted Eden's argument that by "turning on the heat" on Bulgarian cities it might shortly be possible either to provoke a coup d'état or to batter the government into suing for peace.[24] On March 10, Sir Charles Portal told Churchill that he had ordered heavy attacks on Sofia and other Bulgarian cities as soon as possible.[25]

On March 16 and then on March 29–30 the Allies launched the most destructive attacks of all on Sofia, as well as subsidiary attacks on Burgas, Varna, and Plovdiv in the interior, designed to disrupt rail communications and sea traffic for the Turkish trade with Germany. The attacks were aimed predominantly at the administrative city center of Sofia and carried a proportion of incendiaries, 4,000 in all, in order to do to Sofia what had been done so effectively to German targets. The raid of March 16 burned down the royal palace; the heavy raid of March 29–30 by 367 B-17s and B-24s, this time carrying 30,000 incendiaries, created a widespread conflagration, destroying the Holy Synod of the Bulgarian Orthodox Church, the National Theater, several ministries, and a further 3,575 buildings, but killing only 139 of the population that had remained.[26] The last major raid, on April 17 by 350 American bombers, destroyed a further 750 buildings and heavily damaged the rail marshaling yard. During 1944 the death toll in Sofia was 1,165, a figure that would have been considerably higher had it not been for the voluntary evacuation of the capital. The incendiary attacks hastened the disintegration of Bulgarian politics and increased support for the Soviet Union, whose armies were now within striking distance. But only on June 20, 1944, several months after the bombing, did the new government of Ivan Bagryanov begin formal negotiations for an end to Bulgarian belligerency, still hoping to keep Bulgaria's territorial spoils and avoid Allied occupation.[27] By this time the Allies had lost interest in bombing Bulgaria, which slipped further down the list of priority targets as the bombers turned their attention to Budapest and Bucharest in the path of the oncoming Red Army.[28]

By the summer of 1944 the Allies had other preoccupations, and it seemed evident that Bulgarian politics had been sufficiently destabilized by the bombing to make further attacks redundant. Nevertheless, the final assessment of the effects of the bombing was ambivalent. In July the U.S. Joint Chiefs of Staff prepared an evaluation of the Balkan bombings which suggested that the psychological effects desired had largely been achieved; the report nevertheless suggested that the enemy had sustained an effective propaganda campaign about the high level of civilian casualties, which had undermined the prestige of both the United States and Britain in the eyes of the Bulgarian people. The chiefs directed that in the future any attacks in the region had to be confined to "targets of definite military importance" and civilian casualties minimized. The British chiefs of staff rejected the American claim, and, in defiance of what they well knew to be the case, insisted that only military targets had been subject to attack, even if this had involved damage to housing and civilian deaths. Their report concluded that Allied bombers ought always to be able to act in this way and that operations "should not be prejudiced by undue regard for the probable scale of incidental casualties."[29] This was a view consistent with everything the RAF had argued and practiced since the switch to the deliberate bombing of German civilians in 1941.

For the historian the judgment is more complex. Bombing almost certainly contributed to the collapse of any pro-German consensus and strengthened the hand both of the moderate center-left in the Fatherland Front and of the more radical partisan movement. But in the end this did not result in a complete change of government until September 9, 1944, when the Soviet presence produced a Fatherland Front administration dominated by the Bulgarian Communist Party (a political outcome that neither Churchill nor Eden had wanted from the bombing).[30] Moreover, other factors played an important role in Bulgarian calculations: the crisis provoked by Italian defeat and surrender in September 1943; the German retreat in the Soviet Union; and fear of a possible Allied Balkan invasion or of Turkish intervention.[31] Where Churchill saw bombing as a primitive instrument for provoking political crisis and insisted throughout the period from October 1943 to March 1944 that this was the key to knocking Bulgaria out of the war, the American military chiefs continued to give preference to the bombing of Italy and Germany and were less persuaded that a political dividend was certain. For them the bombing fitted with the strategy of wearing down Germany's capacity for waging war by interrupting the supply of vital war matériel and forcing the diversion of German military units from the imminent Normandy campaign. There was also a price to pay for the bombing. In September 1944, following the Bulgarian surrender, some 332 American air force prisoners of war were sent by air shuttle to Istanbul and then on to Cairo; some had been shot down while bombing Bulgaria, others on their way to or from attacks on Romanian targets. An American report suggested that the prisoners had been badly maltreated. Two air force prisoners were killed by the Bulgarian police, and an estimated 175 American war dead were presumed to be on Bulgarian territory, although only eighty-four bodies could be located.[32]

The bombing of Bulgaria re-created in microcosm the many issues that defined the wider bombing offensives during the Second World War. It was a classic example of what has come to be called strategic bombing. The definition of strategic bombing is neither neat nor precise. The term itself originated in the First World War when Allied officers sought to describe the nature of long-range air operations carried out against distant targets behind the enemy front line. These were operations organized independently of the ground campaign, even though they were intended to weaken the enemy and make success on the ground more likely. The term "strategic" (or sometimes "strategical") was used by British and American airmen to distinguish the strategy of attacking and wearing down the enemy home front and economy from the strategy of directly assaulting the enemy's armed forces.

The term was also coined in order to separate independent bombing operations from bombing in direct support of the army or navy. This differentiation has its own problems, since direct support of surface forces also involves the use of bombing planes and the elaboration of target systems at or near the front whose destruction would weaken enemy resistance. In Germany and France between the wars, "strategic" air war meant using bombers to attack military and economic targets several hundred kilometers from the fighting front, if they directly supported the enemy's land campaign. German and French military chiefs regarded long-range attacks against distant urban targets, with no direct bearing on the fighting on the ground, as a poor use of strategic resources. The British and American air forces on the other hand thought long-range bombing was the real revolution in air warfare and gave a secondary role to support of surface operations. Over the course of the Second World War, however, the distinction between the more limited conception of strategic air war and the conduct of long-range, independent campaigns became increasingly blurred for the Western Allies too. Distant operations against enemy military, economic, or general urban targets were carried out by bomber forces whose role was interchangeable with their direct support of ground operations. The aircraft of the U.S. Army Air Forces in Italy, for example, bombed the monastery of Monte Cassino in February 1944 in order to break the German front line, but also bombed Rome, Florence, and the distant cities of northern Italy to provoke political crisis, weaken Axis economic potential, and disrupt military communications. Allied bombers attacked German oil stocks in France and the Low Countries during the invasion of 1944 but also bombed oil production targets in the distant regions of occupied eastern Europe. The Normandy campaign saw strategic bombers used for what were evidently tactical targets. For the unfortunate populations in the way of the bombing, in Italy or France or Romania, there was never much point in trying to work out whether they had been bombed strategically or not, for the destructive effects on the ground were to all intents and purposes the same: high levels of death and serious injury, the widespread destruction of the urban landscape, the reduction of essential services, and the arbitrary loss of cultural treasures. Being bombed as part of a ground campaign could, as in the case of the French port of Le Havre in September 1944 or the German city of Aachen in September and October the same year, produce an outcome considerably worse than an attack regarded as strategically independent.

No sharp dividing line is drawn between the different forms that strategic air warfare took in what follows, but the principal focus of this book is on bombing campaigns or operations that can be regarded as independent of immediate surface operations on either land or sea. Such operations were distinct from the tactical assault by bombers and fighter-bombers on fleeting battlefield targets, local troop concentrations, communications, oil stores, repair depots, or merchant shipping, all of which belong more properly to the account of battlefield support aviation. This definition makes it possible to include as "strategic" those operations that were designed to speed up the advance of ground forces but were carried out independently, and often at a considerable distance from the immediate battleground, such as those in Italy or in support of the Red Army in 1944 and 1945 (including the attack on Dresden). However, the heart of any history of the bombing war is to be found in the major independent bombing campaigns carried out to inflict heavy damage on the enemy home front in order to undermine military capability and demoralize the population and, if possible, to provoke a political collapse. In all the cases where large-scale strategic campaigns were conducted—Germany against Britain in 1940–41, Britain and the United States against Germany and German-occupied Europe in 1940–45, Britain and the United States against Italy in 1942–45—there was an implicit understanding that bombing alone might unhinge the enemy war effort, undermine popular war willingness, and perhaps even force the politicians to sue for peace before the need to undertake dangerous, large-scale, and potentially costly amphibious operations. These political expectations of bombing are an essential element in the history of the Anglo-American bombing war.

The political imperatives are exemplified by the brief aerial assault on Bulgaria. The idea of what is now called a political dividend is a dimension of the bombing war that has generally been relegated to second place behind the more strictly military analysis of what bombing did or did not do to the military capability and war economy of the enemy state. Yet it will be found that there are many examples between 1939 and 1945 of bombing campaigns or operations conducted not simply for their expected military outcome, but because they fulfilled one or a number of political objectives. The early bombing of Germany by the Royal Air Force in 1940 and 1941 was partly designed, for all its military ineffectiveness, to bring war back to the German people and to create a possible social and political crisis on the home front. It was also undertaken to impress the occupied states of Europe that Britain was serious about continuing the war, and to demonstrate to American opinion that democratic resistance was still alive and well. For the RAF, bombing was seen as the principal way in which the service could show its independence from the army and navy and carve out for itself a distinctive strategic niche. For the British public, during the difficult year that followed defeat in the Battle of France, bombing was one of the few visible things that could be done to the enemy. "Our wonderful R.A.F. is giving the Ruhr a terrific bombing," wrote one Midlands housewife in her diary. "But one thinks also of the homes from where these men come and what it means to their families."[33]

The political element of the bombing war was partly dictated by the direct involvement of politicians in decision making about bombing. The bombing of Bulgaria was Churchill's idea, and he remained the driving force behind the argument that air raids would provide a quick and relatively cheap way of forcing the country to change sides. In December 1943, when the Mediterranean commanders dragged their feet over the operations because of poor weather, an irritated Churchill scribbled at the foot of the telegram, "I am sorry the weather is so adverse. The political moment may be fleeting." Three months later, while the first Bulgarian peace feelers were being put out, Churchill wrote, "Bomb with high intensity *now*," underlining the final word three times.[34] The campaign in the Balkans also showed how casually politicians could decide on operations whose effectiveness they were scarcely in a position to judge from a strategic or operational point of view. The temptation to reach for airpower when other means of exerting direct violent pressure were absent proved hard to resist. Bombing had the virtues of being flexible, costing less than other military options, and enjoying a high public visibility, rather like the gunboat in nineteenth-century diplomacy. Political intervention in bombing campaigns was a common feature during the war, culminating in the decision eventually taken to drop atomic weapons on Hiroshima and Nagasaki in August 1945. This (almost) final act in the bombing war has generated a continuing debate about the balance between political and military considerations, but it could equally be applied to other wartime contexts. In the evaluation of the effects of the bombing of Bulgaria and other Balkan states, it was observed that bombing possessed the common singular virtue of "demonstrating to their peoples that the war is being brought home to them by the United Nations."[35] In this sense the instrumental use of airpower, recently and unambiguously expressed in the strategy of "shock and awe," first articulated as a strategic aim at the U.S. National Defense University in the 1990s and applied spectacularly to Baghdad and other Iraqi cities in 2003, has its roots firmly in the pattern of "political" bombing in the Second World War.

Bombing was, of course, much more than a set of convenient political tools, and much of what follows describes the organizations, the forces, and the technology that made bombing operations possible. Strategic bombing was a military activity that had to be organized very differently from the operations of the army and navy, and it was one fraught with difficulty under the technical conditions of the time. Air force commanders wanted to deliver what the politicians wanted, but as a consequence bomber forces were always trying to run before they could walk. All the major air services faced a long learning curve during the war as they struggled to overcome a whole range of inherent problems and limitations, but none more so than the RAF and the U.S. Army Air Forces as their offensives grew in scale and complexity. Power was generally projected onto distant cities or industrial installations and in most cases involved long and hazardous flights, hampered by fickle weather, by enemy defenses, and by complex issues of navigation and effective bomb aiming. Fixed bases had to be secured near enough to enable the bombing to take place. The rate of loss of aircrew was high, though not exceptional if a comparison is made with other frontline forces. The most distinctive feature of bomber operations was the capacity of aircraft to penetrate enemy airspace and to inflict damage on the domestic economy, military capability, and population according to the prevailing directives. No other service could project power in this way, so by default the bomber became the supreme instrument for waging what was defined at the time as total war. The belief that modern, industrialized war was now to be fought between whole societies, each mobilizing the material energies and willpower of their entire population for the task of fighting, arming, and supplying the mass armed forces of the modern age, took root in the generation that grew up after the Great War. While it was generally understood by the air forces themselves that bombing enemy populations for the sake of exerting terror was contrary to conventional rules of engagement, attacking and killing armaments workers, destroying port facilities, or even burning down crops could all be construed, without too much sophistry, as legitimate objectives of total war.

Before the coming of the Second World War those air forces that had considered the implications of war against the enemy home front had to choose a set of targets that made strategic sense. This was essentially a British and American story, and it deserves telling in some detail. The concept of the independent strategic air offensive as the potentially decisive means to undermine the enemy war effort took root between the wars only in Britain and the United States. Even here the idea was hedged about with restrictions, not only as a result of the dubious legality of a campaign waged against the civilian home front, but because of pressure from the two senior services, army and navy, to make airpower conform to the general aim of the armed forces to defeat the enemy army and navy in the field. In the United States the air forces remained a part of the army, subject to army doctrine. In the "Fundamental Principles for the Employment of the Air Service," published by the War Department in 1926, air force organization and training was based "on the fundamental doctrine that their mission is to aid the ground forces to gain decisive success."[36] A board established in 1934 to reassess the role of what was now called the Army Air Corps was told by the army deputy chief of staff, Major General Hugh Drum, that in the army's opinion no operations should be undertaken by air forces that did not contribute directly to the success of the ground forces. "Battle is the decisive element in warfare," Drum continued, whereas independent air operations "would be largely wasted."[37] In 1935 the army agreed to the establishment of a General Headquarters (GHQ) Air Force, an independent component of the Air Corps, but its object was to bring additional reserve airpower to bear at decisive points in repelling an unlikely enemy invasion, not to conduct strategic operations distant from the battlefield.[38] In the absence of any real danger and faced by an unhelpful Treasury, the Air Corps mustered an exiguous force. In 1932 there were just ninety-two light bomber aircraft on hand.[39]

Under these circumstances American airmen found themselves

compelled to elaborate an unofficial theory of strategic bombing in tandem with the formal commitment to support the operations of the army. The American airmen who had witnessed the bombing of London in 1917–18 were more impressed by its results than their German counterparts. In the early 1920s the chief of the Air Service, Major General Mason Patrick, publicly supported the idea that "decisive blows from the air on rear areas" might end future conflicts, even while he endorsed his service's formal commitment to direct army support.[40] His deputy, Brigadier General William "Billy" Mitchell, was an even more outspoken advocate of airpower as a new way of war. His enthusiasm for an autonomous air arm was based on his conviction that attacks on "transportation and industrial centers" with high-explosive, incendiary, and gas bombs could prove to be a decisive contribution to victory. Mitchell elaborated the concept of the "vital centers" in the enemy's civilian war effort, whose destruction from the air might render surface operations by the army and navy redundant.[41] Although these views were not turned into doctrine—Mitchell was court-martialed in 1925 for his outspoken demands for an independent air force—they survived in air force circles as an unspoken commitment to the idea that in a future war between modern, highly urbanized and industrialized states, airpower could uniquely destroy the key targets that kept that sophisticated network in being.

The idea of the vital centers lay at the root of the future elaboration of American bombing strategy in the Second World War. The commander appointed to the GHQ Air Force in 1935, Major General Frank Andrews, privately supported the idea that independent air operations against factories, refineries, power plants, utilities, and centers of population were the most effective way to use bomber aircraft. The concept was elaborated and taught at the Air Corps Tactical School in the 1930s by a number of officers who were to become prominent organizers of the American bombing effort in the 1940s. Unlike European air forces, American airmen argued that attacking the more vulnerable home front made greater strategic sense. "Civilization has rendered the economic and social life of a nation increasingly vulnerable to attack," ran one lecture in 1935. "Sound strategy requires that the main blow be struck where the enemy is weakest." The will of the enemy population, it was argued, could be broken only by assaulting the "social body," a metaphor for the elaborate web of services, supplies, and amenities that held modern urban life together. In a list of factors that represented the capacity of a nation to sustain a war effort, the military system was placed fourth, behind the "social, economic and political systems" that nourished the military effort in the first place.[42] Major Harold George, who later drafted the plan for the American air offensive against Germany, argued not only that modern industry had created an "economic web" that could be interrupted by bombing, but that the moral effect on an enemy population "by the breaking of this closely-knit web" might end the war on its own.[43] To confirm these speculations, the Air Corps Tactical School commandant, Major Muir Fairchild, conducted an elaborate exercise in April 1939 on the vulnerability of New York and its surrounding area as a model for all cities, "the most important and the most vulnerable" element of the modern state. The conclusion was that two squadrons of bombers, attacking with 100 percent precision, could knock out the entire electricity-generating system in New York and paralyze the whole city at a stroke.[44]

The Air Corps operated in a vacuum in the 1930s in the absence of permissive air doctrine and the necessary aircraft equipment to justify the idea of a strategic offensive. In 1933 the Air Corps was allowed to explore the development of a four-engine bomber in order to ensure that military air technology kept abreast of the more rapid developments in civil aviation. The development contract was won by the Boeing Airplane Company, which by 1935 had produced a prototype designated the XB-17, forerunner of the B-17 Flying Fortress, with a range of 1,800 miles, carrying 4,000 pounds of bombs.[45] The army had approved the project only as a defensive aircraft for the long routes to Panama, Alaska, and Hawaii, but in 1936 army thinking changed and the production order was canceled. The army, impressed by the results of frontline support operations in Spain, thought medium bombers promised "greater efficiency, lessened complexity and decreased cost."[46] The development of the B-17 was squeezed to the slenderest of margins. It was saved only by a sudden revolution in political support for the Air Corps. In late

1938, President Roosevelt authorized a large-scale increase in American military spending, including a major commitment to the expansion of the air force (partly to ensure that France and Britain could be supplied with aircraft for the growing crisis in Europe). An Air Board appointed in March 1939 strongly supported the idea of a heavy bomber, and the B-17, from a single development model, became overnight the heart of American air strategy. Plans were developed to build 498 by 1941 and 1,520 by the end of 1942, the first commitment of any air force to the employment of a heavy four-engine bomber.[47]

One of the companies asked to produce the B-17, the Consolidated Airplane Company, instead designed its own bomber model in 1939 capable of carrying up to 8,000 pounds of bombs, with a higher speed and a maximum range of over 2,000 miles. This was accepted by the Air Corps after trials and modifications in 1940 and became the B-24 bomber, nicknamed "Liberator" by the RAF when a number were sent to Britain in 1941. It eventually became the standard American bomber, with 18,400 produced by 1945. The new bomber designs, together with the revolutionary M-4 Norden stabilized bombsight, first developed by the Dutch-American engineer Carl Norden for the U.S. Navy in the late 1920s, meant that the United States was better placed to operate a strategic air campaign in the early 1940s than any of its potential enemies. In 1939 permission was given to begin development of a "superbomber" with a range sufficient to reach Europe. What the Air Corps still lacked was any plan or doctrine that would allow it to use its enhanced power for what most airmen assumed was the primary function of the air force: to assault the "social body" of the enemy.

In Britain, commitment to some form of an independent bombing offensive was kept alive throughout the twenty years that separated the unfought air campaign against Germany in 1919 and the onset of a second war in 1939. In this case too, the RAF did not enjoy unlimited opportunity to develop either the doctrine to support an air offensive or the technology necessary to sustain it. In the 1920s there was relatively little thinking about the nature of an air offensive beyond speculation on the assertion by the chief of air staff, Sir Hugh Trenchard, about the probable vulnerability of civilian morale in any future conflict. When in the late 1920s the Air Ministry explored the possibility of a "Locarno" war against France to help the Germans repel a possible French invasion in violation of the 1925 Locarno Pact, it was argued that even if the French bombed London, "we can count on our superior morale and striking power to ensure that the Frenchman squeals first."[48] In 1928 the British chiefs of staff insisted on securing a firm description from the RAF of the war object of an air force. In the meetings that followed, the navy and army chiefs of staff made it clear that in their view the vague commitment to attacking the enemy economy and population was not only contrary to international law but departed from the traditional principle of war that the main effort had to be devoted to defeating the enemy in the field. An uneasy truce was established between the services on the basis that the aim of the air force, "in concert with the Navy and Army," was to break enemy resistance, and to do so "by attacks on objectives calculated to achieve this end." This left Trenchard and the RAF with substantial leeway in defining just what those objectives were and how they might be attacked.[49]

Although the other services wanted the RAF to develop a balanced force, capable of offering them support and defending the country against air attack, the air force itself remained dominated by the idea that bombing defined its purpose as a modern force capable of revolutionizing warfare. In a survey of RAF development written after the end of the Second World War, Robert Saundby, deputy commander of Bomber Command during the war, claimed that the air staff in the 1920s "saw clearly that the bomb was the offensive weapon of the Air Force"; and indeed in the first edition of the RAF *War Manual*, published in 1935, it was claimed that "the bomb is the chief weapon of an air force and the principal means by which it may attain its aim in war."[50] When it came to thinking about what the bomb or bombs might be used for, RAF leaders continued to rely on unverifiable assumptions about the social fragility of the enemy. In the 1928 discussion organized by the chiefs of staff, Trenchard, like American airmen, had suggested that airpower would have to be exerted against the "enemy's vital centres," where the enemy "is at his weakest," but he made little effort to define what those might be.[51] For much of the decade that followed, those

British airmen who followed the "Trenchard doctrine" fell back on bland metaphors about the social body, using, like American airmen, an anatomical language that created a deliberate abstraction in place of the real bodies that bombing would damage.[52] The RAF *War Manual* claimed that all modern states "have their nerve centres, main arteries, heart and brain." By attacking them, air forces would delay, interrupt, and disorganize the vital centers to such a degree that the enemy's "national effort" would collapse, not only through injury to the social body, but by the effect this might have on the collective mind, as the *Manual* explained:

> Moral effect—Although the bombardment of suitable objectives should result in considerable material damage and loss, the most important and far-reaching effect of air bombardment is its moral effect. . . . The moral effect of bombing is always severe and usually cumulative, proportionately greater effect being obtained by continuous bombing especially of the enemy's vital centres.[53]

The conviction that bombing must cause the physical and mental collapse of an enemy state dominated British air theory, as it dominated public anxieties about total war.

One reason why the RAF stuck with the idea that a powerful striking force of bombers would be the most effective way to exploit the potential of airpower can be found in the nature of the combat experience enjoyed by British airmen in the interwar years. Instead of drawing lessons from the Spanish Civil War about the advantages of close-support aviation and air superiority, which was the conclusion drawn by most other air forces, RAF doctrine was mainly informed by the experience of what was called air policing in the empire or Afghanistan.[54] The use of aircraft to enforce local control against rebel tribes and tribesmen (described in the *Manual* as war against "semi-civilised peoples") was taken as a paradigm to explain what might happen if a civilized state was subjected to a heavier level of bombing. Even tribal communities, it was argued, had vital centers that governed their existence; target intelligence on those centers would allow the small light bombers allocated to the operation to destroy them and, in doing so, to compel compliance from unruly subjects. John Slessor, director of plans in the Air Ministry in the late 1930s, gave a brutally frank description in his memoirs of why air policing worked: "Whether the offender concerned was an Indian Frontier tribesman, a nomad Arab of the northern deserts, a Morelli slaver on the border of Kenya, or a web-footed savage of the swamps of the southern Sudan, there are almost always some essentials without which he cannot obtain his livelihood."[55] A model example for the RAF was the bombing undertaken in Ovamboland in southern Africa in 1938, in which rebel chieftain Ipumbu of the Ukuambi tribe was brought to heel by three aircraft that destroyed his kraal (camp) and drove off his cattle. In this case, and others, emphasis was put on the "moral effect" of coercive bombing, as well as its material impact.[56] The practice of air policing using bomber aircraft as a "strategic" tool was shared by all those who later held high RAF office in the Second World War: Charles Portal, wartime chief of the air staff; Arthur Harris, commander in chief of Bomber Command; Richard Peirse, his predecessor as commander in chief; and Norman Bottomley, Portal's wartime deputy. Later, in September 1941, Portal used the analogy to explain to Churchill the nature of the assault on the "general activity of a community" in Germany: "In short, it is an adaptation, though on a greatly magnified scale, of the policy of air control which has proved so outstandingly successful in recent years in the small wars in which the Air Force has been continuously engaged."[57]

This perception of bombing serves to explain the wide gap between the strategic vision at the heart of the interwar RAF and the reality of British bombing capability and defense strategy in the 1930s. Imperial air policing was undertaken in conditions of clear visibility, little or no opposition, and low-level attack, none of which would be true of an aerial offensive undertaken in Europe. As a result, colonial practice did not persuade Britain's military leaders to bank everything on the bomber. Indeed, fear of bombing, particularly once Hitler's Germany had been identified in the mid-1930s as the most likely potential enemy, acted as a powerful spur to change British priorities in the air to one that was more appropriately defensive. When the military Joint Planning Committee

was asked in 1934 to estimate the probable effects of a German "knock-
out blow" from the air, it was assumed that a week of bombing would
produce 150,000 casualties and render millions homeless. Later estimates
by the chiefs of staff continued to assume that these statistics were
realistic—more than a match for the alarmist literature of the age.[58] In
1937 the newly appointed minister for the coordination of defense, Sir
Thomas Inskip, told the RAF that the role of the air force was not to
inflict a knockout blow on the enemy (which it was incapable of doing)
"but to prevent the Germans from knocking us out."[59] The Committee
of Imperial Defence spelled out guidelines for air strategy in which the
air force would have to support the navy and army, defend the mainland
United Kingdom from air attack, and try to inflict aerial damage on the
enemy's strike force. Instructions were given to prepare for a possible attack on German industry in the Ruhr, but only if political permission
was given and only after the RAF had met its other commitments. Instead of a force dominated by a large component of bombers to assault
the enemy's war effort, the British defense chiefs insisted on a balanced
force, a view with which a number of senior airmen agreed, despite the
prevailing culture that bombing was what the RAF should do. Between
1937 and the outbreak of war this meant devoting the lion's share of
resources to Fighter Command, the air defense network, and civil defenses. As a result, RAF strategy seemed increasingly schizophrenic,
half of it emphasizing the strategic value of bombing, the other half
preparing plans to defend successfully against it.

For all the emphasis in air force circles on the value of a strike force,
the technical preparations for an offensive were almost nonexistent. Instead of the massed bomber fleets assumed to be necessary to inflict serious damage, the force was composed of a modest number of light and
medium bombers, most of them incapable of reaching beyond the
fringes of western Germany. More problematic was the absence of serious thinking about problems of navigation, bombing training, bombsights, and bombing accuracy, reflecting an air force culture that played
down the importance of technique and tactics.[60] The RAF made gener-
alists of the senior staff, who moved regularly between command in the
field and office duty in the Air Ministry, discouraging the development

of a corps of technically qualified airmen to match the Technical Office of the German Air Force. The British scientist Sir Henry Tizard chaired a committee set up in 1938 to give scientific advice to the RAF on bombing, but found senior commanders unenthusiastic about collaborating with science.

When an Air Ministry Bombing Policy committee was finally set up in March 1938 to explore the problems of how to reach, find, and hit a target, it was acknowledged that a great deal more needed to be done to be able to do any of them. The bombsight was little different from those used in the First World War and navigation was undertaken either visually by day or by the stars at night. At the committee's first meeting, the pessimistic conclusion was reached that new technical equipment was unlikely to produce any marked improvement in navigation or accuracy. Opportunities for accurate nighttime bombing were expected to be "rare."[61] Bombing trials showed that with high-level bombing by day, the form most favored, only 3 percent of bombs were likely to hit their target, and in a shallow dive, 9 percent.[62] By March 1939 the Air Ministry planning department bemoaned the failure to mobilize all the country's scientific resources to produce a better bombsight, and suggested that political pressure should be exerted on the United States to provide the Norden gyroscopic model, but it was largely a problem of their own making.[63] A month before the Munich crisis in late September 1938, the commander in chief of Bomber Command, Air Chief Marshal Edgar Ludlow-Hewitt, told the Air Ministry that under present circumstances it would be best to rely on the North Sea and air defenses in the event of war with Germany. The attempt to bomb Germany "might end in major disaster."[64]

The many practical and conceptual difficulties faced in trying to get the armed forces and governments in Britain and the United States to accept a strategic bombing capability reflected fundamental differences of opinion over what aircraft could actually achieve and anxious concern about the legitimacy of campaigns that might raise serious moral objections if civilians were put in the front line. These concerns survived long into the war itself. Air force commanders as well as politicians were reluctant to endorse operations that could not demonstrate some clear military or war-economic purpose, however broadly the net of total war might be spread, or however forceful the political pressure. Even in Bulgaria, the brief political directive from Churchill was watered down to give it a spurious military justification when it was passed on to the military chiefs: "Sofia is a centre of administration of belligerent government, an important railway centre, and has barracks, arsenals and marshalling yards."[65] The unwillingness of the air commanders on the spot to carry out the bombing of Bulgaria with the single-mindedness demanded by Churchill reflected their view that bombing was not likely to achieve very much in practical terms, while the bombing of, for example, Romanian oil supplies or the Viennese aircraft industry could clearly have significant consequences. The short campaign against Bulgaria illustrated the tension that existed between the exaggerated expectations of politicians and the public about the likely political and psychological results from attacking an enemy from the air and the demonstrable value in military and economic terms of doing so. This ambiguity underlay many of the wider wartime arguments between politicians, airmen, and the military chiefs over what bombing could or could not deliver, and it helps to explain a feature characteristic of all bombing campaigns: the escalation of the degree of indiscriminate damage.

The pattern of bombing in Bulgaria, from a limited raid on Sofia's railway facilities and the Vrajedna airfield in November 1943 to the final raids in March and April 1944 when the extensive use of incendiaries produced much higher levels of urban destruction, was not an accidental progression. In all the major campaigns in Europe (and in the campaigns mounted in eastern Asia) there occurred an evident escalation the longer the bombing went on and the more uncertain were its results. Air force commanders had an urgent need to demonstrate that their operations were militarily useful in the face of hostile criticism from the other services or the impatience of their political masters. Perhaps the best example is the shift in British planning from the 1939 Western Air Plans for limited attacks on Ruhr industrial installations to the decision taken in 1941 to attack the central areas of German industrial cities with large quantities of incendiaries to destroy working-class housing and to kill workers. The reasons for escalation differ in historical detail from case to case. Nevertheless, they suggest a common process dictated partly by technical frustration at poor accuracy and navigation or high losses; partly by political frustration at the absence of unambiguous results; partly by air force anxiety that failure might reflect badly on its claim on resources; and finally, and significantly, by the slow erosion of any relative moral constraints that might have acted to limit the damage to civilian targets. Among the many questions about the military conduct of the campaigns, the issue of escalation and its consequences remains the most important. It has significant implications for the current exercise of airpower in the wars of the twenty-first century.

For the societies that suffered bombing during the war there was only one reality that mattered: "The bomber will always get through." The famous remark by the British deputy prime minister, Stanley Baldwin, on the eve of his departure for the Geneva disarmament talks in November 1932, that the man in the street ought to understand there was no power on earth yet available to stop him from being bombed, has usually been taken for deliberate hyperbole to scare delegates at Geneva into accepting a ban on bomber aircraft. Yet though it proved possible during the war to detect aircraft with radar and to intercept them by day and increasingly by night, and to inflict high-percentage rates of loss on an attacking force, in the context of the Second World War, Baldwin was right. Most bombers did reach the approximate target area and disgorge their bombs with limited accuracy on the ground below, turning wartime civilian society into an effective front line. That this would be so was widely expected by the 1930s among the populations of the world's major states, who saw bombing fatalistically, as something that would define future conflict. "It is the height of folly," wrote the British air minister, Lord Londonderry, to Baldwin in July 1934, "to imagine that any war can be conducted without appreciable risk to the civil population."[66] Brought up on a diet of scaremongering fiction and films, and subjected by the 1930s to regular drill or instruction or propaganda for air-raid precautions, civilian society came to take for granted that it would become an object of attack, even that there might be some degree of democratic legitimacy to bombing if all of modern mass society had to be mobilized for war.

The concept of civilian society, primarily urban society, as a new front line in war was in reality a novel, indeed unique, phenomenon in the context of the modern age. It gave the strategic bombing war a second political dimension because it raised the problem of maintaining social cohesion and political allegiance in the face of extreme levels of direct military violence against the home front. The survival of positive "morale" became central to the concerns of those governments whose populations were attacked. Morale as such was poorly defined at the time, was difficult to measure in any meaningful way, and was subject to a great many other pressures besides the effects of bombing. A British Air Ministry report in the summer of 1941 confessed that since "morale is itself a thing of opinion and not of fact, there is no likelihood even of experts agreeing on the matter."[67] Yet it was the bombing war in particular that was popularly believed by rulers and ruled to have a fundamental impact on the war willingness and psychological state of any population, and it featured regularly in home intelligence reports on the public mood in every bombed state. Judging the mood of an enemy population was an equally difficult assessment to make for those doing the bombing. They tried to estimate with some precision what effect their attacks might have on the state of mind of those they bombed, but the answers were more often than not contradictory or confused. The JIC report on the bombing of Bulgaria, produced in January 1944, highlighted social effects that were "out of proportion" to the modest scale of the attack, but still concluded that the political results had been negligible.

There can be little room for doubt that the experience of bombing was deeply demoralizing for many of those who survived it, though it could also provoke sudden moments of exhilaration, or induce a profound apathy, but the difficulty in drawing any clear causal links between bombing and popular response is simply that the response was as varied, irregular, unpredictable, and diverse as the society that made it. The social reaction to bombing is often treated as if it must be uniform, but it differed widely between states and within communities. This was a reality seldom appreciated by those doing the bombing, for whom "Germans" or "Italians" or even "Bulgarians" became simply a generic description of the human target. One of the key questions still debated about the bombing war is why the bombed societies did not collapse at once under the impact, as conventional wisdom before 1939 suggested they would. This is too simple an approach. Bombing did place enormous strains on local communities, and some did experience a cumulative or temporary social breakdown as a result, but it was always a long step from local social crisis to the complete collapse of a war effort. To understand why "morale" did not collapse in Germany in any meaningful way, but evidently declined in Italy prior to surrender in 1943, is to engage with complex issues of social cohesion defined by regional differences, the intensity of the bombing experience, the nature of the prevailing state and local administration, the peculiar structures of local society, and the cultural impact of propaganda. Any narrative of the bombing war has to address issues of social, psychological, and cultural response as well as the conventional military reality: the view from below as well as the view from above. This dual approach has featured only rarely in the existing history of the bombing campaigns, yet it is the one sure way to assess just what effects bombing actually had on the target communities, and to suggest what those effects might be in any future war.

The story of the civilian front line in the air war is an aggregate story of loss of extraordinary proportions: an estimated 600,000 killed, a million seriously injured, millions more hurt less severely; millions dispossessed through bomb destruction; 50–60 percent of the urban area of Germany obliterated; countless cultural monuments and works of art irreparably lost. It is only when these costs are summarized that the unique character of the bombing war can be properly understood. The dead were not accidental bystanders but the consequence of a technology generally incapable of distinguishing and hitting a small individual target, and which all sides knew was incapable of doing so with the prevailing science. This raises serious questions about why the states that endorsed bombing never reined back campaigns with such a high civilian cost and in particular why the major liberal democracies, Britain and the United States, ended up organizing strategic bombing campaigns that killed around 1 million people in Europe and Asia during the course of the war.

This is one of the most important paradoxes raised by the fact of the Anglo-American bombing war. Both were liberal states committed in the 1930s to trying to keep the peace, both were states in which there was widespread public condemnation of bombing civilians, whether in Ethiopia, China, or Spain, yet in both the idea of destroying the "vital centers" or the "social body" was most fully elaborated. Part of the explanation lies in the geopolitical and military realities confronted by both states. Force projection for both had seldom involved a large army, and the army remained, even after the Great War, a component of the defense establishment rather than its driving force, as it was in France, Germany, or the Soviet Union. In conjunction with large navies, on which home security had been dependent, airpower could be projected overseas with greater flexibility and potential striking power than overseas expeditionary forces. In Britain, defense of the empire against threat meant that Germany was not the only potential enemy. In the discussions surrounding the development of the "Ideal Bomber" in the mid-1930s, range was called for that could reach targets in Japan or the Soviet Union (in case of a communist threat to India), as well as provide empire reinforcement in areas as geographically distant as Canada or Sierra Leone. The threat from Soviet long-range bombers—anticipating the later Cold War—was expected to spread to British interests in the Middle East and eventually to menace British cities. The only response was expected to be a British strike force for use against Soviet cities.[68] In the United States, the arguments from the Air Corps for the survival of a heavy-bomber program were all based on the idea that force might have to be projected across oceans to American Pacific possessions, and even against targets in Europe from American airbases.

There was also in both Britain and the United States a real attraction for the idea that air warfare was a more modern and efficient form of fighting than the recent experience of a grueling and costly land war. Since both were democracies, with political elites sensitive to popular anxieties and expectations, airpower was intended to reduce the human cost of war on the ground. Arthur Harris famously argued that the army would fail next time to find "sufficient morons willing to be sacrificed in a mud war in Flanders," but for Germany, France, or the Soviet Union, a ground army and effective ground defenses were essential elements in their security planning.[69] The idea that modern technology and science-based weaponry enhanced military efficiency was central to the American view of the potential of a bombing war. At the Air Corps Tactical School, airmen emphasized that airpower was "a new means of waging war," one that would supply "the most efficient action to bring us victory with the least expenditure of lives, time, money and matériel."[70] Airpower also appealed because it could make optimum use of the technical and industrial strengths of the two states, while minimizing casualties. In the United States, planning for possible industrial mobilization of resources to support large-scale air activity began in the 1920s and by the early 1930s produced detailed mobilization planning for 24,000 aircraft a year; in Britain plans for industrial mobilization dated from the mid-1930s with the development of so-called shadow factories, ready to be converted to military output if war broke out. In both cases, extensive manufacturing capacity and advanced technical skills were regarded as a critical dimension of future warmaking, particularly in the air.[71] The modernity of airpower was emphasized in other states as well, for propaganda reasons as well as military ones, but much less autonomy was allowed to those air forces to campaign for strategies that could be presented as more efficient and less costly than traditional surface combat with armies and ships.

One important consequence of the equation of airpower and modernity was the willingness of airmen in Britain and the United States to accept that modern "total war" reflected a changed democratic reality, that war was between peoples as well as armed forces. In an age of modern industry, mass political mobilization, and scientific advance, war, it was argued, could not be confined to the fighting front. Although the term "total war" was first popularized by Erich Ludendorff, the German general who had masterminded much of Germany's war effort between 1916 and 1918, it was appropriated as a description of whole societies at war much more fully in Britain and America than it was in continental Europe. "There can be no doubt," wrote the British aviation journalist Oliver Stewart in 1936, "that a town in any industrial civilisation is a military objective; it provides the sinews of war; it houses those

who direct the war; it is a nexus of communications; it is a centre of propaganda; and it is a seat of government."[72] As a result, he continued,
"blind bombing of a town as a town might be logically defended." In a
lecture to the Naval Staff College, also in 1936, Air Vice Marshal Arthur Barratt asked his audience to recognize that it was no longer possible "to draw a definite line between combatant and non-combatant."
This was, he claimed, a result of the "power of democracy"; the more
governments depended on the support of the governed, the more the
morale and resources of the civil population became a legitimate object
of attack.[73] The U.S. air force also based its argument in favor of offensive bombing on the nature of a modern democratic state, as the following extract from an Air Corps Tactical School lecture reveals:

> Where is that will to resist centered? How is it expressed? It is cen-
> tered in the mass of the people. It is expressed through political
> government. The will to resist, the will to fight, the will to progress,
> are all ultimately centered in the mass of the people—the civil
> mass—the people in the street. . . . Hence, the ultimate aim of all
> military operations is to destroy the will of those people at home. . . .
> The Air Force can strike at once at its ultimate objective; the na-
> tional will to resist.[74]

It may be that in both Britain and the United States popular public
fears about a war from the air were more powerfully and publicly expressed, given the previous geographical immunity both states had enjoyed before the coming of the airplane and full freedom of expression,
and that as a result popular phobias fueled military speculation that
bombing the home front would have immediate results. But whatever
the source of this conviction, it governed the expectations of both the
British and American air forces about how the next war should be
fought.

Seventy years after the event, the British and American decisions to
mount bomber offensives seem out of place with the stated aims of liberation and the defeat of dictatorship. But there is a sense in which

current moral concerns about what bombing represented are anachronistic. The willingness to embark on campaigns with such a deadly outcome can only be properly understood by reconstructing the terms in which the moral imperatives of war were perceived at the time. The assault on civilians signified an acceptance, even by the victim populations, of shifting norms about the conduct of war; what had seemed unacceptable legally or morally in 1939 was rapidly transformed by the relative ethics of survival or defeat.[75] It is easy to deplore the losses and to condemn the strategy as immoral, even illegal—and a host of recent accounts of the bombing have done just that—but current ethical concerns get no nearer to an understanding of how these things were possible, even applauded, and why so few voices were raised during the war against the notion that the home front could legitimately be a target of attack.[76]

The contemporary ethical view of bombing was far from straightforward, and often paradoxical. It is striking, for example, that among those who were bombed there was seldom clear or persistent hatred for the enemy; there was a sense that "war" itself was responsible and "modern war" in particular, as if it enjoyed some kind of existence independent of the particular air fleets inflicting the damage. There could even be a sense that bombing was necessary to purge the world of the forces that had unleashed the barbarism in the first place, a blessing as much as a curse. A young German soldier captured and interrogated in Italy early in 1945 told his captors, "In the long run your bombings may be good for Germany. They have given her a taste, bitter though it may be, of what war is really like."[77] The moral response to bombing and being bombed was historically complex and sometimes surprising. Issues that seemed black and white before the war and seem so again today were colored in many shades of gray during the conflict. Nonetheless, the figures on death, injury, and destruction are shocking, like the statistics on other forms of mass death of civilians in the Second World War. The grisly consequences of the bombing war would have outraged opinion in the 1930s just as they have attracted current opprobrium among historians and international lawyers.[78] Exploring how it was possible for the

British and American military and politicians to legitimize this scale of damage in the brief span of total war between 1940 and 1945 forms the fourth element in the narrative alongside the political context that shaped the development of the aerial conflict, the military operations that defined its precise character and extent, and the administrative, social, and cultural responses it evoked from the communities subjected to it.

Chapter 1

The Sorcerer's Apprentice: Bomber Command, 1939–42

On September 1, 1939, President Franklin D. Roosevelt sent an appeal to all the major European powers involved in the crisis over Poland to give a public undertaking that they would abstain from any air attacks against civilians or unfortified cities. The same day, Hitler told the American chargé d'affaires in Berlin that this had always been his preference and assured Roosevelt that German aircraft would attack only military objectives. The British prime minister, Neville Chamberlain, gave his guarantee the same day; a joint Anglo-French declaration followed on September 3, only reserving the right to act as they saw fit if the enemy failed to observe the same restrictions.[1] The Polish ambassador in Washington, whose country was already at war, agreed that Polish pilots would be told not to bomb open cities as long as the enemy did the same.[2] None of these expressions of goodwill were legally binding in international law.

The idea that bombing warfare could somehow be "humanized" had been explored by a British committee set up in July 1938 with the cumbersome title "Limitation of Armaments Committee, Sub-Committee on the Humanisation of Aerial Warfare." The discussions of the committee, chaired by Sir William Malkin, went round in circles. The terms for a possible international agreement on limiting bombing to military objectives suffered not only from the realistic objection that such terms would be unenforceable in a real war, but also from the difficulty of defining what was meant by a military objective. In the end the committee proved more useful in giving the Air Ministry the opportunity to defend the idea that bombing arms factories and armaments workers was as legitimate as a naval blockade than it was in finding grounds for a diplomatic solution.[3] In the absence of international agreement, the RAF was told to abide by the Hague Rules for air warfare, first drafted in 1923 but never ratified, but to do so only as long as the enemy did the same. The rules were spelled out in a cabinet decision and repeated regularly up to and beyond the outbreak of war: intentional bombing of civilians was illegal; only identifiable military objectives could be attacked from the air; and any such attack must be undertaken without negligent harm to civilians. In August 1939 the Air Ministry concluded that attacks on targets difficult to identify through cloud or at night would also be illegal, as would any operation in which the civil population, hospitals, cultural monuments, or historic sites were targeted. An interdepartmental committee, set up the same month to draft detailed instructions on rules of engagement for the British armed forces, stipulated that "it is clearly illegal to bombard a populated area in the hope of hitting a legitimate target."[4]

These legal limitations reflected decisions taken in military staff talks between the British and French high commands in the spring of 1939 as they planned for a possible war. In April the two military staffs had agreed only to attack military targets in the narrowest sense of the term, at sea or at the fighting front. British bombers were to be used to help the battle on land, not to attack distant targets in Germany. The French were insistent that the RAF should not attack German cities while the balance of air resources so obviously favored Germany and French industry was not yet adequately protected.[5] A few days before the outbreak of war the chief of the British air staff, Sir Cyril Newall, warned Air Chief Marshal Edgar Ludlow-Hewitt, commander in chief of Bomber Command, that his activities were bound to be restricted "for political reasons," though Ludlow-Hewitt knew that Bomber Command's small size and operational difficulties were enough on their own to inhibit offensive action.[6] Newall worried that even if the RAF bombed legitimate objectives, the Germans would claim that they had killed civilians. There was strong political pressure to ensure that the democracies were not seen to violate the bombing proscription first. It was decided in October 1939 that only if German aircraft started to kill large numbers of civilians from the air—"promiscuous bombardment," as it was called— would the RAF "take the gloves off."[7]

Both sides at first stuck to their pledge not to attack targets in each other's cities where civilians were at risk (though this did not prevent the German Air Force from killing noncombatants during its operations in Poland). Chamberlain had no interest in provoking German bombing of British towns, despite appeals from the Polish government in early September to begin bombing Germany as a gesture of assistance.[8] It was nonetheless the case that for the first months of the war Bomber Command strained at the leash to be able to do what years of planning had prepared it for. A halfhearted agreement was reached with the French high command to initiate bombing of the German Ruhr-Rhineland industrial region—usually capitalized in British documents simply as the RUHR—if a sudden German attack threatened Belgium or menaced Franco-British forces decisively, but the French remained cautious about risking German retaliation, even during the invasion in May 1940.[9] In the end it was the British who ended the international embargo agreed to in September. On the night of May 11–12, two days after the German invasion in western Europe, thirty-seven medium and light bombers attacked industrial and transport targets in the Rhineland city of München Gladbach (now Mönchengladbach), killing four people, including an Englishwoman who happened to live there. British raids were to continue throughout the war. The last was made on May 2–3, 1945, on the north German port of Kiel, just thirty-six hours before Allied troops occupied the city.[10]

"Taking the Gloves Off," 1939–40

The political and legal restrictions imposed on Bomber Command were consistent with the widely held view in Britain that indiscriminate bombing was the hallmark of barbarism, whereas self-restraint was a feature of being civilized. Yet there were also powerful prudential arguments for not undertaking bombing from the start of the war, as the French realized. In the autumn of 1939, Bomber Command was not yet ready to launch any major offensive campaign. For all the talk in the 1930s of developing a "striking force" capable of taking the fight to the enemy heartland, progress in developing the technology of aircraft, bombs, bombsights, and navigation aids had been painfully slow. One of Chamberlain's more desperate acts before the war was to ask Roosevelt on August 25, 1939, a week before the president's appeal, to supply the American Norden bombsight for British use. Roosevelt declined, not because it would compromise his subsequent appeal to abstain from bombing, but because agreeing to this request would make it seem that the United States had taken sides in the conflict.[11] At the outbreak of war Ludlow-Hewitt was well aware of the deficiencies of his force, which had already been exposed when the Air Ministry in 1938 at last began to consider the practicalities of long-range bombing. The gap between ambition and reality was remarkably wide for a force committed to a bombing strategy, a reflection of the poor technical experience of much of the RAF leadership and the failure to define doctrine clearly. There were too few airfields capable of handling heavier aircraft, little experience in bombing training, a shortage of maps of northwestern Germany, and a total of only 488 bombers of all kinds, including light bombers destined to form part of the Advanced Air Striking Force when it was sent to France in late 1939. "Unrestricted air warfare," ran an Air Ministry instruction, "is not in the interests of Great Britain."[12]

RAF Bomber Command dated from the reorganization of the air arm in 1936. In contrast to the German Air Force, all bomber units were grouped together under a single commander in chief, based at Bomber Command headquarters near High Wycombe, northwest of London. This had important implications for the identity of the command, because its sole function was to bomb. As a force it was only offensive, and its main duty was to define what targets to bomb, to produce the technology to enable those targets to be destroyed, and to train the manpower to do it. This functional identity encouraged Bomber Command to construct a doctrine and a force independent of the army and navy, capable of striking a potential enemy at what was perceived to be its most vulnerable point. The command was disinclined to accept the role of auxiliary to the requirements of surface forces, and there was almost no planning for army cooperation to match German Air Force doctrine. Right up to the outbreak of war and beyond, the RAF argued that its contribution to the battlefield would be of little significance: attacks on railway communications were regarded as difficult and ineffective, while raids against marching columns of men were deemed to be a waste of bombing resources.[13] Instead the Air Ministry drew up what were known as the Western Air Plans, a series of sixteen individual plans, some of which committed the bomber force to assist the Admiralty in the war at sea, but none of which committed the bombers to help the army in the field. Only two of the plans were seriously prepared for: W.A.4 involved long-range attacks against communications targets in Germany to slow a German advance; W.A.5 was for attacks on the German industrial economy, particularly the Ruhr area and the German oil industry.[14] An Industrial Intelligence Centre, first established in 1931 under Desmond Morton (later Churchill's intelligence adviser), drew up lists of vulnerable targets in German industry. Most of them could not be hit from British bases with existing aircraft, but they formed the basis for the RAF insistence that the most efficient use of bomber aircraft was against the enemy home front, not its armed forces.[15] Yet vulnerable targets on the home front could not be hit as long as the government insisted on the letter of the law.

The bomber force was organized in September 1939 in five groups, spread out across east-central England and East Anglia, each group made up of between six and eight squadrons, a total of thirty-three in all. Although some of the aircraft were called heavy bombers at the time, the groups were actually equipped like the German Air Force with twin-engine light or medium bombers. The light bombers made up sixteen squadrons, ten consisting of the Fairey Battle, six of the Bristol Blenheim IV. The Battle emerged from a 1933 requirement for a monoplane light bomber but was obsolescent by 1939 and unsuited to daylight raiding; its operational function was unclear and its striking power negligible. They were sent to France as part of the air expeditionary force but were sitting ducks for German fighters. On May 14, 1940, as many as forty out of a force of seventy-one Battles were shot down in a single disastrous operation against the crossings at Sedan in the Ardennes, close to the Belgian border. The Blenheim was developed from 1935 as a fast medium bomber. It was weakly armed but could reach a maximum speed of 266 miles per hour. It could carry only 1,000 pounds of bombs around 700 miles. Its limited range and small bomb load made it unsuitable for a strategic role, and it played a larger part in the antiship-ping war along the German-occupied northern shores of Europe. Light bombers were sensibly phased out as the war progressed.[16]

Bomber Command had three principal long-range bombers in 1939: the Vickers Wellington, the Armstrong Whitworth Whitley, and the Handley Page Hampden. The Hampden came from a 1932 specifica-tion, the Whitley from 1934, making them both considerably older than their German counterparts. The Hampden had a top speed of 255 miles per hour and could carry up to 4,000 pounds of bombs around 600 miles; the Whitley Mk V with Rolls-Royce Merlin engines was the mainstay of Bomber Command in the first year, with a range of 800 miles with 3,000 pounds of bombs and a top speed of 222 mph. They were lightly armed and easy prey on unescorted sorties by day. The most successful of the medium bombers was the Vickers Wellington Mk IC (succeeded in 1941 by the Mk II and III), which made up more than half of Bomber Command's strategic force by 1942. It was powered by Bris-tol Pegasus engines, had a top speed of 235 miles per hour, and could carry 4,500 pounds of bombs some 600 miles. Its geodetic construction—a lattice-like fuselage shell—made it exceptionally robust compared with the Hampden and Whitley, and later marks of the Wellington re-mained in service throughout the war.[17] What the medium bombers lacked were effective navigational aids to match the German electronic systems (navigators and pilots were still taught astral navigation), power-ful armament to be able to defend themselves against fighter assault, and bombs of sufficient destructive power. The standard British 250- and 500-pound bombs had a low charge-to-weight ratio (around one-quarter was explosive, against one-half in German bombs), but they also con-tained less destructive explosive content, without the addition of alumi-num powder (standard in German bombs), and were prone to fail to detonate. The standard incendiary bomb was the four-pound Mk I magnesium bomb, which remained in production, with small modifica-tions, throughout the war. Larger "firepot" bombs were developed in 1939 and 1940, designed to distribute a high number of incendiary de-vices, but they were plagued with technical difficulties. Only later in the war did Bomber Command acquire heavier oil-based incendiaries.[18] The technical level of the force that went to war in 1939—aircraft, bombs, and equipment—can be described charitably as unsophisticated.

The early experience of the bomber force during the "Phoney War" confirmed the wisdom of not pressing for an immediate bombing offensive. The political restrictions confined the RAF to attacks on German naval vessels at sea and naval targets on the North Sea islands of Sylt and Helgoland, and on the German coast at Wilhelmshaven. Even these limited operations brought insupportable casualty rates: a small raid on the German coast on September 4 cost 23 percent of the bomber force; a raid by Hampdens against Helgoland on September 29 cost half the force. In October 1939 the "heavy bombers" were ordered to operate chiefly at night, as the Air Ministry had always expected.[19] The only operations permitted in German airspace were propaganda runs dropping millions of leaflets. Some aircrews, struggling to cope with the excessive cold, chucked out the heavy bundles without cutting them first, making them a potentially more lethal weapon than had been intended. By March 1940 it was reported that the morale of Bomber Command crews was close to cracking after long and dangerous propaganda operations that seemed to contribute nothing to winning the war and exposed crews to excessive risk of accident.[20] The nighttime flights posed all kinds of difficulties. Interviews with operational crews confirmed that intense cold and long, risky flights over sea were compounded with the difficulty experienced over Germany itself, which they found to be "very black." It proved almost impossible to find and hit a specific target in the midst of the blackout, even with leaflets, a fact that RAF planners had already realized some months before when drawing up a "Night Plan" to accommodate the shift from daylight to nighttime operations, in which it was admitted that hitting anything "will be largely a matter of chance."[21] In late March, shortly before the campaign in Norway, the chiefs of staff concluded that Bomber Command was too weak and unprepared to be able to do anything effective in the foreseeable future.[22] In April, just prior to the German invasion of the Low Countries and France, the new head of Bomber Command, Air Marshal Charles Portal, who replaced Ludlow-Hewitt in March, told the air staff that he had only 260 serviceable bombers and 384 crews; he estimated that they would be capable of dropping 100 tons of bombs in the first week of bombing operations but only thirty tons by week three. Because of the high rate of loss anticipated, the force would be capable of only thirty-six sorties a day after two weeks of conflict.[23] This was a negligible effort on the eve of the German offensive.

It is all the more surprising under these circumstances that the RAF should have decided to take the gloves off in May 1940 when the German invasion began. The decision to permit British bombers to attack military-economic targets on German soil close to civilian populations was not an invitation to undertake the heavy city bombings of the later war years, if only because Bomber Command was manifestly incapable of inflicting them. But it was a threshold that had to be crossed consciously, given the heavy weight of political and ethical restrictions laid on the force from the start of the war. What was judged to be illegal in August 1939 had to be presented as legitimate when it was undertaken in the summer of 1940. Most explanations for the start of the British campaign have assumed that it was a response to the German bombing of Rotterdam on May 14, but the first raid, on Münchengladbach, had already taken place three days before, while Rotterdam was not mentioned in any of the cabinet discussions about initiating the bombing of German targets. The decision was taken because of the crisis in the Battle of France, not because of German air raids.[24] The actual circumstances surrounding the onset of bombing were more complex. By chance the German attack in the west on May 10, 1940, began on the same day that the Chamberlain government was replaced by a new one headed by Winston Churchill. Chamberlain had always opposed the use of bombers against urban targets, but Churchill had no conscientious or legal objections. As minister of munitions in 1917, he had been a prominent supporter of an independent air force and a campaign of long-range bombing against German industrial objectives. Later, as minister for air after the war, he had played a key role in securing the independent future of the RAF. He accepted the argument that bombing could be expected to produce important strategic results. A government headed by Churchill rather than Chamberlain was always more likely to endorse a bombing campaign.[25]

One of the first issues discussed by Churchill's new War Cabinet on May 12 was the virtue of initiating what was described as "unrestricted air warfare." It was agreed that the RAF should no longer be bound by any moral or legal scruples to abstain from bombing; Germany's wartime actions, Churchill claimed, had already given the Allies "ample justification" for retaliation. The chiefs of staff had since the outbreak of war approved the idea that if urgent military necessity made bombing imperative, it should not be limited by humanitarian considerations. On May 13 the cabinet considered again whether the crisis in the Battle of France was severe enough to justify bombing. Though there were arguments against running the risk of German retaliation, approval was given for a bombing attack against oil and rail targets in Germany on the night of May 14–15. On May 15 the cabinet finally took the decision to approve a full bombing strategy against German targets where civilians might be casualties, as long as they were "suitable *military* objectives."[26] The driving force behind the decision was the deputy prime minister, Clement Attlee, who had been absent from the earlier cabinet discussions but who strongly favored raids on Germany, and continued to do so throughout the war. Churchill was anxious about the effect on American opinion if Britain began the bombing war, but the dire state of the ground campaign turned the tide. It was hoped that German bombers would be forced to strike back at Britain, while German fighters would be withdrawn from the land battle to defend Germany, though neither eventuality materialized. On the night of May 15–16, Bomber Command launched its first large-scale raid, with ninety-nine medium bombers on targets scattered across the Ruhr. To prevent further heavy losses of bombers in the land campaign in France, the air staff decided on May 19 to use the medium bombers only for attacks on Germany; on May 30, as the front in France collapsed, Bomber Command was ordered to stop using any bombers for direct support of the land battle and to concentrate on German industry, an admission of just how disastrously the British light bombers had performed in battlefront conditions against an air force that had advanced air technology and a sound doctrine for aircraft use.[27]

The change in priorities necessitated a revision of the rules on the

conduct of air warfare laid down in August 1939, which had made it illegal to attack targets in which civilians might be "negligently" killed.
On June 4, 1940, the Air Ministry issued new guidelines for Bomber
Command, canceling the earlier instructions. The intentional killing of
civilians was still regarded as a violation of international law, but attacks
could be made on military targets "in the widest sense" (factories, shipyards, communications, power supply, oil installations), in which civilian casualties would be unavoidable but should be proportional.[28]
"Undue loss of civil life" was still to be avoided, which meant returning
to base or jettisoning bombs safely if the target could not be properly
identified.[29] Nevertheless, the ethical restraints imposed at the start of
the war were eroded step by step as a result of the decision to initiate
"unrestricted" bombing of targets in urban areas. In July, Bomber Command war orders were modified to allow pilots discretion in choosing
any military or military-economic target (defined increasingly broadly)
if the primary target was obscured or difficult to find, a policy almost
certain at night to involve extensive damage to civilian life since, as Portal reminded the Air Ministry, a high percentage of bombs "inevitably
miss the actual target."[30] The final restraints were lifted in September
and October 1940 after the heavy German attacks on London, which
began on September 7 and continued almost without interruption for
three months. The onset of the German "Blitz" is often regarded as the
trigger for British attacks on German urban areas, but there had already
been growing pressure from Bomber Command to be allowed to bomb
less discriminately.[31] In September the policy of bringing back unused
bombs was suspended in favor of bombing anything that could be found
worth bombing, though not merely at random. On October 30, Bomber
Command was directed to focus on enemy morale by causing "heavy
material destruction in large towns" to teach the German population
what bombing could do.[32] In setting aside the political and legal limitations that had operated during the Phoney War, this decision brought to
an end the first stage, and it paved the way for the escalation of the RAF
campaign during 1941 and 1942 into full-scale city bombing.

The onset of the RAF bombing campaign in the summer of 1940
can certainly be explained by the change in government and the

military necessity imposed by the German breakthrough and triumph in the west, but neither argument is entirely convincing. Unrestricted (though not yet unlimited) air warfare against Germany owed its genesis partly to the intense pressure applied by the RAF from the start of the war to be allowed to commence bombing operations over Germany regardless of the possible human cost. Military expediency also played a part, for RAF leaders had a force whose chief purpose was long-distance bombing; used in any other way, the strike force would no longer give the RAF the chance to demonstrate what strategic bombing could achieve. Bombing policy was predicated on offensive action and nourished by the idea, widespread among RAF leaders, that total war, if it came, would see the erosion of any distinction between the fighting man and the civilian war worker.[33] In the first few months of the war senior airmen argued repeatedly for attacks on the Ruhr as Germany's Achilles' heel. It was always recognized, by politicians as well as airmen, that such attacks would involve heavy civilian losses, as a War Cabinet paper in October 1939 made clear:

> Germany's weakest spot is the Rhur [sic], the heart of which is about the size of Greater London, and in which is concentrated approximately 60% of Germany's vital industry. It contains, moreover, a population which might be expected to crack under intensive air attack. Such attacks would involve a heavy casualty roll among civilians, including women and children.[34]

A planning document in October 1939 claimed that Bomber Command could, if allowed, bring industry in the Ruhr *"practically to a standstill"*; about a month later the Air Ministry produced a precise schedule of sorties needed to "K.O. the Ruhr" in a matter of weeks.[35] By the spring of 1940 there was a chorus of demands to allow the Ruhr plan to be put into action. Early in May, Viscount Trenchard, the doyen of the bombing lobby, expressed his regret to Portal that bombing had not yet been attempted "when I and others think it would probably have ended the war by now." Portal himself, two days before the start of the German invasion, pressured Newall, the chief of the air staff, to reserve Bomber

Command for attacks on German industry rather than fritter it away in direct support for the army.[36] All such views were represented by Newall to the chiefs of staff and the War Cabinet. The decision in May was clearly influenced by the widespread but unverifiable assertion that bombing would achieve something worthwhile.

The bombing lobby rested its case on a number of evident exaggerations. Both the accuracy and power of British bombing and its capacity to inflict decisive material and psychological damage on Germany were presented in terms quite incompatible with the reality of Bomber Command's strength, range, and capability. The detailed study on the Ruhr bombing suggested that somewhere between 1,000 and 4,000 sorties were all that were required to knock it out. Calculations suggested that eight bomb hits would eradicate a power plant, sixty-four hits destroy a coking plant, and twelve hits destroy an aqueduct; average bombing error was given as seventy-five yards (sixty-nine meters) from low level and 300 yards (276 meters) from high altitude, figures that had never been verified under combat conditions (and proved entirely unattainable in practice).[37] It would take Germany months, so it was claimed, to recover from such an assault. There was no sense in this, as in other planning documents, of the exceptional operational and technical difficulties that would be encountered in carrying out such a program.

The effect that these operations would have had on the German war economy and German morale, even if they could have been executed, was subject to similar distortion. In the late 1930s intelligence assessments of German economic capacity for war almost all emphasized the fragility of an industrial economy regarded as taut and overburdened. Planners in the Air Ministry assumed that they faced an enemy whose strength was a façade, "politically rotten, weak in financial and economic resources," and that the results of bombing were likely to be "decisive" for the outcome of the war.[38] This remained the prevailing view for much of the war despite all evidence to the contrary. It also colored the first overoptimistic reports of the impact of RAF raids in summer 1940 once the gloves were off. A Foreign Office intelligence report compiled from neutral eyewitnesses on May 30 suggested "terrible effects" in the Ruhr and a serious crisis of morale spreading through the German home front; a second report sent on to Churchill in early June by the foreign secretary, Lord Halifax, talked of the profound depression in Germany caused by the "violence and efficacity" of British bombing.[39] An Air Intelligence evaluation suggested "general dislocation of rail traffic" throughout Germany. The RAF planning staff considered that the first three weeks of bombing had produced "valuable results," apparently justifying the decision to start it in the first place.[40]

There was also the moral dimension. To abandon the principle that killing civilians from the air was wrong owed a good deal to the British perception of the German enemy. The legal issue involved was sidestepped by two arguments: first, that the Germans had begun unrestricted bombing and would do it again, given the chance; second, that Hitler's Reich represented such a profound menace to Western civilization that the greater moral imperative was to use every means available to destroy it. The view that the Germans were responsible for bombing civilians first had a long pedigree, stretching back to the Zeppelin and Gotha raids of the First World War, which many RAF commanders had experienced as young officers just over twenty years before. During the 1930s, popular prejudices revived about German science and the German military conniving to produce lethal weapons of mass destruction to be unleashed from the air on an unsuspecting opponent.[41] The bombing of the Basque town of Guernica in April 1937 by the German Condor Legion was popularly regarded in the West as evidence that the Germans had once again abandoned any pretense of civilized behavior. The campaign in Poland was scrutinized for evidence that German bombers were deployed for terrorizing and murdering civilians. Although the evidence was ambiguous, since it was understood that the German raids were directed at military targets as part of a combined-arms ground campaign, the RAF preferred to assume that the Germans had bombed indiscriminately. A report published by the RAF Tactical Committee in October 1939 of a speech made by a German air staff officer on the Polish campaign claimed that on the Germans' own admission their operations went beyond the terms of the Hague Rules.[42] That same month Newall told the commander of the Advanced Air Striking Force in France that because of German action in Poland, "we are no longer bound by restrictions under the instructions governing naval and air bombardment. . . . Our action is now governed entirely by expediency."[43] Churchill himself later came to cite the German bombing of Warsaw and Rotterdam as moral justification for what was to be done to the German civilian population.

The assumption in all the discussions about restricting bombing was that it had force only so long as the enemy observed the same limitation, and in this sense Poland played an important part in paving the way for British action. Of course, German bombers had not yet bombed British cities, so the argument for attacking Germany came to be based on preemptive retaliation. Even before the war the RAF had taken for granted that the German Air Force would be bound by no scruples and would be "ruthless and indiscriminate" when the time came for a knockout blow.[44] When a German raid on the Royal Navy base at Scapa Flow in March 1940 killed a nearby cottager (the first civilian casualty of the war), Churchill angrily berated the Air Ministry for not giving it maximum publicity as the likely start of "deliberate horror raids on civilians," for which the Germans would carry the blame.[45] In April the propaganda department of the new Ministry of Economic Warfare recommended describing German reconnaissance missions as frustrated bombing raids—"driven off before they were able to drop their bombs"—so as to justify any British retaliation.[46] In May 1940 one of the arguments for bombing Germany was that sooner or later German leaders would do the same when it suited their strategic interests. "Do [the government] think," wrote one bombing lobbyist, Marshal of the RAF Sir John Salmond, "that Hitler, who does not consider for a moment the slaughter of thousands on the ground and of devastating countries with which he has no quarrel, will shrink from killing civilians in this country?"[47] In the cabinet discussion on May 15, Sir Hugh Dowding, commander in chief of Fighter Command, argued in favor of anticipatory attacks because he felt convinced that sooner or later the German Air Force would start indiscriminate bombing.[48] Yet very soon the argument that Germany started the bombing became the standard version, both among the wider public and in the RAF, and it has remained firmly rooted in the British public mind ever since.

The view that German crimes, or potential crimes, made British bombing legitimate was legally dubious, since it amounted to claiming that two wrongs make a right, but it was morally rooted in the belief that German bombing was just one manifestation of the profound threat that Hitler and the National Socialist movement represented to the survival of the West. The terms of the contest in 1940 were easily presented as a struggle of light against dark, civilization against barbarism, to a public anxious not to see the war as a repeat of the pointless slaughter of 1914–18. The claim to the moral high ground gave an ethical purpose to British strategy that could be used to justify an air policy that in the 1930s would have been widely regarded as a moral lapse, like the Italian bombing of Ethiopians or the Japanese bombing in China. Churchill was among the foremost champions of the idea that every effort should be made to root out the source of Europe's political poison. "The whole world is against Hitler and Hitlerism," he announced in a radio broadcast in November 1939. "Men of every race and clime feel that this monstrous apparition stands between them and the forward movement that is their due, and for which the age is ripe."[49] And although Churchill sometimes made the distinction between "Nazis" and "Germans," he commonly used the pejorative "Huns" to describe the enemy, a term deliberately chosen in the First World War to contrast German barbarity with Western civility.

There was also widespread popular support for the argument that Hitler's Germany was so wicked that any methods, even if they were morally questionable, should be used to destroy it. This was true across the political spectrum, even among those who had campaigned for peace in the 1930s. In an article on "Nazism and Civilisation," Sir Charles Trevelyan, who had once advocated mass resistance to war, defined the war as a necessary crusade against a barbarous system that had discarded "all moral, international and public law" and had bombed women and children.[50] Philip Noel-Baker, director of the International Peace Campaign in the late 1930s, observed that the bombing of Germany, of which he approved, was almost civilized "compared to the concentration camp and to the Himmler terror." In a newspaper article just after the onset of the Blitz he pointed out that Hitler had smashed "every last remnant of the Laws of War" and that British hands were now free to take any measures to "bring his monstrous aggression to an end."[51] A leading member of the Women's League for Peace and Freedom, which had publicly condemned bombing in the 1930s, abandoned her pacifism in 1940 on the grounds that "Nazism is a menace of evil corruption and lying and of all the forces of evil," which could only be eradicated by the use of force. When pacifist clergy lobbied the archbishops of Canterbury and York in 1940 to condemn the British use of bombing, they received the following reply: "The moral issue involved in the victory of the allies is of greater importance than the harsh fact of fighting by methods that one deplores."[52] Many prominent churchmen, politicians, and intellectuals who might have condemned bombing under different circumstances supported it as a necessary evil. For people who were already predisposed to see the German threat in crude moral terms, it was a relatively simple step to the argument that the greater moral obligation was to secure the continued freedom of the West than to abstain from killing German civilians.

The British government and the RAF leadership were nevertheless aware that it was necessary to present the bombing as distinct from German practice to avoid the accusation that the British were no less barbarous than the Germans. In late April 1940 the minister for air, Sir Samuel Hoare, stated in a radio broadcast that the British would never imitate the enemy's "dastardly conduct": "We will not bomb open towns. We will not attempt to defeat the Germans by terrorizing their women and children."[53] When the decision was finally taken on May 15 to start bombing, Churchill advised the Ministry of Information to publish a discreet press release on German killing of civilians from the air in France and the Low Countries, but to say nothing about British retaliation.[54] Pilots were at first instructed to ensure they could identify and hit specific targets before bombing them. Emphasis was put in every subsequent discussion on RAF bombing that it was directed only at military targets, even though the term was stretched almost to meaninglessness by the long list of economic and social objectives eventually classified as military, and the decision in October 1940 to permit the targeting of morale through attacks on city areas.[55] Throughout the war the public presentation of the bombing offensive in Parliament and in the press never deviated from the claim that the RAF bombed only military targets, unlike the enemy. When attacks against "industrial populations" were included in a draft directive in August 1942, the Air Ministry insisted that the term be altered to "industrial centres" to avoid the impression that civilians were deliberate targets, "which is contrary to the principles of international law—such as they are."[56] When Air Marshal Harris tried to persuade the Air Ministry in the autumn of 1943 to be more honest in its publicity about bombing by showing that killing civilian workers was a stated aim of the bombing campaign, the ministry refused to change. "It is desirable," ran the reply, "to present the bomber offensive in such a light as to provoke the minimum of public controversy."[57] Discretion was always observed in describing British bombing as directed at military targets, even to the crews who could see the real results of the later raids that obliterated whole cities.

Much of the argument about whether to bomb or what to bomb was rendered void by the reality of Bomber Command's offensive across the summer months of 1940. The optimistic intelligence reports were belied by the evidence of just how little Bomber Command could do with limited numbers and a small bomblift. Taking the gloves off revealed not a clenched fist but a limp hand. In late May priority was given to oil (Western Air Plan W.A.6) and communications targets, since their destruction was expected to affect the campaign in France directly. After the French defeat the priority given to oil remained in place, but a new directive on June 20 added the German aircraft industry to the list and proposed the firebombing of forests to induce a food crisis in Germany. It was argued, implausibly, that game driven from the forests by fire would be forced to eat the crops on the surrounding farmland. On July 30, Bomber Command was also directed to hit electric power stations where they could be located easily by night, while over the whole summer raids had to be carried out on targets in the ports from which an invasion might be launched.[58] Between June and August the modest bomb load of 2,806 tons was divided between these eight different objectives, spread across northern France, the Low Countries, and northern Germany, a little under one-quarter of the tonnage directed at enemy airfields.[59] The constant shifts in priority prevented the command from focusing on any one target system. Most operations had to be conducted in unfavorable conditions when the primary target was obscured by haze or cloud or shrouded by the blackout. Irregular, small-scale, dispersed, and difficult to assess, the early raids had the sole merit of forcing large numbers of Germans in northwestern Germany to seek shelter during the summer nights until ways were devised by German civil defense to minimize the time lost because of the alarms.

The large number of German targets and sudden shifts in allocation required a tactical approach that reduced even further any prospect of serious damage. In most cases only twenty to thirty aircraft were dispatched to each location, and only a fraction allocated to each specific target on the assumption that a handful of bombs dropped by five or six aircraft would be enough to do effective damage. Out of eighty-nine attacks made on Hamburg in 1940, fifty-eight were made with fewer than ten aircraft.[60] Most bombs carried were high explosive; incendiaries were spread in small quantities throughout the attacking force, which eliminated any prospect of a concentrated fire-raising operation. The number of bombers available for sorties declined over the summer months after the losses sustained in the Battle of France and because of the need to divert bomber aircraft to training units. The total number of sorties carried out between June and August was 8,681, but over 1,000 were against targets in France and the Low Countries, and around two-fifths were light bomber sorties. The tonnage of bombs dropped was just 0.9 percent of the tonnage dropped by Bomber Command in the same months in 1944.[61]

It soon became clear that the bombs were dropped with no particular accuracy. In the absence of electronic navigation or an effective bombsight, Portal's claim that bombing would be inherently inaccurate proved entirely justified. A photographic survey of bombing raids on the German aircraft industry in July 1940 found that out of ten attacks only a couple of hangars had been destroyed; out of thirty-one oil installations bombed, only one appeared damaged.[62] An American eyewitness account of an RAF attempt to bomb a Daimler-Benz factory in Stuttgart highlighted the exceptional efforts bomber pilots made to identify their target, circling the city for half an hour, but reported that not a single one of the bombs they subsequently dropped hit the plant.[63] One Bomber Command pilot later wrote that precise objectives in summer 1940 "were pointless" when crews could not even find the city they were supposed to target.[64] Most RAF bombs fell in the German countryside, but even those deliberately dropped on forests between June and August 1940, following repeated pressure from Churchill to try to burn down German woodlands, failed to ignite a fire. Experiments with setting fire to woods or crops continued for more than a year, until it was finally conceded that even under ideal climatic conditions most incendiaries burnt only the few inches around where they landed.[65]

Little of this problem was due to German defenses. As the British were themselves to find when they tried to combat German night bombing in the opening weeks of the Blitz, little preparation had been made by the German Air Force for defense against nighttime operations. German antiaircraft fire could force enemy aircraft to fly higher at night, but could only hit them mainly by chance, and this despite a formidable array of antiaircraft weapons. By June 1940 there were 3,095 heavy guns, 9,815 light guns, and 4,035 searchlights organized into defensive zones around the vulnerable industrial areas. Guns were moved back from the frontier areas following the defeat of France, strengthening the home defense even more. Yet between January and June 1940 only two aircraft were claimed from antiaircraft fire, and in August and September not a single one. The principal effect was to force the attacking bombers to break formation, exacerbating the existing dispersion of the British effort.[66] Most of Bomber Command's problems were self-inflicted. A postwar presentation of the early bombing effort by an official of the British Bombing Survey Unit in 1946 concluded that the forces were too small, the weapons incapable of a high degree of damage, targets could not be found, and too much effort was devoted to subsidiary operations: "great call on Air Force," ran the lecture notes, "to attack and destroy targets beyond its power."[67]

Under these circumstances it is perhaps surprising that the offensive was continued at all. Its survival owed much to the confidence of Bomber Command's new commander in chief, Charles Portal, that bombing would eventually deliver strategic dividends. Portal was a successful career airman who began flying in the First World War and was among the first to drop bombs on German soil. He played a key part in building up RAF strength in the late 1930s as director of organization. He was in charge of training when he was called to command the bombing war in April 1940. He was widely respected—"honest and unprejudiced," according to one former colleague, "not much small talk," according to another—and liked by Americans for his straightforward character and shrewd intelligence. A shy man who lunched alone day after day at the same London club, the private man was sealed off from his staff. He was convinced that bombing was a more effective way to wage modern war and remained a staunch defender of the bombing force when he was appointed chief of the air staff in October 1940.[68] He argued steadily through the summer months that Bomber Command should be allowed to do what it had been prepared for despite all the operational difficulties, and he shielded the force from criticism through the years that followed.

The second factor was the unstinting support of Churchill, whose interest in bombing waxed through the months after the fall of France. He asked to be informed about the operational performance of Bomber Command and intervened in every aspect of its activities, from the supply of bombers and bombs to the plan to burn down forests. His enthusiasm for bombing was a creature of the emergency facing Britain during the summer and autumn of 1940 when British forces had to demonstrate to the United States and to the peoples of occupied Europe that they still had some capacity for offensive action, however limited. It was also necessary to impress the British public that military action against Germany had not been abandoned after the evacuation from Dunkirk in late May and early June.[69] On July 8, Churchill wrote to the minister of aircraft production, Lord Beaverbrook, summing up his view of how bombing could help decisively in the overthrow of Hitler: "But there is one thing that will bring him back and bring him down, and that is an absolutely devastating, exterminating attack by very heavy bombers from this country upon the Nazi homeland."[70] The choice of words was unfortunate, and Churchill's comment has contributed to the recent debate about whether the bombing campaign from the outset had a genocidal purpose.[71] This is almost certainly not what Churchill had in mind, since he wrote the letter months before the onset of the Blitz (which *did* prompt in him a rhetorical language of violent retribution). He was also content to reproduce the letter in his later history of the war, when he had had time to reflect on what to leave out, and indeed deliberately omitted much of the story of British bombing and his part in it.[72] But it did express Churchill's desperate hope that bombing Germany was perhaps, as RAF leaders had repeatedly asserted, one possible means to compel Hitler to abandon invasion plans, or even to dislocate the German war effort decisively. Harris kept a copy of the Beaverbrook letter with him after the war. "That was the RAF mandate," he told the biographer Andrew Boyle in 1979, shortly before his death.[73]

From the point of view of British strategy, approval of bombing was a decision that came at a high price. Bomber Command achieved negligible results against German targets and invited German retaliation. In early September, Hitler finally responded to British attacks by permitting a campaign against London and other cities that dwarfed anything that could be done in return. Between September 1940 and June 1941 more than 57,000 tons of high-explosive and incendiary bombs were dropped, principally on British port cities, which absorbed 85 percent of the tonnage. Around 43,000 people were killed in the ten-month campaign, more than ten times as many as were killed by RAF raids on Germany in the same period. It is possible that the Blitz would have been launched anyway, as British air leaders had expected, but it is also possible that without a British bombing campaign over the summer of 1940, British cities might have been spared the full horrors of the winter of 1940–41.

German Lessons, 1940–41

The onset of heavy German night bombing in September 1940 showed Bomber Command at last what a serious bombing offensive looked like. Attacks were made with hundreds of bomber aircraft concentrated

against a single target, while diversionary or nuisance raids were made
to confuse the defenses and create widespread disruption. Heavy use of
incendiaries contrasted with the British preference for high-explosive
bombs, and produced widespread area damage. At first the RAF
thought the German campaign was flawed, because it assumed the attacks were designed to terrorize the population. "Notes on the Lessons
to Be Learned from German Mistakes," a survey produced two weeks
after the first heavy raid on London, concluded that "the indiscriminate
attack of cities is invariably uneconomical," a view with which German
air commanders would have concurred.[74] But it soon became clear that
the pattern was to attack ports, food supplies, and the aircraft industry,
and the evident ability of German bombers to attack at will and achieve
a relatively high concentration of hits turned the RAF toward the idea of
learning lessons from what the Germans got right. After nine months
the Air Ministry arrived at the view that regular "Blitz" attacks on German city areas demonstrated the most profitable use to which Bomber
Command could be put.[75] The shift in 1941 and 1942 to a policy of
"area" bombing came about not as a result of the poor accuracy achieved
in attacks on specific objectives, as is usually suggested, but by copying
the Germans.

    The German offensive was from this point of view a valuable learn-
ing tool, since it was difficult to evaluate clearly what Bomber Command was itself achieving over Germany. From June 1940 onward,
Britain was cut off from Europe by German military successes. Until the
autumn the RAF relied on hearsay and occasional news reports to form
a picture of the effects of British bombing. The sustained German attacks could now be used to assess with greater scientific, technical, and
statistical precision exactly what an air raid might achieve. The program of evaluation began almost immediately. In late September 1940
the Research and Experiments Department of the Ministry of Home
Security supplied a detailed study of the effects of German bombs on
different types of targets—oil storage, gasworks, power stations, aircraft
factories, and so on—and arrived at a conclusion that was to have far-
reaching consequences for the development of Bomber Command's offensive. "It is axiomatic," ran the report, "that fire will always be the

optimum agent for the complete destruction of buildings, factories etc."
The department recommended using high-explosive bombs to create
the "essential draught conditions" in damaged buildings, followed by
heavy incendiary loads, and completed with more high explosive to
hamper the enemy emergency services.[76] The evidence that concentrated use of incendiaries was the most effective form of air assault
against large industrial centers gradually emerged as the key lesson to be
learned from the experience of the Blitz. It was the seed from which area
bombing slowly germinated during the year that followed.

The work of the Research and Experiments Department made an
essential contribution to understanding what bombing could achieve.
The department was set up in spring 1939 to help the Home Office evaluate the effects of bombing and was run by the former director of the
Building Research Station, Dr. Reginald Stradling. He co-opted scientists and statisticians onto the staff, including the zoologist Solly Zuckerman and the physicist (and former pacifist) J. D. Bernal. In November
1941, Bernal established division RE8 to supply the Air Ministry directly with calculations on the effects of German bombs on British cities,
the productive loss caused by bombing, and the likely impact of British
bombing on German cities.[77] This work was supplemented by the Air
Warfare Analysis Section, which looked at the weight and type of bombs
to be dropped, and by the work of the Road Research Laboratory and
Building Research Laboratory, both of which helped to estimate the nature of bomb damage and the vulnerability of German building structures.[78] Bombing research was in its infancy during the Blitz, but it
benefited from the experience gained in the 1930s in recruiting senior
scientists to work on particular aspects of air warfare.[79] Although the
relationship between scientists and airmen was never formalized, the
Air Ministry knew that it needed scientific input not only to provide effective technology (particularly radar and navigation aids) but also to
make better sense of operations. Research questions were usually framed
by the air staff and the subsequent expert reports circulated to those who
needed them; sometimes it was the experts who took the initiative. This
was particularly the case with the German-born Oxford physicist Frederick Lindemann (later Lord Cherwell), who was recruited by Churchill

in 1939 to form a small Statistical Section in the Admiralty, and then followed Churchill to Downing Street in 1940. Lindemann took a special interest in bombing and was perhaps more responsible than anyone in keeping Churchill abreast of the many problems faced by Bomber Command in its early years.[80] His Statistical Section began at once in September 1940 to produce accurate figures on the damage inflicted by German bombs and to relate those figures to the density of urban population in different city zones. These figures were then applied to German cities to try to determine the areas where the highest damage could be done in terms of lives lost and houses destroyed.[81] Why Lindemann was so committed to the idea of destroying the country of his birth has never been clear, but he played an important part in deriving conclusions about German bombing and projecting them onto potential German targets.

Of all the lessons drawn from what was thought to be German practice, the possibility of urban destruction was the most important. It was gradually understood that the German intention was to undermine British morale by inflicting concentrated attacks on ports and industrial cities, reducing the will to work by the destruction of services, amenities, and housing, and reducing food supplies. Planners at the Air Ministry described German bombing as the direct opposite of British practice: instead of attempting to hit precise targets, the German Air Force carried out attacks on particular industrial or commercial areas where multiple targets were clustered; German raids were concentrated but too inaccurate for any purpose, it was argued, other than "the 'blitzkrieg' of fairly extensive regions."[82] Studies of British cities also confirmed that the critical level of damage was inflicted by incendiary bombs dropped in large numbers. Particular attention was paid to the German bombing of London, Coventry, and Liverpool, but special studies were commissioned of the bombing of Hull and Birmingham with a view to understanding how fire combined with high explosive affected areas of different housing and population density. Damage was heaviest in the congested working-class districts, which suggested that these were optimum targets. A draft directive from the Directorate of Bomber Operations in the Air Ministry in June 1941 drew heavily from this research on the Blitz: "The output of the German heavy industry depends almost exclusively on the workers. Continuous and relentless bombing of these workers and their utility services, over a period of time, will inevitably lower their morale, kill a number of them, and thus appreciably reduce their industrial output."[83]

These arguments signaled an important change in the way "morale" was interpreted. The politicians, Churchill included, generally understood morale in political terms: heavy pressure from bombing would induce a social and political collapse, perhaps even a revolution. The German attacks on morale were more clearly economic in intent. In May 1941 the Ministry of Economic Warfare, which had been monitoring the ineffective impact of Bomber Command on precise economic objectives in Germany, sent a memorandum recommending that the RAF abandon military targets and focus instead on economic warfare against major industrial concentrations or "whole cities." The idea stemmed from the effects of German bombing on the British workforce: "British experience leads us to believe that loss of output . . . through absenteeism and other dislocation consequent upon the destruction of workers' dwellings and shopping centres is likely to be as great as, if not greater than the production loss which we can expect to inflict by heavy damage."[84] Although the hope for a political dividend from bombing was not abandoned entirely, particularly by Churchill, the Air Ministry came to view morale as a barometer of productive performance rather than political outlook. The same term was used to cover both, but by the time morale became a specified objective in July 1941, it was used as a description of economic attrition—a form of "industrial blockade"—in which the working-class population was attacked as an abstract factor of production whose deaths, disablement, or absence would have economic consequences.[85]

By the spring of 1941, the arguments in favor of imitating what was thought to be German practice had come to be widely broadcast and from a variety of different sources. The debt owed to German bombing was evident in the choice of the term "Blitz" to describe the nature of the new strategy. In April 1941 a review of bombing policy recommended "carefully planned, concentrated and continuous 'BLITZ' attacks delivered on the centre of the working-class area of the German cities and towns." Notes produced in the Directorate of Bomber Operations in the Air Ministry a month later on the use of the bomber force also stressed "continuous blitz attacks on the densely populated workers [*sic*] and industrial areas."[86] Later in 1941, when calculations were made of the ratio between weight of bombs and expected deaths among German workers, the measurements were given as "1 Coventry," "2 Coventries," and so on; an attack on the scale of "4 Coventries" was expected to yield 22,515 German deaths.[87] It is important to recognize that the emphasis on killing German workers and destroying their milieu was deliberate, not an unintended consequence of bombing factories. In November 1940 a memorandum on bombing policy, almost certainly penned by Harris, asked whether the time had not come to strike in full force "against the people themselves." In May 1941 the director of Air Intelligence welcomed an attack on "the livelihood, the homes, the cooking, heating, lighting and family life of that section of the population which, in any country, is least mobile and most vulnerable to a general air attack—the working class." The chiefs of staff in June finally endorsed morale attacks that induced "fear of death and mutilation."[88] The idea of collateral damage had been turned on its head: instead of the death of workers and the destruction of their housing being a side effect of hitting factories, damage to factories was a collateral effect of destroying working-class neighborhoods.

However, deliberate attacks on densely populated areas aimed at killing workers and disrupting civilian life once again raised awkward moral questions. A further memorandum drafted in May 1941 by the director of bomber operations pointed out that since October 1940, Churchill had freed Bomber Command from having to bomb with discrimination, so that "attacking the workers" was now permissible. "We do not mean by this," he continued, "that we shall ever profess the German doctrine that terrorism constitutes an effective weapon of war." Nevertheless, he recommended that no announcement of the policy should be made, and the details of plans for attacking the population should have very limited circulation; in the wrong hands, "all sort of false and misleading deductions might be made."[89] In late November

1941, Sir Richard Peirse, the then commander in chief of Bomber Command, addressing a sympathetic audience of the Thirty Club, explained that for almost a year his force had been attacking "the people themselves" intentionally. "I mention this," he continued, "because, for a long time, the Government for excellent reasons has preferred the world to think that we still held some scruples and attacked only what the humanitarians are pleased to call Military Targets. . . . I can assure you, Gentlemen, that we tolerate no scruples."[90]

There were also lessons to learn about how a Blitz attack should be carried out. An air staff memorandum on area attack pointed out how unwise it would be "if we fail to pick the brains of an enemy who has had so much experience in developing the required technique."[91] The method consisted of a high concentration of incendiary bombs dropped in a short period of time with the use of a target-marking force to indicate the urban area to be devastated. The proportion of incendiaries carried by German bombers was known to vary between 30 and 60 percent, concentrated in the first attack groups, while RAF bombers carried between 15 and 30 percent, diluted throughout the force. The critical problem was how to drop enough incendiaries to create fires that ran out of control, which meant smothering an area with firebombs. The attack on the City of London on December 29, 1940, was used as the model. The raid started twenty-eight conflagrations, fifty-one serious fires, 101 medium fires, and 1,286 small ones, and it was this level of assault that could be expected to overwhelm the emergency services.[92] Detailed evidence from Britain's other blitzed cities suggested that incendiary bombs had five times the destructive potential of heavy explosive per ton. They were best used, it was suggested by Air Intelligence, against cities with narrow streets and wooden structures. Germany's old town centers were "ideal targets for large-scale incendiary attack" because German urban areas were denser and taller than their British equivalents. A salvo of 30,000 British four-pound incendiaries dropped in twenty minutes was regarded as a necessary minimum, though much larger quantities were found to be necessary later on. High explosive was needed to reduce the water supply and ventilate the buildings.[93] It was realized in the Air Ministry by the summer of 1941 that to maximize the effect of firebomb attack the equivalent of the German Kampfgruppe 100 was required, skilled in navigation so that it could carry out a fire-raising attack that the following bombers could use for their own navigation.[94] Portal used Kampfgruppe 100 as his example when he suggested in August 1941 to the government scientific adviser, Sir Henry Tizard, the need to move to a target-marking system as soon as possible.[95]

These lessons were learned in the end both slowly and piecemeal. The structure for decision making in the RAF and the Air Ministry made it difficult to change quickly, while there remained honest differences of opinion about the most effective use for bombers. Major changes in policy over bombing required the approval of the chiefs of staff and Churchill's Defence Committee. They had to be properly formulated and presented to the Air Council and the air staff in the ministry before they could be presented to higher authority. Much of the work on trying to understand German strategy and tactics was dispersed among different departments and usually written up in the first instance by junior staff. This situation improved when a Directorate of Bomber Operations was finally set up under Air Commodore John Baker in September 1940, at the prompting of the then deputy chief of the air staff, Air Marshal Harris. While strategy was decided at the highest level, the operational conduct of Bomber Command was left largely to the discretion of the commander in chief, who could modify or ignore instructions from the air staff with which he disagreed. Bombing policy was also subject to external civilian influence. The Ministry of Economic Warfare under the Labour minister Hugh Dalton and the ad hoc Lloyd Committee, set up in 1939 under Geoffrey Lloyd to deal specifically with the German oil situation, could make recommendations to the politicians that simply bypassed the RAF.[96] Air policy was not entirely haphazard, but it moved in the first years of war in fits and starts, trapped between exaggerated expectations and a beleaguered reality.

Portal's successor as commander in chief of Bomber Command in October 1940 was Sir Richard Peirse, a senior career airman, who had been vice chief of staff before his appointment. He was a supporter of precision bombing, though more of a realist about what could be achieved, and not in principle opposed to area bombing. He stuck to the directives that called for attacks on oil, communications, and the air-craft industry, but his force remained small and divided between numer-ous targets. The number of sorties per month fell steadily, exacerbated by the slow supply of bombers and crew and the deteriorating weather, which grounded bombers on both sides through much of December and January. In September 1940 there were 3,597 sorties, by November only 2,039, and in January 1941 only 1,131. Even by the summer of 1941 the figures were little better than they had been a year before, reaching a peak of 3,989 in July.[97] The RAF also experienced, like the German Air Force, a high rate of wastage, due chiefly to accidents. The Bomber Command groups had 290 serviceable bombers at the beginning of Oc-tober 1940, but only 212 at the end of November. Peirse told Portal that for every aircraft shot down by the enemy, he was losing six to accidents.[98] Part of the problem he attributed to the declining skill of bomber crews, too many of whom were rushed from the Operational Training Units (OTUs) to the frontline squadrons. The decision to accelerate promo-tion to allow sergeants to pilot aircraft produced evidence, so it was claimed, of "slackness and inefficiency." A report from 7 Group in Janu-ary 1941 highlighted poor discipline among recruits from the OTUs: "unpunctuality and absence without leave . . . some of them seem to think they can turn up when they like."[99] For many crewmen in the win-ter of 1940–41 the reality was to fly long, dangerous operations over German territory in poor weather, with inadequate equipment, return-ing to bomber stations that were still improvised and poorly lit, and in the knowledge that most of the target photographs they took were of somewhere other than the place to which they had been directed.

The poor performance of Bomber Command owed a good deal to the priorities that had been given to home defense during the summer and autumn of 1940. But since this was one of Britain's few offensive op-tions, its deficiencies were very public. In early November, Churchill complained to Portal that bomb tonnage on Germany was "lamentably small," given the amount of money and matériel devoted to it: "I wish I could persuade you to realize that there is a great failure of *quantitative delivery*." In December 1940 he returned again to attack the "stagnant con-dition" of the command and its "deplorable" operational performance.[100]

Peirse was sensitive to the accusations and continued to insist that his force would be a cardinal factor in reducing Germany's war economy and will to war by the spring of 1941, while paradoxically explaining that weather and poor training were likely to inhibit anything his force could do.[101] Churchill's frustration contributed to pushing Bomber Command slowly toward a strategy that favored city bombing. He tried unsuccessfully to insist that Bomber Command attack Berlin in October. He told Peirse that he hoped his command would soon be bombing "every 'Hun corner' every night."[102]

In late November 1940 the War Cabinet endorsed a decision to retaliate for the attack on Coventry on November 14–15, when 503 tons were dropped on aero-engine plants, destroying much of the city center at the same time and killing 554 people. It was decided that a German city should be bombed indiscriminately in retaliation, although Coventry was evidently a military-economic target, scattered though the bombing had been. Portal supplied a list of four cities—Hannover, Mannheim, Cologne, and Düsseldorf—and told Peirse to mobilize every aircraft he could, even from the training units. Bombing was to continue all night, replicating the German practice of heavy incendiary attack, followed by high explosive, and then further incendiaries. For an operation code-named Abigail Rachel, Peirse chose Mannheim as his target and attacked it on December 16–17 "based on the experience we have gained from Coventry, Bristol etc." But because of poor weather only 101 out of a planned 235 aircraft could be sent. Most claimed to have bombed the target, but in fact the advance group of Wellingtons failed to mark the center of the city, while other bombers scattered their loads widely over residential areas. There were thirty-four deaths and 476 houses were destroyed. When Peirse asked whether he could conduct a similar raid against Hannover, Churchill was noncommittal.[103]

The city attacks were not repeated, though not from any moral qualms. The Blitz had finally eroded any serious concern about the morality of bombing the civilians of a state whose air force had killed almost 30,000 British civilians in four months. They were held in abeyance by the striking news given to the cabinet in mid-December that the small effort against German oil targets had probably reduced German supplies by 15 percent. The figure was a gross distortion of reality, as photoreconnaissance intelligence of plants bombed in December made clear, but Portal snatched at the news as a chance to redeem Bomber Command at one of the many critical moments in its survival over the early war years. The air staff worked out that there were enough aircraft to knock out seventeen oil plants and that the attacks could be repeated every four months to ensure that they remained inoperable.[104] The chiefs of staff approved the policy on January 7, 1941, and the War Cabinet a week later, with the rider that in adverse conditions area attacks might be made instead. The decision to focus on a single target made little sense in the light of what had already been learned about the pattern of German bombing, and the failure of the plan was evident within weeks. At the end of February 1941, Peirse had to confess to Portal that he had only been able to attack oil targets on three nights in the whole of January and February; towns had been attacked six times, but most of Bomber Command's effort had in fact been devoted to German naval and port targets, which were easier to find and hit.[105] The oil plan was a peculiar fantasy given the current technical capability and evident inaccuracy of the bomber force. Its failure was masked by the sudden decision taken by Churchill in early March to focus the effort of Bomber Command entirely on the Battle of the Atlantic to try to break the blockade imposed by German sea and air attacks. Portal lacked Hermann Göring's political muscle and could not resist the diversion. Naval priorities prevailed, and for four months Bomber Command began a largely fruitless campaign against German submarine pens and warships.

By the time Bomber Command was permitted to return to priorities in Germany, the weight of opinion inside and outside the RAF had consolidated in favor of morale attacks on working-class urban areas. Early in June 1941 the Air Ministry produced a new discussion document rejecting oil as a primary target. What was proposed was a compromise between what remained of the principle of precision and the desire to replicate German area attacks. Using material supplied by the Ministry of Economic Warfare, a concerted attack on railway transport in the Ruhr-Rhineland area was proposed. Precise targets were to be located in city areas so that "'shorts and overs' [which constituted most British bombs] will kill." For most nights, however, it was proposed that the bomber force be used to attack the industrial workforce in the same Ruhr area.[106] Following German practice, it was also suggested that city targets on or near water would be more suitable to make sure that a sufficient proportion of the attacking force could find them. On July 9 the new proposals were issued as a directive to Bomber Command, after the phrase "the morals of the German people" had been altered to read "morale." A list of suitable railway targets was appended with the caveat that for 75 percent of any month bombers would not be able to see their targets clearly enough for precision; for three-quarters of each month Bomber Command was expected to undertake "heavy, concentrated and continuous attacks of working class and industrial areas."[107] There was no certainty how long this directive would remain in force. Peirse complained to Portal about the constant changes in priority: "I do not feel I am fully in touch with your ideas. I may be working with you or against you, I am not sure. But it is certainly difficult to work to any plan with this ever-changing background."[108] Peirse came to accept that winning the bombing war required "attack of the German people themselves," and this part of the directive remained in place, in one form or another, for the rest of the war.[109]

The one lesson that the RAF and the government failed to learn from the German experience was, paradoxically, the reality of relative failure. German bombing did not dislocate the economy seriously, nor did it undermine civilian commitment to the war effort, as the Air Ministry could clearly see. Calculations were made which showed that potential output in the British economy was reduced by no more than 5 percent; even in cities heavily bombed, economic activity was restored to previous levels in between three and eight days.[110] It was also difficult to argue that German "morale" would somehow crack if British morale had remained intact after nine months of remorseless assault. When the new directive was shown to the American chiefs of staff at the Argentia meeting between Churchill and Roosevelt in August 1941, they found it hard to reconcile the morale bombing of Germany with the "valorous experience" of the British people under German bombardment.[111] The

RAF could not ignore this paradox. It was resolved by suggesting that the Germans lacked the qualities of endurance and pluck displayed by the British under fire. The general prejudice among senior airmen was that the German people, as one intelligence report put it, "will not stand a quarter of the bombing" dished out to Britain, though there were few sensible grounds for believing it.[112] A report in July 1941, following a meeting in Lisbon with American diplomatic personnel from Germany, suggested that the average German worker was a fit target because he displayed a "lack of moral fibre."[113] An air staff memorandum produced in September 1941 accepted that in the British case bombing tended to stiffen rather than weaken morale, but went on to argue that the Germans had based their campaign on judging the poor morale of their own people. Made of sterner stuff, British morale had not given way, but, the report concluded, "the wheel has gone full cycle, and it has become increasingly clear that one of the most (if not *the* most) serious chinks in the German armour is the morale of the civil population."[114] The paper concluded with an unambiguous statement of the purpose that now lay behind the British bombing offensive:

> The ultimate aim of the attack of a town area is to break the morale of the population which occupies it. To achieve this we must achieve two things: first, we must make the town physically uninhabitable and, secondly, we must make the people conscious of constant personal danger. The immediate aim is, therefore, twofold, namely, to produce:
>
>   (i) Destruction, and (ii) The fear of death.

Here was a German lesson to be taught to the Germans.

Bomber Command in Crisis, 1941–42

By the time the July 1941 directive was issued, the war had suddenly changed its character. Heavy German bombing of British cities stopped in early June, and on June 22 as many as 4 million Axis soldiers poured across the Soviet border in the largest invasion in history. That same evening Churchill broadcast to the nation, pledging British support for the Soviet Union against "the bloodthirsty guttersnipe" who had now unleashed war against another suffering people. He announced that he had offered Stalin all technical and economic assistance, but the one military pledge he made was to promise "to bomb Germany by day as well as by night with ever-increasing measure" to give the German people a taste of their own medicine.[115] On July 7, Churchill sent a telegram to Stalin explaining that the best Britain could offer as direct military assistance was bombing; this, Churchill continued, would force Germany to divert fighters to the west, and ease the pressure on the Soviet front.[116] Churchill hoped privately that the new campaign would prompt Soviet bombers to attack Germany from the east: "A lot of German war industry should be vulnerable especially if we are bombing from the other side." Stalin replied that he would prefer Britain to open a second front in northern France or Scandinavia.[117]

Churchill exaggerated what Bomber Command was capable of achieving and misunderstood the nature of Soviet air strategy, which favored ground support over long-range bombing. But Bomber Command used the German-Soviet war as a way to improve its low political stock. On July 21, 1941, Churchill and Attlee were invited to view a demonstration by the heavy bombers that were scheduled to come into large-scale service over the coming year. The party watched as five heavy four-engine bombers flew past at low altitude: a Short Stirling, an Avro Lancaster, a Handley Page Halifax, and two American bombers promised to Britain under the Lend-Lease scheme authorized in March 1941, the Boeing B-17 Flying Fortress and the Consolidated B-24 Liberator. The party was impressed in particular by the Lancaster, but there were reservations in the RAF about the American bombers with their more limited bomb loads.[118] The political imperative of supporting the Soviet war effort suited Bomber Command in summer 1941 because it gave the command a prominence that its poor operational record scarcely warranted. Churchill needed bombing as something to trade with Stalin. Later in the war, Air Vice Marshal Richard Peck, in a speech surveying the course of British bombing, reminded his audience that in the summer of 1941 the air forces were given the task of supporting

Russia by bombing Germany: "Not everyone has appreciated," he continued, "the extent to which the bomber offensive was applied to aid the Russian armies."[119]

The political imperative masked the operational reality. On June 22, the night of the German invasion, seventy medium bombers raided the north German port of Bremen; it was covered in haze and the bombing was scattered. The following night sixty-two bombers raided Cologne, where a few bombs fell on the city but there were no reported casualties; forty-one bombers raided Düsseldorf with no clear result; twenty-six aircraft attacked Kiel with little effect and one death.[120] These were no larger than the attacks still being mounted by the exiguous German force left in northern France after the end of the Blitz—raids on Birmingham with 94 and 88 aircraft, on Hull with 78, 64, and 114, on London with 60—and considerably less destructive.[121] Most RAF attacks were still being made on targets on the French coast. On July 7, Churchill complained to Portal that he should stop bombing these Battle of the Atlantic targets and concentrate on "the devastation of the German cities" to take the weight off Russia. The war diary written up at Hitler's supreme headquarters failed even to mention any of the British raids.[122]

Summer 1941 was not the first time that bombing had been promoted for political reasons, but the fear that Germany might defeat the Soviet Union and turn back to Britain with all the resources of Eurasia at its disposal gave bombing an added urgency. It also made the operational inadequacy of Bomber Command more obtrusive. In early July, Churchill complained to Lindemann, Portal, and the air minister, Sir Archibald Sinclair, that the bomber force was little larger than it had been the year before, though it was supposed to be "indispensable for victory."[123] High losses and the slow buildup of bomber production had indeed reduced the plans for expansion. There was worse to come. In July 1941, Lindemann asked Bomber Command whether he might investigate bombing accuracy by analyzing photographs taken during operations. This was a project that had only become possible since the early summer. When the war broke out, the RAF had day cameras but none suitable for night photography. Trials were carried out with the standard F.24 camera using a shutter mechanism and a large flash unit released manually through the bomber's flare chute. When the flare was at maximum intensity, one of the bomber crew had to close the shutter. The result was a complex operation designed to be undertaken at the most dangerous point over the target. Research began on an automatic night camera, but it was not ready until 1942. The force had to make do in 1941 with a simplified camera with no shutter, which produced a poorer image but one regarded as adequate. In December 1940 there were still only thirteen cameras available; Peirse asked for five hundred so that most bombers could carry them. By March 1941 there were seventy-five, by September two hundred.[124] Taking an effective photograph was always difficult, with the ground obscured by smoke and the camera confused by flares, gunbursts, and searchlights. Pilots disliked the order to keep a level flight path while the picture was taken. Nevertheless, from June 1941 a growing stream of images became available for the first time, interpreted by a special unit set up at RAF Medmenham. Now that a fuller photographic record was possible, Portal willingly agreed to Lindemann's request, perhaps not fully aware of what the results might show.[125]

Lindemann instructed a young economist on his staff in the Statistical Section, David Bensusan-Butt, to examine 650 photographs taken from 100 raids between June 2 and July 25, 1941. The report was ready by August 18. The analysis showed that in general only one in five of all bomber aircraft sent on a mission reached within five miles of the assigned target; of those recorded as actually bombing, the proportion was one in four over Germany, one in ten over the Ruhr industrial area, and on moonless or hazy nights one in fifteen.[126] Churchill was alarmed by the revelations: "It is an awful thought," he wrote to Portal, "that perhaps three-quarters of our bombs go astray."[127] The RAF response was, not surprisingly, defensive. Portal pointed out that weather over Germany had been very poor in June and July; that the Butt Report covered only one-tenth of Bomber Command sorties; that inexperienced navigators probably took images too long after the release of the bombs (almost certainly the case, given the difficulty of operating the camera and seeing the bomb burst below); and, above all, that German raids tracked over Britain showed only 24 percent of German bombers reaching the target area. Even Lindemann admitted that conditions had not been ideal for photographic analysis in the summer months.[128] Portal was no doubt correct to argue that the Butt Report was subject to substantial methodological flaws, but the RAF's own operational evidence gathered since 1940 had consistently shown a very wide margin of error between what the crews reported and what had actually been bombed. Given Bomber Command's continued practice of sending raids to two or three cities on the same night, and in relatively small numbers, the aircraft likely to be hitting a particular aiming point in Germany on any one raid would be in single figures.

The Butt Report has generally been regarded as a turning point in the British bomber offensive, but its significance can easily be exaggerated. Peirse had asked the Air Ministry in December 1940 to speed up camera supply so that a proper survey of accuracy and bombing effort could be made.[129] Detailed examination of photographic evidence had already been carried out by Bomber Command in April 1941, and again in June, each time showing how overoptimistic were the reports of the crews and how wide the margin of error. Exaggerated reports were common to both sides in the bomber war, but the sober reality was well understood by the bomber crews. Robert Kee, a bomber pilot and future historian, later reflected on what his diary entries from late 1941 showed him:

It read pretty depressingly in terms of successful operations. . . . Here is an attempt to bomb Brunswick, hopelessly dark, bombed some incendiaries at what we hoped was Hanover. Düsseldorf also hopeless, bombed searchlight concentration. Kiel, this is three in succession. Kiel, hopeless again, very bad weather. . . . Mannheim, too much cloud, bombed searchlights.[130]

In October the Operational Research Section of Bomber Command, established at Peirse's request in September under the direction of Dr. Basil Dickens, reviewed accuracy for the three months following the Butt Report. It was found that the average performance was even worse than feared; only 15 percent of aircraft bombed within five miles of the target point.[131]

In truth, the Butt Report highlighted just one of the many problems facing the force in the late summer of 1941, important though it was. Losses began to increase substantially as the result of stronger German defenses, placing a heavier burden on a training program that turned out a growing number of crewmen with limited understanding of what was required of them. "The one failing of the whole training system," recalled a rear gunner, "was that we weren't told more of what to expect. We just learned it strictly from experience." Peirse told the Air Ministry that up to 40 percent of the operational squadrons' work consisted of essential additional training, which resulted in regular accidents. Most of the nonoperational flying was done during the day, which also prepared crews poorly for what to expect of nighttime conditions.[132] In August, Bomber Command lost 525 aircraft destroyed or severely damaged (a wastage rate of 13 percent, many lost to accidents), but received only 106 replacements. In the following three months a further 578 aircraft were written off, many again on nonoperational flights. Raids carried out on Berlin for political effect had losses of 30 percent.[133] Between July and December 1941 the force showed a steady decline in its capability (see table 1.1):

There are many explanations for the crisis now confronting Bomber Command. The new strategy of attacks on city areas was only possible with better equipment, and the directives failed to take sufficient account of what technology was currently available. The most pressing need was for larger aircraft capable of carrying a much greater tonnage, dropped with greater accuracy. This was an obvious solution, and the pressure to accelerate output and improve navigation came from all sides. Yet the heavy bombers that Churchill had been shown in July were still only available in very small numbers because of persistent problems with technical development, while improved navigation was still at the experimental stage despite more than eighteen months of war. The Stirling and the Halifax made their first sorties in February and March 1941. The Short Stirling Mk I was the only one of Britain's wartime bombers designed from the start to have four engines. It was first commissioned in 1936, the prototype made its first successful flight in December 1939, and the first aircraft came into service late in 1940. Powered by four Bristol Hercules engines, the Stirling had a top speed of 270 miles per hour and a range of 590 miles with a full bomb load of 14,000 pounds. It had a limited flying ceiling but good defensive capabilities with three powered turrets, yet it was plagued with technical problems that had to be ironed out in 1941 and early 1942. The same was true for the Handley Page Halifax, which also stemmed from a 1936 specification and was originally designed as a twin-engine medium/heavy bomber. In 1937 it was converted to four Rolls-Royce Merlin engines, and the prototype flew in October 1939. The Halifax Mk I was developed rapidly and was in service by November 1940. Its first operation, against the French port of Le Havre, was made in March 1941. It had a low operational ceiling of 18,000 feet, a top speed of 265 miles per hour, and a range of 1,260 miles with a maximum bomb load

Table 1.1: Bomber Command Statistics, July 1941–February 1942[134]

Month	Bomb Tonnage	Bomber Sorties	Aircraft/ Crews (average)	Aircraft Missing*
July 1941	4,384	3,989	449	152
August	4,242	3,988	486	156
September	2,889	3,021	485	95
October	2,984	2,715	517	86
November	1,907	1,765	507	83
December	1,794	1,582	530	47
January 1942	2,292	2,226	410	56
February	1,011	1,506	374	41

*Aircraft missing are missing on operations. The number damaged or lost to accidents was higher; figures include all heavy, medium, and light bomber operations.

Source: TNA, AIR 9/150, DBOps to DCAS, September 11, 1941; AIR 22/203, War Room Manual of Bomber Command Operations, 1939–1945, 20–21; AIR 41/41, RAF Narrative, "The RAF in the Bombing Offensive Against Germany: Vol. 3," App. C, E1.

of 13,000 pounds. The aircraft exhibited persistent development problems, had slow handling characteristics, and took high losses. Output
continued because it was difficult to disrupt production schedules already laid down, but it was an unpopular aircraft with bomber crews.[135]

The third heavy bomber, the Avro Lancaster, grew out of another
twin-engine development, the Manchester, also first specified in 1936.
The Manchester was designed around twin Rolls-Royce Vulture engines, but these proved to be a constant source of technical delays. The
prototype flew in July 1939, and the first service aircraft were delivered
in November 1940. The first raid was against the French port of Brest in
February 1941, but repeated engine failure led to the cancellation of further production and only 209 were built. In late 1940 a Manchester
Mk III was produced with four Rolls-Royce Merlin engines. It was renamed the Lancaster, and for Bomber Command it was an unexpected
godsend. The Lancaster had a much better performance: a top speed of
287 miles per hour, a ceiling of almost 25,000 feet, and a range of over
1,000 miles even with its heaviest load of 22,000 pounds. The usual load
was somewhere between 14,000 and 18,000 pounds and the range cor-
respondingly farther. Its carrying capacity was larger than that of any
other bomber used in the European theater, and four or five times that
of the standard German medium bombers. Some 6,750 Lancasters were
produced during the war, the mainstay of the later force. Unlike the
Halifax, the Lancaster had a more modest loss rate (3.92 percent compared with 5.75 percent), absorbed less production effort, carried an average of almost twice as much bomb weight, and was easier to service.[136]
But it only began operations in modest numbers in 1942. In 1941 the
small total of heavy bombers dropped only 4,000 tons, against the
31,500 tons dropped by the Wellington medium bombers.[137]

The advent of heavier aircraft would mean that the RAF could take
advantage of both a new generation of heavier bombs under development
and the rapid expansion of bomb production. The prospect of increasing
the aggregate payload was regarded as the critical factor in the offensive,
but it had to be postponed until the heavy bomber force became available. The 250- and 500-pound General Purpose bombs were still

extensively in use in 1941; larger 1,000-, 2,000-, and 4,000-pound bombs, more suitable for the larger bomber models, were developed during the Blitz and brought into use in small numbers. These Medium Capacity (MC) and High Capacity (HC) bombs had a higher charge-to-weight ratio, a thinner metal shell, and a much greater blast effect. However, they still lacked aluminized explosive, which would have increased that effect more than threefold; only later in the war was Lindemann finally able to persuade the RAF to adopt it. The 4-pound incendiary bomb remained standard equipment but was supplemented by the larger 30-pound fire-bomb with a blend of phosphorus, rubber, and benzol gel, 400,000 of which were ordered in June 1941 and 3 million used by the end of the war.[138] All these bombs became available in quantities too large for the existing bomber force to use. In April 1941, 12 million incendiaries were ordered for the rest of the year and 36 million for 1942; because of magnesium shortages, however, output was only 2.2 million in the nine months of 1941 and 11.8 million in 1942, but these figures were more than enough for a force not yet converted fully to mass incendiary bombing. By the end of 1941 there was a surplus of more than 2 million bombs, and monthly production was double monthly expenditure.[139] By the summer of 1941 around 11,000 tons of high-explosive bombs were being produced and filled every month, though Bomber Command had dropped an average of just 948 tons a month between January and April and averaged only 1,884 tons on Germany between July and December. In October 1941 there were unused stocks of 121,000 tons of bombs.[140] This was the reverse of the German problem during the Blitz, when there had been the airplanes but insufficient filled bombs; the RAF had the bombs but not enough heavy and medium bombers to use them.

Both the new aircraft and the new bombs were slow to join Bomber Command in any significant numbers. Only 41 heavy bombers were produced in 1940 and 498 in 1941, compared with an output of 4,703 medium bombers.[141] These were modest figures against the plans drawn up in the spring of 1941 to create a force of 4,000 heavy bombers by the spring of 1943. Bomber production had taken a backseat during the summer and autumn of 1940 when priority went to fighter aircraft for defense against German raids. The minister of aircraft production, Lord Beaverbrook, was later blamed by the Air Ministry for trying to kill off "the Big Bomber programme," but this ignored the serious technical problems encountered in trying to develop and get into service large and complex aircraft in a matter of months.[142] In May 1941, Portal informed Beaverbrook's successor, John Moore-Brabazon, that he did not want any further heavy bombers developed during the war because of the long lead time between designing a bomber and seeing it into service.[143] The "4,000 Plan" was always unrealistic. It called for production of at least 1,000 bombers a month over a two-year period, more than twice the number produced during 1941 and 1942. It was already evident by the summer of 1941 that bomber production had hit a serious bottle-neck. The RAF pinned its hopes on being able to persuade the United States to make up the shortfall.

The efforts to get America to solve Britain's bomber crisis went back to the early spring of 1941, when Lend-Lease was finally approved. The RAF delegation in Washington had the challenging task of persuading the American service chiefs to accept the transfer of substantial quantities of modern aircraft, and in particular heavy bombers, from their own rearmament program. Air Vice Marshal Slessor negotiated the aircraft requirements with the Army Air Corps, commanded by General Henry "Hap" (for "Happy") Arnold. The American offers were enshrined in what became known as the Slessor-Arnold Agreement, a generous commitment, subject to circumstances, to supply Britain on a 50–50 basis from all American aircraft production.[144] The agreement failed, however, to address the problem of the heavy bomber, where Britain's deficiency was most marked and American output still in its infancy. Arnold visited Britain in April 1941 and was told that the British aircraft industry could not produce more than 500 of the 1,000 heavy bombers needed each month. The United States was asked to fill the gap. Arnold agreed that up to four-fifths of American heavy bomber output could go to Bomber Command by the summer of 1942, but this would consist of fewer than 800 aircraft. By then it was evident that the American air force would renege on the original agreement as relations with Japan deteriorated. At the staff discussions at the

Churchill-Roosevelt Argentia summit at Placentia Bay in August 1941, Arnold refused to confirm the American offer. In his diary he noted, "What the British want—my God what a list and what things—no promises."[145] During September the full extent of American withdrawal from the initial Slessor Agreement became clear. The bombers destined for Britain had been fitted with the Norden bombsight, which was still embargoed for British use, and ensured that the bombers could not be released to the RAF. Instead of the 800 bombers expected, the British were granted 238 with no promise of any further deliveries beyond July 1942. It marked the end of the Slessor Agreement and the end of any prospect of developing a force of 4,000 bombers.

The most urgent problem facing Bomber Command was the search for some form of electronic aid for navigation, without which even larger numbers of bombers would still have restricted striking power. In the summer of 1941 the problem was not simply the failure to hit a precise industrial or railway target, but the inability, under conditions of night, poor weather, and German defenses, to find an entire city. Given that these failures almost nullified what Bomber Command was trying to do, the long period that elapsed in trying to find appropriate tactics or technology is difficult to explain. The technology itself was not exotic, and the capacity to interfere with German electronic navigation in the winter of 1940–41 made evident that British science was capable of replicating German practice. The Telecommunications Research Establishment had begun work on a system using radio pulse transmitters in 1938, known as G (for Grid), but usually described as Gee. The system worked by sending pulses from three ground stations that could be measured on a cathode-ray tube carried in the receiving aircraft; where the coordinates intersected it was possible to estimate to between a mile and six miles the aircraft's position. Like the German system, it had limited range and was less accurate the farther away from the ground stations the aircraft was. It worked generally no farther than western Germany. The system was shown to Bomber Command in October 1940, and service trials began in May 1941. The first experimental operation using Gee was conducted by two Wellington bombers on August 11, 1941, but one crashed on German soil. The delay in introducing Gee was partly a result of delays in the production of one of its vacuum tubes, but the main problem was the argument between those who favored putting Gee in a small number of target-finding aircraft, which would lead in the rest of the force, and those who argued that it was something that should be made widely available for the benefit of all. This was to become a central conflict in deciding the best tactics for attacking German cities, and it undermined efforts to develop a more appropriate operational system more rapidly. The use of Gee was postponed until enough sets were available to supply much of the command; its first operational use was not until March 8, 1942.[146]

The arguments over the introduction of Gee also involved the best tactics to adopt to achieve Bomber Command's new objectives and to counter the threat posed by German antiaircraft defenses. Since the summer of 1940, when the German Air Force had relied principally on antiaircraft fire, a more sophisticated defensive system had been constructed combining antiaircraft fire, night fighters, searchlights, and radar. The original air defense system, like that of the British, had been based on the assumption that attacks would come by day. The German defenders soon realized that the pattern of British bombing was difficult to predict. A few daylight raids were made, but most raids were small night attacks defined because of their modest scale as nuisance raids (*Störangriffe*), whose object, it was assumed, was to intimidate the population and disturb the rhythm of industrial labor. Then came heavier raids in the spring of 1941, again scattered and unpredictable but deliberately directed, so the German authorities believed, against "open cities and residential areas" as simple terror attacks.[147] Night attacks meant that antiaircraft fire, without radar assistance, was effectively blind. The decentralized pattern of British raiding made it difficult to know what to protect. German air observation posts were set up around fifteen to twenty kilometers from predicted target areas, but nighttime conditions reduced the prospect of accurate information. The numerous sound detectors used in conjunction with searchlights were found to be vulnerable to the British tactic of throttling back the engines to dampen the noise as aircraft approached a potential danger zone. (British crews also believed that throwing empty milk bottles or beer bottles out of their aircraft confused enemy equipment. The "whistling bottle" was said to interfere with sound location and trigger the searchlights to switch off.)[148] For the German side a concerted defense was difficult to mount, because RAF bombers failed to damage essential war-economic targets, which were guarded by "air defense strongpoints," and instead scattered their loads over an extended area with few evident objectives. The Butt Report could essentially have been written by the Germans months earlier.[149]

On March 3, 1941, the German Air Force established a new command system to cope with the British offensive. General Hubert Weise was appointed *Luftwaffenbefehlshaber Mitte* (air force commander, center) with the task of constructing an effective air defense wall around northern Germany. He centralized air defense by taking over the defensive functions of the *Luftgaue* (air regions) in northern, western, and central Germany. On May 1, 1941, he set up the first dedicated night-fighter organization under General Josef Kammhuber as *Jagdführer Mitte* (fighter leader, center) and integrated it with the searchlight and antiaircraft artillery batteries deployed in northern Germany and the Low Countries. A "Kammhuber Line"—generally known in German as *Himmelbett* (heavenly bed)—was constructed from the Swiss border through the Belgian city of Liège to the German-Danish border, consisting of a series of map "boxes" in each of which a small number of fighters were controlled by a new and improved radar, code-named Würzburg.[150] Only one fighter could be controlled at a time, but once a bomber had been identified, it became with practice easier to direct a fighter to combat position. The night fighters were not yet fitted with AI (Airborne Interception) radar, like British night fighters. But the German version, code-named Lichtenstein, was in the process of development and was finally installed in 1942, though it was not popular with pilots, who assumed the large external antennae would reduce performance. The searchlights were numerous and powerful, but it was found they were wrongly positioned. From mid-1941 they were spaced out at least three kilometers apart to ensure a better prospect of trapping a bomber overhead. The antiaircraft batteries were gradually supplied with the new Würzburg radar, which, like the British experience with antiaircraft radar, proved difficult to operate with poorly trained personnel and was prone to technical problems. As radar-guided fire improved, the batteries found the supply of radar too slow. By the spring of 1942 only one-third of antiaircraft guns had the new apparatus.[151]

The fighters worked in two distinct ways. The first echelon engaged in what was called "dark" night fighting, using radar-equipped ground controllers to guide them to their target; behind the night-fighter boxes was a line of searchlights, soon to have their own radar guidance system, which was used by a second echelon of night fighters for "light" fighting against bombers trapped in a searchlight cone. No dedicated night fighter had been developed before the start of British bombing, but the Junkers Ju88, the Messerschmitt Me110, and the Dornier Do17 (later Do217) were converted to the role in 1940 and formed the mainstay of the force thereafter. The night-fighter force had expanded by the start of 1942 to four groups totaling 265 aircraft, a modest fraction of the total German Air Force establishment. The British tactic of allowing bomber crews to work out their own route to the target meant that the raiding group became spread out in area and time, making it easier for each German night fighter to locate and destroy them in their individual boxes. By September 1941, night fighters assisted by searchlights had claimed 325 enemy aircraft, while "dark" night fighting added a further 50.[152] Antiaircraft fire claimed 439 aircraft shot down between January and September 1941, though many of these, if true, were from daylight operations mounted by other RAF commands.

The steady increase in losses might well have pushed Bomber Command to adopt new tactics. The decision to focus on incendiary bombing of urban areas ought to have encouraged a tactical shift to larger and more concentrated raids. The advantages were obvious: the concentration of the bomber stream would mean that the individual fighter boxes in the *Himmelbett* line and the searchlight wall behind them would be swamped; most bombers would be through the line and to relative safety until they reached one of the inland gun belts. Above all, tight formation and a bomber stream would allow a raiding group to drop all its bombs in a short period of time, maximizing their impact and reducing bomber casualties.[153] Opinion in the Air Ministry and the air staff nevertheless remained divided. Peirse favored retaining the loose, decentralized formations and encouraging the crews to find the best way to their target and back. A tighter formation, it was claimed, would place a heavier burden on pilots, while it would become easy prey for the "dark" night fighters waiting in the Kammhuber Line. Bomber Command had reached an impasse, exaggerating the threat from the German defenses, yet incapable of responding creatively to the new strategic imperatives.

Peirse's lackluster command finally produced a growing chorus of criticism. The Directorate of Bomber Operations insisted that Bomber Command begin serious operational preparations for large-scale incendiary attacks on enemy cities. Assessments were produced by Air Intelligence of the degree of necessary concentration based on German practice. The Air Warfare Analysis Section tested the possible effects of heavy salvos of incendiaries on a large-scale map of the City of Westminster to see what damage might be done. Around 100,000 incendiary bombs were now considered a suitable load to begin a major conflagration. Zone maps of German cities were drawn up showing the most densely populated residential areas (Zones 1 and 2A), the suburban areas (Zones 2b and 3), and the outer industrial areas (Zone 4), with recommendations to deliver the maximum bomb load on the two central zones where large numbers of workers were packed together and to leave the industrial areas alone. In October, Peirse was sent detailed instructions on carrying out an experimental incendiary raid on a German city. The subsequent raid on Nuremberg on the night of October 14–15 proved an inauspicious start: most aircraft bombed a small town outside Nuremberg and only one Stirling hit targets in the city, injuring six people. No major fires were started.[154]

The most dangerous criticism came from the top. In response to a paper from Portal in late September 1941 spelling out the long-term plan for 4,000 bombers, Churchill replied, "It is very disputable whether bombing by itself will be a decisive factor in the present war. On the contrary, all that we have learnt since the war began shows that its effects, both physical and moral, are greatly exaggerated."[155] Portal objected that he saw no reason to regard the bomber "as a weapon of declining importance," but went on to ask Churchill whether the RAF should now be looking for a new strategic concept. Churchill's reply in early October was equivocal. On the one hand he assured Portal that bombing was still a strategic priority, but on the other he played down the likelihood of a satisfactory strategic outcome:

> I deprecate, however, placing unbounded confidence in this means of attack, and still more expressing that confidence in terms of arithmetic. . . . Even if all the towns of Germany were rendered uninhabitable, it does not follow that the military control would be weakened or even that war industry could not be carried on. The Air Staff would make a mistake to put their claim too high.[156]

This was the start of Churchill's growing disillusionment with what bombing could deliver. His initial enthusiasm had been based on a very limited understanding of what bombers were currently capable of achieving. As a politician he was interested in the prospect that air attack might provoke a political reaction in Germany, but the erratic intelligence available suggested that bombing had done very little to undermine German war willingness, while the clearer evidence nearer home showed that the British political system and social structure had survived intact. Morale was now viewed by the RAF less as a means of political pressure, more as a war of economic and social attrition, or, as Portal put it, "interference with all that goes to make up the general activity of a community." But to Churchill, who had imagined a more immediate and politically significant effect from bombing, the idea of long-term and unpredictable attrition was an unexciting prospect.

Peirse made one final effort to redeem his reputation and that of his force. On the night of November 7–8, 1941, he marshaled the largest force yet sent out on operations over Germany, some 392 aircraft, including 43 heavy bombers. The weather forecast was poor but he persisted with the operation. The chief target was Berlin, but of the 169 bombers sent there, only 73 reached the capital, where they distributed their bomb loads with very limited effect. Only fourteen houses were destroyed, nine people killed, and thirty-two injured. Other bombers attacked Cologne, which suffered five deaths and two houses destroyed, and Mannheim, where no bombs fell at all. During the night 37 bombers were lost, more than 9 percent of the force; for the task force sent to Berlin the loss rate was 12.4 percent. One squadron recorded in its diary that the mission was "practically abortive."[157] Berlin was not bombed again until January 1943. Peirse was summoned to see Churchill on the following day and told to suspend the offensive over the winter to conserve his shrinking force. Small raids were carried out when possible, but the assault on morale ordered in the summer of 1941 effectively came to an end with little achieved. The air staff investigated the Berlin raid and concluded that Peirse had been negligent in sending out his force in the knowledge that high winds, storms, and icing would be met by the crews. The decision was taken in December to replace him, and he was finally removed in early January 1942 after Churchill had been shown the documents on the disastrous Berlin raid. On January 8, Peirse was appointed to command Allied air forces in Asia, facing the Japanese. Air Vice Marshal John Baldwin, commander of 3 Group, became his temporary replacement until a new commander in chief was in post.[158]

Bomber Command found itself in a state of limbo in the last months of 1941 and the first two months of 1942. The crews were only too aware of the crisis surrounding their commander in chief and the failures of the force. Over 3,000 had been casualties during 1941. In December the Directorate of Bomber Operations investigated the views of the group commanders about the state of the force and found evidence of a feeling of "hopelessness and ineffectiveness" among the operational units, largely on account of the difficulties in navigating and target marking. When they found a target, the report continued, "they stumbled on it more by luck than judgement."[159] The overwhelming evidence that British raids were still dispersed and ineffective exposed Bomber Command to close scrutiny by the chiefs of staff. The talk in the interregnum imposed by Peirse's redeployment was about the possibility of winding up the offensive. In a note on "Use of the Bomber Force" drafted early in 1942, the government scientist Patrick Blackett speculated that with a few more reverses the navy and army might insist on the "dismemberment of the Air Force as a unit."[160] Sir Stafford Cripps, Lord Privy Seal, told the House of Commons late in February 1942, winding up a debate on the current strategic situation, that bombing strategy was among the things under consideration: "The Government are fully aware of the other uses to which our resources could be put."[161] The day before this speech the new deputy director of bomber operations, Group Captain Sydney Bufton, fresh from command of a bomber squadron and a champion of concentration and target marking, warned his superior of the situation now faced by the command:

> At the present time there is a great deal of criticism of our strategic bombing offensive. This is being voiced not only in Army and Navy circles and in Parliament, but also more generally by members of the public. The criticism cannot be countered by promises of results which we expect to obtain in the future, and rightly cannot be met by evidence of any decisive results which our bomber force has achieved in the past. These results so far have been nebulous, inconsistent and indecisive.[162]

One week before this a new commander in chief had been appointed to Bomber Command—Air Marshal Sir Arthur Harris.

Harris and the Americans

Harris was in Washington on the morning the Japanese navy bombed Pearl Harbor, December 7, 1941. He had been sent in July as a member of the delegation negotiating for American aircraft deliveries to the RAF. His telegrams back to London said much about his personality. In September he dismissed the prospect of American belligerency—"these people are not going to fight . . . they have nothing to fight with"—and thought they engaged in "plain double cross" in reducing aircraft allocations to Britain.[163] Harris complained to Air Chief Marshal Wilfrid Freeman, vice chief of the air staff, about how hard it was to carry out missionary work "with a people so arrogant as to their own ability and infallibility as to be comparable only to the Jews and the Roman Catholics." The problem, Harris continued, was the American conviction "of their own superiority and super efficiency—and of our mental, physical and moral decrepitude."[164] During the morning of December 8 he was summoned to see Henry Stimson, Roosevelt's secretary of war, and Robert Lovett, assistant secretary of war for the Army Air Forces, to discuss supplies for Britain in the wake of the Japanese attack. "They were dazed," Harris wrote to Portal, "and Stimson himself hardly able to speak." The American politicians asked Harris to give back at once 250 aircraft already supplied to the RAF so that they could defend Hawaii. Harris telegrammed Portal for urgent instructions about what to "save from the wreck if wreck is unavoidable."[165] Two weeks later Portal arrived in Washington to attend the first major wartime conference between Roosevelt, Churchill, and the Allied military chiefs. During the first week of January 1942, Portal told Harris that he wanted him to replace Peirse; Harris agreed and Churchill approved the appointment, which was made official from February 22, 1942, after Harris had sailed back to England.[166]

The Japanese attack promised to transform the bombing war more certainly than the German invasion of the Soviet Union, because it brought into the conflict a power capable of colossal military output and an air force already committed to the concept of long-range strategic bombing. Yet the outcome of the Arcadia Conference in Washington between December 22, 1941, and January 14, 1942, left the bomber offensive as one small part of the wider strategic objectives agreed to between the two leaders. On the way to the conference Churchill cabled to Roosevelt a long memorandum on Allied strategy, which included a short passage on bombing asking the United States to send at least twenty bomber squadrons to help boost Britain's offensive. "Our own bomber programme," he added, "has fallen short of our hopes."[167] During the twelve meetings between the British and American teams, however, bombing was discussed only once, when the U.S. side insisted that their bombers would only be manned by American crews, confirming that Britain would get no further heavy bombers from American production.[168] In the list of strategic priorities, bombing was included as a contribution to item "(d)": "wearing down and undermining German resistance by air bombardment, blockade, subversive activities and propaganda."[169]

On January 7, Churchill, briefly in Florida for his health, summed up what the two men had agreed. Bombing hardly featured except for Churchill's fears that the Blitz might be renewed. He assumed that most American airpower, including the bombers, would have to focus on the Pacific War for the coming year.[170] The role of bombing in Allied strategy for the foreseeable future was regarded as modest and peripheral.

The Americans were not unprepared for involvement in the European bombing war. Indeed, as early as 1935 American airmen had begun thinking about building bomber aircraft that could fly across the Atlantic to project long-distance airpower against a hostile state. Writing in 1939, General Arnold, chief of the Army Air Corps, addressed the question "Can We Be Bombed?" and concluded that the answer was yes: "We are vulnerable to bombing. Such bombing is feasible."[171] On the day the German army invaded in the west, May 10, 1940, Arnold proposed the development of a new bomber with a 4,000-mile radius of action capable of attacking European ports to disrupt "the launching of expeditionary forces against the Western hemisphere."[172] During 1940 and 1941 the U.S. Army Air Forces had been instructed by Arnold to collect detailed intelligence information on German industrial and economic targets, much of it supplied by the British Air Ministry. Consistent with air force thinking, this material was designed to support the idea that attacks against the vulnerable industrial web would unravel the enemy's capacity to make war. When Roosevelt instructed the American armed forces to draw up a "Victory Program" in the summer of 1941, the air force was asked to prepare a plan of the resources needed to fulfill a strategic air campaign against Germany. In six stifling days in Washington in August 1941, a team assembled by Lieutenant Colonel Harold George worked day and night to produce a detailed plan for a putative offensive. The result was AWPD-1, a detailed survey of 154 German targets in three key target areas: electric power, fuel oils, and communications. Production of 11,800 heavy bombers, to be employed on precision bombing in daylight, was considered sufficient for the task, though the air force currently had only a few hundred. Unlike the RAF, which had never embraced a serious counterforce strategy, the American planners—like the German Air Force in 1940—assumed that enemy airpower would be an essential intermediate target, whose de-struction would make the obliteration of the primary objectives possible.[173] Morale was not considered a useful target and was not included on the list. Again unlike the RAF, the American planners did not argue about the legality of bombing urban targets or hitting civilians.[174] The German economic web, with its vital centers, was treated as an abstraction; the metaphor of the "social body" created a language that distanced those planning the bombing from the reality of civilian deaths.

Roosevelt was pleased with the plan. He had supported American air rearmament steadily since 1938 and in spring 1941 authorized a schedule of production that included 500 heavy four-engine bombers a month.[175] Despite his appeal in September 1939 to avoid bombing civil-ians, he shared Churchill's uncritical view that bombing was a possible war winner in the face of German aggression. He had a long-standing personal hostility to Germany and the Germans, and an abhorrence of Hitlerism. American reports sent back to Washington at the start of the war in Poland highlighted the ruthless destruction of Polish towns from the air and underlined how shallow had been Hitler's positive response to Roosevelt's plea.[176] Roosevelt, like Churchill, proved susceptible to the extravagant fears of German airpower and scientific ingenuity painted by unreliable intelligence. Since the Munich crisis, when the president had advocated to his cabinet the idea that European states should bomb Germany in concert to halt Hitler's aggression, Roosevelt had retained extravagant notions of what airpower might achieve. His special adviser Harry Hopkins noted in August 1941 Roosevelt's conviction that bomb-ing was "the only means of gaining a victory."[177] In the United States as in Britain, the air forces became the unexpected beneficiaries of political support at the highest level, without which the complaints and blandish-ments of the other services would have been more difficult to resist.

The sudden coming of war with Japan, Germany, and Italy in De-cember 1941 nevertheless exposed how flimsy were the American prep-arations so far. The United States possessed no strategic bomber force and had to build one from scratch. Most of the small number of B-17 Flying Fortress bombers were stationed in Hawaii and the Philippines to protect against possible Japanese aggression. A real fear was the possibility of air attack either on the eastern seaboard from German bases or on the Pacific coast from Japanese carrier aircraft. Civil defense preparations were already in place, organized by the Office of Civilian Defense set up in May 1941, and were activated at once in vulnerable areas on the outbreak of war. War-essential factories in coastal areas were ordered to begin a program of camouflage and to black out windows with black paper and layers of opaque paint. All aircraft plants, even in areas not obviously exposed to risk, had to prepare concealment and obscurement plans, while the American Chemical Warfare Service developed units to distribute a five-mile smoke screen around vulnerable targets.[178] Air-raid wardens patrolled Washington streets to enforce the blackout drills, and in June 1942 it was decided that coastal cities should operate a permanent "dim-out" against the threat of air raids, with veiled vehicle lighting and low-visibility streetlamps.[179]

Strict civil defense instructions were issued for the control of traffic during air-raid alerts, and in August 1942 the Federal Works Agency produced a 173-page air-raid protection code, covering every subject from behavior in air-raid shelters to compulsory fire watching. As in Britain, dispersed sheltering was favored, with no more than fifty people in any one shelter, but unlike the European experience, basements and cellars were regarded as hazardous. In tall buildings with a reinforced skeleton it was recommended that shelters should be constructed on the upper floors, though not on the top floor; the exact position could be calculated by working out the load-bearing properties of the ceiling once debris had collapsed onto it. The structure of the air-raid precautions system resembled that of the British, with volunteer auxiliary firemen, fire-watching units, first-aid volunteers, decontamination, and rescue battalions.[180]

The Office of Civilian Defense, run in 1942 by James Landis, a Harvard law professor, was responsible for organizing the volunteer and full-time personnel. Thousands of Americans spent much of the war period engaged in drills and practices that made increasingly less sense as the war went on, though continued speculation about the possibility of German bombing kept the civil defense force in being. In May 1943 there were fears after the German defeat in Tunisia that Hitler would seek a

propaganda coup by launching bombing aircraft from German submarines against East Coast cities. The gas threat was also an ever-present
anxiety. In June 1943, Roosevelt announced that any use of gas by the
Axis powers would provoke immediate retaliation "throughout the whole
extent of the territory" of the enemy state.[181] As in Europe, civil defense
was also designed to get the American public to identify with the war
effort as democratic participants; since American bombing was predicated on attacking the social and economic web of the enemy, the American people could now be viewed as an active part of the war. The
Civilian Defense journal was deliberately titled *Civilian Front* to reflect
war in the modern age. This rationale was explained by Landis in an
editorial in 1943:

> Civilian Defense is more than insurance for ourselves. It is a mili-
> tary duty. Modern war is not confined to battle lines. It is all the
> arms, resources and production of one people against all the arms,
> resources and production of another. A food warehouse or a ma-
> chine tool plant 3,000 miles from the spot where the land forces
> are locked in combat is as legitimate a military objective as a pill-
> box on the battle line. . . . That is our assignment and it is a mili-
> tary assignment as definite as that given an armed task force
> ordered to take and hold an enemy position.[182]

Imagination rather than reality shaped these views as they had in prewar Europe, but in the eyes of the American public they helped to legitimize American bombing of German urban targets when this began
early in 1943.

The American bombing campaign took a long time to evolve. The
Eighth Air Force was activated on January 28, 1942, in Savannah,
Georgia, under the initial command of Colonel Asa Duncan. Because of
the commitment made at the Arcadia Conference to mount an invasion
of Europe, or possibly North Africa, during the coming year, the Eighth
Air Force was expected to play an air support role as well as prepare for
strategic operations from airfields in England. Arnold sent Colonel Ira
Eaker to Britain to establish contact with Bomber Command and to
learn about its operations. Eaker met Harris in Washington before they

both left in late February, and an immediate rapport was established between the two men, despite the differences in their personality: Eaker was diffident and earnest, Harris opinionated and brusque. Eaker arrived in London on February 21, a day before Harris assumed command at High Wycombe. After a period staying with Harris, Eaker in April set up an American headquarters in the nearby Wycombe Abbey School for Girls, after the pupils had been forced to leave. Code-named Pinetree, the site became the wartime command center for the Eighth Bomber Command, with Eaker (now brigadier general) as its commander, but as yet with no aircraft or personnel.[183] It was made clear from the start that the American force was not under RAF command, though it was expected to learn a great deal from British experience. Eaker wrote to Harris later in the summer that he regarded him as "the senior member in our firm—the older brother in our bomber team."[184] Arnold appointed Major General Carl Spaatz, one of the most senior American airmen, as overall commander of the Eighth Air Force, including its fighter, reconnaissance, and service branches, but Spaatz remained in the United States for five months while the air force organization was established, the training programs initiated, and the service and procurement system organized. He finally took over from Duncan on May 10, 1942.[185] Both Eaker and Spaatz were selected by Arnold because they had shared with him the struggle to establish American air forces during the years of isolation, and both supported his view of the strategic importance of independent airpower. Spaatz had visited Britain in July and August 1940 and had been unimpressed by what appeared to be indiscriminate German night bombing, but impressed by the possibility that daylight bombing in close formation could afford sufficient protection against fighter penetration and achieve greater bombing precision.[186] These were lessons that governed the operational and tactical development of the American bomber force in 1942 and 1943.

The first echelon of American air force personnel arrived on May 11, a second one a week later, but the first 180 aircraft only arrived in mid-July, and just 40 were heavy bombers. American planning, unlike British, had to be based from the start on the assumption that an invasion might take place somewhere in 1942, so that most of the initial aircraft deliveries were of light or medium bombers for army support roles at the expense of a strategic bombing capability.[187] Until the decision taken by Churchill and Roosevelt in July 1942, against strong American objection, to undertake a limited invasion in North Africa (code-named Torch), American air planning had to be based on the assumption that a landing in France would be undertaken before October. The result would have been to divert American aircraft almost entirely to a role in support of surface forces, and this possibility compromised the early efforts to turn the Eighth Air Force into a principally strategic force. The prospect of an invasion of Europe (code-named Sledgehammer) also prompted the head of the American military mission (Special Observer Group) appointed in the spring of 1941, Major General James Chaney, to insist that Eaker and Spaatz integrate with his organization rather than set up a new independent command. The jurisdictional battle was resolved only because Eaker refused to be based in London under Chaney's close supervision. The arguments over invasion also affected relations with the British, who tried to insist for the sake of operational efficiency that American fighter aircraft be absorbed into RAF Fighter Command and that at least 400 American heavy bombers be given in the first instance to Bomber Command, which could utilize them immediately. Arnold visited London in late May 1942 and succeeded in reducing this demand to a tentative 54 but could not promise that American-flown bombers would be in action much before the autumn.[188] He found London very different from his last visit during the Blitz: "Men, women and children have lost that expression of dreaded expectancy," he wrote in his diary, "they have a cheerful look on their faces. . . . Pianos are playing, men are whistling. London is changed."[189] He returned to Washington with enough achieved to prevent the further emasculation of the Eighth Air Force's still nonexistent capability.

Harris arrived in England shortly before Eaker and moved at once to High Wycombe to take up the command left in abeyance by the sacking of Peirse. He remained the longest-serving bomber commander of the war. He began his air career in the First World War when he left Rhodesia, where he had emigrated as an adventurous teenager in 1910, to join the Royal Flying Corps. He became a major and ended a dramatic operational career in 1918 as a training officer. He remained in the fledgling RAF and saw active service in the Middle East, where he helped to define "air policing" methods by using light bombers to intimidate recalcitrant populations in Iraq and Palestine. He held high office in the Air Ministry in the 1930s, and played a key part in planning what was known as the "Ideal Bomber" (the Lancaster was a distant descendant). In 1939 he became commander of 5 Group, Bomber Command, before becoming Portal's deputy when he was appointed chief of staff in October 1940. From June 1941, Harris was in Washington, absent from the ongoing arguments about air tactics and the diminishing impact of the command, though not unaware of the problems.[190]

On most accounts Harris was judged an effective officer, and he impressed many of those who met him with a shrewd intelligence and a mordant wit. He established a working relationship—though not always frictionless—with Churchill and the American air leaders. He gave the impression of a straightforward, no-nonsense personality, who spoke his mind and changed it little. He had scant sympathy with those of his colleagues or his men who displayed any weakness. The crews who followed behind the target markers he termed "rabbits"; the crewmen who expressed doubts about bombing civilians were "weaker sisters." The civilian critics of bombing were "Fifth Columnists," his junior critics at the ministry simply "impertinent."[191] His blunt talk became a hallmark of his relations with anyone who crossed him, however senior. In April 1942, Wilfrid Freeman, then vice chief of the air staff, told Harris after a typically robust exchange that he had spent years getting used to his "truculent style, loose expression and flamboyant hyperbole," but could still be surprised by the level of verbal injury Harris was willing to inflict. So fearsome was Harris's reputation that when in early 1947 the Air Ministry proposed a conference on the wartime bombing campaign based on the critical report of the British Bombing Survey Unit, Claude Pelly wrote to his coauthor Solly Zuckerman that they needed adequate warning if Harris decided to come from retirement in South Africa so that they could "make the best of a couple of Continents' start. Iceland or Southern Pacific?"[192]

Harris had two important prejudices that colored his entire period as commander in chief. He held an exceptional hostility to the Germans, which made it possible for him not only to run a campaign of city bombing with high civilian casualties in mind, but also to relish, in his own choice of words, "this lethal campaign." Harris was known to see the First World War as unfinished business, and he had an instinctive hostility to totalitarian systems, right or left. But neither perhaps explains sufficiently why he regarded the death of ordinary Germans as something to be sought in its own right. "We have got to kill a lot of Boche," he famously wrote in April 1942, "before we win this war."[193] During 1943 and 1944 he wanted the Air Ministry to state unequivocally that killing the German people was what his command was for. In later life he never wavered from his conviction that there was nothing ethically objectionable to killing the enemy civilian in total war, which was a view widely shared at the time, but his complete indifference to the fate of the Germans he bombed, even in Dresden, is more difficult to understand. When the biographer Andrew Boyle asked Harris in 1979 about his "aggressive philosophy where Germans were concerned," Harris did not respond.[194]

His second conviction was his unyielding belief that the heavy bombing of urban areas was the best use to which the current bombing technology could be put. He contested, often bitterly, any attempt to divert the forces under his command to other purposes, and when compelled to do so, he fought to have his bombers returned to what he saw as their only rational function as soon as possible. The destruction of cities, Harris insisted to the end of the conflict, would "shorten the war and so preserve the lives of Allied soldiers," though it cost the lives of half his operational crews.[195] This stubborn refusal to accept that any other strategy might yield more strategically useful and less damaging results made him into the Haig of the Second World War. Harris's reputation, like Douglas Haig's before him, has been a historical bone of contention ever since.

Though Harris's appointment no doubt marked a turning point in the bombing war, he was not, as is so often suggested, the originator of the area-bombing campaign. He arrived at his command after a brief interregnum in which the officers in the Air Ministry in favor of

large-scale incendiary attacks on residential areas had been able to exploit the absence of a field commander to put in place an unambiguous
commitment to the strategy they preferred. A new directive was sent to
Baldwin as acting commander in chief on February 14, 1942, modifying
the directive of July 1941 by removing communications as a primary
target and focusing the force entirely on "the morale of the enemy civil
population and in particular of the industrial workers." A list of cities
was appended to the directive, with the vulnerable central zones highlighted and the bomb tonnage necessary to destroy them recommended.[196]
In February 1942 the Directorate of Bomber Operations, which had
prepared the directive, explored the vulnerability of particular cities to
large-scale conflagration and chose Hamburg (rated "outstanding"), followed by Hannover, Cologne, Düsseldorf, Bremen, Dortmund, and Essen.[197] The zoning system developed in 1941 was now applied to these
cities to show the value of hitting the "closely built-up city centre" (Zone 1)
and the "completely built-up residential area" (Zone 2A). Attacks on
these central zones were estimated to be up to twenty times more effective than attacks on the outer industrial and suburban zones. The damage done to a large working-class area was expected to affect the output
of numerous factories through absenteeism or death, where an attack on
a single factory target would affect only that one.[198] This was the background to the famous minute sent to Churchill by Lord Cherwell on
March 30, 1942, in which he calculated that 10,000 RAF bombers
would by mid-1943 be able to drop enough bombs to dehouse one-third
of Germany's urban population. "Investigation," ran the minute, "seems
to show that having one's house demolished is most damaging to morale." Churchill was so impressed that he insisted on circulating the
minute to the War Cabinet. It generated at the time a great deal of argument from other scientists who criticized the arithmetic (Patrick Blackett
thought it exaggerated by a factor of 600 percent), and it has attracted
much discussion from historians, but in effect it simply advertised a shift
in bombing priorities that had already been agreed upon and was now
in place.[199]

Harris did make a difference when he took over Bomber Command,
because he was an aggressive and single-minded defender of his force

against all efforts to divert it to other purposes or to compromise the directive he had been given. He also argued forcefully against the widespread criticism of the command—"ignorant and uninstructed chatter," he called it—because of the damaging effect on bomber crew morale to be regularly reminded that their efforts were "futile."[200] But Harris did realize how limited bombing still was without a substantial increase in the size of the bomber force and an end to the dispersion of bomber aircraft to other theaters. When he arrived at the command he had at his disposal only a few hundred bombers, of which a large part were still medium Wellingtons. He understood that this force was incapable of achieving what the new city-bombing directive suggested. He complained to Norman Bottomley, deputy chief of staff, that what he needed was a force of at least 2,000 bombers; such a force, he claimed, would not only destroy his list of twenty cities but "knock Germany out of the war."[201]

Harris nevertheless set out to demonstrate what his limited numbers could achieve. On March 8–9, 1942, 211 aircraft (including 37 heavy bombers) armed with Gee navigation attacked Essen and the Krupps complex. Dense industrial smoke obscured the city; no bombs hit Krupps, a handful of houses were destroyed, and ten people were killed. A second raid on Essen two days later killed only five people; the bombs were scattered over sixty-one different villages and towns.[202] A raid on Cologne on March 13–14 proved more effective thanks to better target marking despite a gloomy night. The most successful attack was made against the Baltic Sea port of Lübeck on the night of March 28–29. Although the city was beyond the range of Gee, there was a full moon and good visibility. The 234 bombers attacked in three waves, carrying two-thirds incendiaries against the lightly defended and densely constructed "old town" area. Around 60 percent of buildings in the city were damaged and 312 people killed, the heaviest casualties in Germany so far. A series of four raids were then made against the northern port of Rostock between April 23–24 and 26–27, again aiming for the main city area, 60 percent of which was damaged or destroyed, though thanks to effective civil defense only 216 inhabitants died. These were the first raids where incendiary damage could be inflicted on the central areas of a combustible target along the lines planned in 1941, and they inflicted high levels of urban destruction. They were also the first raids that the German authorities took seriously; following the Rostock raid a special category of "great catastrophe" was introduced to define larger and more destructive attacks.[203]

The reaction to the first Gee raids at the Air Ministry was nevertheless unenthusiastic. The director of bomber operations, John Baker, accused Harris of misunderstanding the nature of the incendiary attacks he had recommended, by carrying too much high explosive. Harris was sent a memorandum summing up the opinion of British fire chiefs about the relative value of high explosive and incendiary, which showed that in almost all cases more than 90 percent of the damage had been caused by fire. Baker suggested carrying at least 200,000 four-pound incendiary bombs to maximize the damage.[204] On May 8, following the Rostock raids, Baker's deputy, Sydney Bufton, also wrote to Harris with the evidence from plotted photographs that his attacks on Essen in March and again in April showed that 90 percent of bombs had fallen from between 5 and 100 miles from the Essen aiming point. Plots of twelve raids on Essen between March and June 1942 showed that in seven of them fewer than 5 percent of aircraft got within 3 miles. The raids on Rostock, which was easier to locate, being near the coast, showed that 78 percent of the photographs taken were not of the town.[205] A few weeks before this, on April 14, the chiefs of staff had asked Churchill to authorize a second study of bombing results by Justice Sir John Singleton, to see what might be expected from bombing over the following eighteen months. The decision was prompted by Cherwell's minute on "de-housing," which suggested very significant consequences by the end of that period with more bombers and greater accuracy.[206] Singleton's report was produced by May 20 using material supplied by Baker and Bufton, though without the statistical foundation used in the Butt Report from the previous August. Singleton concluded that the use of Gee had had mixed results, but that in general, efforts to improve the level of accuracy and concentration had been a failure. He did not believe that over the following six months "great results can be hoped for."[207] Cherwell wrote to Churchill a week later that Singleton had been disappointed, "as any layman would be, by the inaccuracy of our bombing."[208]

On the question of greater accuracy Harris was generally unhelpful. The arguments over developing a target-finding force equivalent to the German Kampfgruppe 100 had begun in 1941 but were still unresolved when Harris took over. He was opposed to the idea of using the introduction of Gee as an opportunity to develop specialized units to find, identify, and illuminate a target city. Together with other senior commanders, he thought the creation of an elite corps would leave poorer-quality crews to follow behind and would sap the morale of the rest of the force. He favored keeping "lead crews" in each bomber group to find and mark the target, and was impervious to the evidence that this practice failed to produce a concentration of bombing effort. At a meeting with group commanders and the Directorate of Bomber Operations in mid-March, Harris made it clear that he entirely rejected the idea of a target force and was supported by all five group commanders.[209] The argument highlighted the extent to which the individual commanders in chief and their subordinate commanders enjoyed independence from the air staff at the ministry in the way they chose to run their campaigns. It was nevertheless difficult for Harris to ignore all the evidence of continued inaccuracy and the political and service pressure to improve it. Failure to do so might, as an air staff memorandum pointed out in May, make it increasingly difficult "truthfully and logically" to resist pressure to divert bombers to other uses.[210] In March, Bufton sent out a questionnaire to squadron and station commanders in Bomber Command asking them whether they approved the creation of a target-finding force. The replies were unanimously in favor. A squadron commander based at Oakington, near Cambridge, told Bufton that the senior officers' First World War experience was valueless in the new conflict: "The crocks . . . must be swept from the board."[211]

Bufton sent the results of the survey to Harris, but it made little difference. Harris found five squadron commanders who were prepared to argue the opposite case. The most he would concede was the idea of raid leaders for each group, which built on existing practice. The crisis point came in June when Wilfrid Freeman, acting on Portal's behalf as vice chief of staff, finally seized the initiative after weeks of fruitless argument with Harris over tactical issues. He told Harris that he would have to accept the logic of a specialized force. Harris met Portal and despite a trenchant rearguard action finally agreed to the establishment of what he insisted on calling the Pathfinder Force to distinguish it from the air staff title of target finding. Even then Harris found ways to obstruct the proper functioning of the new force, which remained short of the most effective aircraft and highly trained crews. An Australian pilot, Group Captain Donald Bennett, was appointed on July 5, 1942, to command the new units; the Pathfinder Force was activated on August 15 and undertook its first operation three days later against the north German coast port of Flensburg. It proved an awkward baptism. Strong winds drove both the Pathfinders and the main force off course, and instead of on the German city, the bombs fell on two Danish towns and injured four Danes.[212] An Air Ministry minute in early August noted that despite the agreement to form a target-finding force, "a lack of enthusiasm and sense of urgency in high quarters permeates the whole command, and will inevitably result in a complete failure of the T.F.F. [target-finding force] at its inception."[213]

Harris found himself, like Peirse before him, fighting against a chorus of criticism both inside and outside the RAF. During May he began to plan a sensational air raid to try to still public criticism and stamp his mark on his new command. He won approval from Portal and Churchill for the plan to send 1,000 bombers against a single German city. It was a risky promise, because it depended on the cooperation of Coastal Command in releasing their bomber aircraft for the raid and the use of aircraft from the training units. Bomber Command itself had just over 400 frontline aircraft. The city chosen was Hamburg, which like Lübeck and Rostock was easily identifiable as near the coast. The object, Harris wrote, was to wipe it out in one night, or at most two. The target was large, near, and "suitably combustible." The aim was to carry every single incendiary possible and to create an "unextinguishable conflagration" by bombing in a continuous stream and in a short period of time, a gesture toward the tactical recommendations made by the Air Ministry.[214]

The code name Operation Millennium, like later code names, betrayed its apocalyptic purpose. By May 23 plans were prepared with details of German defenses and three routes to the target. Coastal Command agreed to release 250 aircraft, only to find that the Admiralty countermanded the offer. Harris had at the last moment to recruit training personnel and trainee pilots to raise his force to a total of just over 1,000. The weather worsened over the week that followed, and by May 26, Cologne was chosen as a possible alternative. Hamburg was finally abandoned as the primary target and waited another year for its firestorm.

After first being approved, then canceled, then reinstated on May 30, the raid against Cologne was authorized by Harris for that night. A total of 1,047 bombers were sent off, but only 868 claimed to have attacked the main target, dropping 1,455 tons of bombs, two-thirds of them incendiaries, though only 800 tons fell on the city itself. The concentrated stream allowed the bombers to complete the raid in just an hour and a half, which may explain why the first reports from the city suggested that only between 50 and 100 bombers had been overhead. A later report from the local National Socialist regional leader confirmed the actual scale: it was, he wrote, "the most successful concentrated enemy air attack to date."[215] Some 3,330 buildings were destroyed and 7,908 damaged; 486 people were killed and over 5,000 injured; 59,100 were rendered temporarily homeless. This represented a loss of 5.2 percent of Cologne's buildings. Heavy though the raid was, it was impossible to wipe a city out, as Harris had hoped.[216] He planned to continue the large raids as long as he had the force of bombers acting together. On June 1–2 another "1,000" raid was made on Essen, with far less success: only eleven houses were destroyed and 15 people killed. The last large "1,000" raid, Millennium II, was against the port of Bremen on the night of June 25–26. Out of a force of 960 aircraft, 696 claimed to have hit the city, but destroyed only 572 buildings and killed 85 people, suggesting that many of the bombs missed the target area altogether.[217] This was the end of the "1,000" plan. Despite the effort to overwhelm the Kammhuber Line by using a concentrated bomber stream, losses were the highest of the war, 123 bombers from the three raids. This threatened to eat into Bomber Command's training system, and the large raids were discontinued. Some of the OTUs were close to mutiny at the loss of training staff and the demands placed on novice crews sometimes forced to fly obsolescent aircraft to make up the numbers on each raid.[218]

The gesture did something to reinstate Bomber Command's reputation, particularly with a British public impatient for more rapid progress, but the situation faced by both Bomber Command and the Eighth Air Force in the summer and early autumn of 1942 was more dangerous to the future of the bombing campaign than the crisis in 1941. The summer of 1942 represented a low point in Allied fortunes. The Pacific and southern Asia were dominated by a rampant Japan, held at bay by the victory at Midway in early June, but a formidable obstacle for sustained counterattack. In North Africa the British Commonwealth forces abandoned most of Libya, lost Tobruk, and retreated into Egypt. Field Marshal Erwin Rommel seemed poised to seize the Suez Canal. The Battle of the Atlantic had reached a critical point, and on the Eastern Front, German forces poured toward the oilfields of the Caucasus and the Volga city of Stalingrad. The many areas of crisis left Allied strategy in confusion, and the bombing offensive was the unwitting victim of efforts to plug the many strategic gaps that were opening up with Axis success. Field Marshal Jan Smuts, recruited to Churchill's War Cabinet, urged the prime minister to send Bomber Command to North Africa where he thought it would do more good.[219] To try to allay these pressures, Harris wrote directly to Churchill to persuade him that Bomber Command was still the potentially war-winning instrument it had hoped to be two years before:

> We ourselves are now at the crossroads. We are free, if we will, to employ our rapidly increasing air strength in the proper manner. In such a manner as would avail to knock Germany out of the War in a matter of months, if we decide upon the right course. If we decide upon the wrong course, then our Air power will now, and increasingly in the future, become inextricably implicated as a subsidiary weapon in the prosecution of vastly protracted and avoidable land and sea campaigns.[220]

Harris appended a document to show that his force had at present just thirty-six squadrons with 584 aircraft, or exactly 11 percent of the entire RAF and Fleet Air Arm, and added that of this percentage half the operational effort went to help the Royal Navy. A few weeks later Harris calculated that his force had dwindled to twenty-two effective squadrons available for bombing Germany.[221]

In the last months of 1942, Bomber Command waited to see what the strategic outcome would be. Harris knew that the command would benefit from a number of technical and tactical innovations that were in the pipeline. As predicted, Gee had had a very short life. It was first jammed by German countermeasures on August 4, and a wide network of stations was set up to interfere regularly with its transmissions. Two new systems had been in development at the Telecommunications Research Establishment. The first was known as Oboe (the transmission noise resembled the sound of the instrument). Two ground radar transmitters, one at Dover and one at Cromer in Norfolk, emitted pulses that were received by an aircraft transmitter and relayed back to the master station, allowing an exact fix of the plane's position. When the aircraft was over the aiming point, the second station sent out a bomb-release signal. The system was accurate but had a range of only 270 miles, covering the Ruhr but little else, and could only be used by one aircraft at a time. The second system was a more radical innovation. Taking advantage of the British discovery of the cavity magnetron, which permitted much narrower radar wavelengths, an airborne radar device, H2S, was devised that gave a map of the ground area by recording stronger echoes from built-up areas. This could be used over longer distances and could not be jammed as beams could be. Both instruments were available for operational use in early 1943. Their potential effectiveness was magnified by the fortuitous development of a new fast twin-engine bomber, the de Havilland Mosquito. Begun initially as a private venture in October 1938, the aircraft was uniquely made of wood, and powered by two Rolls-Royce Merlin engines. It was designed as a light bomber and relied on its high speed to avoid enemy fighter interception. The Air Ministry showed little interest until Air Marshal Freeman, in charge of research and development, saw the aircraft late in 1939 and ordered work on a prototype. It first flew on

November 25, 1940, and saw operational service a year later, when it was used extensively for daylight bombing. It could fly at almost 400 miles per hour (faster than Battle of Britain fighters) and had a service ceiling of at least 28,000 feet. It was so difficult to intercept that it had lower losses than any other Bomber Command aircraft. Its special operational characteristics made it a natural choice for the new Pathfinder units, but in January 1943 there were still only sixteen Mosquitos available.

Bomber Command was nevertheless unable to demonstrate after the Cologne raid of late May 1942 that it merited the kind of strategic profile that Harris had argued for in June. The hope that American entry into the war might soon lead to a strengthened bombing effort was undermined by the slow establishment of the Eighth Air Force, which until July did not know whether there would be time to mount any raids against German targets at all before starting direct preparations to aid a cross-Channel invasion. Even more than Bomber Command, the American bomber force lived in the future. The slow buildup of aircraft and personnel postponed any serious possibility of action against Germany into 1943. Table 1.2 shows the buildup of the Eighth Air Force during 1942, but none of the operations it describes took place over Germany.

As with the German Air Force and Bomber Command, an opera-

Table 1.2: Eighth Bomber Command Operational Statistics, August–December 1942

Month	Sorties	Bomb Tonnage	Operational Bombers	Crews Available	Losses
August	90	135	24	21	2
September	106	215	56	55	7
October	157	334	90	110	11
November	382	612	99	113	14
December	243	417	115	114	34

Source: AFHRA, Maxwell, AL, Eighth Air Force collection, 520.056-188, Statistical Summary of Eighth Air Force Operations, August 17, 1942–May 8, 1945; Richard G. Davis, *Carl A. Spaatz and the Air War in Europe* (Washington, DC: Center for Air Force History, 1993), App. 17.

tional learning curve had to be followed before crews with no operational experience could be released against improving German defenses.
Pressure from Washington insisted that Spaatz and Eaker organize a
demonstration to satisfy American and British opinion, and Arnold named
Independence Day, July 4, as the day to carry it out. Spaatz had no aircraft of his own, so he recruited six Douglas A-20 light bombers serving
with the RAF to make a suicidal attack against four German airfields on
the Dutch coast. The RAF colors were painted over and the six aircraft
sent off on the morning of July 4. By the end, one-third of the force was
lost, seven aircrew were dead and one a prisoner. Three weeks later a
surviving crewman committed suicide. The press on both sides of the
Atlantic made the most of the raid, but it was a futile gesture.[222] Arnold
pressed his commanders to speed up the organization of real operations.
The U.S. bomber offensive was launched on August 17 with an attack
by twelve Boeing B-17 Flying Fortress bombers on the railway sheds at
Rouen in northern France. Eaker flew with the mission, which was protected by RAF fighters. All aircraft returned safely after striking the target. Ten days later, after three more missions over occupied Europe,
Eaker reported to Spaatz the current assessments of accuracy. The
bomb plots seemed to show that 90 percent of the bombs dropped fell
within a one-mile radius of the aiming point, almost half within 500
yards. He concluded from this that daytime bombing with the Norden
bombsight was ten times more accurate than RAF night bombing. Limited though this experience was, Eaker, like Harris, thought that Allied
bombing by day and night would be adequate "completely to dislocate
German industry and communications."[223] But unlike the British and
German learning curve, the early raids convinced the American side
that daylight raids were possible.

While Harris waited for a response from Churchill on the future of
the offensive, the prime minister flew to Moscow on August 12 for urgent talks with Stalin. The object was to explain to Stalin why the Western powers had decided in July to abandon the idea of a cross-Channel
invasion in 1942. The meeting was famously combative: Stalin argued
against every explanation provided by Churchill in insulting terms until
the point when Churchill explained the plans for an Anglo-American

bomber offensive. Roosevelt's representative, W. Averell Harriman, wired back the result to his leader: "Stalin took over the argument himself and said that homes as well as factories should be destroyed. . . . Between the two of them they soon destroyed most of the important industrial cities in Germany."[224] Harris and Spaatz were both fortunate that bombing was still required in the summer of 1942 as a means to placate the Soviet Union over the failure to open a second front. Although Churchill knew about the poor progress of the offensive, it could not easily be abandoned now that there was to be no cross-Channel operation. On August 17, Churchill asked Portal and Sinclair to lay on an operation against Berlin to show Stalin that he had been in earnest, but he was told that Harris regarded the operation as too costly with only 300 serviceable bombers and a great many inexperienced crews. Though Churchill argued angrily in favor of an attack, Harris told Portal that it would seriously damage the expansion of the command. "As I have frequently pointed out to you," he wrote in late August, "Bomber Command is now quite definitely too small for the tasks it is expected to carry out."[225]

As a result, when Harris asked Churchill for a "firm and final decision" on September 4 about the future of the bomber offensive, he received a guarded response. Churchill remained committed to bombing Germany, since he could not easily terminate such a conspicuous element of Britain's war effort, but he thought it would have no decisive results in 1943 nor bring the war to an end; "better than doing nothing," he concluded.[226] This was a view widely shared in military and political circles by the autumn of 1942, for which the chief priority was breaking the submarine blockade, using bombers if necessary, and supporting American participation in the ground offensives planned for North Africa and Europe. Leo Amery, one of Churchill's cabinet colleagues, found the Harris memorandum "entirely unconvincing" and thought bombers should be used for "tactical co-operation with the army and navy."[227] One of the scientists at the Air Warfare Analysis Section warned the Air Ministry that Bomber Command could not hit enough of German industry to do any decisive damage. "I am aware that this view of night bombing," he continued, "is shared by a very large number of thoughtful people."[228] When the chiefs of staff considered the future of the bombing campaign in November 1942, Portal was subjected to a hostile cross-examination by his colleagues. General Alan Brooke, chief of the imperial general staff, thought the air force lacked a clear plan of campaign, underestimated the German defenses, exaggerated the possible bomblift, and overstated the damage likely with blind bombing. The one slim advantage, he concluded, was its political value, bringing "the horrors of war home to the German people."[229]

Harris took out his own frustration on others. He deplored the decision by the Canadian bomber squadrons, which composed a growing fraction of the command, "to huddle into a corner by themselves," even more the prospect of supplying them with Lancaster bombers at the expense of British crews.[230] He was scathing about the American Eighth Air Force, despite the public image of friendly collaboration, for taking airfields in East Anglia away from British squadrons, forcing them to fly dangerous return routes to bases farther west and north, and without contributing "the smallest assistance" to the bombing campaign against Germany. He asked the Air Ministry to challenge American leaders to state categorically "whether it is their intention to proceed with the air bombardment of Germany," and, if so, when it would start. If no adequate answer was forthcoming, Harris recommended taking some of the airfields back, to which the ministry gave qualified agreement.[231] To Portal he sent a bitterly sarcastic denunciation of the efforts to divert his force to what he called panacea targets: "In sum," he concluded, "they spell the end of our effective Bomber offensive against Germany." He spent the rest of the war grimly contesting every attempt by what he called "Panacea Target mongers" and "Diversionists" to prevent him from bombing city areas.[232]

There was little that Bomber Command could do over the autumn months to still the chorus of complaints. Evidence from attacks on Germany showed that despite the advent of the Pathfinders, levels of accuracy were still strikingly low. In December 1942 the government scientist Henry Tizard asked the command for details of its performance in recent weeks against Ruhr targets and was told that in good weather around one-third of bombs were landing within three miles of the aiming point, but in most raids the figure was still 15 percent, and sometimes zero.[233] Surveys of raids on Mainz and Munich showed a wide spread of bombs, with most incendiaries destined for Munich falling in open country. "There is at the present time," wrote Bufton in response to these findings, "a lack of grasp throughout the Command of a common tactical doctrine."[234] There was also no effective way of measuring what impact the bombing was having on the German economy, military machine, and popular morale. During 1942 the command dropped 37,192 tons of bombs on German soil, compared with 22,996 in 1941, but most of these bombs failed to hit the target area, and the raids cost some 2,716 bombers lost on operations or through accident.[235] The first scientific analysis of a major raid was supplied in November 1942 by division RE8 of the Research and Experiments Department, which used British models to calculate the likely degree of homelessness, lost man-months, and financial cost of the 1,000-bomber raid on Cologne six months before. The first statistical assessments of acreage destroyed and of the ratio between high-explosive and incendiary damage were only ready in January 1943.[236] Until then, claims that cities had been wiped out or obliterated were mere guesswork. In fact, during 1942 the damage to the German economy and society remained limited. A small number of spectacular raids in the late spring had not been sustained, and the German civil defense and repair organization coped with the consequences with little pressure. The German economy cushioned the bombing and expanded weapons output by more than 50 percent during the year. Postwar calculations in the United States Bombing Survey suggested a loss of potential overall production of 2.5 percent due to British bombing, or roughly half the impact of the German Blitz on Britain. During the course of 1942, 4,900 Germans had been killed, two for every bomber lost.[237] The one solid achievement was to compel the German enemy to divert aircraft, guns, and ammunition to defense against bombing, when they could have been used for the fighting fronts in North Africa and Russia.

At the chiefs of staff meeting on November 18, 1942, Churchill opened the discussion on bombing with the remark that at the moment it had "petered out." He continued that the answer was not megalomania— a none too oblique reference to Harris—but a more modest and achievable program.[238] There are a number of familiar explanations given for the failure to produce an operationally effective and sustained bomber offensive in the first three years of war—economic restraints on aircraft production, the demands of other theaters, the long program of training and preparation—but none of them is sufficient to understand why evident tactical, operational, and technical changes were not made sooner and consistently or a clear and convincing plan devised (or indeed why the whole strategy was not abandoned in favor of using the resources more productively). By the autumn of 1942 neither the British nor American air forces had a bombing plan beyond destroying working-class districts and attacking a limited number of industrial objectives in western Germany, and no effective effort had been made to evaluate what even this modest program might achieve strategically. The British War Cabinet finally asked the Joint Planning Staff to draw up a bombing plan in late August 1942, but nothing was approved before the end of the year.[239] Roosevelt the same month ordered Arnold to produce a comprehensive plan for the future air war, and the result, AWPD-42, was the clearest outline yet produced of how a bombing offensive should be organized and with what object, though it was still not a definite operational directive. Arnold complained to Harry Hopkins a few weeks later that what was still missing was "a simple, direct plan, tied to a definite date."[240] American frustration at the lack of strategic direction and the slow buildup of the Eighth Air Force made Arnold decide to send Spaatz to join Dwight D. Eisenhower in North Africa with a view to eventually making him overall commander of all American air forces in Europe. Spaatz was reluctant to lose operational control of the Eighth Air Force, which was now taken over by Eaker, while the start of operations in Africa, as had been feared, diverted the bombing effort to the Battle of the Atlantic and postponed even longer the start of American bombing over Germany.[241]

The most remarkable failure in the British offensive was the slow development of target finding and marking, the dilatory development of effective electronic aids, marker bombs, and bombsights, and the inability to relate means and ends more rationally to maximize effectiveness and cope with enemy defenses. The lengthy learning curve cost Bomber

Command 14,000 dead from September 1939 to September 1942. A central explanation is the poorly defined relationship between the Air Ministry, the air staff, and the commanding officers. A great deal of responsibility was delegated to the commander in chief, which in turn was delegated to the group commanders in the field. This created a wide gap between the essential scientific and tactical evaluation available from the staff in the ministry and the officers whose task it was to organize operations. The Ministry of Economic Warfare in a letter to the air minister observed that this gap reduced the prospect of learning from experience and of collectively evaluating the best use to be made of the bomber force. The ministry wanted a greater say in bombing operations, and was thus a scarcely neutral observer, but the predicament was a real one, made worse by Harris's strident defense of his independence.[242] At the same time, directives were worked out by ministry officials for the air staff with too little reference to the commanders in the field on questions of technical requirements and operational feasibility, and with no clearly articulated strategy behind them, since this was not the officials' job. The result, as a memorandum produced in May 1942 suggested, was "considerable criticism and loss of faith on both sides."[243] The crews were caught between these two poles, asked to perform impossible tasks, taking high casualties, and receiving little explanation for the wider purpose of their missions. Bufton, himself a former squadron commander, summed up this sense of frustration: "They feel that they can do more than they are doing; they grope somewhat blindly in an effort to find where the failure lies."[244]

Chapter 2

The Casablanca Offensive:
The Allies over Germany, 1943–44

At lunchtime on January 18, 1943, Air Vice Marshal John Slessor, RAF assistant chief of staff, sat on top of the roof of the Anfa Hotel in Casablanca watching "the long Atlantic rollers breaking on the beaches" while he sketched out a compromise agreement between the American and British chiefs of staff over the future of Allied strategy. Chief of Staff Charles Portal then read it through and changed a few words. In the list of strategic commitments jotted in his notebook, Slessor had included "The heaviest possible bomber offensive from the UK against GERMANY direct."[1] His hastily concocted notes were typed up and agreed to when the Combined Chiefs of Staff reassembled for the afternoon session, and they became the basis for the document on Allied strategy endorsed by Roosevelt and Churchill three days later. Slessor elaborated the idea of a heavy bomber offensive into a full draft directive, and this was presented to the Combined Chiefs on January 21 with only minor changes in the wording. It was approved, and the Casablanca Directive for a joint bomber offensive against Germany was released as policy document CCS 166 two days later.[2]

The Casablanca Conference (January 14–24) came at a critical point for the Allies. Stalin declined to come, being too occupied with the battle for Stalingrad, so the discussions focused on the future of Western Allied strategy. At stake was the balance between expanding the Mediterranean theater of war, which the United States had joined with the landings of Operation Torch in November 1942, and the plan to open a second front in France in 1943 or 1944. For the bomber forces there was more at stake. The conference opened at the end of a period of growing criticism of Bomber Command and the Eighth Air Force; it presented both forces with the opportunity to argue their case for sticking with an independent bombing strategy. This entailed a public relations exercise to sell bombing to a potentially skeptical audience. General Arnold instructed his staff to prepare detailed statistics, maps, reports, and colored charts for him to take to Casablanca, a list of props that ran to over three pages.[3] Harris took pains to ensure that a regular flow of publicity material, including good aerial photographs of damaged cities, reached the American press. The Air Ministry organized an exhibition in Washington in early January 1943, which was visited by Vice President Henry Wallace and later taken to the White House to show to Roosevelt. Wallace, it was reported, was "completely sold on the necessity of bombing Germany" as a result of what he had seen, and keen to pass on his impressions to the president. The RAF delegation in America thought of producing a film to assist Arnold's efforts to present the bombing offensive to the American public.[4] At Casablanca, Arnold fielded a full team with both Eaker and Spaatz in attendance to argue the air force case; Portal had chosen to take Slessor, a sociable air force diplomat with planning experience, rather than Harris, whose bluntness would have been out of place in the delicate discussions to follow.

It is difficult to assess whether these propaganda efforts really affected the final decision to approve a combined offensive. The outcome for the two bomber forces was in the end mixed. The Casablanca Directive was a loosely worded document, a set of hopeful intentions rather than a clear plan "that could have been made by any schoolboy," as one senior RAF officer later put it.[5] Months went by before a real planning document was produced. It was also designed to fit in with the priorities of the other services and the political leadership. Bombing was accepted at Casablanca as one way of weakening Germany before invasion rather than as an independent offensive in its own right, the same role that the German Air Force had had before the aborted Operation Sea Lion, the German plan to invade Britain in autumn 1940. Bombing survived as an option not because it was central to the strategic outlook of the Western Allies, but because it was secondary.

The Casablanca Directive

Straightforward as the final decision for CCS 166 has seemed to later historians, the conference highlighted many of the conflicts and arguments that surrounded the bombing campaign in the last months of 1942. The commitment of the two war leaders and their military staffs to a sustained bombing campaign was not a foregone conclusion. Churchill had shown increasing impatience with Bomber Command since August 1942, when he had assured Stalin on his visit to Moscow that a heavy raid on Berlin was imminent. Harris refused to attack the German capital until he had an adequate force at his disposal, and the eventual raid, code-named Tannenberg, took place only on January 17, in the middle of the conference, long after Stalin too had lost patience with the constant delays.[6] In the end Churchill had to be content with sending Stalin a list of the sixteen German cities that had been attacked between July and September 1942. Not until March 1943, more than six months after Churchill's first promise, did Stalin finally acknowledge the news that Berlin had been raided.[7] There was impatience, too, in both London and Washington, with the slow progress of the Eighth Air Force. Churchill thought that American bombers should be allocated to the war at sea and support for the landings of Operation Torch, and that the Eighth Air Force should abandon plans for a daylight offensive against Germany. In December, Spaatz warned Eaker that the Eighth had to start operations "projected into Germany" or face the prospect of diversion to the Mediterranean theater, but the first American raid on a German target was launched only on January 27, 1943, when fifty-nine bombers attacked the port at Wilhelmshaven three days after the end of the conference.[8] Arnold later reported to his chief of staff that at Casablanca he had been put permanently on the defensive by the British and American delegations "for not having our heavy bombers bombard Germany."[9]

The air forces' case at Casablanca had to be made to a disillusioned audience and it had to be made as far as possible in concert. Yet from the autumn of 1942 there were evident strains in the relationship between the RAF and the U.S. Army Air Forces, despite the public commitment to combined operations. Both air forces realized that bombing had to be presented as a more coherent strategic option than it had offered for much of 1942. In September 1942, Portal and Slessor drew up a paper on "Future Strategy," which argued for a combined offensive that would create the conditions for an easier invasion of continental Europe by weakening German resistance and might knock Italy out of the war entirely, but no effort was made to articulate what kind of bombing was needed and against which targets.[10] Arnold bemoaned the absence of any definite plan from a British air force "without strength in any one place to win decisively."[11] On September 19, 1942, his planning staff in Washington produced a detailed operational plan, AWPD-42, which resembled the British commitment to wearing Germany down prior to a land invasion, but spelled out minutely how this was to be achieved. The American plan committed their bomber force to bomb by day a list of 177 targets vital to the German war effort, dropping 132,090 tons of bombs on 66,045 operational sorties; the seven chosen target systems were the German Air Force, submarine building, communications, electric power, oil, alumina, and synthetic rubber. A counterforce strategy against the German fighter fleet was described as a key intermediate aim, whose achievement would make it possible to complete the rest of the program in time for invasion, but counterforce strategy never appealed to the RAF.[12] Portal told Arnold politely that he had read AWPD-42 "with great interest," but it does not seem to have brought the two sides to a common view except that bombing mattered to ultimate victory. Arnold complained to the American Joint Chiefs at Casablanca that the British in his view seemed incapable of thinking in global strategic terms but simply chased "the next operation"; he did not think the British "had ever had a definite bombing program," and at his insistence the Combined Chiefs of Staff were asked to draft a priority bombing program, which provided the trigger for the Casablanca Directive a few days later. Even this amounted to a compromise between the British statement of general aims about undermining German morale and American articulation of a list of priority targets.[13]

The most awkward issue at Casablanca was the argument over daylight bombing. This had been a running sore through 1942 as the Eighth

Air Force built up its capability. Churchill was strongly skeptical of the claim that daylight bombing would work. Neither the RAF nor the German Air Force had been able to sustain daylight operations against effective fighter and antiaircraft defenses, and until January 1943 the Eighth Air Force had only flown against light resistance in France. Churchill began a sustained campaign in the autumn of 1942 to persuade the American side that day bombing was too risky over Germany: "They will probably experience a heavy disaster," he minuted to Portal, "as soon as they do."[14] Churchill thought it more sensible for American bombers and crew to be converted for night work and integrated with Bomber Command. In October he asked Dwight D. Eisenhower, recently appointed supreme commander for Operation Torch, if American bombers could not be changed over to night fighting.[15] On the advice of both Portal and Sir Archibald Sinclair, the air minister, Churchill restrained himself from pressing the point too far in case the American leadership decided to switch their bombing effort to another theater. RAF leaders waited to see what would happen with daylight attacks before deciding whether to insist that the American air force accept the alternative of night bombing.[16] The American air force delegates at Casablanca knew that this was an argument they had to win. After clearing the request with Eisenhower on January 13, Arnold invited Eaker to fly to Morocco to help him present the case for the American offensive. Arnold warned him at once that Churchill had already suggested to Roosevelt that the Eighth Air Force switch to night bombing under RAF control. Eaker was asked to draft notes for "The Case for Day Bombing"; he prepared a one-page synopsis with seven principal arguments to show to Churchill and a fuller version to help Arnold influence the Combined Chiefs of Staff.[17]

Although it was unlikely that Churchill would get his way, given the weight of British and American opinion in favor of trying out the day-bombing experiment, the risk existed that Roosevelt would be too preoccupied with other issues to notice. At a high-level discussion with the president on January 18, Eisenhower and Spaatz secured agreement that neither bomber force should have the right to "alter the technique or method of operating" of the other. American fears that Harris might be placed in overall command of a joint bomber offensive were set aside by the decision to make Portal, who was a popular choice with the Americans, the nominal director of the whole bombing campaign.[18] On January 20, Eaker was given a brief appointment to see Churchill so that he could present his paper. Churchill greeted him dressed up in the uniform of an RAF air commodore and the two men sat down on a couch to talk. The prime minister read aloud the page-long list of reasons for day bombing. Eaker later recalled that when he came to the sentence about round-the-clock bombing, Churchill "rolled the words off his tongue as if they were tasty morsels."[19] Later that day Churchill was heard to remark, "Eaker almost convinced me," but he had nonetheless agreed to give day bombing over Germany a preliminary trial. At a meeting that evening Roosevelt and the army chief of staff, General George Marshall, also gave daylight bombing their blessing, and the following day Slessor was able to draft his directive for bombing by day and by night, one of the few features of the subsequent combined campaign on which both sides were agreed.[20]

The records of the many discussions held at Casablanca give little hint of the arguments over bombing taking place in the wings. In the minutes of the American Joint Chiefs of Staff the bombing campaign was mentioned briefly only three times; during the plenary sessions bombing was discussed on only two occasions, again at no length. In the list of priorities finally agreed to by the Combined Chiefs the critical issues were the commitment to an invasion of Italian territory in the Mediterranean and an eventual campaign in northwest Europe, for which bombing would be a necessary prelude to maximize the chances of success for a major combined-arms operation. Churchill telegraphed the War Cabinet from Morocco the results of the conference, but included no mention of bombing.[21] The army and navy commanders at Casablanca devoted almost nothing in their memoirs to the arguments over bomber strategy. The projection of airpower against Germany was essentially subsidiary to the wider strategic intention of reoccupying Europe during 1943 and 1944. The Casablanca Directive itself was a brief set of instructions to destroy and dislocate the German "military, industrial and economic system" and to undermine the morale of the German people to the point where the German power of resistance was "fatally weakened." This was worded in terms that were permissive rather than prescriptive, and its force was immediately compromised by the list of other tasks bombing could be called upon to perform: bombing the submarine bases in France; attacking Berlin to keep the Russians happy; a campaign against Italy when required; objectives of fleeting importance (including German naval vessels); and full support "whenever Allied Armies re-enter the Continent."[22] This was a wish list that encouraged the continued dispersion of Allied bomber forces.

When Eaker arrived back in England on January 26 he ordered the first American raid on Germany for the following day, and then dined that night with Harris to discuss what had happened. Two days later Norman Bottomley, the deputy chief of staff, was asked to send the new directive to Bomber Command. His original letter included the decision to make Portal responsible for the strategic direction of the bomber offensive, but Portal thought it more prudent not to advertise the change to his prickly subordinate, and on February 4, Harris was sent only the Casablanca Directive.[23] Although it was suggested that the new directive replaced the one issued to Bomber Command in February 1942, it is clear that Harris did not regard it as anything more than a statement of intent. In his memoirs Slessor described the Casablanca Directive, which he had drafted, as a policy statement rather than a proper directive.[24] Both air forces could read into it what they wanted.

A Combined Offensive? January–July 1943

In the last months of 1942 the term "combined offensive" began to be used more commonly. In August 1942 the Joint Planning Staff had drawn up recommendations for a concerted Anglo-American program of bombing that provided the background for the eventual directive at Casablanca.[25] The preamble to AWPD-42 stipulated that the offensive was "a combined effort" of the two air forces, the Eighth Air Force concentrating on destroying precision objectives by day, the RAF on night bombing of areas to break down morale. The passage was underlined to give it added force.[26] The combination was little more than a marriage

of convenience. American air forces based their planning and preparation on isolating and destroying Germany's key industrial and economic
targets and eliminating German airpower—much as the German Air
Force had done against Britain—while Bomber Command continued,
when able, its unremitting destruction of the central areas of German
industrial cities.

As in any marriage of convenience, the partners had separate beds.
There had been suggestions before Casablanca that there should be a
single commander for the bomber offensive. Arnold wanted a supreme
air commander for the whole European theater, but the British preferred
separate commands in Britain and the Mediterranean, and Arnold
waited for almost a year before appointing Spaatz as supreme commander of all American strategic and tactical air forces in Europe in the
face of British objections.[27] The decision to accept bombing by day and
by night underlined the need for two separate organizations, and although Portal had been given overall responsibility for coordinating the
bomber offensive, he was not in command of either the Eighth Air Force
or Bomber Command. This produced an awkward structure in which it
remained unclear exactly the limits of Portal's power or the degree of
collaboration between the two Allied bomber forces. Eaker had made it
evident well before the Casablanca Conference that he did not regard
the Eighth Air Force as in any sense under British command, though he
did submit plans to Portal for approval and looked to him for protection
from the demands of other theaters and services. "We always feel,"
Eaker wrote to Portal in late August 1943, "that our guardian and greatest friend is away when you are absent."[28] The American air forces in
Britain found the formal command lines all the way back to Washington
difficult to operate smoothly; in turn, air force officials in the U.S. capital were often poorly informed about conditions in Europe, and frustrated by the long distances. Eaker relied on Portal to supply bases and
equipment and benefited from the chief of staff's familiarity with the
offensive and with the political arguments that surrounded it. Harris
had none of these difficulties. He communicated regularly with Portal
and Churchill in defense of his command prerogatives and tolerated as

little interference as possible. The two air forces maintained liaison staff at each other's headquarters, and on occasion collaborated on a common target, but there was no mechanism for shared command. The American mission statement for the offensive described the bombing as "a *joint* assignment, completely complementary," which it was, but it remained combined in name rather than fact.[29]

The divide between the two air forces was explicit on the question of their strategic priorities. The Casablanca Directive required little adjustment for Bomber Command, which had been attacking German morale and destroying industrial cities for several years with the aim of fatally weakening the enemy. Harris remained doggedly resistant to the idea that specific target systems were strategically valuable in themselves and was hostile to the diversion of his force for other purposes. Bomber Command was committed to accruing a growing register of destruction in German cities in the hope that the attrition might at some unspecified point and in an indefinable way weaken to the point of collapse German capacity to wage war. Harris, unlike the American air force commanders, remained convinced that bombing, combined with Soviet pressure, would bring victory in 1944 without the need for an expensive ground invasion.[30]

In the discussions following Casablanca, Harris summed up for the American side his strategic achievements so far and his plans for 1943. Essen, he claimed, was "smashed out of recognition" and was out of action for two months; Berlin, Nuremberg, Munich, Cologne, and Wilhelmshaven were "badly knocked about" but not devastated; Hamburg, Duisburg, and Stuttgart had had "lucky escapes." His plan was to devastate one city and to damage three others badly each month up to September:[31]

This will mean 6 cities "Essenised" and another 18 badly knocked about. Taking cities more or less at random from last year's chief targets, this might work out as follows:–

Devastated Hamburg (counted as two by virtue of its size), Bremen, Duisburg, Wilhelmshaven, Kiel.

Badly Hit Berlin, Bochum, Cassell [*sic*], Munich, Nuremberg, Dusseldorf, Cologne, Leipsig [*sic*], Hanover, Stuttgart, Gelsenkirchen, Brunswick, Emden, Frankfurt, Mannheim, Magdeburg, Dortmund, Essen.

This was a crude strategy, crudely expressed, and it greatly exaggerated what Bomber Command could actually do to a city, including Essen. The ambition was not random only in the sense that most German cities housed some industry and could therefore be subject to attack; it could also be given a scientific gloss by the calculations supplied by the RE8 division and the Ministry of Economic Warfare (MEW) on the estimated economic damage already done and the potential economic gains from further destruction. This had allowed Portal in November 1942 to present the chiefs of staff with the grisly prediction that Bomber Command in eighteen months could kill 900,000 Germans, seriously injure another million, destroy 6 million homes, and dehouse 25 million people.[32] The MEW drew up a detailed list of all the important industrial and commercial targets in the so-called Bombers' Baedeker (after the famous German tourist guides). Each installation was awarded a point score: 1+ for factories of leading importance to the war effort; 1 for major plants in major industries; 2 for minor plants in major industries or major plants in minor industries; and 3 for factories of small importance.[33] These scores were then calculated with population size to produce a league table of German cities that Harris kept with him at his headquarters. The list eventually reached over 100 cities, with "key-point ratings" attached to each one—ranging from Berlin at number 1 with 545 to Wittenberg at number 104 with a rating of just 9. Harris crossed out each city on the list as they were attacked.[34]

American commanders rejected the idea of city bombing and were skeptical of the claim that morale attacks would diminish the German war effort or create a widespread crisis. Portal tried to persuade Eaker in February 1943 that round-the-clock attacks on cities would be strategically valuable—"heavy blows delivered on German cities have far greater effect than they did"—but Eaker would not be drawn in.[35] The gulf between the two strategic conceptions, as has often been emphasized, reflected two very different military cultures. American strategic prac-tice was much closer to the German model than it was to the British. Eighth Air Force officers could be genuinely puzzled by exactly what the British strategic aim was. At a meeting called in the Air Ministry in March 1943 by Sydney Bufton, now promoted to director of bomber opera-tions, the American representative asked for an explanation of what Bomber Command was trying to do: "Was it to kill Germans; to cause them to expend man hours; or was it to do specific damage to some cer-tain installation?"[36] There was an awkward pause until Bufton announced that it was to neutralize German man-hours, a strategic commitment not expressed in any directive. When Eaker sent a draft of the American plans for fulfilling Casablanca to Spaatz in April, Bomber Command's effort was described no fewer than four times as little more than "con-centrated attacks against related areas and cities."[37] The assumption in American planning was that Bomber Command would now help the Eighth Air Force, not the other way around.

Unlike Harris, Arnold and Eaker wanted to build on the Casablanca Directive to produce a strategic directive that made greater sense. The driving force behind American planning was the belief that whatever the air forces did over the coming year, they should contribute to mak-ing the invasion of Europe possible. The air force mission statement de-fined "fatally weakened" as "so weakened as to permit initiation of final combined operations on the Continent," which gave bombing a defined strategic purpose.[38] Arnold asked the Committee of Operations Ana-lysts in Washington, set up in December 1942 under the prominent law-yer Elihu Root Jr., to draft a list of targets whose destruction would contribute to Axis defeat; staffed by men from business and the profes-sions, the committee supplied the data on nineteen industrial target sys-tems by March 1943.[39] Arnold instructed Eaker to work out with Portal the precise number of targets and the degree of operational effort re-quired to destroy them, and by early April the draft plan for a Com-bined Bomber Offensive (CBO) was ready. The final version identified seventy-six key targets, with the aircraft industry at the top, submarines second, and ball bearings third.[40] It was sent on to Bufton by an Air Ministry colleague with a covering note that it was "dull as hell" and needed to be shorter and brighter. It had been drafted chiefly by Eaker and his staff and was based on their fundamental realization that the German air forces had to be defeated first before the subsequent precision bombing of key industrial targets could be carried out without insupportable losses, and it was this argument that separated American from British bombing strategy most clearly. The adoption of a counterforce priority proved to be strategically well founded, as it had been for the German Air Force in 1940.[41] The "intermediate target" became in effect the primary target.

The Air Ministry planning department had already tried to alert Portal to the growing threat of the German single-engine fighter force before Eaker's report was available, so that there was support from both air forces for the shift in priority. Harris sent Eaker a fulsome response, since the new plan was clearly designed for the American market and impinged little on what he hoped to do.[42] The report was sent to Washington for Arnold's approval, and in late April Eaker traveled back to the United States to defend his plan before the Joint Chiefs, who approved it on April 29. This was in some ways a more important moment than the argument at Casablanca, since the whole offensive critically relied on political approval in Washington for speeding up bomber allocation for the Eighth Air Force. Late in May, Eaker was informed from air force headquarters in Washington that the plan had been approved by the president and by Churchill; the Combined Chiefs of Staff endorsed it with Portal's strong support on May 18.[43] The new directive for what was code-named Operation Pointblank was issued to Harris and Eaker on June 10, 1943. The close link with the planning for Operation Overlord, the planned invasion of northern France, was explicit. The Combined Chiefs asked for regular reports on the progress of the CBO to help them judge when conditions for invasion were ripe. Portal set up a regular flow of monthly reports from the Joint Intelligence Committee, while Eaker promised Washington that Arnold would get an analysis every two weeks together with a monthly summary. In September the Combined Chiefs confirmed that the CBO was now the "prerequisite to 'Overlord,'" with the highest strategic priority.[44] Air supremacy was the key to successful invasion, and bombing was its instrument. In

America there was at last a sense that a proper air strategy was in place. Assistant Secretary of War Robert Lovett wrote to Eaker in July that the combined offensive "ought to have the effect of the famous old 'one-two' in prize fighting."[45]

These differences in command and strategy were compounded by the gulf separating the two forces in terms of current striking power. Bomber Command had been slowly expanded and modernized for three years before Casablanca and was closer to being able to redeem some of its tarnished promise in the spring of 1943 than the Eighth Air Force, which was still in the difficult throes of constructing a viable organization. Building up an effective bomber force differed markedly from the development of a major land army. Bomber commands consisted of volunteers with a high degree of long-term, expensive, and specialized training. The initial equipment was complex and industrially demanding. On both counts loss rates had to be kept as far as possible to a supportable minimum. The nature of air battle required numerous well-equipped permanent bases, an extensive maintenance organization, a large stock of spares, and, in the case of the Eighth Air Force, a long transoceanic logistics tail. The sharp end of air combat was supported by a ground organization many times larger than the aircrew on which the campaign rested. There was no supporting infantry in air combat.

Bomber Command became a substantial force only in the spring of 1943 as the changeover from medium to heavy bomber production was finally completed. By March 1943 it was planned to have forty-nine heavy-bomber squadrons, by June as many as sixty out of a worldwide total of 431 RAF units of all types. Heavy-bomber squadrons made up 7 percent of RAF squadron strength in September 1942, 14 percent by the summer of 1943.[46] This was still far short of what Harris had wanted. In January 1943 there were still only an average of 514 heavy bombers and crews operationally ready. Harris's command reached its peak strength in heavy bombers only in 1944 and 1945; the same was true for pilot strength, which was not much greater in 1943 than it had been in late 1941, though each of the heavier aircraft they flew dropped up to four times the weight of bombs (see table 2.1 for the growth of Bomber Command). The overall size of the command was dictated by the need for specialized

Table 2.1: Bomber Command Strength in the United Kingdom, 1939–45

Year	Squadrons (including training units)			Pilots	All Aircrew	Ground Staff	Women's Auxiliary Air Force	Airfields
	LB	MB	HB					
1939 (Sept.)	6	17	—	—	—	—	—	20
1940	6	17	—	1,110	6,702	49,685	2,408	—
1941	9	32	3	2,133	20,633	99,515	10,169	—
1942	9	33	15	1,468	23,003	115,570	22,092	45
1943	10	16	36	2,403	45,330	127,914	34,080	60
1944	5	0.5	60.5	3,747	52,476	134,834	38,157	81
1945	10	0	73	3,501	49,418	136,629	37,292	71

Figures for columns 1–3: January 1 each year. Figures for columns 4–7: July 1940, December 1941–44, May 1945. Column 8: February 1942, January 1943–45.

Source: Compiled from TNA, AIR 22/203, War Room Manual of Bomber Command Operations, 1939–1945, chart 1; AIR 20/2025, Air Ministry Statistics, RAF personnel, establishment and casualties, 1939–45; UEA, Zuckerman archive, SZ/BBSU/3, Exercise Thunderbolt, précis no. 10, "Administrative Aspects of the Bomber Offensive."

ground personnel, which meant by the start of 1943 a combat strength of 23,000 aircrew (including training and OTU personnel) and a supporting force of 138,000 men and women, a ratio of 1:6. As the force of heavy bombers and pilots expanded, the ratio changed. By the end of the war there were 49,000 aircrew supported by 174,000 ground staff, a ratio of 1:3.5.[47] Women made up 17 percent of the force by 1944.

The aggregate figures disguised manpower problems. By the summer of 1943 there were substantial shortages of skilled labor, much of it required by industry or by overseas air squadrons. This included a deficiency of 65 percent of aircraft fitters (I Class), the most important category, and an overall shortage of two-fifths of skilled technicians and more than a third of all other trades.[48] There was also a persistent shortage of construction labor for airfields, for both Bomber Command and the Eighth Air Force. Heavy bombers required larger airfields, solid runways, and extensive depots. In January 1943 there were 32,000 workers building airbases for the American force, 42,000 for Bomber Command. As demands for training facilities also expanded, more new bases had to be built. In addition to the 81 Bomber Command operational fields ready by January 1944, there were also 47 for training purposes.[49] The Eighth Air Force initially calculated that it would need 61 completed airfields by the end of 1943, but eventually built 120, utilizing 1 million man-months of labor and laying 46 million square yards of concrete. The Royal Canadian Air Force No. 6 Group was promised 15 airfields, but ended up with only 10.[50]

The pressure on airfield space was reduced by the decision very early in the war to disperse most of the basic training overseas. It is seldom sufficiently acknowledged that the British bombing effort during the war was in reality a British Commonwealth undertaking. Britain was never "alone" during the Second World War. On December 17, 1939, an agreement had been signed with the Canadian government to set up the British Commonwealth Air Training Scheme on bases in Canada. During the course of the war a peak of seventy-three schools were set up under the scheme, with a further twenty-four under RAF control. The scheme turned out 131,000 trained aircrew, including 49,808 pilots and 29,963 navigators. By 1944 over 3,000 completed training each month.

The majority (55 percent) went into the Royal Canadian Air Force (a high proportion for Canadian units in Bomber Command), while the RAF took one-third; the remainder went to the Australian and New Zealand air forces.[51] Other British aircrew were also posted to training schools in the United States under the so-called Arnold Scheme. In April 1941 the American army agreed to allow British participation in the Southeast Air Corps Training Program in the southern United States, and 7,885 pilots were sent for basic training, together with 1,200 navigators. The program was linked with Canadian training, but the failure rate in the United States was high because of the poor level of scientific education among British recruits, and the scheme petered out in 1942.[52] Although crew were trained for a variety of different combat roles, the most pressing need was for bomber crews, and it was here that overseas training had its greatest impact.

The training program was the prelude to a great expansion of Commonwealth and European participation in the bombing war. There were Free French, Dutch, Norwegian, Czech, and Polish crews in Bomber Command, but by far the largest contingents came from the main Dominion states: Canada, Australia, and New Zealand. Only the Canadian units were large enough to be organized into a separate national organization, because Canada, unlike Australia and New Zealand, was not directly menaced by Axis aggression and could confidently send its forces overseas. The RAF had not initially warmed to the idea of separate national units, partly because the complex training pattern made it difficult to keep crews from the same nationalities together as they went through the system. This was the problem with the limited number of Australians who contributed to the bombing war from British bases. Three Australian squadrons were activated, but even these could not be replenished regularly with only Australian airmen, while two-thirds of the ground personnel were British. In the spring of 1943 an effort was made by the Australian War Cabinet to stimulate creation of a distinctly Australian bomber group; there was resistance from the crews, already integrated with RAF units, and eventually an acknowledgment that the personnel needed to operate a full group could not be freed from the limited labor supply in Australia needed for the Pacific War and wartime industry.[53] The pressure from the Canadian government for the "Canadianization" of the units organized in Bomber Command had more success. On January 1, 1943, an entirely Canadian group, No. 6, was activated under the command of Air Vice Marshal G. E. Brookes. It was spread out across the Yorkshire countryside, with headquarters at Allerton Hall, nicknamed "Dismal Castle" on account of its gloomy aspect. In total, fifteen Canadian squadrons were formed, though like the Australian units they were not composed entirely of Canadians. The exception was the French Canadian squadron, formed in autumn 1942, where a great effort was made to ensure that it received only French-speaking aircrew.[54]

The Eighth Air Force was, by contrast, an almost entirely American effort. The structure of the force set up by Spaatz and then Eaker differed from Bomber Command because it also included its own fighter, training, and air service commands, which were regarded as integral to the bombing campaign. When Eaker replaced Spaatz as commander of the Eighth Air Force late in 1942, he appointed Colonel Newton Longfellow, commander of the Second Bombardment Wing, to take over the Eighth Bomber Command. The force was divided into three air divisions and then into combat wings, each with its own tactical headquarters, each wing made up of three heavy bombardment groups, or squadrons, and modeled, despite the differences in vocabulary, on Bomber Command practice. The force was still very small at the start of 1943, partly because of the decision to take a large component of aircraft and crew to establish the Twelfth Air Force in the Mediterranean theater. Some 27,000 men and 1,072 aircraft were transferred at a critical point in the buildup of the offensive, leaving Eaker temporarily with just 27,000 men and 248 heavy bombers.[55] The diversion left the Eighth Air Force as little more than a skeleton. By April there were still only 250 heavy bombers, of which around half were serviceable at any one time, a reflection of the difficulty in establishing an effective supply organization and the need for extensive modification of the B-17s for actual combat conditions. Even by June 1943 the serviceability rates for heavy bomber units was little more than half.[56] In the second half of 1943, however, the Eighth Air Force began to expand rapidly, reaching its peak strength, like Bomber Command, in late 1944 and early 1945; see table 2.2 for the buildup of the Eighth Air Force.

Even more than the RAF, the American organization relied on very extensive base facilities and a large noncombat cohort to service and maintain the force. Among the many problems facing the Eighth Air Force in the first half of 1943, the issue of supply—everything from aircrew to spare parts—was the most pressing. For Bomber Command the logistics were straightforward. For the Eighth Air Force all the combat matériel, except for heavy aircraft, which could be flown across the northern Atlantic, had to come by ship and be stored in large service depots set up at each bomber base to handle the incoming resources. A truck transport system was established that by the end of 1943 could move 1.5 million ton-miles each month. The seven principal storage depots covered an area of more than 9 million square feet.[57] The most urgent need was for service personnel. In the late spring Arnold sent Major

Table 2.2: The Buildup of the Eighth Air Force, 1943–45

Date	Heavy Bombers Assigned	Heavy Bombers Operational	Crews Available	Officers	Enlisted Men	Service Command
1943 January	225	80	85	4,525	31,716	10,181
1943 July	800	378	315	11,966	89,685	20,236
1944 January	1,630	842	1,113	19,087	137,580	58,557*
1944 July	2,688	2,036	2,007	31,586	168,055	—
1945 January	2,799	1,750	2,295	27,187	148,498	—

*Figure for December 1943.
Source: AFHRA, Maxwell, AL, 520.056-188, Statistical Summary of Eighth Air Force Operations, 1942–1945; CD A5835, "Eighth Air Force: Growth, Development and Operations 1 December 1942–31 December 1943," Personnel Status, Exhibit 1.

General Follett Bradley, inspector general of the Army Air Forces, to England to help organize an effective program to supply the trained manpower necessary to keep the Eighth Air Force flying. The "Bradley Plan" called for 190,000 personnel in the Service Command to match the planned size of the force, but the figures were always behind target in 1943, partly because around 88 percent of the air force had to be shipped across the Atlantic in competition with vital supplies for the Mediterranean and the buildup of forces for the eventual invasion of France.[58] By June 1943 five bomber groups had arrived in England without their ground crews or operational equipment and had to double up on bases that did have them.[59] The Service Command rejected the offer of help from the RAF and insisted that American aircraft should only be maintained by American workmen, but many aircraft arrived in England in need of extensive modification. To Arnold's complaints about the low level of combat readiness of the Eighth Air Force by the summer of 1943, Eaker retorted that aircraft should have been prepared for combat in the United States rather than rely on modification depots in England, which lacked the means to convert aircraft quickly.[60] It took most of the year before serviceability and replacement rates for American heavy bombers could keep more than half the air force flying.

The Eighth Air Force also suffered from the absence of a large corps of trained officers and men from the prewar air force. Some senior airmen had combat experience from the First World War, but most younger officers had never had to fire a gun or drop a bomb in anger. Arnold acknowledged that with only 1,500 regular officers in 1941, spread worldwide a year later, "the experience level is very thin."[61] Tactical thinking about the conduct of long-range bomber operations was in its infancy and relied on learning from both the British and German experience. The large number of volunteers in the United States for service in the air force had not, unlike those in the RAF, witnessed the battles over northern France and southern England or seen what bombing might achieve. Eaker called them "sturdy amateurs," not lacking in enthusiasm or courage, but not the equivalent of a highly trained peacetime force.[62] Brigadier General Haywood Hansell, temporarily in command of the Eighth Bomber Command before Longfellow's appointment (hitherto commander of the First Bombardment Wing), produced a report for Eaker in February 1943 suggesting that the force was simply not ready yet for a major offensive against Germany. Hansell added that for the following months crews should be asked to undertake shallow attacks against German targets to keep losses to a minimum and to practice with the new target-finding apparatus, Oboe and H2S, taken over from the RAF.[63] Nevertheless, the pressure on the command to show that it could produce results made it difficult for Eaker to limit what was done, even when the early raids sustained high losses and resulted in extensive combat fatigue. Between January and April the monthly loss rate averaged almost 7 percent, too high a figure for such a small force.[64] The slow expansion of the bomber units meant that crews arriving together from the United States might be broken up to fill the losses in existing groups. This process, Eaker told Arnold, created "an understandable and definite loss of morale."[65]

The problems faced by the Eighth Air Force in adjusting to new conditions of combat, thousands of miles from the United States with thousands of freshmen aircrew, were exacerbated by the often poor relations between American airmen and the British communities that had to accommodate and service them. The relationship with the air force suffered from the instinctive sense of competition between the Eighth and Bomber Command, since they were the only servicemen actively in battle against the German homeland. The numbers involved were also very large—by December 1943 there were 283,000 servicemen and civilians in the Eighth Air Force—while the irregular nature of air combat gave aircrew long periods when they lived among predominantly civilian communities. One woman, keeping a diary for the British Mass Observation public opinion surveys, condemned Americans as "loud, bombastic, bragging, self-righteous." Opinion polls showed that the British public most disliked American "boastfulness," "immaturity," and "materialism."[66] Though established prejudices might explain some of this reaction, the behavior of mostly very young men a long way from home, learning "British English," contributed to the confrontation. Eighth Air Force commanders were warned in December 1942 that "unbridled speech" was causing embarrassment to Anglo-American relations and that all supplies of alcohol to the command would be suspended if it continued.[67] General Marshall wrote to all senior commanders that American officers had encouraged a "marked hostility and contempt for the British," and great efforts were made to introduce activities that would educate the American servicemen into treating their British hosts with greater respect and dignity. The provost marshal of the Eighth Air Force, in a lengthy report on the conduct of airmen toward the British, complained of the persistent "Limey complex" that made them largely indifferent to their hosts unless there was the prospect of sex. A Special Service Study found that only 2 percent of the American airmen had actually visited a British home.[68] The Eighth Air Force set up a speakers' pool with officers assigned to give talks to British audiences about American customs and manners; between April and September 1943 the speakers averaged fifteen lectures a month, a grand total of 241. Eaker joked that out of the three possible crimes his men might indulge in—murder, rape, and "interference with Anglo-American relations"—the first two might under certain circumstances be pardoned, "but the third one, never."[69]

British criticism was not confined to popular areas of social friction. Over the first half of 1943 there was evidence of mounting frustration from the Air Ministry and Bomber Command over the long apprenticeship and unredeemed promises from the American air force. Harris and Portal both pressed Eaker to collaborate more fully in the renewed offensive in the spring of 1943, though both well knew that Bomber Command had taken three years to reach its current size and capability. There were British complaints about the quality of the B-17 Flying Fortress as a daylight bomber and arguments over the effectiveness of the new American oil-based incendiary bomb, the six-pound M-69. British tests suggested that the new bomb lacked penetration, had an unreliable fuse, and suffered from relatively low incendiary efficiency, and despite American objections to the test results, the RAF continued to use the standard four-pound incendiary.[70] There were strong objections to the British view of the B-17, but the American judgment on the bombers currently employed also accepted that the two main bombers, the Flying Fortress and the B-24 Liberator, were rapidly reaching the end of their useful life.[71] Indeed, the harshest criticism of Eighth Air Force performance came from the American side, not from the RAF. Arnold, whose health deteriorated badly during 1943, finally lost patience with Eaker's force in June 1943. Citing the number of aircraft already sent to Britain, Arnold telegraphed Eaker that the number of bombers sent out on each mission "is not rpt not satisfactory," and told him bluntly to change his commanders and staff to find officers who could organize attacks in "a highly efficient manner."[72]

In the short correspondence that followed, Eaker was defensive about his force and resentful of Arnold's intervention. Arnold ought certainly to have known better, since the ratio between aircraft supplied and aircraft on missions always had to take account of those awaiting repair, modification, or use for training purposes. "Neither of us," Eaker replied, "has been able to accomplish ideal for reasons both should appreciate. We get nowhere with recrimination."[73] Nevertheless, Eaker agreed to make major changes in his command structure, anxious perhaps about the security of his own position. Longfellow, whom Arnold regarded as insufficiently aggressive, was redeployed to Washington; Hansell was passed over (too "nervous and highly strung," according to Eaker); responsibility for the Eighth Bomber Command was given on July 1, 1943, to Brigadier General Frederick Anderson, commander of the Third Bombardment Wing, while Hansell was replaced as commander of the First Bombardment Wing in June. The Third Wing was taken over by a young commander admired by both Arnold and Eaker, Colonel Curtis LeMay, future chief of the Strategic Air Command after the war. Anderson had arrived in England in February, flew his first mission to Rouen on March 15 ("enjoyed it thoroughly"), and in his diary looked forward to the day when a stream of B-17s would be taking off every day "as they carry out their joy, dropping bombs on Germany." He flew regularly with his crews and took the same risks they did.[74] Though Anderson had only been a few months in active service, Eaker judged that he had the right character for high command, though he regretted losing Longfellow, who was a close friend. "This Bomber Command job of ours is a killer," he told Arnold. "It will break anybody down in six months unless he is a very unusual fellow."[75] What had most concerned Arnold during the command crisis was not so much the virtue of the bomber offensive itself and its achievements as the extent to which it represented the claims to a distinct air force identity and a distinct strategy. For Arnold this meant a clear demonstration to the American public that the offensive was producing results that would inspire their "faith in *our way of making war*."[76]

The different force profiles and levels of preparation were no more sharply evident than in the contrast between the operational performance of the two bomber forces over the course of 1943, when Harris launched what have come to be seen as the three major battles of the bomber offensive, against the Ruhr-Rhineland in the late spring and early summer of 1943, against Hamburg in July, and against Berlin in the autumn. The campaign against the Ruhr-Rhineland was not in any sense a new one, since it had been a first priority for bombing ever since the onset of the campaign in May 1940. The difference in the spring of 1943 was the advent of substantial numbers of heavy bombers, particularly the Lancaster. During the months from March to June, when the Ruhr battle took place, the operational strength of Bomber Command averaged 794 heavy bombers, of which 578 (or 73 percent) were serviceable. Each bomber dropped an average of just over 7,000 pounds of bombs, against an average load of 4,970 for the Eighth Air Force throughout 1943.[77] The Pathfinder Force was now fully equipped with the Mosquito Mk IX, which utilized the new electronic aids, Oboe Mk IA and H2S, which were both now available in sufficient quantity, though H2S proved a disappointment over heavily urbanized areas. Raids on the Ruhr had always been subject to the hazards of cloud and industrial smog and the effective use of decoy sites. Navigation equipment no longer dependent on visual sighting was expected to allow a much greater degree of concentration at or near the principal aiming point. Over the target, new systems of marking had been developed using bright white markers when the ground was visible, or red, green, and yellow sky markers when it was not. The colorful flares were known by the code name Wanganui; the German public called them "Christmas trees." Once at the target the new Mk XIV bombsight could be used even when the aircraft took evasive action.[78] Radio countermeasures were available to block the German Freya radar, code-named Mandrel, and to interfere with

German ground-control transmissions, known as Tinsel, while new airborne devices to warn of German night fighters and radar ("Monica"
and "Boozer") were finally being used, though again with only mixed effect.[79] All of these many technical and tactical innovations made Bomber
Command a much more formidable threat. In a speech later in the war,
Harris admitted to an army audience that the bomber offensive only
started seriously in March 1943.[80]

The first major raid on the Ruhr was made on the night of March
5–6 against Essen. A force of 442 aircraft attacked with 1,014 tons of
bombs, two-thirds of them incendiaries. The Pathfinders worked well
and an estimated 75 percent bombed within three miles of the city center, which was the principal aiming point. The apparent success of the
raid gave Harris his verb "to Essenise" the target, but the next raid on
Essen was less successful, and a major raid on Duisburg on March 26–
27 was scattered, largely because five out of nine of the Pathfinder Mosquito aircraft had to turn back with technical problems. A major raid on
Berlin, conducted at Churchill's suggestion, lost direction and hit the
capital with only ten high-explosive bombs; the next raid missed the city
altogether. Although the Ruhr plan was the first time Bomber Command had concentrated on a single coherent target, major raids were
also made on more distant cities, reducing the impact on the Ruhr-
Rhineland to no great effect. Attacks on Munich and Stuttgart recorded
between one-fifth and one-third of bombs within three miles of the aiming point, levels of accuracy not significantly better than the year before.[81]
Between March and June, when the battle against the Ruhr came to an
end, Bomber Command had launched twenty-eight raids against cities
in the Ruhr-Rhineland area, but another eighteen raids against targets
in central Germany, Italy, and France. Though the pattern of destruction varied widely between the different operations, the attacks on the
Ruhr-Rhineland were the first raids to inflict serious levels of destruction on the urban area.[82]

The reaction from the German side was to search for new ways to cope
with the sudden escalation of RAF capability. Hitler was preoccupied with
stabilizing the war in Russia and North Africa but angered by what he saw
as the continued failures in air defense. His air adjutant Nicolaus von

Below recalled long evening conversations with Hitler about the inadequacy of antiaircraft fire, the incompetence of Göring, and the shortage of modern aircraft designs, but Hitler remained, according to von Below, "at a loss" on questions of airpower.[83] To stifle widespread popular anxiety, Joseph Goebbels, "Minister for Popular Enlightenment and Propaganda," ordered the press and propaganda agencies to stop using the word "mood" to describe public attitudes, which could evidently be widely variable, and to write only about "high morale."[84] Security Service intelligence reports showed the population in the bombed regions dismayed and restless at the apparent absence of effective defense, while exaggerated rumors of the extent of the destruction and casualties in the Ruhr were in circulation throughout the unbombed areas and could not be stopped. "Even sensible people," ran one report, "have given these rumors credence."[85]

The German defenses against night bombing were nevertheless stronger than they had been a year before. General Josef Kammhuber had around 400 night fighters, double the level of the previous year, organized in five wings. There were around 500 day fighters in the Western theater protecting the Reich against daylight incursions. Each box in the *Himmelbett* system now had enough radars to control three fighters at a time, and had developed the means to pass on information to neighboring boxes, but the rigid nature of the fixed line of air defense made less sense against large concentrations of heavy bombers that could routinely swamp the line as they crossed into Germany. Kammhuber proposed a single central authority to control the whole night-defense system and a fivefold increase in the night-fighter force, but the proposal was rejected by Hitler in favor of strengthening antiaircraft and searchlight defenses around the vulnerable inland areas.[86] As a result the night-fighter force stagnated, taking losses of 282 aircraft during the period of the Ruhr battle, against an overall loss of 600 RAF bombers from all causes. Pressure to change to a more flexible system of defense was rejected. The idea of using ground-control stations to direct night fighters into the bomber stream so that they could fly with it, shooting down any bomber that came within range, a tactic known as Zahme Sau ("Tame Boar"), was turned down because it would drain resources away from the Kammhuber Line; a second proposal from Major Hans-Joachim

Hermann to use single-engine day fighters at night against bombers illuminated by searchlights, flares, and target markers, known as Wilde Sau ("Wild Boar"), arrived too late for the spring attacks and was again difficult to integrate with the existing system.[87] Kammhuber's insistence that his aerial fortification was the only way to combat the bombers brought him into conflict with Göring and his deputy, Erhard Milch, and in November he was finally relieved of his command and sent to run the rump Air Fleet 5 in Norway.

In the midst of the campaign against the Ruhr, Harris was compelled to organize an operation of which he fundamentally disapproved. The engineer Barnes Wallis had begun work in 1940 on the kind of explosive device needed to breach a major dam wall. In March 1941 an Air Attack on Dams Committee was set up to study the possibility, using the Road Research Laboratory as a base. In April 1942, Wallis developed the idea of a cylindrical bomb, dropped from a low height, to bounce across the water and drop to the foot of the dam wall; codenamed Upkeep, the bomb tests represented a real technical challenge but were convincing enough by February for the air staff to approve a possible operation against the German Möhne, Sorpe, and Eder dams.[88] When the report was passed to Harris, he scrawled at the bottom, "This is tripe of the wildest description . . . not the smallest chance of it working."[89] Nevertheless, more trials were conducted to determine whether the "bouncing bomb" was a viable operational proposition. A squadron of Lancasters under Wing Commander Guy Gibson, no. 617 squadron, was activated on March 21, 1943, and trained rigorously for an operation against the reservoir dams that supplied water for the Ruhr. Harris remained adamantly unconvinced: "As I always thought," he minuted in April, "the weapon is balmy [sic] . . . get some of these lunatics controlled or if possible locked up."[90] His skepticism was ignored. On the night of May 16–17, under the code name Operation Chastise, nineteen Lancasters were dispatched, of which twelve attacked the three dams, breaching the Möhne and the Eder, but doing only superficial damage to the Sorpe. Two-thirds of the water escaped from the reservoirs and 1,294 people were drowned in the inundation, including 493 foreign workers. The destroyed dams lost an estimated 25,000–30,000 tons of masonry, but both were repaired by October, while the long-term damage to the industrial water supply was less than had been hoped.[91] Further attacks were ruled out, partly because of the high loss rate. Only eight Lancasters returned from the raid and 56 out of the 113 aircrew were lost.

The early raids against the Ruhr were regarded by Harris as less than satisfactory. The proportion of aircraft dropping bombs within three miles of the aiming point varied greatly. The experiment with sky marking showed that out of eleven raids that used it, one resulted in severe damage, one in considerable damage, eight in "scattered damage," and one in no damage at all. The photoreconnaissance evidence on major raids showed that the percentage of hits within three miles varied from 80 percent to 25 percent, with most less than 50 percent.[92] Harris assumed that "weaker brethren," as he called them, were failing to press home attacks, while he singled out the tactic of violent evasive action (an instinctive response to intense searchlight and antiaircraft activity) as a key culprit. In early May 1943 he circulated a tactical memorandum to groups on "Evasive Action by Bombers" to replace existing instructions, which had given pilots advice on what forms of evasion to take under different circumstances. The new memorandum insisted that most forms of evasion were "useless," since an antiaircraft barrage was indiscriminate and inaccurate (a claim scarcely justified by the 1,496 bombers damaged by antiaircraft fire during the campaign). Evasion, the report continued, increased the chance of collision, kept bombers longer in the danger zone, and placed serious strain on the aircraft structure. Crews were told to fly "straight and level" through the target area to increase the concentration of bomb hits.[93] Whether crews really did respond to the instruction, or whether the growing experience of the Pathfinders and the surviving pilots reduced losses and increased concentration, the major raids carried out between May and July against Cologne, Duisburg, and Wuppertal-Barmen resulted in the most destructive and lethal attacks so far.

These last raids produced very heavy damage to the centers of the cities, and in the case of Barmen, attacked on the night of May 29–30 by 719 bombers, created a major conflagration that consumed four-fifths of the built-up area and killed 3,400 people, the largest number in any one raid until then. Wuppertal, the other half of the town of Wuppertal-Barmen, was raided on June 24–25 by 630 aircraft and 94 percent of its urban area was destroyed or damaged, with 1,800 deaths. In the four months of the heavy "crash raids," as they were called, an estimated 22,200 were killed, almost twice the number killed in the whole period since May 1940. Some 55,700 buildings were rendered for the moment uninhabitable. "They had ruined the Ruhr," complained Hitler in June, though only 5 percent of buildings were actually destroyed.[94] The exact nature of the damage could not be known to Bomber Command, but intelligence estimates of the damage to the Ruhr were constructed in the summer to give Harris the necessary matériel to defend his city-bombing campaign. This was difficult to do and had to be based on extrapolation from the detailed statistical surveys of housing damage and man-hour losses in British cities bombed in 1941 and 1942. The Joint Intelligence Committee estimated that 9 percent of the population of the most heavily raided cities were homeless (422,500) and 38.5 percent (1,816,000) had housing damage. The committee estimated that 68,750 houses had been destroyed, a figure closer to the reality than might be expected from simple photoreconnaissance. Estimating the impact on the economy was more difficult. The Krupp works in Essen were thought to have lost between one-quarter and one-half of planned output over the summer. The MEW estimated a total loss to German production of 10–12 percent from attacks on the Ruhr-Rhineland (including 2–2.5 million tons of steel) and a bad state of morale.[95] A study by the RE8 department two months later of the impact of the raids on Essen, based on studies of British workers during the Baedeker raids on historic British cities in the spring of 1942, concluded that if German workers reacted in the same way as British workers to the loss of housing and amenities, then Essen lost the equivalent of fifty city-days of work. None of these efforts at calculating what Bomber Command was achieving were coordinated or consistent. Nor could they confirm whether bombing was a strategically sensible use of British resources.[96]

Alongside the night bombing, the Eighth Air Force, as one senior American commander put it, "can only nibble at the fringes of German strength."[97] There were three small raids on German territory in March;

one in April (a mission to Bremen that cost the loss of 15 percent of the force); six attacks on the north German coast in May; and three in June, including the only attack on the Ruhr, against the synthetic rubber plant at Hüls on June 22, where the loss rate was almost 9 percent.[98] The two forces were at quite different stages. In the first six months of 1943, Bomber Command dropped 63,000 tons of bombs, the Eighth Air Force only 8,400 more. For the American command, Operation Pointblank had not yet started; in contrast, the RAF, as the director of plans explained in March 1943, hoped that bombing "may well produce decisive results this year." There was nevertheless no prospect that the two bomber forces would constitute what the Joint Intelligence Committee called after the Ruhr offensive "an organic whole," because of continued American resistance to the idea that bombing cities was strategically useful. The Ruhr battle was one of a long line of Bomber Command campaigns in which the Eighth Air Force was largely absent.[99]

Operation Gomorrah: The Destruction of Hamburg

Back in November 1941 the Directorate of Bomber Operations in the Air Ministry had concluded from a study of urban targets in northern Germany that Hamburg was the city that presented the best general conditions for a large-scale incendiary attack. Since the area was large, "saturation point" would be harder to achieve. The report continued that if Hamburg was selected for special incendiary attack, "the whole of the effort should be confined to the congested city and housing areas North of the Elbe." To get a clear picture of what saturation point might look like, the directorate used a map of central London as a model, placing transparencies with a typical incendiary bomb salvo printed on them over the London streets to work out how widely the bombs would spread and how vulnerable the buildings might be.[100] Over the winter of 1941–42 a great deal of effort went into working out how to create a major conflagration with the existing technology. In February 1942 a further memorandum on choosing a German city to burn down had Hamburg at the top of the list, its vulnerability rated "outstanding."[101]

Harris might well have tried to exploit that vulnerability in May

1942 when he planned the first 1,000-bomber raid, but poor weather prevented it. Had he done so, Hamburg would certainly have sustained far less damage and loss of life than proved to be the case when Harris finally decided, on May 27, 1943, that it would suffer next what he was inflicting on the cities of the Ruhr-Rhineland. What resulted in a series of raids appositely titled Operation Gomorrah was the single largest loss of civilian life in one city throughout the whole European war, exceeded only by the 250,000 Japanese killed in the firebombing of Tokyo and the atomic attacks on Hiroshima and Nagasaki. The destruction of Hamburg in an uncontrollable firestorm on the night of July 27–28, 1943, is often presented as if it were an accident, the result of exceptional meteorological conditions and the failure of German defenses, and not a product of deliberate intention. This is to misunderstand entirely the purpose of the city-bombing campaign, which was predicated from the start on causing as much general damage and loss of life as possible by means of large-scale fires. The firebombing of Hamburg was not exceptional. Not for nothing was its vulnerability rated "outstanding"; it was expected to burn well.

To understand the capacity of Bomber Command to inflict a conflagration of such intensity on Hamburg, it is useful to place it in the context of the long operational and scientific effort devoted by the Air Ministry to understanding how incendiarism worked. When the RE8 department was established in the summer of 1942, one of the first tasks given to it by the Air Ministry was research into the spread of fire and the role of wind speeds in turning a strong blaze into a conflagration. It was assumed that city fires could be acted upon much as a pair of bellows on a domestic hearth if the wind speed and direction were favorable. "Once a large conflagration has become established," wrote one of the department's scientific advisers, "the 'fire-storm' which it induces is sufficient to ensure its further spread."[102] On the advice of J. D. Bernal, wind trials were conducted by the Porton Down Experimental Station in Wiltshire using models of urban areas, while the RAF Photo-Interpretation Section provided night photographs to help in identifying the factors that accelerated the spread of fire.[103] It was also necessary to determine scientifically the vulnerability to firebombs of German urban structures, in particular town houses and apartment blocks, and the quantity and mix of bombs necessary to overwhelm the fire services in a single raid. Work on German structures began in 1942 and was more or less complete by the time of the final RE8 report on "German Domestic Architecture" issued early in 1943. Tests on models of different kinds of German roofs were carried out at the Road Research Laboratory at Harmondsworth, outside London, while material on German staircases and stairwells was supplied from a German publication on "Residences and Houses of the Middle Classes."[104] The study of German architecture had involved a good deal of argument over the average thickness of wood beams and the penetrative power of the standard four-pound incendiary bomb, which had only been resolved by recruiting émigré German architects, including the Bauhaus founder, Walter Gropius, to confirm the details of construction. The conclusion from studies of roof coverings, joists, and floor density typical of construction in northwestern Germany and Berlin was that "a German house will burn well."[105]

The most important issue was to decide what mix and weight of bombs would best achieve a conflagration that was beyond the control of the ground defenses. The quantity of incendiary and high-explosive bombs judged to be necessary to destroy each square mile of the target city was cranked up regularly during the two years before Operation Gomorrah. Initial research suggested that between 100,000 and 200,000 four-pound bombs would swamp any fire-watching and firefighting force, but they had to be dropped in large salvos, not in small packets.[106] By late 1942 incendiary technique was better understood. Its purpose, as one Air Ministry report put it, was "the complete destruction by fire of the built-up area of a city." This required a fire-raising group to isolate the target and start fires pronounced enough for the follow-up force to drop 25,000 incendiaries for each square mile attacked as well as high-explosive bombs to destroy windows, crater the streets, and intimidate civil defense and fire workers. In order to start a conflagration the target area had to be the most densely packed residential areas of the city center, Zones 1 and 2A on the zone maps supplied to Bomber Command. Igniting the "terraces of box-like buildings dating from the Middle Ages" was, according to the Bomber Directorate, expected to "yield good dividend."[107]

To prevent effective firefighting, the incendiary load had to contain not only regular incendiaries but also the delayed-action explosive incendiary, capable of maiming or killing enemy civil defense workers and deterring them from action. These devices were deliberately timed to detonate at irregular intervals, some after three minutes, a small proportion only after ten.[108] In late 1942 a small antipersonnel high-explosive bomb with a trigger fuse was developed, which could be activated by any object, even a jet of water, and would kill those immediately around it without warning.[109] It was suggested that a high proportion of delayed-action bombs should be used in "incendiary attacks on virgin towns" to create a powerful deterrent effect on the enemy emergency services.[110] There was also considerable argument about the merits of complementing the conventional magnesium bomb with larger oil-based incendiaries, which were also subjected to rigorous scientific testing. The result was the selection of the thirty-pound Mk II containing a mix of white phosphorus and benzol gel, capable of greater penetration than the four-pound incendiary, and effective in spreading fire quickly over a wider area.[111] All of these bombs were eventually produced and used in substantial quantities over the last three years of the war, peaking in 1943 (see table 2.3).

There was strong American interest in the development of incendi-

Table 2.3: Incendiary Bombs Dropped by the RAF, 1940–45

Year	4-lb. bomb	4-lb. explosive bomb	30-lb. bomb	No. 14 IB Cluster (106 × 4-lb.)
1940	508,993	—	—	—
1941	2,082,669	—	758	—
1942	8,010,920	—	309,200	—
1943	25,898,290	1,469,853	1,728,949	—
1944	18,392,077	1,498,723	979,182	6,288,460
1945	6,761,544	690,523	—	3,764,670

Source: TNA, AIR 22/203, War Room Manual of Bomber Command Operations, 1939–1945, 54.

ary bombing. The conventional view that the Eighth Air Force used predominantly high-explosive bombs for precision air attacks in contrast to the fire-raising tactics of Bomber Command is not borne out by the evidence. The Bomber Directorate in the Air Ministry collaborated closely with the American Office of Scientific Research and Development, which produced studies on the "Theory and Practice of Incendiary Bombing" and supplied the British with illustrated volumes on major conflagrations in American cities, which were more common and more destructive than in Europe. The photographs resemble closely the aftermath of the major city bombing in Germany.[112] In December 1942, America's foremost expert on fire in foreign countries, Boris Laiming, filed a report that was passed on to the Air Ministry in December 1942. He argued that the only way to start a major conflagration under conditions normally prevailing in Germany was to start a great many smaller fires simultaneously on long strips of urban territory on a day when there was a reasonable wind and low humidity.[113] In the United States, experiments were made at the Chemical Warfare Service depot in Utah in burning down different kinds of structures and at a facility in New Jersey on penetrating simulated German roofing with incendiaries.[114] American expertise was also invited to Britain. Horatio Bond, chief engineer of the National Fire Protection Association, visited London for four months in late 1942 to give advice on large-scale fire destruction, followed a few months later by James McElroy, another senior NFPA engineer, who worked for the rest of the war at the RE8 headquarters at Princes Risborough in Buckinghamshire, first producing so-called fire division maps of German cities, showing each urban "cell" that needed to be set alight, then going on to produce vulnerability maps of major industrial targets for the Eighth Air Force Operational Research Section, to show what proportion and what type of incendiary bomb should be carried by aircraft.[115]

The American air force was impressed by British incendiary practice. In April 1943, Arnold spelled out for his assistant chief of staff for matériel the ways in which the Eighth Air Force would be expected to use incendiary bombs: first, for burning down precise industrial targets when a greater degree of destruction was possible using fire; second, by

starting fires "in the densely built-up portions of cities and towns" to create a beacon for RAF attacks at night on the same city or town; third,
for burning down densely built-up areas "when the occasion warrants."[116]
American forces used principally the 4-pound incendiary (renamed the
M-50), the M-17 110-bomb cluster, the M-47 70-pound oil and rubber
bomb, and the M-76 473-pound oil bomb. Extensive plans were laid in
1942 for incendiary bomb production, 39 million bomb cases in that
year, 107 million in 1943, divided between the different services and
Lend-Lease supplies for Britain.[117] Extensive research on the effects of
incendiary bombing resulted in a set of recommendations for the Eighth
Air Force in September 1942, which differed from RAF practice principally by preferring the 473-pound oil bomb over the 4-pound incendiary
and identifying weather as a vital condition: "A high wind is still the best
weapon." Bomb patterns were to be dense enough "to *guarantee* real conflagrations."[118] Extensive experiments were carried out in Britain on the
use of oil bombs of different weights, and in April large quantities were
finally shipped to American bases for operational use. They were first
employed extensively in July 1943, the month of Operation Gomorrah.
By the end of the war the Eighth Air Force had dropped a total of 90,357
tons of incendiaries and incendiary clusters, totaling 27 million 4-pound
bombs and 795,000 heavy incendiaries.[119]

The two-thirds load of incendiary bombs aimed at the residential
areas in Hamburg north of the river Elbe to try to stimulate an uncontrollable conflagration was thus no accident. The choice of Hamburg is
not difficult to explain. The Air Ministry Target Committee in April
1943 defined Hamburg as "No. 1 priority" because of its shipbuilding
industry.[120] It had been attacked repeatedly since 1940, usually in small
raids that inflicted light damage on Germany's second-largest city.
There were 127 small raids between 1940 and the end of 1942; the 10
raids in 1943 before Gomorrah resulted in just 142 deaths and the destruction of 220 buildings.[121] Hamburg was fourth on the MEW list, behind Berlin, Duisburg, and Bochum, all three of which had been
attacked in the late spring. The MEW rankings in the "Bomber's Baedeker" had twenty-one industrial targets ranked 1+ or 1 and twenty-five
ranked 2, substantially more than most other cities.[122] The vulnerability

of Hamburg was magnified by its proximity to British bases, the conspicuous coastline, and its sheer size. In a survey of German cities already subject to incendiary attack, the ratio of incendiary to high-explosive damage in Hamburg was judged to have been 13:1, higher than any other except the nearer port of Wilhelmshaven.[123] It is not clear whether Harris was ever shown these figures, but his desire to launch a spectacular operation fitted with the geographical pattern of the new attacks and Air Ministry ambitions. Not to have attacked Hamburg in force would have been more difficult to explain.

The decision was nevertheless not easily endorsed and rested in the end on Churchill's approval. The chief argument concerned the decision of whether to use a simple tactical device to temporarily blind all German radar, known by the code name Window. The tactic consisted of dropping very large quantities of small aluminized strips that would create a confused blur of echoes on enemy radar screens and make accurate detection of the bomber stream impossible. It was first developed in late 1941 by Robert Cockburn at the Telecommunications Research Establishment in Malvern, and early trials led to the manufacture of the material with a view to using it against German radar in May 1942. Frederick Lindemann persuaded Portal to cancel the instruction, and a fresh set of tests showed that the latest British ground and airborne radar was highly susceptible to Window if the Germans retaliated with it. Lindemann insisted that it should not be used operationally until an antidote could be found. The Germans did develop the same technique, known as Düppel, but, like the RAF, hesitated to develop and use it. However, by late 1942 new British AI radar for night fighters and GCI (ground-controlled interception) radar for ground control, together with a new American airborne radar, SCR-270, all had the capacity to survive a Window assault. American experiments also showed that maximum effect would come from a large number of narrow strips, about half as long as the wavelength of the German Würzburg radar, which controlled the German air defenses. Window was manufactured in 30-centimeter (12-inch) strips, 1.5 centimeters (0.6 inch) wide, with paper on one side and aluminum foil on the other, in bundles of 2,000 for release from each aircraft in the bomber stream.[124]

The combination of improved British defenses and the weakness of the German bomber arm in the west finally persuaded Portal to approve the employment of Window, but now the chiefs of staff objected to its operational use before the invasion of Sicily in early July, in case the German Air Force used it to confuse Allied air support during the landing. As a result its use was postponed until Operation Gomorrah, following approval by Churchill on July 15.[125] A few days later Churchill was faced with another objection, this time the choice of Hamburg as a target at all. Henry Tizard, the government's chief scientific adviser, wrote to Churchill and Portal deploring the planned destruction of Hamburg on the grounds that it would be a useful capital for the Allies to occupy when they ran postwar Germany, and that its population was "anti-Russian, anti-Prussian and anti-Nazi," and might soon be "anti-war." Churchill sent the letter to the chiefs of staff, but Portal had already answered Tizard, explaining that Hamburg was too important a target to ignore. "It is a moot point," he continued, "whether bombing produces a more desirable effect when directed upon anti-Nazis than upon the faithful," but he was content for Harris to find out whether Hamburg's anti-Nazi sentiment would be stung into action by bombing. Churchill took this for approval.[126] By then the first of the Gomorrah raids had already taken place.

The operation against Hamburg, like the heavy bombing of Cologne in late June and early July, was spread over ten days from the first RAF raid on July 24–25 to the final raid on August 2–3.[127] The opening night-bombing raid by 728 aircraft was the first to use Window. Around eighty miles from the target the Pathfinder Force and the main force that followed emptied bundles of foil strips at the rate of one bundle a minute. The strips worked perfectly, creating numerous echoes on the cathode-ray radar screens and presenting German night fighters with a confusion of false information. Searchlights and antiaircraft artillery had to improvise a barrage of light and fire in the hope that bombers might be deterred anyway. In just under one hour 2,284 tons of bombs were dropped, including an average of 17,000 incendiaries for every square kilometer.[128] Although fewer than 50 percent of the bombers hit the three-mile aiming zone, the rest hit the large central and northwestern residential districts, killing, according to the Reich Statistical Office, 10,289 people, three times more than the worst raid so far.[129] Over the following two days the Eighth Air Force attacked targets by day in northwest Germany. On July 24, 218 bombers bombed shipbuilding targets in Hamburg and Kiel, losing 19 aircraft in the process; on July 25, 96 aircraft attacked Hannover and 54 raided Hamburg, with the loss of a further 18 aircraft, a rate over the two days of more than 10 percent, an indication that the warnings about the dangers of daytime bombing voiced at Casablanca had not been misplaced. The two American raids killed 468 people in Hamburg.[130]

The RAF raid that followed on the night of July 27–28 was a textbook example of the incendiary planning of the previous two years. It was helped by the prevailing meteorological conditions. There had been rainfall on July 22, but the remainder of the week was dry. Humidity levels, which had been high earlier in the month, fell abnormally, reaching 46 percent on July 25 and only 30 percent on July 27. Temperatures soared in the last week, reaching 32°C (90°F) on the evening of July 27; low humidity and high temperatures remained over the following two days. These summertime conditions favored the chances of a major conflagration.[131] The Pathfinder Force dropped markers several miles east of the center of Hamburg, but the 729 aircraft concentrated their 2,326 tons well on the packed working-class districts of Hammerbrook, Borgfelde, Hamm, Billwerder, Hohenfelde, and Rothenburgsort. The raid lasted just over an hour. The concentration of approximately 1,200 tons of incendiaries on an area of two square miles created numerous major fires that soon merged together into a roaring inferno. Water shortages caused by the earlier heavy raid hampered firefighting. Many emergency workers and vehicles were farther west in the city still coping with the aftermath of the first fires where the civil defense control room had been destroyed. Efforts to stem the fires proved useless. What followed, in the words of Hamburg's police president, was a "hurricane of fire . . . against which all human resistance seemed vain."[132] The illusion of a hurricane was caused by the scale and intense heat of the conflagration, which caused fire winds that drove the flames across natural firebreaks. The inferno created a pillar of hot air and debris that rose quickly to a height of more than two miles above the city. Greedy for more oxygen, the fire drew in cold air from the surrounding area with such force that the new winds reached hurricane-force strength in the area of the fire, collapsing buildings, uprooting trees, and sucking human bodies into the flames where they were swiftly incinerated or mummified. Acting like giant bellows, the winds created temperatures in excess of 800°C that destroyed everything combustible barring brick and stone. Oxygen was sucked out of the thousands of basement and cellar shelters, leaving their inhabitants to die slowly of carbon monoxide poisoning.[133] An estimated 18,474 people died during the night. An area of more than twelve square miles was burnt out.

This was not the end for Hamburg. Harris's intention of destroying the city brought two more major raids on July 29–30 and August 2–3. The first, carried out by 707 bombers, dropped a higher tonnage than the firestorm night, but did not create a second thermal hurricane. Large residential areas were again burnt out and an estimated 9,666 killed. The final raid in August was abortive. Large thunderstorms protected Hamburg. The Pathfinder force failed to mark the city and most aircraft dropped their bombs over northern Germany or in the North Sea. The final raid killed 78 people. The cumulative total for Operation Gomorrah calculated by the local police authorities by November 1943 was 31,647; the figure was revised in May 1944 to 38,975, which is close to the figure currently favored of 37,000.[134] Around 900,000 people evacuated the city and 61 percent of Hamburg's houses and apartments were destroyed or damaged, together with 580 industrial premises and 2,632 shops. The RAF bomber force lost only 87 aircraft, or 2.5 percent of all sorties, thanks partly to the use of Window, partly to the shock effect on Hamburg's defenses. The post-raid report noted that smoke obscured much of the evidence of destruction but confirmed that the "amount of residential damage is very great."[135]

The consequences for the German air defense system were profound. The catastrophe at Hamburg even more than the raids on the Ruhr catapulted the German Air Force into abandoning the principle of the fixed front, embodied in the Kammhuber Line and heavy reliance on antiaircraft fire, and substituting instead a much larger fighter force based on new forms of combat. Even before the conflagration at Hamburg, Göring, despite his anxiety to begin offensive air operations against Britain, admitted to his staff that "air defense is now in my opinion decisive." The terrible events in Hamburg accelerated the shift to priority for fighter production and intense efforts to combat the scientific lead in radar and radio countermeasures that the Allied air force had established over the summer months.[136] By October, Göring's deputy, Erhard Milch, had drawn up firm plans for the output of more than 3,000 fighter aircraft a month, and more speculative plans for 5,000 fighters every month during 1945, at the expense of further bomber production.[137] By simplifying production methods, reducing the large number of aircraft types, and abandoning the habit of regular modification, Milch calculated that the output could be achieved without a large increase in labor.[138] He had already taken over central responsibility for radar and radio development in May and had begun an immediate acceleration of research and production. In July a new office for high-frequency research was set up under Dr. Hans Plendl, which drew in 3,000 scientific personnel to combat the variety of devices that had fallen into German hands during the Ruhr battle, thanks to the recovery of equipment from crashed bombers.[139]

After the success of Window, priority was given by the Germans to developing radar that would be more immune to its effects in order to increase as rapidly as possible the hitting power of the German fighter force. Permission was now given to build up units trained for Hermann's Wilde Sau technique, while on the day following the final heavy raid on Hamburg, July 30, the Zahme Sau tactic of controlled infiltration of the bomber stream was approved by Milch and Hubert Weise, overall commander of the German home-front air defense. The result was a substantial diversion of guns and aircraft away from the fighting fronts where they were needed more than ever by the summer of 1943. By late August there were over 1,000 fighter aircraft stationed in Germany, 45.5 percent of all German fighter strength, and a further 224 in northern France. Over the same period the number of heavy antiaircraft guns on the home front increased from 4,800 before Gomorrah to over 6,000 by the end of August, including more of the heavier 105-millimeter and

128-millimeter models. Shortages of skilled personnel hampered the antiaircraft effort throughout the year, and for the first time substantial numbers of women and young people were recruited as *Flakhelfer;* on Hitler's orders training began in August 1943 for 250 units of Reich Labor Service boys to undertake air defense duty in the year before they joined the armed forces.[140]

In Britain the Hamburg raids were treated as a great success. The director of intelligence in the Air Ministry thought that the operation confirmed the superiority of incendiary over high-explosive bombs: "The complete wipe-out of a residential area by fire is quite another and better conception. May it long continue!"[141] Robert Lovett wrote to Eaker from Washington that the War Department was keen to see the photoreconnaissance images of Hamburg's destruction as soon as possible: "The pasting Hamburg got must have been terrific." Eaker replied that the raids had "a tremendous effect."[142] For Harris, Operation Gomorrah was more than he could have hoped for. The post-raid assessments, now based on RE8 research on man-months lost and acreage destroyed, transformed the statistical image of Bomber Command's achievements and gave Harris the weapons he needed to argue the case that bombing was capable of knocking Germany out of the war. If there had been a defensiveness about Bomber Command strategy before Hamburg, the new evidence could be used to strengthen Harris's hand. On August 12 he wrote to Portal, who was with the Combined Chiefs at the Quadrant conference in Quebec, that in his view the bombing war was "on the verge of a final show-down." Harris was certain that with the same concentration of effort "we can push Germany over by bombing this year."[143]

The results of Operation Gomorrah could only be assessed by the crudest measurements, since the detailed effects were not yet known even to the German authorities. This meant chiefly an assessment of the acreage of Zones 1 and 2A, the inner-city residential areas, "devastated" predominantly by incendiary attack. The Hamburg raid had the effect of doubling the amount of damage inflicted on German cities so far. Up to the end of June it was estimated that 12.27 percent of the inner-city areas had been destroyed; by the end of September this figure had increased to 23.31 percent, 18,738 acres against 9,583.[144] The intelligence staff at Bomber Command headquarters used this material to present a statistical way of measuring success based on the following three criteria:

Tons of bombs claimed dropped per built-up acre attacked = "Effort"

Acres of devastation per ton of bombs claimed dropped = "Efficiency"

Acres of devastation per acre of built-up area attacked = "Success"

On this basis it could be demonstrated that "success" (acres destroyed per acres attacked) had increased from 0.001 at the end of 1941, 0.032 at the end of 1942, to 0.249 at the end of October 1943. The acres of Germany's central urban area devastated had increased by a factor of 24 in the course of 1943.[145] These figures gave no indication of what effect this was likely to have either on Germany's war effort or on the state of mind of those bombed. The MEW warned the Air Ministry that it was hard to judge German conditions. They estimated that Operation Gomorrah had cost Hamburg the equivalent of 1.25 million man-months, or 12 percent of the city's annual production. The cumulative effect of all Bomber Command's attacks during the late spring and summer was estimated at a more modest 3 percent of Germany's potential production effort.[146]

Evidence soon became available to show that the damage was not as crippling as had at first been hoped. The port of Hamburg, which had been less severely damaged than the city, was estimated by MEW to be operating at 70 percent of its capacity again by the end of August; intelligence on the Blohm & Voss shipyards, one of the principal targets for the Eighth Air Force, suggested that they had not been destroyed and were still functioning.[147] By November the city was back to 80 percent of its pre-raid output. When Göring was captured at the end of the war with a train full of possessions, the American army found among them a presentation folio of more than a hundred charts and graphs on the remarkable recovery of Hamburg.[148] The one statistic that could only be guessed at was the number of dead. This was not a measurement used by Bomber Command, whose calculations of "effort," "efficiency," and "success" became increasingly more abstract as the war went on. The acreage destroyed was released to the British press as early as August 6, though the RAF communiqué emphasized that the damage "particularly covers the principal manufacturing districts and the docks and wharves."[149] Sources in Sweden suggested the figure of 58,000 dead, which was reprinted in British newspapers later in August. News of the firestorm became available from a correspondent of the Swiss paper *Basler Nachrichten* only in November 1943, when it was circulated among the antibombing lobby in Britain and published in the *New Statesman*. The claims that 20,000 bodies had been found, incinerated to a degree not even found in a crematorium, were contested by British scientists who were shown the material. They dismissed the description of the firestorm as scientific nonsense, an "intrinsic absurdity."[150]

Stalemate over Germany

In the aftermath of Operation Gomorrah both Allied bomber forces expected a growing success rate and both were impatient to achieve it. There was a growing confidence that the aims laid down at Casablanca might now be operationally in their grasp. Lovett wrote to Eaker in early July about the wave of optimism surging through the United States "that the Air Forces will knock Germany over by Christmas."[151] A report on the combined offensive produced by Eaker in early August 1943 talked of knocking out the industrial props of Germany one by one until "the German military machine comes closer and closer to collapse."[152] Harris telegraphed Portal at the Combined Chiefs of Staff conference in Quebec in mid-August that the combined efforts of the two forces should be enough, once again, to "knock Germany stiff."[153] Portal was keen for Harris to attack Berlin with the same force as Hamburg: "In present war situation," he telegraphed from Quebec, "attacks on Berlin on anything like Hamburg scale must have enormous effect on Germany as a whole." Harris explained that this would need 40,000 tons of bombs and good weather, but Berlin was to be next on his list.[154]

For both bomber forces there was a race against time. The Eighth

Air Force needed to be able to show that it was meeting the Pointblank requirement to undermine the German Air Force in time for the projected invasion of France in May 1944. Whatever the American public expected of the bombing campaign, Eaker's directive was to use airpower to prepare the way for the ground armies, and the progress of the combined offensive was regularly measured against this requirement. The Quadrant conference in Quebec in August 1943 reiterated that destruction of German airpower was to have "the highest strategic priority."[155] By October it was evident that the German fighter force was growing in strength and that the efforts to reduce it had been ineffective. The Eighth Air Force was directed to speed up its assault on its list of essential German targets; out of 128 attacks on Europe, only 50 had so far been against Germany.[156] Throughout the last weeks of 1943 and the first months of 1944, Eaker, and his successor in January, Brigadier General James Doolittle, were told insistently by Arnold and Spaatz that Pointblank "must be pressed to the limit." In January 1944 the chiefs of staff wanted the offensive to focus only on German fighter strength during the preparatory period for Operation Overlord, as the German Air Force had been asked to do before Sea Lion in 1940.[157]

Harris and Bomber Command ran a different race. He wanted city bombing to bring the war to a conclusion without an extensive and costly ground invasion, and this meant doing such severe damage to Germany's urban population and environment in the months after Gomorrah that the German war effort would crumble. A joint report on the progress of the combined offensive drawn up in November 1943, but clearly influenced by Harris, played down the impact of American raids and highlighted the significance of area attacks on industrial cities, which had already reduced German war potential, it was claimed, by 10 percent and "may well be fatal" if the figure could be doubled in the next few months.[158] Harris drew up a list the same month of the different urban target areas (with Berlin the priority) for "the continuation and intensification" of the offensive, each city defined as "largely destroyed," "seriously damaged," "damaged," or "undamaged," and with the added hope that the Eighth Air Force would soon join in the bombing of the German capital.[159] In December, Harris used the urban damage figures in a report to Portal and Sinclair in which he claimed that the physical destruction of 40–50 percent of the urban area of the principal towns of Germany would produce, by April 1944, the month before Overlord, "a state of devastation in which surrender is inevitable."[160]

The two ambitions were not easily compatible, and in the event difficult to achieve. Over the course of the late summer and autumn both forces carried out major raids that became large-scale air battles of increasing severity and intensity as German defenses were strengthened and the German Air Force was freed at last to pursue more effective operational tactics. On August 12, 133 B-17 Flying Fortresses attacked Bochum in the Ruhr-Rhineland and lost 23 out of 133 aircraft (17 percent of the force). The next major battle came on August 17, deliberately chosen as the anniversary of the Eighth Air Force's first mission in 1942. The object was to inflict a spectacular blow. The targets selected were the ball-bearing works at Schweinfurt and Messerschmitt Me109 fighter production at Regensburg. For this raid American bombers were divided up; those destined for Regensburg under the command of Curtis LeMay would continue on to North African bases, those for Schweinfurt, commanded by Brigadier General Robert Williams, had to fight their way there and back. Both cities were the farthest the Eighth Air Force had yet flown into German airspace and involved the largest number of bombers so far dispatched, a total of 376 B-17s—a reflection of a sudden escalation in the supply of both crews and aircraft. The Messerschmitt works produced 18 percent of all Messerschmitt Me109 production; the ball-bearing works at Schweinfurt produced 45 percent of the supplies of German ball bearings. The aircraft set off in the late morning of August 17 and were attacked by German fighters from the moment Allied fighter cover ended, at Antwerp on the Channel coast. The group destined for Regensburg reached the target near midday and dropped 298 tons, killing 400 people and causing the temporary loss of 20 percent of fighter output. On the way there 12 B-17s were shot down, and 12 more were lost in the aftermath as they flew on across the Alps to Tunisia. Poor repair facilities in North Africa left more bombers grounded, and after a long return flight with further losses, only 55 out of the original 146 returned to English bases.[161]

The First Bomber Division faced an even greater battle. For more than three hours in the afternoon flight the bomber stream was subjected to persistent fighter attack, losing a total of 36 aircraft. Around three o'clock, 424 tons of bombs were dropped on the Schweinfurt works, killing 141 people, destroying two works completely, and seriously damaging a number of others. The German Armaments Ministry recorded a temporary loss of 34 percent of ball-bearing production, though large reserve stocks were available to cushion the blow.[162] For the Eighth Air Force the cost for just two targets on their list was exceptional. Together with the 60 aircraft shot down, 176 were damaged and 30 remained in North Africa. Including those lightly damaged, the casualty rate was 71 percent; counting those destroyed, severely damaged, or out of theater, the loss rate was 31 percent, levels that could scarcely be sustained for more than a few more raids. The German Air Force lost 28 fighters to the concentrated fire of the B-17s, though in common with almost all air-to-air engagements, American aircrew claimed to have shot down a remarkable 288 enemy aircraft.[163] In September a raid on Stuttgart, undertaken while Arnold was visiting Britain, saw the loss of 65 bombers (19 percent) out of a force of 338, with little damage to the city itself.

The Eighth Bomber Command nursed its wounds for more than a month before beginning a new series of deep-penetration attacks in October. A raid on the coastal city of Anklam on October 9 cost 18 bombers out of a force of 106, but the most famous battle of the bomber war took place during a second raid on Schweinfurt on October 14, when 65 bombers were lost out of an attacking force of 229, a total loss rate of over 28 percent of the force. Fighters accompanied the aircraft as far as Aachen, thanks to the addition of extra fuel tanks, which pushed their range to 350 miles, but after that the bomber stream was subjected to hundreds of attacks with rocket and cannon fire from enemy fighters. Eaker wrote to Arnold after the raid, "This does not represent disaster; it does indicate that the air battle has reached its climax."[164] But so severe was the risk on any raid past fighter cover that for the next four months operations were only carried out with increasing numbers of bombers on cities within easy range. As a result, Kiel, Bremen, Wilhelmshaven, and Emden—already the victims of the first year of Bomber Command raids thanks to their proximity—became the recipients of occasional heavy bombing, while the majority of American attacks now took place once again over France. The Eighth Air Force, like the German Air Force and Bomber Command years before, began to think about the possibility of night attacks, and in September 90 B-17s were converted for practice and training in night flying.[165] In three months of raiding, the Eighth Bomber Command lost 358 B-17s in combat, suffering the highest loss rate of the war in October. The campaign did not come to a complete halt, but the next raid deep into Germany was made only on February 20, 1944, in very different circumstances.[166]

Bomber Command also began to experience higher losses and, despite the advent of the target-finding apparatus Oboe and H2S, continued to hit urban targets with intermittent success. The rate of expansion in the first half of the year was not sustained: operationally ready aircraft within the command increased by more than two-thirds between February and June, but only by another quarter between July and December. Pilot strength was 2,415 in June, 2,403 in December.[167] On August 17–18, Harris was ordered to mount a more precise attack on the German Air Force research station on the Baltic coast at Peenemünde. The raid by 560 aircraft dropped 1,800 tons mainly of high explosive on the research stations and accommodations (also killing 500 Polish forced laborers in a nearby labor camp). Extensive damage was done to the rocket research program in one of the few "precision" raids attempted by the command in 1943, but 40 aircraft were shot down, a loss rate of 6.7 percent. Harris then shifted his focus to Berlin. The first raid on August 23–24 missed the center of the capital and hit the southern suburbs, killing 854 people and destroying or damaging 2,600 buildings. The loss rate of 7.9 percent was the highest on any raid since the start of the offensive. A second raid on August 31–September 1 cost 7.6 percent of the attacking force, while H2S marking was erratic, causing the bomber stream to drop bombs up to thirty miles from the aiming point. Only 85 houses were destroyed in Berlin and 68 people killed. So heavy were the losses to Stirling and Halifax squadrons that the third attack, on September 3–4, was made only with Lancasters, but not only did the

H2S marking once again miss the main aiming point, but 7 percent of the Lancaster force was lost. The first "Battle of Berlin" petered out until November in favor of less dangerous targets.[168] On the night of October 22–23 a second firestorm was created in the small city of Kassel, where H2S marking was for once accurate. The raid report noted that the whole city area "was virtually devastated."[169] The death of an estimated 6,000 people was a higher percentage of the city population than in Hamburg. Some 59 percent of Kassel was burnt out and 6,636 residential buildings destroyed. Armaments production was hit heavily by the destruction of the workers' quarters, but like Hamburg's it revived after two or three months to around 90 percent of the pre-raid level.[170] The raid put Kassel for the moment at the top of Bomber Command's list of the proportion of city buildings destroyed or damaged, ahead of Hamburg, 58 percent to 51 percent.[171] But Bomber Command lost 43 aircraft, 7.6 percent of the force, a steady attrition of its strength. Over the course of 1943 the command lost 4,026 aircraft, 2,823 in combat.[172]

The high losses of the autumn months created a growing sense of urgency and uncertainty in both bomber forces, despite the brave face turned to the outside world. The claims that had been made from Casablanca onward served the cause of service politics as well as Allied strategy; the stalemate developing in late 1943 as the balance shifted away from offensive toward defensive airpower exposed the bomber force to the risk of relative failure. Although both forces advertised their success in diverting ever-increasing numbers of German fighters to the defense of the Reich, this was in some sense a Pyrrhic victory, since the bomber forces were now subject to escalating and possibly insupportable levels of loss and damage. Lovett reminded Eaker in September that if Germany did not collapse over the winter, the public would think "our 'full-out' offensive doesn't work."[173] A paper prepared for Portal in October argued that a failure to demonstrate what strategic bombing could do would have "dangerous repercussions upon post-war policy."[174] Both forces wanted the other to help more in pursuit of what was seldom a common ambition. In October, Portal told Eaker and Harris that the Pointblank aim to eliminate the German Air Force as a preliminary to a more sustained offensive had so far failed. "Unless the present build-up of the G.A.F. fighter force is checked," he continued, "there is a real danger that the average overall efficiency and effectiveness of our bombing attacks will fall to a level at which the enemy can sustain them." The operational evidence showed that Bomber Command had so far devoted only 2 percent of its effort to fighter aircraft assembly plants (as by-products of area attacks), and Harris was now instructed to launch operations against six principal cities associated with fighter production.[175]

Harris treated the request as he had treated other "panacea" targets. In July he had been briefed to attack Schweinfurt as the most vulnerable link in the chain of German war production. Alongside claims for its importance he scribbled "sez you!" in the margin, and no night raid was made. In December he was told again that his command should bomb Schweinfurt at night. He rejected the idea on the grounds that his force even now could not hit a small city with any certainty, and would not waste time on a single target when there were bigger cities to destroy and "only four months left!"[176] To the Air Ministry's complaints that Bomber Command should have done more to support the Eighth Air Force campaign against German airpower, Harris retorted that he would not do their job for them. The two forces could not be regarded as complementary, Harris continued, since his command had dropped 134,000 tons in 1943 and the Eighth Air Force only 16,000, much of it on less important targets.[177] When RE8 researchers suggested that Bomber Command attacks had by their estimate actually done little more than reduce German economic potential by 9 percent in 1943 (even this figure turned out after the war to have been overoptimistic), Harris responded angrily that in the cities his force had devastated the proportion must self-evidently be higher. Even this devastation, as the Air Ministry reminded him, had affected only 11 percent of the whole German population, but Harris was a figure difficult to gainsay even over an issue of real strategic significance.[178] He stuck to area bombing in preference to selected targets and as a result made Pointblank harder to achieve, while paradoxically contributing to the stalemate he was trying to break.

While the two forces argued over priorities, the greatest battles of the bomber war were being played out in the skies over Germany. In all cases the majority of bombers succeeded in carrying out their bombing mission; there was never a point when the bomber did not get through. Although the bomb loads were often spread over areas widely distant from the actual target, wherever they landed they did serious damage to the home population, in town or countryside, on which they fell. These aerial battles were nevertheless distinct from the bombing itself. They were fought between the enemy defensive forces—guns, night- and day-fighter aircraft, searchlights, decoys, and barrage balloons—and the intruding enemy. At this stage of the war the problems facing both sides, though they were supported by increasingly sophisticated scientific and technical equipment and weaponry, remained the same as they had been since the onset of the bombing war in 1940: weather conditions, bombing accuracy, the balance between defensive and offensive tactics, operational organization, and force morale. These factors profoundly affected what the two bomber commands were capable of achieving.

In an age where radar aids to navigation and electronic guidance systems were in their infancy, weather continued to play an arbitrary and intrusive role in the conduct of air warfare. The final United States Bombing Survey report on weather effects regarded them as "a major controlling factor" in the operation of Allied bomber forces. For the Eighth Air Force, which relied more on visual bombing, weather prevented any operations for a quarter of the time, while 10 percent of all aircraft that did take off aborted because of weather conditions. It was calculated from unit records that the operational rate of the Eighth Air Force was only 55 percent of the potential effort because of the effects of northern Europe's rainy climate. Low cloud and fog were the main culprits.[179] Calculations by the Army Air Forces' director of weather in late 1942 found that the average number of days per month when the sky over the target was absolutely clear was 1 or 2 in the winter months, rising to a peak of 7 in June, a total of 31 days in the year. Days when the major limiting factors of high wind, ice, or more than three-tenths cloud cover were absent were more numerous, but still numbered only 113 out of the year, again with a low of 6 in the winter months and a peak of 12 in June.[180] The air force weather service developed a sophisticated pattern of weather prediction, based on the experience of the burgeoning civilian airline business in the 1930s, providing regular climate data, forecasts of current weather trends, and a precise operational forecast for particular missions.[181] Even with reasonably accurate forecasting, weather conditions could alter rapidly and unexpectedly. The combat diary of the 305th Bombardment Group in 1942–43 can be taken as an example: November 23, Lorient "covered by cloud"; December 12, Lille, "cloud cover at the target"; January 23, Brest "obscured by the cloud cover"; February 4, Emden, "no bombs were dropped due to the clouds"; and so on.[182]

Bomber Command was less affected by the weather because area bombing could be carried out in weather conditions that were less than ideal, but British experience also showed that "average good visibility" was only available between five and nine nights in the summer months and three to five during the winter.[183] To the end of the war, Harris continued to cite the weather as a principal explanation for why Bomber Command could not switch to attacks on precise target systems.[184] With the arrival of electronic aids to navigation, bombing could be carried out through cloud and smoke, though the return to a base suddenly shrouded in fog caused regular accidents. Weather did make severe demands on pilots as they struggled at night to cope with the elements, as the following recollection of the last night of Operation Gomorrah illustrates:

> We set course north to the targets and flew into thunderstorms resulting in heavy icing. We could hear the ice breaking off the sides of the aeroplane and the propellers, and then we were losing power virtually on four engines with heavy icing and I then lost control of the aeroplane. . . . It started to descend with the weight of ice and at that stage we were hit by anti-aircraft fire. . . . The aeroplane by this stage was completely out of control with icing . . . a very frightening experience.

On this occasion pilot and crew survived.[185]

Of all the problems posed by the generally poor weather conditions over Germany, maintaining adequate levels of bombing accuracy was the most significant. For the Eighth Air Force, clear weather was essential if precise targeting was to survive. In ideal conditions the early raids on France showed an average error range of 1,000 yards, but conditions were seldom ideal. An investigation carried out in February 1943 highlighted problems of poor accuracy and, alongside weather and enemy defenses, blamed poor onboard teamwork and inexperienced pilots. It was found that the method of bombing in squadron (or group) formation reduced accuracy substantially for the last formations to bomb because of the smoke and fire on the ground; up to July 1943 an average of only 13.6 percent of bombs fell within 1,000 feet of the aiming point, but for the last formation to bomb the figure fell to only 5 percent.[186] Anderson pressed his commanders to focus all their efforts on putting more bombs "on the critical points of the targets." "It is evident," he continued, "that our bombing is still not up to the standards that it can be."[187] Cloud, industrial haze, and smoke screens made this inevitable. The American offensive began without a Pathfinder Force and no electronic aids to navigation. In March 1943, Eaker had asked Portal to supply both the Oboe and H2S equipment for use by the American formation leaders. Portal offered equipment for only eight aircraft and training facilities for the crews. By the early autumn there were three Pathfinder units forming, one with H2S, two with the American version of the technology, known as H2X.[188] Eaker found the temptation irresistible to use the new guidance system to allow bombing when the target was obscured. In September 1943 the Eighth Air Force undertook its first deliberate blind-bombing attack on the German port of Emden. The bombing was scattered around Emden and the surrounding region, but the fact that it was now possible to arrive over the area of the target in poor weather introduced the American air forces to area bombing.

Escalation in this case *was* dictated by the technical impossibility of bombing accurately for more than a few days a month. From September 1943 onward, American bombers were directed to attack city areas through cloud in the hope that this would hit the precise targets obscured by the elements. Sensitive to opinion, the raids on city areas were defined, as with Bomber Command, as attacks on industrial centers or, increasingly, as "marshaling yards."[189] The distinction for most, though not all, American raiding from British area bombing was intention. The civilian and the civilian milieu were never defined as targets in their own right, even if the eventual outcome might make the distinction seem merely academic. Around three-quarters of the effort against German targets between 1943 and 1945 was carried out by blind bombing using H2X equipment; from October to December 1943 only 20 percent of bombs dropped using radar aids came within five miles of the aiming point, an outcome little different from Bomber Command's in 1941–42.[190] High levels of accuracy were reserved for primary industrial targets in good weather, where accuracy levels increased from 36 percent within 2,000 feet in July 1943 to 62 percent in December. American practice became one of selective precision when visibility was good, and less discriminate attacks when visual conditions were poor.[191] The result, as with Bomber Command, was to increase the number of German civilians killed and houses destroyed by American bombers, which now carried much higher incendiary loads for blind-bombing raids. Even precision bombing resulted in widespread damage to the surrounding civilian area. The USAAF in-house history of radar bombing was more candid than the public image: "Neither visual nor radar bombing ever achieved pin-point bombing; both methods were, in effect, methods of area bombing in the sense that a certain percentage of bombs fell within an area of a certain size, the rest falling without."[192]

The problem for Bomber Command was different. Here unacceptably inaccurate bombing had to be improved to achieve higher concentrations on the chosen urban areas. The introduction of Oboe and H2S contributed to raising the average accuracy of the attacking force, but concentration could be lost if the weather deteriorated or the Pathfinder Force missed the aiming point, or German decoys were successful in diverting a proportion of the attacking force. In raids using Oboe in 1943, the number of aircraft that bombed within three miles of the target ranged from 77 percent against Cologne in July to 32 percent against Bochum in September, but poor weather prevented evaluation of at least half the raids. Oboe certainly proved to be the more successful of the two methods but could only reach as far as the Ruhr-Rhineland. For H2S operations the scale of accuracy was even longer: 86 percent against

Kassel in October to 2.1 percent against Berlin on August 31. The average for the twenty-three H2S raids that could be plotted was 32 percent, a substantial improvement on the Butt Report evidence, but still a low level of concentration.[193] Research on the first large-scale blind-bombing raid using H2S in poor weather, against Mannheim-Ludwigshafen on November 17–18, estimated that perhaps 60 percent of the attacking aircraft had hit the conurbation itself. These figures indicated that the force had at last adopted a technology and tactics that might reduce the amount of wasted effort. This was partly due to the additional training for Pathfinder navigators organized by the Bombing Development Unit, set up in late 1942, consisting of flights over British cities. These simulated raids showed wide deviation from the putative aiming point, but an average of 50 percent of "hits" within a three-mile radius (four miles for London). The trials showed that H2S worked well over certain urban targets, but poorly over sprawling urban areas or cities surrounded by hills, as had already been found over Germany. The Operational Research Section of Bomber Command calculated that this was probably the best to be hoped for when bombing cities. Improved though Bomber Command accuracy was from the poor state of 1941, every second bomb was still miles from the aiming point.[194]

The problems of weather and bombing accuracy highlight a factor about the bombing war that is seldom given the weight it deserves in assessing what was and was not possible for the forces at the Allies' disposal. The operations mounted week after week during the last two years of war were of unprecedented scale and complexity, employing some of the war's most sophisticated equipment. For both air forces the pre-raid preparation required all the conventional demands of battle—tactical, logistical, and technical; the intelligence and operational research reports had to be factored into each calculation and the weather closely monitored. Organizing a raid with hundreds of aircraft coordinated over long distances promised all kinds of hazards. Pilots had to create formations while avoiding accidents and to synchronize their flights with the escorting fighters as far as their range would allow. Along the target run and over the target itself there were precise instructions about combat, evasion, target recognition, heights, and speeds. On return there was the process of debriefing crews, coping with casualties, and estimating the outcome of the raid. Each battle was self-contained, but for commanders and their crews the campaign was continuous, more so than for almost any other form of combat over the four or five years of war.

The typical instructions for a Bomber Command raid illustrate the close attention to planning detail and the range of demands made of the crews. Aircraft from four or five bomber groups were given instructions about force size, composition of the bomb load, routes to the destination target (or for the decoy attacks), and the timing of each of five waves of attacking aircraft, which had to drop their bombs within a twenty-minute period to maximize impact. There were instructions on Window, on the Mandrel jammer, radar and wireless use, and the chosen target-marking pattern, which could be either ground marking with illuminating flares followed by red and/or green target indicators or sky marking with red and green star flares. The master bomber and the supporting Pathfinders had to drop their markers and repeat markers over an eleven-minute period, while the main force had to watch for the markers, bomb the center of them if they could, and then make for home. The whole combat force typically extended for twenty miles, was six miles wide, and flew in staggered formation, the highest aircraft some 4,000 feet above the lowest. Crews had to fly low over England, then climb to 14,000–15,000 feet, then increase speed and fly at 18,000–20,000 feet for bombing, finally falling away from the target zone to 12,000 feet, back to 18,000 feet for the return flight across Germany, 12,000 feet again at the European coast, and not below 7,000 feet on crossing back over English territory. Then came the debriefing interviews and the post-raid assessments.[195]

The Eighth Air Force derived a lot from British experience, but its typical raid preparations and combat showed an even greater awareness of the complexity of the task. The principles guiding target selection dwarfed the simple list of cities and their industrial importance given to Harris. Target selection involved assessing the strategic importance of a target, working out the degree of "cushion" in the economy for substituting or dispersing output, calculating the depth of a target system (how far away a product might be from frontline use), judging the recuperative possibilities of a target, and weighing up its vulnerability and the capacity of the air forces to destroy it by researching its potential structural weaknesses and susceptibility to damage.[196] The material was collected and evaluated by the Enemy Objectives Unit based in the American embassy in London under the leadership of Colonel Richard D'Oyly Hughes, a former British officer who had taken American citizenship in the early 1930s. His team of economists visited British industrial plants to work out the most vulnerable part of each type of target and then applied the knowledge to detailed photographic material on the German equivalent. In the evenings they relaxed from their efforts by working out fruitless statistical teasers—"How many sheep are there in Bavaria?" "What is the most economical land route from Gdansk to Gibraltar?"[197] Their labors proved most effective with assessments of damage to capital-intensive targets such as oil refineries or synthetic oil and rubber producers. This material was taken and put into operationally useful form for air force units.

The typical Eighth Air Force operational procedure reflected a managerial ethos that was quite distinct from British practice. American officers had in many cases been drafted into the air force from business and professional backgrounds, which prepared them for the vocabulary and categories typical of modern managerial practice. The formal procedure laid down in July 1943 reflected that culture: a conference of key personnel at four in the afternoon before the operation at which the prospective weather determined the target to be attacked; target folders checked; fighter escort informed; calculation of type and weight of bombs and number of aircraft; notification of assigned combat groups; finally, determination of axis of attack, rendezvous point, route out, initial point (near the target run-in), altitudes, aiming point, rally point (just outside target area), and route back. The resulting field order was then sent by teletype to the combat units involved.[198] A second procedure then took place at the airbases of the different bombardment wings, with an operational briefing for all commanders and crew for approximately two and a half hours covering the following: plan for formation (general), approximate time for turns, sun position, power settings, intelligence information, and weather prospects. Detailed planning was essential because in daytime bombing the force had to fly in tight formation. The Eighth Air Force flew at 25,000 feet, each wing flying in three staggered combat boxes, covering a height of 3,000 feet to maximize the firepower of the group, before breaking into bombing formation in approach to the target. Separate briefings were then held for pilots and copilots (sixteen items), navigators and bombardiers (six items), gunners and radio operators (three items). Watches were then synchronized. At 8 a.m. on the morning of the operation a decision to go ahead or postpone had to be taken based on the current state of the weather. Commanders had an obligation, according to a manual on tactics, "to work out each mission in *minute* detail. The struggle here is of the life and death variety."[199]

Somehow or other all the detailed calculations, operating plans, and contingencies had to be mastered and put into effect by the expensively trained crews. There was always to be a gap between the ideal operation laid down by the military bureaucracy that ran the offensives and the reality of combat. Unanticipated factors of all kinds, not least the extent and combativeness of the enemy forces, undermined the best-laid operational procedures. Given the technical sophistication of much of the equipment, the large number of freshman crews to be initiated on each operation, and the vagaries of weather and navigation, it is perhaps surprising that bombing operations achieved as much as they did. Almost all the flight crew were between the ages of eighteen and twenty-five, a large number of them between eighteen and twenty-one; a few who lied about their age flew heavy bombers aged just seventeen. Almost nothing of what they experienced in training could prepare them for what happened by day or by night over Germany. For Bomber Command crews there was extreme cold for much of the time unless they wore layer upon layer of protective clothing; there was a numbing tiredness on operations that could last eight or nine hours, using up the body's natural adrenaline supplies and requiring chemical stimulants (commonly amphetamines); with the decision taken in the spring of 1942 to have just one pilot, the crew had to hope that one of their number had enough basic flying skills to get them to their target and back if the pilot was killed or incapacitated. There was the constant fear of night fighters and antiaircraft fire or of being coned by searchlights, to which large night-time formations added the danger of collision or bombs from the invisible aircraft above in the bomber stream.

The Eighth Air Force crews had some advantages; the B-17 Flying Fortress was less cold to fly in, and they were provided with good thermal clothing; each aircraft had a pilot and copilot; attacking aircraft were more easily visible, though the limited range of the B-17 machine guns meant that rocket- and cannon-firing fighters could damage the bombers before facing risk themselves. Other factors were shared. The experience was frightening and the accounts of a great many airmen understandably recall fear as a very primary emotion. "I was scared all the time," recalled one veteran, "but I was more scared of letting the rest of the crew see." Aircrew were commonly sick as a result of the long, bumpy flights. Their priority was to complete the mission and return to base. "You bombed a target and got the hell out and got home, there wasn't much glamour about it," remembered another. Their primary loyalty was to the other crews about them. "I never worried about the people down below," said one pilot. "I was more concerned with the ones in the air." This was perhaps an understandable moral concern. The permanent dangers to which an aircrew was exposed and the sheer mental and physical demands of combat, surrounded at times by dead or dying companions, with jammed guns or engines knocked out, created a temporary nightmare world in which the one hope was that their aircraft and crew would not be next. After the Regensburg raid one American commander who reached Tunisia reported that he and his crew "felt the reaction of men who had not expected to see another sunset." He recommended reducing the standard tour of thirty operations to twenty-five if crew were not to collapse from the psychological pressure. "Survival was our thing," concluded one veteran.[200]

The success of bombing operations depended almost entirely on the quality and training of the crews, but the pressures to which they were subjected placed often insupportable demands on their psychological equilibrium. This situation arose not only because of the natural stresses of combat, but because of the curious social situation in which bomber crews found themselves. Although they were regularly called upon for

operations that provided hours of tension and endeavor, once back at
base there might be days, sometimes longer, before the next operation.
In that interval crews were free to go to the local town, meet girls, re-
unite with wives or partners, and enjoy a variety of forms of recreation.
Cinema attendance at Eighth Air Force bases reached a million a month
by November 1943, stage-show attendance 150,000.[201] This meant that
bomber crews had a cycle of relief and anxiety distinct from the emotional pattern of ground combat troops. In the first years of the offensive, survival rates were low, so that life at base was also about reconciling
the loss of companions, relishing survival, and anticipating the next operation. Casualties were high not only from combat but because of routine flying accidents. In Bomber Command some 6,000 crew were killed
in accidents in 1943–44; the Eighth Air Force suffered in 1943 as many
as 8,800 losses in combat and a further 2,000 from noncombat accidents.[202] Death or German imprisonment was more common than serious injury, which numbered only 1,315 in the Eighth Air Force up to the
end of 1943, mostly to the hands, neck, and head. The American statistical record described those who had finished their tour of thirty operations and returned to the United States as "Happy Warriors"; they were
certainly lucky warriors, constituting less than one-fifth of the crews sent
to Europe.

The one form of often hidden casualty that bombing encouraged was
psychiatric. The stress of combat, or combat fatigue, was not in doubt.
Questionnaires from the USAAF Psychological Branch to squadron
commanders found that they valued "judgment" and "emotional control" far higher than practical skills among cohorts of incoming pilots.[203]
The psychological reaction to flying stress depended partly on the personality of the individual crew member, partly on the nature of the experiences or dangers to which he had been exposed. Most crew on a tour
of twenty-five or thirty operations died before they reached their total.
Of those who survived, a small proportion became medical casualties as
a result of stress, but almost all suffered from some degree of fear-induced
anxiety, which was observed to get worse the longer the operational tour
lasted. American psychiatrists reported heavy drinking, psychosomatic
disorders, and long periods of depression among crew who carried on

flying.[204] In Bomber Command the tendency was to blame any exaggerated state of anxiety on "lack of moral fibre" (LMF), a stigma designed as an emasculating deterrent to any sign of weakness. Harris thought that among his crews only a quarter were effective bombers, the rest merely there to give German antiaircraft guns something to shoot at.[205] Air force medical staff, on the other hand, found that there were very few records of cowardice, despite the popular fear among aircrew that they might be regarded that way if they broke down. In both the RAF and the Eighth Air Force it came to be recognized that regular air operations induced particular forms of neurosis that had little to do with a lack of spirit and everything to do with the harsh experiences of daily flying. Eighth Air Force was instructed to rest and rotate tired crews but to isolate those whose behavior might contaminate the efficiency of their unit. These cases were divided between the categories of "flying fatigue" and "lack of moral fibre." To the former there was no stigma attached, but the latter were to be removed from flying status, stripped of their commission, and sent home in disgrace.[206] Those who developed serious psychoneurotic symptoms were sent to special hospitals to undergo narcosis therapy, and many were subsequently returned to duty, including combat flying. By early 1944 it was found that around 3 percent of flying officers (of those who survived) were removed from flying status before completing a tour of twenty-five operations.[207]

In Bomber Command the treatment of flying fatigue could be much harsher if unit commanders were prejudiced against the idea of psychiatric casualty.[208] But like the Eighth Air Force, a system of classification came into use that allowed the neuropsychiatrists in the RAF medical service to distinguish between those with neurotic conditions capable of diagnosis and possible treatment and those classified as "waverers," defined as fully fit but fearful. Flying stress was accepted as an understandable reaction to "severe combats, crash landings, 'bale-outs' and 'shaky-dos' in general." Those who ended up in front of the psychiatrist were classified in four categories based on a predisposition to neurotic behavior (usually defined by character assessments or family history) and degree of flying stress. Those with a high predisposition or a high level of stress were deemed to be medical casualties and withdrawn from flying without penalty. Those with low predisposition but marked flying stress or those with neither predisposition nor serious evidence of stress were defined as lacking in confidence, and a judgment had to be made about whether they were also guilty of "lack of moral fibre." It was never easy, as one RAF psychiatrist put it, to tell "whether a man's inability to continue flying is his fault or his misfortune, whether in fact it is due to simple lack of confidence or of courage, or whether it results from nervous predisposition or illness outside his control."[209]

These were fateful decisions for the men involved, since those deemed not to be medical cases (approximately 25 percent of those referred for assessment) were dealt with by an executive board that tended to assume cowardice on the part of the men in front of them. Yet the medical casebooks show that individuals were often subjected to a series of traumatic combat experiences sufficient to challenge the mental stability of even the toughest character:

> Flight engineer, 20 raids, 150 operational flying hours: "He had been badly shot up on four occasions. On the last of these, after being attacked by a night-fighter, the port engine of his machine caught fire, the mid-upper gunner was badly injured and the rear gunner was killed. . . . The rear-gunner's body was burning and motionless. . . . He had to use an axe to hack off bits of the blazing turret and also parts of the rear-gunner's clothing and body, finally letting the slip-stream blow them all away. . . . The wireless, the hydraulics and the tyres had all gone and a crash-landing was made. . . . 10 days later he was in a nervous state with tremulous hands and sweaty palms. He had some headaches, felt unable to relax, was depressed, preoccupied and unable to concentrate. His appetite was bad. . . . When I asked him how he would sum up his feelings in one word, he said 'fear.'"[210]

On this occasion the decision was made to allow the officer a spell of noncombat duty, rather than assume cowardice. But there were other cases where fear was imputed by the psychiatrists, often unjustifiably, with the result that an airman could be stripped of his commission and the right to fly. In the RAF, 8,402 aircrew were examined for neurosis from 1942 to 1945, of whom 1,029 were declared LMF, 34 percent of them pilots. The best postwar estimate has suggested that Bomber Command crews provided one-third of those figures, which works out at perhaps 20 per month, a remarkably small proportion of all those regularly exposed to the stress of combat flying.[211] Most medical reports on the air forces indicated high morale despite the high casualty rate. Eaker claimed that morale was not affected so much by losses as by the knowledge that a raid had been ineffective.[212] Psychiatrists nevertheless found that one of the most important motivations was the desire to make it through to the end of the tour still alive. Since only one in four completed one tour, and one in ten a second one, survival remained a primary drive despite the stresses. Research in the Eighth Air Force found that a large proportion of men returning to the United States after a completed tour of duty displayed "subjective anxiety" symptoms: "weight loss, insomnia, severe operational fatigue, and loss of efficiency."[213]

These were the men sent by night and by day against German targets in the context of steadily increasing losses on the major raids. During 1943, Bomber Command lost 15,678 killed or prisoners of war, while the Eighth Air Force lost 9,497, almost all of them in missions against German targets.[214] The escalating costs of the offensive presented the bomber commanders once again with questions about the strategic value of what they were doing. The reality of tactical stalemate coincided by chance with a revival of the hope, largely abandoned since 1941, that bombing might induce a social or political crisis so severe that it would critically undermine the German war effort. Though Harris saw area bombing chiefly as a form of economic attrition, he never entirely excluded the possibility that his bombing might provoke a political bonus, even to the point of German surrender, and he was happy to fuel such speculation if it strengthened his hand. Air Intelligence, for example, was impressed by his claim that the destruction of half the German urban area would provoke collapse, even if the Gestapo and the SS (Schutzstaffel) were determined to "prevent insurrection."[215] For some months political intelligence in Britain, encouraged by German difficulties on the Soviet front and in the Mediterranean, had been suggesting that there might be a positive answer to the question "Will Germany crack?" and that bombing could supply it. In September 1943 the Joint Intelligence Committee prepared a long paper on the "Probabilities of a German Collapse" in which Germany's situation in the autumn of 1943 was compared with the historical reality of the collapse of the German home front in the autumn of 1918. The JIC thought the conditions of life in the bombed cities much worse than in 1918 and the signs of revolutionary discontent increasingly evident despite the brutal nature of the dictatorship.[216] In November 1943 an even more optimistic evaluation was produced by the British Political Warfare Executive on the creation in bombed cities of a "new proletariat" with a communist mentality, which might yet create a revolutionary crisis in Germany before the winter was over. In January further intelligence was sent to Churchill on social unrest in Germany which suggested that "the more we bomb, the more satisfactory the effect." Churchill underlined the sentence with his trademark red pencil.[217]

For Churchill the promise of a German collapse revived the confident assumptions about the political impact of bombing that he had harbored ever since the offensive began in 1940. The evidence in the autumn and winter of 1943 was nevertheless slender, based to some extent on imagining what bombing on such a scale might have meant if it had been British rather than German cities under the hail of bombs. American political intelligence was in general dismissive of the idea that bombing alone could generate a German collapse. Spaatz rejected entirely the value of popular war willingness as a target: "Morale in a totalitarian society is irrelevant so long as the control patterns function effectively."[218] American assessments of the revolutionary potential of the German working class focused on the "negative character of its assumption of power" in 1918, following the kaiser's abdication, and the failure of the German left to stop Hitler. Arnold asked a "Committee of Historians" for their analysis of the prospects for German collapse. The nine historians included distinguished names—Bernadotte Schmitt, Edward Mead Earle, Louis Gottschalk—with experience of writing the history of war and revolution. They concluded that although German morale had deteriorated during 1943, the existence of Nazi control "gives no encouragement to the supposition that any political upheaval can be anticipated in Germany in the near future." They acknowledged that there was a superficial resemblance to the final days of 1918, but their report concluded that Allied insistence on unconditional surrender, the lack of any effective avenue for popular discontent, and the contrast in the military situation "make the seeming analogy invalid."[219] The key problem identified by all the critics of the idea that Germany would imminently crack was the exceptional capacity of a totalitarian state to exact obedience. If the German people were "discouraged, disillusioned and bewildered," as intelligence reports suggested, they still appeared to have a fear of state terror more powerful than the fear of further bombing.[220] "Even when public morale is desperately low," remarked Portal's deputy, Norman Bottomley, in a speech in the spring of 1944, "general collapse can for a long while be staved off by a ruthless and desperate party system and a corps of brutal Gestapo hangmen and gangsters."[221]

These projections were, as it turned out, broadly correct. The bombing made the German population more rather than less dependent on the state and the party. Like the Blitz, Allied bombing created largely passive responses to the problem of survival. In its monthly news digest in March 1944, American air intelligence published a translated article on the air offensive from the German *Berliner Börsen-Zeitung*, which seemed to sum up the frustrating reality of an attrition war in the air:

> A war with its focal point centred in the air is not the shortest, as was once believed, but on the contrary the longest and most meaningless in its accumulation of destruction . . . particularly as even the greatest terror gradually wears off or corresponding countermeasures are found. Thus the time when it was thought that air offensives alone could force Europe to capitulate and that the Anglo-Americans could then march in with music had disappeared into the dim distance.[222]

The Committee of Historians concluded from their assessment of Allied strategy and German staying power that the defeat of Germany was only possible with continued Soviet pressure from the east, continuous bombing from Britain and Italy, and one or more large-scale invasions of German-occupied western Europe. "It seems clear," continued the report, "that bombing alone cannot bring about that defeat in the spring of 1944."[223] The stalemate in the bombing war could only be reversed by military means. "Our first objective," wrote General Doolittle to his commanders on assuming control of the Eighth Air Force in January 1944, "is to neutralize the German fighter opposition at the earliest possible moment."[224]

Chapter 3

The "Battle of Germany," 1944–45

In June 1943, Robert Lovett, assistant secretary of war responsible for the air force, wrote a long memorandum for Arnold in which he analyzed the problems facing the American air offensive and suggested solutions. The most important issue he identified and emphasized was "supply *long range fighter* protection to help the B-17s." He suggested designing built-in additional fuel tanks for American fighter aircraft but in the interim adding two wing tanks to the new P-51 Mustang fighter. He concluded, "This is a 'must.'"[1] The P-51 did not see long-range service over Germany until the spring of 1944, by which time other fighter aircraft converted to longer range were already in service to protect the American bombers part of the way to their targets. But it proved to be a critical explanation for eventual victory in what Major General Frederick Anderson, Spaatz's deputy from January 1944, called "the battle of Germany."[2]

The need for long-range fighters matched the need the German Air Force had experienced in the Battle of Britain in 1940 but had failed to solve. Success in defeating the German Air Force in their own airspace— the "Battle of Germany"—depended on establishing air supremacy, and this in turn relied on the extent to which the Eighth Air Force could use large fighter forces to destroy enemy airpower over Germany itself. Fighter-to-fighter combat and counterforce bombing was the solution not only to the expansion of the bomber offensive but also to the eventual success of Allied invasion in the west and success on other European fronts. What the Eighth (supported by the Fifteenth Air Force flying from Italy) was now engaged in was less a strategic air offensive, more the conduct of a "grand tactical" air battle that resembled in many ways the campaign waged by the German Air Force in 1940. It was belated recognition that even in a modern strategic air war, destruction of the enemy air force and its resources rather than destruction of the enemy home front was the essential condition for eventual victory.

"The Arithmetic of Impending Ruin"

There has been since the war much discussion of why it took so long for the U.S. air forces to develop fighter aircraft with long-range capability able to contest air superiority over Germany. Spaatz had been a witness to the German raids on England in 1940 when the need for fighter cover to protect German daylight bombing had been self-evident. The planners in 1941 who drew up AWPD-1 emphasized that the development of escort fighters that could fly as far as the bombers was "mandatory."[3] Arnold as early as February 1942 had asked for all new fighters to be developed with auxiliary tanks. In June 1943 he ordered a crash program to ensure that full bomber escort could be provided by early 1944.[4] There was no shortage of high-quality fighter aircraft designed with longer range than the British Spitfire (which had supplied limited fighter escort in 1943). The Lockheed P-38 Lightning, a radical twin-engine, twin-boom fighter, was a prewar development that had long-range extra fuel tanks built into the design. Its development was delayed and it entered service in the summer of 1942; it was used in North Africa as a low-altitude battlefield aircraft, a role that suited it poorly. Late in 1943 two groups were allocated to the Eighth Air Force and at once extended potential escort range as far as Leipzig, though in numbers too small to transform the offensive, and with persistent technical problems with the engine. The mainstay of the Eighth Fighter Command in 1943 was the Republic P-47 Thunderbolt, a high-performance fighter/fighter-bomber designed in 1940 around the Pratt and Whitney R-2800 radial engine. It could carry two external fuel tanks to boost range as far as the German frontier when drop tanks were first installed in July 1943, but little effort went into modifying the P-47 so that it could reach far into Germany. Eaker gave auxiliary tanks a low priority among his many other problems. Yet with larger tanks the P-47 could by the spring of 1944 fly as far as Hamburg, where before it had been confined to an arc that reached little farther than the Low Countries and the German border.[5]

The one aircraft that promised to transform the air war over Germany was the North American P-51 Mustang recommended by Lovett. Originally designed to meet a British requirement in 1940, it began service with the RAF (under the name Apache) in November 1941. British engineers fitted it with a Rolls-Royce Merlin engine and revolutionized its performance, increasing speed, rate of climb, and maneuverability. News reached Washington via the American embassy in London and Arnold immediately saw the aircraft's potential. By November 1942 he had placed initial orders for 2,200, fitted with Merlin engines made under license in the United States.[6] Since the P-51 was supposed to fulfill British orders, Arnold had once again to renege on the agreement. After a stormy exchange with Portal in the late autumn of 1943, he got his way.[7] The P-51 entered service in early December 1943 with drop tanks that could take it 475 miles into Germany; when it finally came onstream in significant numbers in the spring of 1944 its range, with new tanks, could take it farther than Berlin and even as far as Vienna. Most accounts of the battle for air supremacy credit the P-51 with the destruction of German fighter defenses, but rather like accounts of the Battle of Britain, in which the Spitfire has always been privileged over the Hurricane, the sturdy and less glamorous P-47 Thunderbolt bore the brunt of the first months of the Battle of Germany. On the day the P-51 was introduced to combat against targets in France, December 5, 1943, there were 266 P-47s but only thirty-six P-51s. Three months later, on the first deep daylight raid into Germany against Leipzig, there were 688 P-47s and just seventy-three P-51s. By the end of March 1944, the point that some historians have seen as the moment when air superiority passed to the Eighth Air Force, there were still more than twice as many Thunderbolts as Mustangs.[8]

The explanation for the slow evolution of a long-range fighter capability lies not with the technology but with the Eighth Air Force commanders. Eaker had always believed in the self-defending capability of the large daylight bomber formation. The prevailing tactical assumption in operations was "the security of the force"; the larger the bomber stream, the more secure it would be.[9] The Eighth Fighter Command under Brigadier General Frank Hunter shared Eaker's view that unescorted bomber operations were possible, and for much of the summer and autumn, when Eighth Bomber Command losses were rising, he ordered fighter sweeps across northern France and the Low Countries that on some occasions encountered no German aircraft at all. When it was insisted that the P-47s escort the bombers more effectively, the range was still too short to provide more than limited assistance, and made shorter still by the order to fly a weaving route next to the bomber formation to match its speed. In August 1943, after the first Schweinfurt raid, Arnold insisted on sacking Hunter and replacing him with Major General William Kepner, a dedicated fighter general, popular with his crews, who saw the role of his command to fly deep into Germany in order to destroy the German fighter force. Eaker opposed the change of commander and remained lukewarm about the effort to use fighters, rather than his bombers, to achieve the air superiority required from the Pointblank offensive. Destroying enemy fighters he saw as "the secondary job"; the primary task was dropping bomb loads as accurately as possible on strategic air force targets.[10]

Arnold's persistent dissatisfaction with the performance of the Eighth Air Force speeded up the decision to activate the Fifteenth Air Force in the Mediterranean to attack Pointblank targets from the south, where the weather was better. Without notifying Eaker, Arnold asked the Combined Chiefs at their meeting on November 18 to approve the reorganization of American air forces by appointing an American strategic air commander for both European theaters, responsible for the Eighth, Fifteenth, and Ninth Air Forces and, if possible, Bomber Command. The Combined Chiefs agreed to the rearrangement on December 4 (with the exception of Bomber Command, which Portal refused to hand over), and Arnold got support from Roosevelt and Churchill.[11] Arnold asked Spaatz to return to Britain to take up the post of commanding general, strategic air forces, on January 1, 1944. He brought with him Major General James Doolittle, commander of the Northwest African Strategic Air Force, and a firm advocate of bomber escorts. Spaatz took over Eaker's headquarters, while Doolittle commanded the Eighth from "Widewing," up until then headquarters for Anderson's Bomber Command. Anderson became chief of operations to Spaatz. Arnold had been insensitive enough to notify Eaker of the change in command by telegraph back on December 19, rather than in person, consistent with his testy treatment of Eaker earlier in the summer. Eaker objected vehemently to the change, but his objections were overruled; on January 6, Doolittle took over the Eighth and Eaker left to command strategic forces in the Mediterranean at just the point when large numbers of bombers and escort fighters were at last coming through the pipeline to transform the capability of the air force Eaker was compelled to abandon.[12]

In any assessment of the success in establishing air superiority over Germany, the change in American leadership is clearly central. Spaatz, Doolittle, and Kepner shared a common strategic outlook on the importance of combining the indirect assault on air force production and supplies through bombing with the calculated attrition of the German fighter force through air-to-air combat and fighter sweeps over German soil. Spaatz spent some weeks reviewing the offensive in January 1944 and then told Doolittle that destroying German fighter strength and increasing the tempo of attacks on German aircraft production was "a critical deciding factor in Germany's defeat."[13] Doolittle was from the start eager to use his large force, now with more than 1,000 bombers and 1,200 fighters, to destroy the German air arm. Commenting to Spaatz on the plans for completing the Combined Bomber Offensive, he was critical of the idea of pursuing "economic" bombing, and argued for making attacks on the enemy fighter force in the air and on the ground the "primary consideration," as it had been when he was a commander in the Mediterranean.[14]

Kepner had already begun to transform the tactics of fighter support before Doolittle's appointment. The key was to allow the fighter escorts to engage the enemy fighter force and not simply protect the bombers; this had been the dilemma facing German fighters in the Battle of Britain, when they were eventually compelled to fly as close support for the bomber stream and lost their combat flexibility. From January 1944 onward, American fighter units were ordered to "pursue the Hun until he was destroyed."[15] The new tactic of "Free Lance" allocated some fighter planes to abandon the bombers entirely and seek the German force wherever it was to be found. The escort aircraft, flying in loose groups of four, ranged up to seven or eight miles away from the bomber stream in search of combat. On the return flight they were encouraged to fly at a low level to strafe German airfields or attack German fighters taking off or returning to base. To maximize combat time, a system of escort relays was set up in which each stage of a bomber's flight would be protected by fighter units assigned to a particular stretch, so that they could fly direct to the rendezvous point rather than lose precious fuel flying slowly with the bombers. P-47s guarded the first and last legs of the route, P-38s the intermediate stretch, and the very long-range P-51s the area close to the target zone. The success of the change in tactics depended first on a much-enlarged supply of fighter aircraft and pilots, with improved levels of maintenance, and the exploitation of the RAF "Y" radio-intercept service, which made it possible for American fighters to be directed to the point where German aircraft were themselves assembling in formation.[16] The object was to leave the German enemy no respite from the threat of combat and to impose an insupportable level of attrition by deploying more fighter aircraft than the enemy. "The arithmetic in itself," Anderson told Arnold in February 1944, "spells impending ruin."[17]

The German Air Force did not remain passive in the face of the growing American threat. The driving force behind the reorganization of air defense and the expansion of fighter output was Göring's deputy, Erhard Milch, who understood more clearly than his master that "the homeland is more important than the front."[18] The allocation of priority to the defense of the Reich and to fighter production brought about not only a regular process of tactical and technical readjustment, but a major change in command and organization as well. In August 1943 the chief of staff, Hans Jeschonnek, who effectively carried the weight of high command in Göring's increasing absence, found the constant criticism and abuse from his commander in chief over the bombing offensive impossible to withstand. On August 19 he shot himself, leaving behind two letters for Hitler's air adjutant condemning Göring's incompetent leadership. Jeschonnek was not entirely blameless, since he had continually emphasized the importance of airpower at the fighting front rather than defense of the home territory.[19] He was replaced by Colonel General Günther Korten, whose relationship with Göring was better, but unlike Jeschonnek, he was committed to the idea of strengthening home air defenses and had Hitler's support for doing so. In November, Kammhuber was removed from his post, one of the remaining obstacles to reorganizing the defensive system. In northern Germany, Fighter Corps I (Jagdkorps I), responsible for the fighter defense of most of western and central Germany, was expanded and placed under the command of Lieutenant General Josef "Beppo" Schmid, best known for supplying overoptimistic intelligence during the Battle of Britain. From a single fighter wing in January 1943, Schmid's new command had eleven wings and twenty fighter groups by the end of the year. In December 1943, Hubert Weise, *Luftwaffenbefehlshaber Mitte*, was replaced by Colonel General Hans-Jürgen Stumpff, the former commander of Air Fleet 5; on January 27 the command was renamed the Reich Air Fleet (Luftflotte Reich), now responsible for the coordinated control of the entire defensive air war against the Allied bombers.[20] The process of creating a single centralized air defense of Germany was completed in February 1944 with the transfer of antiaircraft artillery and the German air-warning system to direct control by the Reich Air Fleet and the local fighter divisions. The system now more closely resembled the centralized control structure set up by Fighter Command in Britain in 1940. From Stumpff's headquarters in Berlin it was possible, using the radar information from Fighter Corps I, to communicate a running account of the air battle to the fighter units to ensure a concentrated response; for his part, Schmid had no fewer than 148 direct telephone lines to fighter stations and control centers.[21]

The German Air Force knew a remarkable amount about the British and American air forces. Most of the information came from downed Allied aircraft and interrogated prisoners. The bombers' predictable tactics and long flying time over German territory in the last months of 1943 had contributed to the escalating loss rates imposed on each bombing mission.[22] The electronic war, which had swung briefly in the Allies' favor with the use of Window over Hamburg, was more evenly balanced by the end of the year. German researchers quickly discovered ways to neutralize the effects of Window with two devices, Würzlaus and Nürnberg, which allowed the more skillful radar operators to distinguish between Window echoes and an airplane; by the end of the year, 1,500 Würzburg radar devices had been modified. The German Telefunken researchers came up with a new air radar device, code-named SN-2, that could operate impervious to Window interference, and a crash production program was begun. The new Allied H2S radar navigation could also be tracked by the end of 1943 using a new homing device, Naxos-Z, which enabled German night fighters to track the RAF Pathfinder Force; it also proved possible to get a bearing on the Allied bombers that were not carrying H2S by using their Identification Friend-or-Foe mechanism. Both breakthroughs contributed to Bomber Command's escalating losses. The Eighth Air Force began to use Window (codenamed Chaff in the United States) on December 20, 1943, at the same time as introducing a Würzburg jammer known as Carpet to reduce losses by radar-guided antiaircraft fire. Here again German radio engineers found a partial solution by introducing a modification known as Wismar, which allowed the radar to switch frequencies and avoid the effects of Carpet, though by this time the tactical battle between the two air forces had rendered electronic protection less important.[23]

The keys to German air defense were assumed to be production and manpower. To meet the threat of daylight bombing, the antiaircraft artillery was substantially increased in early 1944, with 1,508 heavy batteries (5,325 guns), 623 light batteries (9,359 guns), and 375 searchlight batteries (5,000 lights of 200- or 150-centimeter diameter). Output of antiaircraft guns reached a peak in 1944 of 8,402 heavy and 50,917 light guns, but the wastage rate of barrels doubled over 1943 because of the increased bomber activity.[24] An additional 250,000 personnel had to be found in 1944, mainly recruited from Soviet prisoners of war, Italian volunteers from Mussolini's Italian Social Republic, air force wounded, and young German volunteers. This represented a damaging dilution of the quality of antiaircraft personnel. By the spring of 1944 some 111,000 women also served in the German antiaircraft defense system. To navigate the regime's confused stance on employing women, posters reminded the female volunteers, "The woman in a soldier's post but still a woman!"[25] The antiaircraft batteries by 1944 were organized increasingly in large groups of heavy guns—*Grossbatterien* made up of three regular batteries—to produce more concentrated fire, but this made heavy demands on a less skilled and less robust workforce. Yet over the course of the year antiaircraft artillery came to replace the fighters as the main means for destroying or damaging enemy aircraft; the major industrial targets were protected by defensive strongpoints of no fewer than three *Grossbatterien.*[26] Throughout the campaigns of 1943 and 1944, antiaircraft damage to Allied aircraft was extensive. An American raid on Berlin on March 6, 1944, resulted in damage to 48 percent of the 672 bombers that reached the target. Only faltering supplies of ammunition prevented antiaircraft fire from being more effective.[27]

The accelerated production of fighter aircraft also faced problems in late 1943, partly because aircraft production was still controlled by the Air Ministry while the rest of the armaments economy had been centralized under Albert Speer's Ministry of Armaments and War Production, and partly because of Göring's renewed efforts to revive German offensive airpower by switching resources to bombers again in the winter of 1943. The current plans for producing more than 30,000 fighters in 1944 and 48,000 in 1945, drawn up by Milch's planning staff in the German Air Ministry, also lacked realism, not least because of the problem of fuel supply. Yet the figures matched what the crisis in the skies over Germany seemed to require.[28] Milch collaborated closely with Speer and the head of his technical office, Karl-Otto Saur, to reduce the different models of each aircraft type—eventually reducing the models from forty-two to five—and to speed up dispersal programs. But the problems posed by Göring's revival of bomber plans pushed Milch, for political as well as practical reasons, to offer control over aircraft production to Speer to achieve a long-overdue rationalization of the whole production structure.[29] In February the two men reached an agreement to run together an emergency "Fighter Staff" (Jägerstab) with Saur as its director, and it was established with Hitler's agreement on March 1, 1944. As a result, in 1944 three times as many fighters were produced than in 1943, in the hope that this would be sufficient to hold back the Allied bombers long enough to allow the whole German aircraft program to revive and expand.[30]

It was nevertheless evident by the end of 1943 that sheer numbers of

German fighter aircraft were not the entire solution. The production of aircraft had to be balanced against losses, and despite the success rate of German day and night fighters against the major raids of the autumn and winter, the cumulative attrition of the fighter force made it difficult to expand overall force strength despite the very substantial increases in output. Although 3,700 day and night fighters were produced between September and December 1943, the force at Stumpff's disposal when he assumed command in December numbered just 774 day fighters and 381 night fighters, with serviceability levels of 60–70 percent because of shortages of spares and skilled ground personnel.[31] This paradox can be explained in a number of ways. Fighter aircraft were compelled to fight in poor weather conditions against bombers now using blind-flying techniques. Commanders sent aircraft out in dangerous conditions (though not usually in fog or heavy cloud), with the result that the accident rate rose sharply again. Icing and misting of the cockpit windows was a particular hazard. Between September and December 1943 the German fighter force lost 967 aircraft in combat, principally with the American P-47 Thunderbolt, but a further 1,052 to accidents.[32] The second factor was pilot strength and quality. The high loss rates could not easily be made good by the flying schools, which were under intense pressure to supply crew to every combat theater. The result was a sharp reduction in the length of time devoted to training, which was exacerbated by the careful use of fuel. The hours devoted to training for a new German fighter pilot fell from 210 in 1942 to 112 by 1944; operational training was reduced from 50 hours to 20, and crews could be sent to squadrons with only a few hours' training on the frontline aircraft they were to fly in combat. Pilots who returned from combat on the Eastern Front found it difficult to adjust to dogfighting with skilled opponents, while pilots drafted in from other branches of the air force, or from air ferrying, were not the equal of enemy crew who enjoyed dedicated fighter training in an entirely bomb-free environment.[33] The result was that by early 1944 the German fighter force was obtaining an average net gain every month of only twenty-six new pilots. The stalemate inflicted on the bomber forces in the autumn created the illusion of German success. In reality the German Air Force was a brittle shield.

The declining skills and rising losses of the German day-fighter force were magnified by the insistence that the object for the force as a whole was to destroy the enemy bomber. This, too, had been a problem for RAF Fighter Command in 1940, when the choice had to be made between stopping the German bombers or fighting their intruding fighter force. German Air Force tactics worked effectively as long as their fighters could seek combat in areas where the bomber force was unescorted. The introduction of longer escort runs in late 1943 transformed the battlefield, though the German Air Force was slow to adapt to the changed reality. Göring famously insisted that the first long-range American fighters to crash near Aachen must have drifted there with the prevailing wind.[34] The existing German fighter force was divided between the Me110/Me410 "destroyer" aircraft, armed with rockets and cannon against the Allied bombers, and the more versatile Me109 and Fw190 fighters that were responsible when necessary for air-to-air combat with enemy fighters. Once American escorts appeared, the slower twin-engine German "destroyers" were sitting ducks. The first reaction was to move defense units farther into Germany in the hope that Allied escort fighters would still have a limit to their range. But the heavier destroyers now had to be escorted by the single-engine fighters, which meant that they too would be tied to a role in which they would be at a persistent disadvantage. In March the destroyers were finally withdrawn altogether after one wing of forty-three aircraft lost twenty-six in one raid, but the prevailing German view was still that their single-engine fighters had to try to get close to the enemy bombers to inflict damage, leaving those fighters easier prey to the increasingly aggressive Americans.[35] The more flexible the tactics of the Eighth Fighter Command became, the more inflexible the tactical demands on the German Air Force.

These weaknesses were cruelly exposed when Spaatz unleashed his campaign for air superiority over Germany. The eventual success of this campaign could not be taken for granted, not because of the German enemy but because of arguments over strategy among the Allies. There was no question that undermining the German Air Force was now a top priority. But Spaatz had to achieve Pointblank in competition with the demands for the "Crossbow" operation authorized by Allied leaders in late 1943 against the V-weapon silos and installations, and the early on-set of bombing tactical targets in support of Operation Overlord, which was expected in February 1944 to absorb at least three months' bomb-ing effort by the strategic air forces.[36] The tension between pursuing Pointblank targets in Germany and the diversion to targets in occupied Europe more directly related to invasion was evident to Spaatz and his commanders. It resulted in prolonged arguments over target priorities, which were finally resolved at a meeting between Eisenhower and the senior Allied commanders in Europe on March 25, 1944, in favor of the "Transportation Plan" for interrupting German rail traffic in northwest Europe. Spaatz was able to start his assault on the German Air Force before these arguments had been properly formulated and resolved—and in the event between January and May 1944 the Eighth and Ninth air forces based in Britain dropped 111,546 (75 percent) tons of bombs on strategic targets against 38,119 (25 percent) on tactical ones.[37] The real problem for Spaatz was the difficulty in persuading Harris to share in the task of defeating the German Air Force.

Harris was determined in early 1944 not to abandon the city attacks for a more concentrated assault on German Air Force targets. In Janu-ary his command was asked directly to abandon indiscriminate area attacks (Harris scrawled "never has been" in the margin of the memo-randum) in favor of raids on ball-bearing factories and fighter output as a contribution to the Eighth Air Force effort to establish "free deploy-ment" for the day campaign over Germany.[38] Figures were produced by Bomber Command intelligence to show that over one-third of German man-hours had been lost in the bombed cities. Harris told the Air Min-istry in early March 1944 that if his force stopped city bombing, Ger-man industry would quickly recover and nullify all the efforts his force had made over the previous year.[39] When the air minister, Sir Archibald Sinclair, asked Portal for the opinion of the air staff on Harris's strategy, Portal replied candidly enough that the effort to calculate when Ger-many might collapse under a certain weight of bombs was "little more than a waste of time"; the air staff, he continued, preferred a strategy of isolating and attacking the vulnerable points in the German structure, whereas Harris just believed in "piling the maximum on the whole structure."[40] Portal nevertheless made little effort to get Harris to comply with the American plan to hit air force targets, until pressured to do so by Sydney Bufton, director of bomber operations. Harris was finally ordered to bomb Schweinfurt by a special directive, and Bomber Command obliged on February 24–25. Target marking was generally poor and the damage to the city and its ball-bearing industry "nominal"; only twenty-two bombs fell within the city boundaries, the rest in open country. In this sense Harris's fear that his force could not hit a small urban target effectively was right.[41]

Further raids were made to support the American campaign against Leipzig, Augsburg, and Stuttgart, where there were aircraft and component firms, but the raid on Leipzig missed the Erla aircraft works entirely at a cost of 11 percent of the attacking force, while the raid on Augsburg did little industrial damage but burnt out the whole medieval center of the city. The raids on Stuttgart, mainly through cloud, were scattered, though a lucky hit was made on the Bosch magneto plant. Throughout the period when Spaatz was attacking the German Air Force, Harris persisted in continuing the Battle of Berlin, where losses remained high and the impact limited. An assessment of the attacks on the capital between November 1943 and February 1944 by RE8 showed that only 5 percent of residential buildings and 5 percent of industrial plants had been damaged in heavy raiding.[42] The attacks made in March on Berlin still brought loss rates of between 5 and 9 percent of the force on each raid. The last major British raid of the war on Berlin, on March 24–25, experienced high winds and resulted in scattered bombing across 126 villages and townships. Some 72 aircraft were shot down, 8.9 percent of the force. In April the final city raid against Nuremberg before the switch to the Overlord campaign showed the persistent limitations of area bombing. A total of 95 aircraft were lost out of the 795 dispatched, the highest loss rate of the war, 11.9 percent. At least 120 aircraft bombed Schweinfurt by mistake, but missed the main area of the city; the remainder bombed a wide area of the German countryside north of Nuremberg, killing sixty-nine villagers. Harris at last recognized that the effectiveness of the German night defenses, as he told the Air Ministry, might soon create a situation in which loss rates "could not in the end be sustained."[43] Between November 1943 and March 1944, Bomber Command lost 1,128 aircraft for little evident strategic gain. Losses among the expanding German night-fighter force were also high, but by the spring they could see that they were gaining as close to a victory as air war would allow.[44]

In the end the defeat of the German Air Force was an American achievement. Spaatz divided the campaign into three elements: Operation Argument to undermine German aircraft production; a follow-up campaign against the German oil industry to starve the air force of its most precious resource; and finally, continuous counterforce attacks against German fighters and their organization. The attack on the aircraft industry, which came to be known as Big Week, was postponed regularly through late January and early February 1944 by poor weather. Attacks were carried out against targets in France and a few deeper raids into Germany, but cloud and snow kept German fighters grounded and increased the risk of accident to American aircrews. On February 19 the weather finally cleared, and for the week until February 26 the Eighth Air Force flew 6,200 sorties against eighteen aircraft assembly plants and two ball-bearing factories. The raids on the first day, February 20, divided the bombers between twelve major targets in Rostock, Brunswick, Leipzig, and half a dozen other smaller towns. The losses totaled only 15 bombers from the 880 that attacked—a rate of only 1.7 percent—and 4 fighters. Losses climbed as the German Air Force grasped the pattern of attacks, and the cost during the week was eventually 158 for the Eighth Air Force (imposed when, for some reason, escorting lapsed) and 89 for the Fifteenth, which attacked from Italy entirely without escort. Only 28 American fighters were lost from the large numbers dispatched on each raid, but the German Air Force lost one-third of its single-engine fighters during February and almost one-fifth of its fighter crew. By contrast, the number of P-51 Mustang fighters available was 90 percent higher at the end of Big Week than it had been at the beginning.[45]

The damage sustained by the German aircraft industry was difficult for the Allies to gauge, not least because air intelligence estimates of German production by this stage of the war greatly understated the reality. The MEW estimate of German fighter production for the first half of 1944 was 655 a month, whereas the reality was 1,581 and rising steadily.[46] The aero-engine industry, more difficult to disperse and more vulnerable, was not attacked, a failure that Göring later pointed out to his postwar interrogators.[47] The attacks accelerated the further dispersal of the industry and prompted a program for underground construction in which aircraft had a priority, a planned 48 million square meters of floor space out of a provisional total of 93 million.[48] Output nevertheless continued to increase rapidly despite the bombing, and this has encouraged the view that Operation Argument effectively failed. The figures show, however, that the Allied attacks, which continued intermittently thereafter, did reduce *planned* fighter output substantially below expectations. Between January and June 1944, 9,255 German single-engine fighters were produced instead of the planned 12,667, a shortfall of 27 percent. The heaviest loss was experienced in February 1944 with a shortfall of 38.5 percent of planned output.[49] Not all of this loss was due to bombing, since many other factors affected industrial performance by 1944, but the impact in February almost certainly was. The problem for Allied calculations was the failure to apprehend the rapid conversion in Germany to fighter priority and the successful rationalization and reorganization of aircraft production.

Spaatz also planned to attack oil facilities, particularly those producing aviation fuel, which were more vulnerable than aircraft assembly halls because of the large capital plant involved and the difficulty of dispersing or concealing them. Intelligence on German oil supplies was the reverse of aircraft production, consistently overestimating German synthetic production and imports. Reluctance to renew an oil offensive after the RAF failures of 1940 and 1941 was based partly on the belief that Germany had large concealed stocks available. By the spring of 1944, however, Allied intelligence indicated a growing oil vulnerability in Germany. Spaatz set up a planning committee in February 1944 composed of members of the Enemy Objectives Unit to report on other target systems that would accelerate German Air Force decline, and the committee report, presented to him on March 5, highlighted oil as the principal factor, followed by rubber and bomber production. The economists calculated that enough damage could be done to current oil production to force the German armed forces to consume remaining stocks and that this was the quickest way to undermine fighting power.[50] Spaatz willingly accepted the argument and used the new oil plan to make his case, unsuccessfully, against the diversion of his resources to the tactical Transportation Plan. The aim to destroy or immobilize twenty-seven key oil targets was presented to Portal and Eisenhower as a surer way to undermine German military mobility at the front line, but the estimate that it might take three months to do so made oil plants, in Portal's view, a long-term objective. Instead, the Transportation Plan won the day.

In the end Spaatz succeeded in undertaking attacks on German oil targets by sleight of hand. In April 1944 the Fifteenth Air Force began a number of raids against the Romanian oil-producing city of Ploeşti, nominally against "marshaling yards." In fact the raids hit the oilfield, as intended, and in early May, Eaker gave tacit approval for further attacks on Romanian oil production. Spaatz managed to persuade Eisenhower that German Air Force dependence on oil made it effectively a Pointblank target too and got a verbal assurance that on days when he was not attacking French targets, he could attack synthetic oil production.[51] On May 12, Spaatz finally sent 886 bombers escorted by 735 fighters to attack six major oil plants across Germany. The force lost 46 bombers (32 of them from a bomber division whose escort failed to rendezvous correctly), but the swarms of American fighters destroyed 65 enemy aircraft for the loss of just 7 planes. The high-level Ultra intelligence, produced at Britain's code and cipher center at Bletchley Park from intercepted German messages, revealed the following day an urgent German order to move all available antiaircraft artillery to protect the synthetic oil plants, including guns that until then had been guarding the aircraft industry. The next raid on May 28 was even more devastating, temporarily destroying output at the oil plants at Leuna and Pölitz in eastern Germany. Spaatz was proved right: the oil targets not only encouraged fierce defense by the German fighter force, but quickly proved debilitating to German forces reliant on a shrinking supply of fuel. Production of aviation fuel was 180,000 tons in March, but had fallen to 54,000 tons in June. So successful were the first attacks that on June 4, two days before the invasion of France, Eisenhower gave formal approval for the oil offensive.[52]

All the while, Spaatz was driving the Eighth Air Force to impose insupportable levels of attrition on the enemy fighter force. When there were no bomber raids, Kepner was encouraged to send his long-range fighters in wide sweeps over German territory, attacking German airbases and seeking opportunities for combat. For bombing operations Spaatz chose long-distance targets that would compel German fighters to attack the bombers. In March he launched a number of major raids against aircraft production in Berlin, briefly overlapping with the battle Harris had been waging since November. The raids were among the costliest of the Pointblank campaign. On March 6, 730 bombers and 801 fighters left for the first raid on the capital. Fierce battles erupted over the city so that not only was the bombing inaccurate but the raid cost the Allies 75 bombers, though only 11 escorts were lost for the destruction of 43 German fighters. Raids continued throughout March and April, culminating in a final assault on Berlin on April 29 in which the bombing was ineffective and 63 bombers were lost. The German Air Force had reacted to the advent of the long-range escort fighter by creating large concentrations of up to 150 fighters—the "Big Wing" used in the last stages of the Battle of Britain—that were designed to batter their way through to the bomber stream, or, when opportunity presented, to focus entirely on bombers whose escort had failed to materialize. The results for both sides were the highest losses of the war. In April the Eighth Air Force lost 422 heavy bombers, 25 percent of the total force; the German fighter force lost 43 percent of its strength in the same month.[53]

The arena of daylight air combat over Germany was among the harshest of the air war. American commanders expected a great deal of their crews. "Greater risks are justified," wrote Anderson to Arnold, "and high losses are to be expected."[54] They were able in the end to accept high losses only because a generous spring tide of aircraft and crew was now flowing across the Atlantic. For the German fighter force, high losses made it difficult to keep more than 500 serviceable fighters in the Reich Air Fleet at any one time. The result was that in air-to-air combat, fighter to fighter, the German force was completely outnumbered and the concentrations easily broken up. "An enormous number of us arrived, a crowd of 30, 50, sometimes 60 aircraft," a captured German fighter wing commander explained, "but each pilot simply attacked wildly at random. Result: each of them was shot down wildly at random."[55] The same officer described the decline in German pilot morale over the spring of 1944 as the order persisted to attack only the bombers, when their instinct was to protect themselves by engaging the enemy fighters first. One of Germany's surviving pilots, Heinz Knocke, later published a vivid diary account of what air combat was like for German pilots in the spring of 1944:

> During the ensuing dogfight with the Thunderbolts my tail-plane was shot full of holes, and my engine and left wing were badly hit also. It is all I can do to limp home to our field. . . . Immediately I order a reserve aircraft to be prepared for me to take off on a third mission. It is destroyed during a low-level strafing attack. Two of the mechanics are seriously wounded. No. 4 flight places one of its aircraft at my disposal. . . . When we attempt to attack a formation of Liberators over Lüneberg Heath, we are taken by surprise by approximately forty Thunderbolts. In the ensuing dogfight our two wingmen are both shot down. After a wild chase right down to ground level the Commanding Officer and I finally escape with great difficulty.

Knocke sat in the crew room that evening with the one remaining pilot from his squadron.[56] Declining morale was not difficult to explain with a one in two chance of surviving, repeated sorties each day, regular and unpredictable low-level attacks, irregular supplies, and little chance of leave. Missions for German pilots became all but suicidal by the time of the Normandy invasion, when hundreds of fighter aircraft were sent west from Germany against odds even greater than the ones they had met in the spring.

For American aircrews the situation was less rosy than German accounts might suggest. Morale dropped for them too during the spring offensive, partly because of high losses, partly because of the demands made on the crews from bad-weather flying. In March and April 1944, eighty-nine bomber crews chose to fly to Swiss or Swedish bases for internment. Conditions were made worse by the decision to abandon automatic repatriation of crews to the United States after twenty-five missions in order to keep up the number of experienced aircrew available.[57] German interrogation reports of crashed American aircrew found a deep fear of antiaircraft fire, and a strong dislike of the order to conduct low-level attacks against German airfields because of light flak and the tactic of stringing thick steel hawsers (*Drahtsperre*) across narrow valley approaches to slice into an attacking fighter.[58] A major hazard was the return flight with battle damage and the difficulty of landing away from base. The crew of one B-24 Liberator bomber, hit by antiaircraft fire over Brussels, bailed out over Kent at the last moment before the damaged aircraft exploded: "I broke an ankle and incurred internal injuries," recalled the pilot. "The navigator hit a tree and broke his back. . . . The flight engineer had a scalp injury from hitting his head on a rock. In all, we were pretty lucky."[59] The high casualty rate made it difficult for American aircrews to form any sense of whether they were winning the battle or not. In the period from January to the end of May 1944 the Eighth and Fifteenth air forces lost 2,605 bombers. Between March and May the American fighter forces lost 1,045 aircraft over Germany and France.

Success only gradually became evident in May and June when Allied bomber losses suddenly fell sharply from the peak in April. By the summer the percentage of attacking bombers actually hit by enemy fighters fell from 3.7 percent in March and April to only 0.4 percent in July and August.[60] The reason can be found in the corresponding German statistics. Between January and June, German aircraft losses on all fronts equaled 137 percent of established strength, 6,259 lost in combat, 3,608 due to accidents, predominantly due to poor weather or pilot error. Despite fighting much of the time over German territory, the German Air Force also lost 2,262 pilots. Most of the losses occurred in Germany or on the Western Front in France and the Low Countries. In June 1944 losses totaled 3,534, only slightly less than the 3,626 aircraft of all types produced that month.[61] This was an insupportable attrition cycle of both German matériel and manpower: even with the increases in fighter output that peaked later in the year, new production was sucked into a whirlpool of rapid destruction. Fighter pilots waited for the Me262 jet fighter, which first flew in March, in the hope that, produced in volume, it might turn the tide.

The point at which Allied air supremacy was established in German airspace is difficult to establish because of the continual, fluid, and incoherent nature of air combat. Some historians date it from the first attrition battles in March 1944, others from the early attacks on oil installations. The head of the Historical Section of the German Air Force, Major General Hans-Detlef von Rohden, argued in a postwar assessment that Allied air supremacy over Germany had been achieved by the time of the Normandy invasion: "Germany had lost the struggle for Air Control."[62] A Joint Intelligence Committee evaluation in August 1944 concluded that the German Air Force "can no longer affect the military situation on any front," which was not entirely true, but did reflect the exceptional degree of operational flexibility now available to American and, increasingly, British aircraft over Germany.[63] No date is entirely satisfactory, but by June, when German reserves were sucked into the aerial maelstrom in France, the attrition cycle was, for the moment, complete. This was a situation the German Air Force wanted to reverse. In September 1944 a staff paper reflected on the lessons of the Battle of Britain: "We must try to achieve what England achieved in 1940."[64] The larger question posed by the "Battle of Germany" is why the German Air Force failed where in 1940 the RAF—by a narrow margin—succeeded.

There are certainly grounds for comparison. The German Air Force had a substantial fighter force with technology at the cutting edge, particularly after the Me109 fighter was refitted with the more powerful Daimler-Benz 605A engine; aircraft production was concentrated on an emergency fighter program; a large pool of more than 2,000 fighter pilots was regularly available; there was a complex advance-warning system based on sophisticated radar equipment; and the organizational reforms during the winter of 1943–44 created a central control and communications system not unlike the centralized structure available to Hugh Dowding in 1940. The German Air Force had good intelligence warning of incoming attacks and a thorough understanding of enemy tactical weaknesses. Like Fighter Command, the men who fought in the

German fighter force were defending their homeland and prepared to take high losses in doing so. As in the Battle of Britain, the German Air Force leaders believed that success in the air was at that point "the most decisive precondition for victory."[65]

The comparison is nevertheless a superficial one. Germany's strategic position in 1944 was very different from Britain's in 1940, fighting as it was on two major fronts in the Soviet Union and Italy and facing growing resistance in other areas of German-occupied Europe. The German priority was not simply to frustrate the Allied search for air superiority but to try to defend a fortress area in central Europe against overwhelming material superiority on all fronts. The strategic crisis explains the emergency program of fighter production, like the British crisis of the summer of 1940. German fighter output reached its wartime peak between the last months of 1943 and the autumn of 1944, though this was achieved in an environment of heavy and continual bombing. As a result, the gap between German fighter production and Anglo-American fighter output (produced in an almost entirely bomb-free environment) was not as significant as the gap in economic resources might suggest. British and American fighter output between January and June 1944 was 11,817; German production over the same six months was 9,489.[66] In both cases this production was spread among a number of fighting fronts. Yet the Eighth Fighter Command had more than twice the number of fighters available when compared with the Reich Air Fleet, as well as additional support from RAF Fighter Command and the Ninth Air Force. In May 1944 the Reich Air Fleet had 437 serviceable fighters, the Eighth Air Force 1,174. The explanation lies partly in the difference between the two training regimes already noted, which put novice German pilots at a permanent disadvantage. There was also a major contrast in serviceability rates, which were higher for Allied aircraft once the American logistical system was working effectively. Under constant air attack and a manpower shortage, the production and distribution of spares and the supply of adequate ground engineering staff all declined in Germany. More than 9,000 German aircraft in 1944 were lost in transit to Allied air attack before they reached the combat squadrons.

These contrasts were reflected in rates of operational readiness and rates of loss. During the Battle of Britain the peak loss rate for Fighter Command reached 25 percent in September 1940. German Air Force monthly fighter losses were already 30 percent of the force in January 1944 and more than 50 percent by May (see table 3.1). Numerical inferiority was then compounded with the demand that German fighters seek out the Allied bombers rather than fighters, which made them more vulnerable at the moment of attack, and by the decision to assemble large numbers of fighters together (like Douglas Bader's "Big Wings" in the Battle of Britain); this meant time lost in flight to assembly points and, for pilots who had flown on the Eastern Front in pairs or loose groups of four, a difficult adjustment to flying in larger formations.[67] The RAF in 1940 avoided both of these operational handicaps by using Spitfires against enemy fighters, Hurricanes against the bombers, while Dowding judiciously resisted the switch to "Big Wings." The difference between the two sides was not simply a product of economic resources, as is usually argued, but stemmed from operational and tactical choices that rested in the end with those in command.

German Air Force commanders were also quick to point out to their interrogators after the war that the principal problem they faced was

Table 3.1: Comparative Fighter Statistics, German Air Force and Eighth/Ninth U.S. Air Forces, January–June 1944

Month	German Air Force		Eighth/Ninth Air Forces	
	Strength	% Loss Rate	Strength	% Loss Rate
January 1944	1,590	30.3	2,528	2.7
February 1944	1,767	33.8	2,998	3.4
March 1944	1,714	56.4	3,419	5.6
April 1944	1,700	43.0	3,685	7.6
May 1944	1,720	50.4	3,382	10.0
June 1944	1,560	48.3	3,046	17.7

Source: Calculated from Richard G. Davis, *Carl A. Spaatz and the Air War in Europe* (Washington, DC: Center for Air Force History, 1993), App. 9, 22–24; Horst Boog, Gerhard Krebs, and Detlef Vogel, eds., *Das Deutsche Reich und der Zweite Weltkrieg. Band 7: Das Deutsche Reich in der Defensive* (Stuttgart: DVA, 2001), 105.

leadership. This is more difficult to assess, and air force commanders were scarcely without prejudice. Most accounts blamed the air force commander in chief, Hermann Göring. Minutes of the regular meetings in late 1943 and early 1944 show a commander full of irate bluster and frustration, prone to impulsive gestures and trite solutions. Though he was capable of sudden bursts of activity, his subordinates found him a bizarre, sadly comical figure. A paratroop general, secretly tape-recorded in captivity in October 1944, entertained his fellow officers with a description of a recent interview with Göring at Karinhall: "There stood the figure and I thought: is it Nero II or a Chinese mandarin? [*laughter*]. . . . A cloud of all the perfumes of the orient and occident met you half-way exuding over the fat cheeks . . . [All: *laughing helplessly*]."[68] Göring, however, blamed Hitler: "You had a great ally in your aerial warfare—the Führer," he told interrogators in June 1945.[69] From 1942 onward, and particularly after the failure of the air force to supply the encircled forces at Stalingrad, few major decisions in the air war could be taken without Hitler's approval or intervention. Yet Hitler did many things right in relation to the air war: he did not in the end obstruct the shift to fighter priority, favored a heavy antiaircraft defense, authorized the dispersal of industry underground, and bullied the air force into prioritizing improvements in electronic warfare.

Göring aside, the other leadership problems stemmed from lower down the air force tree. The coordinated aerial defense of German territory in 1944 fell to an organization that for years had been accustomed to conducting operational air warfare at the fighting fronts. The shift of three-quarters of the fighter force to Germany and the sharp decline in the bomber arm forced a rapid adjustment to an unfamiliar air environment. Stumpff, Schmid, and Korten were relatively inexperienced for the kind of contest they fought in the Battle of Germany. Spaatz, Kepner, and Doolittle had solid experience with just the kind of battle they faced in 1944 and suffered little direct interference from Arnold or Roosevelt in Washington. Although Arnold was also capable at times of irate bluster, he quickly grasped key technical and organizational issues—the importance of the P-51 fighter, the absolute priority for extra fuel tanks, the critical role of logistics—which made his style of management more effective than Göring's was in 1944 or had been in 1940.[70] One factor did link the Battle of Britain and the Battle of Germany: the German Air Force did not admit that they had lost either one. In the same document that reflected on how the German Air Force should emulate Fighter Command in 1940, optimistic plans were sketched out for a possible revival of effective fighter defense and a renewed bombing effort, despite the profound crisis now facing German airpower: "The war can only be brought to a satisfactory conclusion if we take the offensive."[71]

Releasing the Hurricane, September 1944–May 1945

The combined offensive was formally reactivated in September 1944 after three months in which the priority for Allied air forces had been supporting the invasion of France and the defeat of German armies in the west. Eisenhower eventually relinquished control of the strategic air forces on September 14, 1944, though he retained the right to request help with the land war when needed. Both bomber commanders were eager to return to what they saw as their primary mission. Spaatz reported to Arnold on the revival of the preinvasion command structure with the comment that "the Hun has still got a lot of fight left in him . . . we must concentrate to kill him off."[72] By July, Harris was impatient to restart full-scale bombing because he expected Germany to have recovered fully in five bomb-free months. In August, Portal warned Churchill that there were evident signs of German revival, which would have to be snuffed out by a bombing policy of "continuous attrition."[73]

What followed from September 1944 to May 1945 was an Allied campaign with the heaviest weight of bombs and the highest level of German casualties of the war. Over the eight months until German surrender the Eighth and Fifteenth air forces together with Bomber Command dropped three-quarters of the wartime bomb total against a deteriorating German defense; approximately half of all German deaths from bombing occurred over the same period. It is the extravagant power of this final bombing campaign, and its massive damage to Germany's civilian population, urban infrastructure, and cultural heritage, that has occasioned most postwar criticism of bombing strategy. To understand

Bomber Command commander in chief Sir Richard Peirse at Bomber Command headquarters in 1941 with his deputy, Air Vice Marshal Robert Saundby. This image is more familiar with the figure of Air Chief Marshal Arthur Harris at the desk.

A flight of Armstrong Whitworth Whitley bombers in 1940. The Whitley was one of the mainstays of Bomber Command in the early months of the RAF campaign against Germany, though its performance was limited and it was poorly armed.

Political warfare leaflets are loaded onto an RAF bomber for delivery over occupied Germany. During the war, more than 1.4 billion leaflets were dropped by aircraft in the propaganda war against the Axis, and a further 95 million by balloon.

An RAF bomb store in October 1940. Rows of 500-pound bombs are waiting to be loaded onto Bomber Command aircraft for another night raid against Germany after five months of almost uninterrupted operations against German targets.

The Combined Bomber Offensive in action. The picture shows British and American air leaders at dinner in 1943. Seated facing the camera from left to right are Carl Spaatz, Charles Portal, Frederick Anderson, Ira Eaker (standing), Arthur Harris, and James Doolittle. In the center foreground is Trafford Leigh-Mallory.

Though relations between the RAF and the U.S. Eighth Air Force could be strained, publicity stunts, like this one on an RAF base, were designed to ease the tension. Here, members of a U.S. aircrew write messages on a British bomb destined for Germany.

Women workers at a Boeing plant in Seattle assemble electrical components for the B-17 bomber. As men were recruited to the services, women came to play a vital part in American war production.

In the United States, the outbreak of war brought active civilian defense regulations. Here, the head of the Office of Civilian Defense, Professor James Landis (seated left), is shown a demonstration stirrup pump designed to douse house fires caused by incendiaries.

Two RAF crewmen after their return from a combat mission. The strain from operations that resulted in the death of almost half the men who flew is evident. Fear was the emotion most commonly remembered by those who survived, and courage their chief characteristic.

The dangers faced by bomber crews came from enemy fighters, antiaircraft fire, and the weather. Here, a stricken B-24 Liberator bomber in the Eighth Air Force, on fire and damaged by antiaircraft shells, struggles to keep flying.

The "Battle of Germany." The U.S. strategic air forces aimed to destroy German aircraft production and defeat the German fighter force in the air. Here, two German officials survey the smoking ruins of the Fieseler aircraft plant at Kassel.

A rare image of a fighter kill in the air battle over Germany. A German fighter crashes into fields, as photographed by the pursuing aircraft. By May 1944, German fighter pilot losses were running at more than 50 percent a month.

An artist's impression of RAF Lancaster bombers flying low over the Ruhr city of Essen to destroy industrial targets. The caption claimed that this would "ensure accuracy." In reality, raids were made from safer heights against whole cities rather than factories.

The reality of inaccurate bombing can be seen in the ruins of this farm, bombed during a raid on the Ruhr city of Dortmund on May 23–24, 1943. German farmers were under instructions to douse lights at night and to keep civil defense equipment at hand.

A Boeing B-17 bomber over the German city of Ludwigshafen, where an oil facility has been attacked. During 1944, German aviation fuel production was cut by 95 percent.

While the Eighth Air Force attacked from bases in Britain, the Mediterranean Allied Air Forces struck from Italy. Here a B-24 Liberator in RAF markings waits to be bombed up on a field in southern Italy for a raid on German-occupied Europe.

Two German women, surrounded by civil defense personnel and fire engines, wander through the haze and devastation of a raid on Ebenfurth in September 1943. Nine million Germans eventually joined the stream of evacuees from the stricken cities.

Women and girls played a large part in the German civil defense effort. Here, a young member of the German Girls' League (BDM) works alongside civil defenders during a raid on Düsseldorf in July 1943.

A rare photograph of the Hamburg firestorm on the night of July 27–28, 1943. The fire consumed more than twelve square miles of the city area and killed over 18,000 people.

Male and female German civil defense workers rescue a man from the ruins of his house during the bombing of Hamburg. Soldiers, firemen, and air raid wardens worked together in German cities to cope with the rising scale of casualties.

Two circus elephants recruited in the aftermath of Operation Gomorrah against Hamburg help to move a car destroyed in the raids, which killed an estimated 37,000 people over a week of heavy bombing.

Concentration camp workers, wearing the familiar striped suits, work to clear the piles of rubble left in the aftermath of the bombing of Hamburg. Prisoners came to play an important part in the emergency repair services and the clearing of debris. By summer 1944, there were over half a million camp prisoners in Germany.

The Minister for Public Enlightenment and Propaganda, Joseph Goebbels, in his role as coordinator for air raid emergencies, visits the ruined city of Kassel after the firestorm of October 22–23, 1943.

The grisly aftermath of the Kassel firestorm. Incinerated bodies and body parts have been laid out among the ruins. An estimated 6,000 died in the raid, a higher proportion of the city's population than in the heavy raids on Hamburg.

Girls of the Italian civil defense organization (UNPA) pose for the camera in the northern Italian city of Brescia in 1939. Volunteers were hard to find, and when war broke out many disappeared.

The ruins of a railway marshaling yard in Rome after the American raid of July 19, 1943. Though the damage was extensive, rail communications were soon reestablished, and Rome did not fall to the Allies for almost a year. The Fascist Party symbol can clearly be seen on the front wall of the ruined station.

Workers watch as the Fiat plant at Lingotto goes up in flames in March 1944. Although Italy had surrendered in September 1943, the bombing of industry and communications continued in the German-occupied north.

... a dir le mie virtù basta un sorriso...

Two Italian Fascist propaganda posters show Stalin and Roosevelt as the malign instigators of city bombing in Italy. The image of Stalin gloats over British and U.S. bombs on the Vatican, while Roosevelt grins over a well-known slogan from an Italian toothpaste advertisement: ". . . to tell of my virtues, a smile is enough . . ."

One of many ex-voto paintings put up in Italian churches to thank local saints or the Madonna for surviving a raid. This one at the Basilica Madonna della Consolata in Turin dates from April 28, 1945, just before the end of the war.

French opinion turned against the bombing of urban targets in 1943–44 because of high-flying and inaccurate raiding. This image of bombs falling on Paris shows the impossibility of hitting a small target with any accuracy.

An ironic image from among the ruins of the French port city of Le Havre, devastated by heavy raids in September 1944. The monument to the dead of the First World War still stands erect between lampposts decorated with the flags of the Allies from the Second.

Improvised shelter for the homeless in liberated Naples in 1944, following years of bombing. Shantytowns like this grew up all over Europe to cope with the large numbers of homeless, refugees, and displaced persons.

why the offensive was continued on such a devastating scale it is necessary to reconstruct the strategic situation as it seemed to the Western
Allies in the autumn of 1944.

The most obvious answer is that there was no compelling reason after the rapid victory in France to ease the pressure on an enemy who, it
was hoped, might be defeated before Christmas. There was wide popular endorsement of the bombing campaign among the home populations. The percentages in favor of bombing German civilians expressed
in British opinion polls rose from less than half in 1940 to almost two-
thirds by 1944, a reflection of popular anxiety to end the war quickly
and a growing familiarity with bombing as a central pillar of Allied
strategy.[74] The BBC air commentaries in 1944 by "Squadron Leader
Strachey" (the left-wing politician John Strachey, now a temporary
member of Bufton's Bomber Directorate) had record radio audiences.[75]
There was little reason for Churchill or Roosevelt to shut down the
bombing offensive given the exceptional commitment to its organization
and supply, and both leaders were by now eager to accelerate an end to
the conflict and frustrated by an enemy whose willingness to continue
fighting showed little sign of wilting. When Churchill was shown yet
another political intelligence report confirming that the German people
lacked the "energy, the courage or the organization" necessary to overthrow Hitler's dictatorship, he asked to be spared any further reports on
German morale.[76] From the military point of view, bombing was now
part of the combined-arms offensive to defeat Germany on the ground,
and although the targets were distant from the front line in eastern
France, the Combined Chiefs of Staff understood that bombing would
be used in general against targets that promised to expedite the army's
advance. The achievement of air superiority in the summer of 1944 required constant and vigilant defense against any prospect of German
recovery, since superiority was always relative. It was feared that if the
German war effort was not suppressed, the conflict might run on well into
1945, or might even reach stalemate. There was always the persistent
fear, going back many years, that the German leadership might be able
to turn the tide of war by jumping a stage ahead in the race for new
science-based weapons.

Of all the factors that encouraged the final months of heavy bombing, the fear that the German military situation might be reversed by new weapons, secret or otherwise, kept bombers at their task. Though some of these fears might appear with hindsight as mere fantasy, the launch of the German V-weapons in the summer of 1944, and the first employment of the Me262 jet fighter/fighter-bomber, confirmed the Allied view that Germany's military situation might abruptly improve. The so-called vengeance weapons hit British targets indiscriminately, first the V-1 flying bomb, which was first launched in mid-June, and then the V-2 rocket, which first fell on London in September. The Me262 was a crude fighter, easily adapted to mass production, but with its high speed it appeared capable of posing a serious challenge to the bomber fleets had it been available in sufficient numbers. The few units equipped with the Me262 by the end of the war claimed to have shot down 300 heavy bombers. The new aircraft was certainly welcomed by German air leaders as a possible war winner. Evaluations of the war situation produced in September 1944 and January 1945 by German Air Force intelligence presented the possibility of a "final victory" given the apparent decline in Anglo-American military capability and enthusiasm since the summer and the clutch of dangerous new technical developments available to Germany; these included the Wasserfall ground-to-air missile (V-4), proximity fuses, jet fighters (Me262 and Heinkel He162), jet bombers (Arado Ar243), rocket fighters (Me163), and equipment for nonvisual detection and destruction of enemy aircraft.[77] Some of these developments were well known to the Allies, others merely speculation. The correspondence between Spaatz and Arnold on the threat of the German jet fighters reveals the extent to which the Allies feared for the future of the bombing offensive. Spaatz wanted top priority for the development of the American jet fighter, the Lockheed P-80, and suggested the possibility that American bombers would have to change to night bombing or shallow penetration raids to keep losses to jet fighters within acceptable limits.[78] Doolittle told Arnold in August 1944 that he was not "awed" by German potential, and proposed to challenge jet and rocket-propelled fighters by head-on attack and superior turning. But by October he warned that jet aircraft and enhanced weaponry, including the powerful 30-millimeter cannon, might well "overwhelm our defenses" in attacks on Germany.[79] Anglo-American air intelligence confirmed, as Harris had warned, that by the autumn the German single-engine fighter force would be larger than at any point in 1944. Hence the arguments in favor of continued heavy bombing of German industrial and military targets.

The greatest fear was that the German leadership, like some wounded stag at bay, would unleash what are now called weapons of mass destruction. The U.S. Chemical Warfare Committee in January 1945 warned that although German leaders had not yet authorized the use of gas, the strategic situation they faced had changed for the worse: "The Germans are now fighting with their backs to the wall, on their homeland, and may out of zealousness, in defense of their own soil, or the fanatical desperation of the Nazi leadership, resort to the gas weapon."[80] These fears had a long pedigree. Extensive preparations had been made by the RAF during the Blitz to prepare for a gas campaign against Germany. When the United States entered the war, gas warfare plans were coordinated between the two allies.[81] In late 1943 these anxieties revived. Intelligence from a captured Italian diplomat suggested that Germany had large stocks of gas but would only use them "in a last resort." Churchill, who had been the motor behind expanding Britain's gas capability in 1941, underlined on the report the words "Gas," "no new gas has been produced," and "Germans would not use" as evidence of his continued concern.[82] A report from the Analysis of Foreign Weapons Division in October 1943 to the War Department concluded that "Germany is well prepared with the necessary weapons and agents to start gas warfare at any moment," using a variety of new toxins and means of delivery. This was indeed the case: by the beginning of 1944 the German armed forces had thousands of tons of chemical weapons on hand, including the deadly agents sarin and tabun.[83] In December the Joint Chiefs of Staff were supplied with full details of the toxic gases available to American forces for the conduct of gas warfare from the air in both the European and Pacific theaters, and in 1944 an accelerated program for the production of gas bombs was set in motion. In January, Arnold's headquarters could confirm that the air force "can be effectively employed for waging gas warfare."[84]

British preparations for gas warfare were much further advanced and more likely to be used. In January 1944, Portal told Churchill that he was toying with the idea of using gas to attack preliminary V-weapon installations that had been identified in France and the Low Countries, but hesitated to do so because the repercussions of starting gas warfare "would be far-reaching." The RAF was nevertheless alert for the first whiff of German gas in order to activate its extensive plans for airborne gas attacks. The War Cabinet was notified by the air staff the same month that if Germany should ever use it, the air force would immediately unleash six area attacks with mustard gas and two with phosgene every month. The attacks were to be divided between lighter, harassing raids and heavy concentrated raids using a mix of gas bombs, incendiaries, and high explosive, which would have to be repeated regularly "on the most densely populated centres."[85] The air staff understood that even if the German forces used gas against the invading troops in June 1944, Churchill favored gas attacks not only on enemy troops but also on "the cities of Germany." A list of suitable cities was drawn up in case such attacks were needed, fifteen for Bomber Command, thirty for the Eighth Air Force, and fifteen for American bombers from Italy. For the Normandy landings Bomber Command planned 11,000 sorties using gas and other bombs against a variety of military and civilian targets.[86] The stalemate in Normandy and the onset of the V-weapons campaign brought further pressure from Churchill to use gas to speed up German defeat: "I want a cold-blooded calculation made," he wrote on July 6, "as to how it would pay us to use poison gas . . . we could drench the cities of the Ruhr."[87] But the chiefs of staff remained opposed to the risk, while all the available intelligence suggested that there were no German plans to use it (though it was certainly discussed by Hitler and other German leaders during 1944).[88] Nevertheless, by early 1945 the American Chemical Warfare Service had sufficient stocks of gas in theater to maintain a campaign equivalent to 25 percent of the total available bomblift. Almost all gas attacks would be made from the air.[89]

Less well known are the plans for biological warfare against Germany developed in 1944–45. These too were the result of growing fears that a desperate enemy might utilize bacteriological warfare, possibly projected by some form of rocket propulsion. In 1942, Roosevelt authorized a War Research Board directed by George Merck, with an advisory board of prominent scientists, disguised simply as the "ABC Committee," whose first task was to work out ways to protect the American population from a possible German or Japanese bacteriological attack. In late 1942 the work was taken over by the Chemical Warfare Service, which set up a research facility at Camp Detrick in Frederick, Maryland. As with gas warfare, intelligence began to appear in 1943 that suggested Germany was planning the use of biological warfare agents, and in particular "bacillus botulinus" (now known as *Clostridium botulinum*, the cause of botulism), which was impossible to detect in an airborne attack, caused symptoms in four to five hours, and death by embolism in most cases. The assumption was that Germany would only hesitate to use biological weapons because of the threat of "instant reprisal," and as a result a program to produce lethal pathogens was accelerated. A further report in January 1944 warned that rocket or air attacks using bacteria might be imminent, and their effects "devastating." This included the probability of using anthrax spores directed at human populations.[90] Three plants were set up for experiment and production in Mississippi, Indiana, and Utah; sixty workers were inadvertently infected, but none died.[91] Before biological agents became available in sufficient quantities, which would not be before April 1945, it was recommended that retaliation should be with gas.[92]

Would the Allies have used either gas or germ warfare? The question was never tested, since Hitler was opposed to their use and more concerned about defense against a possible Allied biological attack.[93] But the development of both Allied programs shows the extent to which perception of the German enemy colored the decision to continue heavy bombing in case worse weapons were to hand. The most significant factor is that fear of chemical and biological weapons prompted the Allies to think in terms of retaliation against civilian populations on a large scale, turning interwar fantasies about gas and germs into potential reality. The RAF staff thought that incendiary and high-explosive raids were more strategically efficient, in that they destroyed property and equipment and not just people, but in any of these cases—blown apart, burnt alive, or asphyxiated—deliberate damage to civilian populations was now taken for granted. This paved the way for the possibility of using atomic weapons on German targets in 1945 if the war had dragged on late into the year, a fact that is easily forgotten. Echoes can be found in the later extravagant planning for second-strike nuclear destruction during the first decades of the Cold War, when up to 80 million Soviet citizens were expected to be casualties.[94]

It is against this strategic background that sense can be made of the decision to intensify the bombing offensive to be certain of securing German defeat. The summer diversion to the ground war, however, had done nothing to settle the inter-Allied arguments over bombing strategy that had surfaced in the early months of 1944. Indeed, a renewed eagerness to demonstrate what air forces were now capable of gave them fresh impetus. The first step following the decision to return the bomber forces to air force control was to change the overall command structure to more properly reflect the balance of power between the two Allied bomber forces. This was now heavily tilted toward the Eighth and Fifteenth air forces, which had on hand between them more than 5,000 heavy bombers in the European theater and could call on over 5,000 fighters, including by November around 2,000 P-51s. One major Eighth Air Force raid late in 1944 employed 2,074 bombers and 923 fighters. Against this Harris could field around 1,400 heavy bombers, mainly Lancasters, a fraction of what had been hoped for.[95] Spaatz refused to return to Portal's direct control and preferred to retain his close relationship with Eisenhower. Under pressure from the British chiefs of staff, Arnold agreed to relinquish the link with Supreme Headquarters Allied Expeditionary Force (SHAEF), but only on condition that he would now be the representative of the Combined Chiefs of Staff for directing the American strategic and tactical air forces in Europe rather than Portal. To mollify the British, Spaatz was also formally appointed as Portal's deputy chief of staff, together with Norman Bottomley. In practice Spaatz was left free to organize an independent campaign; he left Anderson in London and based himself in a forward headquarters next to Eisenhower, first in Paris, then Rheims. He told Arnold in late September that he preferred to keep the two forces separate.[96] Harris also understood that the change would give him once again more control over his force; since he was now the junior partner after years in which Bomber Command had been the senior manager, the guardianship of his campaign loomed larger than ever in his mind.[97]

The changed command structure made a common plan for the strategic air war less likely. The Bomber Directorate in the Air Ministry in August 1944 argued for a major operation against German morale, code-named Thunderclap, for "laying on a 'Rotterdam'" in the center of Berlin. The aim was to shatter any German hope of sustaining the war effort by "the *obliteration* of the visible signs of an organized Government," using 2,000 tons of bombs dropped in accurate concentration on a 2.5-square-mile area of central Berlin. The likely shock effect on German morale was compared with the shock effect on the Dutch government in 1940, which surrendered the day after the Rotterdam raid.[98] The proposal came, for the moment, to nothing. The Combined Chiefs of Staff preferred to wait until German morale was evidently at its most fragile. The two bomber forces continued for the moment to attack what they had targeted before Normandy, Harris against city areas, Spaatz against oil and air force targets. During September, Spaatz searched for a combination of targets that would put maximum pressure on the German military war effort. Since it was now evident that the Allies, sitting on the German frontier, would not find it as easy to invade as had been hoped, Spaatz preferred a strategy that would maximize the help the air forces could give to Eisenhower. His staff worked on a program to attack major military industries and communications in the Ruhr-Rhineland, Saarland, and southwest Germany to create the maximum dislocation and demoralization of the military and administrative structures. The plan was divided in two parts: "Hurricane I" was to be directed in general at areas that contained valuable targets in western Germany during periods when visual bombing was difficult; "Hurricane II" was for precise attacks in good weather on oil installations, motor transport depots, and communications. The directive was issued on October 13 to both Harris and Spaatz, but persistent poor weather rendered "Hurricane II" unworkable, while "Hurricane I" was too amorphous in ambition and was largely ignored.[99]

The search for an agreed plan did not stop the Allied bomber forces from heavy and regular attacks on German targets, almost all of them nonvisual on account of the deteriorating weather. On October 18 the two forces agreed to set up a Combined Strategic Targets Committee, chaired jointly by Bufton and Colonel Maxwell from Spaatz's staff, to work out a better set of priorities. Air Marshal Arthur Tedder, Eisenhower's deputy, was invited by Portal to contribute to the evaluation process. Tedder deplored what he described as a "patchwork quilt" of targets with no comprehensive pattern and recommended concentration on oil and communications as the two targets most likely to undermine German capacity to wage war. Tedder had been a firm supporter of the transport plan in Italy in 1943–44, then in the invasion of France. He was strongly supported by Solly Zuckerman, who had been responsible for working out the Italian plan, and was now advising SHAEF.[100] Tedder's intervention proved decisive. Ultra intelligence in late October confirmed that attacks on transportation had already had a substantial effect on coal movements. A meeting at SHAEF headquarters on October 28 agreed on priority being given to oil targets and communications, and a new instruction, Strategic Directive No. 2, was issued on November 1 to Spaatz and Harris. The new directive, however, was a compromise, as most directives had been since the Casablanca Conference. Alongside oil and transport, the directive allowed attacks on "important industrial areas" when visual bombing was impaired, as well as policing attacks on the German Air Force organization and, when required, direct support of land operations.[101] Bombing preferences in fact remained divided: Spaatz, Doolittle, and Bufton preferred the oil campaign; Tedder and Zuckerman sponsored communications; Harris, who had a strong personal antipathy to Zuckerman ("the 'expert' Mr. Solly Zuckerman") and to Bufton ("one of my ex-Station commanders"), remained wedded to the idea that oil and transport were expensive, dangerous, and futile objectives when the destruction of cities could be more easily accomplished.[102] In a famous exchange of letters with Portal (his were drafted by Bufton) in December 1944, Harris rejected the oil plan on the grounds that it would need a quarter of a million tons of bombs and months of effort to achieve it.[103]

The effect of differences of opinion can be exaggerated. Allied airpower was now so overwhelming and technically sophisticated that attacks anywhere contributed to the cumulative collapse of the German war effort, and could be carried out with small losses. Harris diverted some of his area raids to the Ruhr-Rhineland synthetic oil installations in November and December, and ordered a heavy attack on Leuna-Merseburg on December 6–7 that, though deep in German territory, cost only 5 bombers from a force of 475. From 6 percent of its bombing total on oil in October, Bomber Command increased the total to 24 percent the following month. That same month the Eighth Air Force devoted 39 percent of its total on oil targets, the Fifteenth Air Force 32 percent. Despite justified fears that German efforts would be focused entirely on reconstituting oil production, the long-term trend of the oil attacks since the beginning of the year was to create a critical level of loss, whose effects on German military mobility and airpower were indeed fundamentally debilitating (see table 3.2). Most of Harris's attacks

Table 3.2: German Oil Production and Imports, 1944 (in thousands of tons)

Month	Synthetic Production	Oil Refined in Germany	Imports	Total
January 1944	498	175	179	852
February 1944	478	160	200	838
March 1944	542	191	186	919
April 1944	501	157	104	762
May 1944	436	170	81	687
June 1944	298	129	40	467
July 1944	229	115	56	400
August 1944	184	134	11	329
September 1944	152	113	11	276
October 1944	155	124	34	313
November 1944	185	105	37	327
December 1944	164	108	22	294

Source: Calculated from Charles Webster and Noble Frankland, *The Strategic Air Offensive Against Germany* (London: HMSO, 1961), 4:516.

were nevertheless devoted to night raids on urban targets, particularly on smaller cities that had not so far been the object of attack. Between October and April, when area attacks were ordered to cease, Bomber Command launched heavy attacks against cities across Germany. Some contained important rail junctions or marshaling yards, some chemical and oil plants, but most of the time the heavy bomb loads destroyed wide urban areas or continued to fall in open ground. Although a number of daylight raids were made, Harris refused to convert his force to day bombing, perhaps to ensure that the contribution of his command remained distinctive to the last.

By contrast, American bombing, though intended to be directed at oil and transport targets, was often little distinguishable from area raiding. Much of the air policing of the German Air Force and attacks on targets of opportunity on the German transport network were carried out by fighters and fighter-bombers, which swarmed over Germany. The heavy bombers focused on major industrial and rail targets, but poor visibility for much of the winter meant that most bombs again fell widely scattered. Of every hundred bombs dropped on an oil plant, eighty-seven missed the target entirely and only two hit the buildings and equipment.[104] A conference on bombing accuracy called in March 1945 confirmed that most bombing since September 1944 had been blind bombing, much through complete cloud cover. From September to December 1944 only 14 percent of bombing was done with good to fair visibility, a further 10 percent visually aimed with poor visibility; 76 percent was carried out nonvisually, using a variety of electronic aids. In good visibility, at least four-fifths of bombs were found to fall within one mile of the aiming point, but through 10/10 cloud cover only 5.6 percent.[105] The instructions given to the Eighth Air Force in October 1944 on bombing procedure encouraged attacks in poor weather on any towns visible with the aid of H2X, for the reason that they were certain to contain some vital military targets. The effect, like the directives to Bomber Command three years before, was to encourage escalating damage to the civilian milieu and higher civilian casualties.[106]

Whatever the operational drawbacks to flying in poor weather against heavily defended targets, enough bombs struck the oil plants and transport network to cause sufficient disruption. The transport plan was put into effect by the Eighth Air Force in early September, but serious assaults on the main rail junctions and marshaling yards began in October against Cologne, Hamm, and Duisburg. The Rhine was blocked at Cologne by a lucky strike on the Cologne-Mülheim Bridge, which collapsed into the water, blocking one of Germany's main traffic waterways. By November the German Railway was down to eleven days' supply of coal, by December 12 down to five days. Southern and eastern parts of Germany were starved of coal; locomotives and wagons were routinely strafed by fighters and fighter-bombers. Out of 250,000 goods wagons available, almost half were inoperable by late November. Total rail freight traffic fell by 46 percent from September 1944 to January 1945. In the Ruhr, rolling stock available for daily use was by late October half the level of September. Rolling stock was withdrawn farther away from the attacks in western Germany, but the result was to block supplies of coal and coke from the Ruhr and force a reduction of one-third in electricity generation.[107] Serious damage to the Mittelland Canal, the main link between the Ruhr and central Germany, left it unusable for much of October and November. Coal traffic on inland waterways was 2.2 million tons in September, but 422,000 in December.[108] Hitler ordered the transfer of 1,000 heavy and 2,000 light antiaircraft guns to defend key transport junctions, but as a result denuded the defense available to other vital war industries. Ultra intelligence decrypts kept the Allies regularly aware of the impact the transport plan was having and encouraged its expansion.[109]

Somehow or other, amid the accumulating chaos of smashed rail lines, burnt-out cities, and crumpled factories, the German Air Force continued to sustain a threat to the ubiquitous enemy. Despite the long battle of attrition, there were 2,500 serviceable fighters and night fighters still available by December. Moreover, Allied losses on a number of daylight raids began to mount again: 40 bombers were lost in raids on oil targets on October 7, 40 again on November 2. But most of the raids recorded in the Eighth Air Force war diary show negligible losses and in many cases no losses to combat at all. Overall loss rates fluctuated between 1 and 2 percent throughout the period from September 1944 to the end of the war, an increasing number due to antiaircraft fire. Allied fighter losses were never high (the peak in September 1944 was only 1.9 percent of sorties); losses amounted to just 1.37 percent of all sorties in the last eight months of the war.[110] Meanwhile, the German Air Force remained trapped in the attrition cycle set in motion earlier in the year. Combat in large formations proved dangerous even to experienced pilots. The Allied raid on November 2 that lost 40 bombers cost the German fighter force 120 planes. The collapse of aviation fuel supply played an important part; training was cut back even further and strict instructions were given on flight times and procedures to reduce fuel consumption. Both day-fighter and night-fighter squadrons found they had a surplus of pilots with available aircraft, but they could not fly because of the restrictions. The enthusiastic expectations of the Me262 jet fighter were disappointed by the slow pace of development and continued technical problems with the jet turbines. Although 564 jets were produced in 1944, the first fighter squadron armed with the new model began operations only in November.[111]

The situation for the night fighters was also seriously affected by fuel shortages. Bomber Command losses fell dramatically from the high point of the summer when attacks were still suffering average losses of 6–7 percent. Over the last months of the war, loss rates dropped to an average of 1.5 percent. In 1943 a Lancaster bomber had lasted on average for twenty-two combat sorties, whereas by 1945 the figure was sixty.[112] The more experience crews got, the better their chances of survival. The German night-fighter force, on the other hand, was hit by the collapse in fuel supply in a number of ways. It was essential to be able to run full training programs for crews in the use of the complex scanning equipment, the SN-3 and FuG218, now available to locate the bomber aircraft. The dynamos needed to charge the radar equipment could not be operated because of fuel shortages; electricity supply to the radar stations was intermittent by the winter months of 1944, which also reduced training time on the new detection instruments.[113] Most night fighters were now the high-quality Junkers Ju88G, fitted with SN2 and Naxos equipment, and the Flensburg detector used to home in to an Allied bomber's "Monica" signals. By chance this equipment fell undamaged into British hands when a disoriented German night-fighter pilot landed in error on a Bomber Command station at Woodbridge in Suffolk in July 1944. Extensive testing soon showed that the simple expedient of turning off both the Monica tail radar and the H2S set would blind the enemy night fighters. New devices—"Perfectos," "Piperack," and "Serrate IV"—were developed to give warning of enemy fighters and to confuse German radar.[114] Although a new round of research began in Germany, there was too little time or opportunity to profit from it as the infrastructure collapsed. The seesaw electronic war ended in the Allies' favor. By 1945 the night-fighter force was a wasted asset.

In November 1944 the crisis in the German Air Force reached a peak. Göring found himself caught between two poles, Hitler's harsh accusations over the failure of the air force and the stark reality of Allied air supremacy. He took out his own frustration by blaming his aircrew for lack of courage and loyalty. On November 11, Göring convened a tribunal ("Aeropag") in Berlin with his senior air force commanders at which he announced that German airpower had failed and asked for solutions. It became, recorded one of those present, "a dreary forum which harped on about National Socialist influences within the Luftwaffe" but resolved nothing.[115] The anxieties in the West about the revival of German airpower now scarcely reflected the reality. The air force relied increasingly on gestures. New *Sturmjäger* (storm fighter) units were created from skilled pilots who flew their aircraft, armed with heavy new 30-millimeter cannon, straight at the bomber stream, regardless of the powerful fighter escort. The suicidal tactics were occasionally accompanied by ramming, despite Hitler's disapproval of the idea of German kamikaze. To cope with the impossibility of day-to-day combat in small formations—usually groups of ten or twenty aircraft, now directed mainly at fighter-bombers and fighter-intruders rather than the bomber stream—Adolf Galland, the general of fighters, organized a plan for a "Great Blow" by building up a reserve of fighters and fuel to release a sudden devastating attack on a large bomber stream. By November 12 there were 3,700 fighters of all kinds available, around 2,500 assigned for the blow. The object was to shoot down at least 400 bombers in one raid to try to deter the Allied offensive and buy time for the buildup of modern air equipment, "the shock the enemy needed," one of the pilots later told his American captors, "to make them cease their inroads into the heart of Germany."[116]

At just the point that Galland and his commanders were waiting for the weather to clear, the units were ordered westward to the Ardennes to take part in Operation Autumn Mist (Herbstnebel), better known as the Battle of the Bulge. The reserves were lost and later decimated in Operation Bodenplatte, directed against Allied airfields in early January, when almost 300 German fighters were shot down. Galland was sacked by Göring a week later on suspicion of instigating a pilots' rebellion against his leadership. A mutiny finally surfaced in a grim confrontation at the Air Ministry after Karl Koller, the successor to Korten as chief of staff, sent a delegation to meet Göring to request changes in command, the reequipment of fighter units with the Me262 jet, and greater respect for what the fighter arm was trying to do. Göring threatened them with court-martial, but in the end the ringleaders were simply posted away from Berlin. Hitler, however, finally conceded that the jet ought to be used as a fighter rather than an ineffective fighter-bomber. Galland was sent to lead one of the first converted Me262 squadrons. On his last mission, flown on April 26, eleven days before the end of the war in Europe, he was attacked by an undetected Mustang and limped back to his base with a smashed instrument panel and both turbines damaged. As he arrived, the airfield was being bombed and strafed by Thunderbolts. He landed among them and dived into a bomb crater from his battered aircraft. Two weeks later he was explaining to his American captors the most effective way to put airfields out of commission.[117]

By January 1945 there was accumulating Ultra evidence that the choice of oil and the transport network as targets had been sensible. The stabilization of the front after the Battle of the Bulge made it evident that German forces were near the end of their fighting power, yet the assault on Germany itself promised a costly finale. The possibility of using Operation Thunderclap as a way to bring about sudden collapse was raised again. The Bomber Directorate wrote to SHAEF suggesting a bombing operation of exceptional density designed to provoke "a state of terror by air attack" in which any individual in the vicinity of the raid would realize that the chances of escaping death or serious injury "are extremely remote."[118] This was one of a number of voices raised over the winter in favor of punitive raids designed to spread the bombing over wider sections of the population. The Joint Intelligence Committee at SHAEF suggested in October 1944 that surplus bombing capacity before German surrender might be usefully employed in attacks against parts of Germany that had not yet been affected, "in order to bring home to the whole population the consequences of military defeat and the realities of air bombing."[119] Postwar interpretations of the last three months of bombing on a collapsing German war effort and a disoriented population have also come to regard the final flourish of bombing against a weakened enemy, with overwhelming force, as merely punitive, neither necessary nor, as a result, morally justified. The American air forces alone between January and April 1945 dropped more than four times the bomb tonnage used by Germany during the ten-month Blitz on Britain. For both Allied air forces the fact that it was now possible to demonstrate the full potential of airpower at a critical point of the European war played some part in their willingness to push the offensive to the maximum, in case airpower really could deliver the coup de grâce. But the calls for punitive attacks were not reflected in the prevailing directives, which still presented German resistance, particularly after the crisis in the Ardennes, as substantial enough to merit unrelenting attack. Robert Lovett wrote to Arnold early in January 1945 that despite everything, Germany showed no signs of cracking, while the German forces were fighting with such "skill and fanaticism" that it might produce "a type of dug-in, trench warfare which will be slow, costly in lives and difficult to synchronize with the increased demands of accelerated Pacific operations." Only airpower, Lovett concluded, could break the stalemate.[120]

The story of the last months of desperate German resistance is now well known, but at the time the intelligence picture for the Allies was less coherent and full of potential menace. Persistent rumors of German plans to build a "redoubt" in southern Germany or the Alps were taken more seriously than they deserved. The capacity of the Red Army to complete its victory on the Eastern Front was regarded as more

imponderable than it should have been. These uncertainties help to explain the decision that led on the night of February 13–14 in the Saxon
city of Dresden to a third major firestorm, which killed approximately
25,000 people in a few hours. No other raid of the war, not even Operation Gomorrah, has generated so much critical attention. Harris has
regularly been blamed for conducting a needlessly destructive and strategically unnecessary raid against Dresden, but the irony is that the purpose on this occasion was dictated by the conditions of the ground war
rather than the bombing campaign. It was Dresden's misfortune to be
not only in the path of the oncoming Soviet armies, but also a possible
transfer route for the phantom last stand of German armies in the south.
Although the city was ranked number 22 on the MEW list of target
cities, with a key-point rating of 70, Harris had not yet attacked it in
force, partly because of the long distance, but almost certainly because it
contained no major industries linked to the current directive.[121] By the
autumn of 1944, Dresden was also routinely included on target lists issued to the Fifteenth Air Force stationed in Italy, along with other targets in southern and eastern Germany, but had not yet been attacked.[122]
When the Combined Strategic Targets Committee met in late November 1944, it listed cities for possible area attack when blind bombing was
necessary, with an "x" to indicate oil targets present and "+" to indicate
a key communications center. All thirteen cities in western Germany
had one or both targets indicated; of the eleven selected in eastern Germany, seven were marked "+" but four—Dresden, Leipzig, Dessau, and
Danzig—had no key target marked.[123]

The origin of the decision to bomb Dresden has been obfuscated by
the long postwar debate over who should accept responsibility or blame
for what happened. The historical narrative seems, however, clear
enough. The possibility of an area attack on Dresden first surfaced in
October 1944 when Portal responded to a request from Churchill for a
list of "area targets" that the advancing Soviet air force might be able to
bomb, which included Dresden among the seven suggested.[124] Discussion about bombing cities in eastern Germany was always related to the
progress of Soviet forces and the possibility of helping their advance by a
display of Allied airpower. In mid-January 1945, Tedder met with Stalin

to discuss the progress of the campaign against oil targets. Stalin showed great interest in the effects of bombing on German military fuel supplies and then showed Tedder the Soviet plans for the main Oder operation, launched five days later, on January 20.[125] This discussion seems to have prompted two separate responses. The JIC on January 25 announced that the Soviet offensive would be greatly helped by heavy attacks on Berlin, though priority was still to be assigned to oil targets. Portal and the air staff assessed the evidence but were unconvinced, and on January 26 their preference was still for attacks on oil and jet-fighter targets.[126] However, the same day, Churchill, who must have read the report, asked Sinclair whether there were any plans to help the Soviet offensive. Dissatisfied with Sinclair's equivocal response, he dashed off a note on January 26 demanding to know whether Berlin "and no doubt other large cities in East Germany" were now to be considered valuable targets. Sinclair replied on January 27 that Berlin, Dresden, Leipzig, and Chemnitz were all now on the list for possible attack when the weather had improved.[127] The next day Portal wrote to Churchill that oil targets remained a key priority of the bombing war, but added the following: "We also intend, as you know, to apply as much bomber effort as we can to the cities of Eastern Germany, including Berlin: but oil must come first."[128] Two days later Portal and Churchill both traveled to Malta for discussions with the Americans before going on to the conference at Yalta.

The second response was to set in motion actual operations. On January 27, Bottomley sent Harris the JIC report and asked him to prepare attacks on Berlin, as well as the three principal Saxon cities: Dresden, Leipzig, and Chemnitz.[129] He then drafted a paper for the chiefs of staff meeting, due to convene in Malta on January 31, which effectively summarized the grounds for the bombing:

Evacuation Areas: Evacuees from German and German-Occupied Provinces to the East of Berlin are streaming westward through Berlin itself and through Leipzig, Dresden and other cities in the East of Germany. The administrative problems involved in receiving the refugees and re-distributing them are likely to be immense. The strain on the administration and upon the communications must be considerably increased by the need for handling military reinforcements on their way to the Eastern Front. A series of heavy attacks by day and night upon these administrative and control centres is likely to create considerable delays in the deployment of troops at the Front and may well result in establishing a state of chaos. . . . It is for these reasons that instructions have been issued for heavy scale attacks to be delivered on these centres at the earliest possible moment.[130]

The initiative now passed to Tedder at Eisenhower's headquarters in Paris. After discussions with Spaatz and Bottomley, he drew up a planning document on January 31 incorporating the city attacks that would involve both British and American bombers. Spaatz, who thought that Operation Thunderclap was now the plan, preferred a heavy attack on Berlin, with high casualties, but he did not demur at a broader program.[131]

The only barrier to carrying out the raids was raised by the Soviet delegation at the Yalta Conference. The Soviet side demanded agreement on a formal "bombline" in eastern Germany, running through Berlin, Leipzig, and Vienna, beyond which Western air forces would not bomb for fear of hitting Soviet forces and equipment. The discussions at Yalta were resolved on February 7 by agreeing on the term "zone of limitation" to describe areas that either side could currently bomb, freeing Dresden and other cities from the Soviet proscription. It has often been argued that the Soviet side at Yalta asked for raids on Berlin, Leipzig, and Dresden, but the discussion with the Soviet chief of staff, Marshal Aleksei Antonov, recorded in the minutes, only mentions the bombing of Berlin and Leipzig; Portal seems to have insisted on including Dresden, since this was already on the list of cities suggested by the Air Ministry.[132] Though Harris later argued at the height of the Cold War that the request to bomb Dresden had come "from the other side of the Iron Curtain," there can be no doubt that the plan was always a Western one.[133] On February 7 the American military representative in Moscow, General John Deane, was notified by Spaatz that the bombing had been planned, and Soviet leaders were finally told five days later that the raid on Dresden was imminent. On February 8, SHAEF issued a formal operational instruction to Bomber Command and the Eighth Air Force to attack cities in eastern Germany when the weather was favorable.

The question for Dresden and the other cities of eastern Germany was not why they were attacked, which conformed with Allied policy on raids in support of the ground war, from Monte Cassino to Le Havre, but the way in which the raids were conducted and the weight of attack. Consistent with the new directive, Spaatz ordered a major daylight raid on Berlin on February 3, 1945, with 1,000 B-17 Flying Fortresses and almost 1,000 fighters. For once he ordered the aircraft to attack the center of the city along the lines first suggested in Operation Thunderclap, despite Doolittle's unhappiness about the deliberate targeting of civilian areas. On the operational directive Spaatz scrawled, "Beat 'em up!" (though much later he chose to remember the raid as just another military target). The toll was high for an American raid, indeed the highest German death toll from any of the raids on the capital. An estimated 2,890 were killed and 120,000 rendered temporarily homeless. A second heavy raid on Berlin with 1,135 bombers was made on February 26.[134] On February 6, Chemnitz was also hit, by 474 American bombers; on February 14–15 a second attack was made by Bomber Command with 499 Lancasters, though cloud obscured the city and most bombs fell wide of it; a further raid was made by the Eighth Air Force on March 2. Seen from this perspective, it is evident that the raid on Dresden was made as part of a series of agreed attacks on the cities of eastern Germany. All of these raids, and not just the attack on Dresden, were undertaken in the full knowledge that these cities were filled with civilian refugees from farther east, and that their destruction was likely to cause not just dislocation but high casualties as well.

The Dresden raid on February 13–14, 1945, was carried out by Bomber Command in two successive waves with 796 Lancasters, carrying 2,646 tons of bombs (including 1,181 tons of incendiaries). Dresden's light defenses resulted first all from the transfer of antiaircraft artillery to the Eastern Front and second from a successful diversionary raid that attracted the nearby night fighters away from the city. The first wave was not very effective, but the follow-up raid with the bulk of the Lancaster force in clear conditions achieved an exceptional level of concentration. Low humidity and dry, cold weather, combined with a very large number of small fires quickly started, proved ideal conditions for the generation of another firestorm. The flames consumed fifteen square miles of the city, an area that exceeded the damage at Hamburg. Recent estimates from a historical commission in Dresden have confirmed that the original figure suggested by the city's police president in March 1945 of approximately 25,000 dead is the best available estimate. Out of 220,000 homes, 75,000 were destroyed.[135] The firestorm, like the Hamburg conflagration, left bodies mummified or reduced to ash, making the final count difficult. A further 1,858 skeletons were unearthed when the city was slowly rebuilt after 1945. The aiming point in this, as in all area attacks, was the historic city center, which was entirely burnt out. The next day the Eighth Air Force carried out its first raid on the marshaling yards of the city, but the smoke from the previous night's bombing obscured the target and the 700 tons of bombs destroyed more of Dresden's hapless streets. In the afternoon 210 B-17s, unable to bomb their primary oil target, blind-bombed the city with another 461 tons. In all, almost 4,000 tons of bombs were dropped on a single target in less than twenty-four hours.

Unlike any of the other major raids in the last months of the war, the Dresden attack had immediate repercussions on Allied opinion. Two days after the raid an RAF officer at SHAEF headquarters gave a news conference in which he talked about bombing cities deliberately to cause panic and destroy morale. An Associated Press correspondent, Howard Cowan, filed a report successfully past the SHAEF censor, and by February 18 the American press was full of the news that the Allies had at last decided "to adopt deliberate terror bombing." Arnold was compelled to run a campaign to reassure the American public that Dresden had been attacked, like Chemnitz, as a major communications center, entirely consistent with American bombing policy.[136] It was hard to stifle the debate. Goebbels released to the neutral press news that 250,000 people had been killed in Dresden (by the judicious addition of an additional zero to the provisional casualty estimate). In Britain and America news of the death toll was soon public knowledge. The Bombing Restrictions Committee in London publicized the figure of 250,000 at once and provoked a furious correspondence accusing the committee of acting as the mouthpiece for German propaganda. Air Ministry statements in the House of Commons dismissed the accusations of terror bombing by claiming that no one, air marshals or pilots, was trying to work out "how many women and children they can kill."[137] But for the first time the real nature of area and blind-bombing attacks came under public scrutiny.

This may explain Churchill's now well-known decision to send a minute to Portal on March 28, 1945, protesting that the policy of bombing "for the sake of increasing the terror, though under other pretexts, should be reviewed." He asked Portal to focus on oil and transport, as the strategic directives had intended, instead of "mere acts of terror and wanton destruction." Harris was told of the document by Bottomley, who suggested that Churchill might have been worried about the shortage of German building materials, but Harris was outraged. He replied that city bombing had always been strategically justified because it would shorten the war and save the lives of Allied soldiers, an assertion difficult to reconcile with the five long years of British bombing. Portal persuaded Churchill to moderate his original minute for the chiefs of staff, which he did, but area bombing's days were now numbered. Churchill did not indicate his motives, and the entire episode of Dresden is missing from his history of the Second World War. It is possible that the publicity surrounding bombing as a result of Dresden worried Churchill as he contemplated a general election at some point in the next few months; it probably reflected his persistent ambivalence about bombing ever since its first disappointments in 1940 and 1941; or it may be that he finally realized, as Allied forces now poured into the broken cities of the Ruhr, just what bombing had done (on March 26 he lunched on the banks of the Rhine with General Bernard Montgomery, commander of the British 21st Army Group) and was affected by its enormity, as he had been when he wandered through British cities during the Blitz. Harris much later in life dismissed the episode as unimportant; he told his biographer that Churchill's attitude to him did not alter "in any perceivable way" between 1942 and 1945. But the rift was important enough to be suppressed until its publication in the official history in 1961.[138]

Whatever Churchill's misgivings, British city bombing continued in ways that were evidently punitive in nature and excessive in scale. Just ten days after Dresden, Bomber Command attacked the small town of Pforzheim. The marking worked well and the bombers dropped their loads from just 8,000 feet (instead of 18,000–20,000 feet on raids against defended targets); the subsequent conflagration consumed 83 percent of the city area, until then the worst in any raid of the war, and killed an estimated 17,600 people, though the death toll, the third highest in the European bombing war, has never had the publicity accorded to Dresden. The ruins of Cologne, hit by more than 250 wartime raids, were raked over again by a massive Bomber Command attack on March 2 by over 700 Lancasters, just four days before it was occupied by American forces. Essen suffered the same fate on March 11, with a macabre finale by over 1,000 bombers dropping 4,661 tons on a desolate landscape only hours before it fell to the advancing army. On March 24, Bomber Command headquarters portentously announced that, thanks to bombing, the "Battle of the Ruhr," then in its last furious days of ground combat, "is already over—and Germany has lost it."[139] On March 16–17, 1,127 tons of bombs were dropped on the small medieval city of Würzburg, killing between 4,000 and 5,000 people and destroying 89 percent of the city, a wartime record. Hildesheim was half destroyed on March 22 (the town center "should make a good fire," the crews were told).[140] The small city of Paderborn was destroyed on March 27, and half of Plauen on April 10–11. The final catalog of area attacks could not be restrained even by Churchill. On April 4, Portal, spurred perhaps by Churchill's minute, had notified the chiefs of staff that area attacks on industrial districts for the sake of destruction would now cease. When Harris destroyed Potsdam in a devastating raid on April 14–15, Churchill wrote angrily to Sinclair, "What was the point of going and blowing down Potsdam?" Portal replied a day later assuring the prime minister that Harris had already been told to discontinue industrial area attacks.[141] The directive sent to Harris on April 16 for the first time since February 1942 no longer contained industrial areas or morale as dedicated objectives.[142]

The American air forces wound down operations in April 1945. Much of the bombing since the February attacks was tactical in nature, directed at almost any target that could be deemed an element of German resistance. Operation Clarion was carried out with mixed success against a range of smaller communications targets. On April 5 all objectives were defined henceforth as tactical, but American bombing of the shrinking German area reached a crescendo, with 46,628 tons dropped in nineteen days of raiding, almost the same weight dropped during the German Blitz, but in just three weeks. The last raid by the Eighth Air Force was made on April 25 against the Skoda works at Pilsen; the last by the Fifteenth was on April 26 against the Austrian city of Klagenfurt.[143] Spaatz attended the surrender ceremony in Berlin on May 8 as the senior air commander in Europe. The Soviet delegation, however, refused to allow him to sign as the equal of Marshal Zhukov, the conqueror of Berlin, and he had to add his name underneath as a witness.[144]

Spaatz already knew that the Eighth Air Force was destined to go to the Pacific under his command to help complete the defeat of Japan. British bombers were also expected to contribute, and preparations were in hand to undertake operations against Japanese cities that had already been reduced to ash in a series of extensive incendiary attacks carried out by the former Eighth Air Force divisional commander, Curtis LeMay. RE8 produced a report on May 25, 1945, two weeks after the German surrender, titled "Area Attack Against Japan," recommending that since everything easily combustible had already been burned down, Bomber Command should use 4,000-pound blast bombs to destroy any urban areas or industrial targets still standing. From previous analysis carried out on the vulnerability of Japanese housing, it was calculated that each bomb would destroy more than ten built-up acres, whereas in Germany the figure had been only 1.5.[145] The air war in Europe was over, but Japan was soon to profit from its grim lessons.

Surveying the Wreckage, 1945

In August 1944, Spaatz had asked his air force commanders to speed up the defeat and surrender of Germany so that a special committee could review what bombing had achieved in Europe in order to apply their conclusions to the war against Japan.[146] The idea of undertaking a serious scientific survey of the bombing campaign had first been aired in the spring of 1944 and was enthusiastically supported by Spaatz, who approached Arnold and Lovett on the subject in April. Arnold wanted an independent assessment of the question "Was strategic bombing as good as we thought it was?" With Lovett's strong support, the air force put together a plan that they presented to the president in September. Roosevelt approved the project and asked the secretary of war, Henry Stimson, to establish the new office. Arnold chose a businessman, Franklin D'Olier, president of the Prudential Life Insurance Company, to head a board of professional economists, academics, and analysts, and on November 3, Stimson formally set up the United States Strategic Bombing Survey (USSBS), based in London; a forward base was set up after the end of the war in the resort town of Bad Nauheim, with branches in other German cities. Approval was given to enlist 300 civilians and 850 officers and men from the armed forces.[147] Their task was to produce comprehensive reports not only on the results of American bombing but also on the RAF offensive. The survey began its operations before the end of the war, as German territory was gradually captured.

The RAF also began to plan for a possible survey in the spring of 1944. The British side assumed that they would collaborate with the Americans, and on August 10, 1944, the chiefs of staff authorized the Air Ministry to prepare an inter-Allied survey organization. Arnold was solidly opposed to any joint venture, though it did not stop the USSBS from commenting at length on British bombing. By the time Sinclair finally proposed a survey to Churchill in December 1944, it was to be a British project. Churchill brusquely dismissed the idea of what was now called the British Bombing Research Mission, partly because of the assumption that it would take at least eighteen months to report, and hence be of no use in the war against Japan, but also because he deprecated tying up "the use of manpower and brainpower on this scale."[148] Instead of the large staff envisaged by the ministry, Churchill recommended a limited group of twenty to thirty people. His intervention invited months of bureaucratic wrangling over who should take part and at what cost, until Portal finally lost patience, abandoned the idea of the mission, and recruited a small unit already established at SHAEF, the Bombing

Analysis Unit, as the core of a British Bombing Survey Unit (BBSU). The new organization was formally launched on June 13, 1945, months after the American survey had begun its work.[149] The unit was to be run by an air force officer, Air Commodore Claude Pelly, and the SHAEF target adviser, Solly Zuckerman, assisted by staff from the RE8 division of the Ministry of Home Security, which was to be closed down when the war ended.[150] Both men were committed enthusiasts of the attack on communications, and their work and the subsequent reports reflected their bias. Their terms of reference were to examine the effects of bombing on German fighting capacity, the effectiveness of German defenses, and the accuracy of assessments of damage.[151] Already hostage to the small size and limited resources of the new unit, the BBSU became a vehicle for Zuckerman to argue his transport case in contrast to the disinterested analysis sought by the American air force. Much of the work of the BBSU was reliant on American research and expertise, a reflection of the rapid shift in the balance of power between the two air forces.

The process of collecting files and statistics and interrogating senior German personnel began at once. By the end of May a great many of the key figures had already been interrogated, including Göring, whose transcripts reveal an almost boyish desire to share his knowledge of the German Air Force with the victors. The provisional conclusions among the cohort of German airmen, engineers, and ministerial staff subject to interrogation were almost unanimous. A British intelligence assessment, "Factors in Germany's Defeat," produced by May 17, included an interrogation with Adolf Galland, who ranked the offensive against transport, then oil, then the air force as the most decisive.[152] In mid-June a full report of interrogation extracts was produced by the director of American air force intelligence at SHAEF, George C. McDonald. They also showed that the three critical targets were considered to be oil facilities ("The general opinion of the German leaders is that the attack on synthetic oil was the decisive factor"), communications ("brought about the final disruption of the German war effort"), and the German Air Force—achieved through attacks on aircraft production, airfields, and combat attrition.[153] Göring thought the collapse of oil supply to be the single most critical factor—"without fuel, nobody can conduct a war"—while

Albert Speer, Hitler's minister for armaments and war production, ranked communications at the top of the list of critical targets. Erhard Milch, Göring's deputy at the Air Ministry, ranked "synthetic oil plants and railway communications" together.[154] On area bombing the German judgment was largely negative. It did not "cause the collapse of the German people" and was regarded, according to McDonald, as "the least important of the major target complexes." When Göring was asked in one of his first interrogations on May 10 whether precision or area bombing was more effective in Germany's defeat, he replied, "The precision bombing, because it was decisive. Destroyed cities could be evacuated but destroyed industry was difficult to replace."[155] In a USSBS interview on May 24 with Karl Koller, the last German Air Force chief of staff, Koller claimed, not altogether plausibly, that without precision attacks "Germany would have won the war." He confirmed that oil and transport facilities were fatal targets for Germany.[156]

In general, Allied assessments reached the same conclusion. The USSBS produced over 200 detailed reports on every aspect of the bombing war, but the "Over-all Report" reflected the views of those interrogated. The survey board had an interest in arguing that in the Western theater airpower was decisive, thanks chiefly to the air victory achieved over Germany in the spring and summer of 1944, "which made devastating attack on [the German] economy possible." The report highlighted the relative failure of area attacks, which "had little effect on production," while singling out oil and communications as critical. The attack on Ruhr steel in late 1944 was also added as a key factor, but the choice of this period rather than Harris's "Battle of the Ruhr" in 1943 added weight to the implication that it was American bombing that had been decisive. The treatment of city attacks (4 pages out of 109) minimized their impact on economic output. Statistics were presented showing that city attacks, overwhelmingly by the RAF, cost only around 2.7 percent of German economic potential in the target areas. It was calculated that the combined offensive cost 2.5 percent of potential German output in 1942, 9 percent in 1943, and 17 percent in 1944 (figures that were roughly consistent with the claim that 5 percent of British output was lost during the lighter Blitz). Since area bombing in 1944 experienced diminishing returns, ton for ton, by dropping on previously destroyed areas, the implication again was that most of the production loss was due to American bombing of selected target systems.[157]

Perhaps more surprisingly, this was the conclusion also arrived at by the BBSU when its main report was finally completed in draft in June 1946, almost a year after that of the USSBS. There were months of delay in arguments with the senior commanders who had been responsible for the offensive, except Harris, whose views were not canvassed. Unlike the USSBS reports, which were easily available, the BBSU final survey and subsidiary reports were given only a limited circulation. The final report was critical of almost all phases of Bomber Command's activities except the final phase against oil and communications targets. A good deal of the report was devoted to demonstrating that the final industrial and military crisis in Germany was a result of the disintegration of rail and water traffic: "Enough has been said to show that the collapse of the German transport system . . . was the fundamental and main reason for the contemporaneous collapse of German war industry."[158] This fitted with Zuckerman's own prejudices. Even the assessment of oil supply, which the report regarded as critically disabling, concluded that the offensive against transport was responsible for preventing the recovery of Germany's oil position.[159] The judgment of the report on area bombing of German cities was even more damning than that of the USSBS. Using methods pioneered earlier by the RE8 department, Zuckerman's team calculated on the basis of twenty-one heavily bombed industrial cities that area bombing reduced potential war production by 0.5 percent in 1942, 3.2 percent in the first six months of 1943, 6.9 percent in the second six months of 1943, and then approximately 1 percent throughout 1944, when bombing again brought diminishing returns and area bombing was only one of the factors affecting output. The figures were lower than the USSBS estimates (which had been speculative extrapolations) because they were based on careful research across a range of cities and because they measured potential loss against a rising trend of output. In all twenty-one cities studied, war production expanded faster than it had done in a control cohort of fourteen cities not subject to attack.[160]

Damning though this indictment was, and partial though Zuckerman's position appeared to be, it fitted not only with the interrogation evidence but with the views among Air Ministry officials and RAF commanders in the two years after the war when hard thinking had to be done about what had been achieved by Bomber Command, rather than the combined offensive as a whole. Sydney Bufton, once an advocate of incendiary attacks on cities, produced a long critical assessment of area bombing in January 1945, in which he admitted the failure at Hamburg in 1943 as an example of misplaced confidence in the economic or morale effects of heavy urban destruction.[161] Norman Bottomley, Portal's deputy for the last three years of the war, and Harris's successor as commander in chief at Bomber Command, contributed an assessment of British bombing at a workshop organized by Tedder, now chief of staff, in August 1947 under the code name Exercise Thunderbolt. The effect of area attack, he concluded, was "great but never critical," nor was enemy morale ever "critically undermined," a fact he blamed on poor intelligence. "Offensive against oil and transportation proved most effective," he wrote, but only after the achievement of the vital precondition of air superiority.[162] A lecture given in 1946 by one of the RAF officers on the British survey highlighted air force attrition, oil, and transport again, but argued that "little worthwhile" had been achieved by area attacks before 1943, and thereafter the resistance of the German population and the reserve capacity of German industry made them "resilient to area attack."[163] Given the uniformity of opinion on both the German and Allied side, the one based on experience, the other on extensive research, it is surprising that the effects of bombing have occasioned so much debate ever since. The proximate causes—defeating the German Air Force and emasculating oil supply and transport—are unlikely to be undermined by further research.

The statistics nevertheless require some explanation about why the overall impact of bombing for much of the war period should have been so much lower than expectations. At its simplest level, as Henry Tizard put it after the war, "You can't destroy an economy."[164] American economists drafted in to advise the U.S. war effort in Europe were critical of the idea that bombing either areas or specific industries would of itself produce cumulative damage. The Hungarian émigré economist Nicholas Kaldor, a member of the USSBS team, argued that the critical factors in choosing economic targets were the degree of "cushion," the degree of "depth," and the degree of "vulnerability." The first was governed by the existing elasticity of the economy in terms of finding additional or substitute resources for those lost to bombing; the second measured the extent to which a particular product or resource was close to actual military use, since the farther back in the production chain, the longer the time before bombing would affect military performance; the third was governed by the extent to which concentrated, and relatively inflexible, capital industries could be effectively destroyed from the air.[165] Kaldor and his economist colleagues argued that for most of the war period Germany had a large cushion of resources of capital stock, labor, and raw materials that could be allocated to sustaining war production. His conclusion was based partly on the assumption, now generally regarded by historians as invalid, that Hitler did not order full-scale mobilization until 1944. The degree of allocation of productive resources to war purposes was in fact high from the start of the war, but many of the economies of scale characteristic of large-scale industrial production became effective only by 1942–43, while the unanticipated length of the campaign against the Soviet Union distorted war production plans at a critical juncture in 1941–42.[166]

Yet Kaldor was not wrong to argue that a cushion existed. The index of armaments output showed that German production increased threefold between 1941 and 1944, despite all the bombing; some individual categories of weapon expanded more than this, fighter aircraft by a factor of thirteen, tanks by a factor of five, heavy guns by a factor of four.[167] As a result of the conquest of much of continental Europe, Germany had access to large resources beyond her borders. Although this also involved economic costs to Germany, occupation meant that over 119 billion marks were contributed to Germany's war budget, one-quarter of all the costs of the armed forces; 7.9 million forced workers and prisoners of war were compelled to work in Germany, while an estimated 20 million more worked on orders for the German war effort in the occupied zones.[168] Moreover, German technical and organizational ingenuity made it possible to find substitute products or productive capacity even for "bottleneck" industries like ball bearings, where, as Kaldor argued, the target had "run away" by the time the Allies attacked it again in 1944.[169] The German economy, wrote the USSBS economist John Kenneth Galbraith in an early evaluation, was "expanding and resilient, not static and brittle."[170]

For most of the Allied bombing offensive these factors were either insufficiently known or not understood, and bombing, as a result, was relatively ineffective. Only in 1944, with the American decision to focus on enemy airpower, oil, and transport, were three targets chosen that fortuitously matched Kaldor's calculation. The attack on the German aircraft assembly industry, as part of the assault against enemy airpower, was the least successful because of the substantial cushion that existed in dispersing the final stages of production; all German leaders claimed, however, that repeated attacks on aero-engine production would have been critical. Oil and transport facilities, on the other hand, had poor cushioning possibilities once heavy attacks began, were highly vulnerable to sustained attack, and had a positive "depth" factor because both were needed almost immediately by the armed forces and by industry to sustain fighting capability and output. The campaign against the German Air Force was indeed a precondition for the success of the campaigns against oil and transport, and was a direct result of the changing tactics of day bombing and the high priority given by Spaatz to suppressing German airpower as fully as possible. When German oil installations and air force operations both threatened a limited revival in late 1944, Spaatz shifted once again to priority oil and counterforce attacks. It is difficult not to argue that the U.S. air forces had a surer strategic grasp and a clearer set of strategic objectives than did Bomber Command. Counterforce operations and the search for target systems that would unhinge the enemy's military efforts were central elements in American wartime air doctrine. The RAF, by contrast, thought of airpower more as a form of blockade, and was never enthusiastic about counterforce operations or attacks on transport, though both had been adopted in the Mediterranean campaign. The defeat of the German Air Force over Germany and the massive dislocation of German transport were primarily American achievements.

Area bombing was nevertheless, despite its critics, not entirely without impact on the German war effort. The random and scattered nature of much of the city-bombing campaign had evident opportunity costs for the German war effort, in addition to the effects of substantial civilian casualties and damage to housing. Consumer goods production had to be increased in 1943, against the trend of total war mobilization, to meet the needs of bombed-out families. The night bombing interrupted utility services and hit shops and occasionally factories, necessitating the allocation of additional resources of manpower to cope. There is no way in which these kinds of costs can be computed, any more than there was in Britain as a result of the Blitz. The real question concerns assessment of the damage done to the German industrial working class, since this was the whole rationale behind the campaign. It has never proved possible to calculate the number of workers killed, rather than nonworkers (elderly, women with families, children, etc.), but some sense of the limitations of any such assessment can be found in the death statistics in Hamburg, where on the night of the firestorm in 1943 that killed over 18,000 people, only 280 were killed in the factory district, away from the main area of bombing.[171] Workers were not always the most likely victims, but even if the estimated total of 350,000 German dead from bombing were all workers, that would still have represented only 1.6 percent of the German industrial and rural workforce, some of whom would have been killed by American daytime bombs rather than by the RAF.

The other argument for area bombing was the high level of absenteeism it would induce, though the British evidence, on which the strategy was based, was scarcely convincing. German records show that absenteeism as a direct result of bombing made up 4.5 percent of hours lost at the height of the bombing in 1944; an additional 10.8 percent of hours were lost due to illness or leave, though these may well have been a response to circumstances caused by bombing. Figures of hours lost due to bombing were higher in targeted industries (7.9 percent in shipbuilding, 10.6 percent in vehicle production), but much of this loss was the result of precise attacks by day rather than by Bomber Command at night.[172] The state of "morale" among the German population, which was also a stated objective, will be examined in greater detail in the next chapter.

The emphasis that has usually been put on the economic impact of bombing, in part a result of the very full economic data supplied by the bombing surveys, has had the effect of avoiding the more important question about the effect of bombing on the German military effort. Here the impact is more evident, though it would be prudent not to take at face value the USSBS claim that bombing was decisive. The air war over Germany was, in Albert Speer's phrase, "the greatest lost battle."[173] But it was a battle that was won alongside the Allied armies and navies; no particular service was decisive on its own. At the end of the war, Bufton observed that the whole purpose of the bombing offensive in 1944 "has been designed to weaken the German war machine as a whole so that it could not resist successfully when the Allied Armies made their final attack."[174] One of the principal criticisms of the BBSU report made by Portal (now Lord Portal of Hungerford) was the failure of its authors to grasp that "from 1941 onwards, if not before, the object of the bomber offensive from the U.K. was to weaken Germany to such an extent that an invasion of the Continent would succeed."[175] The problem with such claims is to be able to find a way to calculate the extent to which bombing really did inhibit German fighting power. As in the British case, the critical factor was the distorting effect that bombing had on German strategy once it became necessary to divert large resources to the military combat against the air offensive. Bombing, as Speer recognized, really did come to constitute a "Second Front" by 1943, preventing German military leaders from using airpower effectively at the fighting front as they had done in all the campaigns from 1939 to 1941. Failure in Russia, in the Mediterranean theater, and against the Allied invasion of France owed a great deal to the fact that German fighter aircraft, guns, ammunition, and radar equipment were tied up in the Reich. This had not necessarily been the Allied intention, which focused on unhinging the domestic war effort, but it undoubtedly contributed to the military outcome at the fighting fronts throughout the last three years of war and compensated for whatever weaknesses might have existed in Allied combat experience or skills.

There are two ways in which the effects of bombing on Germany's military effort can be directly measured. The combined offensive distorted German military strategy by imposing a heavy cost in active and passive antiaircraft defense. One of the keys to Germany's early battle-field successes was the employment of fighters, fighter-bombers, and me-dium bombers in support of ground forces. The Allied bombing forced the German leadership to switch aircraft back to the defense of the Reich and to reduce sharply the proportion of output devoted to front-line bombers and fighter-bombers, as table 3.3 demonstrates. This had the immediate effect of limiting severely the offensive airpower available on the battlefield.

In early 1943, 59 percent of German fighters were in the Western theater facing the bombing; in January 1944, 68 percent; by October 1944, 81 percent. At the beginning of 1944 German aircraft available on the Soviet front were little more than the number a year before, in the Mediterranean theater they were 40 percent fewer, but in defense of Germany the number increased by 82 percent. The same was true for the distribution of antiaircraft guns: in the summer of 1944 there were 2,172 batteries of light and heavy antiaircraft artillery on the home front, but only 443 batteries in the Mediterranean theater, and 301 on the

Table 3.3: German Fighter and Bomber Strength and Production, 1943–44

Date	Fighter Output	Bomber Output	Fighter Strength	Bomber Strength
March 1943	962	757	2,028	1,522
June 1943	1,134	710	2,403	1,663
September 1943	1,072	678	2,220	1,080
December 1943	1,555*	522*	2,172	1,604
March 1944	1,638	605	2,261	1,331
June 1944	2,449	703	2,301	1,089
September 1944	3,375	428	3,002	929
December 1944	2,630	262	3,516	528

*Figures for January 1944.

Source: Calculated from Charles Webster and Noble Frankland, *The Strategic Air Offensive Against Germany* (London: HMSO, 1961), 4:494–95, 501–2.

whole of the Eastern Front.[176] This situation left German armies denuded of air protection at a critical juncture of the ground war on the
Eastern and Mediterranean fronts, while the diversion to the defense of
Germany created just the conditions the American air forces needed to
be able to overcome the German Air Force in the "Battle of Germany,"
perhaps the single most significant military achievement of the offensive.

For the German war effort the costs of all forms of air defense by
1943–44 were substantial in terms of both manpower and equipment.
The antiaircraft service absorbed 255,000 people in 1940, but 889,000
at its peak in 1944; the 14,400 heavy and 42,000 light guns by 1944 required production of 4,000 new guns a month, and antiaircraft units
consumed one-fifth of all ammunition, half the production of the elec-
tronics industry, and one-third of all optical equipment.[177] The passive
civil defense personnel numbered around 900,000 (supported by 15 million members of the Air Defense League); the numbers involved in post-
raid clearance fluctuated over time, but they totaled by 1944 in the
hundreds of thousands. Civil defense and medical equipment had to be
maintained in the face of wide losses, hospitals had to be built and repaired, and fire services expanded. Few of those involved would have
been potential soldiers, but many would have been potential war workers, if they were not already combining civil defense activities with paid
work. This does not mean that civilians were ipso facto legitimate targets, but as in the British case, it shows that bombing compelled German
resources to be allocated in ways that directly affected German military
potential at the fighting front and the pattern of strategic choices. Without bombing, Germany would have been as free to optimize the use of
resources and to conduct the military war effort as was the United States.
The military consequences of the bombing campaign were clearly more
important than the economic, psychological, or political ones.

This still begs the question of what it meant for the Allies. Galbraith,
one of the USSBS team, later wrote in his memoirs that the man-hours,
aircraft, and bombs "had cost the American economy far more in output than they had cost Germany."[178] Both air forces were sensitive to this
charge and calculated themselves what proportion of the national effort

could be attributed to the bombing. In the British case the proportion was calculated to be 7 percent of all man-hour equivalents, in the American case an estimated 12 percent of wartime expenditure, both figures that did not distort exceptionally the structure of either war effort, unless account is taken of just how wasteful much of the bombing was.[179] Moreover, these were positive choices made about the allocation of resources, where in the German case the choice was involuntary, an addition to the other choices made about the distribution of strategic resources. Nevertheless the cost in manpower and aircraft lost in combat was substantial. In RAF Bomber Command, 47,268 were killed in action (or died as prisoners of war) and 8,195 in accidents. According to Harris, an estimated 135,000 flew in combat with Bomber Command, a loss rate of 41 percent. Total RAF dead during the war from all causes totaled 101,223, so that Bomber Command deaths amounted to 54.7 percent of all RAF losses.[180] Of these, the largest non-British contingent was composed of Canadians, 9,919 of whom died in Bomber Command.[181] Total wastage of Bomber Command aircraft from all causes was 16,454.[182] American heavy bomber losses against Germany totaled 10,152 between 1942 and 1945, and the total killed in all theaters against Germany was 30,099.[183]

Balancing the Allied losses against the German figures for aircraft and personnel says little about the final outcome. The costs were modest compared with the 9 million Soviet military dead and 5 million German dead, reflecting the priority of both Western Allies to avoid repeating the losses of the Great War for publics likely to be less tolerant of the escalating human cost to themselves than were populations under dictatorship. For Britain and the United States, the political advantages of preferring bombing to other forms of combat were to be found in the desire to limit the cost to the home population while maximizing the use of advanced technology and large manufacturing capacity to impose insupportable costs on the population, economy, and military structure of the enemy. Bombing could be used to maintain domestic morale and to exert leverage on the enemy in ways that were rendered easily visible in the democratic media. That the campaign could have been conducted differently, at lower cost (to both sides), and with greater efficacy is not in doubt, but it is evident from the historical record why these opportunities, strategic and technical, were missed or ignored or misunderstood, or incompetently attempted. War is always easier to fight looking backward.

Chapter 4

The Logic of Total War: German Society Under the Bombs

After the war in Europe ended in May 1945, many of those who had helped direct the bombing of Germany were curious to see the destruction for themselves. General Spaatz flew to Augsburg in Bavaria on May 10 to meet Hermann Göring, who had just been captured by American troops. The American official historian, Bruce Hopper, was with Spaatz and recorded the two-hour interrogation in a small office in the Augsburg Riding School in which Göring reflected on why his air force had failed to halt the bombing. It was, Hopper wrote, a historic meeting of the "Homeric Chiefs of the Air War." All around was evidence of the destruction of the national economic and civil life of a great nation, doomed, so he thought, to be set back by a century as a result. "That," he added, "has never happened before in history."[1]

Other senior American airmen visited the German ruins. General Anderson flew around the captured areas of western Germany, landing where he could and unloading a jeep to get a better look. The diary record of his trip—"Jeeping the Targets in a Country That Was"—recorded a shocking catalog of destruction: "Mainz, a shimmering shell. . . . Darmstadt, a shambles. . . . Frankfurt. Largely roofless. Looks like Pompeii magnified. . . . Ludwigshafen. Frightful, fantastic spectacle." Anderson flew across the Ruhr-Rhineland industrial basin where the language he used to describe the spectacle was stretched to extremes: "Dusseldorf, not even a ghost . . . all ruins begin to look alike. . . . Cologne, indescribable. One gets a feeling of total horror: nothing, nothing is left." His plane took him back to France five days later. His diarist breathed a sigh of relief: "escape from Götterdamerung [*sic*] back to civilization."[2] Sydney Bufton went to look at Hamburg and was "greatly

impressed," but shocked at the sight of people living in wrecked buildings "into which I would not care to venture."[3] Around the same time
Solly Zuckerman, the British government scientist and champion of the
Transportation Plan, visited the same Ruhr cities, where he witnessed a
similar desolate landscape: "so much destruction one longed for open
fields and to get away from the trail of our bombs." Here and there he
saw women sweeping the pavement in front of houses that were no more
than neat piles of rubble; in the eradicated city of Essen he observed
people who looked neat and tidy and in no obvious sense dejected. He
was puzzled by this behavior, so at odds with what he had expected.
"How the German civilians stuck the bombardments," he wrote a few
days later, "is a mystery."[4]

The survival of German society under the bombs has generally attracted less attention than explanations of British survival during the
Blitz. Yet the German population of the major cities had to endure more
than four years of increasingly heavy bombardment, fighting a war that
was evidently lost long before its end. Despite Germany's growing de-
bilitation, industrial production, food supply, and welfare were all maintained until the very last weeks when Allied armies were on German soil
and Allied bombers were pounding ruins into ruins. The capacity of the
state and the National Socialist Party to absorb this level of punishment
and manage its consequences demonstrated some remarkable strengths
in the system, as well as its harsher characteristics. The question asked
by the Allies before 1945 was typically, "When will Germany crack?"
For the historian the issue needs to be approached the other way round.
As for Zuckerman, the real issue is how German civilian life, trapped
between remorseless bombardment and a suicidal dictatorship, adapted
to the material and psychological pressures of progressive urban obliteration.

Community Self-Protection

In 1935 the German Reichsluftschutzbund (Reich Air Protection League)
published a poster featuring a stern-faced Hermann Göring above the
slogan, "Air defense fighters have as much responsibility and as much

honor as every soldier at the front!" The civil defense structure built up in Germany in the 1930s was from the outset more military in character than its British counterpart. The purpose of preparations for a possible bombing war was not simply to provide adequate protection from gas and bombs but to use air-raid precautions as a form of collective social mobilization. Civil defense was a community obligation that matched the wider claims of the German dictatorship to have created a rearmed and psychologically reinvigorated people after years in the democratic wilderness. By 1939, 15 million Germans had joined the Luftschutz-bund; by 1942 there were 22 million, almost one-quarter of the population.[5]

The formal civil defense structure in Germany was intentionally military in nature because it was set up and commanded by the German Air Force when the armed forces were reconstituted in March 1935 in defiance of the Versailles Treaty. From 1933 to 1935 air-raid defense was an office in the German Air Ministry, first set up in September 1933 with Göring as minister. In March 1935 it became part of the new air force structure, and on July 4 the Air Protection Law was published, defining the responsibilities of the new organization. The Air Protection Department was run by Dr. Kurt Knipfer, an air-protection expert previously with the Prussian Ministry of Commerce, who held the office down to 1945, despite numerous changes in the organization of the ministry and the nature of civil defense activity. In 1939 the department was placed under Air Force Inspectorate 13 (Air Protection), but Knipfer was able to avoid too much interference from the military side of the air force, which regarded civil defense as a passive subsidiary to the combat role enjoyed by the rest of the service. With the creation of twelve Regional Air Commands (Luftgaukommandos) in 1938, a territorial structure was established for running air-raid protection at the local level. The regional commands were responsible for all active and passive air defense in their area, including the Air Raid Warning Service (Luftschutzwarndienst), emergency repairs, medical aid, decontamination squads, blackout, camouflage policy, and fire protection.[6]

The question of organization was in practice far from straightforward. The Reich Interior Ministry, which had hitherto been responsible for air-raid protection, objected to the changed ownership of civil defense, and retained some responsibilities in areas of public health, civil administration, and post-raid organization that survived until well into the war, though without very clear definition.[7] More significant was the claim made by the leader of the SS, Heinrich Himmler, when he was appointed chief of German police in June 1936. At the local level the responsible leader of air-raid protection was usually the city police president, together with a committee composed of the local heads of the various emergency services. In smaller towns or the countryside the control post could be assumed by the local mayor, or rural officials, but in the threatened urban areas, the regular Order Police assumed responsibility. Himmler claimed that the police, rather than the air force, should run the fire service, provide medical help (in collaboration with the German Red Cross), organize gas decontamination, and coordinate the emergency rescue services (Sicherheitsdienst und Hilfsdienst). Confusion was temporarily set aside by an agreement between Göring's deputy, Erhard Milch, and Himmler in 1938, which confirmed that the Regional Air Commands had overall responsibility for active and passive air defense, but the Order Police would operate the rescue and welfare services once an air raid had taken place. The arguments over responsibility continued into the war as Himmler sought to exploit civil defense as an instrument for internal security as much as civil protection.[8] The emergency services were in July 1942 turned into the Air Protection Police (Luftschutzpolizei) to make clear that they served the police authorities, not the air force. Such dualism was characteristic of the institutional competition provoked in the Third Reich by the efforts of the party and the SS to penetrate or subvert or substitute conventional forms of authority.[9]

The creation of a national fire service was a typical example. The fire service was decentralized before 1933, the responsibility of local cities or provinces, with no technical compatibility between the different forces in equipment, hydrants, or hose couplings, and was dependent on a large number of volunteer auxiliaries. In 1933 the Air Ministry began a program to encourage manufacturers to standardize fire-service equipment. In Prussia, the largest German province, fire and police services were tied more closely together and instructions on standardized practices and technical standards were introduced; these were confirmed in the 1935 Air Protection Law. In 1936 the Interior Ministry planned to extend the Air Ministry guidelines to other provinces in order to promote national standards. Himmler, however, wanted the fire service under his control as chief of police and prepared legislation to create a National Fire Service, run on standard lines defined by the police authorities and including both professional firemen and volunteers. A National Fire Service Law came into force on December 23, 1938, dissolving all existing fire services and placing the new national organization under the control of the Order Police. Firemen were now to be known as fire defense police (*Feuerschutzpolizei*), the volunteers as police auxiliaries.[10] By 1940 standard and interchangeable equipment was available, including a single model light-alloy hose coupling that could be used for all types of hoses, and three standard pump appliances.[11] In the end, the contest for jurisdictional control did not inhibit the development of a more effective service to meet the needs of a future air war. The German model was the example used when a national fire service was created in England in 1941.

The German public was largely free of these jurisdictional conflicts. Unlike most other European states, the principal aspects of air-raid protection were to be undertaken by the German population on its own behalf. The Luftschutzbund very quickly established itself as the national agent for educating, training, and supervising the community in every aspect of air-raid protection. By 1937 there were 2,300 local branches with over 400,000 officials and 11 million members. By 1942–43 there were 1.5 million officeholders and 22 million members. They paid just one mark a year in subscription. In return, members attended one of 3,400 air-raid schools, or local courses in first aid, self-protection, and firefighting.[12] For potential leaders there were Air Protection Academies to attend. In May 1937 the public's civil defense role was defined in a law on "Self-Protection." Three distinct forms of self-help were identified: "self-protection" (*Selbstschutz*), "extended self-protection" (*Erweiterter Selbstschutz*), and "work protection" (*Werkluftschutz*). Individual householders were expected to create their own "air-protection community" in each house or apartment block, responsible for creating an air defense room (a cellar or basement if possible), providing effective escape routes through adjoining walls, and maintaining in good working order a complete set of tools and equipment for post-raid assistance. These generally had to be paid for by the householders but were a statutory requirement; they included rope, a fire hose, ladders, a home first-aid kit, sand buckets, water storage, an axe, a shovel, and armbands for those who were "lay helpers" or wardens.[13] The intention was to ensure that all citizens assumed responsibility for their own protection, in their own homes; if required, they would have to help protect the immediate neighborhood as well. This was an extreme form of decentralization, but at the same time a commitment by every member of the "people's community" (*Volksgemeinschaft*) to a common defense of the nation. Self-protection was voluntary in only a limited sense, since Luftschutzbund officials were supposed to check every household to make sure that blackout materials, anti-incendiary equipment, and a secure air-protection room were available. Failure to comply with civil defense regulations could involve a fine or imprisonment.

The other forms of self-protection involved sites outside the home. "Extended self-protection" was designed for all those buildings that were unoccupied in the evening or at weekends, including commercial offices, warehouses, museums, theaters, and administrative buildings. The system was not needed until war broke out, and it took time to establish, but it ensured that empty buildings did not become easy targets when incendiary bombing began. Work air-raid protection was placed in 1937 under the supervision of Reich Group Industry (Reichsgruppe Industrie). Each factory or plant had its own air defense unit, usually headed by a manager in charge of an emergency organization. Factories had to provide their own shelters and organize lookout schemes, and each one was linked by telephone with the main police control center in the city.[14] Again the object was to ensure that a high degree of community commitment would minimize damage and casualties and remove much of the air-protection burden from the public authorities. In the event that a building or workshop was bombed or set on fire, the local self-protection community had to tackle it first, then notify the local officials if it was too difficult to master, only finally receiving intervention from the police and emergency authorities when the incident was too serious. The onus in defending a locality from the effects of a bombing raid lay in the first instance, despite all the claims of the police and the air force, on those who lived and worked there.

The key figure in self-protection was the air-raid warden (*Luftschutz-wart*). These were generally volunteers, men or women, most commonly members or officials from the Luftschutzbund, responsible for a group of apartment houses or a street. Their function was to ensure that air-raid rooms had been prepared, equipment was up to date and available, the blackout was observed, attics and cellars were cleared of waste and rubbish, air supply and escape routes were adequate, and behavior in the shelters orderly. They lacked the power of arrest, but did enjoy the right to compel local people to help with bombing incidents, even while the bombing was still going on.[15] Before the war many of the wardens combined their role with that of local party "block leader," responsible for checking on each block of houses or apartments to make sure that party instructions and propaganda were disseminated and no visible signs of dissent expressed. But by the time war broke out the role was generally divided to make sure that both functions could be performed effectively, adequate civil defense and adequate party surveillance. With military mobilization in 1939, male wardens had to be replaced by women. Regular appeals were made in the early years of the war for female volunteers; at least 200,000 Luftschutzbund officials were women. The air-raid warden was to be chosen for evident qualities of leadership, an obsessive requirement in a system dominated by the "leadership principle." The definition of typical leadership qualities produced early in 1942 presented a formidable range of requirements: "Personal example, involvement of the leader at the site of greatest danger, superlative capability, firm will, calmness, steadfastness and confidence in the most difficult situation, trustworthiness, pleasure in responsibility."[16] Regular circulars were sent around in the war with stories of heroic individuals displaying, it is to be supposed, some or all of these characteristics.[17] This was the front line on the German home front: ordinary people called upon to perform, if they could, extraordinary acts of heroism.

Nonetheless, the introduction of civil defense measures before the outbreak of war was far less extensive than the large organization and popular propaganda of civic mobilization might have suggested. This was partly a result of geography. Though the object was to involve the whole population, the Reich was divided into three zones to reflect the degree of imminent danger from air warfare. Zone I included all the major industrial cities in Germany, ninety-four in total, with augmented civil defenses; Zone II covered 201 air defense sites (*Luftschutzorten*) of lesser importance; and Zone III included small towns and rural areas, or regions too far distant for existing enemy aircraft to reach.[18] Only those communities in Zone I were promised state financing to fund civil defense preparations. In late 1938 the association of municipalities complained to Göring that a lack of money for Zones II and III made it difficult either to build public shelters or to provide firefighting equipment, but the Air Ministry remained adamant and local Regional Air Commands were told to reject applications for less urgent air-raid facilities.[19] Not until November 1941 was the order reversed and funds were made available for exceptional expenditures in areas still designated Zone II or III.[20] Air-protection facilities and expenditures were targeted at the key areas only; the countryside had almost no organization, though its inhabitants were required to observe the blackout regulations. Only 12 million gas masks were distributed, again on the assumption that most people would not need them. A further explanation for the slow and uneven spread of air-raid protection lay in the air force conviction that antiaircraft fire would be sufficiently concentrated to deter enemy aircraft even if they succeeded in penetrating Reich territory, a judgment largely shared at first by the wider German public. For all the fear earlier in the decade that Germany was exposed to a circle of hostile states capable of bombing the German heartland, preparation on the home front came later and on a more limited scale than in either Britain or France.

The most obvious deficiency came in the provision of public air-raid shelters and the supply of matériel to make the air defense room (*Luftschutzraum*) a safe and reliable refuge. The quality of the "room" varied a great deal: sometimes it was an extensive cellar under an apartment block, sometimes little more than a small storeroom or a corridor. Most

German industrial regions were of recent construction and the communal housing was large in scale and concentrated, though there was usually a basement or cellar. Older housing varied, though the evidence suggests that few people in the threatened cities did not have access to local domestic shelter of some kind. Guidelines were regularly published about the ideal "room," which had to be gasproof, blastproof, clearly indicated, clear of obstructions, and provided with lighting and seating: "Everything prepared for the emergency!"[21] In the summer of 1939, the Air Ministry calculated that it would cost 50 reichsmarks (RM) per person to provide adequate shelter for the 60 million people who needed it, a total of 3 billion marks for which the money was simply not available.[22] The gap between ideal and reality was difficult to breach, and cellars and basements had to be slowly improved over the war years. The same problems existed with public shelters. In late 1939, for example, it was discovered that the shelter program for schools was well behind schedule, particularly in the areas outside Zone I. Many schools in more remote areas had neither cellar nor basement and had to be provided with trench shelters covered with concrete, or a strengthened ground-floor room, when the materials were available.[23]

The provision of shelter varied from area to area, since there was no common policy, but in 1939–40 the number of places available was far below what would eventually be required. In Hamburg in September 1939 there were just 88 public shelters for 7,000 people, by April 1940, 549 shelters for 51,000 out of a population of 1.7 million. Building work was directed at the 80,000 cellars in the city, of which three-quarters were provided with shoring and blast protection.[24] In the west German town of Münster, likely to be in the path of incoming bombers, there were by April 1940 public shelter places for just 4,550 people, 3.3 percent of the population. Only by the end of the year was this increased to 20,000, with room for an estimated 40,000 in private air defense rooms.[25] Most public shelters were designed for those who were caught in the street during a raid; the preference was to ensure that people returned if they could to their house shelter in order to carry out their "self-protection" duties. The one major difference between German practice and that of other European states was the legal compulsion to seek shelter during a raid, which almost certainly contributed to reducing casualties in the first war years. The wartime version of the Air Protection Law of 1935 carried the legal requirement to seek an air defense room or trench as soon as the alarm sounded, or to ask the nearest warden for help in finding a shelter place. In July 1940, after the first few RAF raids, the Luftschutzbund included in its regular bulletin for members a reminder that failing to take shelter was an offense: "The police have been instructed to take steps against offenders and report them for punishment."[26] Although it is unlikely that this happened in more than a few of the many cases, and merited little more than a nominal fine, shelter discipline was regarded as a serious question. Shelterers had to observe the simple rules of community: not smoke in the shelter, or drink alcohol, or bring in animals except dogs for the blind. To ensure that the local wardens or "self-protection" leaders could monitor the households for which they were responsible, formal notice had to be given of any overnight absence from home and copies of keys for all locked doors deposited with the officials. Once the bombing started in the summer, the rules became a ready instrument, with legal force, to control who would or would not have access to particular shelters.[27]

Rules for the blackout and evacuation also showed less immediate concern with the threat of bombing than had been apparent in Britain before the declaration of war. Blackout preparations in Germany had been insisted upon from the mid-1930s, when extensive blackout exercises were held in major cities, though with mixed success. The main law covering the blackout was issued on May 23, 1939, with a subsidiary order on domestic lighting issued on September 1, the day Germany attacked Poland.[28] All householders had a responsibility to ensure that the blackout was effective; in offices or commercial buildings one designated person was held to be responsible, in multistory apartment blocks one person was required to extinguish the lights in the halls and stairwells. In the first months of the war blackout discipline was variable. Building sites and factories showed more light than permitted; street lighting was 60 percent gas-fired and more difficult to turn off and on than electric lighting, so in many cities dim lighting remained. Helpful propaganda and advice were liberally supplied to help the population cope with the sudden plunge into darkness. In March 1940, Himmler, as chief of police, issued detailed guidelines on blackout behavior that included walking on sidewalks no more than two abreast, and avoiding excessive alcohol: "Drunk pedestrians bring not only themselves, but others into danger." Blackout infringements brought regular fines of up to 150 RM, but later on householders could also have their electricity supply cut off as a reminder not to leave a light showing.[29]

State-sponsored evacuation against bombing was, by contrast, almost nonexistent. In October 1939, Göring announced that there would be no assisted evacuation from the threatened urban areas, though plans could be made to transfer schoolchildren if necessary. Voluntary evacuation was neither prevented nor encouraged. Decisions on evacuation were reserved for Göring himself.[30] The initial wartime movements of population were away from the frontier (Red Zone) opposite France, only loosely connected with the bombing threat. Not until October 1940, more than a year after the start of the war, and six months after the start of British bombing, did the first trainloads of children leave Berlin at Hitler's instigation. They went as part of a scheme authorized in late September 1940, under the direction of the head of the Hitler Youth, Baldur von Schirach, as an extension of the existing program to send city children for invigorating breaks in the countryside (Kinderlandverschickung, or KLV), first begun in the late nineteenth century. In 1938 alone, 875,000 had benefited from the peacetime scheme. Now, to reduce public alarm, the pretense was kept up that what children subjected to regular air-raid alerts needed was an extended rest in rural areas, rather than permanent life in a bomb-free region. The first cities where the program was introduced were Berlin and Hamburg, followed some months later by cities in the Ruhr. The children, all aged between ten and fourteen, flowed out to youth hostels, summer camps, and small guesthouses, a total of 2,500 destinations with 100,000 places, where they stayed for up to six months, unless cold, homesickness, or the severe routine of the Hitler Youth sent them home sooner.[31]

The "Phoney War" period in the air war in Germany lasted a shorter time than in Britain. On May 10, 1940, the first bombs fell on the south German city of Freiburg im Breisgau, killing fifty-seven people, including thirteen children. The German press deplored the evidence of Allied butchery, but the town had been bombed in error by three German aircraft that had lost their way on a flight to attack the French town of Dijon on the first day of the German offensive. Freiburg was later bombed twenty-five times by Allied aircraft.[32] It was the following night, on May 11, that the first British bombs fell on the Rhineland; from then on across the summer months bombs fell on a German urban target almost every night. Since the raids were small and the bombing was scattered, the principal effect was to trigger the alarm system over wide parts of western Germany, compelling the population to seek shelter. In Münster in Westphalia there were 157 alarms in 1940, lasting a total of 295 hours, all but 7 of them at night.[33] The onset of bombing did not, however, signal the onset of a frontline mentality. Bombing was geographically restricted and distributed in small packets over villages as well as major cities. German propaganda immediately began to condemn the attacks as simple terror bombing, but this was also the view of the German Air Force, which assumed on the basis of the random pattern of the bombs that the British object must be to terrorize the population rather than attack the war economy. This thinking dominated German perception of the Allied offensive for much of the rest of the war. The propaganda apparatus played down the actual effects of RAF raids, but suspicious foreign journalists soon discovered for themselves almost no evidence of damage in Berlin or the Ruhr cities, and what small damage occurred there was quickly repaired or covered by wooden fencing.[34]

The absence of a clear urban front line fitted oddly with the large organization dedicated to civil defense and the prevailing image of the Third Reich as an embattled "people's community." The Security Service (Sicherheitsdienst, or SD) reports of the first few raids indicated that the population kept calm, except in places where the air-raid sirens failed to sound.[35] Air-raid discipline proved at first to be shallower than anticipated from the endless training courses and the 4- to 5-million-strong army of trained civilian "self-protection" helpers. In May 1940 it was observed that out of simple curiosity people stayed out on the street to watch the bombing, or stood at open windows or on balconies. The Luftschutzbund circulated warnings in May and July that as soon as searchlights and antiaircraft gunfire began it was an obligation to seek shelter, even more to ensure that no light was left visible given the plan-less character of British aircrew who "threw their bombs wherever they saw a light."[36] But when the bombing spread to Berlin in late August, the same pattern became evident and sterner warnings had to be issued. In September the president of the Luftschutzbund, Lieutenant General Ludwig von Schröder, announced that anyone who sustained injury while deliberately failing to shelter would not be given any state medical assistance. A propaganda campaign was launched to advertise the air-raid room as the safest place to be in a raid and to highlight the numbers still being killed in the open, but the official complaints disappeared in 1941 as the bombing became heavier and more deadly.[37] During the summer and autumn of 1940 the population viewed the war differently from the embattled British under the German Blitz; buoyed up by the sense of a historic victory and expecting Britain soon to abandon the war, they did not seem to view the bombing with the same sense of battle.

The regular bombing nevertheless forced the German government to accelerate the program for better protection and to ensure regular welfare. Since the attacks were small and irregular, the costs could be absorbed with relative ease. From the start the government agreed that compensation would be paid for injuries or losses sustained as a result of enemy air action, perhaps unaware of what such a commitment might mean in the long term. After the first raid in mid-May 1940 the Interior Ministry reminded all local authorities that compensation for bomb damage, or loss of livelihood or removal of personal possessions, was a direct charge on the Reich.[38] The question of loss of earnings was more difficult, since it would mean paying workers for doing nothing while they sat in the air-raid shelter or took time off while their work premises were repaired. Random though British bombing was, the social geogra-phy of the raids showed that the key targets were industrial and port cities, and the majority of victims likely to be workers. The air-raid legis-lation of September 1, 1939, promised payment of 90 percent of wages lost, but this had not anticipated the long periods of alarm when there were no attacks. One solution was to change the alarm system to ensure that as little time as possible was lost from productive work, and eventually the two-tier system of general alarm, followed by all-clear, was changed in favor of a series of step alarms in which the local civil defense would be notified first, followed by a "raid possible" siren, then a general alarm. Industries were expected to work through the general alarm until a final six-minute warning was sounded to give workers time to get to the shelters.[39]

In the summer of 1940 it was decided that the 90 percent wage compensation should be changed into an obligation to work extra time to make up for lost production or to help in repair and debris clearance after a raid, to make sure that workers were being paid for actual work. But this decision produced many anomalies and provoked working-class resentment, as had other restrictions on pay introduced with the onset of war.[40] Salary earners, for example, were paid 100 percent loss of earnings, while in February 1941 the Ministry of Labor agreed that porters and ancillary staff were also entitled to pay during alarms, but could not be expected to make up lost time for nonproductive work. By contrast, it was decided that home workers were entitled to nothing since they could work extra hours when they chose.[41] The consequence was that some workers were paid compensation for doing nothing, whereas others were paid nothing and made to work extra hours. It was evident that the escalating air attacks in 1941 made working-class morale a critical issue. A meeting in October between the Labor Ministry, the giant Labor Front union (representing 26 million workers), the Propaganda Ministry, and the Party Chancellery concluded that morale was more important and insisted that the Labor Ministry find ways of improving compensation and assistance for workers who faced increased travel costs or short-term unemployment as a result of bombing, though not before the Labor Ministry representative had argued that workers saved money sitting in the shelters because there was nothing for them to buy there.[42] The issue remained unresolved, since firms were free to interpret themselves whether workers ought to be paid at all for interruption of their work or should earn only by working more. Pressure was applied increasingly by the party through the local *Gau* economic offices to ensure that the law was not applied at the workers' expense. By late 1943 there had been nineteen different pieces of legislation to try to cope with the consequences of work interrupted by bombing.[43]

Anxieties about compensation for German workers and German households were not extended to Germany's Jews. A decree in December 1940 instructed all local labor offices to ensure that no compensation for loss of earnings would be paid to Jewish workers, on the grounds that the war "to a not inconsiderable extent can be traced back to the influence of World Jewry."[44] A second order on July 23, 1941, excluded German Jews or Jewish-owned businesses from making any claim for damage compensation under the "War Damage Order."[45] Efforts were made from early in the RAF campaign to help the bombed-out (*Obdachlose*) by housing them in apartments owned by German Jews. In the Rhineland city of Soest the decision was taken in the late autumn of 1940, and although the Interior Ministry highlighted the possible legal problems with doing so, the policy of replacing Jewish householders with "Aryans" became established by the time of the heavy raids in the spring of 1942.[46] In Cologne the Jewish occupiers were removed to crude barracks while Jewish houses and apartments were redistributed. The Party Chancellery confirmed in April 1942 that if British raids continued, "we will pursue this measure completely and clear out all the Jewish homes."[47] By this stage the preparations were well under way for transporting Germany's Jews to camps in the east and seizing the remaining Jewish housing and assets. Rules published in November 1941 made it possible to sell expropriated Jewish furnishings and possessions to survivors in bomb-damaged cities. Between October 1941 and March 1942, 60,000 German Jews were sent east, most to their deaths, and in the next three months a further 55,000.[48]

The bombing also forced the pace in providing more effective shelter and protection. Because of the poor accuracy of British bombing, many bombs fell in the open countryside or on villages, a result that had not been anticipated when planning air-raid protection. By the summer of 1940 it was evident that the emergency services would have to supply units to help with rescue, bomb disposal, and repairs "even in small, or the smallest localities, and outside them."[49] Villages were helped by the local police, but the rural population was expected to form "rural air-protection communities" as well, even in outlying areas with scattered homesteads. The blackout was strictly enforced in rural areas, though villagers could sometimes be the victims of bomb attacks on the many decoy sites set up across western Germany in country districts.[50] For farmers, the Reich Air Protection Law provided a statutory veterinary first-aid chest, one for the first ten animals, two for more than twenty, and three for farms with over forty horses, cattle, or pigs.[51] The destruction of housing, in town and countryside, was relatively small-scale in 1940 and 1941 because the RAF was not yet using incendiaries systematically on a large scale, but the regime was sensitive to the need to show that rehabilitation was an urgent priority. On September 14, 1940, the general plenipotentiary for construction, Fritz Todt, published a decree on repair to bomb-damaged housing, which gave it top ranking ahead of the list of urgent war-essential construction projects, as long as the repairs could be carried out quickly and the labor and materials found easily from local contractors. Todt's deputy for construction in Berlin, Albert Speer, promised in December 1940 that all lightly damaged houses (windows, roofs, etc.) would be repaired in thirty-six hours, and all plasterwork repaired in four days. These were promises not difficult to fulfill as long as the damage remained modest.[52]

The onset of bombing highlighted particularly the inadequate protection offered by the converted air-raid room and the modest amount of public shelter. In Hamburg an emergency program was started that saw the number of places in public shelters expand from 51,000 in April 1940 to 233,207 a year later; by the time of Operation Gomorrah, the bombing of the city in July 1943, around three-quarters of the cellars had been converted to air-raid rooms.[53] In other cities, schemes were set up to strengthen the air-raid rooms by providing a reinforced ceiling, props, and escape routes, but shortages of matériel and labor made it difficult to complete the work. In Münster around 5,000 cellars were improved between the autumn of 1940 and the spring of 1941, but a survey in early 1942 showed that still only 4.7 percent of the population had rooms that were considered entirely safe in a raid.[54] In Berlin in the autumn of 1940 only one-tenth of the capital's population had air-raid rooms, partly on the assumption that it was relatively safe from long-range bomb attack, which it was not. Following the first raids on the city in August 1940, Hitler ordered a program to build between 1,000 and 2,000 bunkers in Berlin, each capable of holding 100 people. He told the air-protection authorities that "damage to property was bearable, but in no case were human losses." Every house had to have its own air-protection room, if possible with light, heating, and somewhere to sleep, and the cost would now be borne by the state.[55] On October 10, Hitler finally published an "Immediate Program" empowering the Air Ministry to undertake an extensive program to ensure that the urban population had access to a proper air-raid room, as well as bunkers and shelters for businesses, schools, museums, galleries, and ministries.[56] The cost in labor, cement, and iron in an economy already facing rigorous restrictions and priorities proved impossible to meet, and in mid-1941 and again in December that year, work on larger bunkers was curtailed where possible in favor of blastproof trenches and reinforced cellars.[57]

Nevertheless, concrete bunkers were built both above and below ground in the major threatened cities, particularly in the Ruhr-Rhineland. In Cologne a total of at least 58 were built between 1940 and 1942, 15 of them concentrated in the inner city center.[58] In all, some seventy-six cities undertook to construct a total of 2,055 bunker shelters between November 1941 and 1943, of which 1,215 were finished by early 1942, though not yet fully equipped. Shortages of matériel and the competing claims of armaments production, the Atlantic Wall defenses (which consumed twice as much concrete as the bunker program), and the giant concrete pens for submarines meant that much of the program remained incomplete by the time the heaviest raids began in 1943.[59] Even this number of new shelters could provide only a fraction of the population with protection. The first wave of building up until the summer of 1941 provided places for 500,000; a second, smaller wave resulted in places for 740,000 by the summer of 1943, or only 3.87 percent of the population in the seventy-six cities involved. There were in addition converted cellars and air-raid rooms for 11.6 million, though many were scarcely bombproof. For millions of Germans there was no immediate prospect of secure shelter, particularly in the cities ranked in Zones II and III, which became the object of heavy attacks in the last year of the war.[60]

A few weeks before the "Immediate Program," Hitler had also ordered the construction of six vast "Flak-towers" in Berlin. The extraordinary scale of the buildings appealed to his sense of the architecturally gigantic, like the plans for the rebuilding of the capital. Their solid design, modeled on a towered Gothic castle, was deliberately intended to express both grim defiance and grotesque physical power, a blend of function and ideology, "like a fantastic monstrosity," one eyewitness wrote, "from a lost world, or another planet."[61] They were planned to provide not only enhanced antiaircraft fire but protection for up to 20,000 people, artworks, museum collections, essential defense services, hospitals, and a Gestapo office. Towering above the surrounding Berlin townscape, coated in green paint to make them less visible from the sky, the colossal towers were prestige buildings. Their cost in labor and resources was prodigious, the "Berlin-Zoo" tower consisting of almost 200,000 tons of concrete, stone, and gravel. The first was completed by April 1941, the second by October, and the third by the spring of 1942. Hitler approved two more tower sets to guard the port in Hamburg; one was finished by October 1942, a second just before Operation Gomorrah, in July 1943. Between them they could hold 30,000 people. Two more tower pairs were built in Vienna in 1943 and 1944, capable of holding not only the cultural treasures of the city, but at least 40,000 of its inhabitants. The Vienna towers were to be literally monumental; the ornamental marble to cover the exterior walls was quarried in France but in the end could not be shipped because of the Allied invasion of Normandy in June 1944.[62]

The development of effective protection and compensation was a reaction to the onset of British bombing, rather than a result of advanced planning for the possibility. Until well into 1941, while there was still a prospect that Britain would abandon the war, the plans for civil defense might still be regarded as temporary; the war against the Soviet Union made it clear that Hitler had abandoned the prospect of defeating Britain quickly and that the bombing offensive was likely to increase in intensity before German forces were free once again to concentrate on the

British enemy. This strategic reorientation made it more important for the German state and the party to be able to provide sufficient support to prevent bombing from damaging domestic support for the war effort. In 1940 only 950 people had been killed in all the bomb attacks (which suggests that the air-raid cellar offered better protection than the authorities feared). In 1941 the level of civilian casualties and damage to property began steadily to increase. In Münster there were 24 raids between July and December 1940, which killed 8 and wounded 59; just 3 raids in July 1941 killed 43 and injured 196. In Hamburg, 69 attacks in 1940 had resulted in 125 deaths and 567 injured; a further 143 raids up to the time of Gomorrah in July 1943 killed 1,431, injured 4,657, and left 24,000 temporarily homeless.[63] In 1941 an estimated 5,029 were killed and perhaps 12,000 injured in a total of 295 raids. Small though these statistics are by comparison with the casualties of the Blitz, it represented the first serious loss of civilian life for a population more accustomed to the roll call of the military dead.[64]

During 1941 the pattern of RAF bombing also changed. From spring onward, bombers carried a higher proportion of incendiaries and began to concentrate them more effectively. Training in fighting incendiaries had been part of routine civil defense education, but now detailed pamphlets were issued on every type of British incendiary device with instructions on how to tackle them, including the recommendation to wear a gas mask. The schedule for self-protection classes was changed so that almost all the practical elements were devoted to fighting fire and extinguishing incendiaries. Training centers had an "air-protection exercise house" where trainees learned to overcome any anxieties about tackling a real fire by exposure to a controlled blaze.[65] Göring put his name to a list of ten principles to observe when combating incendiaries, under the slogans "Incendiary bombs must be tackled immediately!" and "Everyone fights for his own property and goods!"[66] A greater effort was made to get householders to remove clutter and stores from all attic spaces to prevent the rapid spread of fires. Hitler Youth groups and other party organizations were detailed to carry out house-to-house clearance of all unnecessary stocks and furnishings, while local civil defense authorities were instructed to remove stored grain and foodstuffs from endangered storerooms. Air-raid wardens were instructed to set up small gangs of two or more residents to go out, even before the all-clear, to check on fires and try to get them under control. Anyone who refused to help was liable in the worst cases, according to the Air Ministry, to a spell in a concentration camp. No house was to be left empty and unwatched.[67] In March 1941, Hitler's Supreme Headquarters issued an order to local military commanders to establish an Armed Forces Emergency Service to provide military assistance in cases of major raids where the local civil defense and police units were not sufficient to cope with the scale of the damage or where fires threatened to destroy militarily important stocks or buildings. Armed forces stationed at home were to become an important source of emergency assistance over the following three years.[68]

The impact on popular opinion of the increased bombing is difficult to gauge in a state where the media was centrally controlled and public expressions of anxiety were likely to bring severe reprimand. In the spring of 1941 the authorities began to think about more formal programs of evacuation from the most bomb-threatened regions, though the preference was for movement to safer suburban areas of the same city, or to the immediate rural hinterland. It was only available for women, children, and the elderly, but not for any German Jews, for whom no official provision was allowed.[69] Evacuation remained voluntary and was presented to the population as a welfare measure, run exclusively by the party through the National Socialist People's Welfare (National-sozialistische Volkswohlfahrt, or NSV), another vast party organization, with 15 million members, mostly volunteers and predominantly female. The first wave of evacuation from Berlin, Hamburg, and the Ruhr cities involved only a small fraction, perhaps 10 percent, of the children and mothers who qualified. Most parents preferred to wait and see what the risks were or were unenthusiastic about handing their children over to party organizations.[70] The SD reports for 1941 show a declining concern among the wider public over the air raids, but regular interest in the wider news of the war, particularly the successful campaigns against Yugoslavia and Greece and then against the Soviet Union from June 1941, all of which once again raised the possibility of a rapid end to the conflict, which would make all the effort at air-raid protection suddenly redundant. Bombing nevertheless persisted whatever was happening elsewhere in Europe. In July 1941 von Schröder sent a report to all Luftschutzbund officials praising the "decisive bravery" and "will to resist" of the German population subjected to bombing. The aim, he continued, was to overturn the "legend" that the English held the record for steadfastness by demonstrating to the world the inner resolve of the German people.[71]

"Great Catastrophes," 1942–43

The German home front was suddenly rocked in March 1942 by the first concentrated and heavy incendiary raid on the coastal town of Lübeck. Two-thirds of the 400 tons were firebombs, dropped from only 2,000 feet on the old city center, which consisted of half-timbered houses. Rumors immediately circulated in the surrounding area that 3,000 had been killed and 30,000 rendered homeless (just over 300 died in the raid, the worst casualties so far); reports to Berlin observed an immediate improvement in air defense discipline in other cities.[72] The raid was swiftly followed by a series of devastating incendiary attacks on the port of Rostock, which produced for the first time an outcome classified under the term "great catastrophe."

The first attack on Rostock, on April 23–24, was relatively limited. The gauleiter reported to the Party Chancellery that the population was calm and the raid well under the control of party and state authorities. But three more raids in quick succession imposed more serious dislocation, damaging or destroying three-quarters of Rostock's 12,000 buildings. A state of emergency was declared and troops and SA (Sturmabteilung) men were brought in from the surrounding area. By the third day 100,000 of the population had been evacuated or had fled into the surrounding countryside. Rumors began to spread that Sweden had suddenly declared war on Germany and bombed Rostock as the first act.[73] When on the fourth day an alarm went off in error in the afternoon, the population began to panic and armed SS men were called in to make sure order could be maintained. Two looters were caught and one condemned to death within a day. Loudspeaker vans toured the area to call for calm while supplies of chocolate and butter (both commodities that had almost disappeared) were handed out from stocks found hoarded in the city. Fifteen military field kitchens were brought in to hand out hot meals, while an emergency supply column with 100 tons of food was sent to the stricken city from the "catastrophe stores" kept for just such an occasion.[74] By May 2 the population was starting to return to collect goods stacked in the street while groups of hand workers were brought in to begin work on reroofing and reglazing damaged buildings to make them habitable again. It was observed that among the 165 dead so far recorded were 6 Hitler Youth, 8 local National Socialist political leaders, and 3 SA men. The regional authorities found little evidence of "hostile opinion against Party or state." Their aim was rapidly to re-create "the normal conditions of daily life in every area."[75]

Although the authorities in Rostock judged that the civil defense services had coped well with the consequences of the raid, the onset of "catastrophic air attacks" prompted a fundamental overhaul of the way civil defense and post-raid welfare was organized. The driving force behind the change was the party hierarchy, which understood that the social and psychological consequences of heavy bombing were likely to have wider ramifications for social cohesion and war willingness. During 1942 the balance in the air-protection structure swung heavily toward the party and away from the Air Ministry and the police. The key figure was the Minister for Popular Enlightenment and Propaganda, Joseph Goebbels. In late April, Hitler agreed to give him special responsibility as commissar for organizing immediate help measures for those areas where the local authorities could not cope. All local party *Gaue* (and not the Regional Air Commands or the Order Police) were to notify Goebbels's ministry at once if help was needed. Goebbels told the gauleiters that the watchwords were "unity and planning."[76] The choice of the new commissar was not an obvious one, and his actual powers, as so often in the Third Reich, were poorly defined, though he evidently benefited from direct and regular access to Hitler. Goebbels's principal claim was his concern with monitoring and molding popular opinion, which his local propaganda offices watched closely. Reports on raids were routinely sent to his office as party Reich leader of propaganda, which left him better informed about the national picture than most other political or military leaders. Moreover, Goebbels was a gauleiter himself, representing Berlin; his new office was designed to ensure that the local party leadership should play a fuller part in managing bombed communities. His appointment confirmed the increasing "partification" of the whole civil defense project.

The roots of this new configuration could be found much earlier in the war. The Party Chancellery, directed by Rudolf Hess, had a Mobilization Department (*Abteilung-M*), which drew up guidelines for the role of party organizations in the event of war. The NSV was detailed to take on responsibility for providing post-raid welfare, including evacuation, and to wear green armbands with "Luftschutz-NSDAP" sewn on them to show that they were independent of the air force or police. In the autumn of 1940, Martin Bormann, Hess's deputy, drew up a list of nine civil defense activities formally under Göring's authority, in which the party claimed a role. They included controlling behavior in shelters, checking on the blackout, supplying candidates for air-raid warden who possessed impeccable racial and party credentials, and providing moral support when it was needed.[77] These claims had at first a nominal value, given the limited raiding activity and the extensive civil defense organization already in place. But party insinuation was insidious and remorseless. By the time Goebbels was granted his new powers, the party had already made itself conspicuous in supplying SA and SS assistance when needed, Hitler Youth as messenger boys, the NSV as the organizers of evacuation, and the necessary pomp and ceremony at the burial of bomb victims. The post of Reich defense commissar (*Reichsverteidigungskommissar*), established on September 1, 1939, and generally given to the local gauleiter as a largely nominal title, was elevated by the war into an instrument for party leaders to play a fuller part in home-front mobilization. On November 16, 1942, the posts of commissar and regional party leader were formally merged and the *Gau* became the administrative unit for the home front. The gauleiter of Munich later recalled that from 1942 onward his work came to consist almost entirely of "defence from the enemy air war, activation of civilian air protection."[78]

The claims of the party had the paradoxical effect of demilitarizing the home front, as the air force role was confined progressively to the more evidently military aspects of air defense. Goebbels was to be the direct beneficiary of this process, though Bormann, now director of the Party Chancellery following Rudolf Hess's flight to Scotland in May 1941, resented Hitler's choice and took every opportunity to increase his influence over post-raid policy. The other competitor was Göring, whose role as general overseer of air defense was challenged by Goebbels's new powers. In May 1942, Goebbels, Göring, and Wilhelm Frick, the interior minister representing the interest of the police and local authorities, drew up a formal document confirming the new pattern of responsibility between them. "Pure air defense" was left in the hands of the air force and the police; all civil administrative tasks were the province of the Reich defense commissars (usually the local gauleiter); the job of managing the care and morale of the population in the face of bombardment was the sole responsibility of the party. Goebbels was confirmed in his new capacity as emergency commissar, for when the existing system could no longer cope.[79] The arrangement made explicit the shift of responsibility toward the party and the collapse of the air force monopoly, but the demarcation left a great many gray areas. In December 1942, Göring issued a further directive to try to make the setup clearer: in the event of a catastrophic raid, beyond the scope of the Reich defense commissar or the air protection leader, help should be requested from the Party Chancellery, the Propaganda Ministry, and the Interior Ministry. But this arrangement merely confirmed a state of improvised confusion.[80] At the beginning of 1943, Hitler finally agreed to set up an Inter-Ministerial Air Protection Committee (ILA), based in the Propaganda Ministry, with Goebbels as nominal head. The object was at last to create a single, national clearinghouse for all emergencies, with no new powers and limited organization, but with a sufficient overview to be able to send resources in a crisis where and when they were needed.[81]

The struggle over competency between the power brokers of the dictatorship proved less damaging than it might have been, because intervention from the center was confined principally to the most conspicuous and damaging raids, where the role of the party or the political leadership could be effectively advertised. At the local level the onset of heavy raiding provoked a greater effort to ensure that the local administration and party organs were better prepared to meet the demand to provide effective welfare and emergency rations, rehouse the homeless, and compensate those who had lost everything in the raids. The watchword was *Einsatz,* a difficult word to render in English, suggesting action that is decisive and purposeful. After the bombings of Lübeck and Rostock, cities were encouraged to develop an "action mentality" by creating an *Einsatzstab* (action staff) under a designated *Einsatzführer* (action leader), who was to be chosen from among the local air protection leaders as an individual of outstanding merit. The staff was to consist of representatives of all the local state and party offices for welfare, food, building, repair, transport, and local economy, but the leader was the key figure, given temporary emergency powers to get help from within and outside the raided area and to apply it swiftly and ruthlessly to the catastrophe.[82] "Self-protection" was to be strengthened by creating local "self-protection squads" (*Selbstschutztruppen*) run by yet another lower-level *Einsatzführer* whose job was to tackle raids on streets and small communities in a more coordinated and vigorous way. An "action plan" was made a legal requirement for all *Einsatzführer* in October 1942. In August 1943, service in a self-protection squad was made a legal obligation for every German citizen, man and woman.[83] In practice, not everyone was required to serve, but the proportion could be very substantial. In the small Rhineland town of Bingen, with a population of 16,600 people, 4,783, more than one-quarter, were enrolled as active civil defenders.[84]

According to yet another Hitler decree published in August 1943 after Operation Gomorrah, the aim of all the new emergency arrangements for coping with air raids was "the restoration of normal life as quickly as possible."[85] Though this was not easy in the few major cities where repeated heavy bombing began in 1943, the object of the new "action culture" was to make sure that one way or another the problems of welfare, compensation, rehousing, damage repair, and evacuation allowed an adequate community life to continue. A good example of how this worked was the post-raid activity in the Berlin suburb of Schöneberg, bombed heavily on March 1–2, 1943, leaving 11,000 temporarily homeless. They were gathered first in the seventy-one emergency rest centers, with room for between 25,000 and 40,000 people in converted cafés, schools, restaurants, and boardinghouses.[86] There they were given food, spirits, cigarettes, substitute ration cards, and a provisional sum, in cash or vouchers, for the most urgent replacement clothing and household goods. Those who could not be placed with friends or relatives at once could be found substitute housing, particularly former Jewish homes, with priority for families with children whose houses had been completely destroyed. Evacuation was recommended only in exceptional circumstances, and then to areas if possible within the same urban region, or the same *Gau*. Over 7,000 were rehoused within two days. The salvaged goods had to be left in the street, clearly marked (to prevent looting), where they were collected in municipal street-cleaning trucks or military vehicles and stored in requisitioned warehouses or shops. Glass from the shattered windows was quickly cleaned up and returned to glassmakers for recycling.[87]

The guidelines for rehousing, house repair, and compensation were laid down in a number of decrees issued by the Interior Ministry and the Organisation Todt in the course of 1941.[88] In Schöneberg, housing was tackled at once by a special unit (*Baugruppe Pfeil*) organized by the city mayor. The unit turned up the morning after a raid to classify all housing into four categories of totally destroyed, badly damaged, partially damaged, and lightly damaged. The first had to be made secure, the second repaired if possible, the last two restored to a habitable state. The Interior Ministry instruction was to do no more than ensure that the buildings could be lived in—roofs covered over with boards or broken slates and tiles replaced.[89] In the aftermath of the Berlin raid there were 300 roofers, 460 glaziers, and 485 bricklayers at work at once, covering over roofs first to protect the rooms exposed to the elements, then covering windows and doors temporarily with card or wood, and covering damaged walls with a coat of paint instead of wallpaper. Though there were complaints about the standard, most of those rehabilitated, according to the official report on reconstruction, showed the necessary resoluteness in returning to homes that were now far less comfortable places to live.[90] Most of the light damage from Allied bombing consisted of broken windows and damaged roofs. Three raids on Nuremberg in 1942 and 1943 destroyed 1.75 million square meters of glass and 2 million square meters of roofing; but out of 19,184 bomb-damaged buildings, only 662 were totally destroyed and 973 severely damaged, making it possible for those rendered homeless, as in Britain, to return to where they had lived after first-aid repairs were completed.[91] It was calculated that 324,000 homes had been destroyed or badly damaged throughout Germany by November 1943, but by then 3,184,000 people had been successfully rehabilitated or rehoused.[92]

The most complex procedure was to provide compensating goods for those who had lost some or all of their possessions and to calculate the extent of war-damage compensation to which people were entitled. The evidence from Schöneberg shows that the population took this issue more seriously than any other and that it gave rise to a greater degree of friction.[93] The procedures were time-consuming and the regulations irksome to those who saw themselves as victims. At the emergency centers, the bombed-out were given preliminary vouchers for clothes, shoes, soap, and laundry detergent, without having to make a formal written application. Clothes included a suit or a dress, underwear, stockings, handkerchiefs and nightwear, and one pair of sturdy shoes. In March 1943 the welfare offices handed out 10,432 textile vouchers and 10,810 for shoes and 750 furniture certificates. So complex was the rationing system in Germany set up in September 1939 that bomb damage could destroy cards for household articles, furniture, coal, petrol, soap, and tobacco, all of which had to be queued for, often for hours, in order to argue for a replacement. The new card or voucher was an entitlement only, whose redemption depended on the local supply of goods. Schöneberg was fortunate since there were stocks of secondhand goods and Jewish possessions, as well as goods from occupied or Axis Europe, France and Hungary in particular. In the spring of 1943 Hitler had ordered that labor and materials needed to overcome bomb damage and losses should be secured first from the occupied territories.[94] Berlin still had a large number of small traders and manufacturers who could supply what else was needed, and the stocks used up in March 1943 were soon replenished.[95]

The claims for financial compensation were altogether more fraught. A report from the Schöneberg regional office explained that the officials and the claimants worked in different directions, the first seeking to limit what had to be paid out only to genuinely verifiable losses, the victims with an interest in setting their claim as high as they could. Forms had been distributed to householders so that they could list in detail all their possessions in anticipation of a raid.[96] Some filled out the claim form in only the most general terms, while others supplied a detailed description of what was lost, including, at times, photographs of the missing objects. Where the owner had been killed, legatees gave their own description of what they had expected to inherit. The officials based their assessments on the credibility of the claimant, including estimates of social class and likely earnings, as a guide to what a claimant might possibly own. One Berlin toolmaker claimed 12,000 RM of furnishings from a one-room apartment, including 143 separate items; the claims office dismissed the claim and paid out 1,500 RM. A building engineer living in a four-room household with his wife and four children claimed a loss of 50,000 RM, including a table valued at 4,800 RM (around three times the annual wage of a semiskilled worker); he was granted just 6,000 RM pending further investigation. The harassed office staff treated few claims as deliberately false, but the bombed-out all over Germany inflated the value of their losses once their possessions could no longer be checked.[97] The total number of cases involved and the sums claimed represented a major administrative and financial effort for the state to cope with in the middle of a major war. In Nuremberg alone, there were 27,977 claims for compensation by the spring of 1943, amounting to 44.8 million marks; of this sum 8.8 million were paid out in cash, 14 million in kind.[98] By late 1943 payments at the national level were running at over 700 million RM a month; claims totaling 31.7 billion RM had been filed, of which 11.6 billion had already been paid out.[99] These were sums that could never have been imagined when the initial commitment was made to pay for the direct costs of the bombing war.

The greatest test of the evolving civil defense and emergency structure came with the bombing of Hamburg in July and August 1943. The

137 small raids (and 782 air-raid alarms) up to July 1943 had given Hamburg more experience than most cities in coping with the consequences of bombing.[100] The idea of an action staff for catastrophic raids had been pioneered there. By July 1943 public shelter was available for 378,000 people; attics had been cleared, fire-risk stocks had been stored safely, and a program of fire-retarding wood treatment—the "Fire Protection Chemical Scheme"—had been ordered in spring 1943 for completion by the summer. There was a large cohort of 9,300 Luftschutzpolizei, and a citywide fire-watching scheme, which involved 15,000 people in the dock area alone. There had been 11,000 demonstrations organized in the city on how to extinguish incendiary bombs. Some 70,000 men and women had been trained for first aid by the German Red Cross. Hamburg's police president later in the year described the city as "one large Air Protection community."[101] The heavy British raids on other cities earlier in the year gave little indication of what Hamburg could expect in Operation Gomorrah. An attack on Stuttgart on April 14–15 had killed 118; a heavy raid on Dortmund on May 23–24 left 345 dead; another on Krefeld in June resulted in 149 deaths.[102] Hamburg itself had suffered 626 deaths in forty-two raids in 1941, 494 deaths in fifteen raids in 1942, and 142 deaths in ten small raids in 1943. The first reports to reach Berlin of the Hamburg bombing gave little indication of how much more serious the raids in Operation Gomorrah proved to be.[103]

Hamburg was not unprepared for its ordeal, but the scale of the three nights of attack on July 24–25, 27–28, and 29–30 overwhelmed the thousands of trained personnel. After declaring a state of emergency, the Reich defense commissar, gauleiter Karl Kaufmann, called in mutual assistance from outside the city from as far away as Dresden. At the height of the crisis there were 14,000 firefighters, 12,000 soldiers, and 8,000 emergency workers, but although they were able to achieve limited containment of the fire area, the conflagrations soon grew out of control, consuming everything in their path.[104] The firestorm caused by the second raid fed on the oxygen in the thousands of cellars used as "air-protection rooms," where people sat slowly asphyxiating from carbon monoxide poisoning or were burnt so completely that doctors afterward had to estimate the number of dead by measuring the ash left on the floor. Others died with apparently no external injuries because their body temperature rose above 42 degrees Celsius (107.6 degrees Fahrenheit), causing the body's natural regulator to collapse from "over-warming."[105] By the end of the year it was estimated that 85 percent of deaths in German cities were caused by fire rather than high-explosive bombs.[106] The Hamburg police president later wrote that "speech is impotent" to describe the scene that he confronted after the fire had ebbed away, but the description in his official report is vivid enough:

> The streets were covered with hundreds of corpses. Mothers with their children, youths, old men, burnt, charred, untouched and unclothed, naked with a waxen pallor like dummies in a shop window, they lay in every posture, quiet and peaceful or cramped, the death-struggle shown in the expression on their faces.[107]

By the end of November 1943, records had been compiled to confirm 31,647 dead, of which only 15,802 could be identified; a further 2,322 were known to have died outside the city. The final death toll will never be known with certainty, but it is generally assumed to be between 37,000 (shown by police records) and 40,000 (the figure widely used in Germany before the end of the war). The Hamburg Fire Department calculated that all the wartime bombing in Hamburg, from 1940 to 1945, resulted in the deaths of 48,572 people.[108]

The aftermath of the raids saw an awful calm descend on the damaged city. Nine hundred thousand people fled unorganized over the course of the week and had to be absorbed into the surrounding countryside and small towns; 315,000 houses and apartments were destroyed or badly damaged, 61 percent of the city. Over the course of the war 902,000 people in Hamburg lost all their possessions, including the novelist Hans Nossack, who by chance had gone to a summer cottage outside the city just before the raids began. He watched the columns and truckloads of refugees, some still in their nightwear: "They brought with them an uncanny silence . . . crouched and remote. . . . No lamenting anywhere, no tears." Nossack returned to the city a few days later, losing his way in the ruined landscape and the swarms of rats and flies, "insolent and fat."[109] The heat that had allowed the firestorm to take hold persisted after the bombing. Another eyewitness, Gretl Büttner, found the contrast uncanny between a deep blue sky dotted with pretty white clouds and the "image of unending misery and terrible devastation," made starker by the fickle weather. She joined hundreds of others searching through the corpses, laid out in neat rows in squares free of debris, to try to find her companions.[110] The police set up a record-card index divided into four categories: identified and registered dead, unknown bodies and their place of discovery and burial, property salvaged and assigned to bodies, and articles found but unclaimed. Any goods that were not claimed were sold secondhand to the homeless. There were hundreds of orphaned children, or children separated from their parents, who had to be identified and housed. In the aftermath of the Hamburg bombings the Inter-Ministerial Committee made it compulsory for all children up to age four to wear a wooden or cardboard tag with their name, date of birth, and address.[111]

The most urgent need in Hamburg in the first days after the firestorm was to supply clean drinking water and to avert a health disaster as refugees began to return to the devastated areas and in some cases to reoccupy the ruined remains of their homes. The drinking-water system was destroyed in the raids and regular water sources contaminated. The emergency services brought in disinfected street-cleaning trucks filled with fresh spring water immediately after the bombing had ended. Water trucks were sent from as far afield as Stettin, Breslau, Berlin, and Leipzig, mostly cleaned and converted gasoline tankers. The level of hygiene was poor and the population was warned to boil water even from the trucks. Two days after the last raid the local Hygiene Institute laboratory was working again, monitoring the quality of water from the main springs and the wells that were opened up for use. Epidemic illness was avoided.[112] The medical conditions in the city were nevertheless far from ideal. Instead of the usual 20,000 hospital beds, there were now only 8,000 following the destruction of twenty-four hospitals. Emergency medical stations were set up to give immediate treatment. The many corpses were covered in quicklime and buried in mass graves, or doused with petrol and burned.[113] The most damaged areas of the city were walled up to prevent people from returning to areas where there was a risk to health; buildings that had been checked for bodies and cleared were marked with a blob of green paint.[114] Much of the gruesome work was carried out by camp prisoners whose survival worried the authorities less. Looters were few since the penalties were severe. By August 5 the first seven had been sentenced to death; in total, thirty-one cases were tried in the four months following the raids and fifteen looters executed.[115]

Operation Gomorrah represented a profound challenge to German society and the German war effort, but not one that could not in the end be met. Hermann Göring visited Hamburg on August 6 to an apparently enthusiastic welcome, though informers also heard widespread criticism of his leadership of the air force. The SD report following the raids spoke of the "exceptional shock effect" across the whole country, but also recorded the still widespread belief that Germany had the means to "end the war victoriously."[116] Albert Speer famously recalled in his memoirs his claim at the time that after six more Hamburgs, Germany would be finished. But he also remembered Hitler's reply: "You'll straighten it out again."[117] Following the raids, Speer was authorized by Hitler to set up yet another emergency organization based on three Air Raid Damage Staffs stationed in Hamburg, Berlin, and Stuttgart. In the event of a new catastrophe, he would move in mobile columns of workers, relief supplies, and equipment to get workers provided for as soon as possible and damaged industry and utilities working again.[118] Over the course of the year following Gomorrah, 50,000 emergency homes were built for Hamburg's workforce. Small (between 30 and 40 square meters, or 300 to 400 square feet) and crudely built, the new housing clustered near the factories, which supplied the workforce with subsidized electricity at one-fifth of the regular price.[119] The number of households in Hamburg fell from 500,000 to 300,000, reducing pressure on local amenities and housing so that within months around 90 percent of the remaining population could be accommodated in regular housing.[120] The social consequences of the raids, which had killed around 2.4 percent of the city's population, were gradually absorbed as services were restored, the rationing system reinstituted, and urgent house repair completed.

There were important lessons to be learned from the worst of Germany's air raids. Although he concluded that the city's civil defense system was basically sound, the police president added to his report twenty pages of helpful advice on practical and technical improvements to aspects of air-raid protection. His most urgent recommendation was to ensure that there were adequate escape routes, known to all shelter users, to prevent the mass deaths that had occurred in apparently safe air-raid rooms. The problems this presented were advertised in a Luftschutz-bund report in July 1943 about a woman who succeeded in the nick of time in saving her fellow shelterers:

> There was darkness in the cellar. We were all thrown on top of each other. The light failed. If we had only put ready an axe for opening up the breakthrough at a fixed point on the wall, we would have saved ourselves fearful minutes of alarm. We found the axe only after a good quarter of an hour. As the air in the cellar quickly became worse, I bashed at the breakthrough like someone possessed. Now it got its revenge, because we had never bothered particularly about the added bit of wall. Only after 20 minutes had I cut a hole just large enough to slip through.[121]

In the months after the bombing of Hamburg, air-protection instructions sent out monthly by the Air Ministry to local police authorities emphasized repeatedly the need to keep cellar shelters clear of obstacles, with a clearly marked breakthrough point, made of shallow mortar. More difficult was the realization that the constant repetition of the slogan earlier in the war that "the air-protection room is the safest place" was no longer always the case. Air-raid wardens and action leaders were now encouraged to teach their communities the right moment to leave a shelter if a fire threatened to run out of control. When leaving a cellar in a firestorm, people were advised to wear a coat soaked with water and a damp hood. A coat, it was claimed, was more difficult for the fiery wind to tear off the body.[122]

After the experience of Hamburg, priority was given to finding more effective ways to prevent or to fight a firestorm, challenging though this was. Civil defense and firefighting units were instructed to start attacking fires as soon as they appeared, even during the raid, since casualties were certain to be lower than they would be once a firestorm took hold. "The first half hour is of decisive importance in the development of fires," ran the Air Ministry instructions. "It is possible to prevent the genesis of a major conflagration, under circumstances where the fires started by the bombs are extinguished along whole streets."[123] If a firestorm took hold, firefighters were told to concentrate on the area around the edges, where buildings were not yet completely on fire, in order to contain it; at the same time they were encouraged to search for pathways through the waves of fire that could be opened up to allow some of the trapped inhabitants to make their escape. In Hamburg, a few of the population engulfed by the hurricane of fire survived relatively unscathed in blast-proof surface shelters.[124] All self-protection leaders were charged with making sure that householders in every building or apartment kept adequate quantities of water available to tackle a small fire before it spread. The more water stored, the better; use was to be made of "*all* available containers whatever, not only buckets, pails, bathtubs and rain barrels, but even washbasins, washtubs etc." Water could even be removed from central heating systems.[125] Each air-protection room now had to contain its own supplies of water and sand. Self-protection units also had to appoint groups to go out during a raid to spot fires and tackle them at once; empty buildings were no longer obliged to observe the blackout, so that fires could more easily be identified through the uncovered windows. "Fires," ran one piece of Luftschutzbund advice, "always look much worse than they are, and are much easier to extinguish than appears in the first moment."[126]

How effective civilians were in tackling a fire clearly varied from case to case, and it placed a heavy responsibility on householders, whose first thought was often for their own family and possessions. A Cologne journalist recorded in his diary how well his neighbors coped with the 1,000-bomber raid in May 1942: "The incendiaries which clattered down around our house: one on the balcony of our neighbor Feuser, immediately extinguished by our neighbor Brassart, one in front of the garage of our neighbor Uhlenbruck, which the coal merchant snatched up, one by the garage of neighbor Gessert, which the householder put out."[127] For the regular fire service, the onset of heavy firebombing raids placed a strain on units that were already depleted by regular culls of manpower for the armed forces. In September 1943 a second national inspector was appointed for the fire service, Hans Rumpf, who made it his job to visit more than 150 fire-service units over the following year, checking their equipment and practices. The system depended increasingly on volunteer firefighters, around 1.7 million by 1944. After the heavy fire raids in 1943, the local volunteers were organized in "firefighting emergency units" so that they could be summoned at once from the surrounding area to help with fires in the major cities, an estimated 700 units made up of 100,000 firefighters. They were all brought under police jurisdiction, and those who were also members of the SS were permitted to wear the familiar silver runes on their uniform. The numbers of German men in the service fell steadily, so that during 1943 it became necessary to recruit foreign workers—Poles, Czechs, and Ukrainians—into the fire service. In Hamburg by the end of the war around one-quarter of the regular fire service was made up of Ukrainians. A more radical departure was the call in April 1943 for women to volunteer for the fire service, not only in auxiliary roles but as regular firefighters. From October 1943 they could be subject to compulsory mobilization, and by autumn 1944 an estimated 275,000 female firefighters, aged between eighteen and forty, took their part in combating Allied incendiarism.[128] The popular myth that German women did nothing more than guard hearth and home during the war is demonstrably untrue for this most dangerous of activities.

Hamburg also signaled the onset of widespread urban evacuation following the first two years of war in which it had been discouraged or temporarily indulged. The veiled evacuation of children permitted under the KLV organization tailed off during 1942 and 1943; from a peak of over 160,000 children in organized camps in July 1941, there were only 40,000 by May 1942, and a similar number in the spring of 1944. The peak figure accounted for only 2 percent of all eligible ten- to

fourteen-year-olds. Most stayed for no more than a few months in the
Hitler Youth camps before returning home because the accommodation
was not suitable for winter; mothers and younger children sent away to
the country also stayed for short periods or tried to find friends or relatives to stay with as an alternative to close supervision by the National
Socialist People's Welfare. Altogether the party organizations accounted
for around 2 million temporary refugees from the cities, but not for a
system of permanent evacuation.[129] In July 1942 local authorities were
reminded that "rehousing" (rather than evacuation) would be approved
and covered by public funds only if it was necessary to remove the population from areas of severe bomb damage or unexploded ordnance, or in
cases where population transfers were socially useful, and only with
Göring's approval.[130] In February 1943, Hitler finally agreed that whole
school classes could be evacuated from danger areas, but insisted that
parents should have the choice whether or not to split the family. The
number of schoolchildren formally evacuated remained small. In August 1943 in Berlin out of 260,000 eligible schoolchildren, only 32,000
were in organized evacuation, 132,000 placed with relatives or acquain-
tances.[131]

Only in the spring of 1943, with the onset of the heavy bombing of
the Ruhr-Rhineland, did evacuation begin on any scale. On April 19
the Interior Ministry published a decree on organized evacuation (*Umquartierung*), either to accommodation in the same city or in the rural
hinterland, or, for the population not essential for the war effort, transfer
to a more distant and safer region.[132] There were no firm plans in place
to cope with the growing stream of refugees from the heavily bombed
areas who were evacuating themselves. To avoid a growing chaos, the
Interior Ministry finally published in July 1943 a list of city populations
scheduled for evacuation and quotas for the regions (based on the party
Gaue) where the evacuees—mainly the old and the very young—would
be sent. It was the crisis in Hamburg that shocked the German population into greater acceptance of evacuation as a clear necessity. Up until
June 1943 the German railway authorities estimated that no more than
140,000–150,000 people had been moved under formal schemes to
more distant areas; by the end of 1943 more than 2 million people had

been transferred under official programs.[133] The immediate evacuation of 900,000 from Hamburg was a result of the panic that occurred as Operation Gomorrah intensified. By the end of September 1943, 545,000 had been settled in regions across Germany, more than one-quarter in the neighboring rural areas of Schleswig-Holstein, almost one-third in and around the south German town of Bayreuth.[134] The firestorm in Hamburg provoked widespread fear that Berlin would be next. From a marked reluctance to accept transfer away from the city, Berliners now flooded out, 691,000 by mid-September. Around 1.1 million altogether left the German capital, one-quarter of the prewar population.

The urban exodus provoked widespread problems, not least because it had not been systematically planned for, as it had been in Britain, and finding and allocating spare accommodation—often just a room in a village house—had to be improvised at short notice. There were obvious sources of friction between a small-town and rural population, not yet much exposed to the physical effects of the bombing war, and an urban population used to different standards or from a very different social milieu. A report sent to the Party Chancellery from Upper Silesia in May 1943 highlighted some of these issues:

> The attitude of these racial comrades towards the guest region appears incomprehensible, for it must be observed that at the moment the women, scarcely having set foot on the soil of Upper Silesia, exclaim: "If I have to come to a nest like this, then I'd rather go back to a heap of ruins"; another woman declared, "I am surprised that the sluttish wives that crawl around here can still attract men." . . . The Germans from the west have often criticized the "Heil Hitler" greeting with the remark that people don't greet each other like that in the old Reich.[135]

In August 1943, Goebbels's Inter-Ministerial Committee sent recommendations out to all gauleiters to combat the "spiritual depression" evident among the evacuee populations in their new surroundings, including the provision of a well-heated community room, with a radio, games, magazines, and newspapers from the evacuated cities, as well as film shows using equipment salvaged from bombed cinemas.[136] But the temptation to return home was strong. By the end of November 1943, 217,000 Berliners had returned despite efforts of the authorities to use compulsory ration-card registration in the evacuation areas as a means of ensuring that the rail network would not be overburdened with those who chose to return. In some areas the quota for evacuees from the major cities had to compete with local evacuation from small towns and cities not yet threatened. In Württemberg in southern Germany, out of 169,000 evacuees in February 1944, at least 52,000 (and perhaps as many as half) had abandoned the region's own towns for safety in the countryside. In other areas, the number of evacuees threatened to overwhelm small communities, which were expected to accommodate evacuee populations that were not far short of the number of permanent residents. In some cases, an apparently safe rural retreat was bombed anyway by aircrews who could not see where they were aiming, making both inhabitants and evacuees into refugees together.[137]

The evacuation crisis following Operation Gomorrah also exposed the serious state of the German medical service as it wrestled to cope with a much-reduced medical profession, the destruction of hospitals and clinics, and a sudden increase in the number of casualties, many of them serious, brought about by the intensified bombing. After the Hamburg firestorm, many doctors and nurses left with the evacuees; clinics and medical practices were destroyed, leaving doctors with few alternatives but to find occupation away from the stricken city. When evacuation set in elsewhere, doctors were among those who accompanied the transferred communities. By late August an estimated 35 to 40 doctors a day were leaving Berlin, some with the evacuees, some with the 11,500 bedridden patients who were transferred to hospitals in safer areas.[138] The evacuation from the Ruhr-Rhineland had been carried out too quickly to match medical needs to the evacuee community, and since the majority were children, old people, and women, many of them pregnant, the need for doctors, child nurses, and midwives was more rather than less urgent. In the reception areas the problem was made worse by the fact that the armed forces had taken many of the doctors from the zones classified II or III, not having realized the extent of the later bombing threat.[139] The aim of the Reich health chief, Leonardo Conti (one of those responsible for the T4 "euthanasia" program), was to try to keep an acceptable proportion between the population and the number of doctors, but by October 1943 the profession was down to 35,000 for the whole population, from a prewar level of 80,000. Around 5,500 were too old to practice effectively, and 3,883 died between 1939 and 1942, some in military service. The ideal of one doctor for every 2,000 or 2,500 people could not be met, and of those available, many were themselves the victims of overwork, tiredness, and illness. For evacuees Conti's aim was only one doctor for every 10,000.[140]

The onset of heavy bombing made it necessary to find a solution or risk a breakdown of effective medical services. Military casualty rates rose sharply during 1943 and 1944, making it more necessary to find ways to rationalize the civilian system. Trucks and vans were requisitioned as less than adequate ambulances, while efforts were made to find hotel or guesthouse accommodation to use as hospitals. Doctors were ordered to place their instruments and medicines in bomb-safe basements every evening to avoid damage, while equipment from ruined clinics was given or sold to doctors still practicing.[141] The German Red Cross, which controlled most of the ambulance service, instructed local branches to set up an emergency controller in major cities, with responsibility to call in emergency medical columns, prepared in advance with trucks, temporary barracks, beds, stretchers, sanitary materials, and water filters, and a staff of one or two doctors and up to six nurses. Most bomb victims who survived were only lightly injured, a great many with eye injuries from glass, smoke, soot, and dust from debris. It was decided that these walking wounded would have to be treated in first-aid centers rather than hospitals, which would be used for the serious cases. Operations were suspended for hopeless cases so that resources could be devoted to those who might survive.[142] The main shortage was hospital space, since both military and civilian victims competed for this. In August 1941, Hitler authorized construction of emergency hospitals in bomb-threatened areas at the expense of the state.[143] The scheme made slow progress, and in May 1943, Hitler approved the appointment of one of the doctors on his staff, Karl Brandt, as general commissar for sanitary and health issues, with responsibility for creating additional emergency hospital space and planning its distribution. Conti immediately objected, since Brandt's appointment trespassed directly on his own role, but the purpose of the new appointment was to focus on hospital beds rather than areas of general medical policy. Brandt immediately bustled about planning nineteen new hospital sites and 54,000 more hospital beds, but the "Brandt Action" cut across existing planning, creating, in Conti's words, "a permanent state of chaos." Allocation of hospital space continued on an improvised basis.[144] The one area where extra provision proved unnecessary was psychiatric casualty. As in Britain, the assumption at first was that bombing was bound to increase the degree of serious mental disorder, particularly as many of those subjected to bombing were female. Yet it soon became clear that although fear and nervous anxiety were widespread, this did not lead to evident psychotic states. Psychiatric casualty was generally nursed in the privacy of family and friends. Only after the war were the traumatic consequences of exposure to the bombing threat eventually observable.[145]

Along with the evacuees came not only problems of welfare and medical provision but a treasure trove of rumors spread by an urban population that suddenly found itself the center of attention in the reception areas. Rumors performed a number of functions: they gave the evacuees a sense of temporary importance as they regaled their hosts with overblown accounts of the horrors of being bombed; they were a safety valve for people whose opportunity for criticizing the authorities was severely circumscribed; and they acted as an instant form of information and communication for communities that were starved of anything other than the official line peddled by German propaganda. Responsibility for controlling and combating rumors lay with Goebbels's Propaganda Ministry. As in Britain during the Blitz, the decision about how much information to release was a difficult one, not only because the effect on the public had to be monitored, but because hard information could be used by the enemy. The heavy raids on the Ruhr-Rhineland in the spring of 1943 immediately opened up, according to the party propaganda office, "the worst outcome, a flood of rumors."[146] In areas that had not been bombed, rumors often reinforced a self-interested sense of immunity. Common rumors centered on the invulnerability of a region thanks to unspecified British interests in leaving it intact, or the depth of industrial and urban smog covering the area, or the excessive distance from British bases. Others focused on the most likely time to be bombed—on Fridays, on national festivals, on Hitler's birthday, on days specified in Allied leaflets.[147] One rumor involved lurid tales, which spread across Germany, of people stuck in melted asphalt and burned alive, or ignited by some form of phosphorus rain, half-truths from the sight of those struggling against the firestorm.[148]

In other cases rumors took on a more solid shape. In Munich following a heavy raid in September 1942, strong rumors were overheard, first that it was Germany's fault that civilian bombing had begun in the first place; second, and more significant, the view that bombing was God's punishment for having "pushed the Jews over the frontier and thrown them into poverty."[149] In July 1943 the rumor took root that volcanoes were to be bombed to bring about the end of the world. Rumors about the apocalypse were, Goebbels thought, quite understandable when faced with the sight of dead children laid out after a raid, but had to be contested nonetheless.[150] One child, hearing adults talking about "the end" in a shelter, was unsure whether they meant the end of the war or in fact "the end of the world."[151] The summer of 1943 encouraged a sense of extremes. The news from Hamburg, which reached Bavaria in August, was, wrote one diarist, "beyond the grasp of the imagination . . . streets of boiling asphalt into which the victims sank . . . 200,000 dead." He witnessed a group of Hamburg refugees trying to force their way into a railway car, until one battered suitcase carried along by "a half-crazed woman" dropped open to reveal clothes, a toy, and the shriveled, carbonized body of a child. He reflected that the terrible news from Hamburg meant the end of the old world for good: "This time those riders now saddling their black steeds are none other than the Four Horsemen of the Apocalypse."[152]

The issue of rumors was bound up with the more profound question of how to sustain popular commitment to the war effort and avoid a more serious social or political crisis. These issues came to the forefront only in 1943 when casualty lists grew longer and the means to obstruct

Allied bombing became clearly ineffectual. In the Ruhr-Rhineland in the spring of 1943 the first evidence of possible social crisis emerged as the authorities struggled to cope with homelessness and temporary unemployment. Information fed into the Propaganda Ministry highlighted a growing sense of desperation. The raid on Duisburg on March 19–20, 1943, left thousands homeless, destroyed the city's major department stores, and left just two restaurants still functioning for 200,000 people. The local population complained that the promise of revenge against British cities had not been met, while the Ruhr was reaching the breaking point: "We see no end. We cannot keep this up for long. How will it go?"[153] Even Goebbels was affected by the evidence of the first really sustained bombing campaign. On March 13 he wrote in his diary that "air warfare is at present our greatest worry. Things simply cannot go on like this."[154] The difficulty for those charged with the psychological welfare of the population—the party called it *Menschenführung*—was to separate out the different factors affecting the public mood, of which bombing was just one. In February 1943, Goebbels had delivered in Berlin his famous speech about total war to a selected party audience, an oration designed to reinvigorate the war willingness of the population after the defeat at Stalingrad. But its impact was limited and failed to address the question of how to cope with the consequences of air attack upon morale, though the speech was popular with the armed forces, who wanted the civilian population to grasp the true dimensions of the conflict.[155] The SD reports showed that some of the population blamed the intensified bombing on Goebbels's speech, which seemed to be an invitation to the enemy to wage unrestricted war against the German people. Resentment against Berlin as the source of the "total war" idea provoked a verse that soon had wide currency in western Germany: "Lieber Tommy fliege weiter / wir sind alle Bergarbeiter. / Fliege weiter nach Berlin / die haben alle 'ja' geschrien" ["Dear Tommy fly on farther / we are all miners here. / Fly farther to Berlin / they have all screamed 'yes'"].[156]

From the spring of 1943 onward the regime for molding opinion in Germany struggled to find a method to influence the response to bombing in ways that were more positive for the German war effort. Rumors were tackled by insinuating SA or party officials into crowds and queues with instructions to challenge the substance of rumors; some rumors were deliberately started by propaganda officials to counter a local mood of depression or hopelessness; home intelligence regularly recommended dealing with rumors at the source by publicly announcing their false nature and providing some nuggets of more plausible information.[157] The difficult thing was to gauge how much hard information should be given out. The formal policy, approved by the high command, was to announce no details about the number of casualties and the damage to buildings. In March 1943 a brief but clear communiqué was given about a raid on Berlin, which immediately won wide public approval.[158] But only in the case of the raid on the Rhineland dams were precise casualty figures given, to stop the rumors that 10,000–30,000 people had died.[159] Rather than yield to public pressure to give precise information, public anxiety was to be mediated by propaganda that highlighted the achievements of the German Air Force against the bomber offensive. Propaganda companies from the military propaganda arm began to work in the bombed cities from June 1943 to provide local stories on successful air defense or air-to-air combat. Goebbels had already orchestrated a campaign to convince the public that the German Air Force was taking revenge on the enemy population and would do so with new, powerful but secret weapons in the near future.[160]

The idea of vengeance (*Vergeltung*) was itself problematic, since it depended for its propaganda success on more than just promises. In 1943 the German Air Force's activity against British targets reached its lowest point. Goebbels hoped that the successful test launch of the V-1 and the V-2 by early 1943 indicated a rapid move to large-scale revenge attacks; the substantial time lag meant that the public became first skeptical, then widely critical of the regime's promises. In late April 1943 the SD reports noted widespread longing for the "revenge announced 'already so often,'" and popular calls for revenge punctuated all the weekly reports throughout the year. By September the following joke was in circulation in the Ruhr and Berlin: "The English and the Americans were given an ultimatum: if they do not cease the air war at once, another vengeance speech will follow."[161] By then rumors about a new missile

were in circulation and there were popular hopes that a definite dead-
line would be announced for its use. Goebbels had by then realized that
vengeance propaganda was counterproductive, and on July 6, 1943, he
ordered the German press to stop using the term, though it retained its
public currency. The armed forces' propaganda branch set up a commission to study the potential of the new weapons and concluded that
they were not capable of turning the tide of war and should no longer be
used for propaganda purposes.[162] Instead Goebbels used the Jewish
question both as a way to explain the bombing war and as an instrument
to encourage German resistance. In a speech on June 5, 1943, he de-
nounced British bombing and the "Jewish instigators" behind it. After
Operation Gomorrah, party propaganda played on "the Jews' will to
extermination" expressed through the "bombing murder of the Jewish-
plutocratic enemy," and called for a fanatical defense of German race
and culture.[163]

On some issues the German public felt strongly, though it is not
widely evident that the struggle against "world Jewry" meant very much
to the population in the front line against bombing. There were strong
demands that the dead in bombing raids should be marked in the newspapers with an iron cross, like the military dead. The Propaganda Ministry approved of the idea in December 1941, but it was overturned by
Hitler in January 1942 (who did not want women to be honored that
way) and rejected by the armed forces, who thought that it would diminish the value of the symbol for the military dead.[164] Attempts to describe
the bomb victims with the military terms "fallen" or "wounded" (*Gefallene* or *Verwundete*) were also rejected by the armed forces, since many of
those who died did so from willful failure to seek shelter, including a
notorious case in Bremen when fourteen partygoers were killed because
they wanted to finish their food and drink before going down to the cellar. In the end a compromise was reached, allowing civil defense workers of either sex who died while carrying out dangerous duties to have
their death notices marked with an iron cross. They could also be described as "fallen" for the Fatherland, but the rest of the bomb victims
could not, a distinction confirmed by Goebbels in May 1943.[165]

Opportunity for more serious political or social dissent was limited, given the willingness of the regime to impose severe punishment on any open or dangerous forms of protest; where it existed, political resistance was fueled by ideological difference rather than by bombing. Nevertheless, a growing pessimistic realism about the future jostled in public opinion with evidence of a firmer resolve and persistent confidence in Hitler's capacity to stabilize the situation. The SD reports speculated, as did British intelligence, that the mass of homeless and disgruntled evacuees might be a possible source of an "inner collapse" if the bombing got worse, but an estimated one-third of the evacuees returned home. Those who remained, mainly women and children, were unlikely instigators of revolt, though there were isolated acts of protest against the treatment of evacuees or the withholding of ration cards. The most famous case was in October 1943 at Witten in the Ruhr, where the police refused to intervene.[166] In some ways bombing actually created a safety valve for popular disaffection. Rumors could represent a surreptitious challenge to prescribed public discourse without amounting to serious dissent. In the shelters it was sometimes possible for the small communities that inhabited them to complain about their hardships or to satirize the regime without fear of punishment. In one Berlin bunker, Hitler was always referred to as "The Hitler," an intentionally less flattering epithet than "our Führer." The local warden turned a blind eye both to this and to harsher complaints directed at the dictatorship.[167] For the bombed-out, the opportunity to let off steam could also be tolerated. One generic story, cited by a number of observers, told of a hysterical woman evacuee challenging the police to arrest her for some trivial offense because at least she would have a roof over her head. In each version of the story, the police do nothing.[168] The SD reports noted a widely circulating rumor in August 1943 that the Allies had promised to stop the bombing if the government was changed; this was a brave rumor to pass on, but it was overheard in towns as far apart as Innsbruck and Königsberg.[169] It was also evident that the anxieties and fears generated by bombing in particular affected not only the home front but the fighting front as well. Censors intercepted letters giving painful details of the effects of heavy raids; soldiers on leave could see these effects for themselves. An SD report in early September 1943 described a typical frontline response:

"What is the point in defending the homeland at the front if everything at home is smashed to pieces and there is nothing left afterwards when we come back."[170] Efforts were made to ensure that news reached soldiers quickly to allay their fears. Special "bomb postcards" could be written from raided towns with express delivery to military units.[171]

The heavy bombing of 1943, and the shock effect of the destruction of Hamburg in particular, did not in reality provoke serious political or social crisis, though it prompted growing public criticism and anxiety and occasional local acts of grumbling protest, which could be tolerated by the authorities. There is no single explanation for this, since the response varied a great deal between different regions and cities, between different social groups and public organizations, but a number of factors played a part. The bombing was still geographically concentrated in 1942 and 1943, principally on the coastal towns and the industrial regions of western Germany, though an estimated half of British bombs fell in open country. Although regular warnings, compulsory sheltering, and waves of morbid rumors affected much of the rest of the population, bombing was not directly experienced. For those who were principally affected, the chief concern was to survive the catastrophe, to find adequate welfare, food, and shelter, and to protect and reestablish the private sphere. Hans Nossack found among his fellow Hamburgers a preoccupation with the mundane: "If by chance a newspaper came into our hands, we didn't bother to read the war bulletins. . . . We would immediately turn to the page with the announcements that concerned us directly. Whatever happened outside of us simply did not exist."[172]

Since the regime was exaggeratedly anxious about the state of public opinion, the duplication of effort by the air force, the local authorities, the party, and the police meant that whatever jurisdictional friction might be generated, problems were identified and tackled. The plethora of mobile emergency columns, bringing food or medical care or construction teams, meant that none of the afflicted cities was likely to be short of some form of effective assistance. The range of civil defense activities was extensive, and the mobilization of more women and young people in 1943 spread the mantle of responsibility over a large fraction of the urban population. The combination of state, party, and community initiatives helped German society to cope with the rigors of a long-term bombing campaign and dampened any prospect of social disquiet. "Everything went on very quietly," wrote Nossack, reflecting on the absence of latent rebellion, "and with a definite concern for order, and the State took its bearings from this order."[173] Only in 1944–45, when bombing overwhelmed German society, was the search for order challenged.

Economic Miracles

It has become fashionable in recent accounts of the German economy during the Second World War to dismiss the idea that there was anything very miraculous about its ability to expand war production continuously between 1939 and 1944.[174] All war economies did this, the German more slowly at first than the others, then more rapidly toward the end of the war. The difference is that German industrial cities were subjected to heavy bomb attack from at least the spring of 1943 onward, and in 1944 to a weight of bombs many times greater than the Blitz on Britain. In September 1944, Hitler addressed the leaders of German war production on what had been achieved "despite the growing damage from air attacks." The new peak in war production achieved in August, he continued, showed that German industry could be trusted, even in the shrunken and battered area still remaining to Germany, to concentrate everything on war production "in order to be able to increase yet further the output of the most important weapons and equipment."[175]

If the "miracle" of expanded German production has very material explanations in the effective exploitation of both capital and labor and efforts to rationalize the distribution of resources, the ability to sustain exceptional levels of war production in the face of the bombing offensive cannot be taken for granted. If bombing eventually placed a ceiling on what could be produced, the performance of the key sectors of German industry over the last two years of war did have something of an "economic miracle" about it. Above all, it was the exact reverse of what the

Allies thought would be possible once the offensive got going, as the statistics in table 4.1 make evident. Whatever the other resource and organizational issues confronting the German war economy, which is not the
subject here, the extent to which German war economic potential could
be safeguarded against the impact of bombing became a central concern of the German war machine and allowed the armed forces to
continue fighting forlorn campaigns well into 1945.

The geography of German industry at the outbreak of war had something in common with the British pattern. Older industrial sectors—
coal, steel, machinery—were concentrated in the Ruhr-Rhineland and
Saar basins, but had been supplemented in the 1930s by expanding domestic production in new greenfield sites, particularly on the Salzgitter
orefield in Brunswick, and the seizure of additional iron-ore, steel, coal,
and machinery production in Austria, the Sudetenland, and Bohemia/
Moravia. Modern industrial sectors, however, including chemicals, elec-
tronics, radio, the aeronautical industry, and motor vehicles, were sited
away from the old industrial regions, in Bavaria, Württemberg, Berlin,
Saxony, and a fringe of smaller industrial cities. After 1933, with the
new regime's emphasis on military and economic rearmament, con-
scious efforts were made to disperse industry away from the more exposed industrial regions behind the western frontier and to place it in

Table 4.1: Selected Statistics on German Military Production, 1940–44

Weapon Type	Unit	1940	1941	1942	1943	1944
Munitions	Tons	865,000	540,000	1,270,000	2,558,000	3,350,000
Armor	Tons	37,235	83,188	140,454	369,416	622,322
Artillery	Over 75mm	5,964	8,124	14,316	35,796	55,936
Aircraft	Number	10,250	11,030	14,700	25,220	37,950
Submarines	Tons	—	162,000	193,000	221,000	234,000

Source: IWM, S363, Saur papers, "Auszug aus dem Leistungsbericht von Minister
Speer, 27.1.1945."

relatively bomb-safe areas in central, southern, and eastern Germany, a process known as *Verballung*, literally, breaking up the industrial "ball." German territorial expansion in 1938–40 ensured that the balance of industrial output in the enlarged "Greater Germany" tilted farther east, creating a cushion to absorb any potential damage done to the Ruhr-Rhineland. The Ruhr supplied three-quarters of German iron and steel output in 1939 but less than two-thirds by 1943.[176] The vast Reichswerke "Hermann Göring," a state holding company for iron, steel, coal, and armaments set up in 1937, controlled 71 firms in Germany but 241 in occupied Austria, Czechoslovakia, and Poland. Until 1944 a proportion of German war production was protected by its geographical dispersal and the long aerial ranges needed to reach it.

The vulnerability of German industrial and service sectors to bombing was well understood, and "work self-protection" (*Werkluftschutz*) featured in the 1937 "Self-Protection" law. But like air-raid protection in general, the factory system was introduced piecemeal; those plants farthest from the bombing threat were less inclined to introduce rigorous air-protection procedures for their workforce, provide them with effective shelters, or install blast protection for machinery and equipment. When the Heinkel aircraft plant in Rostock suffered damage in the raids in 1942, it was found that the firm had not followed the Air Ministry's advice in building protective bomb walls.[177] In the cities in Zone I effective work protection was mandatory. From 1939 onward, vulnerable firms were asked to transfer some of their production to less endangered areas, and an effort was made, as in Britain, to ensure that vital components or even whole products (aircraft, aero-engines, tanks, etc.) were produced in at least three geographically distinct sites. Some of this early dispersal was effective—the Weser aircraft works at Bremen moved one-third of its production of the Ju87 Stuka to Berlin; the Focke-Wulf plant, also in Bremen, was decentralized to three separate sites farther east in 1940 and 1941; the Blohm & Voss flying-boat production was transferred from Hamburg to Bodensee, in south Germany, while new capacity was built in areas far removed from the current bombing threat. In 1938–39, Messerschmitt Me109 production was set up at Wiener-Neustadt outside Vienna (five other assembly plants in Austria and Bohemia were added later); another production center was established at the Erla works in Leipzig. None could easily be bombed until 1944.[178]

As in Britain, a program of camouflage and decoy sites was set up to confuse bombers trying to identify industrial targets in difficult nighttime conditions. The largest and most effective site was at Essen, where the vast Krupp works was reproduced in effigy in the countryside outside the city and sustained, according to German Air Force estimates, around three-quarters of the bombing attacks aimed at the real plant. Decoy sites outside Stuttgart and Karlsruhe attracted well over half of all bombs in 1941.[179] In Berlin elaborate efforts were made to disguise the government quarter to avoid the danger of bombing. The Brandenburg Gate was reconstructed along with mock ministries farther from the center while prominent landmarks were concealed. The east-west axis road in the center of Berlin was covered with a canopy of wire netting and green gauze, while lampposts were covered with green material to look like trees. A lake in west Berlin was covered with green netting with a length of gray material laid across it to resemble a road.[180] Outside the city, sixteen major dummy industrial sites were set up, which attracted British bombs throughout the war. When firebombing became the principal RAF method, the German Air Force set up fire sites in small walled enclosures to mimic the appearance of blazing buildings. These too proved highly effective for much of the war. To accentuate the disruptive effect of industrially generated smog, the air force also introduced artificial smoke to screen vulnerable targets. Once daylight raids began in earnest in 1943, the program was expanded so that by the end of the war there were 100 smoke companies composed of 50,000 men and women.[181]

Of the many problems faced by the German economy between 1940 and 1942, bombing was not one of them. Small-scale, incidental damage could be compensated, while dispersal and decoys reduced what limited prospect there was of accurate raiding against economic targets. The German economy from 1939 onward experienced a rapid and extensive transfer to war production priorities, cutting private consumer spending by one-quarter by 1942 (against a 14 percent reduction in Britain) and increasing the percentage of workers in manufacturing who produced goods for the armed forces, from 28 percent in May 1939 to 70 percent in May 1942.[182] Arms production expanded steadily in the first years of war, though not without considerable difficulties. These were not caused, as has often been argued, by an unwillingness on the part of the regime to commit to large-scale economic mobilization for war—indeed it is possible to describe as early as 1941 a problem of *over*mobilization—but by poor facilities for national planning of resource use, competition between the three services, and a fraught relationship between the military and industry; the one was concerned with rapid innovation and constant tactical alterations in design, the other with finding profitable ways to convert the large resources of allocated manpower and machinery to an efficient and uninterrupted mass production. Productive performance was held back as much by poor planning as by potential resource bottlenecks, which only really inhibited war production in Germany at the end of 1944 when bombing, the collapse of the economic New Order, and the disruption of trade finally reduced German access to key materials. The effect of production politics in the first years of war was to hold back the full rationalization of war production. The gradual introduction of a system of production rings and committees in 1941–42 to oversee each branch of production, together with the establishment in March 1942 of an organization for coordinated resource allocation, known as Central Planning, saw the creation of a framework within which the substantial earlier investment in war output capacity could be used to expand the supply of armaments exponentially over the last three years of war.[183]

Bombing became one of the factors that German industry had to take more fully into account only during 1943 and early 1944, as a result of the RAF campaigns against the Ruhr, Hamburg, and Berlin, and the American attacks on aircraft production and ball-bearing factories. Although the Ruhr campaign led to a temporary reduction in iron and steel supply, it failed to halt the upward direction of German war production, which reached new peaks during 1943. The main Krupp works in Essen lost only 7.6 percent of its planned output in 1943; the giant August-Thyssen concern produced more iron in 1943 than in either of the previous two years.[184] At the same time sales of iron and steel from the new plants in central Germany and occupied eastern Europe controlled by the Reichswerke "Hermann Göring" expanded by 87 percent between 1941 and 1943 to compensate for declining Ruhr production. The Reichswerke supplied one-fifth of all iron and steel, one-quarter of German coal.[185] Bombing, as already noted in chapter 3, only reduced potential German industrial output by around 9 percent in 1943. That loss has to be set against a threefold expansion of war production between 1941 and 1944 evident for all major classes of weapons. Total munitions output for large-caliber artillery was 100 percent greater in 1943 than 1942, production of tank guns 60 percent higher, aircraft output up by 61 percent; in 1944 these statistics were once again exceeded by a wide margin. Bombing caused local and temporary dislocation, but could not prevent German industry from adapting to the pressures and expanding output.[186] The central problem facing the German war economy in the last years of war was not the bombing but the escalating loss rates at the fighting front. In the first years of the war, losses of both manpower and equipment had been relatively low; from the Stalingrad battles on the Eastern Front to the collapse of Axis forces in North Africa and the rising attrition in the Battle of the Atlantic, the toll on Germany's armed forces escalated sharply. The demand for higher production reflected higher losses and the subsequent demands from the armed forces for more rapid and extensive replacement of stocks. Army stocks of tanks and self-propelled guns on hand were by 1944 almost four times greater than in 1941; stocks of antitank guns five times greater than in 1942; the supply of aircraft, both new and repaired, expanded from a monthly average of 1,381 in 1940 to an average of 3,609 in 1944.[187] The continuous campaigning in 1943 and 1944 for greater rationalization and concentration of production was driven by the military necessity of supplying the fighting fronts, including the antiaircraft defenses, with larger quantities of weapons in a context of high wastage. Hitler's response to losses was always to call on the industrial economy to produce more; the priority for German industrialists and planners was to meet those demands, irrespective of the impact of the bombs.

   Clearly production would have been easier to organize and have imposed a lesser toll on managers and workers alike in an entirely bomb-free environment. Bombing inhibited the wartime development of new technologies, though it did not prevent it. Indeed in some well-known cases—

the Heinkel He177 heavy bomber, for example—the problems were self-inflicted. Improvisation proved successful, but it also came at a cost in organizational effort and problem solving that did not affect managers in the United States or the far Soviet Union. As the bombing grew heavier in 1943 and 1944, the initial attempts to offer protection or immunity to German industry were extended and consolidated. The first possibility was to provide better protection on site. Antiaircraft guns were concentrated in special defensive zones around the most threatened areas of war production. Special "action units" were established for industry, which, like their urban counterparts, were sent to bombed industrial sites to try to restart production as rapidly as possible. In August 1943, following the Hamburg raids, Speer was authorized to declare emergency "damage regions" (*Schadensbereiche*), which would receive priority in the restoration of productive activity.[188] Individual plants were encouraged to develop comprehensive protective installations for their machinery and to increase the level of training for their workforces in simple air-raid protection procedures. Factories that had been bombed but were still able to function were told not to put on a new roof but to construct a black cover below roof level to simulate an empty building; fire-damaged external walls were kept in place to make it look as though the plant had been abandoned. Other undamaged buildings had camouflage damage painted on the sides.[189] All combustible stores of materials had to be moved to safer storage sites, and by the autumn of 1943 the Economics Ministry was able to report that the policy was working well. Stocks were moved to the edge of the endangered cities and stored by small firms more remote from the threat of attack.[190] The result was that even in cities badly hit, it was still possible to maintain a large proportion of pre-raid production. In Augsburg, for example, where industry was among the most heavily damaged, the average value of monthly production was 964,000 RM in the last five months of 1943; in the five months of heavy raiding in 1944 the average was 814,000 RM. In Hagen, hit by four heavy attacks in 1943, the pre-raid average value was 5.2 million RM, the post-raid value 5.17 million. Much of any loss was absorbed by cutting consumer production and concentrating on war-essential products.[191]

The second necessity was to ensure that the working population in the bombed cities could be assisted enough to ensure that labor productivity was maintained and absenteeism kept to a minimum. This was a more complex problem by 1943 because of the introduction of an increasing number of foreign compulsory workers and the rising proportion of women in the workforce, though in both cases work discipline could be imposed more ruthlessly by male German supervisors. Foreign workers were treated as effective captives; they had restricted access to air-raid shelters or had to make do with slit trenches, so as to emphasize the difference in status between them and skilled German workers. In a controlled economy, with no right to strike and heavy penalties for dissent, worker unrest could still be displayed through slow working or sabotage. It remained in the interest of employers and the state to ensure that the German labor force was given both stick and carrot to keep it productive. Priority was given to repairing workers' housing or replacing it with temporary barracks. Workers engaged in repair work following a raid were given a bonus of between 52 and 65 percent an hour depending on their particular skills.[192] Workers who were rendered homeless had to report to their employer within two days to qualify for compensation and to be allowed a brief period of compassionate leave.[193]

Other rewards or bonuses were introduced to sustain worker loyalty despite the long hours and greater danger. Hourly wage rates for all German workers were increased to 25 percent extra for overtime, 50 percent extra for Sunday work, and 100 percent extra on holidays. Firms were encouraged to set up nurseries for working women, hostels for workers, and midday hot meals. The Daimler-Benz company increased its "social spending" on workforce facilities and bonuses from 1.6 million RM in 1939 to 2.1 million in 1944; in the last year of war, 4.6 million RM were spent on air-raid protection.[194] In October 1942 arrangements were made to provide additional food rations for the population in raided cities, predominantly in the western industrial areas: fifty grams of extra meat a week for a minimum of four weeks, and extra fats and bread at the discretion of the local Reich defense commissar. Later in the war, when overtime incentives were declining, special "Speer recognition" awards were made for exceptional efforts, usually paid in kind—alcohol and tobacco for men, health tonics, canned vegetables, and condensed milk for women and youths. But at the same time German workers were subject to closer discipline. In the Ruhr cities "labor control" units were organized by the German Labor Front, checking on attendance and hours worked, granting leave to bombed-out workers, and searching out workers absent without leave to return them to work. Thought was given to militarizing the labor force as "soldiers on the home front," but although the term was regularly used in propaganda, it was not carried through from fear that it would make labor less rather than more efficient.[195] In the summer of 1944 instructions were given to compel workers aged over eighteen to serve ten times a month (eight for women) in the works' self-protection squads to make sure there were enough people to fight the fires, though for much of the war the factory was almost certainly a safer place to be than at home.[196] Yet in the end the greatest incentive for workers to remain at work was the need for regular wages to support them and their families, and the fear that defeat would usher in a return to the Depression days of high unemployment and short-time working and the possible dismemberment of Germany. Bombing gave them no incentive to give up.[197]

The most common response to the increased bombing was some form of dispersal. For several years production had been dispersed to different units in order to expand capacity. From the summer of 1943 dispersal policy was designed to provide substitute sites, not extra capacity. On June 28, 1943, Hitler issued a decree for securing factory space and accommodation for workers in those areas where production was to be dispersed.[198] Two weeks later Speer's ministry sent out orders implementing the decree, which included a prohibition on any "wild dispersal" undertaken without approval and an injunction not to move everything to the eastern regions just because they were still beyond range of regular air attacks. Instead firms were encouraged to disperse into local rural areas, which would allow them to keep their workforce intact and maintain links with local service and component contractors.[199] The Air Ministry had already begun a program of dispersal in October 1942, when orders were issued to move all production out of the most endangered areas and to ensure that each product was manufactured in at least two or three different places. Sometimes by chance the same component was bombed simultaneously in two separate places—a Ju87 component, for example, in two raids on Bremen and Osnabrück in 1942—but in general multiple production gave an added cushion of flexibility. By November 1942 most of the 290 businesses producing 100 percent for the air force west of the line Stettin-Berlin-Munich had dispersal plans prepared.[200] Over the following months much aircraft production was moved to the Protectorate, Slovakia, Poland, Silesia, and Saxony, but there still remained much to be done by the time Hitler published his decree in June 1943. The next month, Göring, as "Plenipotentiary for the Four-Year Plan," ordered complete "evacuation of war-essential industry from the core of major cities."[201]

The success of the dispersal policy, which allowed German production to expand significantly despite the escalating bombardment, can best be illustrated by looking at the two industries chosen by the U.S. Eighth Air Force as potential bottlenecks: ball bearings and aircraft assembly. Both cases demonstrate the substantial cushion available in a heavily industrialized state when manufacture needed to be decentralized. The potentially disruptive effects of this process were mitigated by the simultaneous insistence, laid down in regular orders from Hitler himself, on simplifying and standardizing production and design, concentrating on a narrow range of model types, searching for substitute materials or parts for those in short supply, and eliminating any production, whether civilian or military, that was classified as less essential. Bombing forced the German productive system to become more flexible and improvisatory in ways that the Allied air forces had not anticipated. The attack on the production of ball bearings at Schweinfurt failed in its purpose for just this reason. Four days after the attack, Speer flew to Nuremberg on Hitler's orders to inspect the damage; the following day, October 19, 1943, Philipp Kessler, a member of Speer's Armaments Advisory Council, was appointed "General Commissar for Restarting Ball-Bearing Production." Disliking the rather ponderous title, he established a "Ball-Bearing Rapid Action" (Kugellager-Schnellaktion) organization under his direction. Schweinfurt represented only 45 percent of available ball-bearing production; stocks were immediately taken over from the other producers and from contractors who held substantial reserves, a total equivalent to two months' production. The careful husbanding of stocks meant that by January 1944 reserves of ball bearings were three times greater than in January 1943. Machine tools for production at Schweinfurt were by January 1944 back to 94 percent of requirements. Production was decentralized so that less than half was left in Schweinfurt itself, the rest spread out among twenty other producers. The whole ball-bearing industry in Germany was served in the end by forty-nine dispersal plants; only 20 percent of national production remained in Schweinfurt a year after the main attack. The output of aircraft and tanks, which relied extensively on ball bearings, was affected hardly at all thanks to design changes. By the time ball-bearing supply was back to its pre-raid level, aircraft production was 58 percent greater, tank production 54 percent.[202]

The dispersal of the aircraft industry indicated another cushion of productive capacity, even if in some cases in 1944 assembly or repair had to be improvised in farm barns, wooded shelters, or road tunnels. The second wave of dispersal following the planned decentralization in 1942–43 came after the Allied air attacks in "Big Week" in February 1944. Although the production loss was small and soon made good, the decision was taken by the German Fighter Staff to decentralize all aircraft and aero-engine production even further in case the campaign intensified. The 27 main assembly plants were divided among 729 smaller units, though in the end only around 300 were used; aero-engine output was divided from 51 plants (in many cases already dispersed once) to 249 new sites. Up to the end of 1943 some 3.3 million square meters had been made available as dispersed capacity, but the new programs involved a further 2.4 million.[203] The result was a complex mosaic of productive sites for each of the main producers. The Erla works in Leipzig, making up one-third of Me109 production, was split up among 18 dispersal plants, 13 component plants, and 5 main assembly points, and although output was temporarily safeguarded, the six-month transfer of production lines cost 2,800 lost aircraft. The Me109 production at Wiener-Neustadt also had to be decentralized in the spring of 1944, and once again was undertaken with mixed success because sites were chosen where too much new installation and reconstruction was needed. Efficiency was hit by the requirement to have no unit capable of producing more than 150 aircraft a month. Nevertheless, the company managed to build 50 percent more fighter aircraft in 1944 than in 1943. By contrast, Me110 production at the Gothaer Waggonfabrik in Gotha was more successfully dispersed after the raids in February, so that full production was restored after only a few weeks.[204] The whole dispersal policy ensured that aircraft output would reach a peak of almost 40,000 aircraft in a year when 1 million tons of bombs were dropped on German and German-occupied targets. Bombing might have prevented higher output, but the aircraft industry would anyway have faced limitations from raw materials and labor supplies in trying to produce more, with or without bombing.

The decentralization of production did come at a cost, and no doubt overall output would have been higher in 1943 and 1944 without it. The success of the transfer to aboveground sites ensured that overall output could continue its upward trajectory. For those who had to undertake the reorganization, or for the workers forced to transfer to different sites, almost 850,000 by late 1944, the social and psychological costs were considerable. For one thing, managerial and technical personnel had to be distributed among additional small plants, increasing individual responsibility and diluting a firm's leadership corps; more workers were engaged indirectly on military orders for which they had not been trained, or other workers (usually foreign or camp laborers) had to be transferred from one camp barrack to another; shorter production runs undermined the time and cost savings of large-scale assembly; tools and jigs had to be supplied in multiples, though in this case the large number of general-purpose machine tools available in Germany made the transfer to fragmented production easier to carry out. Above all, dispersal placed strains on the communications system and in particular on the carefully controlled distribution of equipment and parts run by the Armaments Ministry, designed to ensure that components and tools only arrived at the time and in the quantities needed. With an exceptional amount of organizational and laboring effort, German industry succeeded in maximizing production despite the obstacles presented by dispersal. The object, as one manager put it, was for "the impossible to be made possible."[205]

Doing the impossible might well have described the coincidence of

peak bombing and peak production. The factors that kept war production expanding during 1942 and 1943 played a critical part in sustaining
the expansion of output during 1944. The concentration of production
on the most essential equipment reached its high point in the spring of
1944 as older models of weapons and equipment were eliminated and
standard models introduced. Types of light infantry weapons were to be
reduced from fourteen to five, antitank weapons from twelve to just one,
antiaircraft guns from ten to two; the number of vehicle models was reduced from fifty-five to fourteen; and so on.[206] All inessential or non-
military manufacture was combed through one more time to weed out
unneeded production: the 117 firms still making carpets were reduced to
5; the 23 firms making 300 types of prismatic glass were reduced to 7,
making just 14 types; the 900 machine-tool firms were reduced to 369.
Where possible, the floor space and labor were allocated to direct military output. In the machinery industry, 415,700 workers were freed by
early 1944 to work directly on war matériel.[207] Rationalization, defined
by the regime as extracting as much military equipment as possible from
existing machinery, materials, and labor, was pushed to its limits during
1944. The major constraint on the German war effort, labor supply, was
ameliorated by drawing in resources from occupied Europe, exploiting
camp labor more extensively, and finding ways to get women with children to undertake part-time work or work at home. To cope with the
large-scale movement of the population as a result of bombing, the
plenipotentiary for labor, the gauleiter of Thuringia, Fritz Sauckel, issued an order on January 17, 1944, obliging those who had been evacuated and were not yet working to report to local labor offices for work.
The first order produced only 65,000 volunteers, but as the number of
evacuees increased, the second and third "report orders," which applied
to women with children under seven and women aged forty-five to fifty,
reaped a larger harvest. By October 1944, 1.6 million had registered,
out of whom 303,000 were given work, three-quarters of them half-day
shifts in dispersed factories. Almost all of these were women, joining the
3.5 million female workers already on half shifts. Women constituted
more than 50 percent of the total German workforce by the end of the
war.[208]

The changing composition of the industrial workforce brought advantages and disadvantages for German war production. The foreign
workforce made up 1.6 million (15 percent) of industrial labor in July
1942, 2.7 million (22 percent) in July 1943, and by the summer of 1944,
3.2 million (29 percent). Their presence could present problems of language, discipline, and training, and there was anxiety that they would
not cope as well as German workers under the pressure of bombing. At
Daimler-Benz, thirty-one different nationalities were recorded in the
workforce, including one lone Afghan and one Peruvian.[209] Women came
to make up a growing proportion of the labor force, many of them forced
laborers from the east. Female employment raised problems about family care, physical exhaustion, and the struggle to secure rationed goods,
but the economy would not have functioned without them. Efforts were
made to sustain their productivity too with bonuses or extra rations and
appropriate training. Of the total of 6.2 million employed in the arms
industry, more than half of all industrial employment by October 1944,
35 percent were women, 37 percent foreign workers or prisoners of war.[210]
This heterogeneous labor force was subject to persistent and heavy
bombing throughout 1944 and the first months of 1945.

The assumption for Allied planners was that urban destruction
would create a growing problem of absenteeism, which would contribute
to undermining armaments production. Yet the statistics show that
bombing contributed only a small proportion of lost hours in 1944. According to records compiled by the Economics Ministry, in October
1944 only 2.5 percent of hours lost nationally were attributed to air
raids. Absenteeism was a result of illness, leave, truancy, or workplace
problems—a total of 16 percent lost work hours—but was not directly
caused by bomb attack.[211] The aggregate figure nevertheless disguised
wide variations from one branch of industry to another, and between
different areas of the Reich. The absenteeism rates for the main industrial groups between March and October 1944 are set out in table 4.2.

Absenteeism rates were higher in the western areas of Germany, in
Hamburg and in Munich. Yet over the course of 1944, despite the losses,
the total number of hours worked in the 12,000 war production firms
surveyed by the ministry actually increased from 976 million in March

to 1,063 million in October.[212] One explanation is that the large proportion of foreign, prisoner of war, and concentration camp workers made it possible to use coercion to keep them working. At the Ford works in Cologne, absenteeism was a problem only among German workers. In 1944 it was estimated that 25 percent of the German workforce was absent on average over the year, whereas the figure for the eastern workers (Russians, Poles, Ukrainians) was only 3 percent. German workers either absented themselves permanently—a total of 1,000 at Ford in 1944, two-thirds of them women—or returned slowly after a raid, one-tenth after one to two days, two-thirds after two weeks.[213] For the German war economy one of the major advantages of exploiting captive labor on a large scale in 1944 and 1945 was the possibility of controlling their work effort even in the adverse conditions imposed by heavy bombing.

The large captive workforce also made it possible to contemplate from summer 1943 onward a more radical solution to the policy of dispersal by placing the most important war production under the ground, either in converted mines, caves, and tunnels or in new purpose-built underground facilities, coated with up to seven meters of concrete. Interest in the program was generated from a number of quarters. In July 1943, Hitler asked that production of the new A4 rocket (the later V-2) should be made as safe as possible from bombing, preferably underground;

Table 4.2: Hours Worked and Hours Lost in German Industry, March–October 1944 (%)

Industrial Branch	Hours Worked	Hours Lost	Air Raids	Illness/ Leave
Iron and steel	84.7	15.3	5.1	10.2
Machinery	83.3	16.7	6.2	10.5
Vehicles	77.0	23.0	10.6	12.4
Aircraft industry	85.6	14.4	4.6	9.8
Shipbuilding	82.2	17.8	7.9	9.9

Source: BA-B, R 3102/10031, Statistical Office, "Vermerk über die Auswirkung der feindlichen Luftangriffe auf die Arbeiterstundenleistung der Industrie," January 27, 1945.

Himmler undertook to carry it out because he had access to a rapidly expanding concentration camp population for the supply of labor. The Air Ministry had already asked the mining section of the Economics Ministry to compile a list of all potential sites in Germany and the nearest occupied territories with underground floor space for the aeronautical industry to escape the raids.[214] The list of possible sites ran to twenty-two pages, fifteen with German locations, seven more for those identified in Hungary, Slovakia, Bohemia/Moravia, and Poland. Limited progress was made in 1943, but in the spring of 1944, with the onset of more targeted bombing of key industries, comprehensive plans were drawn up for a colossal construction program to embrace eventually 93 million square meters of underground room, to include additional programs for oil and SS projects, among them the A4 rocket. The distribution of underground plants, planned, completed, and in hand, is set out in table 4.3.

The plans were by 1944 difficult to implement, though the SS con-

Table 4.3: Programs of Underground Construction, November 1944 (m²)

Industry	Planned	Abandoned	Under Construction	Completed
Airframes	20,766,800	645,000	16,570,400	3,550,800
Air components	6,391,400	—	5,347,700	1,043,720
Aero-engines	20,992,700	1,345,000	15,871,000	3,776,800
Tanks	2,109,000	—	1,818,400	290,500
Motor vehicles	2,808,360	—	2,711,500	96,800
V-weapons	1,538,700	—	387,400	1,151,300
Shipbuilding	1,775,400	—	1,248,200	527,200
Weapons	2,173,500	—	2,119,720	53,800
Machine tools	7,101,600	—	6,079,400	1,022,200
Total	**65,657,460**	**1,990,000**	**52,153,720**	**11,513,120**

Source: TNA, AIR 10/3873, BBSU, "German Experience in the Underground Transfer of War Industries," 12.

trol of slave labor in the camps provided a ready-made supply of workers for the rocket program, set up in the notorious Mittelbau-Dora works at Nordhausen. Only 17 percent of the program was completed by the end of 1944, and not all of that was occupied or functioning by the end of the war. The initial program was designed to get aircraft production into shelters so that increased output of planes could be used to turn back the bombers and perhaps render the rest of the program redundant. By May 1944 some 10 percent of aircraft construction was underground, more by the end of the year. Saur developed a plan to create large underground sites in Hungary, first for fighter aircraft, then one for fuel oil, finally an integrated plant for weapons, munitions, and vehicles, even though the Red Army was now within striking distance. The underground program has always been viewed as a waste of resources: "burrowing away from reality" was the judgment of the British Bombing Survey Unit.[215] It is true that most of the dispersal underground was wasted effort. The transfer of BMW aero-engine output into salt mines began in May 1944 and was scheduled for occupation by December, but was not in the end utilized. The access shafts were narrow, the subterranean corridors only ten to thirty meters wide, the salt a threat to the workforce and the machinery. Many of the underground installations suffered from poor ventilation, condensation, and the danger of rockfalls; conditions for workers were so poor that preference was given to using the captive workforce, which in the case of BMW made up 13,000 out of 17,000 at the main plant. By the time the vast Volkswagen works at Wolfsburg was ordered to disperse underground in August 1944, only 15 percent of its 17,000 workers were German.[216] It is nonetheless difficult to see what other long-term solution remained to a regime that refused to surrender and overoptimistically assessed the prospects of survival into 1945 and 1946. When Allied bombing was finally directed at oil production in May 1944, the threat to the vulnerable capital-intensive sectors of German industry could only be solved by either finding effective ways of sheltering it from the bombs or giving up the conflict.

Allied bombing was at its most dangerous in 1944 when it targeted large capital projects in oil and chemicals that could not easily be moved or substituted, unlike ball bearings or aircraft. Following the first bombing, Hitler on May 31, 1944, approved the appointment of Edmund Geilenberg as yet another emergency manager, this time as general plenipotentiary for emergency measures, with the task of putting fuel production underground or moving it into less exposed aboveground installations. The plan was to create ninety-eight dispersed sites, twenty-two of them under the earth, capable of producing up to four-fifths of all aviation fuel and 88 percent of diesel fuel for tanks. By the end of the war around three-fifths of the preparatory work had been done, but only a small amount of equipment had been installed. German fuel supply relied in the end on being able to repair quickly enough the damage to the existing plants.[217] The problems posed by trying to repair damage and supply replacement components were critical in explaining the final collapse of the German war economy under the remorseless punishment inflicted in the last months of the war. Even before the onset of the transportation bombing in September 1944, random interruption to an overstretched communications system led to regular holdups in getting damaged plants repaired, machines replaced, or vital components and equipment supplied. The weekly reports on economic conditions produced by the Economics Ministry throughout 1944 reiterate the problems presented by interrupted rail lines and damaged rolling stock.[218] The department heads from Speer's renamed War Production Ministry all highlighted in their postwar interrogations the damage to production imposed because repairs could not be effected or components and parts supplied.[219] This situation was exacerbated by the decision to disperse production often long distances from the main plant. At the Henschel aircraft works, 200 couriers were on hand to collect and distribute vital materials and parts to and from subcontractors in order to keep production going at all.[220]

Given the artificial concentration on war production at all costs, the chronic stress on the workforce laboring sixty to seventy hours a week, and the rapid contraction of the European supply base, there were limits to how far the German war economy could be pushed, even without the effects of bombing. The economist John Kenneth Galbraith, drafted to assess the German economy at the end of the war, judged that in 1944 German production, bombing or not, was approaching "what might be called a *general* bottleneck."[221] The weight of attack from September 1944 on a taut economic structure confirmed that the German war economy had reached its limit. There was a sudden increase in the number of firms reporting air-raid damage. In July there were 421, of which 150 were totally or severely damaged; in September there were 674, with 253 in the worst categories; in November 1944, 311 out of 664 firms had suffered total or severe loss.[222] The economy kept going during the last eight months of war using accumulated stocks to compensate for the slow decline in the supply of basic materials—steel, iron, aluminum, machine tools—and the cumulative effect of the loss of rail and water transport for the supply of coal. As a result, peak wartime production for artillery, armored fighting vehicles, and fighter aircraft was actually reached in the last three months of 1944.[223] After that, production collapsed rapidly as the encircling armies and the enveloping air fleets tightened their noose around the German neck.

The German leadership continued, nevertheless, to throw emergency solutions at a collapsing structure. On August 1, 1944, an armaments staff responsible for eight priority production programs was established, bringing together under the direction of Speer and Saur twenty-five department heads with supreme authority to squeeze what weapons they could out of the shrinking economic base. In December 1944, Germany was divided into seven armament zones (*Rüstungsbezirke*), in each of which an autonomous military economy was supposed to flourish. Production declined by more than half. During the last weeks of the war the system continued to hover between fantasy and reality. The army planned a slimmed-down "storm program" for army weapons, deciding what the forces could do without while still able to keep on fighting successfully.[224] In early March, Speer set up an emergency "transport staff" to coordinate all communications; on March 8 he finally established three armaments plenipotentiaries in areas he thought were suitable for an "autarkic economy." One was based in Heidelberg, one in Prague, and one in the Rhine-Ruhr, just days before its surrender.[225]

Bombing critically affected the German productive economy only during the last months of the war, but even though a ceiling was placed on further expansion, war production continued to increase until the crisis provoked by the loss of territory, the failure of the dispersal schemes, and the collapse of the repair cycle. A combination of effective work protection, control of the workforce, concealment and deception, dispersal of key production, and insistent policies on concentration and rationalization had succeeded in limiting the damage that air attack could inflict on industry, though not on the cityscapes and urban populations that surrounded it. On March 19, 1945, Hitler published his "scorched earth" decree, in which he ordered the destruction of all that remained of Germany's industry, transport network, and food supplies. It was never implemented, thanks partly to the intervention of Albert Speer, but it would certainly have imposed a higher level of damage on the industrial economy and infrastructure than the bombing. Hans Rumpf, chief inspector of the German fire service, later observed that the dismantling and reparation regime established by the Allies in the occupied zones of Germany after the war's end took a much higher proportion of German industrial capacity than the fraction destroyed by bombing. Of German engineering capacity, 20 percent was destroyed from the air, 70 percent by Allied requisitioning.[226]

"Will Germany Crack?": 1944–45

In February 1944, Heinrich Himmler, appointed minister of the interior in August 1943, in addition to his other offices, announced that "no German city will be abandoned" as a result of bombing.[227] The situation facing Germany's urban areas in 1944 was nevertheless a daunting one. In the last seventeen months of the war three-quarters of all bombs were dropped and approximately two-thirds of all bombing deaths were caused. In Munich, 89 percent of bombs on the city fell in 1944 and 1945; in Mainz, 93 percent of the deaths from bombing occurred in the same two years.[228] By the spring of 1945, no part of the contracting German empire remained untouched. Bombing by day and by night did not affect every area simultaneously, and many towns were bombed just once. But bombing and its social and cultural consequences came to dominate the daily lives of millions of Germans, a majority of them female. One young schoolgirl in Berlin, Waltraud Süssmilch, subject to compulsory civil defense training and playground demonstrations, surrounded by bombed areas of the city, straining to distinguish the different rush and explosion of each type of bomb, later recalled the bizarre wartime world in her memoir: "Bombs belonged to my life. I was confronted with them daily. I could not do otherwise. . . . I was no longer a child."[229]

The presence of Himmler as minister of the interior as well as chief of German police continued a process begun in the 1930s to extend the responsibility of the SS and police system over all areas of air-raid protection and civil defense policy. During 1944, Himmler continued to undermine the position of the Air Ministry, and in August the Air Force Inspectorate 13, responsible for air-raid protection, was abruptly abolished at Hitler's insistence. Responsibility for air-raid protection and the air-raid warning service was transferred unconditionally to the SS and police. On February 5, 1945, just weeks before the end of the war, Himmler also succeeded in removing the Regional Air Commands from any responsibility for civil defense, leaving only a handful of mobile "Air Protection Regiments" under air force control.[230] His new role introduced a fresh element of menace into the regular work of civil defense. On April 14 he published a decree threatening tough punishment for civil defenders who failed in their duty. While most citizens were said to display an "exemplary self-sacrifice," the slackers and feckless were to be dealt with sharply under the terms of the Air Protection Law. Persistent negligence, malice, or deliberate defiance was to result in a court appearance, which by 1944 meant facing a justice system dominated by a narrow ideological outlook and a search for vengeance.[231] For many of those engaged in civil defense, whether Ukrainians in the fire service or camp prisoners detailed to clear up urban debris, the SS was effectively their lawless master.

Goebbels found it difficult to maintain his position in the face of Himmler's ambitions. In December 1943, frustrated that the Inter-Ministerial Committee had too little power, Goebbels persuaded Hitler to make him Reich inspector for civil air protection. With the gauleiter of Westphalia-South, Albert Hoffmann, as his deputy, and a collaborator from the committee, Alfred Berndt, as his office director, Goebbels used his new position to review civil defense all over Germany and to insist on improvements in self-protection organization and communal services.[232] By this stage the local responsibility for coping with the after-math of raids had passed entirely to the Reich defense commissars, with whom Goebbels kept in close contact. In September 1944 the commissars were formally acknowledged as the key coordinating figures in the defence of the Reich, at which point the party also assumed the public political role of preparing the German people for their final ordeal. By this time Goebbels had abandoned the inspectorate, which had done little more than report the state of affairs rather than initiate action; on July 25, 1944, he was named "Reich Plenipotentiary for Total War," another emergency appointment that bore little relation to the conditions on the ground for which he was now ostensibly responsible.[233] It is questionable whether Goebbels's initiatives did anything more than simply confuse the existing structure for air-raid defense. In February 1944 the gauleiter of the Sudetenland complained that there was "an alarming confusion" of orders issuing from a system that had become "more and more bureaucratic." The Reich defense commissar in Hannover-East pointed out in August that he was the subject of five separate streams of instructions on air-raid questions, producing simply a "flood of paper" rather than a single, clear administrative path.[234]

The evidence on the ground suggests that the real responsibility for coping with air raids and their consequences still lay principally with local authorities and the millions of civilian volunteers who fought as best they could against the rising tide of destruction and demoralization. In August 1943 the police authorities issued an order compelling every resident or visitor in an air-protection zone to take part in self-protection action during a raid. Every street and apartment block had its wardens, self-protection troop, house fire defenders, lay helpers, and messengers, led by the local leader of the self-protection area.[235] In January 1944, Hitler approved further measures to increase the active participation of the population in their own defense, despite the growing risks they faced. He compared their experience with the frontline soldier who had to get over his fear of attacking tanks at close quarters: "The one who has actually seen and practiced extinguishing incendiary bombs loses a large part of his fear of this kind of weapon."[236] The schoolgirl in Berlin whose life was dominated by bombs was expected to tackle and extinguish one of a number of types of Allied incendiary. ("Would you trust yourself to extinguish such a bomb?" asked the fireman demonstrator. "Yes," she replied.)[237] In May the Luftschutzbund issued instructions to air-protection officials to undertake home visits to every house and apartment in their sector to provide up-to-date information for each householder, to ensure that every resident was materially prepared to assist, and to try to strengthen the "spiritual resolve" of the community for the difficult task ahead.[238]

The priority by 1944, with heavy raids on Berlin and other cities deeper in German territory, was to try to save as much as possible of German urban life and the populations still living there. Even while Allied aircraft remorselessly reduced the habitable areas of major cities, the effort to repair or recondition damaged housing continued so that workers who remained could have some kind of shelter. The repair of bomb-damaged housing was governed by two decrees issued by Speer as general plenipotentiary for construction on September 15 and 16, 1943, which gave priority to getting working-class housing habitable again to reduce lost work time. Only those houses that could be repaired easily and immediately were to be tackled; nothing was permitted that took more than three months.[239] Local repair was allocated to a construction team organized by the Reich defense commissar, with help from mobile columns of skilled workers organized by the Reich Group Handwork. These motorized emergency units—for doors/windows, roof repair, shop windows, and room interiors—were functioning by October 1943 and fully funded by July the following year. They arrived in a bombed town, parked their vehicles in undamaged streets or squares, and began work on reconstruction at once.[240] The quantity of residential housing destroyed in 1943 was estimated at 5 percent of the housing stock, but during 1944 the figures mounted sharply, making it difficult to keep pace with the program of repair. In the most heavily bombed cities, houses that were lightly damaged in one raid might be hit again in the next more seriously. In the Ruhr city of Bochum residential damage by the spring of 1944 was 147 percent of all homes, in Düsseldorf 130 percent, in Essen 126 percent, a result of counting some repaired houses two, three, or more times.[241] Between January and October 1944 the number of destroyed or heavily damaged residential buildings was

311,807 against 119,668 in the first nine months of 1943, leaving 3.5 million people temporarily, or in some cases permanently, homeless.[242] From the autumn of 1944 it became difficult any longer to construct an accurate statistical picture of housing losses. The last recorded figures, in November, showed the loss of 57,000 buildings in one month.[243]

The urban population also depended on the survival of services— gas, electricity, and clean drinking water. The problem of water supply became acute by the summer of 1944 and emergency measures were prepared for a population that had to share water with the fire service. In all cities under attack the authorities were told to put up notices indicating where people could find a stand-tap with clean water, and warnings where water was not drinkable and would have to be boiled.[244] The Interior Ministry drew up a list of all tanker trucks available nationally to help distribute clean water; the Reich inspector for water and energy sent out detailed instructions in August 1944 on how to keep the water supply going by protecting or establishing plants that could filter and purify contaminated water.[245] In Berlin the local association of brewers was asked in the autumn of 1943 to supply a complete list of the water sources (springs, streams) used in brewing and mineral water production; by June 1944, 286 usable sources had been identified. The same month the Interior Ministry drew up an inventory of unused bottles that could be requisitioned to supply water, which included 357,000 beer bottles and 312,000 used for Coca-Cola.[246]

Gas supply, on which a large number of German households depended, faced the same problems of random but cumulative damage to the gas network. It was found in 1943, even in heavy raids, that the loss of supply could be kept within manageable boundaries. Surplus capacity in the network actually exceeded by a significant margin the damage done by bombing. A heavy raid on Berlin on September 3–4, 1943, resulted in the loss of gas in some districts for only a few hours, in others for only a day. It was possible to find supplies from other parts of the network when local gasworks were damaged; after the raid on Leipzig on December 3–4, 1944, the main gasworks, supplying 250,000 cubic meters of gas, was temporarily put out of action, but long-distance supply managed to restore 90 percent of what was needed.[247] But the expanded raiding in 1944 resulted in widespread and unpredictable damage to both the gas and water networks. By June 1944 there were ninety-four badly damaged gasworks and waterworks countrywide; by the autumn gasworks were forced to cease operation in many places because of the loss of vital pieces of equipment that could no longer be supplied.[248] Millions of householders found that by 1945 gas supply was nonexistent or confined to a slender stream. "The gas is running on a tiny, dying flicker," wrote one Berlin woman in her diary in April 1945. "The potatoes have been cooking for hours. . . . I swallowed one half-raw."[249]

The damage done to German cities in 1944 and 1945 was extensive and indiscriminate. Goebbels ordered lists to be compiled of the destruction of all cultural monuments and cultural treasures. Church authorities sent in regular reports of damage to ecclesiastical property.[250] Table 4.4 shows the tonnage of bombs dropped by both Allied air

Table 4.4: Bomb Tonnage Dropped on Major Urban Targets in Germany, 1940–45

City	Bomber Command	USAAF	Total
Berlin	45,517	22,768	68,285
Cologne	34,712	13,302	48,014
Hamburg	22,583	15,736	38,319
Essen	36,420	432	36,852
Duisburg	30,025	510	30,535
Kiel	16,748	13,198	29,946
Frankfurt am Main	15,696	12,513	28,209
Bremen	12,844	12,669	25,513
Mannheim	18,114	7,067	25,181
Stuttgart	21,014	3,905	24,919
Dortmund	22,242	2,541	24,783
Nuremberg	13,020	7,381	20,401
Munich	7,858	10,993	18,851

Source: Olaf Groehler, *Bombenkrieg gegen Deutschland* (Berlin: Akademie Verlag, 1990), 432.

forces on major German cities (by comparison total tonnage on London in the Blitz was 18,800 tons, and on the second most heavily bombed urban area, Liverpool/Birkenhead, only 1,957 tons). The detailed histories of individual cities show the extent of the cumulative losses inflicted in the final raids. Munich, untouched for the first three years of war, suffered thirty major raids from September 1942. This involved the loss of 10,600 residential buildings; only 2.5 percent of all buildings in the city remained completely unscathed by the bombing. Some 45 percent of the physical substance of the city was destroyed, an average figure that disguises wide differences: areas of the central old city were three-quarters destroyed, but in the industrial zone of Munich-Allach only 0.4 percent. Of cultural and religious buildings, ninety-two were totally destroyed, 182 damaged, including the cathedral, the old town hall, the council room, the state library (losses of half a million books), the Residence, the Maxburg, the National Theater, and so on. In total, Munich had 7.2 million cubic meters of rubble that needed clearing away at the end of the war.[251] These statistics could be repeated for almost all German cities or towns by the war's end, large or small. The small community of Bingerbrück, on the Rhine, had 470 buildings; 327 were destroyed or heavily damaged, and only two avoided any damage at all.[252]

The heavy destruction of the infrastructure and residential districts of German cities and towns made it increasingly difficult to protect the population from death, injury, and enforced displacement. The evacuation program was expanded rapidly to try to reduce the risk to sections of the population that were not regarded as essential to the war effort. It was now evident that nowhere was safe, so the proportion of the population that might need to move was unmanageably large. In January 1944, Hitler told Goebbels that not everyone eligible to move could go, since this involved an estimated 8 million children, mothers, and the old from the 32 million inhabitants of every city over 50,000 people.[253] The following month Himmler sent out guidelines on evacuation with the object of limiting it as far as possible in order to avoid too much pressure on reception areas that in some cases were already full, and to ensure that work and air defense could be maintained. City dwellers were encouraged to move away from city centers, where the majority of deaths from fire were caused. In an ironic reversal of the RAF zoning system, Himmler ordered local authorities to move people away from the inner zone, with its narrow, tightly packed streets, to the less densely populated outer zones, the commuter suburbs, and the farthest "weekend commuter" belt; the priority was to ensure that most evacuees stayed close to the cities they had left.[254]

In practice, restrictions were difficult to enforce and the rising tide of urban casualties accelerated the pace of both official and unofficial evacuation. Arrangements had to be made between the party regions to see how many people could be accommodated and what transport was available for them, but by September 1944 there were 5.6 million evacuees, by November 7.8 million, and by the beginning of 1945, 8.9 million. Not all of these were evacuees from bombing. Of the final figure for 1945 an estimated 1.76 million had evacuated themselves, while 2.41 million had been compulsorily evacuated or had fled from the frontier areas imminently threatened with invasion, and 841,000 had been moved with dispersed factories.[255] No figures are available for those who remained in the suburbs or commuter belts of damaged cities, but in Hamburg the numbers displaced from the destroyed central areas to other parts of the city numbered half a million, leading to a sudden increase in the level of population density in the unbombed zones.[256] During the last half of 1944 and the first months of 1945, Germany was an exceptionally mobile society; Germans moved westward from the threat of Soviet invasion, eastward from the approaching Anglo-American armies, away from the bombed cities and, in an unknown number of cases, back again. Accommodation became rudimentary, food and welfare supplies exiguous, and pilfering and petty crime more widespread. Those who returned to living in familiar cellars and ruins could tell themselves that life was preferable there, for all the risks and violence of the air war. "My cellar home in Hamburg," wrote a woman evacuated to Linz, "was a thousand times better."[257]

For those who remained in the cities, fighting the raids and their consequences was only one of the problems confronted in the last year of the war. The problems of poor health, the difficulty of obtaining rationed goods, long hours of work, and declining transport all owed something to the effects of bombing, but were also derived from the exceptional demands made in the last year of war to sustain war production and military campaigning from an exhausted people. For almost 8 million forced foreign workers and prisoners of war, and the 700,000 concentration camp prisoners, there was no choice about running the risks of being bombed or the dangers of its aftermath. German cities changed their social geography markedly over the last year of war. The population of major cities in the Ruhr-Rhineland shrank to a fraction of their total before the bomber offensive: Essen, Düsseldorf, and Frankfurt had less than half their prewar population by May 1945, but Cologne had just 20,000 left out of 770,000. The population of Munich declined by 337,000 (41 percent) between 1939 and 1945, the population of Berlin by 1.7 million (40 percent), that of Hamburg by half a million (35 percent).[258] Among those who remained were a rising proportion of non-Germans, or of German workers transferred from other industrial sites, but a shrinking number of young and middle-aged men. This was the population that suffered the high casualty rates of the last eighteen months of the war.

The exact figure of deaths up to the end of the war has never been established with certainty, partly because of the sudden influx of refugees from the eastern regions in the last weeks of the conflict, partly because figures for casualties were collected by a number of different agencies— the Air Ministry, the Interior Ministry, the Economics Ministry, and the Party Chancellery—and partly because in the final weeks of the war accurate recordkeeping was no longer possible. The statistical series collected during the war differed from one another because some distinguished between civilian casualties, uniformed casualties, POWs, and foreign workers, whereas others listed only civilian casualties. In August 1944, for example, Air Ministry records show 11,070 dead, but Economics Ministry records show 8,562; the first includes all categories of bomb victims, the second only civilians.[259] Table 4.5 shows the full record for November 1944 provided by the Air Ministry Air Protection Staff.

This record was used by the United States Bombing Survey after the war to estimate German casualties. The total number of dead for 1943 and 1944 from Air Protection Staff records was 100,107 in 1943, 146,300 for 1944, and 13,553 for the month of January 1945. The overall figure for those injured is 305,455. No further aggregate statistics are available for the last three months of the war. Using the same proportions as November 1944, it can be estimated that of this 259,960 total, approximately 80 percent were German civilians.[260] There are also archive records to show deaths from bombing in the years 1940 to 1942, a total of 11,228, of whom 6,824 died in 1942 and approximately 4,000 in 1941.[261] Based on these archive sources, the figure for those who died from May 1940 to January 1945 comes to 271,188. No doubt this does not include all those who were killed or died of wounds, but it does include uniformed personnel, POWs, and foreign workers, and it applies to the whole of the Greater German area, including those territories incorporated from March 1938 onward.

It is difficult to reconcile these figures with the much larger totals arrived at in postwar calculations. The difference can largely be explained by the speculative nature of the estimates made for the number who died in the last four months of heavy bombing. In 1956, Hans Sperling

Table 4.5: The Dead and Seriously Injured from Bombing, November 1944 (Greater German Area)

Category	Dead	Injured
Armed forces	1,118	1,680
Police/Air protection	129	161
Civilians	14,590	22,145
POWs	371	372
Foreign workers	1,232	1,677

Source: BA-B, R 3102/10031, Air Ministry, LS-Arbeitsstab, "Übersicht über Luftangriffe und Bombenabwürfe im Heimatkriegsgebiet," November 1944.

published in the German official statistical journal *Wirtschaft und Statistik* (*Economy and Statistics*) a detailed account of his reconstruction of the dead from bombing. His total of civilians killed came to 570,000 for the wartime German area. Together with 23,000 uniformed dead and an estimated 32,000 POWs and foreign workers, his sum reached 625,000, the figure commonly quoted today for the total killed in Germany by Allied bombing.[262] Sperling's figures rested on speculations about the number of German civilians and foreign workers who died in the last four months of war, and in particular on the number of refugees fleeing westward into the path of the raids. He guessed that 111,000 of them died between January 1945 and the end of the war, including the greatly inflated figure of 60,000 dead in Dresden. This would mean that around 300,000 people were killed in Germany in the final flourish of bombing, a statistic that has no supporting evidence. In 1990 the East German historian Olaf Groehler published revised figures. Although acknowledging the speculative nature of some of his own calculations, particularly for those who died in 1945, Groehler suggested a much lower figure of 420,000 for all categories of victim and for the enlarged German wartime area.[263]

There are ways to arrive at a more plausible total. If it is assumed that the figure of 271,000 dead by January 1945 is a realistic, if not precise, total (and there are archive figures that suggest a lower sum), it is possible to extrapolate from the last five months of heavy raiding for which records exist (September 1944 to January 1945) in order to find a possible order of magnitude for deaths in the last three months of the war. The average death toll for these five months was 18,777, which would give an aggregate figure for the whole war period of 328,000, though it would not allow for the exceptional casualty level at Dresden, confirmed by the latest research at approximately 25,000. Adding this would produce a total figure of approximately 353,000, representing 82,000 deaths in the last months. Detailed reconstruction of deaths caused by Royal Air Force bombing from February to May 1945, though incomplete, suggests a total of at least 57,000.[264] If casualties inflicted by the American air forces are assumed to be lower, since their bombing was less clearly aimed at cities, an overall death toll of 82,000 is again statistically realistic. In the absence of unambiguous statistical evidence, the figure of 353,000 gives an approximate scale consistent with the evidence. It is a little over half the figure of 625,000 arrived at in the 1950s.

The lower figure of 353,000 still represents an exceptional level of unnatural deaths compared with the impact of bombing elsewhere, and with the much lower level of casualties in Germany up until the summer of 1943. The obvious explanation is that repeated raids with 600 or 700 heavy bombers will eventually overwhelm the capacity of civil defense to limit casualties. This was certainly true for smaller cities hit just once, such as Pforzheim or Hildesheim, but also large cities such as Hamburg, whose defenses could not cope with the firestorm, though they could cope effectively with raids of lesser intensity. But there are other reasons for an escalating level of casualties. Shelter provision had never been ideal, but in 1943 and 1944 resources were no longer available for a comprehensive shelter program. Towns in Zones II and III became victims of bombing with inadequate public shelters. The air-protection room yielded mixed results, but in areas already heavily bombed, the cellar or basement under a heavily damaged building offered much less protection than a shelter under an intact building. Medical aid, despite the exceptional efforts of the profession, was a declining resource in 1944 and 1945, increasing the risk of death from infection or loss of blood. Finally, the mobile population was more exposed to risk, particularly once Allied aircraft began routine strafing of vehicles and trains, and evacuees found themselves in areas thought to be safe from bombs but now subject to random attack. With at least 9 million people accommodated away from their homes, where they had had air-protection rooms and established self-protection routines, the risks of higher casualty levels increased. People who stayed in Berlin, despite the bombing, had established shelters to which they could go. "Finally we're in our shelter," wrote the Berlin diarist, "behind an iron door that weighs a hundred pounds, with rubber seals around the edges and two levers to lock it shut . . . the people here are convinced that their cave is one of the safest. There's nothing more alien than an unknown shelter."[265]

The reaction of the population to this wave of destruction was never uniform. Over the last year of war ordinary people had many different pressures with which to cope, so distinguishing what was particular about the bombing war from wider fears about defeat, dread of the arrival of the Soviet armies, fear of the security apparatus, and anxiety about the mounting military losses is historically complex. Popular opinion was diverse and fluctuating. On bombing, the SD reports in late 1943 and early 1944 show a pendulum swinging between hopes that the air terror would be ended by German retaliation and pessimistic realization that it was likely to get worse. In April 1944, for example, home intelligence found, alongside anxious fears for survival and doubts that the war would end well, the hope expressed that fate would still take a hand in Germany's favor because "one simply cannot believe that everything had been in vain."[266] For much of the year the principal source of anxiety was the state of the war on the Eastern Front; from June 1944 onward the invasion from the west temporarily eclipsed it. Popular concern with bombing briefly revived with the onset of the V-weapons campaign in the summer, but the unrealistic expectation that it would reverse the tide of the air war was at once disappointed, and by late June the intelligence reports found a widespread skepticism that anything could stop the bombing. By July, when every German front line had collapsed, in Belorussia, Italy, and France, "pessimistic opinion" prevailed everywhere. It was judged that this did not mean that the "will to resist" had evaporated, simply that there was widespread doubt that it would be of any use.[267]

The German population lived through this period with a sustained sense of drama in which the experience of bombing played only a part. The party played increasingly with the idea that the German people were bound in a "community of fate" (*Schicksalsgemeinschaft*), in which the final struggles would test their racial qualities to extremes. Some of this propaganda may explain the evidence of a popular mentality of "victory or death" detected by the SD, but most of the home intelligence reports over the last year of the war show that ordinary Germans felt themselves to be trapped between a rock and a hard place—unable to give up because of the consequences expected from a coercive and vindictive dictatorship, but fearful of the consequences of defeat, particularly at the hands of the Red Army. There is little evidence from the intelligence reports that bombing as such strengthened the resolve of the urban population to hold out longer or fight harder. Bombing was a demoralizing and exhausting experience: "nervous anxiety," "fear," "worry," "running around after life" punctuate the reports of popular reaction to the air raids.[268] Regular air-raid alarms forced civilians to shelter for hundreds of hours in what were often uncomfortable and airless rooms. The American postwar morale survey found among the cohort of interviewees that 38 percent experienced "intense fear, nervous collapse," 31 percent "temporary or less severe fright." One woman gave a vivid account of her ordeal: "I saw people killed by falling bricks and heard the screams of others dying in the fire. I dragged my best friend from a burning building and she died in my arms. I saw others who went stark mad."[269] These experiences were no doubt what the survey was looking for. In answer, however, to the question about why people thought the war was lost, only 15 percent identified air raids as the reason, 48 percent military defeats.[270]

What bombing did do was to increase the dependence of the population on both the state apparatus and the party organizations responsible for welfare, reducing even further the space for more serious dissent. Survival depended on not challenging the system. Throughout the heaviest period of bombing, both state and party, assisted increasingly by the armed forces stationed in the Reich, were able to sustain the supply of replacement goods, the distribution of food and water, planned evacuation, and rehabilitation, though transport difficulties and the declining access to European food supplies meant that living standards continued to fall throughout 1944.[271] Indeed, for most of the urban population official sources were the only ones available. The risks from black marketeering and looting grew greater as the war drew to a close, and the terror more arbitrary for the German people; military policemen shot or hanged those they caught on the spot. Even in Berlin in the last days before the Russians arrived, hungry survivors were able to find supplies of food dispensed by whatever authority was still functioning. It proved impossible at this stage to reestablish "normal life" as had been attempted earlier in the war (and had been the aim in Britain, too, during the Blitz), though routines did not break down completely. Rather than greater communal resolve, accounts of the bombed populations show a growing apathy and demoralization: "A weight like lead hangs on all our actions," wrote one diarist in January 1945.[272]

The more surprising result of the bombing was the absence of sustained popular hatred directed toward those who were carrying it out. A long report on popular attitudes to the enemy produced in February 1944 indicated occasional evidence of anger directed at British aircrew, but concluded that "hatred against the English people in general cannot be spoken of." The Soviet people were feared rather than hated, driven by "an alien and incomprehensible mentality." Paradoxically, wide popular hostility was reserved almost exclusively for the Italians for betraying Germany in 1943 by surrendering to the Allies.[273] There were, nevertheless, acts of spontaneous violence directed by the bombed population against aircrew who were caught after they had to bail out and land on German soil. The number of airmen who became victims of "lynch murder" has been estimated at between 225 and 350, a small fraction of the total of air force prisoners of war. The first recorded incident was during Operation Gomorrah on July 25, 1943, when two American airmen were killed. The pressure from above for people to take the law into their own hands increased during 1944 after Hitler endorsed popular vengeance against pilots guilty of strafing civilians, trains, or hospitals. The peak of popular lynching occurred in March 1945, with thirty-seven killings.[274]

The violence is not difficult to explain. Official propaganda had always described Allied bombing as "terror bombing" and the aircrew as gangsters or air pirates. The word "vengeance" had become part of the public vocabulary of the air war. On May 27, 1944, Goebbels published a widely read article in the party newspaper calling for "an eye for an eye, a tooth for a tooth" in subjecting Allied fliers to German "self-justice," echoing views expressed by Hitler as early as the autumn of

1942.[275] Many of the cases of lynching were associated with party members or SA men, or policemen, who expected not to be punished. Spontaneous popular violence was rarer, though again explicable because of the level of destruction and casualties imposed in the last years of war. What is surprising is that the violence was not more widespread given the increasingly lawless character of German justice. Reports after Goebbels's article indicated public concern that killing captured Allied aircrew would result in the killing of captured German airmen too in retaliation. The uniformed services would not endorse the killing, and Allied survivors attested to the intervention of soldiers or policemen in saving them from angry crowds. In the aftermath of heavy bombing, violent reaction against its perpetrators seems often to have taken second place to the relief at having survived and concern for others. Hans Nossack observed in Hamburg in the days after Operation Gomorrah that "no-one comforted himself with thoughts of revenge"; the enemy was at most, Nossack continued, "an instrument of unknowable forces that sought to annihilate us."[276]

Somehow the German civilian population survived under the sharply deteriorating conditions of daily life, in a milieu that became progressively more abnormal. The civil defense structure built up and renewed over the course of the war proved in the end sufficiently flexible to continue the task of combating the raids and coping with their consequences. "Self-protection" is evident in the hundreds of photographs that survive of civilians forming human chains to supply water or to remove rubble, of volunteer firemen and salvage workers struggling to contain the flames. After the heavy raid on Stuttgart in July 1944, one girl recalled how her father had saved their home: "Our row of houses only remained standing because my father had dread of being installed just anywhere after the loss of his house. His view was: 'If I cannot save my home, I have nothing left in life.' So during the raid he stayed up on top so that he could throw the incendiary bombs straight onto the street."[277] Waltraud Süssmilch found herself with other classmates after each all-clear joining a long human chain passing buckets filled with water or sand by hand to the next person, or in school hours packing parcels for the bombed-out, or visiting the wounded.[278] Throughout 1944 advice on firefighting and training for self-protection continued to be published and distributed; blackout regulations were insisted upon and air-raid instructions issued for areas where until late 1944 there had been very little air action and little familiarity with the pattern of air-raid crises.

Right to the very last days of the war, air-raid protection continued to function. The record of two of the air force Air Protection Regiments, mobile units designed to bring immediate assistance to bombed cities, even at considerable distance, illustrates the extent to which positive efforts continued to be made to combat or ameliorate the effects of remorseless daily bombing. Regiment 3, based in Berlin, in action almost every day, traveled 190 kilometers in response to the bombing of Magdeburg on August 5–6, 1944. One company tackled the damaged Krupp-Gruson plant. It succeeded in extinguishing the blazing coal bunkers, rescuing the machinery, putting out the large fires threatening the matériel stores, and saving cellars full of military supplies. A second company worked in the burning city, extinguishing 5 small fires where the bombs fell, 6 roof fires, 11 story fires, 14 "total fires" (preventing them from spreading), 6 burning provision stores, and 5 larger conflagrations. It handled 63 civil defense first-aid cases, 402 civilian injuries, sent 138 off in ambulances, and recovered 38 buried bodies and 33 people still alive.[279] Two weeks later Regiment 3 sent three companies to Stettin, where the raid had devastating effects. They rescued 501 people alive, and dug out 53 dead, extinguished 127 smaller house fires and 29 "total fires," fought 12 industrial and commercial blazes, and prevented 18 fires from spreading any farther. The narrow streets in Stettin made it difficult to get equipment into the heart of the blaze, and only after three hours was it possible to create a corridor covered with water jets to get through to the shelters. There they found 50 dead near the shelter entrance who had tried to escape through the fire by their own efforts, their corpses "completely carbonated." In the last weeks of bombing in 1945, Regiment 7 reported a grueling schedule of operations starting with a major fire raid on Nuremberg on February 20–21, where the unit extinguished 119 small and 60 major fires, and extracted 36 bodies from the rubble, followed by summons to a further seventeen raids between February 27 and March 21.[280] As the military fronts contracted, so it proved possible for technical troops from the armed forces to be deployed more extensively in trying to protect the remaining urban areas, working side by side with the surviving civil defenders.

One of the cities in need of urgent aid in 1945 was the Saxon capital at Dresden, destroyed in a firestorm on the night of February 13–14. Dresden had already experienced two American daylight raids, on October 7, 1944, and January 16, 1945, which had killed 591 people. Little effort had gone into constructing adequate public shelters, and one witness recalled that the sirens failed to sound that night. The day before the February raid was, according to Victor Klemperer, a German-Jewish philologist who had survived in Dresden married to a non-Jew, one of "perfect spring weather."[281] By a strange historical quirk, Klemperer was among the small population of surviving Jews in Dresden who that same day had been ordered to turn up seventy-two hours later to be transported away for "outside labour duty." When the main raid began in the middle of the night he ran at once to the Jewish shelter but scrambled on through the fires and bombs when the shelter became too hot. He managed to get down to the Elbe River, battered by the wind of the firestorm, slipping on the black rain that fell from the condensation caused by the rising column of hot air. He joined the flow of refugees the following morning with his wife, who had been saved only because someone had pulled her from the Jewish into the "Aryan" shelter below their apartments:

> Fires were still burning in many of the buildings on the road above. At times, small and no more than a bundle of clothes, the dead were scattered across our path. The skull of one had been torn away, the top of the head was a dark red bowl. Once an arm lay there with a pale, quite fine hand, like a model made of wax such as one sees in barbers' shop windows. . . . Crowds streamed unceasingly between these islands, past these corpses and the smashed vehicles, up and down the Elbe, a silent, agitated procession.[282]

Klemperer was fortunate to survive. He was treated by first-aid workers that morning as American aircraft returned to bomb what was

left of the city. By the evening food arrived and then water. The following morning the refugees were moved to the nearby towns of Klotsche
and Meissen, where there were plentiful bowls of soup. Klemperer tore
off the yellow star all Jews were required to wear and survived the war.

Klemperer's story is a reminder that the system being bombed still
practiced its lethal racism to the very last weeks of the war, though it also
demonstrates that even wearing the star he could get medical attention
and food and emergency accommodation. Dresden became for the authorities a major emergency. The general of technical troops, Erich
Hampe, was sent from Berlin on the morning of February 14 to super-
vise the reestablishment of rail communications over the surviving railway bridge. He found the burnt-out area of Dresden utterly deserted,
except for a llama escaped from the Dresden zoo. Within only two days
an emergency rail service had been set up and the wounded could be
moved to hospitals in nearby cities.[283] Altogether 2,212 were severely
wounded and 13,718 lightly, but the death toll was much higher. By mid-
March the police president reported that 18,375 dead had been accounted for, but estimated the final figure as likely to be 25,000, the
number recently agreed as the upper limit by a historical commission set
up by the mayor of Dresden in 2004. The bodies were collected in large
pyres and those not already incinerated were burned quickly to avoid a
health crisis.[284] Out of 220,000 homes in Dresden, 75,000 were totally
destroyed and 18,500 severely damaged; there were 18 million cubic
meters of rubble. By the end of February, Dresden, a city formerly of
600,000, housing an unknown number of refugees from the east, had
only 369,000 inhabitants left. It was subjected to two further heavy attacks by 406 B-17s on March 2 and 580 B-17s on April 17, leaving a
further 453 dead.[285]

By this stage of the war the bombing had to compete with fear of the
oncoming Soviet forces, whose offensive the bombing of Dresden had
been supposed to serve. Victor Klemperer noted in his diary, once he
was safe in emergency housing, that he shared with those around him
fear of bombing but also their profound fear of the Russians, confirmed by the long trails of refugees in carts and buggies making their

way westward against the tide of German forces moving the other way. Another survivor wrote two weeks after the firestorm, "Why are we still living? Only to wait until the Russians come."[286] Other diaries show that growing horror at the thought of Soviet occupation, fueled by grim rumors of the primitive behavior of Soviet soldiers, put into perspective the bombing, whose dimensions and effects were more familiar. "Masses and masses of fugitives are crossing the Oder," wrote one eyewitness in February 1945. "Dead people have been temporarily buried in the snow. The Russians are coming! Napoleon's retreat from Moscow must have been child's play by comparison."[287] The Berlin schoolgirl, Waltraud Süssmilch, was fascinated and horrified by the stories brought by the tide of refugees from the east that flowed into Berlin in the last weeks of war. One story of the sadistic murder of a pregnant woman by Red Army soldiers filled her with complete dread, even though almost every day bombs were exacting a brutal physical toll all around her.[288] In the last week before the end of the war Berliners stayed in their shelters, which doubled as protection from Soviet shelling, since here, as over most of Germany, the bombing had ceased, in order to prevent the bombers from hitting Allied forces by mistake. The Berlin diarist found the population of her shelter still agitated and nervous, as though they were waiting for a bombing raid. Some of them speculated that the Russians might not be as bad as German propaganda had painted them. A refugee from the east camped out in the shelter began to shout: "Broken sentences—she can't find the right words. She flails her arms and screams. 'They'll find out all right,' and then goes silent once again."[289]

One of the final raids of the war touched a small town that had been spared the bombing, despite its notoriety. Berchtesgaden, where Hitler had his Bavarian headquarters and retreat, was bombed by British aircraft on April 25, 1945, with considerable accuracy, leaving behind "a chaotic brown-and-black mess" in place of the pretty Alpine woods and the smart modern villas of the party elite. The town itself was not hit, an outcome that local people treated as a miracle, apparently evidenced, as one young eyewitness later wrote, by the sign of the cross visible in the sky. She was puzzled by this: "Why of all places should He protect Berchtesgaden, when all of Europe was in ashes?" Her neighbors expected Hitler to arrive at any moment to make his operatic last stand.[290] But Hitler was cut off in Berlin, amid the ruins of his new chancellery building. Thousands of Berliners crowded into the vast flak towers for safety from the battle going on all around them, though the bombing of the capital was now over. Waltraud Süssmilch and her family had taken shelter in the tower but had to leave when it began to fill with water. The sight of the ruined city, even after years of bombing, struck her as extraordinary. Like General Anderson, former commander of the Eighth Bomber Command, when he toured the bombed cities later that summer, she thought that the bombed-out houses, burning roofs, and broken windows looked like the picture of Pompeii in her school history book.[291]

The bombing imposed on Germany exceptional demands for organizing the home front, quite different from the experience of the First World War. The dictatorship relied on sustaining a high degree of participation, willing or otherwise, in the organizations and institutions that were supposed to bind together the new "People's Community." Any explanation for the capacity of German society to absorb bombing destruction and levels of casualty on this scale must include the willingness of millions of ordinary Germans, in addition to all the other pressures of wartime work and survival, to participate in schemes of self-protection, civil defense work, first-aid organization, and welfare provision, without which the consequences of bombing could not have been sustained, however coercive the regime or however narrow the space within which social protest could operate. The effect of bombing was not, in the end, as the Allies hoped, to drive a wedge between people and regime, but the opposite, to increase dependence on the state and the party and to prompt willing participation by civilians in structures designed for their own defense with a remarkable degree of social discipline. The experience of being bombed did indeed create widespread anxiety, demoralization, social conflict, and limited political criticism, but it was balanced in the end by the capacity of the dictatorship to exploit racial policy unscrupulously to its advantage (redistributing Jewish apartments and furnishings, using camp and foreign labor to clear up debris, etc.), while ensuring that minimum levels of social provision, flexible propaganda, administrative competence, and targeted coercion would prevent anything like collapse.

Chapter 5

Italy: The War of Bombs and Words

Italy was bombed for only a month less than Germany during the Second World War. Yet the story of the bombing of most of Italy's cities failed to attract the attention of the wider world in 1945 and has remained on the margins in most narratives of the conflict ever since. As many Italians were killed by bombing as died in the Blitz on Britain; more tons were dropped on Rome than on all British cities put together. Moreover, the damage to Italy's ancient heritage filled two volumes when it was investigated by a British committee in 1945, set up to preserve for future generations the "artistic wealth" that Allied aircraft had been busy bombarding only months before.[1]

Italy's part in the bombing war was more complex than that of any other European state. For at least three years, from June 10, 1940, when Benito Mussolini declared war on Britain and France, the Italian Air Force (Regia Aeronautica) had carried out an active bombing campaign: briefly against targets in France (before the French sued for an armistice in June 1940), against England in the late autumn of 1940, and throughout the Mediterranean and North Africa until final defeat there in May 1943. Some of this air activity had been carried out in loose collaboration with German air forces. Throughout this period, though not continuously, Italian territory was itself bombed by the RAF, from bases in England as well as bases in Malta and North Africa. On September 8, 1943, following an Italian request for an armistice, the Italian state ceased to be an Axis enemy and became, after a short interval, a co-belligerent with the United Nations and an enemy of Germany, whose forces now occupied two-thirds of the Italian peninsula. For the next two years, the few Italian pilots and aircraft remaining in the area not occupied by the Germans were used to attack German forces in the

Balkans and the Ionian Islands, the first raids taking place against targets on Corfu and Cephalonia as early as September 1943.[2] Meanwhile, in the occupied zones of central and northern Italy a new government under Mussolini was installed under German protection in what was called the Italian Social Republic, and here a small Italian contingent, the National Republican Air Force (Aeronautica Nazionale Repubblicana), fought in German aircraft against the Allies.[3] Since German forces were in occupation, northern and central Italy remained a target for Allied bombing up until the very last days of the war, while the southern liberated zone was subject to occasional German air raids. The bulk of the Italian population was the object of air attack first as an enemy people, then as a population waiting to be liberated. The only constant in the Italian experience of war was the threat from the air.

"Great Delay to the Trains": Allied Bombing, 1940–43

The possibility that Italy might take advantage of the Allies' war with Germany to open up a new theater in the Mediterranean was evident long before Mussolini finally seized the opportunity of imminent French collapse to join his Axis partner. The prospect presented the RAF with additional bombing opportunities to consider if, or when, bombing targets in enemy cities was permitted. In the last week of April 1940, the commander of British air forces in France, Air Marshal Arthur Barratt, wrote to the Air Ministry suggesting that bomber forces could operate from bases in southern France against industrial cities in northern Italy.[4] After the War Cabinet on June 1, 1940, had considered ways to cope with Italian belligerency, Barratt was instructed to begin planning the supply and maintenance of British bombers on southern French bases. In case of war, Italy was to be attacked "without warning."[5] By the time Italy declared war on June 10, "Haddock Force," as it was known, had operational bases, fuel, and supplies on two southern French airfields. On June 11 a dozen Wellington bombers arrived, but the French military authorities were now opposed to any bombing of Italy that might provoke retaliation against French cities, and they parked trucks on the runway to prevent takeoff. Only after days of inter-Allied argument did a force of eight aircraft set off on the night of June 15–16 to bomb the port of Genoa, but only one found it; the following night six out of nine managed to locate and bomb Milan. Then the order came to evacuate following the French surrender and the 950 men of Haddock Force left on ships from Marseille on June 18, leaving all their stores and equipment behind.[6] Only on the eve of the armistice between France and Italy did French aircraft attack Italian targets in Sicily on June 23 and 24, killing forty-five people in a gesture of pointless defiance.[7]

The decision to begin bombing Italy—a campaign that continued uninterrupted in one form or another for five years—brought none of the anxieties over legality or retaliation that had governed the decision to begin bombing Germany four weeks earlier, in mid-May. From the outset it was assumed that Italian morale under Fascism was likely to be a more brittle target than German society under Hitler. Bombing could hence be justified by the expectation of rapid and significant political consequences rather than slow economic attrition. The first raids on northern Italy carried out by Bomber Command from British bases in June and August 1940—three in all involving only seventeen aircraft— were reported to have had "a 'stunning' effect on Italian morale."[8] Intelligence fed to the RAF leadership suggested that Italy was "the heel of Achilles" in the Axis war effort, short of resources and with a population unhappy about having to fight Mussolini's war.[9] Since Italy was difficult to reach from British bases or from bases in Egypt with existing aircraft, heavy bombing was not yet an option. But since Italy was regarded as politically fragile, a leaflet war was mounted to try to persuade the population to give up the fight; a total of 4,780,500 leaflets were dropped between 1940 and 1942.[10]

Leaflets could easily be delivered by small numbers of aircraft operating out of RAF airbases on the island of Malta, a British colony situated only fifty-eight miles south of the coast of Sicily. Italian aircraft had already bombed the island, starting with a small raid on June 11, 1940, on the morning after the Italian declaration of war, but the hesitant nature and small scale of most Italian raids thereafter failed to eliminate the threat from the RAF, small though it was at first. In December 1940 the RAF commander on Malta was ordered to begin a concerted propaganda campaign since leaflets were considered for the moment to be "more effective than bombs."[11] One of the first leaflets drafted on Malta in November 1940 called for an Italian uprising: "On hearing the great signal all of you on to the Square—armed with whatever you can lay your hands on, hoes, pickaxes, shotguns, even sticks." The text called on Italians to create a civilized and democratic Italy and to be ready for the call (in block capitals) to "COUNTER-REVOLUTION."[12] Much of the leaflet campaign linked the call for Italian political resistance with the threat of bombing. A leaflet printed in January 1941 asked Italians to choose—"Mussolini or bombs?"—and 100,000 copies were flown from Luqa airfield to cities in southern Italy. In April 1941 a new leaflet under the headline "ROME IS IN DANGER" threatened to bomb the Italian capital if Mussolini ordered the bombing of Athens or Cairo.[13] By this time a handful of Italian fighter and bomber aircraft had taken a brief and inglorious part in the late stages of the Battle of Britain, and British leaflets promised the Italian population that Mussolini would be paid back in kind for helping Hitler.

Nothing in the end came of the political initiative, and the bombing was in reality small-scale and intermittent, a "small switch," as Charles Portal put it, rather than "a big stick."[14] Throughout 1940 and 1941 there were twenty-four small raids by Bomber Command (only four of them in 1941) and ninety-five raids from Malta, most of them by hand-fuls of Wellington bombers, seldom more than ten at a time, on their way to bases in the Middle East.[15] In November 1940, for example, six Wellingtons attacked Naples, where they reported a poor blackout, no searchlights or enemy aircraft, and inaccurate antiaircraft fire. A raid on Taranto by ten Wellingtons on November 13–14 could be carried out from 5,000 feet because there were once again no searchlights, aircraft, or barrage balloons, and inaccurate gunfire. The blackout was poor in all areas and trains could be seen running between towns fully lit.[16] There were points in 1941 at which intensified bombing of Italy was considered, but the priority in the Mediterranean was to prevent Axis victory in North Africa and to keep the sea lanes open, and this ab-sorbed all the RAF effort in the theater. In October 1941 the Foreign Office suggested that at the right moment, when Italian morale was judged to be cracking, a heavy bomb attack might prove to be "a knock-out blow," but Portal insisted that the war in Libya took priority.[17] The Foreign Office suggested again in January 1942 a surprise raid on German field marshal Albert Kesselring's headquarters at Frascati, near Rome, but the Air Ministry again demurred in favor of military targets in North Africa.[18] In the first nine months of 1942 there was only one Bomber Command raid on Italy, in April against Savona on the Ligurian coast, and thirty-four small raids from Malta against airbases and ports, despite the heavy Axis bombing of the island. For most of the period from late 1940 to the late autumn of 1942, much of Italy was spared anything more than damaging nuisance raids.[19] What Portal did allow was for RAF bombers from Malta to hit "centres of Italian population" if the primary military or economic target could not be hit, a policy already applied in the bombing of Germany.[20]

This situation changed suddenly and dramatically for the Italian population in late October 1942 when the war in North Africa turned in the Allies' favor at El Alamein, followed by the invasion of northwest Africa in November. Imminent Italian defeat encouraged the view, as Churchill put it in early December, that "the heat should be turned on Italy."[21] Portal assured him that Italy would become "Bombing Target No. 1," absorbing the same tonnage of bombs against the main ports and industrial cities as Germany.[22] Bomber Command was ordered to begin area bombing of northern Italian cities as the weather deteriorated over Germany. In the last two months of 1942 six area raids were made on Genoa, seven raids on Turin, and one daylight raid against Milan. There was negligible resistance to the daytime raid, by eighty-eight Lancasters, and bombs were released over Milan from as low as 2,500 feet, though the post-raid report indicated that there had been too few incendiaries dropped to cause the kind of fire damage common in area attacks on Germany. Indeed, detailed research by the RE8 department for the Air Ministry showed that Italian architecture was less prone to either lateral or vertical fire damage than German because of the extensive use of stone and marble, the solid stone flooring, the thickness and mass of the walls, and the wide courtyards and streets. RE8 recommended dropping high explosive on modern multistory apartment blocks, which were more vulnerable than traditional pre–nineteenth century construction, and where a lucky strike in the enclosed courtyard would maximize the blast effect of a bomb.[23] The Air Ministry nevertheless remained confident that incendiary damage in Italian cities would still be greater than damage from high explosive, as long as fire-bombs were dropped accurately enough on the most congested city-center areas, Zones 1 and 2A, and included a proportion of explosive incendiaries to discourage the firefighters.[24]

The onset of the air offensive in October 1942 revealed the extent to which the Italian armed forces, the Fascist Party, and the civil defense organization were unprepared for the effective protection, either active or passive, of the civilian population, and of the economic and industrial resources sustaining Italy's war effort. The Italian Air Force had devoted little effort to constructing a network of air defenses to match the system in Britain or Germany. Its posture had been offensive from the start, still strongly influenced by the legacy of the Italian air theorist Giulio Douhet, who twenty years before had advocated large-scale bombing as the core of air strategy. After three years of war the chief of the air staff, Rino Fougier, was forced to admit that Italy was "in practice without effective defence."[25] Most fighter aircraft had been used in support of the ground armies in Greece and North Africa, while a night-fighter capability scarcely existed despite the fact that most raids until 1943 were by night. By September 1942, Italian night fighters had flown only 380 hours on operations, compared with 158,100 hours for day fighters.[26] Searchlights, antiaircraft batteries, and radar were available in limited quantities, but were not integrated into a national system of communication to cope with identifying and challenging incoming aircraft (even the daylight raid on Milan had prompted the air-raid alarm only after the bombs were already falling). Italian air defenses relied heavily on light 20-millimeter guns, which could not reach high-flying bombers; the plans for 300 batteries of 90-millimeter guns were never met.[27] Fighters were supposed to provide protection during the day, when there were few, if any, raids, while antiaircraft fire was supposed to defend at night, but neither operated at local level under a coordinated command, since antiaircraft artillery was a branch of the army.[28] There were severe shortages of aviation fuel and of modern aircraft, while air-to-ground radio communication had still not been introduced by the end of 1942. Reports from fighter units in the south, now facing daylight raids by American air forces, showed that in many cases scrambled fighters arrived too late to intercept bombers, or in other cases lacked the speed to catch them. One squadron in January 1943 was compelled to send aircraft out just one or two at a time; another group was forced to operate six different types of fighters, some biplanes, some monoplanes, one of them German and eight of them French, with all the problems of coordination and maintenance likely to arise from a hybrid unit.[29]

Following the first major raids in late 1942, an effort was made to find a way of disposing the limited defensive resources to maximize their effectiveness. It was decided that the German system should be carefully investigated to see whether lessons could be drawn for the Italian air defense system; in June 1943, Josef Kammhuber, commander of the German air defenses, came to Italy to discuss how to set up a collaborative air defense structure using Italian and German units and radar. By the summer only one Italian radar station had been completed, while the rest required between six weeks and two months before they would be available.[30] Some Italian pilots were sent for night-fighter training in Germany, but on their return found it difficult to cope with the very different conditions on an Italian airbase.[31] The organization of an integrated and unified air defense system had still not been agreed on when the Mussolini regime collapsed in July. As Italy's military capability evidently declined from late 1942, so German forces stationed in the peninsula came to rely more on their own antiaircraft defenses. By 1943, 300 German antiaircraft batteries had been transferred to Italy, but German forces refused to allow Italian troops to man them, as had been agreed. By June 1943 the German Air Force had night-fighter bases and radar installed along Italy's coastline in thirty-three "boxes," imitating the Kammhuber Line in Germany; two months later there were also ten German night-fighter units protecting Turin, Milan, Genoa, and other north Italian cities as far as Brescia and Venice.[32] This situation could produce its own friction. In Milan in February 1943, German antiaircraft guns opened up on four Italian fighters, forcing them to abandon their operation. When the local Italian commander complained, the German antiaircraft unit told him that as far as they were concerned Italian fighter pilots flew at their own risk.[33]

Italian Air Force leaders had counted from at least 1941 onward on German assistance in supplying aircraft, aero-engines, and advanced machine tools for the Italian aviation industry, but supply never matched requirements. A total of 706 German aircraft were delivered to Italian units over the whole course of the war, some 448 in the period when Italy was an Axis ally. The figure was a fraction of German output, and was divided among fifteen different types, of varying quality. Some 300 were Me109s, but most of these were supplied in 1943 and 1944 to the new National Republican Air Force; there were 155 Ju87 Stuka dive bombers, but the rest were small packets of aircraft for airborne operations or bombing. The Italian Air Force was supplied with only 14 night fighters for the campaign against night bombing.[34] Italy also relied on German supplies of radar equipment. In the course of 1942, five Freya and ten Würzburg sets were made available, a fraction of what was needed. When a new air observation system was organized in the summer of 1943, the Italian Difesa Contraerea Territoriale (DICAT), which had hitherto employed an observer corps based on acoustic devices, was supposed to operate a system of radar "boxes" alongside German radar, but it had to wait for the slow supply of equipment from the German Telefunken manufacturer in order to be able to protect even the major target areas of Milan, Naples, Rome, Turin, and Genoa.[35] German reluctance to supply more was based on a number of considerations. When the Italian Air Force asked for machinery to help them modernize the aircraft industry in the summer of 1941, the German Air Ministry replied that supplies were placed in three categories: essential equipment for German industry; essential machinery for industry in occupied Europe working directly to German orders or for neutrals supplying vital raw materials; and inessential orders, including Italian. The German side took the view that if they helped Italy, they would be assisting a potential competitor when regular commercial activity restarted after the war.[36]

The failure of Italian air defense was matched by the poor state of preparation of civil defense and the welfare and rescue services on which it relied. By a law of March 5, 1934, the provincial prefects, representing the state rather than the Fascist Party, were to assume responsibility for all local civil defense measures. Comprehensive instructions on all aspects of civil defense, including evacuation, shelters, antigas preparations, and firefighting, were first issued in 1938 by the War Ministry.[37] In 1939, to avoid confusion between military and civil responsibilities, the War Ministry confirmed that the prefects rather than the local commanders of Italy's military zones had to organize the protection of the population under the Ministry of the Interior, but instructions continued to be sent from the War Ministry department Protezione Antiaerea on into the war, creating regular arguments over jurisdiction between the two ministries. Each local prefecture had a Provincial Inspectorate for Anti-Air Protection to oversee civil defense measures, but action in the 1930s was slow and piecemeal.[38] For one thing, the funds available were severely limited, around one-tenth of the sums allocated to active air defense. Given these limitations, the state had to decide on an order of priority. It was assumed that major industrial and military targets should be protected, but in case of total war it might be necessary to protect "all the centres of population, based on a scale of the number of inhabitants."[39] Since there was neither the money nor the materials and equipment to provide universal civil defense, resources were concentrated in the most likely target areas. Gas masks, for example, were produced in 1939 for only 2 million out of a population of 45 million, the majority allocated to Rome, Milan, Turin, Genoa, and Naples, the rest to just eleven other cities. The shelter program had scarcely begun in 1939, with places in public shelters for just 72,000 people and in domestic shelters for a further 190,000.[40] Not until the day war was declared, June 10, 1940, did the War Ministry send out to prefects a list of cities ranked in order of priority for civil defense activity, including the blackout. Category "P" included twenty-eight major ports and industrial centers, where civil defense measures were to be introduced "with maximum intensity and speed"; category "M" covered twenty-three smaller cities where civil defense provisions could be introduced "with a slower rhythm and lesser intensity"; category "S" left forty-one cities (some of

which, like Grosseto, were to be almost completely destroyed by bombing) where the authorities were free to carry out measures if they wanted
to, "within the limits of possibility."[41]

Unlike National Socialist Germany, Fascist Italy failed to mobilize a
large mass movement for voluntary civil defense. Instead a more modest
Unione Nazionale Protezione Antiaerea (UNPA) was set up in August
1934 under the direction of the War Ministry to educate the civilian
population on how to observe civil defense requirements, to prepare for
the blackout, to convert cellars and basements into improvised air-raid
shelters, and to train volunteers for post-raid welfare and rescue work.
By 1937, UNPA had recruited only 150,000 volunteers, in contrast to 11
million in Germany, and was constantly short of adequate funds.[42] UNPA
organizers had to be members of the Fascist Party and local block or
house wardens (*capi fabbricato*), responsible for organizing civil defense in
their neighborhood buildings, were also appointed directly by the party
from among UNPA members. Most of them were men over forty-five
(all younger men were reserved for the armed services), women, or
youths; they had in many cases only limited training, and numerous
civil defense exercises before 1940 demonstrated a persistent confusion
between the responsibilities of the police, civil defense workers, and the
military air defense authorities.[43] There can be little doubt that Italy
entered the Second World War with inadequate resources to protect the
civilian population and a civil defense organization uncertain of its functions and short of trained personnel. The inadequacies were fatally exposed when nine RAF bombers arrived over Turin and two over Genoa
on the night of June 10–11, 1940, to find both cities entirely illuminated
despite a plethora of instructions on operating the blackout in priority
areas and regular blackout practices for years. Although detailed orders
for observing the blackout had been distributed in May, there were regular complaints throughout the early period of raiding about its inadequacy, conspicuously so on air force bases and in ministry buildings in
Rome. When Ciampino airbase, near the capital, was asked in October
1940 to explain the bright lights visible through a large window, the
commandant replied that they had been unable to find a curtain large
enough to cover it.[44]

The first raids were militarily insignificant, but they prompted an immediate sense of crisis among a population unprepared for the realities of war. On June 18 the prefect of Genoa complained to the Interior Ministry in Rome that the raids and alerts (three raids and seventeen aircraft) "have caused great delay to the trains."[45] It was immediately realized that alerts had the effect of halting production for long periods as workers scrambled to use the factory shelters or disappeared for hours in panic, leaving machines unattended and electricity and gas switched off. Factories working on war orders received stern instructions to treat each worker "like a soldier, who has an obligation to stay at his post in front of enemy fire."[46] Although factory workers were not in the end militarized, the UNPA personnel found themselves transformed into the status of "mobilized civilian" in August 1940 to maintain standards of discipline and to prevent members from trying to abandon civil defense responsibilities in the face of the real menace of bombing. The *capo fabbricato*, by a law of November 1, 1940, became a public official to emphasize the role of serving the community.[47] For most of Italy beyond the major ports in the south and Sicily serving the Axis armies in North Africa, the bombing ceased to be a serious threat almost at once. Throughout 1941 and the first nine months of 1942 there were almost no raids, and as a result much less pressure to speed up effective civil defense preparations. Shelter provision remained poor (the War Ministry told prefects to let civilians use shelters in factories and public buildings because of the evident deficiency in domestic shelter), while basic protection for industry, including blast walls or sandbagging, depended on the funds available or the good sense of the owner. The same problem confronted the effort to organize the protection of Italy's vast artistic and architectural heritage. Decrees and instructions on protection were regularly published from 1934 onward, but a general law on the Protection of Objects of Artistic or Historic Value was only published by the Ministry of Education in June 1939.[48] Its provisions had scarcely begun to be introduced when on June 6, 1940, just days before the declaration of war, the local superintendents responsible for the artistic heritage were instructed to begin packing up and moving any portable artworks and putting sandbags and cladding over major churches and buildings.

Around 100 depositories were established in Italy and hundreds of monuments given minimum protection, enough to cope with shrapnel or a distant blast, but not enough for a direct hit.[49]

All of this changed with the start of the Allied offensive in the autumn of 1942. The poor level of preparation for attacks on this scale helps to explain their substantial material and psychological impact compared with raiding on Germany. The bombing of Turin, particularly the heavy raids of November 20–21 and 28–29 by aircraft of Bomber Command, which hit both the industrial zone and the city center, resulted in extensive and random destruction. Over 100 firms indicated some damage, but in important cases the loss was almost total. A radar workshop was "entirely destroyed" along with 90 percent of its machinery; a firm producing magnetos for aero-engines was almost completely eliminated by just one bomb; a major aircraft repair factory, Aeronautica d'Italia, was burnt out, leaving only one production line still operating. A report on the raids on Genoa on November 13–14 and 15–16 listed damage to rails, electric power lines, and tunnels, much of which could be repaired, but at the Marconi radio works, production was "completely paralyzed" and had to be transferred to a nearby town.[50] The threat to Italian production, already suffering from severe shortages of materials and equipment, was immediate. The War Ministry on November 15 circulated to all ministries a warning that war industry would now have to be decentralized and dispersed to areas where it could continue to function without the threat of paralyzing air attack.

A few days later the Supreme Command agreed to a comprehensive dispersal program from the main industrial regions. Firms were to try to find tunnels or underground facilities nearby to prevent too much disruption to work patterns or the loss of workers; where these were not available, decentralization into smaller firms in the locality was recommended; in extreme cases a radical transfer to a different zone was required where inessential plants could be closed down and their labor and factory space used by the evacuated firm.[51] For businesses that could not easily be moved—steel production, for example—efforts were at last to be made to supply more antiaircraft batteries, smoke generators to obscure the zone, and a program of camouflage. A special committee was set up in December 1942 composed of representatives from the defense ministries and the Ministry of Corporations to draw up lists week by week of firms that were then ordered to disperse their production. Most went to towns or villages nearby, some into caves or man-made caverns. The dispersal provoked its own problems: shortages of trucks for transport, inadequate rail links, a shortage of skilled workers to assist the transfer, arguments with the Finance Ministry over subsidies and compensation for bombed-out businesses.[52] Italian war production continued to decline during 1943 as firms tried to cope with the sudden demand to improvise the transfer of their production or with the continued heavy bombing of the industrial regions. Firms that had chosen to stay put, like Alfa Romeo, were forced by the summer of 1943 to move, in this case to the Grotte di San Rocco, a system of caves where, despite the stale air and high humidity, it was hoped that the workforce would be more productive than had been possible with regular alerts.[53]

The psychological and physical shock to the Italian population was much greater, as the British had hoped. Secure from the bombing war since the small raids in late 1940, the home front had not developed the infrastructure for civil defense or the mind-set to cope with sudden heavy raiding. Much of the damage was done to residential areas, since these were intended to be area raids. In Turin some 3,230 residential buildings and forty-six schools were destroyed or heavily damaged in the November raids. The local prefect of Turin, whence some 400,000 had fled by December 1942, reported that the demoralized population was "depressed, nervous, irritable and alarmed" not only by the bombing but by a general "sense of exhaustion at the length of the war."[54] Evacuees made their way out to the surrounding countryside or more distant provinces. Iris Origo, an Anglo-American married to an Italian marquis, recorded in her diary the sight of families arriving in Tuscany from Genoa after living for weeks in tunnels under the city "without light, without sufficient water, and in bitter cold," displaying a "healthy, elementary resentment" against those dropping the bombs but a profound anger at the incompetence and mismanagement of the Fascist system that had exposed them to bombing in the first place.[55] The failure to prepare for or to oppose the raids was regarded as a standing indictment of the Mussolini regime. The workers who stayed behind in Turin, according to one report, had calmed down after displaying an "understandable agitation" at being bombed; but they remained in a continued state of anxiety largely because Allied aircraft could regularly be seen circling low over the city by day quite undisturbed. According to another report from Varese, north of Milan, the absence of any effective Italian defense against two Allied aircraft casually photographing the area below left the population "perplexed and alarmed."[56] Leaflets dropped during the raids in November and December listed major cities slated for future bombing (including the ones already bombed) and an appeal to "evacuate the cities" as soon as possible while casualties were still by comparison "very few." Perhaps to rub the message home, small stickers were dropped printed in red letters with the single word "Merda!" ("Oh shit!").[57]

Evacuation was not by 1942 an easy option. In the 1930s evacuating the population from the major cities had been seen as a way of reducing the threat of casualties in the absence of shelters or gas masks. A plan had been distributed to prefects in 1939 designed to halve the city population by encouraging voluntary evacuation where possible and insisting on the compulsory evacuation of children, the elderly, and the sick (as well as convicts, a category more difficult to understand). Those who remained were generally obliged to do so because of the nature of their work or responsibilities. In June 1940 the scheme was virtually abandoned. Voluntary evacuation was uncontrolled, and soon led to prefects insisting that people return home. In the absence of persistent or heavy bombing, urban populations generally remained where they were.[58] The first raids in October 1942 transformed the situation overnight. In November new regulations governing evacuation were drawn up and circulated to all prefects; once again there were compulsory categories, help for voluntary evacuees, and provision for a new category of "evening evacuees" who worked in the city during the day and returned in the evening to families in nearby suburban or rural areas. On December 2, Mussolini publicly endorsed the new wave of evacuations as a "duty" to the community.[59] The mass exodus in November and December was largely unorganized, though Fascist Party workers, mainly youths and women, helped provide food and find accommodation. Since many Italian city dwellers had family or friends in nearby rural areas (an estimated 40 percent in Turin), the social problems were less severe than they might have been, but the problem of overcrowding, the difficulty of organizing regular transport for the "evening" evacuees, and shortages of food soon made themselves felt. Protests from the prefects in March 1943 led to a reversal of policy and evacuees were encouraged instead to return home and run the risk of being bombed. The appeal had little effect. Half of the population of Turin remained away from the city at night, 55 percent in the hinterland, 45 percent in other provinces. A second wave of evacuation occurred in the summer of 1943, reaching two-thirds of the city population, many of the newcomers sleeping in woods and fields in conditions of deteriorating hygiene and widespread hunger.[60]

The crisis induced by bombing was more severe than anything experienced in Germany. As intelligence information filtered through to the Allies, the idea of bombing Italy out of the war suddenly became less fanciful. Sinclair told Churchill in late 1942 that Fascist morale would be badly rocked by bombing war industry and transport but that a final flamboyant attack on Rome "might bring the Fascist state toppling down."[61] An intelligence report to the American Office of Strategic Services (OSS) in April 1943 from Lisbon claimed that the Italian ambassador "expects revolt within a month." A second report a few weeks later passed on news that Pope Pius XII was unhappy about the bombings and now hoped that the generals might seize power and take Italy over to the side of the Allies.[62] As a result the political war on Italy was stepped up in the first months of 1943. American aircraft of the Ninth Air Force, which joined the campaign in December 1942, interspersed the bombing of Italian cities from North African bases with massive leaflet drops, 64 million items in the first eight months of the year. Their purpose, according to the Psychological Warfare Branch (PWB), was to "harden Italian opposition to Mussolini, to Germany and the war." Bombing strengthened the message. There was, the PWB claimed, a special connection between airpower and propaganda.[63] The leaflets explained that bombing was necessary as long as Italy fought at

Germany's side. "Why We Bomb You," dropped in late 1942, challenged the Italian people "to refuse to fight the war of Hitler and Mussolini," but warned them that the innocent would suffer if they did not.[64] This propaganda effort did not go unopposed. Side by side with the leaflets, the Allies were accused by the Italian authorities of dropping explosive pencils to kill Italian children: "in one hand a hypocritical lying message," wrote the *Gazzetta del Popolo,* "in the other a vile death trap."[65] The Fascist press issued its own leaflet accusing the Americans of using black airmen, "the worst men . . . the new tribes of savages."[66] A number of Allied leaflets were sent to Mussolini in July 1943 by his Interior Ministry with the assurance that Italians who read them remained calm and unaffected. Allied propaganda, so it was claimed, "has not produced any effect on public order."[67]

The most difficult thing for the Allies to judge was the right moment to bomb Rome. The idea of bombing the Italian capital went back to the start of the war but was postponed again and again on political, cultural, and religious grounds. When bombers were based in Malta in the autumn of 1940 the practical possibility of hitting the city was hard to resist. On October 28, 1940, following the Italian invasion of Greece, the British Air Ministry immediately ordered the bombing of Rome in retaliation, but the following day the instruction was canceled. Churchill was happy to order the bombing of Rome ("let them have a good dose"), but only when the time seemed appropriate.[68] In the spring of 1941 the Air Ministry told the RAF headquarters in the Middle East that Rome could be bombed at once, without further authorization, if Italian aircraft bombed the center of Athens or Cairo. When an Italian aircraft eventually dropped bombs on an army depot at Abbassia on the outskirts of Cairo in September 1941, the RAF command in the Middle East wanted to bomb Rome without delay, hitting Mussolini's official residence in the Palazzo Venezia and the central railway station, but again the War Cabinet demurred from fear of heavy reprisals against the Egyptian capital.[69] "The selection of the right moment to bomb Rome," wrote Portal to the Foreign Office, "is clearly a matter of some delicacy."[70]

The arguments about bombing Rome rested in the end on its

exceptional symbolic status. Rome was the heart of the Catholic world, home to the neutral Vatican City, whose neutrality had to be respected or risk worldwide condemnation from Catholic communities. It was the heart of the classical Roman Empire, taught to generations of British schoolboys, including those who now commanded the wartime RAF, as a model for the greater British Empire. It was also a primary center of European culture, packed with treasures from the classical world to the age of the high baroque. "Liberal opinion," complained Sinclair to Churchill in December 1942, "regards Rome as one of the shrines of European civilization. This liberal opinion is a bit sticky about bombing."[71] Portal told Sinclair that reluctance could even be found among Bomber Command crews to bombing not only Rome but also Florence or Venice. Sinclair, though a Liberal politician himself, had no cultural scruples—"We must not hedge our airmen round with meticulous restrictions," he scribbled at the side of a memorandum on bombing Rome— but even he could see that there were political risks in damaging "churches, works of art, Cardinals and priests" until the moment when a sudden blow might produce political dividends that outweighed the disadvantages.[72] Anthony Eden, the foreign secretary, was strongly opposed to bombing Rome except as a last resort; he resisted several offers from Arthur Harris to use the 617th Squadron (the "Dambusters") for bombing Mussolini's official residence, the Palazzo Venezia, or his private Villa Torlonia, on the grounds that the attacks were unlikely to kill him and more likely to reverse the decline in popular support for the dictator.[73]

The long hesitation over whether or when to bomb Rome was finally ended in June 1943 as the Allies prepared to invade Sicily after final victory in North Africa on May 13. To prevent German reinforcement, Eisenhower's headquarters in Algiers favored bombing two important rail marshaling yards at Littorio and San Lorenzo, the second close to the ancient basilica of the same name. Churchill wrote to Roosevelt on June 10 asking whether he approved the raid, and four days later Roosevelt replied that he was "*wholly* in agreement" as long as the crews were given the strictest instructions to avoid dropping bombs on the Vatican or on papal property in Rome.[74] This did not end the political arguments. At the Combined Chiefs of Staff meeting a few days later, the prospect of damaging Rome's monuments and churches was discussed again. General George Marshall, the U.S. Army chief of staff, endorsed the raid on the ground that after the bombing of St. Paul's, Westminster Abbey, and the churches on Malta, the United States would "have no qualms about Rome," and the chiefs sent Eisenhower their approval.[75] In early July the archbishop of Canterbury, William Temple, wrote to Sinclair asking for assurance that the ancient and medieval centers of Rome, Florence, and Venice would be excluded from the risk of attack. The Air Ministry told Sinclair that the lives of Allied soldiers should not be placed in jeopardy for the sake of a sacred edifice—"are we to place the monuments of the past before the hopes for the future?"—and two days before the operation to attack the marshaling yards Sinclair told Archbishop Temple that the Allies could not refrain from bombing a military objective even if it was near old or beautiful buildings.[76]

Warnings were dropped by air on Rome on July 3 and 18, and on July 19, 150 B-17s and B-24s from the Northwest African Strategic Air Force, accompanied by 240 B-26s of the U.S. Ninth Air Force, dropped around 1,000 tons on the railway at San Lorenzo and Littorio, and the two airbases at Ciampino. Since the bombing of the marshaling yards was from altitudes of between 19,000 and 24,000 feet, there was extensive damage to the surrounding area. Only eighty bombs were observed to hit the target area around Littorio, and a post-raid interpretation showed that there was heavy damage to the Basilica of San Lorenzo and across twenty-seven residential streets.[77] The following day the pope drove in his black Mercedes through Rome, the first time during the war that he had left Vatican City. The population greeted him with hysterical enthusiasm while aides distributed money among the crowd. There were over 700 dead reported by the emergency services, many in the working-class areas around San Lorenzo, the least Fascist quarter of Rome, but later estimates put the number killed between 1,700 and 2,000.[78] When the king, Victor Emmanuel III, visited the ruins he was met by a sullen crowd that blamed him for the war. "The population is mute, hostile," wrote an aide, "we pass through tears and an icy silence."[79]

Rome's symbolic status ensured that the raid would attract wide publicity. The Combined Chiefs sent Eisenhower instructions that he was to publish a communiqué promptly after the bombing, attesting to the fact that only military objectives had been hit, in order to avoid accusations that the "Shrine of Christendom" had been violated.[80] According to an OSS report, cities in northern Italy welcomed the fact that Fascists in Rome "were getting their medicine at last," and there was evident dour satisfaction among populations already bombed that the cause of their ordeal was suffering too.[81] The papacy, which had appealed several times to turn Rome into an "open city," used the bombing as an opportunity to launch a major diplomatic offensive over the months that followed to try to secure immunity from further attacks. The most significant consequence was the fate of the Mussolini dictatorship, for Rome also symbolized the heart of the Fascist regime. Mussolini had been meeting Hitler at Feltre in northeast Italy on the day Rome was bombed. A "pale and agitated official" had interrupted the two men with the news and Mussolini had hurried back to the capital. The days immediately following the bombing witnessed an atmosphere of mounting political tension. On the evening of July 24 a meeting was summoned of the Fascist Grand Council to which Mussolini was to report on the state of the Italian war effort. That afternoon, Mussolini later wrote, the tension was so acute that "Rome turned pale."[82] At the meeting he admitted that he was for the moment the most loathed man in Italy, but defended his record. By the morning of July 25 there had been a palace revolt; senior Fascists, army commanders, and the king withdrew their support, and Mussolini's rule abruptly ended. The American Psychological Warfare Branch drew an obvious though speculative inference: the bombing of Rome on July 19 meant that by July 25 "the Government was out."[83]

Did bombing bring about the collapse of Mussolini's regime? A good case can be made that the sudden intensification of bombing in 1943 provoked a people already tired of war and fearful of its consequences to reject twenty years of Fascism and to hope for peace. The bombing from the winter of 1942–43 was on an unprecedented scale, 1,592 tons in 1942 but 110,474 tons in 1943, twice the tonnage dropped in the Blitz on Britain.[84] From modest losses in the early raids, the destruction of housing escalated dramatically, 122,000 buildings by March 1943.[85] Most of the operations were now carried out by American air forces that flew high and bombed with poor accuracy. The small town of Grosseto, for example, was largely destroyed when twenty-four B-17s were sent to attack an air force base but hit the residential districts instead, leaving 134 dead. Attacks on the airbase at Foggia, near the east coast, provoked an extraordinary crisis when bombs destroyed the town. After the raid on May 31, some 40 percent of the population fled, leaving shops and factories without manpower and services in disarray. The prefect reported that his city was a spectacle of desolation, "infested by the fumes from putrifying bodies not yet recovered."[86] The ports of the south were heavily bombed in anticipation of the Allied invasion of Sicily: forty-three raids on Palermo; thirty-two on Messina; forty-five on Catania. Naples was struck repeatedly throughout the war, small raids at first from Malta, but from the first heavy raid on December 4, 1942, there were repeated strikes that left 72,000 buildings damaged or destroyed by the spring of 1943. Neapolitans reacted to the bombing as a new war against the home front. "My war started," wrote one, "on the 4 December." The raid, recalled another, "grew infinitely in the memory . . . a monstrous roar of engines seemed to enter the room, in the brain, in every fibre of the body . . . everyone was resigned to die."[87] In Naples and elsewhere in Italy the raids exposed the failure of the regime to provide enough shelter space, to organize effective post-raid welfare, to train sufficient civil defenders, or to mount a serious defense against Allied incursions. Protests dated from the first raids in 1941 against poor food supply, long queues, and the inequality of sacrifice; the decline of support for a failing state long predated the raid on Rome on July 19, 1943.[88]

The evolution of popular disillusionment with the regime can certainly be linked to the more general failure of the state to cope with the consequences of the new offensive. In the spring of 1943 at the Fiat works in Turin spontaneous strikes erupted between March 5 and 8 in protest at the failure to provide an indemnity for all bombed workers, not just for those "evening" evacuees who went back and forth to their families in the countryside. Mingled with protest at rising prices and poor food distribution, the strike movement spread to other factories and eventually as far as Genoa and Milan, until they petered out in April. In Genoa protests against the lack of shelters had already followed the first raids, when crowds of angry women tried to storm the bunkers belonging to the rich.[89] During 1943 a stream of reports reached Rome from provincial prefects indicating the growing demoralization and hostility of the population, though only some of this was due to bombing and much to do with Italy's ineffective war effort. A report from Genoa in May 1943 indicated that "public morale is very depressed" due to food shortages and the complete incapacity of the Italian military effort, as well as the material and morale damage caused by the bombs. From Turin it was reported that workers could no longer see any point in working for a failed system but displayed instead "apathy and indifference." Palermo, hit repeatedly by bombing in 1943, reported in May that almost all civilian activities were paralyzed, the population terrorized and the streets deserted. Even the reports from Rome, not yet bombed, indicated a population that was now "mistrustful and desperate," awaiting a political upheaval of some kind: "Faith in victory seems to be almost completely lost . . . the conviction of the uselessness of past and present efforts is almost general."[90] Iris Origo, listening to discussions going on around her in Tuscany, complained that it was all "talk, talk, talk, and no action," reflecting a "dumb, fatalistic apathy" among a people no longer willing to go on with the war, but unable to find a means to end it.[91] Ordinary Italians turned to religion or superstition to help cope with the dilemma of being trapped between a remorseless bombing and a failed state. In Livorno (Leghorn) the absence of bombing until late May 1943 was attributed to the protection of the Madonna of Montenero (though it was also rumored that Churchill had a lover in the city, which explained its immunity). In Sardinia a prayer was composed against the bombing: "Ave Maria, full of grace, make it so the sirens do not sound, the aeroplanes do not come. . . . Jesus, Joseph, Mary, make it that the English lose their way."[92]

The bombing of Rome was neither the occasion nor the cause of the overthrow of Mussolini, but a symptom of a state in the final throes of disintegration. In a body racked with ailments, it is not always easy to identify the precise cause of death. Moreover, the fall of the dictator brought neither peace to the Italian people nor an end to the bombing.

Indeed, a better case can be made for the argument that bombing accelerated the decision of Mussolini's successor, Marshal Pietro Badoglio, together with the king, to seek an armistice in early September to take Italy out of the war after the initial decision to continue it. At first the Allies were uncertain how to react to the news of Mussolini's fall and bombing was briefly suspended. But on July 31, after a four-day respite, Portal told Air Marshal Arthur Tedder, commander of the Mediterranean Air Force, to start bombing Naples and Rome again in order to pressure the Badoglio government to seek "peace terms."[93] BBC Radio Algiers broadcast the news to Italian listeners that bombing would start again on August 1. Three million leaflets were distributed suggesting that abandoning the Germans was better than more "iron and fire"; another 6 million dropped in mid-August explained that as long as the government in Rome continued the war, so the bombing would continue.[94]

The situation was confused by the request from the Badoglio regime in late July to make Rome an open city. American bombing was halted while the implications were examined. On August 2, Marshall drew up the American War Department's view of what constituted an open city—removal of all Italian and German forces, evacuation of all government agencies, cessation of all war production, and no roads or rail links to be used for military purposes—but a day later the War Cabinet in London rejected any idea of allowing Rome this status, even if the rigorous American demands could be met, as long as the war in Italy continued. On August 13, Eisenhower was notified that bombing could start again and Rome was bombed once more, the first of fifty-one further raids. The pope again visited the damaged area, accompanied by shouts from the crowd of "Long live peace!"[95] Bombing spread out from Rome to other cities in central Italy. Pisa was struck on August 31 by 144 aircraft, leaving 953 dead and wide destruction in the residential areas of the city. Foggia was struck again, leading to its almost complete evacuation. On August 27, Pescara was bombed, with 1,600 dead. American intelligence reports suggested widespread rioting and anti-Fascist demonstrations once the bombing had restarted.[96] On September 3, Badoglio bowed to reality, despite the looming menace of German occupation, and signed an armistice. On September 8, news of Italy's surrender was formally announced, but for most Italians the war at the side of Germany was simply exchanged overnight for a war under German control.

"Certainly Bomb": The Liberation of Italy

The bombing campaign in Italy from September 1943 until the end of the war had not been planned for. The sudden collapse of Italian belligerency provoked an immediate and violent reaction from the large German armed forces now stationed throughout the peninsula. The Italian armed forces were disarmed, interned, and in most cases sent north to Greater Germany as forced labor. Italy became an occupied country, like France, with the difference that in this case a new Mussolini regime, the Italian Social Republic (usually known as the Salò Republic after the town on Lake Garda) was set up following Mussolini's dramatic rescue by German special forces from imprisonment. It was in effect a puppet government, entirely subservient to the military requirements of the German commander in chief south, Field Marshal Albert Kesselring, but a number of Italian airmen and soldiers remained loyal to Fascism and served alongside German forces. German leaders were not so much concerned with re-creating the Fascist state as they were with preventing the Allies from reaching central Europe, but for the Italian people Fascist government remained in place, widely unpopular and despised, until Mussolini's death at the hands of Italian partisans in late April 1945.

For the Allies, Italy presented both problems and opportunities. The priority from September 1943, after the conquest of Sicily and the first tentative landings on the toe of the peninsula, was to defeat the German armed forces and, if that could be done quickly, to liberate Italy and prepare to assault the German empire from the south. If it could not be done easily, as soon appeared the case, Allied air forces would be used to support the land war and to bomb when necessary more distant targets. Even a limited presence on mainland Italy, however, presented the opportunity of raiding German targets from the Mediterranean that were difficult to reach from British bases. These differing aims required a reorganization of the confused mix of air force commands that had grown up with the expansion of the Mediterranean and North African air forces, both British and American. In early 1943 targets in Italy were hit by the Northwest African Strategic Air Force and the combined Tactical Bomber Force, made up of some RAF units together with the American Twelfth and Ninth air forces. RAF units under Air Marshal Tedder formed the Mediterranean Air Force, which had operated chiefly in the desert war, but had begun to raid Italy after the defeat of the Axis in Tunisia in May 1943. In the autumn of 1943 these forces were amalgamated into the Mediterranean Allied Air Forces (MAAF), including both British and American air units. The British component was limited in size; the American element was enlarged to create a Fifteenth Air Force for long-range bombing missions, first under General Doolittle (until he replaced Ira Eaker in Britain as commander of the Eighth) and then under Major General Nathan Twining. The Twelfth Air Force under the command of Major General John Cannon was assigned to tactical missions, including bombing, to replace the Ninth, which was sent to support the Normandy invasion of June 1944. The overall command of MAAF, which was activated on December 10, 1943, was given to Eaker, who took up his post in January; his deputy was the British air marshal John Slessor. On January 4, 1944, the American component of MAAF came formally under the control of General Spaatz when he was appointed overall commander of all American strategic and tactical air forces in Europe, but in practice only the strategic Fifteenth Air Force was responsible to Spaatz, while the tactical air forces answered to the Mediterranean supreme commander—first, Eisenhower; then, from January 1944, General Henry Maitland Wilson. The Fifteenth Air Force was activated on November 1, 1943, with its headquarters near the ruined town of Foggia. Its squadrons were spread over a dozen bomber bases from where they flew missions to Austria, southern Germany, and the Balkans, as well as against Italian targets. The RAF strategic force, composed mainly of medium Wellington bombers, was based at Brindisi.[97]

A clear distinction between strategic and tactical bombing was difficult to make, since there were occasions when strategic forces were needed to support the ground war or to destroy communications far in the rear of German armies, while for the rest of the time they were expected to raid German targets. In December 1943, for example, out of a list of forty-eight strategic targets for Operation Pointblank supplied by the American Economic Warfare Division, only seven were in Italy, and only two (both ball-bearing factories) were included on the list of priorities.[98] In November 1943 the operations director at MAAF, Brigadier General Lauris Norstad, ordered the tactical air forces to concentrate on supporting the ground war and bombing communications targets up to a line from Civitavecchia (near Rome) to Ancona on the east coast; the strategic air forces, by this time principally the Fifteenth Air Force, were to bomb all communications targets north of this line, using either Martin B-26 Marauder medium bombers or their B-17s and B-24s when necessary.[99] The line shifted with the fortunes of the ground battle, but not until March 1, 1945, did the tactical air forces assume responsibility for the whole area of northern Italy still under German occupation.[100] The difference between a tactical and a strategic raid often made little difference to the population around the target, but the distinction was maintained in air force records. Out of 124,000 tons dropped on Italian targets in the first five months of 1944, 78,700 were deemed to be strategic, the rest tactical.[101]

Most of the raiding in the last twenty months of the war was carried out by American air forces. The statistical breakdown of air raids by the different Allied air forces is set out in table 5.1.

The American raids were usually larger than those of the RAF, since at Brindisi the British kept only a small number of Wellingtons for strategic tasks. By the end of the campaign in the spring of 1945 there were over 1,900 American heavy bombers based in the Mediterranean out of an overall total of almost 4,300 American combat aircraft. Heavy bombers flew a total of 18,518 sorties in 1943, 90,383 in 1944, though some of their bomb load was directed at German or Balkan targets. From 1943 to the end of the war, American heavy bombers stationed in the Mediterranean dropped 112,000 tons on Italian targets and 143,000 tons on Greater Germany and German-occupied central Europe; tactical bombers dropped a further 163,000 tons on Italian targets, a grand total by Allied air forces on Italy of 276,312 tons.[102]

For the bomber crews flying in Italy the dangers were considerably less than in Germany, though the weather remained a persistent hazard despite the claim made by Harris that bombing could be conducted on all but 8 percent of days in the Mediterranean in January and 5 percent in July (compared with 51 percent and 21 percent lost days flying from English bases).[103] In late 1942 the Italian Air Force had only forty-four serviceable night fighters, most of them biplanes incapable of effective intervention.[104] The opposition from Italian antiaircraft and fighters disappeared in autumn 1943, to be replaced with a large concentration of German antiaircraft artillery around key targets. But the overwhelming air superiority enjoyed by Allied forces following the Axis defeat in Africa and the conquest of Sicily meant that by 1943 there was little effective fighter opposition from the German Air Force, with the result that higher levels of accuracy were possible than could be achieved over Germany. Bomber Command raids in summer 1943 using H2S radar dropped between 70 and 87 percent of bombs within three miles of their target, while most raids on Berlin at the same time could only achieve 30 percent—not precise by any standard, but more concentrated and hence

Table 5.1: Raids on Italy by British and American Air Forces, 1940–45

Year	Bomber Command	RAF Med.	U.S. 9th	U.S. 12th	U.S. 15th
1940	20	15	—	—	—
1941	4	92	—	—	—
1942	15	40	5	—	—
1943	13	136	92	145	27
1944	—	76	—	73	164
1945	—	22	—	12	42
Total	**52**	**381**	**97**	**230**	**233**

Of the 381 raids by the RAF Med., 135 were small raids mounted from Maltese bases.

Source: Calculated from Marco Gioannini and Giulio Massobrio, *Bombardate l'Italia: Storia della guerra di distruzione aerea, 1940–45* (Milan: Rizzoli, 2007), Web site appendix.

more destructive.[105] By late 1943 there were only 470 German aircraft dispersed between Sardinia, mainland Italy, and the Aegean. Maintenance problems meant a low level of serviceability, while numerical inferiority, a result of the diversion of aircraft to defend the Reich, provoked a constant attrition cycle that could not be reversed. By the summer of 1944 there were only 370 serviceable aircraft in the theater, most of them single-engine fighters flown by both German and Italian pilots.[106] American bomber losses in 1944 and 1945 were largely due to antiaircraft fire or accident, 1,829 against 626 credited to fighter interception.[107] Not for nothing was Joseph Heller's antihero in *Catch-22*, a novel of the American air experience in Italy, afraid of the "goddam foul black tiers of flak . . . bursting, and booming and billowing all around."[108]

Though the defensive threat was less, the question of what to bomb was not easily answered, partly because detailed intelligence on Italian industry and communications after the German occupation in September 1943 was difficult to acquire and partly because of the persistent uncertainty surrounding the fate of Italy's historic heritage. There were disagreements not only over what to bomb, but what not to bomb. In contrast to the British attitude, Washington recognized that it was politically expedient to preserve Italian culture from unnecessary damage in order to limit accusations of Allied barbarism. On August 20, 1943, Roosevelt gave his approval for the establishment of the American Commission for the Protection and Salvage of Artistic and Historic Monuments in Europe. The commission was advised by an academic working group set up by the American Council of Learned Societies, which produced 160 detailed maps of Italian cities using the Italian Baedeker guide, with most cultural monuments clearly marked. These were sent to MAAF and added to the dossiers for briefing officers when organizing an operation.[109] In April 1944 a list was distributed to all Allied air forces in Italy, listing cities in three categories for bombing purposes. The first category comprised Rome, Florence, Venice, and Torcello, which could only be bombed with specific instructions from the high command; the second category of nineteen historic cities, including Ravenna, Assisi, Pavia, Parma, and Montepulciano, were not regarded prima facie as militarily important, but could be bombed under circumstances of military necessity; the third category was made up of twenty-four cities, most with architecturally outstanding city centers, such as Brescia, Siena, Pisa, Bologna, and Viterbo, which were deemed to contain or be near military objectives. These could be bombed freely "and any consequential damage accepted."[110] If any city in categories two and three was occupied by the enemy in a zone of operations, no restrictions were to be observed. Otherwise crews were instructed only to bomb objectives by day if not obscured by cloud, and by night if illumination made the precise military objective sufficiently clear. The rules gave a great deal of discretion to the individual pilot, and in practice, given the wide inaccuracy of high-level bombing, in Italy as elsewhere, protection for cultural monuments was observed only within wide operational limits.

Even the cities in category one came to be bombed when military circumstances dictated. "Nothing," wrote Eisenhower for the Allied forces in Italy, "can stand against the argument of military necessity."[111] In February 1944, MAAF headquarters decided that the rail center at Florence would have to be bombed as part of the effort to cut German communications. British air marshal John Slessor told the Air Ministry that only the most experienced crews would be used. He pointed out that the famous Duomo was at least a mile distant from the target: "It would be very bad luck if any of the really famous buildings were hit." On March 1, Churchill was asked for his view; he scribbled on the letter, "certainly bomb," and the following day the chiefs of staff approved the raid.[112] Luck stayed with the bomber crews this time and the Duomo remained intact. They were told that some damage to the city was inevitable, but should not be construed as "limiting your operations," which explains the damage to two hospitals and the death of 215 Florentines.[113] On April 20, 1944, bombs fell on Venice for the first time, contrary to instructions. An investigation showed that fifty-four American bombers, finding their targets in Trieste covered by cloud, defied orders and bombed the port of Venice as a target of opportunity from 24,000 feet. Once again, luck was in their favor; the city's historic heart suffered no damage.[114]

This was not the case with the efforts to avoid bombing Vatican City.

The bombing of Rome continued despite the persistent efforts by the papacy, the Badoglio government (now based in southern Italy in the Allied zone), and even Mussolini's new Salò regime to get the Allies to accept the status of open city for the capital. Roosevelt, with a large Catholic minority in the United States, was more inclined to discuss the possibility, but Churchill worried that if Rome were made an open city, it would hamper Allied military efforts to pursue the Germans up the western side of the peninsula. The Combined Chiefs discussed the issue in late September but remained deadlocked.[115] Then on November 5 four bombs were dropped on the Vatican, causing serious damage to the Governatorato Palace, the seat of Vatican government. The first reaction from the British ambassador to the Vatican, Sir Francis D'Arcy Osborne, was to blame the Germans for the raid as a propaganda stunt, but a few days later investigations showed that one American aircraft, bombing at night, had lost contact with the rest of the force and dropped bombs in error.[116] Roosevelt once again tried to revive British interest in the demilitarization of Rome, but the British remained adamant that it would place too many restrictions on the Allied ground campaign, and on December 7, Roosevelt finally conceded that it was "inadvisable" to pursue the matter any further.[117] Rome continued to be bombed and over 7,000 Romans died in the course of the year from the first bombing in July 1943 to the Allied capture of the city in June 1944. The accidental raid on the Vatican showed how difficult it was under conditions of night, poor weather, or human error to avoid widespread damage to Italy's cultural heritage even with the best of intentions.

There was nevertheless nothing accidental about the most controversial raid of all, against the fourteenth-century Benedictine abbey on the mountaintop overlooking the small town of Cassino on February 15, 1944. The building dominated the Liri valley position where the Allied armies were attempting to unhinge the German defenses along the so-called Gustav Line, which stretched from the coast north of Naples to Ortona on the Adriatic coast. On November 4, 1943, Eisenhower wrote to the Allied Fifteenth Army Group that the Monte Cassino abbey was a protected building; the pope asked both the Germans and the Allies to respect its sacred status. When Eisenhower was replaced by Wilson as

supreme commander in January 1944, the principle that historic buildings would only be hit under conditions of "absolute necessity" still prevailed, though it did not prevent the bombing of the papal estate at
Castel Gandolfo on February 11, which destroyed the convent and killed
twenty-seven nuns.[118] At Cassino all attempts to dislodge the German
forces from the small town or the hilltop had failed, and it is not difficult
to understand why frustration with the slow progress of the campaign
and the likelihood of high casualties encouraged the local army units to
ask for air assistance. There were strong rumors (but no hard evidence)
that the abbey was already occupied by German forces. On February
11, the 4th Indian Division, planning its assault, made a request for "intense bombing" of the hilltop and its surroundings, including the monastery; on February 12 the commander of the division, Major General
Francis Tuker, insisted that the monastery should be destroyed whether
it was occupied by the Germans or not, since it would easily become a
strongpoint if the Germans chose to use it.[119] The decision should have
been made at the highest level by the Combined Chiefs of Staff and
agreed to by Spaatz, but in the end it was made by General Harold Alexander, overall army commander, and endorsed by Wilson. Eaker was
instructed to launch an attack on February 15 using both strategic and
tactical forces. He flew in a light plane over the abbey the day before and
later wrote, to justify the attack, that he could see it was full of soldiers,
radio masts, and machine-gun nests, though his initial judgment was
quite different.[120] The following day, wave after wave of heavy and medium bombers pounded the monastery with 351 tons of bombs, killing
230 of the Italian civilians who had taken refuge in the abbey precincts.

The destruction was welcomed by the troops on the ground, who
were seen to cheer as the bombers flew in, but the results of these raids
(and attacks by Kittyhawk and Mustang fighter-bombers during the two
days that followed) were mixed. The vast abbey walls remained intact,
in places to a height of thirty feet, making the gutted building ideal for
the German forces who now obligingly occupied it as a hilltop fortress
from where they repelled the Indian and New Zealand efforts to dislodge them. The operation suffered from the usual bomb pattern, some
bombs destroying the headquarters of the local Eighth Army commander,

General Oliver Leese, three miles from the abbey, and the French Corps headquarters twelve miles away.[121] The publicity surrounding the destruction, much of it hostile, forced the chiefs of staff to investigate who had ordered the bombing and why. On March 9, Wilson replied that the abbey building was undoubtedly "part of the German main defensive position" and had to be eliminated to ensure success.[122] Slessor, Eaker's deputy, recalled in his memoirs that no one among the troops would have believed for a moment that the Germans were not using the building as a fortress, "so the Abbey had to go," but he was critical of what the bombing actually achieved given that it took more months to capture the hilltop, now fully occupied by the enemy.[123] A War Office investigation in 1949 into the circumstances of the bombing finally confirmed that there had been no evidence of German occupation to justify the raids, except for an unsubstantiated claim that a telescope had been glimpsed from a window. Eyewitness accounts were collected from Italian women who had sheltered in the abbey during the bombing. "Even allowing for the excitable tendencies of women of Latin race," ran the report, their testimony gave a credible if "prosaic" account of what happened. Some 2,000 from the population of Cassino had sought shelter on German advice in the church of San Giuseppe behind the abbey; on February 3, after angry protests from the crowd of evacuees, some of whom had been wounded by shellfire, the monks let them into the abbey. There were no German soldiers or equipment to be seen, except for two German medical officers tending to the wounded Italians. After the bombing, the civilians made their way where they could. The four women who gave accounts of the abbey reached Allied lines and were interviewed less than two weeks after the raid had taken place.[124]

The Monte Cassino raid was one of the few times that the strategic bombers were asked to support a ground operation directly. A few days later they also obliterated what was left of the town of Cassino itself. In both cases the result was to hinder army efforts to profit from the bombing. On April 16, 1944, Slessor wrote to Portal to complain about how counterproductive heavy bombing was on the battlefield itself: "We hamper our own movement by throwing the debris of houses across roads and making craters that become tank obstacles . . . we are inevitably bound—as we did at Cassino—to cause casualties to our own people."[125] Most of the bombing that took place in 1944 and 1945 was directed farther away from the battlefront, designed to impede German communications throughout Italy and to destroy Italian industries working directly to German orders. The communications campaign was the more important. Italian geography worked both for and against the Allies. The narrow peninsula with its mountainous spine meant that communication by road and rail was mainly confined to narrow channels running down the eastern and western coasts of Italy. These channels represented tempting targets for interruption. On the other hand, the Allied armies were also confined to the hilly coastal zones where there were innumerable natural barriers to favor a defending army. In the winter, mud, heavy rain, and snow slowed up any ground advance, while poor weather restricted air attacks on transport and allowed the enemy time to restock and reinforce.

The origins of the planning for a systematic campaign against communications lay in the hurried survey of the bombing of Sicily carried out by Solly Zuckerman, who among his many duties had been allocated in 1942 to the British Combined Operations headquarters as a scientific adviser. In January 1943 he was sent out to the Mediterranean theater to investigate how Rommel had managed to escape across Libya despite massive Allied superiority on the ground and in the air. Zuckerman stayed on in an advisory role and was asked to supply evaluations for the invasion of Sicily in July 1943, for which he recommended attacking the "nodal points" of the Sicilian and south Italian railway network, and particularly railway repair shops, depots, and shunting yards. His advice was followed and his eventual report, based on a survey of the results in Sicily and southern Italy, suggested the campaign had been "an outstanding success."[126] Early in 1944, MAAF discussed the possibility of applying the Zuckerman model to the railway system in central and northern Italy to cut Kesselring's forces off from their supply chain. The preference was for attacks on rail centers rather than bridges and viaducts, which Zuckerman thought were too difficult to destroy, but there was considerable support among American planners for bridge bombing using fighter-bombers and medium bombers for a task that called for effective precision. In the end, the communications campaign targeted both.

On February 18, Eaker issued a directive for the communications campaign, detailing the northern marshaling yards for the strategic air forces and the rail links farther south for the tactical forces.[127] The Fifteenth Air Force targets were the main railway yards at Padua, Verona, Bolzano, Turin, Genoa, and Milan, with secondary targets at Treviso, Venice Mestre, Vicenza, and Alessandria. The tactical air forces were detailed to attack rail facilities in central Italy, at least 100 miles from the German front line, to maximize the strain on enemy road traffic.[128] The campaign was given the code name Operation Strangle, to indicate its purpose, and lasted from March 15 until May 11 using every kind of aircraft available. The heavy bombers dropped 10,649 tons, the tactical air forces a total of 22,454, for a total loss of 365 aircraft, chiefly fighter-bombers and mainly to antiaircraft fire.[129] Of the bomb total, two-thirds were dropped on communication lines. In April a second campaign was ordered to coincide with an Allied ground assault designed to push the German army back past Rome. This operation was code-named Diadem and lasted to June 22, by which time Rome was in Allied hands and German forces were retreating rapidly toward a new defensive "Gothic Line" north of Florence. This time 51,500 tons of bombs were dropped, 19,000 by the Fifteenth Air Force, for the loss of only 108 bombers, a rate of only 0.4 percent of all sorties. Of this total tonnage, three-quarters fell on transport targets.[130] The outcome was again mixed. The destruction of bridges and viaducts proved more effective than the assault on marshaling yards, which could be used for through traffic even when there was extensive damage. A disappointed evaluation by the MAAF Analysis Section showed that repairs were quickly carried out on rail centers in northern Italy and through tracks reopened. "Military traffic was not hindered to a significant degree by these attacks," the report concluded. Nor did they cause "complete internal economic collapse."[131] Kesselring, when interviewed in August 1945 after the end of the war, confirmed that the transport plan had not been a great success. Bridges were quickly replaced by pontoon bridges, camouflaged in some way; urgent countermeasures had been taken to restore road and rail links.

An air strategy exclusively centered on cutting off supplies, Kesselring concluded, was not likely to be effective.[132]

The second set of targets for strategic attack lay in the surviving industry of the area occupied by German forces in northern and central Italy. As soon as the Italian surrender was certain, Albert Speer, the German minister for armaments and war production, was appointed on September 13, 1943, as plenipotentiary for Italian war production; General Hans Leyers acted as his permanent deputy in Italy.[133] The decision to exploit Italian production was taken for a number of reasons: first, to be able to supply German forces in the field with finished or repaired weapons; second, to supply Germany with additional equipment, resources, and raw materials; and third, to act as a large subcontracting base for components, engines, or subassemblies where there was a shortage of capacity in Germany. A number of committees were established to oversee the transition of Italian industry to German orders, but the priority was the exploitation of the Italian aircraft industry. Four companies made parts for Focke-Wulf, Heinkel, Messerschmitt, and Junkers, while Alfa Romeo, Fiat, and Isotta Fraschini produced the Daimler-Benz DB605 and the Junkers Jumo 213 aero-engines. Once it was evident that production could be continued rather than have the machines and labor transferred to Germany, Italian producers cooperated with the German occupiers; workers, though in general hostile to both the Germans and the new Mussolini republic, had little choice but to work or face unemployment or deportation.[134] In some cases German intervention encouraged industrial modernization and increased productivity in an industry that had failed to adapt to the needs of war, but the revival of production faced numerous obstacles in the supply of materials, transport facilities, and machinery and once it had begun, the major industrial regions again became targets for the Allied strategic air forces. Heavy raids were made in the spring and summer of 1944, hitting a total of 420 plants, particularly in the armaments, engineering, and steel sectors, and Italian oil depots at Trieste, Fiume, and Marghera.[135] Extensive damage was done to industrial buildings, but a regular toll of Italian civilian lives was exacted with each raid, including deaths from low-level strafing of workers. One of the worst was the raid on Milan on

October 20, 1944, which resulted in some of the aircraft dropping their bombs in error on residential districts, killing 614 people, including 184 pupils and 19 teachers at the Francesco Crispi school, more than three times the number killed in all the other seventeen raids on the city in the course of the year.[136]

The renewal of bombing prompted the German authorities to continue the program of dispersal that had begun in haste in the winter of 1942–43 and been suspended with the armistice. Advantage was taken of the extensive road tunnels and caves available in northern Italy. Work on parts for the Me262 turbojet fighter continued in the first months of 1945 in tunnels around Bolzano; the Fiat works moved production to a stretch of tunnel between Riva and Gargnano on the coast of Lake Garda, where 1,300 laborers continued to work until April of that year; Caproni produced parts for the V-weapons and the Me262 in a hydraulic tunnel between the River Adige and Garda. Of the twenty-eight sites chosen for underground dispersal, only ten actually reached the stage of production.[137] From early 1945 onward, before the final offensive to drive the Germans across the Po valley toward the Alps, a renewed communications campaign against rail centers and bridges across northern Italy undermined the frantic efforts of the German authorities to extract what they could from the shrunken Italian industrial economy. By February the MAAF targets committee had difficulty finding any targets left in northern Italy that had not already been hit or were regarded as worth the effort of bombing. Nevertheless, raids continued to be made until the last days of the conflict. As in Germany, Allied air forces by the end of the war possessed a good deal of excess capacity for which there were no longer suitable objectives.[138]

The cost of the bombing campaign to the Italian economy is difficult to compute, not least because of the extensive damage done by artillery and battlefront aviation that resembled the consequences of bombing. The effect on German efforts to extract additional war production in northern Italy has been estimated at a loss of 30 percent in productive performance due to absenteeism and regular alarms. The overall loss of capacity for Italian industry has been estimated at 10 percent, since most industry was not an object of bombing; the loss for war-related industries was much higher, one-half for naval production, 21 percent for the metallurgical industries, 12 percent for machine engineering.[139] By contrast, the textile sector lost 0.5 percent, the electrical industry 4 percent, and the chemical industry 6 percent of capacity. Damage to housing, though heavy in particular cities, has been estimated at only 6 percent of total housing stock. The chief target was the Italian transport system, where two-fifths of the rail network was destroyed along with half the rolling stock and an estimated 90 percent of all Italian trucks. The five years of war reduced Italian national income by 1945 to one-half the level of 1938.[140] This mainly affected not the German occupiers but a large part of the Italian civil population, which endured widespread losses of housing and possessions, unemployment, and food shortages until well after the end of the conflict.

The Italian population was faced in the last two years of war with the bleak prospect of living on a wide and dangerous battlefield, caught between the German occupiers, the new Fascist regime, and the slowly advancing Allies. Most of the casualties from bombing occurred in the period after the armistice, since airpower was the one thing the Allies could project easily into the occupied zones. The Allied powers recognized the nature of the dilemma facing most Italians who had not yet been liberated, but they also wanted them to undermine the German occupation from within by acts of resistance or sabotage. An OSS report on the situation in Italy in September 1943 suggested a propaganda campaign to make Italians realize "that the real people's war of liberation has started for them," and to encourage them to make life miserable for the Germans.[141] It was also recognized that bombing was likely to be politically counterproductive if it seemed to bring liberation no nearer. The ambassador D'Arcy Osborne warned the Foreign Office in March 1944 that bombing was "slowly but surely turning Italian opinion against us" because of the evident disproportion between civilian damage and military results. The Italians, D'Arcy Osborne continued, were beginning to think that German occupation was a lesser evil "than Anglo-Saxon liberation."[142] Eden was sufficiently concerned to ask Sinclair in May to ensure that bombing was carried out with strict precautions against a "friendly population," whose will to resist the Germans was weakened, rather than strengthened, by bombing and who were likely to harbor "bitter memories of our method of liberation."[143] The first priority for both Allies was nevertheless to defeat Germany rather than inhibit military action from fear of alienating Italian sentiments. When in May 1944 news reached London of the bombing of the village of Sonnino, where forty-five people were killed, including thirty children, Churchill complained that the air force should not treat a cobelligerent population the same way as an enemy. Sinclair replied that it was not up to him to tell the air forces in the Mediterranean how to conduct their campaign; the vice chief of the air staff, Air Marshal Sir Douglas Evill, told Churchill that it was the fault of the Italian population for continuing to live near bombing targets.[144] Throughout the campaign the political necessity of defeating Germany overrode any political considerations toward the population held hostage on the battlefield.

There is no doubt that the long experience of bombing did strain Italian support for their imminent liberation. Iris Origo noted in her diary in the summer of 1944 how much British propaganda was resented, with its "bland assumption that peace at any price will be welcomed by the Italians."[145] Corrado Di Pompeo, a ministry official in Rome, recorded in his diary in February 1944 that at first his heart rejoiced "when American aircraft passed overhead," but after regular raiding and the routine sight of blood-smeared corpses, he changed his mind: "Americans are zero; they only know how to destroy and how to kill the defenseless."[146] Nevertheless, the prospects for widespread rebellion against the authority of the Salò Republic or the German armed forces were unrealistic, and throughout the period acts of violent resistance were met by the Germans with atrocious reprisals.[147] Under these circumstances rumor and superstition increased in importance as a mechanism for coping with the real dilemmas of occupation. The most remarkable was the claim, widely repeated, that Padre Pio, the Apulian monk (and now a saint), had safeguarded the region where he lived by rising in the air to the level of the bombers and staring the pilots in the eye until they turned back to base, their bomb loads still on board.[148] In numerous cases, appeals were made to city saints or Madonnas to safeguard buildings and family from bomb damage. The Catholic Church also encouraged a mood of consolation and resignation. When he visited the damaged area of San Giovanni in Rome on August 15, 1943, the pope told the crowd, "Follow the path of virtue and faith in God."[149] Priests in Tuscany, writing of the bombing in 1944, talked of a "Calvary," or "our hour has come," or "for us the hour of trial" as they prepared themselves and their congregations to endure the cruelties of air war.[150] By 1945, with the authority of the Salò Republic collapsing in northern Italy, the church came to play an increasingly important part in the daily lives of many ordinary Italians confronted with the continuous hardships imposed by bombing.

More important in terms of survival was the expansion of civil defense facilities and the widespread flight from the cities. For those who remained in urban areas, air-raid alerts became an almost daily occurrence. In Bologna province, for example, there were ninety-four air raids from July 1943 to April 1945, which killed an estimated 2,481 people, injured another 2,000, and destroyed 13 percent of Bologna's buildings. In 1942 there was one alert lasting 1 hour 29 minutes; in 1943 the alerts lasted for 115 hours, in 1944 for 285 hours, and in 1945, 77 hours.[151] In Bologna, as in many other cities, the provision of shelter spaces had expanded rapidly with the onset of regular bombing. In October 1943 there had been spaces for 26,000 people out of a population of more than 600,000; by the spring of 1945 it was estimated that the 84 bombproof shelters, 15 trenches, and 25 tunnels could accommodate 100,000.[152] In Milan, where trenches, school shelters, and public shelters could hold 177,000 by October 1942, plans were begun to build a further 179 shelters to house another 38,000 people, while 8,000 domestic shelters were in the process of being overhauled to meet shelter standards.[153] Since most raids occurred during the day from 1943 onward, it was important that there was adequate temporary shelter in inner-city areas for daytime workers. In many cases the shelters provided little protection from bomb blasts and suffered from poor ventilation and overcrowding. In two cases overcrowding caused heavy casualties, one in Genoa's Le Grazie tunnel, where 354 people died, and one at Porta San Gennaro in Naples, where 286 perished. There was wide distrust of shelter provision, and with the onset of bombing, millions of Italians either left for the nearby countryside or found refuge in a local cellar or basement.[154] The prefect of Palermo reported in May 1943 that all the public shelters hit had collapsed, leaving the population with "no faith in the remaining ones." The inspector of air-raid protection in Rome, reporting on the raids in July and August 1943, found that no signs had been put up indicating where the shelters were, and that there was no list of domestic shelters, making it impossible to know where their entombed occupants might be.[155]

The response to rising danger in the cities was a widespread wave of largely uncoordinated evacuation from all the threatened cities and towns, accompanied by compulsory evacuation insisted on by the German authorities from major combat zones and the Italian littoral.[156] As in Germany, the Fascist Party used evacuation as a way to try to tie the refugees more closely to the systems for party welfare and assistance, but the often spontaneous and large-scale evacuations were difficult to control, and were often followed by reverse evacuations as people returned to the risks of the city from poorly resourced rural retreats or realized that bombing could happen anywhere there was a railway. Most evacuees found temporary accommodation in nearby villages and small towns. In Turin province the population of nearby towns grew by up to 150 percent as 165,000 people abandoned the city.[157] By May 1944 the number of evacuees in the main northern provinces had reached 646,000, of which 426,000 came from the main industrial cities of Milan, Turin, and Genoa.[158] The total number of evacuees and refugees was estimated at 2.28 million by the spring of 1944, spread out among fifty-one separate Italian provinces.[159] The crowds of evacuees were distrusted by the authorities as a potential source of social protest and closely monitored, but for most the chief issue was to find enough food to survive on. Italy by 1944 was a very mobile society as people sought to find areas of greater safety, or were forced to move from military zones, or tried to return to the liberated south.[160]

Even here in southern Italy safety was not guaranteed, for German aircraft bombed southern towns on occasion, including six raids on the already heavily bombed port of Naples. On the evening of December 2, 1943, a small raid by thirty-five German aircraft on the crowded dock at

Bari led to widespread devastation and, unknown to the local population, the release of a toxic mix of oil and liquid mustard gas. The presence of this deadly mixture was suppressed by British authorities in the post-raid communiqué but was evident on the wounded men taken from the water and tended in the local hospital, where the staff were only notified that gas burns were to be expected when the symptoms were already well established and patients dying.[161] Unknown to the Italian population, the Allies held large stocks of chemical weapons in Italy, ready to be used at a moment's notice. Since Mussolini had been responsible for using gas in Italy's war in Ethiopia, the prospect of a desperate act by the enemy in Italy was not entirely out of the question, but Allied chemical resources in Italy dwarfed the quantities used by Italians in Africa. By 1945, American forces had over 10 million pounds of mustard gas and 3 million pounds of other gases in the theater, to be used principally by the air forces, which had 110,000 gas bombs in store.[162] The air force was ordered to keep on hand sufficient weapons to be able to carry out at least forty-five days of continuous gas warfare from the air, aimed at enemy ports and military installations. In the event of a chemical attack by German or Italian forces in Italy, the Mediterranean Tactical Air Forces were ordered to use gas weapons in the immediate battle area without restriction, and to drop gas bombs on other military targets away from "heavily populated areas" but, by implication, on areas that were nevertheless populated. Stocks of gas weapons were held in store in the area around Foggia, which explains the ship at Bari whose contents were destined to boost existing supplies in southern Italy.[163]

Throughout the peninsula, air-raid protection for the cultural sites threatened by widespread bombing assumed a fresh urgency. In November 1942 the education minister, Giuseppe Bottai, issued directives to intensify the work of protecting cultural buildings and churches, but it proved impossible to provide adequate physical covering that would withstand a direct hit or the effects of large-scale conflagrations. In Naples the destruction of the church of Santa Chiara by fire was only intensified by the protective covering outside, which increased the internal temperature.[164] After Rome tried to claim status as an "open city," other cities followed suit to avoid damage to their historic centers and collections of books and pictures. Padua, attacked forty times, finally submitted its request on February 1, 1945, by which time the damage had been done. With the advancing battlefront it was also decided that much of the movable art and book collections stored in depositories in the countryside were in danger from air warfare and the retreating German armed forces, and the order was issued in October 1943 to bring the collections back to the cities where local art superintendents could safeguard them as best they could in underground storage facilities.[165] In the end the survival or otherwise of cultural treasures was arbitrary, dependent on where the bombs were strewn, or the intelligence of the curators who guarded them, or the attitude of the local German officials of the *Kunstschutz* (art protection) organization. In Turin some thirteen churches had protected status, but only six survived relatively unscathed. In the convent of Santa Maria della Grazie in Milan, Leonardo's fresco of *The Last Supper* survived a direct hit by a miracle, as the rest of the refectory that housed it was demolished.[166] Among the other providential survivals was Botticelli's *Primavera,* spotted by two journalists sent to interview Indian soldiers in a villa outside Florence in sight of German tanks, the painting unboxed on the floor among the men brewing tea.[167] The strenuous efforts made meant that in the end much was saved, but a good deal of an invaluable patrimony was also destroyed or stolen.

The Allied hope that the bombing offensive might encourage Italian resistance to German exploitation, theft, and savagery was as ambiguous as the early ambition to unseat Mussolini by bombing Rome. Opposition to the German occupiers certainly did not need bombing as a spur. Indeed, some case can be made to show that bombing actually harmed the prospects for the resistance and alienated potential supporters of the Allied cause. This was not the case with the strike movement in northern Italy that was linked to the onset of repeated and heavy raids from the autumn of 1943 onward. Strikers at the Fiat works in November 1943 cited bombing as one of the reasons for running the risk of German intervention and Fascist brutality. The risks were substantial. In Turin a German deputy, sent to calm down the social protests, executed the protest leaders and deported 1,000 workers to Germany.[168] In the summer of 1944 further large-scale protests against dispersal plans brought so many workers out on strike that the German authorities were unable to cope. In December 1944 a strike crippled Milan's factories. Among these workers were some who risked acts of sabotage to accompany the bombing, while many workers who refused to be deported to work in Germany disappeared into the mountains to join the partisans. The partisan movement had close contacts with the Allies from 1944, and used these channels to explain that the poor accuracy, high flying, and inadvertent damage caused by Allied bombing alienated potential resisters, particularly as many of the areas hit were working class and anti-Fascist.[169] Partisan protests in late 1944 highlighted many examples where tactical bombing hit neither the Germans nor an evident military target, making a "tragic situation" for the population all the harder. For the Allies this ran the risk, as intelligence information made clear, that the population might turn to supporting Soviet communism rather than continue to identify with the forces responsible for killing them. D'Arcy Osborne, in one of his dispatches from Vatican City, pointed out that many Italians contrasted the Western Allies unkindly with the Red Army, which was "the only one that gets results by fair military means," unlike Anglo-American forces who "compensate their military inferiority by murder and destructive bombing."[170] In this sense bombing had a much greater and longer-term social and political impact in Italy than it had in Germany, and one that fitted imperfectly with the "liberating" image that Allied propaganda sought to convey. Communism continued to thrive in postwar Italy in cities where the housing losses, food shortages, and unemployment compromised the achievements of peace.

The human costs of the bombing war in Italy are difficult to compute, because Sicily and the Italian peninsula were the sites of two years of harsh warfare that raked its way slowly across the whole territory. Damage to buildings, the loss of artworks, deaths and injuries were caused not only by bombing but by artillery fire, rockets, fighter aircraft, and even by naval fire along the coastline, and from both sides, Allied and Axis. The 8,549 deaths in Sicily before the armistice, for example, were the result of all forms of military action, whereas the 7,000 in Rome were due almost entirely to bombing.[171] The postwar statistical record drawn up to show the cause of deaths as a result of the war indicated a

very precise total of 59,796, though other categories of "poorly specified" or "poorly defined" or "various acts of war" count a further 27,762,
some of whom were almost certainly bombing victims.[172] The total number of seriously injured has not been recorded. In cases where urban records provide a list of injured—for example in Bologna—the number is
around the same as those killed, in this case 2,000. The number of those
injured, whether severely or lightly, is not likely to be less than the figure
of around 60,000 killed. Of the number of dead, about 32,000 were
men, 27,000 women, a reflection of the extent of female evacuation and
the compulsory requirement for men to carry on working in the cities on
German orders or to help with post-raid rescue and clearance. That the
level of casualty was not much higher, given that the weight of bombs
dropped in Italy was almost six times the weight dropped on Britain
during the Blitz, may owe something to the fact that many of the objectives for the tactical bombing attacks in 1943–45 were against rural or
small-town targets rather than major cities. It certainly owed little to any
Allied concern to limit damage to Italian society. The Allied view was
that Mussolini had brought this destruction on Italy's head by daring to
attack Britain side by side with Germany in 1940: "He insisted in par-
ticipating in the bombing of England," claimed one British propaganda
leaflet, "and so doing sowed the wind and condemned [Italians] to harvest the tempest." In another leaflet produced in July 1943, the British
Political Warfare Executive (PWE) reminded Italian readers that "the
bombardment of the civil population is an official Fascist theory."[173] In
the war of words and bombs, Douhet, Italy's great theorist of unrestricted strategic bombing, came home to roost.

Chapter 6

Bombing Friends, Bombing Enemies: Germany's New Order

In early 1944 the U.S. Eighth Air Force published a widely circulated publicity booklet, *Target: Germany*. It purported to tell the story of the first year of the American bombing of the German enemy, "raining havoc and destruction on the Nazi war machine." The inside covers show a map of Europe where the force's bombs had fallen: there are nineteen German targets but forty-five in France, Belgium, and the Netherlands. For much of the first year the apprentice American force took the short route across the Channel to bombard military-economic installations working for the German war effort. Most of the photographs in the richly illustrated text are of raids made on France and the Low Countries. The first raid on German territory finally took place late in January 1943, but more accessible European objectives were still seen as a useful way to get the crews to cut their teeth on combat.[1]

The bombing of European targets outside Germany and Italy was in reality more complex than this and was large in scale. The occupied territories of western and northern Europe—France, Belgium, the Netherlands, Norway, and Denmark—absorbed almost 30 percent of the bomb tonnage dropped by the American and British bomber forces. The occupied or satellite countries in eastern Europe and the Balkans absorbed another 6.7 percent.[2] Well over one-third of all Allied bombs dropped on Europe fell on the German New Order, making the experience of bombing in the Second World War a European-wide one. The purpose behind these bombings, and their consequences for the populations caught in the coils of German expansion, are seldom treated as systematically as accounts of the bombing of Germany, yet they cost at least 70,000–75,000 lives, most of them among peoples sympathetic to the Allied cause. The majority of those losses, and most of the bomb tonnage that caused them, occurred in western Europe, principally France. These areas were near enough to reach and in 1944 provided the territorial springboard for the Allied invasion of the western half of the German empire. Much of the bombing in the later period was in a loose sense tactical, intended to achieve a direct military end for the ground forces; but much of it was long-distance and heavy, designed to nibble away at war production for Germany in occupied territory, but also to promote wider political aims. According to the British Political Warfare Executive, set up in 1941, bombing of occupied areas promoted both "morale breaking" and "morale making." Collaborators and Germans would be demoralized by the experience; those who did not collaborate would be encouraged at the prospect of liberation.[3] To be bombed in order to be free now seems paradoxical, but the policy governed much of the bombing that spread out across the entire European continent between 1940 and 1945.

Disordering the "New Order"

The rapid German victories between 1939 and spring 1941 brought most of continental Europe under German control. Neutral states were compelled to work with the changed balance of power, while those states that were allied with Germany—Slovakia, Hungary, Romania, Croatia, Bulgaria—were satellites of the powerful German core. In Berlin the sudden transformation in German fortunes brought a flood of plans and projects for a European New Order that would secure Germany's permanent political and economic hegemony. The conquered states became involuntary participants in this larger project, compelled to provide economic resources, finance, and labor for the German war effort, and doomed to be the battlefields on which the enlarged German empire would defend its borders. Right to the end of the war there were still German forces fighting in the Netherlands, Italy, Hungary, and the Czech lands, alongside the defense of the German homeland.

It was inevitable under these circumstances that Britain, and later the United States, would have to engage the enemy on the territory of occupied or satellite states where German forces were dispersed. Until the Western states were in a position to mount a major land invasion, airpower was regarded as the principal means available to attack Axis military resources across Europe and to undermine the extended war economy established throughout the German New Order. Because of the problem of aircraft range and the danger of flying for long periods over heavily defended territory, it was only possible in the first years of war to attack targets in western and northern Europe. Eastern and southeastern Europe were only struck regularly from late 1943 onward, chiefly by the American Fifteenth Air Force based in southern Italy. An alternative was to rely on local resistance and sabotage, and throughout the period in which air forces bombed targets in New Order Europe, the Allies tried to encourage the occupied peoples to take a hand in their own liberation even while subject to regular bomb attacks. Throughout the war period this resulted in awkward decisions for the Allies about the level of damage that should be inflicted on targets situated among potentially friendly civilian communities forced to work for the German war machine or, in some cases, voluntarily collaborating with it. The erosion of ethical restraints on bombing German industrial cities was a simpler issue than the moral dilemma of causing civilian casualties among those held hostage by German military success.

The debate about bombing friends as well as enemies began as soon as Britain was expelled from the Continent and France defeated. In July 1940 the War Cabinet agreed that any military target could be bombed in the northern and western parts of France occupied by German forces (though not in the unoccupied zone ruled from the new government seat at Vichy).[4] The problem was to decide what counted as a military target since it was already assumed that in the German case this meant industry, utilities, and worker morale alongside more evidently military objectives. On August 17, Air Intelligence provided a list of what were defined as "Fringe Targets" around the edge of occupied Europe that could be subjected to air attack. The fringe included targets up to thirty miles inland in Norway, Denmark, the Netherlands, Belgium, and France. In Scandinavia there were twenty-five targets, consisting chiefly of oil installations and airbases (but including the Norwegian port of Kristiansund, already heavily bombed by German aircraft); in the Low Countries

sixty-one targets were identified, ranging from electricity-generating stations to iron and steelworks; in France thirty-one targets were listed
around the coast from Dunkirk to Bordeaux, including an aero-engine
works at Le Havre, a power station at Nantes, and a marshaling yard
at Lille, a little over thirty miles from the coast.[5] Over the course of the
autumn, additional target information was processed and detailed target maps supplied. The list for France expanded to fifty-eight objectives
located in the thirty-mile zone: nine oil installations, eight chemical
plants, eleven aircraft works, seven blast furnaces/steel mills, eleven
shipbuilding firms, and another dozen smaller targets. The targets were
given star ratings to indicate their importance, three stars for the highest
priority, of which there were seventy-seven by the spring of 1941.[6] In
May 1941 it was agreed that the RAF could undertake attacks on "deep
penetration targets" where these could be reached easily by day without
excessive risk.[7] Conscientious anxieties played little part in these early
raids. Escalation was soon built into the process of deciding what could
be hit and under what conditions.

Many of the early raids around the fringe were tactical bombing operations carried out to forestall the possibility of German invasion and
to hit at targets that supported the German air-sea blockade. They were
carried out not only by Bomber Command but also by Coastal Command aircraft; in 1941, once the invasion threat had receded, Fighter
Command also attacked coastal targets in large-scale fighter sweeps—
the so-called Circus operations—planned to lure the German Air Force
into combat and undermine air force organization. The strategic assault
of economic and military targets nevertheless remained limited at first,
partly from concern over the political implications, partly from the military risks of attacks in daylight (night bombing had not yet been approved for non-German targets) against the large German air forces
stationed across northwest Europe. The reaction of the communities
subjected to fringe bombing was mixed. There was evidence that the occupied peoples positively wanted the RAF to bomb the military and industrial targets in their midst. A Dutch request arrived in August 1940
to bomb the Fokker aircraft works in Amsterdam and a munitions plant
at Hemburg ("working full capacity. Please bomb it").[8] A long letter

from a French sympathizer forwarded to the Foreign Office in July 1941 claimed that many people in occupied France wanted the RAF to bomb factories working for the Germans: "The bombardments not only have a considerable material effect, but are of primary importance for the future morale of the anglophile population."[9] More letters arrived via Lisbon from Belgian sources explaining that the failure to bomb collaborating factories was attributed in Belgium to British "decadence." A Belgian Resistance newspaper, *Le Peuple*, published a report of an informal referendum on bombing taken among workers in factories exploited by the Germans. "Not a single discordant voice," ran the report. "They all wish for the destruction of plants which work for the enemy."[10]

Alongside this more positive evidence, there were regular protests from the localities that were the object of the early fringe bombing and concern expressed by the governments-in-exile in London (Dutch, Belgian, Norwegian) as well as the Free French led by General Charles de Gaulle. The Dutch government-in-exile wanted assurances in 1940 that bombing would not harm Dutch civilians or civilian property.[11] The objections from French sources were a response to the regular small raiding that occurred throughout 1940 and 1941, a total according to French records of 210 raids in 1940 and 439 in 1941 in which 1,650 people were killed and 2,311 injured.[12] In May 1941 the mayors of the coastal towns of Dieppe, Brest, Lorient, and Bordeaux protested through the U.S. legation at Vichy about heavy bombing of residential areas. The British foreign secretary, Anthony Eden, asked the Air Ministry to take every care to minimize damage to civilian property and civilian casualties, but the raids continued nonetheless. Intelligence information suggested that the French population still believed that the RAF bombed only the military targets, while it was the Germans who bombed residential districts to try to stoke up popular hatred of the British.[13] In August the Vichy regime made a formal diplomatic protest to the British government via the British embassy in Madrid about the inaccuracy of British bombing, followed by further representations in September about the continual bombing of the Channel port of Le Havre, where it was claimed that British aircraft had attacked the town fifty-five times in a year (it was indeed a regular RAF target), scattering bombs all over the residential quarters and killing 205 people. The municipal council of Le Havre recognized that the port was "on 'the front' in the war between Germany and England" but also pointed out that "no state of war between France and England exists."[14] The Air Ministry declined to reply to the French protest, but instead told the Foreign Office that accuracy was impossible when operations had to be carried out under indifferent weather conditions and the German habit of generating a smoke screen as soon as the bombers were sighted. The Bomber Directorate suspected that the protests were part of an orchestrated German plot to compel the RAF to reduce their offensive against French targets.[15]

A number of factors explain the escalating scale and lethality of bomber attacks on non-German targets from late 1941 onward. The military situation brought increasing pressure to bomb targets in occupied Europe that served the German submarine and air blockade. The prime targets were to be found in the ports of western France and the airfields and bases across the Channel in northern France and the Low Countries. It was also soon evident that armaments, aviation, and shipbuilding firms in the occupied zones were being utilized by the Germans, either directly taken over or the result of a collaborative agreement.[16] The Ministry of Economic Warfare considered these to be necessary targets for air attack, not only because they were more accessible than most targets in Germany, but because their destruction might reduce the willingness of occupied populations to work for the extended German war effort. On June 23, 1941, the War Cabinet approved the bombing of factories throughout occupied France, but only by daylight, to ensure a better level of accuracy, though the RAF still held back on political grounds from bombing targets far inland, including Paris. Small raids on German shipping at Brest had begun in January 1941, but the first heavy raids against Brest and Lorient, including in this case night attacks, started later in the spring, though these too remained intermittent and ineffective until the War Cabinet recommended a sustained campaign in October 1941 to reduce the dangerous threat to the Atlantic sea lanes, which it failed to do.[17] At the same cabinet meeting Churchill agreed to attacks on goods trains in northern France, which were assumed to be carrying supplies or ammunition for German forces.

Step by step the military imperatives for bombing targets in occupied Europe pushed the RAF across the thresholds established in 1940.

The second factor was political. During the course of 1941, as it became clear that the war was to be a long-drawn-out conflict, the conduct of political warfare assumed a larger place. The Ministry of Economic Warfare, under the Labour politician Hugh Dalton, was at the heart of the indirect strategy laid down in 1940 to use bombing, blockade, propaganda, and subversion as the means to undermine German control of occupied Europe. In the summer of 1941 the minister of information, Brendan Bracken, proposed setting up a separate organization, the Political Warfare Executive (PWE), jointly run by the Foreign Office and the Ministries of Information and Economic Warfare, to coordinate the political initiatives directed at occupied Europe. It was formally constituted in the late summer under Robert Bruce Lockhart, with the journalist Ritchie Calder as director of plans and propaganda.[18] The PWE directors immediately saw the connection between British bombing strategy and political propaganda. The Joint Planning Staff in June 1941 had already indicated that active armed resistance in Europe would never work "until bombing has created suitable conditions."[19] Calder began to lobby for a bombing policy governed not only by military and economic considerations, but by political calculation. He was impressed by the apparent enthusiasm for being bombed expressed in contacts with the occupied populations. The Norwegians in particular wanted to feel that they were still part of the war. Bombing, he thought, would "prove British interest in Norway"; Air Intelligence confirmed that Norwegians were "puzzled and bewildered" by the absence of raiding.[20] In a memorandum for the Foreign Office on the "RAF and Morale-Making," Calder recommended bombing as a way to show the occupied populations that even if Britain could not invade, the German occupiers would not be immune from attack. On the other hand, he continued, "lack of British activity creates the impression that we have 'abandoned' the Occupied Territories." Calder thought that "demonstration raids," as he called them, would counter a mood of "listlessness and despair," and invigorate militant forces among the occupied peoples.[21]

The weapon of political warfare was the leaflet rather than the bomb. Throughout the conflict the political warfare and intelligence establishment remained convinced that propaganda from the air was worthwhile, and millions of small sheets, or pamphlets or newsletters, were jettisoned over the target populations, both enemy and ally. Aircrews seem to have been less persuaded of the value, and the PWE directed some of its propaganda effort to instilling confidence among them that leaflets, or "nickels," as they were known, were just another, and equally effective, tool in the Allies' armory. "They are a weapon aimed not at men's bodies," ran one training manual, "but at their minds."[22] The task of drafting, translating, printing, and distributing the material was enormous. The statistics of RAF leaflet drops are set out in table 6.1; the wartime total was 1.4 billion.

Each piece of aerial propaganda had to be discussed in terms of the current political and military situation, and the language adjusted accordingly. It also had to be considered that for many of those who risked picking up and reading the material, this was the only way they could get news of what was happening in the wider war. Allied confidence in the effects of leafleting was sustained by regular intelligence about the popular demand for more. In Belgium it was reported that children sold the leaflets they picked up for pocket money; French peasants concluded that if the RAF could waste time dropping leaflets, it "must be very strong."[23] On the actual effect of leaflet drops the evidence remains speculative. In Germany and Italy it was a crime to pick them up at all.

There is little doubt that the PWE greatly exaggerated the political effects likely to be derived from a combination of propaganda and judicious bombing. Like the optimistic assessments of imminent social crisis in Germany in 1940 or 1941, every straw of information was eagerly clutched at. Violations of air-raid precautions were particularly highlighted. It was reported that seventeen Dutchmen had been heavily fined in the summer of 1941 for staying out on the street during a raid singing "Who's Afraid of the Big Bad Wolf?" News from Denmark suggested that 20,672 prosecutions for blackout irregularities had been pursued in 1941.[24] British political warfare assumed that the working class would be the most likely to challenge the occupiers because they were by definition supposed to be antifascist. Directives to the BBC European Service

Table 6.1: British Leaflet Distribution by Aircraft by Year and Territory, 1939–45 (in thousands)

Country	1939	1940	1941	1942	1943	1944	1945
Germany	31,095	43,179	29,243	125,536	240,259	176,272	63,762
France	—	21,045	25,870	151,999	282,173	163,330	—
Belgium	—	232	210	5,175	1,888	3,294	—
Netherlands	—	51	463	2,250	6,260	294	960
Denmark	—	—	797	546	856	2,419	1,175
Norway	—	32	700	1,497	1,320	222	6,782
Poland	—	1,421	—	—	—	—	—
Italy	—	891	164	3,726	13,828	—	—
Czechoslovakia	—	2,250	59	—	1,344	—	—
Misc.	—	702	—	665	295	—	—
Total	**31,095**	**69,803**	**57,506**	**291,394**	**548,223**	**345,831**	**72,679**

Source: Calculated from TNA, FO 898/457, PWE, "Annual Dissemination of Leaflets by Aircraft and Balloon, 1939–1945."

in early 1942 asked broadcasters to "take *absolutely for granted* the work-men in enslaved countries are unhesitatingly behind our bombing pol-icy, and will do all they can to help it."[25] Bombing was supposed to suggest that liberation was close behind it and to encourage hatred of the German enemy. The leaflet campaign was deliberately designed to reflect this two-pronged argument. In the spring of 1941 messages to Belgium were to be divided into "Hope—45%," "Hatred—40%," "Self-interest—10%," and "Self-respect—5%." Propaganda aimed at the Netherlands had "Certainty of Allied Victory" top of the list, with 35 percent. In between the leaflets, the idea was to bomb intermittently to keep such hopes alive. In 1941 this appeal was possible. A Belgian woman who had escaped to Britain in October 1941 claimed the raids "were the best propaganda the British had done."[26] The years of apparent inactivity that followed undermined confidence in occupied Europe and damp-ened the hopes of Britain's political warriors.

By the end of 1941 these military and political considerations com-bined to push the RAF toward a more vigorous and less discriminate bombing strategy for the occupied regions. At a War Cabinet discussion in November 1941, the air minister pressed for permission to begin nighttime raids against industrial targets across occupied Europe, in-cluding the major Renault works at Boulogne-Billancourt in Paris. Churchill insisted on postponing any decision until the political out-come was properly evaluated, but following RAF representations early in 1942, which claimed that the morale of the occupied population was better in areas that had been bombed than in those so far neglected, Churchill finally agreed to allow general bombing of European targets, and the cabinet confirmed the change at its meeting on February 5, 1942.[27] The RAF scarcely needed to be prompted. The Air Ministry in November 1941 had already discussed the use of incendiary bombs in attacks on industrial targets in occupied Europe to achieve maximum damage and "to gladden the hearts of all men and women loyal . . . to the Allied cause."[28] In April 1942, Bomber Command was instructed to bomb targets in France, the Low Countries, and Denmark ("knock them about"), so that local people would demand proper protection and hence disperse the German antiaircraft defenses.[29] The PWE reached an agreement with the RAF to ensure that political considerations would play a part in target planning. The link between political propaganda and bombing policy became institutionalized and remained throughout the war a central element in bombing all the areas under German control.[30]

France: Bombed into Freedom

The long arguments over whether or not to bomb targets in Paris were finally resolved by the decision in February 1942 to allow raids against important industrial targets throughout Europe. The raid on the Renault works became a test case of the dual strategy of economic attrition and morale making. On the night of March 3–4, Bomber Command sent off 235 bombers, the largest number yet for a single raid. Flying in to bomb from between 2,000 and 4,000 feet with no antiaircraft fire to distract them, 222 aircraft dropped 419 tons on the factory and the surrounding workers' housing. Much of the factory area was destroyed, though not the machinery in the buildings, at the cost of only one aircraft lost. No alarm had sounded and casualties among the local population were high: French civil defense first reported 513 killed and more than 1,500 injured, but the Paris prefecture eventually confirmed 391 dead and 558 seriously injured, more than twice the number inflicted so far by the RAF on any one night over Germany. An estimated 300 buildings were destroyed and another 160 severely damaged.[31]

The works were bombed not only for the potential damage to German vehicle output in the plant, but also to test how French opinion might react to an escalation of the bombing war. Leaflets were dropped beforehand "To the populations of occupied France," explaining that any factory working for the Germans would now be bombed and encouraging workers to get a job in the countryside or to go on strike for better protection; a BBC broadcast warned French people to stay away from collaborating businesses.[32] The PWE wanted to find out as soon as possible after the raid how French workers had reacted, "because it is the workers who have been killed, the workers who 'go slow' and sabotage."[33] Although the French authorities orchestrated elaborate public funerary events, the British soon received indications that the reaction had not been as adverse as the public outcry might have suggested. A report from Roosevelt's special emissary in the new French capital at Vichy, William Leahy, explained that the propaganda campaign fostered by the regime with German support had been ineffective and that there was little evidence of anti-British feeling either in Paris or in the rest of unoccupied France. Anthony Eden, who had been anxious about the political effect, was pleased with the results of a "well-executed blow," which he believed evoked "admiration and respect" among the people who suffered it. He was now willing to support further raids.[34] In Paris itself the operation was welcomed by many as a sign that liberation might be one step nearer. "Nobody was indignant," wrote one witness. "Most hid their jubilation badly." Blame was directed much more at the French and German authorities for failing to sound the alert, or to enforce the blackout effectively, or to provide adequate shelters.[35] Rumors quickly circulated outside Paris that the Germans had deliberately locked the workers inside the factory or had barred entry to the shelters. It was said that Parisians called out "Long Live Great Britain!" as they lay dying.[36] The raid itself had limited results. Reports reached London in June that only 10 percent of the machine tools had been lost as a result of the bombing and that the Renault works was operating at between 75 and 100 percent of its pre-raid capacity.[37]

The heavy bombing of French targets between 1942 and 1944 by Bomber Command and the Eighth Air Force was undertaken in the hope that casualties could be kept to a minimum to avoid alienating the French population, while serious damage was done to Germany's western war effort. It was unfortunate for the French people that heavy bombers were seen as the necessary weapon for a number of very different strategic purposes for which they were far from ideal.[38] From 1942 onward, bombers were used to try to destroy the German submarine presence on the French west coast by bombing the almost indestructible submarine pens and the surrounding port areas; in 1943–44 bombers were directed at small V-weapons sites that were difficult to find and to damage; in the months running up to the invasion of Normandy, the Transportation Plan similarly directed all Allied bomber forces (including the Fifteenth Air Force in Italy) against small rail targets, many of them embedded in urban areas; finally, the months of campaigning across France in the summer of 1944 led to regular calls from the ground forces for heavy bomber support, producing some of the most devastating raids of the war against French towns defended by German troops. The result was to strain popular French support for the bombing of the enemy in their midst.[39] Although anti-German sentiment was not reversed by the air campaign, there was a widespread belief that a less damaging strategy could have been found to achieve the same end.

The antisubmarine campaign exemplified the many contradictions that plagued the decisions to bomb France more heavily. When Bomber Command was directed to attack German naval targets on the French west coast, the orders were to attack only the dock areas and in conditions of good visibility. In April 1942, Harris wrote to Portal suggesting that the best way to slow down the German submarine war and to drive fear into the French workforce was to carry out "real blitzes" on Brest, Lorient, St.-Nazaire, La Rochelle, and Bordeaux.[40] Portal demurred since this was still contrary to government policy; in October 1942 guidelines were issued to Bomber Command to ensure that the air force would understand that only identifiable objectives in clear weather could be bombed and only if it was certain that heavy loss of civilian life would not result.[41] But when the Atlantic battle reached its climax in late 1942, the Anti-U-Boat Committee, under pressure from the Admiralty, finally recommended abandoning all caution by destroying through area attacks the towns that involuntarily hosted the German submarines. The War Cabinet approved the decision on January 11, 1943, and although Harris by now no longer wanted operational distractions from his attacks on Germany, his desire for "real blitzes" on the French ports could now be fulfilled.[42] Harris described the French interlude in his memoirs as "one of the most infuriating episodes" in the whole bomber offensive and an evident "misuse of air power."[43] He blamed the Admiralty for the change in priority, and there is no doubt that the driving force behind it was the chief of the naval staff, Admiral Sir Dudley Pound, who in this case was able to persuade Churchill and Eden to swallow their scruples over bombing civilians for the sake of the survival of British sea traffic.

There had already been more than twenty attacks on the ports since 1940, which had served to encourage the Germans to take every precaution to protect submarine operations.[44] In the summer of 1942 a British propaganda campaign had been launched from the air against coastal towns from Dunkirk to St.-Nazaire warning the populations to evacuate: "we must carry on a war to the death [*guerre à l'outrance*] against the submarines."[45] Most evacuations did not occur until the bombing started in earnest. The heaviest raiding was reserved for Lorient, where nine major attacks by Bomber Command in January and February dropped 4,286 tons of bombs (including 2,500 tons of incendiaries) with the specific purpose of burning down the town. On one raid the bombers carried 1,000 tons of bombs, the same quantity dropped a few months before by the German Air Force in the major raid on the city of Stalingrad.[46] The French report following the bombing described the raids as an example of a new RAF strategy of "scorched earth"; not a building in the town remained standing or unscathed, a "dead city," except for the submarine pens undamaged by the rain of bombs. In a thirty-kilometer radius from the town thousands of village buildings had been destroyed and farms incinerated.[47] The PWE published an uncompromising statement following the bombing that the innocent must inevitably suffer with the guilty: "The violence and frequency of attacks involving hardship to civilians must increase."[48] Naval Intelligence assessments were nevertheless unimpressed by Bomber Command's strategy "of the bludgeon," which failed to halt the rate of submarine operation significantly in any of the major targets, despite Pound's earlier insistence that it would. In April, Harris was instructed to stop and to turn once again to Germany.[49] The submarine threat was defeated in spring 1943 by using aircraft to attack submarines at sea rather than in their concrete pens. The pens themselves became vulnerable only after the development of two giant bombs—"Tallboy" and "Grand Slam"—both the brainchild of Barnes Wallis, the engineer who designed the bomb used to breach the Ruhr dams. But the first five-ton Tallboy was only used against Brest on August 5, 1944, and Lorient a day later, while the ten-ton Grand Slam was available only for the last month of the war.[50]

Bomber Command was joined by the Eighth Air Force for the submarine campaign, and the round-the-clock bombing gave the local population, most of whom had been evacuated or had sensibly evacuated themselves, no respite from the raiding. Daylight bombing was carried out from a considerable height by crews who were still learning their way. The wide spread of bombs dropped from high altitude and the rising casualty rates that resulted provoked a sudden change in French attitudes during the course of 1943. A French Resistance worker who arrived in Britain in April 1943 warned his new hosts that the population was deeply hostile to high-level American raids, which threatened to undermine irretrievably "the friendly feelings of the entire French population towards the Allies."[51] This shift in opinion coincided with the decision to spread the bombing over all French territory following the German occupation of the southern, unoccupied zone in November 1942. On December 21 the Air Ministry was informed by the Foreign Office that raids on southern French cities were now legally permitted, and on December 29 the BBC broadcast the same warning to the population living there to stay away from military and industrial targets that had been given to the occupied north earlier in the year.[52] The guidelines issued in October 1942 on the conduct of raids now applied to the whole of France, but they were not binding on the Eighth Air Force, and when the Renault works in Boulogne-Billancourt were bombed again on April 4, 1943, by eighty-five B-17 Flying Fortresses, the results were very different from a year before. Just under half the bombs hit the industrial complex, but the rest were scattered over a wide residential area. One bomb penetrated the metro station at Pont-de-Sèvres; eighty corpses were identified there and the unidentified human remains put into twenty-six coffins.[53] There was little antiaircraft fire or fighter pursuit and only four aircraft were lost. The alarm had sounded only one minute before the bombs began to fall, giving the population out on the streets in the hour after lunch little chance to find shelter. The civil defense counted 403 dead and 600 injured; 118 buildings were destroyed and 480 heavily damaged.[54] Two days later, René Massigli, the French ambassador (representing the provisional government in London), met Eden to complain about the "feeling of exasperation" in France caused by civilian losses from careless American bombing. In Brittany, he claimed, the reaction of the population was to cry out, "Vive la R.A.F.!" but also "À bas l'Américain Air Force."[55]

Raids over the summer by both air forces were reined back. The Eighth Air Force was asked to confine raids just to the submarine bases and to try to find an operational pattern that would reduce French civilian deaths. Arnold objected to British requests to restrict what American air forces could do and an agreed list was drawn up of objectives in France that could be attacked after a warning to the population. Massigli was told by Eden that the American air forces would only bomb certain selected targets and would try to do so with greater care, but by the autumn Eaker was keen to extend the Pointblank attacks to aircraft industry targets in France.[56] The French aircraft industry, much of it sheltered in the unoccupied zone until November 1942, produced 668 aircraft for Germany in 1942, 1,285 in 1943, many of them trainer aircraft to free German factories for the production of combat models. German manufacturers used French capacity for their own experimental work, away from the threat of bombs on Germany.[57] As a result, French industry became a military priority for the American air force even at the risk of inflicting heavy casualties on the population. On September 3 and 15, 1943, Eighth Air Force raids on factories in Paris spread damage once again across residential streets packed with workers and shoppers and killed 377 civilians.[58] The raids on the western port city of Nantes on September 16 and 23 exacted the highest casualties so far from French bombing. The targets included a German naval vessel, a French locomotive works, and an aircraft factory, which was hit heavily. On September 16, 131 B-17s hit the town with 385 tons of bombs; on September 23, forty-six out of 117 B-17s dispatched to Nantes in the morning dropped a further 134 tons in poor weather, followed by a less accurate raid by thirty aircraft in the evening.[59] In the first raid the bomb pattern once again spread out over a wide area of the city, destroying 400 buildings and severely damaging another 600. The civil defense authorities counted 1,110 dead and 800 severely injured. While the local emergency services struggled to cope with the damage, they were hit by the two attacks on September 23, which not only struck the ruins but spread out over an area of more than 500 hectares. Because much of the center of the city was already abandoned, deaths from the second two raids were 172, but a further 300 buildings were completely destroyed. This time the population panicked entirely and 100,000 abandoned the city. The raids on Nantes resembled completely the pattern of raids on a German city, with the exception that Eighth Air Force losses were modest, a total of seven aircraft on September 16 and no losses a week later.[60]

The raids of the autumn of 1943 provoked a mixture of outrage and incomprehension in France. Total deaths from bombing in 1943 reached 7,458, almost three times the level of 1942. A French report on public opinion, which reached the Allies early in 1944, highlighted the damaging effect of persistently inaccurate high-level bombing on a people "tired, worn out by all its miseries, all its privations, all its separations, unnerved by too prolonged a wait for its liberation."[61] The French Air Force, reduced under the armistice terms with Germany to a skeleton organization, tried to assess what object the Allied raids could have. Raids on Paris and against the Dunlop works at Montluçon (this time by Bomber Command) puzzled French airmen, who assumed there must be some secondary purpose behind the pattern of scattered bombing that they had not yet worked out.[62] Since the French Air Force could not do its own bombing, much time was spent in 1943 and 1944 observing Allied practice in order to understand the techniques and tactics involved as well as the effects of bombs on urban society, industrial architecture, and popular morale.[63] Many of the reports on individual raids highlighted the sheer squandering of resources involved in a bombing operation when three-quarters of the bombs typically missed the target: "The results obtained," ran a report on the bombing of St.-Étienne, "have no relation to the means employed, and this bombardment represents, like all the others, a waste of matériel—without counting the unnecessary losses in human life that they provoke."[64] The air force worked out the pattern of bombing accuracy to show just how wide the dispersion of effort was. In raids against Lille, the area in which bombs fell was a rectangle 8 by 4 kilometers; against Rouen, 8 by 3 kilometers; a raid on the railway station at Cambrai in 1944 covered an area 3 kilometers in length and 1.5 kilometers wide. The impact varied from raid to raid, but studies showed that many raids covered an area of between 200 and 400 hectares (500 to 1,200 acres), which explained the escalating losses of life and property. The French Air Force was impressed most by low-level dive-bombing and rocket attacks using the American P-47 Thunderbolt and the Hawker 1-B Typhoon, which achieved their object with much greater operational economy, and matched French strategic preferences before 1939.[65]

The French government and population were not unprepared for a bombing war. As in Britain, the French state had begun to plan for passive defense against air attack as early as 1923; a law for compulsory passive defense organization was passed in April 1935, compelling local authorities to begin the organization of civil defense measures. In July 1938 a director of passive defense was appointed in the Defense Ministry to coordinate the protection of civilian lives and property with the committees of passive defense set up in each French administrative *département*.[66] The problem for French civil defense was the sudden defeat and occupation in the summer of 1940. In the area occupied by the Germans, civil defense was likely to be a necessary safeguard against British air activity; in the unoccupied zone, the urgency for continued civil defense seemed less evident. The Vichy government set up the Directorate of Passive Defense in the southern city of Lyon in 1941 under General Louis Sérant, but it was starved of funds and personnel. Spending on passive defense had totaled more than 1 billion francs in 1939 but by 1941 was down to just 250 million.[67] In both zones of France the difficult task was to reach a satisfactory working relationship with the German occupiers. The active air defense of the occupied zone was in the hands of Field Marshal Hugo Sperrle's Air Fleet 3. Following the switch to the war against the Soviet Union, the number of fighter aircraft and antiaircraft guns left in France was seldom adequate for the weight of Allied attack. German priority was given to the protection of the most important military sites, including the submarine pens and German airbases.

Air-raid alarms could only be activated on German orders, though French observers were expected to supply information to allow German officers to calculate whether it was worth sounding an alert. In the occupied zone the blackout was enforced on German orders. Mobile emergency units for air protection were sent from Germany to help with firefighting and rescue work alongside the residual French passive defense organization. They found the French attitude at times lackadaisical. German firemen fighting a blaze in Dunkirk in April 1942 were astonished at the lack of discipline among French colleagues who "stood around on the corners smoking."[68]

The relationship with the unoccupied zone was a constant source of friction for the German air command in Paris and the Italian occupation zone set up in 1940 in southeastern France. The Italian Armistice Commission insisted that Vichy impose a blackout throughout the area abutting the Italian-occupied regions to avoid giving British bombers an easy aid to navigation against Italian targets, but even when the French Air Force agreed, it proved difficult to enforce.[69] In November 1941 the German Armistice Commission in Wiesbaden complained that British aircraft regularly flew over the unoccupied zone without any blackout below: "The contrast between the occupied zone, plunged into darkness, and the unoccupied zone, where the blackout is up to now only intermittent, nicely indicates to enemy planes the frontier of the two zones."[70] The German Air Force demanded complete blackout every night along a cordon 100 kilometers from the occupation zone, and effective blackout over the whole of unoccupied France when aircraft were sighted. French officials regarded the request as "inopportune" and prevaricated for months until August 1942, when the French government finally accepted a blackout of the frontier zones.[71] A German aerial inspection a few weeks later showed that many houses had not bothered to take blackout measures; vehicles could be seen driving with full headlights; in Lyon the blackout occurred only after the antiaircraft artillery had begun to fire.[72] The long delay reflected a more general reluctance on the part of the French military leadership to comply with German demands. Failure to observe the blackout was also a simple way to express noncompliance. Free French radio broadcasts encouraged householders to keep lights on throughout the night to help the RAF find German targets. Only when the whole of France was occupied could the German occupiers insist on the blackout, but even then complaints continued about its inadequacy.

The occupation of the southern zone on November 10, 1942, coincided with the intensification of Allied bombing. As this became heavier, the French authorities recognized that failure to collaborate fully with the German occupiers would expose the population to unnecessary risks. The ambivalence remained, however. When German Air Fleet 3 asked for French antiaircraft gunners in 1943 to man batteries in the north of the country, French officials preferred to site them in central France where they could be used for training purposes rather than to fire at Allied aircraft.[73] In February 1943 the German military command in Paris insisted that a unitary French antiaircraft defense system should be set up covering the newly occupied French territory and working in close collaboration with the thinly spread German antiaircraft resources. The Vichy regime was asked to establish a Secretariat for Air Defense, including a national director for "passive defense," and it was the German intention that the French organization would eventually operate over the whole of France.[74] The new French defenses included antiaircraft batteries that were, unlike their German counterparts, controlled by the army. The German Air Force command in France insisted that the new French units come under air force control, and the army was forced to comply.[75] A new air-raid warning system, the Securité Aérienne Publique (SAP), was activated in February 1943, manned by French personnel under French Air Force control, using a mixture of radar and visual observation. In the southern zone the force numbered 3,800 officers and men; in the northern occupation zone the German Air Force still kept its own system of alerts, but Vichy officials and officers were posted to the main air defense centers to help coordinate air defense measures across the whole country.[76] The system suffered from the same problems found in the northern zone, since alerts could only be authorized by the Germans on information passed to them by French observers, except in more remote areas where there were no German officials.[77] The result once again was that alerts were sometimes sounded only when aircraft were already overhead, minutes before the bombs dropped.

The passive defense system insisted on by the German Air Force already existed in a skeleton form throughout Vichy France, organized by local prefects and mayors. In the southern zone the system had not been properly tested and now required a rapid expansion. The Vichy regime, now led by Pierre Laval as premier, established an Interministerial Protection Service against the Events of War (Service Interministériel de Protection contre les Événements de Guerre, or SIPEG), not unlike the committee established by Joseph Goebbels in Germany the same month, designed to oversee all the policies necessary to maintain economic and social survival in the bombed cities.[78] The Passive Defense Directorate, a branch of the new department of Aerial Defense, held an awkward constitutional position between the German authorities on the one hand and the French SIPEG on the other. One of the things the new organization had to provide was mobile support units to cope particularly with the threat of firebombing on the model already adopted in northern France. Emergency fire and rescue battalions were set up at Avignon, Lyon, Aix-en-Provence, and Montpellier, to be summoned with German approval to any raid where local civil defense could not cope.[79] But they remained short of personnel—there were only 1,500 to cover the whole of southern France—and short of essential equipment because it was being supplied by French factories to meet German orders. When units were sent to help with raids in northern France, the shortages of manpower and equipment were evident, while the population in the south complained that they were not left with adequate protection.[80] In general, French cities were much less well protected than British or German cities, while the tension between the French organization and the German authorities, whose principal interest was in safeguarding German military installations and industries working to German orders, left civilian communities potentially more vulnerable to the effects of inaccurate raiding.

In many cases, however, the German air defense forces cooperated with French civil defense and emergency services. At Lorient the German Air Protection Regiment 34, stationed in northwest France, was called in during January 1943 to try to stem the fires not only in the port area where German personnel were stationed, but also in the residential areas hit by the rain of incendiaries. The local civil defense also summoned help from seven fire services in other towns. The failure to save Lorient resulted not from the lack of effort on the part of both French and German emergency workers, but from the sheer weight of the attack.[81] In Nantes, later in the year, the two forces, French and German, also cooperated in fighting the effects of the raid not only on the port, which the Germans needed, but also on the streets of the town itself.[82] Again it was the scale of the bombing that made it difficult for civil defense to cope with the immediate crisis, but by the day following the heaviest raid, September 17, 1943, there were 800 French and German workers, helped by local miners and teams from the National Youth movement, opening roads, making damaged housing safe, and searching for buried survivors. Eventually 1,500 emergency workers and volunteers worked to restore some kind of order. They were hampered first by the lack of equipment—there were only four mechanical shovels and just fifty trucks—and then by the attacks that followed on September 23. On the following day only 400 men remained to tackle the rescue work, since many workers had fled with their families from the ruined housing. Eventually twice this number could be found, but the French authorities observed that many were German workers, who displayed a greater discipline because they had no personal ties to the city itself.[83]

The disaster at Nantes highlighted the problem of orderly evacuation as a solution to the increased threat from bombing. Evacuation had always been the French state's preference as a way of providing really effective salvation to the urban population, but after the disastrous results of the mass exodus in 1940 during the German attack, priority was given to trying to prevent extensive evacuation and to keeping families together. Here again the German occupiers played a central part in dictating the pattern of evacuations. Following the bombing of Lorient, in which thousands of workers and their families disappeared into the surrounding countryside, the German high command in Paris decided that the vulnerable coastal towns should be evacuated in a planned way, giving priority as in Germany to children, mothers, and the elderly. In Cherbourg the Germans demanded the evacuation of 30,000 out of the 50,000 inhabitants, in Dieppe and Le Havre around one-quarter of the population.[84] The evacuations were carried out despite the reluctance of many inhabitants to leave. In Cherbourg over one-third of the evacuees later returned in the summer and winter of 1943, while the German commanders were lobbied for permission for wives and young children to return to live with male workers regarded by the Germans as indispensable. Once Allied invasion in 1944 became likely, however, the German occupiers insisted that the populations of the northern littoral evacuate as fully as possible to avoid being in the battle zone. There were only 5,000 people left in Cherbourg when the American army arrived in June 1944.[85] The Germans insisted on similar measures on the south coast of France, where it was possible that the Allies might launch a surprise invasion. Since the cities of the south were also now threatened by heavy bombing, evacuation of the coastal zone was seen by the French government as a useful means to reduce casualties. Preliminary plans in January 1944 suggested the transfer of up to 485,000 people for whom transport and accommodation had to be found in inland rural areas unprepared for the exodus. The combination of bombing and imminent invasion forced the French government to produce coordinated plans to move their wartime refugees more successfully than in 1940.[86]

Evacuation had already begun in 1942 on an improvised basis, and by early 1944 over 200,000 children had been moved from the most vulnerable cities. In December 1941 a scheme was established between the bombed city of Brest and the southern city of Lyon in which the bombed-out (*sinistrés*) were to be housed in Lyon and given welfare and funds by the council and population that adopted them. The scheme failed to attract even 100 children, since parents were reluctant to accept separation and the children were reluctant to go.[87] In 1942 other bombed towns either sought or were offered adoption by cities regarded as safe, including Le Havre, which was eventually adopted by Algiers, but much of the aid came in the form of money or clothes or books for the homeless rather than a new home. Most French evacuees moved to family or friends in nearby villages, and French planners insisted, against German objections, that on practical and political grounds it made more sense to house evacuees locally rather than in remote areas in central France. With the heavy bombing of Lorient, St.-Nazaire, and Brest in early 1943, the population flowed out into the surrounding countryside in tens of thousands.[88] On February 4, 1944, Laval issued comprehensive guidelines on evacuation policy following the severe bombing of the winter and the expectation that the military threat would escalate. The guiding principles of the program were the need for an ordered transfer of population and the consent of those to be transferred, "voluntary but organized." The government favored persuasion using a program of posters, radio broadcasts, and public meetings. Priority was to be given to "the human capital of the Nation," above all to children, who carried the demographic future of a postwar France.[89] Mothers and children and pregnant women were the chief categories, though the elderly and disabled were also included; those who remained were classified as "indispensable" (administrators and officials), "necessary" (laborers and white-collar workers, doctors, welfare workers), and "useful" (those who helped to maintain the activity of the indispensable and necessary). Families nevertheless remained unenthusiastic about evacuation; they feared looting if they left their homes, and disliked the loss of independence and reliance on welfare in the destination zones. Eventually around 1.2 million moved as refugees, evacuees, or bombed-out, most in reaction to the urgent imperative of survival.[90]

It has sometimes been remarked that the French failed to exhibit the "Blitz spirit" evident in Britain, and later in Germany, in the face of bombing. In a great many ways the opposite is true. The French population faced an inescapable dilemma that made it difficult to know how to respond to the raids: they wanted the Allies who were bombing them to win, and they wanted the Germans who protected them to lose. Since they were not themselves at war, the sense that they represented a national "front line" against a barbarous enemy could not as easily be used to mobilize the population as it could in Britain and Germany. The bombing was not part of an orchestrated offensive against French morale, and civilians were not supposed to be a target; nor was bombing experienced either regularly or over a wide area, except for the bombing of northern France during the Allied invasion. French towns and cities were nevertheless caught between two dangerous forces, the German occupiers and Vichy collaborators on the one hand, and the Allied air forces (including the B-24 "Liberator") on the other. Resisting the Germans by helping Allied aircrew or sabotaging what had not been bombed meant running the risk of discovery, torture, and execution that no one in Britain's Blitz was expected to face. Lesser infractions—deliberate refusal to observe the blackout, or absenteeism from a civil defense unit—could be interpreted by the occupiers not simply as an act of negligence but as an act of resistance. When evacuees returned without authorization, the local German commanders withdrew ration cards or threatened the returnees with a labor camp. French people exposed to the bombs experienced double jeopardy, both the damage and deaths from raids and the harsh authority of the occupiers.

This dilemma was exploited politically by both sides during the war. The German propaganda apparatus presented the Allied air forces as terror flyers, as in Germany, and the French press was encouraged to focus on the barbarous and indiscriminate nature of the attacks. The Vichy authorities shared this perspective, and may indeed have believed it. Cinema newsreels on the bombing of French targets broadcast by *France-Actualités* carried titles such as "War on civilians," "Wounded France," and "The Calvary continues," while after every major raid there were elaborate official funerals with full pageantry and speeches condemning the massacre of the innocents.[91] Since the Vichy regime was widely unpopular among important sections of the urban population, the bombing was used as a way to show that the authorities cared about the welfare of the damaged communities and to forge links between state and people. The bombed-out were entitled to state welfare at fixed rates; the state paid the funeral expenses of bomb victims; evacuation costs could be met in full for transfers of less than fifteen kilometers' distance; pensions were introduced for those disabled by the bombs, and for those widowed or orphaned in the raids.[92] In addition, bomb victims were entitled to welfare assistance from two voluntary welfare organizations, the Secours National (National Assistance), reestablished in 1940 with Marshal Philippe Pétain as its president, and the Comité Ouvrier de Secours Immédiat (COSI, the Committee for Workers' Emergency Assistance), set up following the Billancourt raid in 1942 under the collaborationist René Mesnard. Both relied on state funds as well as voluntary contributions, and both echoed the propaganda of the Vichy regime in condemning the bombing and highlighting the efforts to aid the victims as a means of binding together the national community. The COSI took funds directly from the German authorities and in reality distributed little of it to the bombed-out and much of it to the officials who ran it.[93] The committee did play a part in redistributing to the victims of bombing some of the Jewish apartments and furnishings confiscated under German supervision, while the money given to the committee by the Germans came from expropriated Jewish assets. The first consignment of Jewish-owned furniture was handed over to COSI in April 1942, and large quantities continued to be diverted to help the bombed-out until 1944, though an even greater volume was shipped directly to the Reich from France and the Low Countries to supply German civilian victims of bombing, a total of 735 trainloads during the course of the occupation.[94]

The Allies, on the other hand, needed to present to the French population a clear justification for the bombing as the key to eventual liberation. This message worked well early in the war when there was hope that RAF raids signaled the possibility of an early invasion, but less well after years of waiting and in the face of rising casualties. The Allies tried to combine the bombing with direct support for the French Resistance, but at the same time to avoid operations that would undermine the credibility of resistance and push the French population toward grudging support for Vichy. Broadcasts from the BBC, which were widely listened to in France, encouraged the French population to see resistance and bombing as two sides of the same coin.[95] The leaflet war was designed to offer clear warnings to the areas scheduled for raiding as well as justification for attacks on German targets or collaborating businesses. Millions of propaganda notices and news reviews were dropped throughout the period, reaching a crescendo in 1943–44. The RAF dropped 155 million in 1942 and 294 million in 1943, the great majority from aircraft, some from balloons sent with the prevailing winds.[96] The Eighth Air Force began leafleting operations in late 1942 only after the initial effects of American raids had been assessed to see what kind of political message should be delivered. A special force of twelve B-17 and B-24 bombers was set up in 1943 tasked with distributing leaflets over the occupied territories as well as across Germany.[97] By February 1944 the Americans had dropped 41 million items, including the French-language paper *America at War*, which was used to explain the course of the conflict and the necessity for bombing French targets. In spring 1944 the quantity increased substantially to 130 million in March on the eve of the transportation campaign against French railways, and more than 100 million each month until D-Day. So heavy was the bombardment of paper that the German authorities in France organized leaflet squads with sharpened sticks to collect them before they were picked up by the local population.[98]

The impact of the leaflet and broadcasting campaign was difficult for the Allies to assess since almost all the public media in Vichy France treated the bombing as an unmediated crime. Allied intelligence was faced with a barrage of information showing that the bombing was defined by its "terror character." One newspaper, the *Petit Parisien*, following the bombing of Paris in September 1943 claimed that "the barbarians of the West are worthy allies of the barbarians in the East."[99] The *Mémorial de St. Étienne* asked, "Will this destructive Sadism have no end? One is appalled before this mounting barbarity, this barbarity behind the mask of civilization." The Allies recognized that the French reaction was not as simple as that, but there was increasing evidence that even among pro-Allied circles the mixed results of bombing raids provoked anxiety and hostility without at the same time undermining the acknowledgment that German targets were both legitimate and necessary.[100] This ambiguity was evident from the reaction to two raids on Toulon on March 7, 1944. The first killed or injured an estimated 900 German soldiers and won wide approval; the second four days later missed the target and killed 110 French civilians to widespread complaints. One of the American crews shot down on the second raid was black, prompting racist comments about the quality and competence of American airmen.[101] American bombing was identified in information from the French Resistance as the major source of resentment because of its apparently "careless and casual" attitude to the communities being bombed: "The Americans make it a sport," ran one report, "and amuse themselves by bombing from such altitudes."[102] In May 1944 the French Catholic cardinals sent an appeal to the Catholic episcopate in Britain and the United States asking them to lobby the air forces to bomb military objectives with greater care and avoid the "humble dwellings of women and children." The archbishop of Westminster replied that his government had given every assurance that casualties would be kept to a minimum.[103]

There was nevertheless widespread resistance or noncompliance prompted by the bombing campaign as well. The Resistance took the view that those killed in Allied bombings were in some sense not victims, but combatants in a war for the liberation and salvation of the nation.[104] Those who chose to operate networks for the escape of Allied airmen certainly ran the risks of any combatant if they were caught. The death penalty was introduced in a decree on July 14, 1941, for helping Allied airmen, but an estimated 2,000–3,000 British and American servicemen were smuggled out of France and back to combat. In cases following heavy bombing, as at Lorient in 1943, some airmen were surrendered to the Germans, but Allied intelligence found that in many cases the Resistance distinguished between the regrettable effects of a heavy bombardment and their view of Allied aircrew as liberators.[105] The Resistance also regarded bombing as complementary to forms of active opposition to the occupiers, though it was seldom integrated as closely as it could have been, despite the insistence of the Resistance that sabotage could often be a more effective tool than bombing.[106] There also existed many lesser levels of protest or noncompliance derived from the bombing war. The funerals of Allied aircrew killed in action attracted large crowds despite German efforts to obstruct them; wreaths were laid by the graveside dedicated "To Our Heroes" or "To Our Allies" or "To Our Liberators" until seized or destroyed by the occupiers. There were numerous public demonstrations under the occupation, 753 in total, some orchestrated by Vichy to protest against bombing, but hundreds directed at shortages of food or adequate shelter.[107] The police reports from the provinces in 1943 found that despite, or because of, the bombings, the population talked openly of their hope for Allied invasion and the horrors of occupation: "No one," ran a report from Charente in northwest France, "believes any longer in a German victory."[108]

The German occupiers found regular evidence of dissent among the French officials and servicemen organizing the air defense system. The slow introduction of French antiaircraft units in the summer of 1943 was blamed by the German Air Force on the existence of a network of Freemasons among the French officials involved. French antiaircraft personnel were made to sign a "declaration of duty" not to reveal military secrets, and both antiaircraft units and the French emergency services were monitored by the German Security Service (SD) for their alleged sympathies with de Gaulle and the Free French.[109] In August 1943, fifteen antiaircraft servicemen abandoned their posts and could not be found; the following month another fifteen men from the Air Force Security School took two cars and a truck and absconded to the Massif Central to join the partisan Resistance. In November 1943 a group of SAP soldiers were caught listening to French broadcasts from Britain; on the wall of their common room a poster was found proclaiming, "Vive les Gaullistes! Vive l'U.R.S.S.! Vive de Gaulle!"[110] German Air Intelligence found that by the autumn of 1943, Allied success in the Mediterranean had changed the attitude of the French population to one of anxious longing for the moment of Allied invasion and celebration of every German defeat. "The expected Anglo-American landing in France," concluded a report in August, "is now the daily topic of conversation."[111]

Allied planning for the liberation of France was indeed far advanced by the autumn of 1943, but from the Allied point of view it was bound to cause high casualties and perhaps compromise at the last moment the sympathies of the French people for the Allied cause. Churchill remained continually anxious, as he told the War Cabinet in April 1944, that preinvasion bombing might create an "unhealable breach" between France and the Western Allies.[112] The principal issue was the decision to use the heavy bomber forces, including the Fifteenth Air Force in Italy, to attack the French transport system before invasion and to support the army as it consolidated its position on the bridgeheads in Normandy in

June and July 1944 and, a month later, in southern France. To this was added the decision to use Allied bomber forces in the Crossbow operations against German V-weapon sites across northern France. Neither Harris nor Spaatz was enthusiastic about using the bomber force this way, since it was not what the bombing was supposed to be for, while the aircraft had not been designed for use against small tactical targets. In January 1944, following an order to intensify raids on V-weapon sites, Harris rejected the use of Bomber Command to attack Crossbow targets as "not reasonable operations of war."[113] His reaction to the idea that bombers should support the ground offensive was just as negative. Bombers used for ground support would, he argued, "be entirely ineffective," leading "directly to disaster" for the invasion force.[114] Spaatz objected to Eisenhower that support for invasion was "an uneconomical use" of the heavy bomber force and preferred to leave the operations to the large tactical air forces assigned to the Allied Expeditionary Air Force under Air Marshal Trafford Leigh-Mallory, whose fighter-bomber and light bomber aircraft were intended to attack small targets and could react quickly and flexibly to battlefield requirements.[115] Both bomber forces wished to be able to concentrate on Pointblank operations against Germany as a more strategically valuable way to limit the German response to invasion. Arnold told Spaatz in late April 1944, after the decision had already been taken to focus on the French railway system, that Pointblank should "still be pressed to the limit."[116] The arguments put forward in favor of the Transportation Plan by Tedder and his scientific adviser, Solly Zuckerman, have already been discussed. Zuckerman's paper produced in January 1944 on "Delay and Disorganisation of Enemy Movement by Rail" formed the basis of the eventual preinvasion plan. On March 25 in a long and hotly debated meeting, Eisenhower finally came down in favor of using the bomber forces, under his own direct command, to attack the French railway system and other strategic targets both before and during the invasion period.[117]

This decision still left unresolved the political anxieties about possible levels of casualty. Portal informed Churchill after the meeting of March 25 that there were bound to be very heavy casualties as a result of the decision to hit seventy-six key points in the French railway network.

Bomber Command suggested a figure of between 80,000 and 160,000 casualties, partly to confirm Harris's argument that heavy bombers were the wrong weapon.[118] Zuckerman calculated on the basis of damage done to British targets earlier in the war a more modest casualty figure of 12,000 dead and 6,000 seriously injured. In a discussion with the Defence Committee on April 5, Churchill deplored a strategy that might result in "the butchery of large numbers of helpless French people," but despite his reservations and the opposition of Eden and General Brooke, chief of the general staff, the campaign was allowed to start on the understanding that casualty levels would be carefully monitored over the weeks that followed and warnings sent to French communities to evacuate the threatened areas.[119] By mid-April casualties from the first nine raids were estimated at 1,103, well within the limits set by Zuckerman's estimate. The Defence Committee was supplied with the outraged French reports ("In Anglo-American eyes, to be European is enough to be wiped off the list of the living"), and Churchill hesitated to give the campaign full approval.[120] Zuckerman and the RE8 department of the Ministry of Home Security continued to monitor reports on a daily basis, and by late April the available evidence suggested that casualties had been approximately 50 percent lower than anticipated.[121] Only after Roosevelt had insisted that there should be no restriction on military action if Operation Overlord were to succeed did Churchill finally on May 11 give his full approval to the campaign.[122] For the four weeks before D-Day a furious crescendo of bombing descended on the French railway system and the unfortunate housing that surrounded its nodal points.

Zuckerman's calculations in fact underestimated French casualties by a wide margin because transport targets were only part of what Allied air forces were expected to bomb in the weeks leading to invasion. French civil defense officials counted 712 dead in March, 5,144 in April, 9,893 in May, and an estimated 9,517 in June. The total of 25,266 over the four months was almost certainly not complete, given the difficulty of constructing exact records in a dangerous war zone; nor did all the casualties come from attacks on rail targets, but also against bridges and military installations, and German forces.[123] They nevertheless represented the overall human cost of the decision to use bombing as the

means to reduce the capacity of the German army and air force to oppose the landings in Normandy. The high casualties resulted chiefly
from the wide dispersion of bombs against relatively small targets and
the large tonnage employed. The 63,636 tons dropped on transport targets exceeded the entire tonnage dropped by the German Air Force
during the Blitz on Britain. The French air defense counted 71,000
high-explosive bombs between January and March 1944, but 291,000
from April to June.[124] Some attacks achieved a high level of precision,
but in many cases bombs were scattered over a wide area. The attack on
the rail center at St.-Pierre-des-Corps on April 11 struck the whole area
of the town; the raid on Lille on April 10 hit an area of thirty-two square
kilometers; that on Noisy-le-Sec on April 18 covered thirty square kilometers; on Rouen a day later, the area was twenty-four square kilometers.[125] In May the French authorities counted a total of 1,284 raids in
which bombs fell on 793 different localities, 630 of them along the northern coast and the area northeast of Paris. Only 8 percent of the attacks
were undertaken at night, which ought to have increased the possibility
of more accurate raiding, but many of the daylight raids were carried
out at heights of 3,000–4,000 meters (10,000–13,000 feet). In some
cases, high casualties resulted from what the Passive Defense Directorate called "imprudence"—people standing at their windows to watch
the bombing, others out in the street, or in their gardens. In a raid on
Nice on May 26, 438 people were killed, two-thirds of them on the
street, one-third in their houses. The shelters, for the most part either
trenches or converted cellars, had uneven fortunes during the raiding;
some stood up well even to direct hits, others, like one at Rouen on May 30,
were blown apart, and most of the occupants killed.[126]

Some of the heaviest losses of life occurred in targets in the former
unoccupied zone, which were hit by American aircraft of the Fifteenth
Air Force operating from bases in Italy. For the crews involved, the
bombing of precise railway targets with a view to reducing damage to
civilian lives and property was very different from the long-range raids
against Pointblank targets in southern Germany, which had been the
main activity of the force since its formation in November 1943. Two

raids, one on St.-Étienne on May 26, 1944, and one on Marseille the following day, resulted in heavy loss of civilian life. At St.-Étienne the alert
sounded in good time; the 150 B-17s attacked in waves from around
13,000 feet, and half the bombs fell in the zone around the rail links. But
there were too few proper shelters for a population unused to the air
threat and more than 1,084 were killed. The effect on rail traffic was
limited. Rail lines remained open and the damage, such as it was, could
be overcome in just four days. The attack on Marseille on May 27, flown
at an estimated 20,000 feet, against stations at St.-Charles and Blan-
carde, both situated in the heart of the city's residential area, scattered
bombs over ten of the city's quarters, destroying 500 buildings and killing 1,752 people. Again Passive Defense observed the "insouciance" of a
population hit by an air raid for the first time and the absence of effective civil defense training. The stations were unimportant (one was a
railway cul-de-sac), but the effect of the raid was to create a crisis of public morale and strong hostility to the air forces that carried out the attack.[127] The scale of the raiding and the damage inflicted brought protests
from the French Resistance and the French authorities in London. The
French Commissariat for Foreign Affairs warned the Foreign Office in
early May that the raids were having a damaging effect on French opinion; in early June a resolution from the Resistance Group Assembly was
passed on by Massigli, calling on the bomber forces to change their tactics and for an active propaganda campaign "to dissipate the growing
ill-feeling" among the victim populations.[128] An OSS report from Madrid relayed the Resistance view that the French population now believed its situation to be no better than that of "the Nazis in Germany."[129]
This knowledge made little difference to Allied operations. In June,
however, the bombing reached its high point as Allied forces poured
ashore on D-Day and spread out into the Normandy countryside.

The results of the Transportation Plan were the subject of keen argument both at the time and since. French investigations showed that by
the beginning of June rail traffic was down to around half the level in
January 1944, and in the key regions of the north and west, down to 15
and 10 percent. There were 2,234 cases of damage to rail lines between

January and June 1944, but as in Britain or Germany or the Soviet Union, these were relatively easy to repair.[130] Much damage was also done by sabotage, which the Resistance thought was a more effective way of achieving the same end, and with fewer losses to the French population, particularly the railwaymen, who were regarded as key Resistance workers.[131] Between January and July, bombing and strafing destroyed or severely damaged 2,536 French locomotives, sabotage a further 1,605. But according to the SNCF (the French national railway), sabotage accounted for 70,000 goods wagons compared with 55,000 from air attack.[132] In the three months from April to June there were 1,020 bomb attacks on the rail network, but 1,713 acts of sabotage.[133] Of these the two most significant causes of delay to traffic were the attacks on repair depots, which created a cumulative backlog of repair to the rolling stock hit by raids or sabotage, and the attacks on rail bridges. Many of these were carried out by the tactical air forces using fighter-bombers and light bombers, and they proved decisive in cutting the key regions off from rapid German reinforcement. Most rail centers could be made operable again in an average of seven days, but bridges took from ten to sixteen days.[134] The German authorities made strenuous efforts to keep the rail system going and succeeded for much of the period of the transport campaign. By suspending almost all civilian traffic and helped by persistent poor weather for bombing, it proved possible to maintain military through traffic up to June (when 535 loaded troop trains could still be deployed), but a slow decline set in from July. Total German ton-kilometers were 300 million for the month to mid-March, 400 million for each of the next three months, but only 150 million in July, by which time the loss of rail traffic compromised the further possibility of effective German defense.[135] The argument from the French viewpoint, however, was not whether German fighting power was affected, but whether the high cost in civilian lives and buildings could not have been avoided by wielding an aerial weapon that was less blunt. French authorities found that major raids by heavy bombers placed between half and four-fifths of the bombs outside the target area; in this sense Harris and Spaatz had been right to insist that large formations of heavy bombers were not the most suitable means to achieve the aim of precise destruction and limited French losses.

This conclusion was even more evident in the efforts of the two bomber forces to destroy the sites from which V-weapons were to be fired rather than raid the factories where they were being made. The first raids against the construction sites and depots in France were made in November 1943 after the Central Interpretation Unit at Medmenham had identified the first V-1 bunkers. The campaign against the V-weapons was code-named Crossbow, but the bombing operations were known as Noball. The quantities of bomb tonnage dropped during the course of the campaign, from early December 1943 to mid-September 1944, exceeded by a wide margin the total devoted to the Transportation Plan, a final tally of 118,000 tons of bombs, 86,000 of which were dropped between June 12 and September 12, 1944, on targets considerably smaller than the marshaling yards and viaducts targeted for D-Day. The first bombings in the winter of 1943–44 were thought to have set back the onset of the V-weapons campaign by six months, but after the first attacks the Germans abandoned the system of "ski-jump" launch sites (so called after their shape) because of their visibility and vulnerability, but let the impression remain that work was still being done on them in order to attract the bombers.[136] Eventually most of the original sites were identified and destroyed, but the newly modified launch sites were hard to find or hit. The German campaign was held up chiefly because of technical problems in producing sufficient operational V-1s to be able to start the offensive sooner.[137] After the first V-1s fell on London from the middle of June 1944 onward, a renewed order went out to both bomber forces to try to stamp out the threat. From December 1943 to May 1944, Crossbow targets had taken 12 percent of the bombing effort, but between June and August 1944 the proportion was 33 percent.[138] This represented a very large diversion of resources from any assistance that could be given to the Allied armies in France against targets that were almost immune to bomb attack. In April 1944, RE8 had explained to the Air Ministry that small sites protected by twenty feet of concrete had a low level of vulnerability.[139] In July, Sinclair instructed Portal to give the Crossbow sites a lower priority because "they are hard to destroy and easy to repair." When Eighth Air Force B-17s attacked ten sites in July, they missed eight and dropped only four bombs on the remaining two.[140] Although Churchill had been keen for Bomber Command to try to blunt the V-weapon assault, the Air Ministry recognized by July that any effects were likely to be ephemeral. An Air Intelligence report in July on the V-1 sites captured by the American army in Cherbourg showed that although they had been heavily bombed, the design of the sites made them almost impervious to bomb damage and easily repaired if a chance hit achieved anything.[141] The bombing continued until September, when most of the sites were captured by the advancing army, but both air forces recognized the limitation of using heavy bombers for what were in effect tactical targets.

The same limitations operated with the decision to use heavy bombers in support of Eisenhower's ground campaign in France. For almost three months, northern France was a battlefield. As in the German attack on France in 1940 or the Soviet Union in 1941, it proved very difficult for the advancing Allied armies and air forces to avoid heavy damage to the towns, cities, and civilians in their path. In northern Normandy, where the battle lasted longest and was at its most intense, 14,000 French civilians died, 57 percent as a result of bombing. Heavy air raids began from the first morning, June 6, after warning leaflets had been dropped at dawn encouraging the Normandy population to "Leave for the Fields! You Haven't a Minute to Lose!" In Caen on June 6 around 600 were killed by an American air raid, another 200 the following day amid the ruins of much of the city; on June 7 a raid by more than 1,000 Bomber Command aircraft against six small towns, including Vire, St.-Lô, Lisieux, and Coutances, eradicated the urban areas almost entirely. In the first two days of the campaign, 3,000 French civilians were killed.[142] The village of Aunay-sur-Odon, bombed to stop the movement of German tanks a few days later, was literally erased from the map. Pictures taken after the raid showed a single church spire in an otherwise entirely level landscape. The French authorities counted 2,307 bombardments in June, 1,016 of them on the north coast provinces, most against railway targets.

In July there were fewer raids, 1,195 in total, in August 1,121.[143] The great majority of the raids were tactical, carried out by the Allied Expeditionary Air Force, but on occasion the heavy bombers were asked to bring overwhelming firepower to bear. Two attacks on Caen, one on July 7 and a second on July 18, were among the heaviest of the Overlord campaign. The raid on July 7 involved 467 bombers dropping 2,276 tons on the northern outskirts of the town. There were few German defenders and the main effect of the raid, which left a moonscape on the approaches to Caen, was to force the British and Canadian troops to clear the roads before any further advance could be made.[144] The raid on July 18 by 942 bombers dropped an extraordinary 6,800 tons on the city and its eastern environs; the result did little to the German defenders, who had largely withdrawn to a defensive line south of Caen, nor to the population, 12,000 of whom eked out a precarious existence in caves outside the town at Fleury, but the raid once again left a ruined landscape that slowed down the advance of ground forces. By the end of the invasion a combination of bombing and shelling had left habitable housing for only 8,000 out of the 60,000 people who had lived there.[145]

The weight of attack that could now be employed by the bomber commands was out of all proportion to the nature of the ground threat and on balance did little to speed up the course of the campaign. The establishment of air superiority over the battlefield was assured by the thousands of fighters and fighter-bombers available to Leigh-Mallory to establish a protective air umbrella over the Allied armies. Occasionally the bluntness of the bombing weapon spilled over to impose friendly fire on Allied troops. On July 24, on the eve of the American breakout into Brittany, code-named Operation Cobra, hundreds of Eighth Air Force bombers were ordered to shatter the German defenses in front of General Omar Bradley's armies. "Ground grunted and heaved as the first cascade of bombs came down," wrote Captain Chester Hanson in Bradley's war diary, "horrible noise and the shuddering thunder that makes the sound of the bomb so different from the artillery." It was followed by the sight of ambulances streaming to the front line to pick up the dead and injured from among the American troops hit by the bombardment, a total of twenty-five killed and 131 wounded. Among the victims was Lieutenant General Lesley McNair, whose mangled body was thrown sixty feet by a bomb and could only be identified by the three stars on his collar.[146] More bombs fell on American troops the following day, bringing the total dead to 101. Eisenhower decided not to use heavy bombers again to support the ground battle but to use them against targets he properly regarded as strategic, but Bradley once again called in heavy bombers to help unblock German opposition in Aachen in November 1944.[147] This time elaborate precautions were taken to ensure that the 2,400 American and British bombers used did not impose friendly fire on American forces. Large panels visible from the air were used as checkpoints in Allied lines to indicate clearly where the army was; a line of vertical radar beams was then set up by mobile units that could be distinguished by onboard radar in the approaching bombers; barrage balloons with special cerise markings flew at 1,500 feet in front of the American line, and antiaircraft guns were set up to fire colored flares at 2,000 feet below the bombers. Despite the most elaborate of precautions, two bomb batches still fell on American troops, but with only one casualty.[148] Aachen was turned into a wasteland.

The gulf separating means and ends in the application of heavy bombers to the campaign in France was no more evident than in the fate of two coastal towns that were obliterated by the Allied bomber commands. Both towns held stubborn German garrisons that refused to surrender even when all France had been liberated. The Channel port of Le Havre, subject to 153 small attacks since 1940, was no stranger to bombardment. It was strategically important as a potential port for Allied supply as Eisenhower's armies moved rapidly eastward toward Germany, but it was defended by a garrison of over 11,000 German troops commanded by Colonel Eberhard Wildermuth. Since Le Havre was heavily fortified and he was under orders to prevent the port falling to the enemy for as long as possible, he rejected a request to surrender on September 3. Bomber Command was then ordered to bombard the city for a week before a ground assault could finally seize the port. A remarkable 9,631 tons of bombs were dropped and 82 percent of the town was destroyed at a cost of at least 1,536 civilian deaths. The German command refused to give up and a brief ground assault soon captured the port and the entire garrison. The post-raid analysis carried out by SHAEF concluded that the bombing had not done much to assist the eventual ground assault, a view that Harris shared.[149] Wildermuth cited artillery as the real source of the Allies' rapid success on the ground; bombing killed only a tiny handful of German soldiers.

The second port was Royan at the mouth of the river Gironde, where the garrison had also refused to surrender when the whole surrounding area had been liberated. The presence of German forces made it difficult for the Allies to use the neighboring port of Bordeaux, and in December 1944, SHAEF was requested by the local American army commander to lay on a heavy bombing to push the garrison to abandon the fight. On the night of January 4–5, 1945, 347 Lancasters dropped 1,576 tons, including 285 4,000-pound "blockbusters"; around 85 percent of the town was destroyed and 490 French civilians (and 47 German soldiers) were killed. Poor communications had failed to alert Harris to the fact that targets outside the town had in fact been requested, not the town itself, while the French authorities had insisted that the civilian population had already been evacuated, which was not true.[150] The raid achieved nothing. The German commander refused to surrender until two further attacks by the Eighth Air Force on April 14 and 15, which dropped another 5,555 tons, destroying everything still standing. The two raids, one of 1,133 bombers, the second with 1,278, were the largest operations mounted against any target in France. The Germans surrendered three days later. A French journalist "defied anyone to find even a single blade of grass."[151]

The overall cost from bombing in French lives and property during the war was exceptionally high, and it resulted in the main from using the overwhelming power of the bomber forces against modest targets that might more easily have been attacked by tactical air forces with greater accuracy. It was this lack of proportionality that attracted most criticism from French sources sympathetic to the Allies and eager that German targets should be bombed. "That which revolts the vast majority," ran an intelligence report from December 1943, "*of whom a great number are members of the Resistance* is the *inaccuracy* of aim."[152] The result of using large heavy bomber forces in level flying from high altitude was to exact forms of damage not very different from the impact on German targets. Table 6.2 shows the overall cost of the bombing on France. The official figures presented here are lower than the figure of 67,000 for overall deaths regularly cited in the postwar literature, and the Passive Defense authorities regarded the initial statistics as a minimum. But although there are minor discrepancies in the figures published by different agencies in 1945, and a more general problem in classifying deaths caused by bombing, tactical air raids, or artillery fire in a battle zone, a figure between 53,000 and 54,000 dead is unlikely to be superseded by anything more precise.[153] The figure for 1940 includes deaths and destruction from the air inflicted by all air forces during the German invasion in May and June.

In the face of the political anxieties regularly expressed in London, why did the Allies use the bomber force in France with such apparent disregard for civilian losses? The bomber commanders were themselves unhappy with what was being asked of them. Spaatz considered the tactical air forces adequate for giving effective ground support. In notes for Eisenhower he argued that strategic bombers would not yield a sufficient strategic return if used for the invasion: "The advantages gained by such use would be very small compared to the effort put forth."[154] The Eighth

Table 6.2: French Losses from Bombing, 1940–45

Year	Deaths	Injured	Buildings Destroyed	Buildings Damaged
1940	3,543	2,649	25,471	53,465
1941	1,357	1,670	3,265	9,740
1942	2,579	5,822	2,000	9,300
1943	7,446	13,779	12,050	23,300
1944	37,128	49,007	42,230	86,498
1945	1,548	692	300	800
Total	**53,601**	**73,619**	**85,316**	**183,103**

Source: BN, Bulletin d'Information de la Défense Passive, May 1945, 4.

Air Force commander, Jimmy Doolittle, told Eisenhower and Spaatz in August that the use of strategic bombers with insufficient training and planning time in support of ground operations was bound to produce errors in execution and admitted that "the fighters have done a better job of supporting the Army than the bombers."[155] The persistent use of the strategic forces has a number of explanations. For the Allied Supreme Command in Europe and the Combined Chiefs of Staff, bombing had evident advantages: it would speed up the invasion after years in which demands for the second front had failed to materialize; it would help to bring the end of the war closer for democratic populations anxious that hostilities should end sooner rather than later; it would make victory in France more certain and less hazardous; and it would finally allow the Allies to cash in the very large investment already made in strategic bombing that had not yet delivered what had been promised from the Combined Bomber Offensive. The bomber commanders also bear some of the responsibility. By making repeated and often strident claims about the capacity of strategic bombing to make a decisive contribution to shortening the war, they invited the ground forces to exploit those claims in a campaign that was regarded as decisive for the war effort. In the end, the balance between operational and political calculation was bound to fall in favor of the anticipated military outcome. When Eaker asked Portal in 1943, before starting the heavy bombing of French targets, how to overcome political objections to French losses, Portal replied that the government "have never shrunk from loss of civilian life where this can be shown to be an inevitable consequence of a considered and agreed plan."[156]

Eastern Europe: Everywhere but Auschwitz

The first time the RAF was invited to bomb the camp at Auschwitz (Oświęcim) in Poland was in January 1941. At that time it was not the extermination and labor complex of Auschwitz-Birkenau, where more than a million European Jews were murdered between the spring of 1942 and the end of the war, but a camp for 20,000 Polish prisoners of war. The request came, according to General Sikorski's Polish army headquarters in Britain, from the prisoners themselves, who would welcome a bombing raid that would allow them to escape en masse. Air Marshal Peirse, commander in chief of Bomber Command, replied that it was impossible. On clear nights every bomber had to be deployed against German industry. The German war economy, Peirse explained, was likely to experience a crisis in 1941. "Sporadic attacks" against a target such as Auschwitz were unlikely to be accurate enough to do more than kill many of the prisoners.[157]

The next time the RAF was asked to bomb Auschwitz was in July 1944, when it was no longer a prisoner-of-war camp, but the center for the mass murder of European Jews. The complex consisted of three main areas: an extermination camp at Auschwitz-Birkenau; a camp for forced labor selected from those deemed fit enough from among the arrivals; and an industrial complex at nearby Monowitz where the chemical giant I.G. Farben was constructing a plant to produce synthetic rubber and other war-related chemicals. On July 7, following an interview with Chaim Weizmann, president of the Jewish Agency, Eden wrote to Sinclair asking whether it was possible to bomb the camp or the rail tracks leading to it. Churchill was keen to pursue this, but Sinclair, like Peirse, was unsympathetic. He told Eden that interrupting rail traffic in France had proved difficult even with the full weight of Bomber Command behind it; to find and cut a single line far away in Poland was beyond the power of the bomber force. Sinclair doubted that bombing the camp or dropping arms to the prisoners "would really help the victims." He thought the American air forces might be in a better position to do it, and promised to discuss the issue with Spaatz, overall commander of American air forces in Europe.[158] Spaatz was sympathetic, but claimed that nothing could be done without better photographic intelligence of the camp itself. There was extensive reconnaissance material on the nearby Monowitz plant and other war-economic targets around Auschwitz, but although some photographs showed areas of the camp, the extermination center had not been the object of a specific reconnaissance operation.[159] Unknown to Spaatz, the War Department in Washington had already been lobbied several times in the summer of 1944 to undertake bombing of the rail lines or the gas chambers but had deemed the operation to be "impracticable." On August 14 the assistant secretary of war, John McCloy, rejected the request (and did so again when lobbied in November).[160] Two weeks later the Foreign Office informed Sinclair that since the deportation of Hungarian Jews to Auschwitz-Birkenau appeared to have been halted, there was no longer any need to consider an operation to bomb it. On September 1, 1944, Spaatz was instructed to pursue the idea no further.[161]

There has been much academic argument over the question of whether an operation against the Birkenau extermination facility or the railway lines was feasible or not.[162] There is no doubt that had it been a priority target for the Allies, it certainly could have been bombed. At just the time that the Allies were considering the requests from the Jewish Agency to undertake the bombing, the U.S. Fifteenth Air Force began a series of raids on the I.G. Farben complex at Monowitz, where the prisoners in the Auschwitz labor camp were marched to work every day. Auschwitz had been on the Mediterranean Allied Air Forces' target list since at least December 1943, when plans were drawn up for attacks on German oil and chemical plants in eastern Europe.[163] The first raid on August 20, 1944, hit Monowitz accurately, a second on September 13 was hampered by enhanced German antiaircraft defenses, the third and fourth attacks on December 18 and 26 did more damage to the plant, and it was finally abandoned in January 1945 as the Red Army drew near. The damage was not extensive and output of methanol (from one of the completed parts of the site) was reduced by only 12 percent. The raids showed, however, that operations over Auschwitz were indeed feasible; only six aircraft were lost despite the strengthening of German defensive measures.[164]

The raids against Monowitz took place against the background of a second request for "political" bombing. On August 1, 1944, the Polish Home Army began an armed rising against the German garrison in Warsaw. The Polish army in London requested help from the RAF in the form of military supplies dropped from low altitude over the city. Churchill was once again keen that something should be done.[165] The Operation Frantic shuttle bombing to bases in the Ukraine had been temporarily suspended at Soviet insistence, which ruled out supply missions by the Eighth Air Force. Although Portal and Slessor, Eaker's second in command in the Mediterranean, regarded the operations as "not practicable" because of the distance and the prospect of high losses, it was decided that the pressure from the Poles and the expectation that the Red Army would soon capture Warsaw were sufficient grounds for undertaking limited operations.[166] The RAF 205 Group, based at Brindisi in southern Italy (considerably closer to Warsaw than bases in England), was ordered to begin nighttime operations. An unofficial mission had already been flown on the night of August 4–5 to drop weapons to Polish partisans, but only six aircraft arrived at the target and four were shot down. On August 8, Moscow was informed that an airlift to the Poles was about to begin, which almost certainly confirmed the Soviet side in the decision not to allow further shuttle bombing until mid-September, when Polish resistance was almost over.[167] On the night of August 8–9 three Polish aircrews successfully reached Warsaw without loss; a total of nineteen missions were flown, the largest on August 14–15 when twelve out of the twenty-seven aircraft dispatched found Warsaw, for the loss of eight aircraft. Total losses were thirty-five bombers (19 percent) out of 195 sorties, but substantial quantities of ammunition and weapons reached the Home Army in the areas of the city where they still held out.[168] In this case the operational conditions were similar to a putative attack on Auschwitz-Birkenau. The difference in the Allied response in the late summer of 1944 can perhaps best be explained in military terms, for the Poles were fighting against the common German enemy. Appeals to help with civilian victims, whether refugees or those slated for genocide, were regarded as outside the remit of Allied military forces, whatever the moral force of the argument. The PWE rejected a Jewish appeal in December 1943 to take action against the Romanians over the killing of Romanian Jews ("considering the constant spate of requests for warning or appeal from Jewish organisations"), but were happy to suggest bombs on Bucharest in March 1944 to speed up the surrender of Romania's armed forces and to help the approaching Russians.[169] In the end, whether bombing Auschwitz-Birkenau would have had any impact on the conduct of a genocide that had almost run its macabre course by August 1944 remains open to speculation.

The arguments about what was possible in the bombing of eastern Europe, and under what operational conditions, highlights the very different circumstances faced by Allied air forces when confronted with the challenges of distance and geography. For at least the first half of the war, targets in eastern and southeastern Europe were difficult to reach from any bases the RAF might have in the Middle East or North Africa. Navigation problems were magnified for flights from desert airfields across inhospitable terrain with poor mapping and reconnaissance, while maintaining heavy bombers in the heat and dust of the Middle East, thousands of miles from the sophisticated maintenance and logistical system in Britain, was a Sisyphean task. From bases in England, however, most aircraft could not reach distant targets; with the advent of the Lancaster and the Mosquito it took time before serious raids could be mounted even against Berlin, and most of the flight was across the heavily defended areas of the Low Countries and Germany. A large-scale offensive against the Balkan states, Austria, Hungary, and Poland became possible only once bases were available in Italy, from the autumn of 1943.

Some sense of how difficult raiding was to be against targets quite remote from the aerial battlefield in western Europe had already become evident when in 1940, and again in 1941, the RAF undertook preparations to bomb the Soviet oilfields in the Caucasus region in order to deny Germany and Italy vital supplies of fuel. The plans in 1940 were prompted first by the French high command, which wanted to strike at Soviet oil not only to undermine the trade with the Axis states but also to create a possible political crisis for the Soviet Union among the Muslim peoples of southern Russia. French military leaders were much happier about bombing the Soviet Union than bombing Germany.[170] The British side agreed with the plan and drew up a detailed study in April 1940 for deploying forty-eight Blenheim light bombers from bases in Syria and Iraq, supported by sixty-five Glenn Martin bombers bought by the French from American production. RAF planners thought little of Soviet air and antiaircraft defenses, and, like the French, hoped that a three-month attack on Batum, Baku, and Grozny might lead sooner or later "to the complete collapse of the war potential of the USSR," as well as disastrous repercussions for Germany.[171] Chamberlain's cabinet thought the campaign too risky, and following the German attack on France on May 10, the French abandoned the idea. But the RAF remained in a state of readiness to eliminate the entire Soviet oil industry in three months, assuming an average margin of error of seventy-five yards, a conclusion entirely at odds with all the bombing trials conducted in 1939 and 1940.[172] The plan was revived again in June 1941 in the knowledge that Germany was about to attack the Soviet Union. There were strong recommendations from the British embassy in Cairo and the chiefs of staff to use two squadrons of Wellington bombers and two of Blenheims for a month of intensive attacks, not only to deny the oil to the Germans but "to remind the Soviet of consequences of acceding to German demands."[173] Planning was completed by August 1941, but once again operational and strategic reality prevented a campaign in which the means were manifestly inadequate for the military and political ends desired. When an impromptu attack was finally made on German oil supplies in Romania on June 11, 1942, by thirteen B-24 Liberator bombers from the airbase at Fayid in Egypt, the result was described by the Middle East RAF headquarters as a fiasco. The aircraft flew singly and independently; not one reached the oilfield at Ploeşti, but instead they dropped their bombs wherever they could; three returning aircraft landed at Ankara airport, two at Aleppo in Syria, one at Mosul, two more at other desert airfields, and only four reached the planned return base at Habbaniya in Iraq. The unlucky thirteenth aircraft was reported missing.[174]

By the summer of 1943 these conditions had altered a great deal. Victory in North Africa in May 1943 opened the way for the invasion and occupation first of Sicily, then of the southern provinces of mainland Italy. Based in Algiers, the Mediterranean high command, first under Eisenhower, then under the British general Henry Maitland Wilson, began to consider at last a full air offensive, combining both political propaganda and bombs, against the Balkan region and more distant targets in central Europe. The North African air forces were transformed into the Mediterranean Allied Air Forces; the American Ninth Air Force (replaced in November by the Fifteenth) was based in southern Italy at Foggia, and the smaller RAF 205 Group at Brindisi. The political offensive mirrored the activity of the PWE and the RAF in western Europe and Germany. It was based on calculations about how populations in the occupied or satellite areas of eastern Europe might react to leaflet propaganda as well as occasional bombing to enhance political pressure. In the Mediterranean, the American Psychological Warfare Branch (PWB) oversaw the production and distribution of most of the Allied political effort in cooperation with officials from the PWE; how that worked in the Italian campaign has already been described. Out of the more than 1.5 billion leaflets produced at the PWB center at Bari and dropped by air or fired in propaganda "shells" whose paper contents burst over enemy lines, hundreds of millions were targeted at Albania, Greece, Hungary, Bulgaria, Romania, Czechoslovakia, and the Yugoslav territories Serbia, Croatia, and Slovenia.[175]

The United States demonstrated the same confident enthusiasm for political warfare as the British. "History may well show," wrote the Eighth Air Force assistant chief of staff, "that no single factor has contributed more to the raising and sustaining of morale in the occupied countries." The combined effect of the British and American leaflet campaigns, he continued, "will shorten the war as a certainty."[176] A pamphlet produced under Spaatz's signature to explain the value of airborne propaganda to American crews (who, like RAF flyers, preferred dropping bombs to paper) claimed that the millions of RAF leaflets had brought "truth, hope and comfort" to the oppressed and sustained the will for sabotage and resistance. "In occupied territory the spirit of rebellion is being fanned," Spaatz continued. "The output of the factories suffers as surely as if they had been struck by bombs."[177] A sophisticated technology was developed to ensure that the leaflets fluttered down over a wide area. A single bomber could carry up to a million leaflets at a time. Two large canisters were installed in the bomb bay, each holding sixty bundles of approximately 16,000 leaflets bound by a cord fixed to a barometric device. On release from the aircraft each bundle tumbled down until the change in air pressure acted on the release mechanism, scattering the individual leaflets over a wide area. The system was not foolproof: sometimes the bundles opened prematurely, scattering the loads in the wrong place; sometimes they failed to open and whole bundles, each weighing around fifty-five pounds, fell dangerously on the target population.[178]

Both the American PWB and the British PWE understood that for eastern Europe the propaganda had to be carefully calibrated to match the circumstances of individual countries, some of which were satellite states of Germany, others the victims of invasion and occupation. For the satellites the propaganda had to suggest the option of abandoning the German alliance and helping the Allies. The leaflet "Take a Decision" dropped in May 1944 on Hungary, Bulgaria, Romania, and Finland had this object in mind. Occupied Czechoslovakia, on the other hand, had to be appealed to differently. Intelligence sources suggested that the Czechs felt abandoned by the Allies as they had been at Munich in September 1938, and the figures show that Czechoslovakia indeed received only a fraction of the leaflet drops made on other areas.[179] Above all, the political initiative had to be related to the possibility or probability of bombing, either as a threat or as a promise. The Czech sources confirmed that workers were waiting for the bombing to start and would add sabotage to anything the bombs failed to destroy. For the satellite states, bombing was seen, like the case of Bulgaria, as a means to bring the war home to these distant and formerly immune peoples. In the summer of 1944 the Western Allies also had to take account of the onrush of the Red Army, which was by now poised to invade central and southeastern Europe. The PWE assessment of bombing Bucharest, for example, pointed out that bombs might increase Romanian "depression," but were unlikely to induce defection from the war as the Romanian army struggled desperately to keep the Soviet invaders at bay. Bombs dropped on Hungary were regarded as more useful, as they would remind the Hungarian government and population that they had to do more to sever their connection with Germany.[180] Even against satellite states, the political warfare officers recommended attacks only on evidently military targets so as to avoid alienating the populations that were to be liberated from German domination. Czech informers made it clear that as allies, the Czech people should not be subjected to area bombing, which would provoke "serious resentment."[181] The Yugoslav partisan armies welcomed precise raids on German targets, but not raids on the major cities. The propaganda made much of Allied claims for bombing accuracy against military targets but was occasionally let down by the translation. A leaflet destined for Axis Bulgaria in late 1943 had the English "blockbuster bomb" (designed to destroy factories or military facilities) translated into Bulgarian as "homewrecker."[182]

These political imperatives were integrated as far as possible with the military planning directed at eastern Europe, although the promise of accuracy was as difficult to fulfill in this case as it had been in the west. For the Western Allies there was only one principal target in eastern Europe once the area came within effective bombing range. The oil-producing region around Ploeşti in Romania supplied around 3 million tons of oil annually to Germany and Italy out of a total production of 5–6 million tons. For Germany, Romanian exports in 1943 amounted to one-third of all German oil products.[183] Since oil was a major target for the Combined Bomber Offensive, the interruption of Romanian supplies assumed a high priority. The RAF had begun to explore the possibility of raiding Ploeşti in the spring of 1942 to aid the Soviet Union, but the operation, at the limit of aircraft range, was regarded as impossible with current strengths. The Combined Chiefs of Staff at the Casablanca Conference in January 1943 called for the immediate bombing of the oilfield, but when Churchill asked Portal to consider the operation he was told that it was still too risky, not only because it would require flying over Turkish airspace to be feasible, but because it would have to be a single heavy and demobilizing strike, which current air strengths in the North African theater could not promise.[184] Although Churchill was willing, as he told Eden, "to put the screw very hard on Turkey" to modify its neutrality for the RAF, the attack on Ploeşti when it came was made by American air forces acting under pressure from the American Joint Chiefs to act quickly to block Axis oil supplies.[185] The British contribution to the opening raid was to supply good maps of the region and large-scale models of the refineries. Portal was keen to allocate three skilled Lancaster crews because he was not confident that American pilots would be able to navigate the 1,850-mile trip successfully, but in the end the raid launched on August 1, 1943, was made only by the B-24 aircraft of the recently constituted Ninth Air Force.[186]

The American operation was first code-named Statesman, then changed in May to "Soapsuds." Churchill disliked the new choice— "unworthy of those who would face the hazards"—and it was eventually christened, with Roosevelt's approval, Operation Tidalwave.[187] The operation required a great deal of preparation. It was originally scheduled for June 23, 1943, but postponed not only because priority was given to air support for the invasion of Sicily in July 1943, but because the period of intelligence research and crew training took much longer than anticipated. For the American airmen involved the raid was a daunting prospect. When a British adviser appeared at the airbase at Benghazi from which the raid was to be mounted, he found the morale of the crew "about as bad as it could possibly be": they told him that they lacked experience of the low-level bombing chosen to maximize the impact of the attack; that they had no previous experience of operations over such long distances; that the countries over which they had to fly were completely exotic, "populated by cannibals" for all they knew. Rigorous training and better information on the value of the raid contributed to overcoming the worst fears, but there could be no disguising that Ploeşti was one of the most heavily defended targets in Europe.[188] American intelligence on German defenses was in general poor, because the target was remote from the main operational theaters. Instead of the 100 antiaircraft guns identified, there proved to be well over 200; instead of a token force of fighter aircraft, there were more than 200 Me109, Me110, and Ju88 aircraft, as well as the Romanian and Bulgarian air forces along the line of attack. The defense of Ploeşti was under the command of Lieutenant General Alfred Gerstenberg, who was also the unofficial German "protector" of Romania. He long expected an Allied attack and introduced regular exercises for the defenses as well as establishing a line of radar stations and a corps of visual observers in the Balkan region. Chemical-smoke battalions were ready to obscure the target, while two dummy sites were constructed northwest and east of the complex to distract any attacker.[189] This was as formidable a defense as any available in Germany itself. For the American crews it meant an operation that was likely to be more suicidal than any they would encounter in western Europe.

The raid on August 1, 1943, began early in the morning. Under the command of Brigadier General Uzal Ent, 177 aircraft flew off on a course designed to take them to the northwest of Ploești, in order to avoid the guns and the barrage of 100 balloons. Over Romania the lead commander turned east at the wrong point, bringing most of the force close to Bucharest, where the German defenders were put on full alert. The force turned north into the teeth of the antiaircraft and fighter defenses. Some small groups flew low into the oil complex and bombed designated targets from 500 feet, but most, on Ent's orders, bombed what they could and escaped. The planned return route was abandoned as aircraft damaged by antiaircraft fire and harried by German fighters flew south in disarray. Only 88 returned to Benghazi; 11 landed in Cyprus, 8 in Sicily, 4 on Malta, 8 were interned at Turkish bases, and 2 crashed into the sea. A total of 54 aircraft were lost, many in acts of extraordinary courage in low-level attacks against massed defenses. Almost all those that returned had suffered damage. Two weeks later the survivors were sent on a further long-range mission against the Wiener-Neustadt aircraft plant in Austria, but on this occasion suffered only two losses against the lightest of resistance.[190]

The results of the Ploești raid fell short of the ambition to knock the complex out for months, but enough serious damage was done to reduce output substantially at three major refineries and to destroy two completely. Spare capacity and rapid repair nevertheless reduced the effects on German supplies of crude oil. The effect on the local population was to produce a sudden exodus into the surrounding countryside, but casualties were relatively low save for eighty-four women killed when one aircraft crashed onto their prison.[191] The oilfield was allowed an eight-month respite during which time the pre-raid levels of output were once again restored. Losses of 40 percent of the force could not be sustained, and the Allied air forces had other urgent priorities in Italy and southern Germany. At a conference on bombing strategy in Gibraltar in November 1943 between Spaatz, Eaker, Tedder, and Doolittle, the main concern was coordinating attacks on German targets from England and Italy. It was agreed that Balkan capitals might make a good morale target, and Sofia was bombed shortly afterward, but oil in southeastern

Europe had for the moment disappeared as a priority.[192] Not until March 17, 1944, was Spaatz informed by Arnold that the Combined Chiefs of Staff favored a renewed attack on Ploeşti when good weather permitted, but the changing strategic situation, with Soviet forces driving on southeastern Europe, gave priority to bombing communications around Bucharest rather than oil, and the target was again postponed.[193] The change back to oil came later after Spaatz lost his argument with Portal over the best strategy for the pre-Normandy bombing and had to accept the Transportation Plan. In order to get at oil surreptitiously, he allowed Eaker to send aircraft not only against the communications targets around Bucharest but to attack once again the Romanian oilfield.

The result was a devastating series of twenty-four raids against Ploeşti between April 5 and August 19, 1944, under the command of Major General Nathan Twining. Twenty of the raids were undertaken by the Fifteenth Air Force, four at night by RAF 205 Group. Between them they dropped 13,863 tons of bombs, all but 577 from American aircraft. German and Romanian defenses had been strengthened since the first raid. Alongside thirty-four heavy and sixteen light antiaircraft batteries and seven searchlight batteries, there were between 200 and 250 aircraft.[194] By the close of the offensive there were 278 heavy and 280 light guns, including the new heavy-caliber 105- and 128-millimeter, supported by 1,900 smoke generators. The oilfield was designated a German "stronghold" and Gerstenberg was appointed by the German high command as "German Commandant of the Romanian Oil Region."[195] But this time the American bombers flew at high altitude, protected by large numbers of long-range P-38 and P-51 fighters. As a result the contest proved more one-sided than the raid in August 1943. Axis air forces managed to mount 182 sorties against the first raid, on April 5, when 13 out of 200 bombers were lost. But by July the sortie rate had fallen to an average of 53 against the five raids that month. On the final raid, on August 19, there was no fighter opposition.[196] Total losses were 230 American bombers, many to antiaircraft fire. Destruction of the refineries was as complete as it could be, with half a million tons of oil destroyed, and more sunk through the successful mining operations on the Danube carried out mainly at night by RAF 205 Group. Some 1,400 mines were dropped and traffic on the Danube was reduced by two-thirds, though 15 percent of the RAF force was lost in raids carried out dangerously at between 100 and 200 feet above the river.[197]

In a final gesture, on the eve of the Soviet entry into Romania, Gerstenberg gathered together any German troops he could find, together with the oilfield antiaircraft division, in a bid to seize Bucharest, where the young King Michael had overthrown the Antonescu government, and bring the capital under German control. To support the coup, the German Air Force mounted a heavy raid on the center of Bucharest on August 24, destroying some of the administrative center around the royal palace. The population, according to the German ambassador, was taken completely by surprise, perplexed by the sudden change from German ally to German enemy. But the German coup was stifled by the Romanian army and the German presence replaced by Soviet forces.[198] In September 1944, Eaker was given permission by the authorities in Moscow to visit Romania, which had been occupied by Soviet forces on August 30. He found the devastation at Ploeşti worse than any photoreconnaissance image he had seen. The information Eaker was given showed that refining capacity had been reduced by 90 percent. By the last attack on August 19, remaining German personnel were only able to transport an estimated 2–4 percent of Romanian capacity. He found his reception cordial and the Red Army commanders astonished at what high-level bombing could achieve. The Romanian people, Eaker reported to Washington, "look upon us as liberators."[199]

In truth the bombing of Romania did not liberate the population but contributed to the collapse of German resistance and half a century of Soviet domination. Whatever the political ambitions to intimidate the Balkan satellites into surrender or to boost the morale of Czechs and Yugoslavs, the pattern of bombing across eastern Europe was to a great extent governed by the military interest of the Allies in weakening German military resistance to the advancing Red Army. The priority given to communications and oil during the course of the summer of 1944 matched the priorities agreed for the bombing of Germany from English bases and brought a great many more locations in Czechoslovakia, Poland, and the Balkans onto the list of key targets assigned to the MAAF.

The strategic commitment to attacking German communications in the region was made in April 1944 when it was realized how successful the Soviet advance had been during the winter months.[200] The MAAF drew up a survey at the end of April 1944 to see what could be done in "giving direct aid to the Russian army," first by cutting German supplies, then by interrupting any German withdrawal in the event of a Russian breakthrough.[201] In May, Portal instructed Spaatz to give top priority to bombing communications in Romania and Hungary and to treat the whole European transport system "as one" when undermining German mobility.[202] Eighteen marshaling yards were singled out for attack, with high priority given to the yards at Bucharest where the Romanian authorities told Eaker later that a Fifteenth Air Force raid had killed 12,000 people, 6,000 of them refugees sitting in trains on the track in the belief that the air-raid siren was only a test. The raid was indeed a heavy one, hitting part of the residential area of the city, but official figures showed only 231 killed and 1,567 buildings destroyed or damaged.[203] From June 1944 oil was finally given a top priority and oil targets in Czechoslovakia and Poland were added to the list of potential targets throughout the region.[204] Right to the end politics played a part in bombing calculations. Strategic attacks against targets in Germany, Austria, and Hungary could be undertaken either by visual or by blind-bombing techniques against any military target defined in the broadest sense, including "targets of opportunity." Over Czech and Polish territory crews were only permitted to bomb the designated military target visually or in exceptional cases by blind bombing, but no opportunity targets were permitted, to minimize the risk of casualties among allied populations.[205]

The most urgent need was to devise a way of ensuring that American and British aircraft did not accidentally bomb or strafe the advancing Soviet lines. In April 1944 a bomb line was agreed, with the Soviet side in southeastern Europe from Constanza, on the Romanian coast, through Bucharest, Ploeşti, and Budapest. Only the last three could be the object of bomb attack, and American airmen were warned to learn the silhouettes and markings of Soviet aircraft.[206] The Soviet forces continued to inform their allies of the changing front line through the Allied missions in Moscow, though the MAAF had also posted representatives informally at the headquarters of the Soviet army group in the Balkans to try to minimize any hazard. A zone of forty miles in front of the advancing Red Army was agreed as the limit for British and American bomber operations, but information about where the line was had to come through a cumbersome process of consultation in the Soviet capital. As the Allied air forces converged from east and west, the danger of inadvertent bombing increased. On November 7, 1944, a force of twenty-seven P-38 Lightnings strafed and bombed a Soviet column in Yugoslavia fifty miles behind the Soviet front line, killing the commander and five others. Three of the nine Soviet fighters sent to protect the column were shot down.[207] Stalin's military headquarters made a strong protest and suggested a bomb line running from Stettin on the Baltic coast down through Vienna to Zagreb and Sarajevo in Yugoslavia, leaving many designated oil and transport targets out of bounds to Western air forces. The Combined Chiefs of Staff refused to accept a bomb line farther north than the Danube, but offered to set up a proper liaison organization with advancing Soviet armies to avoid further mishaps. When Moscow rejected the idea of any collaboration on the ground, Spaatz and Eaker worked out their own bomb line and communicated it to Moscow, sealing Dresden's fate a few weeks later.[208] The Soviet desire to reduce the bombing in eastern Europe was not disinterested, since by that stage of the war Moscow wanted to capture resources, equipment, and plants intact before the strategic air forces obliterated them shortly before they fell into the Soviet sphere. After the war, the formal communist line was to argue that bombing in the teeth of the Red Army advance had been carried out by the agents of capitalist imperialism to weaken the future socialist economy.

Unlike the situation in the western zones of Germany and Austria, it proved impossible for American or British intelligence teams to survey systematically the damage that bombing had done to the industrial and infrastructure targets in eastern Europe, or to establish how effective the political offensive against the satellite and occupied populations had been. An American military mission arrived in Sofia in November 1944, but the Red Army command proved uncooperative. Eaker's visit to Ploeşti in September 1944 was the closest that Allied air commanders got to assessment of the damage, and his judgment that the offensive was "a perfect example of what bombing can do to industry" is supported by the German figures on oil supply.[209] By the end of the war relations between the Allies were already cooling and Stalin was unwilling to allow Western intelligence officers access to the bomb sites in the Soviet-controlled regions of Europe. In July 1945 some of the USSBS team arrived in Berlin, where amid the chaos they tracked down Speer's chief economist, Rolf Wagenführ, who was already working for the Russian occupiers. An American team broke into his house in Soviet East Berlin, dragged him out of bed, and bundled him onto an airplane to the American zone, where he gave advice on German statistics for two weeks before being sent back. A key was also found to the German Air Ministry document safe where additional information was discovered; a discreet foray into the Soviet zone secured more German papers.[210] But all this was little substitute for ground-level reconnaissance of the targets bombed in Czechoslovakia, Poland, and the Balkan states. Assessment of whether bombing had delivered the political dividend in encouraging Axis populations to abandon the link with Germany was open to speculation. In Bulgaria, Romania, and Slovakia the political scene was dominated by the imminent arrival of the Red Army. The resentment and anxiety provoked by sporadic bombing of civilian areas, evident from intelligence sources, paled into insignificance at the prospect of a Soviet empire.[211] This was not the political outcome the West had wished for when the air forces were at last in the position to rain down bombs and leaflets on the distant East.

Rotterdam Once Again

The situation for the smaller states in the German New Order on the northern fringes of Europe—Belgium, the Netherlands, Denmark, and Norway—differed from the fate of France and of eastern Europe. In both these latter cases invasion displaced the German occupier well before the final end of the war in Europe. Belgium was finally fully liberated by November 1944, but not before heavy bombing by the Allies and V-weapon attack by the German side had inflicted wide destruction and casualties. The Netherlands, Denmark, and Norway remained under German occupation until the end of the war. A raid by RAF bombers that hit residential districts of The Hague on March 3, 1945, killing more than 500 people, occurred just weeks before liberation.[212] Over the course of the war the enthusiasm relayed to the Allies by Dutch, Belgian, or Norwegian resisters about bombing German targets became tempered by growing resentment at the cost in lives and livelihoods imposed on those caught in the crossfire of war.

There was also an important political difference in the case of Norway, the Netherlands, and Belgium. Each had a government-in-exile in London, with a miniature apparatus of state. Unlike any other bombed state, the exile governments could represent directly to the British government their views on bombing policy and their objection to or approval of its conduct. This in turn placed considerable pressure on the RAF, and later the U.S. air forces, to ensure that the guidelines governing the bombing of targets in the region clearly expressed its limits. Damage to civilian targets and civilian deaths had to be explained or apologized for, unlike raiding against most other targets in Europe. This was even more the case when bombs intended for a German destination instead fell inadvertently on Dutch or Belgian cities. Both states lay on the flight paths to German targets for the whole war period. The Dutch town of Groningen was bombed by mistake on July 26, 1940, and two people were killed; it was bombed again in error when the German port of Emden was shrouded in fog on the night of September 26–27, 1941, and this time six people died.[213] Maastricht was bombed by mistake for Aachen in February 1942, prompting Dutch protests that the RAF used trainee crews for nearer and easier targets, as they did, making mischance more likely. Raids deliberately targeted against Dutch cities provoked even higher casualties. Operations against targets in Rotterdam in October 1941 and January 1942 cost 177 Dutch lives; a raid in October 1942 on Geelen and one two months later on the Philips electrical works at Eindhoven killed a further 221.[214] Although the British Foreign Office believed that the Dutch took the robust view that "war is war," Eden remained keen to ensure that proper guidelines were drawn up and crews instructed in their observance.[215] Belgian and Dutch targets were governed by the same rules drawn up in October 1942 for bombing occupied France, with the difference that attacks on trains by night could only take place between the hours of eleven o'clock in the evening and four o'clock in the morning rather than throughout the hours of darkness. Military targets had to be identified, and if the prospect of a "large error" occurred that was likely to lead to civilian casualties, the operation was supposed to be aborted.[216]

The systematic bombing of military and industrial targets in the Low Countries only began in 1943 when the Eighth Air Force used its heavy and medium bombers for attacks on targets near enough for fighter protection so that novice crews could be initiated into operational practice with fewer immediate risks, the very policy condemned by the Dutch when bombing started in 1941. The result was an immediate disaster. A daylight raid on Rotterdam on March 31, 1943, cost an estimated 400 lives; an attack that was supposed to hit the German Erla aircraft plant near Antwerp instead devastated the town of Mortsel, killing 926 Belgians, including 209 children in four schools hit by the bombs. The bombing of Mortsel resulted in the worst casualties of the war from a single raid on the Low Countries. No warning leaflets had been dropped and the town was crowded with people. In addition to the dead, a further 1,342 were injured, 587 seriously, while 3,424 houses were damaged or destroyed. In the Erla works, 222 workers were killed.[217] Although heavy damage was done to the aircraft plant, the bombs were strewn over a wide residential area. The Eighth Air Force post-raid assessment showed that only 78 out of 383 bombs dropped came within 2,000 feet (600 meters) of the target.[218] For the residents of the town the raid was a shocking realization of the horrors of aerial war. "I heard the screams of dying schoolchildren," recalled one witness. "I heard the grief-stricken cries of desperate mothers and fathers, searching in the ruins for their beloved children. . . . I saw fires, heaps of ruins and people wringing their hands."[219] A Foreign Office official wrote to the PWE a few days later describing the raid as "catastrophic"; the "bad shooting" of the Eighth Air Force, he complained, had done serious damage to the reputation of Allied air forces in a country that had hitherto welcomed the idea of bombs on German targets.[220]

The poor record of American bombing soon provoked a wider crisis. Eaker was first asked by the Air Ministry to take special care in bombing centers where civilians were likely to be hurt, then told to suspend bombing in occupied areas altogether pending a decision about which specific targets should be allowed. Despite protests from Washington, a list was agreed to between the two air forces, and Eaker and Harris were asked to avoid using freshmen crews against targets in major cities. The twenty accepted targets included only one in the Netherlands and five in Belgium. Bomber Command agreed to use only reliable and experienced crews, but Eaker insisted on the continued right of the American bomber force to use novices.[221] No sooner was the list agreed upon than the new Pointblank directive, drawn up for the Combined Bomber Offensive, apparently reversed the decision by listing targets in densely populated areas of occupied Europe as part of the overall plan. Eaker at once asked whether he was now free to bomb what he liked, but the issue could only be resolved at the highest level. Eden worried that civilian casualties in Belgium and the Netherlands would deeply affect "the morale and spirit" of the local population and asked that radio broadcasts and leaflets should notify the people of impending bombing, but only after agreement had been reached with the Dutch and Belgian governments in London.[222] Leaflets were drafted warning the population that it would be dangerous to work in any factories assembling aircraft, locomotives, submarines, and vehicles or any one of their component parts. On June 25 the Belgian government-in-exile agreed to allow the new targets to be bombed once warning had been given; the Dutch government followed suit on July 15, but only after making it clear that they would only tolerate operations conducted in such a way "as to minimize the danger to the civilian population."[223]

Once again the raiding habit of flying at high altitude against targets that even when visible could not be hit with sufficient accuracy broke the pledge to bomb with greater discretion. The Eighth Air Force began operations with B-17 Flying Fortresses against Dutch targets just two days after receiving approval from the Dutch government. The target chosen was the Fokker aircraft plant in Amsterdam, first bombed by the RAF in 1940 with little effect.[224] The American operation on July 17 killed 185 people and missed the factory. One bomb hit the church of St. Rita, filled with 500 schoolchildren who were singing an "Ave Maria" to ward off danger after the siren had sounded. Eleven were killed in the church; another 29 died when a bomb hit a doctor's waiting room. Around 130 buildings were destroyed.[225] The Dutch government-in-exile immediately protested and Eaker was asked to explain how he was going to avoid a repetition. The Eighth Air Force switched temporarily from using B-17s to using the medium twin-engine Martin Marauder B-26 bombers for attacks on Dutch and Belgian targets from lower altitude. On their second raid, against a Dutch power station at Ijmuiden, all eleven B-26s were shot down.[226] Over the months that followed the B-26s were instructed to fly higher and casualties on the ground mounted again. The bombing of Ghent on September 4, 1943, resulted in 111 dead, that on Brussels on September 7 using B-17s caused a further 327 deaths.[227] An American raid on Enschede on October 10, again using B-17s, killed 150. The damage to the German war effort was limited. The Fokker works completed a program of dispersal and decentralization into forty-three smaller locations scattered around the Amsterdam region.[228] For Dutch workers and producers, as in Belgium and France, the choice of refusing to work for the German military was to run the risk that both the machinery and the workers would be transferred to Germany. In Rotterdam by 1944 over 40,000 workers had been sent to work in the Reich; repeated raids, which killed a total of 748 people in the city during the war, encouraged the German occupiers to move workers to industry in Germany, where there was effective protection and the means to compel compliance.[229]

The inclusion of Dutch and Belgian firms in the Pointblank plan came about as a result of the contribution made by their industries to German aircraft and submarine production, as well as the supply of machinery and steel. There were no complete aircraft produced in Belgium, although hundreds of small firms supplied components; in the Netherlands, however, 414 aircraft were built in 1943 and 442 in 1944, while Dutch shipbuilders supplied an important source of additional capacity for the submarine industry and for the production of smaller naval vessels.[230] By the end of 1943 around 75,000 Belgian and 109,000 Dutch workers were employed on German arms contracts.[231] The transfer of German production to the occupied territories gave the occupiers sufficient reason to provide limited protection from air attack. Antiaircraft guns and fighters stationed in the Low Countries formed, as in France, part of the air defense rampart around the European fortress, which in the Netherlands included ten squadrons of night fighters by 1944 and seventy-four sites for radar and electronic warfare.[232] Regiments of German fire-protection police were also stationed in the Low Countries to supplement the efforts of the local population organized, in the Dutch case, in an Air Protection Service (Luchtbeschermingsdienst) first set up in April 1936 and organized by urban district, street, and housing block. The attitude of the population to the raiding was complex, since many Allied aircraft crashed in the Low Countries, and in many cases surviving crew were helped by the local population or benefited from escape networks. The local press generally condemned the raids with high civilian casualties, although in no occupied territory was the press free from German controls or from the numerous German communiqués on terror bombing they were given. An article in the *Haagsche Courant* on a bombing attack with twenty-two dead carried the headline "That's It: Murder," and ended with the question "Is that not terroristic?" Another article following the bombing of Rotterdam on January 29, 1942, carried the headline "Bloody Work of the English Air Pirates!"[233] British intelligence from Belgium and the Netherlands, however, only suggested that the barometer of popular support for bombing fluctuated as it did in France with the perceived accuracy or inaccuracy of a raid. There was, however, little sign of open resistance as there had been in the early years of war. A report sent to the PWE in November 1943 observed that the people "are just weak and passive."[234]

The most intensive period of bombing came in 1944 with the preparations for the Normandy invasion and the Crossbow raids against sites intended for the V-1 and V-2 missiles. Most of the raids were small tactical raids against rail and air targets carried out by medium bombers

and fighter-bombers. But as Belgium and the Netherlands became involuntary parts of the vast aerial battlefield in northwestern Europe, so the
pace of destruction and loss of life quickened. There descended on both
populations a rain of bombs and leaflets, the second designed to explain
the liberating effects of the first. In April and May 1944 the Eighth Air
Force undertook 1,111 sorties against German airbases in the two countries, and in May 759 sorties against marshaling yards, losing only
twenty aircraft in the process.[235] The preparatory raids by heavy bombers involved some of the highest casualties of the war. In Belgium 252
were killed in Kortrijk on March 26, 428 in Ghent on April 10. The
peak in Belgium came between May 10 and 12, when more than 1,500
died, culminating in a raid on Leuven in which 246 were killed. The
Overlord preparations cost Belgium a total of 2,180 civilian dead.[236]
The Netherlands was bombed less heavily during the late spring, but on
February 22, 1944, it had suffered the severest raid of the war when the
city center of Nijmegen was hit by a group of B-24 bombers returning
from an aborted mission over Germany. The aircrew aimed for a marshaling yard on the edge of the town, still believing that they were over
German territory. Instead the lead bombardier misjudged the speed,
dropping bombs in the crowded city center, followed by the rest of the
combat box. The estimated 800 dead were caught in the open after the
all-clear had been given a few minutes before the bombs began to fall.
Some 1,270 buildings were destroyed or badly damaged. On this occasion the Dutch government, not fully aware of the results of the raid,
lodged no protest.[237] Over the following three months more than 50 million leaflets were dropped on Belgium, 55 million on the Netherlands,
preparing both populations for their liberation but including a leaflet
apologizing for the bombing of Nijmegen and regretting that under the
circumstances of modern air war "sometimes harm and grief was caused
to our friends."[238]

    During the period when the noose was tightened around the Ger-
man New Order, little attention was given to conditions in Scandinavia.
Denmark, like the Low Countries, was astride the bombing runs to targets in Germany and became the inadvertent target from occasional
errors of navigation as well as the site of numerous Allied aircraft that

either crashed or were forced to land. Most of the raiding against German naval targets and airfields was carried out by aircraft of Coastal Command until the end of 1941, when Bomber Command Blenheims and Mosquitos were detailed to attack land targets, while Coastal Command concentrated on targets at sea. The German occupiers collaborated with the Danish civil defense organization, Statens Civile Luftvaern, in observing incoming aircraft. A large number of light antiaircraft guns protected military installations, and when the Kammhuber Line was extended into Denmark to give better protection against RAF raids in 1941, squadrons of German night fighters were also based at Danish airfields.[239] There were almost no strategic Allied air attacks on Denmark. Most bombs were jettisoned or dropped in error, a total of 3,269 high explosive and 22,298 incendiaries counted by Danish civil defense. The only planned attack on an industrial target took place on January 27, 1943, when eight Mosquitos attacked the Burmeister & Wain diesel engine factory in Copenhagen. Some damage was done, and a sugar plant was set on fire. The raid resulted from PWE pressure to undertake an attack on at least one industrial target in each occupied state to discourage collaboration and to reinforce local morale. In the Danish case the raid proved a success: there were few casualties, and in the aftermath Danes took to wearing RAF colors as a mark of sympathy with a distant ally. The only raid by the Eighth Air Force was against Esbjerg airfield on the west coast of Jutland on August 27, 1944, bombed as a target of opportunity following an aborted raid on Berlin. Over the whole course of the war 307 Danes were killed as a result of all Allied air activity and 788 injured.[240]

Operations against Norway were also linked closely to the air-sea war, but Norway differed from Denmark because there were important industrial and raw material resources that the Germans exploited throughout the occupation, particularly aluminum production and the development of "heavy water" for the German nuclear research program. Both were attacked by the Eighth Air Force, the aluminum plant at Heröya on July 24, 1943, the Norsk Hydro plant on November 16. Spaatz was pleased with the result and thought "it was heartening to the Norwegians."[241] Far from being heartened, the Norwegian government complained that the destruction of the Norsk Hydro plant, which produced a large quantity of Scandinavia's much-needed fertilizer, had provoked "bewilderment and dismay" among the Norwegian population as they contemplated declining food output. The small heavy water plant had been successfully sabotaged by the Norwegian Resistance some months before. The Norwegian foreign minister, Trygve Lie, asked the Allies to agree upon a means of collaborating on the choice of targets to avoid further mishaps. It took almost a year of argument before an agreed list was drawn up. British air marshals, Lie complained, were a law unto themselves.[242] When the Air Ministry presented a list of seven targets they would like to bomb, the Norwegian high command responded that some were wrong, some had ceased operating, and others were essential to Norway's economy when the war was over.[243] A second list was worked out with Norwegian advice and finally agreed to on November 2, 1944. But only four days before that, Bomber Command had tried to hit the submarine pens at Bergen in poor weather. The bombs struck the town center, killing fifty-two civilians and burning down Europe's oldest theater. The Norwegian government again warned the Foreign Office that raids without an evident military purpose merely alienated a potentially friendly population. Though on the agreed list, Bergen had been attacked by forty-seven Lancasters, against instructions, through almost complete cloud cover.[244]

For Norway and Denmark the price of remaining occupied was substantially lower than the price paid by Belgium and the Netherlands as they became the focus of the ground campaign from the autumn of 1944. As was the case in France, operational requirements soon came to replace political calculations when deciding on targets to attack. Belgium was caught in between the fighting powers as Allied armies occupied Belgian territory in September 1944. From sites in western Germany, the V-weapons were turned against Allied forces in Antwerp and the surrounding territory, while a few were launched against Paris. The first V-2 rocket fell on October 7 in Brasschaat on the outskirts of Antwerp, the first V-1 flying bomb on October 21. The last V-1 struck on March 28, 1945. Around 12,000 V-1s were launched at Belgian targets, and 1,600 V-2s.[245] The port of Antwerp suffered most. The worst incident occurred on December 16 when a V-2 fell on the Rex Cinema, killing 271 Belgians and an estimated 300 soldiers.[246] Late in 1944 a British civil defense mobile column was sent to Belgium at the request of Montgomery's 21st Army Group, complete with canteens, ambulances, and fire units; three British rescue instructors were sent to Brussels, Antwerp, and Eindhoven to train soldiers for emergency work after a rocket strike.[247] In November 1944 the American brigadier general C. H. Armstrong was appointed commander of Flying Bomb Command Antwerp X, and three belts of antiaircraft guns were set up in a ring around the city to shoot down the flying bombs. RAF Fighter Command set up a Continental Crossbow Forward Unit in December 1944 to add fighter interception of the flying bombs to the effects of antiaircraft fire. By February almost three-quarters of the V-1s were destroyed before they hit the city, a total of 7,412 over the course of the campaign. Only 73 fell in the dock area of Antwerp and only 101 on the built-up area. The effect on the flow of Allied supplies through the port was described in the official account of the campaign as "negligible."[248] Against the V-2 rocket, however, there was no defense; the Belgian population became once again hostage to their geographical location and suffered a heavy toll. In total 6,500 were killed and 22,500 injured in the last flurry of bombardment from the air, almost exactly the same number of casualties exacted by the V-weapon attacks on England. This final German aerial assault greatly increased the overall Belgian casualties from air bombardment during the war. An estimated total of 18,000 Belgians were killed, one-third from German operations.[249]

Since the Netherlands was used as a base for firing V-weapons, the threat of Allied bombing hung over the Dutch population until almost the end of the war. The battle for Arnhem in September 1944 brought further heavy raids against German military targets by both the Eighth Air Force and Bomber Command. The continual bombardment of London by V-2 rockets from sites in the Netherlands finally prompted a decision to try to neutralize the threat by bombing, despite their proximity to residential areas. On March 3, RAF bombers of the Second Tactical Air Force flew from bases in Belgium to bomb a V-2 site in a large park in the north of The Hague. The weather was poor—cloudy and with a strong wind—and the briefing officer had confused the map coordinates, instructing the force to bomb more than a kilometer away from the intended target. The sixty B-25 Mitchell and A-20 Boston/Havoc aircraft dropped sixty-seven tons of bombs on a residential area of the Dutch capital, killing an estimated 520 and rendering 12,000 homeless. A stream of up to 50,000 refugees fled from the area, some of them, one eyewitness wrote, still in their pajamas: "a long procession of people and children crying . . . some were all white from lying under the ruins. Others bled from a variety of injuries, which were half-bandaged or not covered at all. . . . More and yet more."[250] Over the course of the war an estimated total of between 8,000 and 10,000 Dutch deaths came from bombing, around one-tenth of them caused by German raids.[251]

The bombing, so close to the end of the war, provoked a furious response from the Dutch government in London and strong criticism from Churchill. A broadcast apology was made later in the month, promising a full inquiry, but nothing was relayed to the Dutch authorities, who repeated the request in June 1945 for an explanation.[252] The Air Ministry told the Foreign Office at the end of June that the internal investigation had discovered the error in plotting the coordinates for the raid and had court-martialed the officer responsible. There was, however, little sense of contrition. The operation, claimed the ministry, was a difficult one: "The extent of the disaster must to some extent be set down to the mischances of war."[253] Six months later a Dutch woman wrote to King George VI asking him to pay compensation for the total loss of her house and possessions in the March 3 raid. The letter summed up the ambivalence felt by the liberated peoples about being bombed into freedom:

I humbly come to you, first to express my great gratitude for all you, the English Government and the English people have done to deliver us from those awful huns. Second to ask you for help. On March 3 my house (home) with all that was therein, was bombed and nothing could be saved. . . . And now after nearly ten months, I sit here as poor and forlorn as on March 3. . . . It may seem rather impudent from me, to ask you for help, but I know you are righteous and honest, above all, and that in no way you will have a

widow been left in solicitude [*sic*] and affliction, where there is still
a debt for the RAF to be redeemed.[254]

The Foreign Office contacted the Air Ministry for confirmation that
nothing could be done for what was clearly "a hazard of war." The ministry replied that nothing should be done: "If we started paying for this
kind of loss there would be no end to our liability."[255]

In all the bombing of New Order Europe a balance was supposed to be
struck between political calculation and military imperatives, since the
peoples to be bombed were allies or potential allies. The cautious bombing of the first two years of war reflected a balance in favor of political
restraint. In some cases bombing was used as a "calling card," to remind
populations under German domination not to collaborate or to encourage confidence in eventual liberation. In some cases the resistance movements called for bombing because they accepted the airmen's claims
about its accuracy and power. However, by the spring of 1942 and on to
the end of the war, the pendulum swung slowly in favor of military necessity, while European resisters became disillusioned about what bombing might achieve. In June 1943, Sinclair asked Eden to reconsider the
principle that causing casualties to non-German civilians was a sufficient ground for restraint. Eden had a politician's instinct that killing
Allied civilians was the wrong course, but his reply to Sinclair symbolized the shift in priorities: "If the new bombing plan is strategically necessary, I shall not of course stand in its way."[256] American airmen were
in general less affected by political calculation, partly because the State
Department was geographically remote, partly because Americans were
outsiders in the European theater, less aware of the political realities
they faced. As the western war entered Europe, bombing became more
widespread and its effects usually indiscriminate. By 1944, Allied commanders were increasingly "bomb happy," summoning bombing whenever there was a problem to solve. This produced dangerous paradoxes
for the peoples of the New Order: the closer to victory and liberation,
the more deadly became the bombing; as the bombing intensified, so
German antiaircraft resources were spread ever more thinly around the

perimeter of the German empire, exposing the subject peoples more fully to the rigors of bombardment. The occupied states had their own civil defense organizations, but they were in general less well resourced than in Britain or Germany. This would have mattered less if the bombing of military objectives had been as accurate as the Allies claimed (and on occasion achieved). The bombing of Brest, Le Havre, Caen, Mortsel, The Hague, Bucharest, and a dozen or more other cities exposed the hollowness of any claim to operational precision. Bombing was a blunt instrument, as the Allies knew full well, but its bluntness was more evident and more awkward when the bombs fell outside Germany.

Lessons Learned and Not Learned: Bombing into the Postwar World

After 1945 the terms in which a bombing war came to be understood were dominated by the reality of nuclear weapons, which were only used at the end of the conflict in the Pacific War. Until the missile age, the long-range intercontinental bomber was designed to deliver a first- or second-strike nuclear attack of annihilating power against the enemy. This did not rule out the use of conventional bombing (as the wars in Korea and Vietnam made evident), but it forced the Allied air forces to think about the lessons of the Second World War, in terms of both what the campaigns had achieved and projected future war.

On one thing the two major air forces, the RAF and the USAAF, were agreed: the third world war if it came would be another total war of even greater proportions than the last. When the postwar RAF chief of staff—now marshal of the Royal Air Force, Lord Tedder—was invited to give the Lees Knowles lectures on military affairs in Cambridge in the spring of 1947, he assured his audience that in the future "war will inevitably be total war and world-wide."[1] In October 1946, Major General Lauris Norstad, head of the Plans and Operations Division in the U.S. War Department, and a wartime air commander, briefed President Harry Truman on the shape of the postwar American military. He concluded his presentation by repeating what he had already claimed several times: "We must plan for the next war to be in fact a total war."[2] A lecture to the National Industrial Conference Board in the spring of 1947 by General Brehon Somervell, the officer responsible during the war for creating the Pentagon, began from the premise that the next war would be worse than the last: "Let no man question that World War III will be a total war of a destructiveness and intensity never yet seen."[3] It was also understood that this war of the future should not be fought as

if it were World War II. Tedder told his listeners that the fighting services "must discard old shibboleths and outworn traditions"; for future
security "we must look *forward from* the past and its lessons, not *back* to the
past." Norstad told the National War College in Washington, D.C.,
shortly after his briefing of the president that it was a mortal danger "to
cling for security in a *next* war to those things which made for security in
a *last* war."[4]

There were nevertheless important lessons to be drawn. In August
1947, Tedder organized a major RAF exercise code-named Thunderbolt to study the lessons of the Combined Bomber Offensive for the future of war. Senior airmen, government scientists, and politicians were
invited, though Portal and Harris, architects of the offensive, chose not
to attend. There were five senior American air force officers, including
General Kepner, victor of the "Battle of Germany." The conference
opened at the School of Air Support at Old Sarum, near Salisbury, on
August 11 and lasted five days.[5] Although some defense was made of the
bomber offensive, the general tone of the assembly was critical. The failure to destroy the enemy economy or seriously to dent enemy morale
was admitted; so too the slowness of the buildup of Bomber Command
during the war and the failure to exploit science fully enough.[6] The exercise was an opportunity to think about the advent of entirely new weapons, including atomic bombs, and to decide how the air force should be
organized to exploit them. The result was a vision of future air war not
very different from the strategic fantasies of General Douhet, first elaborated in the wake of the Great War in his book *Command of the Air,* which
was finally translated into English in 1942.

Like Douhet, the key priorities identified were the need to be prepared fully for the moment when a war breaks out, to strike ruthlessly
and swiftly using any weapon available, and to target the enemy civilian
population as the key to destroying the will to resist in days rather than
years. Tedder had identified in his Cambridge lectures the key importance of being ready to strike at once when hostilities began, not an "em-
bryo Goliath" like Bomber Command in 1939, which took years to
develop after the outbreak of war, but "a fully grown David, ready to act
swiftly and decisively."[7] This meant choosing weapons that could deliver

a sudden annihilating blow. During Exercise Thunderbolt the possibility was proposed of using atomic weapons, which Britain did not yet possess; Henry Tizard, the government scientist, thought that 500 atomic bombs might bring about a swift end to any war. Norman Bottomley, Harris's successor as commander in chief of Bomber Command, presented a paper on biological warfare as an even more effective instrument for total war since it killed only people rather than destroying cities, as incendiary or atomic bombings had done. Carried in cluster bombs or rocket warheads, biological agents used as a strategic weapon against the civilian population would be, ton for ton, more deadly than poison gas and likely to be available sooner than nuclear weapons.[8] In both cases, nuclear war and biological war, airpower would deliver the rapid and decisive blow it had failed to deliver effectively enough before 1945.

Douhet was even more in evidence in the conclusions drawn by the American military leadership. In his speech to the National Industrial Conference Board, Somervell described World War III in terms every bit as lurid as the scaremongering visions of the 1930s:

> What kind of war would the third world conflict be? Would it be a Buck Rogers affair with atomic bombs bursting everywhere, bacteria of all kinds falling on us from the sky like angry winter rain, rockets moving with uncanny precision thousands of miles to the most remote inland target hidden in a cave in the Rockies, with one-half or two-thirds of our population or that of the enemy wiped out or crawling about maimed by radioactive emanations or crippled by loathsome or incurable disease . . . ? Would it be over as quickly as that, with one or both combatants totally destroyed and their civilization wiped out? God only knows.[9]

Somervell reflected the prevailing postwar view that a future world war would be over quickly, despite all the lessons of the recent conflict, and that it would be even more destructive than the damage inflicted from the air in the wartime offensives. In a speech on "Strategy" to the National War College in January 1947, General Albert Wedemeyer, architect of the American Victory Program in 1941, told his audience that the next war would swiftly assume "the characteristics of a war of extermination" involving ultra-destructive atomic and bacteriological weapons. Since the United States had failed to rearm in the 1930s in the face of Axis aggression, Wedemeyer warned against the typical American attitudes of "indifference and apathy" when confronted by the emergence of yet another totalitarian menace to Europe.[10]

The Soviet Union was regarded as the successor to Hitler's Third Reich, but a state potentially capable of stockpiling weapons of mass destruction and inflicting them in a sudden preemptive strike against the American mainland, which Germany had not been able to do. Norstad told Truman that the Soviet Union was the only possible enemy and that war against communism "is the basis of our planning."[11] American thinking, like that of the RAF, focused on the need to build up overwhelming striking power in peacetime to counter such a threat and to be prepared to use all and any weapons, including bacteriological, chemical, and nuclear payloads, so as to be certain of victory against an apparently ruthless dictatorship. Arnold's final report for the president in 1945 stressed the need in the future for an atomic capability that would allow "immediate offensive action with overwhelming force," which the American air force had demonstrably lacked in 1941.[12] For American planners this meant retaining a strategic air force capable of mounting an immediate air offensive, and in 1948 the Strategic Air Command was activated for this purpose under the former Eighth Air Force wing commander General Curtis LeMay. He welcomed the assignment and had no regrets about wartime bombing. "Enemy cities were pulverized or fried to a crisp," LeMay wrote in 1965. "It was something they asked for and something they deserved."[13] The RAF bomber force was less fortunate after 1945. Bomber Command was almost entirely demobilized, its Air Striking Force reduced to ten squadrons by 1946.[14] By the 1950s Britain could no longer afford to be a major player in the air war of the future. No effective heavy bomber was developed for the postwar force, and in 1950 the RAF had to borrow seventy B-29s from the United States.

The possession of nuclear weapons now made the city-busting strategy of the Second World War a possibility. Though the object of a nuclear arsenal was to deter an aggressor, both Britain and the United States prepared plans for the point where deterrence failed. By the early 1960s

American air forces, using missiles or aircraft, possessed the means to obliterate most Soviet cities and to kill more than 80 million of their inhabitants in a first or second strike.[15] British planners, working with a much more limited nuclear capability, identified fifty-five Soviet cities for destruction. The so-called JIGSAW committee set up in 1960 to investigate the strategy was instructed to consider only the effects on the population, "the aim being to select target cities so as to pose the maximum threat to the greatest possible number of Russian people." The Air Ministry was particularly interested in learning lessons from the bombing of Germany to decide what level of destruction was needed for "knocking out" a city. It was calculated that Hamburg had received the equivalent of a five-kiloton bomb during the war, which encouraged confidence that the large megaton bombs now available really would be able to paralyze a city at a stroke.[16] The principal lesson learned from the bombing campaigns of the Second World War was the need for even greater and more indiscriminate destruction of the enemy if ever World War III materialized.

The experience of the bombing war helped to shape the Cold War confrontation of mutual destruction or mutual deterrence. It was under this shadow that European nations began the process of reconstructing the bombed cities and towns and counting the cost of the cultural damage they had sustained. The programs were ambitious and optimistic despite the threat of nuclear obliteration hanging over them.[17] Recovery was in this sense like recovery from a natural disaster—a volcanic eruption or a major earthquake—in the knowledge that another geological shift might undo the urban rebuilding at a stroke. The reconstruction began at first against a background of economic crisis and legal wrangling over ownership of the ruins, and in many cases the bolder plans were shelved in favor of cheaper or more feasible solutions.[18] The most ambitious building took place in Germany, where more than half the urban area in the major cities had been destroyed. Some thirty-nine cities had at least a million cubic meters of rubble to clear, but in Berlin the figure was 55 million, in Hamburg 35 million, and in Cologne 24 million.[19] Coping with life among the ruins were millions of Germans who lived for years in cellars and shacks, short of food, supplies, and schooling. A delegation of British peace workers visiting Lübeck in 1947 were shown weekly food rations consisting of just two pounds of bread, a half liter of skimmed milk, half a herring, one ounce of butter, and four ounces of sugar. They found 4,000 people in the port still being fed a watery soup daily from a communal kitchen. Accommodation was rationed in Hamburg to 5.6 square meters per person; the water supply was poor, electricity irregular. The women they met expressed strong sentiments "against all forms of militarism or war."[20]

Neither in Germany nor elsewhere in Europe were the heavily bombed and depopulated cities abandoned. In France there was a move to keep the ruined peninsula of the Channel port of St.-Malo as a memorial to the bombing and to relocate the town on the mainland, but tradition prevailed and St.-Malo was rebuilt on the existing site. The only place to be moved as a result of bombing was the Italian town of Cassino. The ruins on the mountainside were declared a national monument and a new and larger town was built on more level ground a mile away from the original site. City centers, where much of the damage had occurred, were also generally restored, with the exception of the heavily bombed British port of Bristol and the German port at Kiel, where there was sufficient bomb damage to allow the relocation of the center to a more geographically convenient quarter.[21] In Germany the reconstruction was slower than elsewhere because of occupation and economic crisis, but here too the cities were all restored on their original sites despite the exceptional level of destruction. This strong sense of belonging, even to a ruined landscape, was explained by a senior German officer to his fellow prisoners of war early in 1945:

If there is such a thing as existence in spirit or will alone, without body or matter, that is the life of the German cities. Only their sentimental appeal still holds them together. Cologne has been evacuated time and time again, but the inhabitants still manage to drift back to the heaps of rubble simply because they once bore the name "home." Past associations are so much more powerful than the necessities of war that the evacuees resent leaving and rush back again long before the danger is over.[22]

Nevertheless, German cities were remodeled after the bombing, while their demographic geography changed. By 1950, cities with more than 100,000 people made up 27 percent of the population in West Germany, whereas they had constituted one-third in 1939; the population of communities with fewer than 20,000 inhabitants increased from 53 percent to 59 percent over the same period. Hamburg, where the damage and depopulation had been among the most extensive, almost recovered its prewar population level by 1950, but experienced a substantial relocation of population within the city limits. The inner zones housed 850,000 people in 1939, but by 1950 only 467,000; the outer zones increased from 848,000 to over a million.[23]

The geographical relocation was typical of much of the postwar reconstruction, since the destruction of older urban environments presented an opportunity to build modern residential housing with less congestion and more amenities. Wider roads and open spaces were regarded by town planners as desirable improvements to old-fashioned and inconvenient urban structures. "The Blitz has been a planner's windfall," wrote the British scientist Julian Huxley about the British experience. "It is the psychological moment to get real planning in our towns."[24] In reality the expense involved and the persistent arguments between local authorities and architects about what was desirable or expedient left many of the plans on the drawing board. The American social scientist Leo Grebler investigated twenty-eight western European cities from four countries in 1954 and found that in general there was little radical urban rebuilding and strong pressures for continuity. The actual amount of damage, even in heavily bombed cities, was less than the immediate images of smashed streets and housing suggested. The temptation for municipal authorities all over Europe (who needed to restore local tax revenues) was to use what was still standing as fully as possible and to rebuild around it rather than engage in further demolition.[25] In Germany the extent of the problem of homelessness was amplified by the large-scale refugee problem as Germans expelled from eastern Europe arrived in the western zones of occupation. This forced migration encouraged the rapid rebuilding and repair of existing structures alongside cheap standard housing built on existing foundations. By 1961, 3.1 million houses had been restored or rebuilt.[26] In no case did Grebler find evidence that the threat of nuclear bombing influenced city planning or house design, a discovery that he attributed partly to "improvidence or defeatism" in the face of the nuclear menace, but principally to the willingness to take high risks for the sake of restoring what had been temporarily sacrificed in wartime.[27]

The physical rebuilding of Europe after 1945 was bound up with the way bombed populations came to terms with the human costs of the bombing war. The psychological impact was difficult to gauge after 1945, and little effort went into analyzing the scale or nature of the traumatic impact on those who experienced air raids. The longer-term effects on civilians have been little studied in comparison with the postwar psychological damage done to soldiers as a result of the stresses of combat. The memory of bombing as an expression of collective public awareness of the victims (though not of the survivors) was also much less developed than the public memory of military losses. Much of that public memory was linked to religious monuments as symbols of the injury to Europe's Christian values in the vortex of total war. In Britain part of Coventry Cathedral was kept in its ruined state as both a local and a national monument; in Germany the Frauenkirche in Dresden was a standing indictment of the firestorm until its rebuilding in the early twenty-first century as a symbol of reconciliation and a final settlement of postwar accounts.[28] The Nicholas Church in Hamburg and the Kaiser Wilhelm Church in the center of Berlin were also left in their ruined state as a visible reminder to the German people of the cost of war against the home front. In Germany the memorializing of the dead from the bombing has been a process shot through with evident ambiguities. For years the memory was suppressed or subdued because of the difficulty of seeing Germans as victims rather than the collective perpetrators of a barbarous European war. The publication in 2002 of Jörg Friedrich's bestseller *Der Brand* (*The Fire*) opened up a new wave of debate over the extent to which the victimhood of ordinary people in the bombing war can be reconciled with a persistent collective guilt for the crimes of the Hitler regime.[29] Outside Germany, the memorialization of victims of bombing has been unevenly applied. Established habits of remembering the fighting man have prevailed over public acknowledgment that in total war civilians are as likely to be victims as soldiers.[30] Only in recent years have lists of the civilian victims of bombing been added to a number of local war memorials in Italy and France.

The ambiguities have also extended to the way in which those who carried out the bombing have been remembered after 1945. The U.S. Air Force established a major monument at Madingley, outside Cambridge, where thousands of American aircrew were buried. But Bomber Command was for decades after 1945 denied a collective monument to the dead. The erection of a statue to Harris in 1992 outside the RAF church on London's Strand provoked widespread criticism, protest, and demonstrations. A memorial to the dead of Bomber Command was finally erected and dedicated only in 2012, in London's Green Park, but once again it provoked renewed debate about whether those who inflicted such damage on civilian communities ought to be remembered in the same spirit in which the "Few" of the defensive Battle of Britain have been lionized in British public history. This is not the only example of a surviving tension in the way the bombers and the bombed are remembered. In Bulgaria, almost a century after the serendipitous invention of the modern bomb by the Bulgarian army captain Simeon Petrov, the U.S. authorities chose in October 2010 to erect a modest stone monument in the grounds of the American embassy in Sofia to the 150 American airmen who lost their lives flying over Bulgarian territory or bombing Bulgarian targets. The event was marked by protests from Bulgarian political parties at what was regarded as an unjustifiable celebration of a murderous policy that resulted in widespread Bulgarian deaths. At a demonstration organized on December 18, 2010, there were placards that read "No to the monument of shame!" A Facebook protest group was organized dedicated "to remove the monument to American pilots who bombed Sofia."[31] Nevertheless, the monument still stands. It performs the conventional function of honoring the military dead who contributed to the well-known history of European liberation—yet it is also a ready reminder that the price of that liberation was not only the death of 1,350 Bulgarians, but of over half a million other European civilians.

NOTES

Abbreviations Used in the Notes

AAF	American air force
ACAS	assistant chief of air staff
ACS	Archivio Centrale dello Stato, Rome
AEAF	Allied Expeditionary Air Force
AFHRA	Air Force Historical Research Agency, Maxwell AFB, AL
AHB	Air Historical Branch, Northolt, UK
AI	Air Intelligence (UK)
BA-B	Bundesarchiv-Berlin
BA-MA	Bundesarchiv-Militärarchiv, Freiburg im Breisgau
BBSU	British Bombing Survey Unit
BN	Bibliothèque Nationale, Paris
BOPs	Bomber Operations
CamUL	Cambridge University Library
CAS	chief of the air staff (UK)
CCAC	Churchill College Archive Centre, Cambridge, UK
CCO	Christ Church, Oxford
CCS	Combined Chiefs of Staff
CD	civil defense
C-in-C	commander in chief
CIOS	Combined Intelligence Objectives Sub-Committee
CoS	chief(s) of staff
DBOps	director of bomber operations (UK)
DCAS	deputy chief of the air staff (UK)
DDBOps	deputy director of bomber operations (UK)
DoI	Department of the Interior
DVA	Deutsche Verlags-Anstalt, Stuttgart
EDS	Enemy Document Section
FDRL	Franklin D. Roosevelt Library, Hyde Park, NY
FIAT	Field Intelligence Agencies Technical
GAF	German Air Force
GL	*Generalluftzeugmeister* (air force quartermaster-general)
HMSO	His/Her Majesty's Stationery Office
IAC	Italian Armistice Commission
IWM	Imperial War Museum, London
JCS	Joint Chiefs of Staff

JIC	Joint Intelligence Committee (UK)
JIGSAW	Joint Inter-Service Group for Study of All-Out Warfare (UK)
JPS	Joint Planning Staff
JSM	Joint Staff Mission, Washington, DC
LC	Library of Congress, Washington, DC
LSE	London School of Economics
MAAF	Mediterranean Allied Air Forces
MAP	Ministry of Aircraft Production
MD	Milch Documents
MdAe	Ministero dell'Aeronautica
MEW	Ministry of Economic Warfare
MoI	Ministry of Information (UK)
NAAF	North African Air Forces
NARA	National Archives and Records Administration, College Park, MD
NC	Nuffield College, Oxford
NFPA	National Fire Protection Association
NID	Naval Intelligence Division (UK)
NSV	Nationalsozialistische Volkswohlfahrt (National Socialist People's Welfare)
OEMU	Oxford Extra-Mural Unit
OKH	Oberkommando des Heeres
OKW	Oberkommando der Wehrmacht (high command of the German armed forces)
ORS	Operational Research Section
OSS	Office of Strategic Services (U.S.)
OT	Organisation Todt
OTU	Operational Training Unit
PArch	Parliamentary Archives, Westminster, London
PWB	Psychological Warfare Branch
PWE	Political Warfare Executive
RAFM	RAF Museum, Hendon, London
RCAF	Royal Canadian Air Force
REDept	Research & Experiments Department, Ministry of Home Security
RG	Record Group
RLB	Reichsluftschutzbund (Reich Air Defense League)
RLM	Reich Air Ministry
RVK	*Reichsverteidigungskommissar* (Reich defense commissar)
SAP	Securité Aérienne Publique
SGDA	Secrétariat Général à la Défense Aérienne
SHAA	Service Historique de l'Armée de l'Air, Vincennes, Paris
SHAEF	Supreme Headquarters Allied Expeditionary Force
TNA	The National Archives, Kew, London
TsAMO	Central Archive of the Ministry of Defense of the Russian Federation, Podolsk
UEA	University of East Anglia
USAAF	United States Army Air Forces
USAFA	United States Air Force Academy, Colorado Springs
USMA	United States Military Academy, West Point, NY

USSBS   United States Strategic Bombing Survey
USSTAF   United States strategic and tactical air forces
VCAS   vice chief of the air staff (UK)

Prologue. Bombing Bulgaria

1 AFHRA, 519.12535, Fifteenth Air Force Operations (Bulgaria), November 1943–July 1944; Wesley F. Craven and James L. Cate, *The Army Air Forces in World War II*, vol. 2, *Europe: Torch to Pointblank* (Chicago: University of Chicago Press, 1949), 584; Marshall L. Miller, *Bulgaria During the Second World War* (Stanford, CA: Stanford University Press, 1975), 166; Rumen Rumenin, *Letyashti Kreposti Nad Bulgariya* (Kyustendil: Ivan Sapunjiev, 2009), 94–95, 204.

2 BA-MA, RL 2/8, German Air Ministry, aircraft deliveries to neutrals and allies, May 1943–February 1944.

3 See Martin van Creveld, *Hitler's Strategy, 1940–1941: The Balkan Clue* (Cambridge: Cambridge University Press, 1973), 109–13, for a full account of the negotiations.

4 Miller, *Bulgaria*, 48–55, 62–68.

5 Richard J. Crampton, *Bulgaria* (Oxford: Oxford University Press, 2007), 272, 275–76.

6 TNA, PREM 3/79/1, minutes of CoS meeting, October 19, 1943.

7 From a leaflet reproduced in Rumenin, *Letyashti Kreposti*, 335.

8 NARA, RG 165, Box 11, Report by the JCS, "The Bombing of Sofia," enclosure B.

9 Ibid., Ambassador Kelley, Ankara, to State Dept., October 18, 1943.

10 TNA, PREM 3/79/1, CCS to Eisenhower, October 24, 1943.

11 Ibid., telegram Eden to Churchill, October 23, 1943; Eden to Churchill, October 29, 1943.

12 Frederick B. Chary, *The Bulgarian Jews and the Final Solution, 1940–1944* (Pittsburgh: University of Pittsburgh Press, 1972), 129–32; Miller, *Bulgaria*, 102–6.

13 TNA, PREM 3/79/1, Churchill to Eden and Deputy Prime Minister Attlee, December 25, 1943.

14 *Akten zur deutschen auswärtigen Politik*, Ser. E, *Band* 7 (Göttingen: Vandenhoeck & Ruprecht, 1979), Ambassador Beckerle to von Ribbentrop, January 23, 1944.

15 TNA, PREM 3/66/10, War Cabinet JIC Report, "Effects of Allied Bombing of Balkans and Balkan Situation," January 29, 1944, 1–2; FDRL, Roosevelt papers, Map Room Files, Box 136, HQ MAAF to War Department, January 10, 1944; Rumenin, *Letyashti Kreposti*, 107–9.

16 Miller, *Bulgaira*, 167–68; Walter Warlimont, *Inside Hitler's Headquarters, 1939–1945* (London: Weidenfeld & Nicolson, 1964), 399. Warlimont was in Bulgaria to discuss Operation Gertrude, a contingency plan for the capture of European Turkey if the Turks joined the Allies.

17 Crampton, *Bulgaria*, 273–74.

18 TNA, PREM 3/79/1, Roosevelt to Churchill, February 9, 1944.

19 FDRL, Map Room Files, CoS to Eisenhower's HQ, March 9, 1944; TNA, PREM 3/79/1, CoS, "Air Operations Against Bulgaria," January 27, 1944; Churchill to General Wilson, January 27, 1944.

20 RAFM, Bottomley papers, AC 71/2/29, note by the air staff for War Cabinet Inter-Service Committee on Chemical Warfare, January 23, 1944, Annex 1.

21 TNA, PREM 3/79/1, Churchill to Roosevelt, February 11, 1944, and February 12, 1944.

22 Ibid., Roosevelt to Churchill, February 12, 1944.

23 Ibid., Lord Killearn (Cairo) to the Foreign Office, February 24, 1944; Lord Killearn to the Foreign Office, February 24, 1944, encl. report from Mr. Howard, 1–3; Crampton, *Bulgaria*, 275–76.

24 TNA, PREM 3/79/1, Eden to Churchill, March 3, 1944, 1–3, 8.

25 Ibid., Portal to Churchill, March 10, 1944.

26 Rumenin, *Letyashti Kreposti*, 125; AFHRA, 519.12535, Fifteenth Air Force Operations (Bulgaria), November 1943–July 1944.

27 Miller, *Bulgaria*, 168–80.

28 FDRL, Map Room Files, Box 136, CoS to Wilson and General Carl Spaatz, March 25, 1944; TNA, PREM 3/66/10, Portal to Wilson and Spaatz, March 28, 1944; Portal to Wilson and Spaatz, April 11, 1944.

29 TNA, PREM 3/66/10, JSM Report, Washington, DC, July 21, 1944, 1–2; CoS memorandum, July 25, 1944.

30 TNA, PREM 3/79/5, War Cabinet minute by Anthony Eden, "Bulgaria," March 17, 1945.

31 Percy Schramm, ed., *Kriegstagebuch des OKW: Eine Dokumentation. 1943, Band* 3, *Teilband* 2 (Augsburg: Weltbild, 2007), 1089.

32 Michael M. Boll, ed., *The American Military Mission in the Allied Control Commission for Bulgaria, 1944–1947: History and Transcripts* (New York: Columbia University Press, 1985), 38–42.

33 Peter Donnelly, ed., *Mrs. Milburn's Diaries: An Englishwoman's Day-to-Day Reflections, 1939–1945* (London: Harrap, 1979), 100, entry for June 14, 1941.

34 TNA, PREM 3/79/1, note by Churchill on telegram Tedder (MAAF) to Churchill, December 29, 1943; note by Churchill on letter from Lord Killearn to the Foreign Office, March 9, 1944.

35 TNA, PREM 3/66/10, JSM Report, Washington, DC, July 21, 1944, 1.

36 Robert F. Futrell, *Ideas, Concepts, Doctrine: A History of Basic Thinking in the United States Air Force* (Maxwell AFB, AL: Air University Press, 1971), 28.

37 NARA, RG 165/888, Maj. Gen. Hugh Drum, "Information on Aviation and Department of National Defense," May 1, 1934, 3.

38 M. Maurer, *Aviation in the U.S. Army, 1919–1939* (Washington, DC: Office of Air Force History, 1987), 325–29; Alfred Goldberg, ed., *A History of the United States Air Force, 1907–1957* (Princeton, NJ: Princeton University Press, 1957), 40–41.

39 NARA, RG 18/223, Box 4, memorandum for the CoS, April 4, 1932, 9.

40 NARA, RG 18/229, Patrick papers, Fort Leavenworth lecture, March 27, 1924, 1–2, 7–8.

41 Ibid., lecture to the Air War College, "Air Tactics," November 1923, 1, 14–15; LC, Mitchell papers, Box 27, "Aviation in the Next War" and "Give America Airplanes"; William Mitchell, *Winged Defense* (New York: G. P. Putnam & Sons, 1925), 4–6, 214–16.

42 USAFA, Hansell papers, Ser. III, Box 1, Folder 1, "Fairchild lecture," December 1, 1964, 8; USAFA, McDonald papers, Ser. V, Box 8, Folder 8, "Development of the U.S. Air Forces' Philosophy of Air Warfare Prior to Our Entry into World War II," [n.d.], 15–16.

43 LC, Andrews papers, Box 11, Maj. Harold George, "An Inquiry into the Subject War," 17.

44 Josef Konvitz, "Représentations urbaines et bombardements stratégiques, 1914–1945," *Annales* (1989): 834–35. Gian Gentile, *How Effective Is Strategic Bombing? Lessons Learned from World War II to Kosovo* (New York: New York University Press, 2000), 16–18; Tami Davis Biddle, *Rhetoric and Reality in Air Warfare: The Evolution of British and American Ideas About Strategic Bombing, 1914–1945* (Princeton, NJ: Princeton University Press, 2002), 161–64.

45 LC, Andrews papers, Box 11, Carl Spaatz, "Comments on Doctrine of the Army Air Corps," January 5, 1935; R. W. Krauskopf, "The Army and the Strategic Bomber, 1930–1939: Part I," *Military Affairs* 22 (1958–59): 94.

46 NARA, RG 94/452.1, General Oscar Westover to General Marlin Craig, December 4, 1936; Henry Arnold to adjutant-general, September 11, 1936; Air Corps Division to the chief of the Air Corps, April 14, 1937; General Embick for CoS, "Changes in Fiscal Year 1938 Airplane Program," May 16, 1938.

47 Ibid., memorandum for CoS (Gen. George Marshall), September 21, 1939; RG 94/580, Gen. George Strong to CoS, May 10, 1940; memorandum, "Army's Second Aviation Objective," February 28, 1941; R. W. Krauskopf, "The Army and the Strategic Bomber, 1930–1939: Part II," *Military Affairs* 22 (1958–59): 211–14. On Roosevelt see Jeffery Underwood, *The Wings of Democracy: The Influence of Air Power on the Roosevelt Administration, 1933–1941* (College Station: Texas A&M University Press, 1991), 135–37.

48 TNA, AIR 9/8, notes on a possible "Locarno War," May 2, 1929.

49 Ibid., CoS paper 156, "Note by the First Sea Lord," May 21, 1928; CAS, "Note upon the memorandum of the Chief of the Naval Staff" [n.d. but May 1928]; "Notes for Address by CAS to the Imperial Defence College on the War Aim of an Air Force," October 9, 1928, 1.

50 RAFM, Saundby papers, AC 72/12, Box 3, lecture, "The Use of Air Power in 1939/45" [n.d.], 2–3; TNA, AIR 9/39, lecture by Air Vice Marshal A. S. Barratt, "Air Policy and Strategy," March 23, 1936.

51 TNA, AIR 9/8, Address by the CAS, October 9, 1928, 5.

52 Richard Overy, "Allied Bombing and the Destruction of German Cities," in Roger Chickering, Stig Förster, and Bernd Greiner, eds., *A World at Total War: Global Conflict and the Politics of Destruction, 1937–1945* (Cambridge: Cambridge University Press, 2005), 278–84.

53 NARA, RG 18/223, Box 1, RAF *War Manual*, pt. I, May 1935, 57.

54 See, e.g., Priya Satia, "The Defense of Inhumanity: Air Control and the British Idea of Arabia," *American Historical Review* 111 (2006): 25–38. A more favorable interpretation is in Sebastian Ritchie, *The RAF, Small Wars and Insurgencies in the Middle East, 1919–1939* (Northolt: Air Historical Branch, 2011), esp. 78–83.

55 John Slessor, *The Central Blue: Recollections and Reflections* (London: Cassell, 1956), 65–66.

56 H. G. Wilmott, "Air Control in Ovamboland," *Journal of the Royal United Services Institution* 83 (1938): 823–29.

57 CCO, Portal papers, Folder 2/File 2, Portal to Churchill, September 25, 1941, encl. "The Moral Effect of Bombing," 1; see too Charles Portal, "Air Force Co-operation in Policing the Empire," *Journal of the Royal United Services Institution* 82 (1937): 343–57.

58 Neville Jones, *The Beginnings of Strategic Air Power: A History of the British Bomber Force, 1923–1929* (London: Frank Cass, 1987), 107–8.
59 Ibid., 123.
60 Ibid., 118–21.
61 TNA, AIR 9/92, First Meeting of the Bombing Policy Sub-Committee, March 22, 1938, 1–2, 6–9.
62 Ibid., note on A.T.S. bombing trial results [n.d.].
63 Ibid., minutes of meeting, deputy director of plans, March 23, 1939.
64 TNA, AIR 14/225, Ludlow-Hewitt to undersecretary of state, Air Ministry, August 30, 1938. See too Charles Webster and Noble Frankland, *The Strategic Air Offensive against Germany* (London: HMSO, 1961), 1:100.
65 TNA, PREM 3/79/1, telegram from British CoS to JSM, Washington, DC, October 20, 1943.
66 CamUL, Baldwin papers, vol. 1, Londonderry to Baldwin, July 17, 1934.
67 TNA, AIR 40/288, AI (Liaison), "The Blitz," August 14, 1941, App. A, "Morale," 1.
68 TNA, AIR 9/8, air staff memorandum, January 15, 1936, 2–3, 5; AIR 9/77, Operational Requirements Committee, minutes of meeting, August 11, 1938, 4.
69 TNA, AIR 9/8, note from Harris to deputy chief of the air staff, September 24, 1936.
70 USAFA, McDonald papers, Ser. V, Box 8, Folder 8, "Development of the U.S. Air Forces' Philosophy of Air Warfare," 3, 15. Michael Sherry, *The Rise of American Air Power: The Creation of Armageddon* (New Haven, CT: Yale University Press, 1987), 53–56.
71 NARA, RG 18/223, Box 4, memorandum for CoS, April 4, 1932; Arnold to the chief of the Air Corps, "Cumulative Production of Airplanes of Mobilization Planning," March 24, 1931. On Britain see Sebastian Ritchie, *Industry and Air Power: The Expansion of British Aircraft Production, 1935–1941* (London: Frank Cass, 1997); George Peden, *Arms, Economics and British Strategy: From Dreadnoughts to Hydrogen Bombs* (Cambridge: Cambridge University Press, 2007), 137–40, 158–61. This is the thrust of David Edgerton, *Britain's War Machine: Weapons, Resources and Experts in the Second World War* (London: Allen Lane, 2011), esp. chap. 1.
72 Oliver Stewart, "The Doctrine of Strategical Bombing," *Journal of the Royal United Services Institution* 81 (1936): 97–98.
73 TNA, AIR 9/39, "Air Policy and Strategy," March 23, 1936, 5–6.
74 USAFA, McDonald papers, Ser. V, Box 8, Folder 8, "Development of the U.S. Air Forces Philosophy," 13–15.
75 On this see Peter Gray, "The Gloves Will Have to Come Off: A Reappraisal of the Legitimacy of the RAF Bomber Offensive Against Germany," *Air Power Review* 13 (2010): 9–40.
76 There is now a very large literature on these issues. See, e.g., Anthony Grayling, *Among the Dead Cities: Was the Allied Bombing of Civilians in World War II a Necessity or a Crime?* (London: Bloomsbury, 2005); Jörg Friedrich, *Der Brand: Deutschland im Bombenkrieg, 1940–1945* (Munich: Propyläen Verlag, 2002); Nicholson Baker, *Human Smoke: The Beginnings of World War II and the End of Civilization* (New York: Simon & Schuster, 2008); Stephen A. Garrett, *Ethics and Airpower in World War II: The British Bombing of German Cities* (New York: St. Martin's, 1993); Beau Grosscup, *Strategic Terror: The Politics and Ethics of Aerial Bombardment* (London: Zed

Books, 2006); Igor Primoratz, ed., *Terror from the Sky: The Bombing of German Cities in World War II* (Oxford: Berghahn, 2010).

77 LC, Eaker papers, Box I.30, Intelligence section, MAAF, "What Is Germany Saying?" [n.d. but early 1945].

78 See the excellent essays in Yuki Tanaka and Marilyn Young, eds., *Bombing Civilians: A Twentieth-Century History* (New York: New Press, 2009).

Chapter 1. The Sorcerer's Apprentice: Bomber Command, 1939–42

1 Heinz M. Hanke, *Luftkrieg und Zivilbevölkerung* (Frankfurt am Main: Peter Lang, 1991), 187–90. Charles Webster and Noble Frankland, *The Strategic Air Offensive Against Germany* (London: HMSO, 1961), 1:134–35, give the wrong dates for the German pledge and the Anglo-French declaration.

2 FDRL, President's Secretary's Files, Box 47, Ambassador Potocki to Cordell Hull, September 1, 1939.

3 TNA, AIR 9/202, first meeting, Sub-Committee on the Humanisation of Aerial Warfare, July 8, 1938; air staff memorandum, "The Restriction of Air Warfare," February 25, 1938; Uri Bialer, "Humanization of Air Warfare in British Foreign Policy on the Eve of the Second World War," *Journal of Contemporary History* 13 (1978): 79–96.

4 TNA, AIR 14/249, "Air Ministry Instructions and Notes on the Rules to Be Observed by the Royal Air Force in War," August 17, 1939, 5–7; AIR 41/5, "International Law of the Air 1939–1945," supplement to "Air Power and War Rights" by the former Air Ministry legal adviser, J. M. Spaight, 7; Joel Hayward, "Air Power, Ethics, and Civilian Immunity during the First World War and Its Aftermath," *Global War Studies* 7 (2010): 127–29; Peter Gray, "The Gloves Will Have to Come Off: A Reappraisal of the Legitimacy of the RAF Bomber Offensive against Germany," *Air Power Review* 13 (2010): 15–16.

5 TNA, AIR 9/105, Anglo-French staff conversations, "Preparation of Joint Plan," April 19, 1939; "The Employment of British Bombers in the Event of German Invasion of the Low Countries," April 21, 1939.

6 TNA, AIR 14/249, Air Ministry to Bomber Command, August 22, 1939; AIR 75/8, Newall to Ludlow-Hewitt, August 23, 1939. Gray, "The Gloves Will Have to Come Off," 22–23.

7 TNA, AIR 75/8, Newall to Gen. Gort, August 24, 1939; War Cabinet Annex, "Air Policy," October 13, 1939; AIR 14/446, Air Ministry minute, August 30, 1939.

8 TNA, FO 371/23093, Sir Hugh Kennard (Warsaw) to Foreign Office, September 11 and September 12, 1939.

9 TNA, AIR 75/8, "Air Policy: Brief for the Secretary of State for Supreme War Council," November 15, 1939, 5–8.

10 Martin Middlebrook and Chris Everitt, *The Bomber Command War Diaries* (Leicester: Midland Publishing, 2000), 42, 702–3.

11 FDRL, President's Secretary's Files, Box 32, Chamberlain to Roosevelt, August 25, 1939; Roosevelt to Chamberlain, August 31, 1939.

12 TNA, AIR 9/131, "The Employment of the Air Striking Force on the Outbreak of War" [n.d. but August 1939], 10. W. A. Jacobs, "The British Strategic Air Offensive

Against Germany in World War II," in R. Cargill Hall, ed., *Case Studies in Strategic Bombardment* (Washington, DC: Office of Air Force History, 1998), 109–10.

13 Richard Overy, "Air Power, Armies and the War in the West, 1940," 32nd Harmon Memorial Lecture, USAFA, Colorado Springs, 1989, 8–12.

14 Webster and Frankland, *Strategic Air Offensive*, 4:99–102, App. 6; Tami Davis Biddle, *Rhetoric and Reality in Air Warfare: The Evolution of British and American Ideas About Strategic Bombing, 1914–1945* (Princeton, NJ: Princeton University Press, 2002), 178–80.

15 TNA, AIR 9/89, Air (Targets) Intelligence: Country: Germany, January 21, 1938.

16 Owen Thetford, *Aircraft of the Royal Air Force Since 1918* (London: Guild Publishing, 1988), 138–41, 273–76.

17 Ibid., 30–34, 313–16, 554–61.

18 Armaments Design Establishment, *The Development of British Incendiary Bombs During the Period of the 1939–1945 World War,* Ministry of Supply, December 1946; TNA, AIR 9/92, Air Ministry, "Bomb Stocks as at 26 April 1939." On the poor quality of bombs see NC, Cherwell papers, G189, Cherwell to Ministry of Supply, January 28, 1942, memorandum, "Bomb Production"; F255, War Cabinet paper, "The Possibility of Improving Efficiency of Blast Bombs," October 6, 1943.

19 TNA, AIR 14/88, Air Ministry to Ludlow-Hewitt, October 27, 1939; AIR 41/5, "International Law of the Air," 1.

20 TNA, AIR 75/5, Slessor to Newall, March 29, 1940; Richard Overy, *Bomber Command, 1939–1945* (London: HarperCollins, 1997), 32–33.

21 TNA, AIR 9/102, Draft Plan W.A.5(d), January 13, 1940; CamUL, Templewood papers, XII, File 2, interviews with officers from Wellington and Whitley squadrons, April 29, 1940.

22 TNA, AIR 41/5, "International Law of the Air," 12–13.

23 TNA, AIR 14/194, Record of a conference with the air staff, April 28, 1940, 3.

24 Martin Gilbert, ed., *The Churchill War Papers*, vol. 2, *Never Surrender: May 1940–December 1940* (London: Heinemann, 1994), 17–18, 24–26, 38–43, War Cabinet minutes, May 12, May 13, May 15, 1940. Randall Hansen, *Fire and Fury: The Allied Bombing of Germany, 1942–1945* (New York: NAL Caliber, 2009), 20, also dates the Rotterdam attack incorrectly.

25 Christopher C. Harmon, *"Are We Beasts?": Churchill and the Moral Question of World War II "Area Bombing"* (Newport, RI: Naval War College, 1991; Newport Papers, no. 1), 8–10.

26 Martin Gilbert, *Finest Hour: Winston S. Churchill, 1939–1941* (London: Heinemann, 1983), 329–30, 334, 342–47; Gilbert, *Churchill War Papers*, 2:17–18, 25, 38–41. War Cabinet minutes, May 13, 1940, War Cabinet minutes: Confidential Annex, May 13, 1940, War Cabinet minutes: Confidential Annex, May 15, 1940.

27 TNA, AIR 14/194, CAS minute, May 19, 1940; DCAS to C-in-C Bomber Command, May 30, 1940.

28 TNA, AIR 14/249, Air Ministry to all commands, June 4, 1940; AIR 41/5, "International Law of the Air," 13.

29 TNA, AIR 14/249, Bottomley (Bomber Command SASO) to all group HQ, June 14, 1940.

30 UEA, Zuckerman archive, SZ/BBSU/56, Portal to Douglas (DCAS), July 16, 1940; TNA, AIR 14/249, Bomber Command war orders, proposed amendment, July 14, 1940.

31 Biddle, *Rhetoric and Reality*, 188–89.

32 TNA, AIR 14/249, telegram from Air Ministry to Bomber Command HQ, September 10, 1940; AIR 41/5, "International Law of the Air," 13; Gray, "The Gloves Will Have to Come Off," 25–26.

33 Richard Overy, "Allied Bombing and the Destruction of German Cities," in Roger Chickering, Stig Förster, and Bernd Greiner, eds., *A World at Total War: Global Conflict and the Politics of Destruction, 1937–1945* (Cambridge: Cambridge University Press, 2005), 280–84; Hayward, "Air Power, Ethics," 124–25.

34 TNA, AIR 75/8, War Cabinet Annex, "Air Policy," October 14, 1939.

35 TNA, AIR 9/79, Air Ministry (Plans), "Note on the Relative Merit of Oil and Power as Objectives for Air Attack," October 16, 1939; AIR 75/8, "Draft Bombing Plans," November 14, 1939.

36 RAFM, Douglas papers, MFC 78/23/2, Trenchard to Portal, May 2, 1940; TNA, AIR 75/8, Portal to Newall, May 8, 1940.

37 TNA, AIR 75/8, "Draft Bombing Plans," November 14, 1939, 3.

38 TNA, AIR 14/194, Slessor (director of plans) to Air Marshal D. Evill, October 22, 1939; "Note on the Question of Relaxing Bombardment Instructions," September 7, 1939.

39 TNA, PREM 3/193/6A, Foreign Office report, May 30, 1940; Halifax to Churchill, June 2, 1940, encl. report, "Morale in Germany."

40 TNA, AIR 75/8, Air Ministry (Plans), "Plans for Attack of Italian War Industry," June 2, 1940; AIR 20/283, Air Ministry (Bomber Operations), "Notes on Bomb Attacks," August 20, 1940.

41 Martin Hugh-Jones, "Wickham Steed and German Biological Warfare Research," *Intelligence and National Security* 7 (1992): 387–90, 393–97; Ulf Schmidt, "Justifying Chemical Warfare: The Origins and Ethics of Britain's Chemical Warfare Programme, 1915–1939," in Jo Fox and David Welch, eds., *Justifying War: Propaganda, Politics and the Modern Age* (Basingstoke: Palgrave, 2012), 148–50.

42 TNA, AIR 14/206, TC 2, "Notes on German Air Operations in Poland," October 19, 1939.

43 TNA, AIR 41/5, "International Law of the Air," 9–10.

44 TNA, AIR 14/194, Bomber Command, "Note on the Question of Relaxing the Bombardment Instructions," September 7, 1939; AIR 14/381, Plan W.1, memorandum for C-in-C, Bomber Command, April 1938, 1.

45 Harold Balfour, *Wings over Westminster* (London: Hutchinson, 1973), 120.

46 TNA, FO 898/311, MEW memorandum, "Bombing of Open Towns," April 19, 1940.

47 CCO, Richards archive, File IV/Folder A, Salmond to Trenchard, May 11, 1940.

48 Gilbert, *Churchill War Papers*, 2:41, War Cabinet minutes: Confidential Annex, May 15, 1940.

49 Gilbert, *Finest Hour*, 81.

50 Robinson Library, University of Newcastle, Trevelyan papers, draft article, "Nazism and Civilisation," March 1943.

51 National Library of Wales, Jevons papers, I IV/85, Noel-Baker to H. Stanley Jevons, November 6, 1940; Noel-Baker, "Reprisals? No," *Daily Herald*, October 2, 1940; Brett Holman, "'Bomb Back, and Bomb Hard': Debating Reprisals during the Blitz," *Australian Journal of Politics and History* 58 (2012): 395–99.

52 LSE, Women's International League of Peace and Freedom papers, 1/16, Executive minutes, July 3, 1940; WILPF 2009/05/04, "Report of Deputation of Pacifist Clergy to the Archbishops of Canterbury and York, 11 June 1940," 2.

53 CamUL, Templewood papers, XII, File 2, transcript of broadcast talk, April 27, 1940.

54 Gilbert, *Churchill War Papers*, 2:42–43, War Cabinet minutes: Confidential Annex, May 15, 1940.

55 CCO, Portal papers, Folder 1, Portal to Churchill, October 27, 1940.

56 TNA, AIR 9/424, Slessor (DCAS) to director of plans, August 17 and August 24, 1942. The final directive (Joint Planning Staff: Anglo-U.S. Bombing Policy) was produced on August 31 naming "industrial centres" rather than industrial populations.

57 RAFM, Harris papers, H47, Harris to the undersecretary of state, Air Ministry, October 25, 1943; A. W. Street (Air Ministry) to Harris, December 15, 1943. There is an extended discussion of this correspondence in Hansen, *Fire and Fury*, 159–66.

58 Webster and Frankland, *Strategic Air Offensive*, 4:111–24. On forests and game see TNA, AIR 40/1814, MEW note, "German Forests," August 7, 1940.

59 TNA, AIR 20/283, Air Ministry War Room, "Tonnage of Bombs Dropped 24 June to 27 Aug 1940." The objectives were oil and fuel, electric power, chemicals and explosives, aircraft industry, enemy aerodromes, aluminum, shipbuilding and docks, and communications.

60 TNA, AIR 9/150, Bomber Command war room, details of raids and tonnages on German port targets to May 1941.

61 Ibid., "Effort Expended by Bomber Command, May to October 1940"; war room to Air Ministry (Plans), details of all sorties, October 11, 1940. The 1944 figures are in Webster and Frankland, *Strategic Air Offensive*, 4:445–46.

62 UEA, Zuckerman archive, SZ/BBSU/56, Douglas to Newall, July 9, 1940; Portal to Douglas, July 16, 1940.

63 CCO, Portal papers, Walter Monkton (MoI) to Portal, November 8, 1940.

64 Edward Westermann, *Flak: German Anti-Aircraft Defenses, 1914–1945* (Lawrence: University Press of Kansas, 2001), 90.

65 TNA, PREM 3/11/1, Churchill note for Newall, July 28, 1940; Newall to Churchill, July 19, 1940, "Note on Attack of German Forests"; AIR 20/5813, "Forestry Report on Incendiary Tests with Different Types of Bombs," July 10, 1941; "Report on a Trial of 'Razzle' in Standing Crops," August 16, 1940.

66 Westermann, *Flak*, 97, 102–3.

67 UEA, Zuckerman archive, SZ/BBSU/2, précis of a lecture by Wing Commander G. Carey Foster.

68 CCO, Richards archive, File VIII, Folder A, interview transcripts with Sir Ian Jacob and Sir Robert Cochrane.

69 Harmon, *"Are We Beasts?,"* 10–14.

70 Winston S. Churchill, *The Second World War* (London: Cassell, 1957), 2:567; Biddle, *Rhetoric and Reality*, 186–87, for Churchill's views on bombing as a "way of winning the war."

71 For instance, Jörg Friedrich, *The Fire: The Bombing of Germany, 1940–1945*, trans. Allison Brown (New York: Columbia University Press, 2006), 62; Douglas Lackey, "Four Types of Mass Murderer: Stalin, Hitler, Churchill, Truman," in Igor Primoratz, ed., *Terror from the Sky: The Bombing of German Cities in World War II* (Oxford: Berghahn, 2010), 134–35, 144–54; Eric Markusen and David Kopf, "Was It Genocidal?," in ibid., 160–71.

72 David Reynolds, *In Command of History: Churchill Fighting and Writing the Second World War* (London: Allen Lane, 2004), 320–22.

73 CamUL, Boyle papers, Add 9429/2c, conversation with Harris, July 18, 1979. Harris also showed the letter to Churchill's biographer, Martin Gilbert. See Gilbert, *Churchill War Papers*, 2:492–93.

74 TNA, AIR 2/7211, "Note on the Lessons to Be Learned from German Mistakes," September 19, 1940, 3.

75 CCAC, Bufton papers, DBOps, "Review of the Present Strategical Air Offensive," April 5, 1941, 5, and App. C, "The Blitz Attack by Night."

76 TNA, AIR 9/132, RE8 report, "Consideration of the Types of Bombs for Specific Objectives Based on Experience of German Bombing in this Country," September 26, 1940, 2–3.

77 UEA, Zuckerman archive, OEMU/50/7, "Notes on the Work of R.E.8," November 18, 1942; TNA, HO 191/203, A. R. Astbury, "History of the Research and Experiments Department, Ministry of Home Security, 1939–1945," 21–23.

78 TNA, DSIR 4/366, Building Research Laboratory, List of Enquiries Aug. 1940–Nov. 1941.

79 For an excellent account see Randall Wakelam, *The Science of Bombing: Operational Research in RAF Bomber Command* (Toronto: Toronto University Press, 2009), 24–33.

80 Hugh Berrington, "When Does Personality Make a Difference? Lord Cherwell and the Area Bombing of Germany," *International Political Science Review* 10 (1989): 18–21.

81 NC, Cherwell papers, F398, Statistical Section, Harrod papers, "Bombs and Deaths," September 30, 1940; G181, "Air Raid Casualties" [n.d. but September 1940]; "House Damage in Air Raids," September 27, 1940; "Bombing of London in September, October and November 1940"; G183, "Notes of a Conversation with Professor Zuckerman," March 26, 1941 (attached two charts of Hannover and Frankfurt with zones of population density).

82 TNA, AIR 9/132, minute by Plans Dept., Air Ministry, January 6, 1941; AIR 20/2264, AWAS Report, "The Bomb Censuses of Liverpool, Birmingham and London," October 29, 1940; AWAS Report, "Bomb Census of Liverpool, Birmingham, London, Coventry, Manchester, Leeds and Special Attacks," April 1941.

83 CCAC, Bufton papers, 3/26, draft directive [n.d. but June 1941].

84 TNA, AIR 40/1814, memorandum by O. Lawrence (MEW), May 9, 1941.

85 See Richard Overy, "The 'Weak Link'?: The Perception of the German Working Class by RAF Bomber Command, 1940–1945," *Labour History Review* 77 (2012): 22–25.

86 CCAC, Bufton papers, 3/48, "The Role of the Long-Range Bomber Force"; "Review of the Present Strategical Air Offensive," April 5, 1940, App. C, 2.

87 CCAC, Bufton papers, 3/13, notes on Plan ZZ, November 19, 1941, App. VI, "Attack on an Area of 150 Square Miles."

88 TNA, AIR 2/7211, bombing policy memorandum, November 19, 1940; AIR 20/25, AI to Baker, May 23, 1941.

89 TNA, AIR 20/25, memorandum on bombing policy by Baker, May 7, 1941.

90 RAFM, Peirse papers, AC 71/13/61-2, notes of a speech by Richard Peirse to the Thirty Club in London, November 25, 1941, 3.

91 TNA, AIR 20/4768, memorandum, September 23, 1941, "The Value of Incendiary Weapons in Attacks on Area Targets," 2.

92 CCAC, Bufton papers, DBOps to the director, June 6, 1941.

93 TNA, AIR 40/1351, AI 3c (Air Liaison), "Air Attack by Fire," October 17, 1941.

94 CCAC, Bufton papers, 3/26, report from BOPs 1 (Sq. Leader Morley), October 18, 1941.

95 Hugh Melinsky, *Forming the Pathfinders: The Career of Air Vice-Marshal Sydney Bufton* (Stroud: The History Press, 2010), 59.

96 Webster and Frankland, *Strategic Air Offensive*, 1:157–64.

97 TNA, AIR 9/150, Air Ministry War Room, Bomber Command sorties May–October 1940, November 1940–April 1941; DBOps to DCAS, September 11, 1941.

98 CCO, Portal papers, Folder 9, Peirse to Balfour, November 27, 1940; Portal to Peirse, November 30, 1940.

99 TNA, AIR 14/291, meeting at Air Ministry, December 10, 1940; HQ no. 7 Group to C-in-C, Bomber Command, January 4, 1941.

100 CCO, Portal papers, Folder 1/File 1, Churchill to Portal, November 1, 1940; Churchill to Portal, December 30, 1940.

101 Ibid., Folder 9/File 1940, Peirse to Churchill, December 24, 1940; Peirse to Portal [n.d. but December 1940]; File 1941, Peirse to Churchill, January 1, 1941.

102 John Colville, *The Fringes of Power: Downing Street Diaries, 1939–1945* (London: Weidenfeld & Nicolson, 2004), 241, diary entry for November 2, 1940.

103 CCO, Portal papers, Folder 1/File 1, Portal to Churchill, December 7, 1940; Folder 9/File 1940, Portal to Peirse, December 5, 1940; Peirse to Churchill, December 24, 1940. Details of raid in Middlebrook and Everitt, *Bomber Command War Diaries*, 111, and TNA, AIR 14/2670, night bomb raid sheets, December 1940, "Results of Night Operations, 16/17 December 1940."

104 Webster and Frankland, *Strategic Air Offensive*, 1:159–60.

105 CCO, Portal papers, Folder 9/File 2, Peirse to Portal, February 28, 1941.

106 UEA, Zuckerman archive, SZ/BBSU/56, "Bombing Policy."

107 Ibid., draft directive, July 9, 1941; Webster and Frankland, *Strategic Air Offensive*, 4:135–37.

108 CCO, Portal papers, Folder 9/File 1940, Peirse to Portal [n.d.].

109 RAFM, Peirse papers, AC 71/13/60, speech to the Thirty Club, November 25, 1941, 11.

110 TNA, AIR 40/288, AI (Liaison), "The Blitz," August 14, 1941, Table 1, "Effects of Blitz."

111 TNA, AIR 41/41, RAF Narrative, "The RAF in the Bombing Offensive Against Germany: Vol. 3," 87.

112 TNA, PREM 3/193/6A, minister of information to Churchill, January 1, 1941, "Conditions in Germany, December 1940," 2.

113 CCAC, Bufton papers, 3/11, "Report on the Interrogation of American Legation and Consular Officials in Lisbon, 24–31 July 1941," 4.

114 TNA, AIR 20/4768, air staff memorandum, September 23, 1941.

115 Foreign Office Historical Branch, "Churchill and Stalin: Documents Collated for the Anglo-Russian Seminar, 8 March 2002," doc. 9, broadcast by Mr. Churchill, June 22, 1941, 1, 3.

116 Ibid., doc. 11, telegram from Churchill to Stalin, July 7, 1941.

117 Bradley Smith, *Sharing Secrets with Stalin: How the Allies Traded Intelligence, 1941–1945* (Lawrence: University Press of Kansas, 1996), 11.

118 Colville, *Fringes of Power*, 363, entry for July 21, 1941.

119 RAFM, Bottomley papers, AC 71/2/29, Peck to Bottomley, April 6, 1944, encl. "Address to Thirty Club, 8 Mar 1944," 1–2.

120 Middlebrook and Everitt, *Bomber Command War Diaries*, 166–67.

121 BA-MA, RL 2 IV/28, Luftflotte 3, Gefechtskalender, "Durchführung und Erfolge Juli 1941."

122 CCO, Portal papers, Folder 2/File 1, Churchill to Portal, July 7, 1941. On the German response see Percy Schramm, ed., *Kriegstagebuch des OKW: Eine Dokumentation. 1940–1941, Band* 1, *Teilband* 2 (Augsburg: Weltbild, 2007), 417–20.

123 TNA, PREM 3/13/2, Churchill to Lindemann, July 7, 1941; Churchill to Sinclair and Portal, July 12, 1941.

124 RAFM, Bottomley papers, AC 71/2/115, "Operational Photography in Bomber Command Sept 1939–April 1945," June 1945, 14–29. Robert S. Ehlers Jr., *Targeting the Third Reich: Air Intelligence and the Allied Bombing Campaigns* (Lawrence: University Press of Kansas, 2009), 96–97.

125 CCO, Portal papers, Folder 9/File 2, Portal to Cherwell, July 29, 1941; Cherwell to Portal, July 30, 1941.

126 Webster and Frankland, *Strategic Air Offensive*, 4:205, "Report by Mr. Butt to Bomber Command on His Examination of Night Photographs, 18 August 1941"; Melinsky, *Forming the Pathfinders*, 43–44.

127 CCO, Portal papers, Folder 2/File 1, Churchill to Portal, September 15, 1941.

128 Ibid., Cherwell to Churchill, September 3, 1941; Portal to Churchill, "Notes on Lord Cherwell's Paper," September 11, 1941.

129 RAFM, Bottomley papers, AC 71/2/115, "Operational Photography," 26.

130 Interview with Robert Kee in Overy, *Bomber Command*, 75.

131 TNA, AIR 41/41, RAF Narrative, vol. 3, 42; Wakelam, *Science of Bombing*, 42–46.

132 Overy, *Bomber Command*, 74, interview with Wilkie Wanless; TNA, AIR 9/150, Peirse to Balfour, September 7, 1941; AIR 20/1979, Bomber Command, aircraft strengths and casualties. Between September 1939 and February 1941, 93,341 nonoperational sorties were flown by day, only 3,157 by night.

133 TNA, AIR 9/150, BOps to DBOps, November 27, 1941; AIR 20/283, Baker (DBOps) to Portal, July 28, 1941.

134 Webster and Frankland, *Strategic Air Offensive*, 4:455; TNA, AIR 9/150, DBOps to DCAS, September 11, 1941.

135 Thetford, *Aircraft of the Royal Air Force*, 317–22, 488–91; Brereton Greenhous, Stephen Harris, William Johnston, and William Rawling, *The Crucible of War, 1939–1945: The Official History of the Royal Canadian Air Force*, vol. 3 (Toronto: Toronto University Press/Department of National Defence, 1994), 604–6.

136 Greenhous et al., *Crucible of War*, 605.

137 Sebastian Cox, ed., *The Strategic Air War Against Germany, 1939–1945: The Official Report of the British Bombing Survey Unit* (London: Frank Cass, 1998), 37.

138 PArch, Beaverbrook papers, BBK/D/329, Air Ministry to MAP, May 4, 1941. On bombs see John A. MacBean and Arthur S. Hogben, *Bombs Gone: The Development and Use of British Air-Dropped Weapons from 1912 to the Present Day* (Wellingborough: Patrick Stephens, 1990), 66–68; Roy Irons, *The Relentless Offensive: War and Bomber Command, 1939–1945* (Barnsley: Pen & Sword, 2009), 190–91, 205–6.

139 TNA, AIR 20/5813, minute, VCS, November 3, 1941; "4lb Incendiary Bomb," BOps 2b, January 2, 1942.

140 NC, Cherwell papers, F222, minute for Churchill from Cherwell, May 1941; G182, H. W. Robinson to Cherwell, October 27, 1941; Chart, "Bombs Dropped on Germany July–Dec 1941"; G189, Cherwell to Ministry of Supply, January 28, 1942; PArch, Beaverbrook papers, BBK/D/330, Air Marshal Courtney to Beaverbrook, May 27, 1941. Details on bombs from Irons, *Relentless Offensive*, 203–5.

141 Cox, *Strategic Air War*, 36.

142 PArch, Balfour papers, BAL/3, "Dunkirk Days–Battle of Britain" (Balfour was undersecretary of state at the Air Ministry). See CamUL, Boyle papers, Add 9429/2C, Boyle to Harris, July 22, 1979, where Beaverbrook was still remembered as "one of the instinctive opponents of bombing Germany."

143 PArch, Beaverbrook papers, BBK/D/329, Portal to Moore-Brabazon, May 10, 1941, 3.

144 Gavin Bailey, "Aircraft for Survival: Anglo-American Aircraft Supply Diplomacy, 1938–1942" (unpublished PhD thesis, University of Dundee, 2010), 183–91.

145 LC, Arnold papers, Reel 199, handwritten notes, Placentia Bay meeting, August 11, 1941.

146 Webster and Frankland, *Strategic Air Offensive*, 4:4–6; Melinsky, *Forming the Pathfinders*, 56–57, 59; Alfred Price, *Instruments of Darkness: The History of Electronic Warfare, 1939–1945* (London: Greenhill, 2005), 97–99.

147 BA-MA, RL 2 IV/101, Vorstudien zur Luftkriegsgeschichte, Heft 8: Reichsluftverteidigung: Teil B, Flakabwehr [n.d., 1944], 12–13, 15.

148 RAFM, Saundby papers, AC 72/12 Box 7, "War in the Ether: Europe, 1939–1945," Signals Branch, HQ Bomber Command, October 1945, 6.

149 BA-MA, RL 2 IV/101, "Flakabwehr," 15–17.

150 Werner Held and Holger Nauroth, *Die deutsche Nachtjagd* (Stuttgart: Motorbuch Verlag, 1992), 115–17.

151 BA-MA, RL 2 IV/101, "Flakabwehr," 18–19, 23; Bill Gunston, *Night Fighters: A Development and Combat History* (Patrick Stephens, 1976), 86–89; Price, *Instruments of Darkness*, 55–59.

152 Westermann, *Flak*, 123–24.

153 TNA, AIR 20/283, minute by DBOps (Baker), November 10, 1941.

154 Melinsky, *Forming the Pathfinders*, 66–67; Middlebrook and Everitt, *Bomber Command War Diaries*, 210.

155 CCO, Portal papers, Folder 2/File 2, Churchill to Portal, September 27, 1941; Portal to Churchill, September 25, 1941, enclosing "Development and Employment of the Heavy Bomber Force," September 22, 1941.

156 Ibid., Portal to Churchill, October 2, 1941; Churchill to Portal, October 7, 1941.

157 TNA, AIR 41/41, RAF Narrative, vol. 3, 111; Middlebrook and Everitt, *Bomber Command War Diaries*, 217–18; Greenhous et al., *Crucible of War*, 559–60.

158 Mark Connelly, *Reaching for the Stars: A New History of Bomber Command in World War II* (London: I. B. Tauris, 2001), 60–62; Webster and Frankland, *Strategic Air Offensive*, 1:254–56; Anthony Furse, *Wilfrid Freeman: The Genius Behind Allied Survival and Air Supremacy, 1939 to 1945* (Staplehurst, Kent: Spellmount, 2000), 199–200.

159 CCAC, Bufton papers, 3/12, "Report of a Visit to Groups and Stations by Wing-Commander Morley, 10 Dec 1941."

160 Royal Society, Blackett papers, PB/4/4, "Note on the Use of the Bomber Force," 3.

161 Webster and Frankland, *Strategic Air Offensive*, 1:328–29.

162 CCAC, Bufton papers, 3/12, minute for DBOps from Bufton, February 27, 1942.

163 PArch, Beaverbrook papers, BBK/D/330, telegram from Harris to Portal and Sinclair, September 18, 1941; RAFM, Harris papers, Harris to Freeman, September 15, 1941, 5.

164 RAFM, Harris papers, Harris to Freeman, September 15, 1941, 2–3.

165 PArch, Beaverbrook papers, BBK/D/330, telegram from Harris to Portal, December 8, 1941.

166 Henry Probert, *Bomber Harris: His Life and Times* (London: Greenhill, 2006), 122–23.

167 Warren Kimball, ed., *Churchill and Roosevelt: The Complete Correspondence*, vol. 1, *Alliance Emerging* (London: Collins, 1984), 296, memorandum, Churchill to Roosevelt, pt. 1, "The Atlantic Front."

168 LC, Arnold papers, Reel 199, Proceedings of the American-British Joint Chiefs of Staff Conferences, December 24, 1941, 2.

169 Ibid., Annex 1, American-British Strategy, 2, 5.

170 Kimball, *Churchill-Roosevelt Correspondence*, 1:314–23, Churchill to Roosevelt, January 7(?), 1942.

171 USAFA, Colorado Springs (USAFA), Hansell papers, Ser. 3, Box 1, Folder 2, "Can We Be Bombed?" [n.d. but late 1939], 22–23.

172 NARA, RG 94.580, memorandum from CAS, May 10, 1940; LC, Andrews papers, Box 11, memorandum for the Executive by Carl Spaatz, January 5, 1935, "Comments on Doctrines of the Army Air Corps," 1.

173 Haywood Hansell, *The Air Plan That Defeated Hitler* (Atlanta: Higgins McArthur, 1972), 53–63, 92–93.

174 Douglas Lackey, "The Bombing Campaign of the USAAF," in Primoratz, *Terror from the Sky*, 41–45; Ronald Schaffer, "American Military Ethics in World

War II: The Bombing of German Civilians," *Journal of American History* 67 (1980): 320–22; Conrad Crane, "Evolution of U.S. Strategic Bombing of Urban Areas," *Historian* 50 (1987): 16–17, 21–24.

175 On Roosevelt see Jeffery Underwood, *The Wings of Democracy: The Influence of Air Power on the Roosevelt Administration, 1933–1941* (College Station: Texas A&M University Press, 1991), chaps. 7–8.

176 TNA, FO 371/23093, Dept. of State communiqué from Ambassador Anthony Biddle, September 13, 1939; FDRL, president's personal files, 554, Biddle to Roosevelt, November 10, 1939.

177 Michael Sherry, *The Rise of American Air Power: The Creation of Armageddon* (New Haven, CT: Yale University Press, 1987), 97–98.

178 NARA, Lovett papers, RG 107, Box 138, memorandum for Lovett, "Blackout Alarms," December 24, 1941; Lovett to Donald Douglas (president, Douglas Aircraft Company), January 27, 1942; Office of Civilian Defense to all regional directors, December 22, 1941.

179 Ibid., Engineer Board, U.S. Army, "Traffic Control During Blackouts," October 5, 1942; Joseph McNarney (deputy army CoS) to vice chief of naval operations, June 5, 1942.

180 Ibid., Box 139, Federal Works Agency, "Air Raid Protection Code for Federal Buildings," August 1942, 13–20, 21–25.

181 Ibid., *Civilian Front*, vol. 11, May 15, 1943, 7; HQ Army Service Forces, Periodic Report to Lovett, 2.

182 Ibid., James Landis, "We're Not Safe from Air Raids," *Civilian Front*, May 15, 1943.

183 James Parton, *"Air Force Spoken Here": General Ira Eaker and the Command of the Air* (Bethesda, MD: Adler & Adler, 1986), 128–34, 149. Eighth Air Force activation in Maxwell AFB, Eighth Air Force, 520.056, Statistical Summary 8th Air Force Operations, 1.

184 TNA, AIR 14/792, Eaker to Harris, July 30, 1942; Bottomley to Portal, February 8, 1942; Baker to Bottomley, February 2, 1942.

185 Richard G. Davis, *Carl A. Spaatz and the Air War in Europe* (Washington, DC: Center for Air Force History, 1993), 67–71.

186 Ibid., 48–53.

187 LC, Arnold papers, Reel 89, Harold George (Asst. CoS) to Arnold, February 25, 1942.

188 John Huston, ed., *American Airpower Comes of Age: General Henry H. "Hap" Arnold's World War II Diaries* (Maxwell, AL: Air University Press, 2002), 1:282–84, 310.

189 Ibid., 1:304, entry for May 30, 1942.

190 Based on Probert, *Bomber Harris*, chaps. 2, 4–5.

191 "Rabbits" in CCO, Portal papers, Folder 9/File 3, Harris to Portal, March 2, 1942; "weaker sisters" in RAFM, Harris papers, H51, Harris to Peck (Air Ministry), May 1, 1942; "Fifth Columnists" in Portal papers, Folder 9/File 3, Harris to Portal, March 5, 1942; "impertinent" in Harris papers, H9, Harris to Bottomley, January 13, 1945.

192 UEA, Zuckerman archive, SZ/BBSU/3, Air Commodore Pelly to Zuckerman, January 8, 1947.

193 RAFM, Harris papers, H53, Harris to Baker (DBOps), April 11, 1942.

194 CamUL, Boyle papers, Add 9429/2C, Boyle to Harris, August 24, 1979.

195 RAFM, Harris papers, H9, Harris to Bottomley, March 29, 1945.

196 Webster and Frankland, *Strategic Air Offensive*, 4:143–48.

197 TNA, AIR 20/4768, memorandum from BOps, February 25, 1942.

198 NC, Cherwell papers, G192, note for Cherwell, February 23, 1942, on German towns; CCAC, Bufton papers, 3/15, memorandum from Morley (BOps 1), "The Employment of H. E. Bombs in Incendiary Attack," November 18, 1942, 1–2.

199 NC, Cherwell papers, F254, War Cabinet, "Estimates of Bombing Effect," April 9, 1942; F226, minute for Churchill from Cherwell, March 30, 1942; TNA, AIR 9/183, comments on Cherwell paper, April 17, 1942.

200 CCO, Portal papers, Folder 9/File 3, Harris to Portal, March 5, 1942.

201 RAFM, Harris papers, H47, Harris to Bottomley, April 9, 1942.

202 Olaf Groehler, *Bombenkrieg gegen Deutschland* (Berlin: Akademie Verlag, 1990), 98.

203 BA-B, R 1501/823, directive from interior minister, May 6, 1942, 1. Details of raids are from Middlebrook and Everitt, *Bomber Command War Diaries*, 246–52, 259–61; Groehler, *Bombenkrieg*, 50–54.

204 RAFM, Harris papers, H53, Baker to Harris, March 21, 1942; Baker to Harris, April 9, 1942; TNA, AIR 20/4768, note from Bufton for Baker, April 6, 1942; Harris to Baker, April 11, 1942.

205 CCAC, Bufton papers, 3/12, Bufton to Harris, May 8, 1942; TNA, AIR 14/1779, chart of attacks on Essen, Duisburg, and Düsseldorf.

206 TNA, PREM 3/11/4, Cherwell to Churchill, March 30, 1942; Sinclair to Churchill, April 6, 1942; Hollis (CoS) to Churchill, April 10, 1942; AIR 9/187, Chiefs of Staff Committee minutes, April 13, 1942.

207 Webster and Frankland, *Strategic Air Offensive*, 4:231–38, "Report by Mr. Justice Singleton, 20 May 1942"; TNA, PREM 3/11/4, Singleton to Churchill, May 20, 1942.

208 TNA, PREM 3/11/4, Cherwell to Churchill, May 28, 1942.

209 CCO, Portal papers, Folder 9/File 3, Cherwell to Portal, February 27, 1942; Harris to Portal, March 2, 1942; Melinsky, *Forming the Pathfinders*, 68–69.

210 CCAC, Bufton papers, 3/12, "Tactical Direction of the Bomber Force," May 16, 1942, 1.

211 Ibid., Bufton to all squadron and station commanders, March 1942; H. Graham to Morley (BOps 1), April 1, 1942.

212 Melinsky, *Forming the Pathfinders*, 72–78; Furse, *Wilfrid Freeman*, 205–8; Middlebrook and Everitt, *Bomber Command War Diaries*, 297–98, 301.

213 CCAC, Bufton papers, 3/12, minute by the assistant CoS (operations), August 2, 1942.

214 TNA, AIR 14/276, Portal to Harris, May 19, 1942; Harris to Coastal Command, Flying Training and Army Co-Operation, May 20, 1942; Harris to Philip de la Ferté (Coastal Command), May 23, 1942; Bomber Command Operational Order, no. 147, May 23, 1942.

215 BA-B, NS 18/1058, report, Leiter IV, Party Chancellery, May 31, 1942; Groehler, *Bombenkrieg*, 65–66.

216 Groehler, *Bombenkrieg*, 66–67.

217 Details from Middlebrook and Everitt, *Bomber Command War Diaries*, 274, 280–81; Groehler, *Bombenkrieg*, 69.

218 Greenhous et al., *Crucible of War,* 621–22.

219 CCO, Portal papers, Folder 3/File 3, Smuts to Churchill, June 30, 1942; draft telegram Churchill to Smuts, July 4, 1942, rejecting the proposal.

220 RAFM, Harris papers, H11, memorandum for the prime minister, June 17, 1942 (revised August 20); TNA, PREM 3/19, Harris to Churchill, June 17, 1942.

221 RAFM, Harris papers, H63, App. A, "Approximate Allocation of Air Resources, June 15, 1942"; TNA, PREM 3/19, Churchill minute to Harris, July 6, 1942; Air Ministry to Cabinet Office, August 12, 1942; CCO, Portal papers, Folder 9/File 3, Harris to Portal, August 20, 1942. Out of forty-two squadrons on establishment, Harris reckoned that six were on loan, six were reequipping or forming, four were operationally limited (Polish squadrons "almost useless"), and five others were unavailable.

222 Parton, *"Air Force Spoken Here,"* 166–67.

223 LC, Spaatz papers, Box 76, Eaker to Spaatz, August 27, 1942, "Accuracy of Bombardment," 2, 4.

224 FDRL, Map Room Files, Box 12, telegram from Harriman to Roosevelt, August 14, 1942.

225 TNA, AIR 8/435, Churchill to Sinclair and Portal, August 17, 1942; Portal to Churchill, August 20, 1942; Harris to Portal, August 29, 1942.

226 TNA, PREM 3/19, Harris to Churchill, September 4, 1942; Churchill to Harris, September 13, 1942; "better than doing nothing" in CCO, Portal papers, Folder 3/File 1, Churchill to Sinclair, March 13, 1943.

227 TNA, PREM 3/19, Amery to Churchill, September 1, 1942.

228 CCAC, Bufton papers, 3/12, L. A. C. Cunningham to Morley (BOps 1), October 14, 1942.

229 Royal Society, Blackett papers, PB/4/4, minutes of CoS discussion, November 18, 1942.

230 CCO, Portal papers, Folder 9/File 3, Harris to Portal, September 24, 1942. On the arguments over the size of the Canadian component see Greenhous et al., *Crucible of War,* 599–600.

231 TNA, AIR 14/792, Harris to Balfour, November 12, 1942; Bottomley to Harris, November 28, 1942.

232 CCO, Portal papers, Folder 9/File 3, Harris to Portal, October 21, 1942.

233 TNA, AIR 14/1779, Air Vice Marshal Saundby to Tizard, December 2, 1942.

234 CCAC, Bufton papers, 3/15, minute for Baker from Bufton, November 2, 1942.

235 TNA, AIR 22/203, War Room Manual of Bomber Command Operations 1939–1945, chart 4, chart 9.

236 UEA, Zuckerman archive, OEMU/50/2, REDept, "The 1000-Bomber Raid on Cologne," November 3, 1942.

237 BA-B, NS 18/1063, Partei-Kanzlei, Abt. PG, "Angaben über die Verluste durch Fliegerangriffen," October 2, 1942; R 3102/10031, Reich Statistical Office, "Die Tätigkeit der feindlichen Luftwaffe über dem Reichsgebiet," January 10, 1945; USSBS, "Overall Report, European War, 30 Sept 1945," 74, 81.

238 TNA, AIR 9/424, note from Churchill for the CoS Committee, November 18, 1942.

239 Ibid., War Cabinet, JPS, "Anglo-US Bombing Policy," August 18, 1942.

240 LC, Spaatz papers, Box 66, directive from Roosevelt to Marshall, August 24, 1942; Arnold to Harry Hopkins, September 3, 1942, encl. memorandum, "Plans for Operations Against the Enemy," 2.

241 Davis, *Carl A. Spaatz,* 113–16.

242 TNA, AIR 40/1814, MEW to Sinclair, May 2, 1942; see too Balfour, *Wings over Westminster,* 103, who wrote that the division he found between service officers and civil servants in the Air Ministry resulted in "processes of administration and decision [that] were cumbersome and slow."

243 CCAC, Bufton papers, 3/12, memorandum by Wing Cdr. A. Morley, "The Tactical Direction of the Bomber Force," May 20, 1942, 2.

244 CCAC, BUFT 3/15, memorandum for DBOps from Bufton, September 6, 1942.

Chapter 2. The Casablanca Offensive: The Allies over Germany, 1943–44

1 TNA, AIR 75/11, Slessor papers, pencil notes, "Conduct of the War in 1943."

2 Ibid., draft by Slessor, "The Bomber Offensive from the United Kingdom: Note by the British Chiefs of Staff," January 20, 1943; draft, "Casablanca Directive," January 21, 1943; John Slessor, *The Central Blue: Recollections and Reflections* (London: Cassell, 1956), 445–46.

3 LC, Arnold papers, Reel 200, Arnold to Gen. Wedemeyer, December 30, 1942.

4 RAFM, Harris papers, H28, Arthur Sulzberger, *New York Times,* to Harris, September 21, 1942; Harris to Francis Drake, January 1, 1943; Robert Lovett to Harris, November 24, 1942; Harris to Lovett, December 24, 1942; H51, Richard Peck (Air Ministry) to Harris, December 22, 1942; telegram from air attaché, Washington, DC, to Air Ministry, January 11, 1943.

5 UEA, Zuckerman archive, SZ/BBSU/29, Air Commodore Pelly to Zuckerman, January 14, 1946.

6 TNA, PREM 3/14/2, cipher telegram, Churchill to the Air Ministry, August 17, 1942; Portal to Churchill, August 20, 1942; Stalin to Churchill, January 19, 1943. For Harris's views see AIR 8/435, Portal and Sinclair to Churchill, August 18, 1942; Harris to Portal, August 29, 1942.

7 TNA, AIR 8/435, Stalin to Churchill, March 3, 1943; CCO, Portal papers, Folder 3/File 3, Churchill to Portal, September 10, 1942; Churchill to Stalin, September 11, 1942.

8 CCO, Portal papers, Folder 3/File 3, Churchill, "Note on Air Policy," October 22, 1942; Folder 3/File 4, Churchill to Portal, October 26, 1942; Portal to Churchill, November 7, 1942; LC, Eaker papers, Box I.20, Spaatz to Eaker, December 9, 1942; Eaker to Spaatz, January 29, 1943.

9 LC, Arnold papers, Reel 200, Arnold to Gen. Stratemeyer, February 26, 1943.

10 Slessor, *Central Blue,* 438–39; TNA, AIR 75/11, draft, "Future Strategy," September 25, 1942; draft for the CoS, "Anglo-American Bomber Offensive against Italy and Germany in 1943."

11 LC, Spaatz papers, Box 66, Arnold to Harry Hopkins, September 3, 1942, encl. memorandum, "Plans for Operations Against the Enemy."

12 Ibid., AWPD-42, "Requirements of Air Ascendancy," 6–7.

13 FDRL, Map Room Files, Box 165, Folder 6, JCS minutes of meetings, January 13 and January 14, 1943; LC, Arnold papers, Reel 200, JCS, minutes of meetings, January 14, 1943, 11–12.

14 CCO, Portal papers, Folder 3/File 4, Churchill to Harry Hopkins, October 14, 1942; "Note on Air Policy," October 22, 1942; Churchill to Portal, Sinclair, and Harris, October 26, 1942.

15 TNA, PREM 3/19, Churchill to Harris, September 18, 1942; AIR 9/424, air staff minute, October 10, 1942.

16 CCO, Portal papers, Folder 3/File 4, Sinclair to Churchill, October 23, 1942; Portal to Churchill, October 28, 1942; Portal to Churchill, November 7, 1942; Tami Davis Biddle, "British and American Approaches to Strategic Bombing: Their Origins and Implementation in the World War II Bomber Offensive," in John Gooch, ed., *Airpower: Theory and Practice* (London: Frank Cass, 1995), 119–20.

17 LC, Spaatz papers, Box 97, "Casablanca Notes," January 15, 1943; John Huston, ed., *American Airpower Comes of Age: General Henry H. "Hap" Arnold's World War II Diaries* (Maxwell, AL: Air University Press, 2002), 1:462; AFHRA, CD A5835, "Eighth Air Force: Growth, Development and Operations," Air Force Plans, exhibit 3, "The Case for Day Bombing"; James Parton, *"Air Force Spoken Here": General Ira Eaker and the Command of the Air* (Bethesda, MD: Adler & Adler, 1986), 217–20; Tami Davis Biddle, *Rhetoric and Reality in Air Warfare: Evolution of British and American Ideas About Strategic Bombing, 1914–1945* (Princeton, NJ: Princeton University Press, 2002), 214–15.

18 LC, Spaatz papers, Box 97, "Casablanca Notes," January 17 and 19, 1943; FDRL, Map Room Files, Box 165, Folder 7, ANFA Meeting minutes, January 18, 1943.

19 Parton, *"Air Force Spoken Here,"* 221. The sentence ran, "It keeps German defenses alerted around the clock, 24 hours of the day."

20 LC, Spaatz papers, Box 97, "Casablanca Notes," January 18 and 20, 1943; Henry H. Arnold, *Global Mission* (New York: Harper & Row, 1949), 395–97; Parton, *"Air Force Spoken Here,"* 221–22.

21 TNA, AIR 8/1076, Churchill to Attlee, January 21, 1943.

22 Charles Webster and Noble Frankland, *The Strategic Air Offensive Against Germany* (London: HMSO, 1961), 4:153–54, "Combined Chiefs of Staff Directive for the Bomber Offensive from the United Kingdom."

23 LC, Spaatz papers, Box 97, "Casablanca Notes," January 25 to January 31, 1943; TNA, AIR 8/425, Bottomley to Harris, February 4, 1943.

24 Slessor, *Central Blue*, 448.

25 TNA, AIR 9/424, note by director of plans, August 24, 1942; JPS, "Anglo-U.S. Bombing Policy," August 18, 1942.

26 LC, Spaatz papers, Box 66, Report on AWPD-42, September 19, 1942.

27 LC, Portal papers, Folder 4/File 1, Arnold to Portal, December 10, 1942; Portal to Churchill, December 20, 1942.

28 LC, Eaker papers, Box I.20, Eaker to Portal, August 30, 1943.

29 LC, Spaatz papers, Box 67, "Status of the Combined Bomber Offensive from U.K.," August 7, 1943, 1.

30 TNA, AIR 14/739A, Harris to Eaker, April 15, 1943.

31 Ibid., Harris to Portal, April 9, 1943, encl. "The United States Contribution to the Bomber Offensive in 1943," 2.

32 Ibid., War Cabinet, CoS, "An Estimate of the Effects of an Anglo-American Bomber Offensive against Germany," November 3, 1942.

33 TNA, FO 837/1315, "Bombers' Baedeker: Guide to the Economic Importance of German Towns and Cities," January 1943 edition.

34 RAFM, Harris papers, Misc. Box A, Folder 4, "One Hundred Towns of Leading Economic Importance to the German War Effort."

35 LC, Eaker papers, Box I.20, Portal to Eaker, February 28, 1943.

36 TNA, AIR 14/1779, minutes of meeting in the Air Ministry, March 1, 1943, 2.

37 LC, Spaatz papers, Box 67, Eaker to Spaatz, April 13, 1943, encl. Air War Plans memorandum, "The Combined Bomber Offensive from the United Kingdom."

38 Ibid., "Status of Combined Bomber Offensive," August 7, 1943, 1.

39 Ibid., memorandum from Arnold to Spaatz, "Report of the Committee of Operations Analysts with Respect to Economic Targets within the Western Axis," March 8, 1943.

40 LC, Eaker papers, Box I.20, Eaker to Portal, April 2, 1943; TNA, AIR 8/1103, Arnold to Portal, March 24, 1943; Portal to Eaker, April 9, 1943; Parton, *"Air Force Spoken Here,"* 250–53.

41 CCAC, Bufton papers, 3/42, Bufton to Portal, April 8, 1943; "The Bombing Offensive from the U.K.," and covering note from RAF liaison at Eaker's HQ; Stephen McFarland and Wesley Newton, *To Command the Sky: The Battle for Air Superiority over Germany, 1942–1944* (Washington, DC: Smithsonian Institution, 1991), 92–94.

42 TNA, AIR 8/1103, Harris to Eaker, April 15, 1943. For Air Ministry views on German fighters see AIR 9/423, memorandum, director of plans, March 22, 1943.

43 LC, Eaker papers, Box I.16, Col. C. Cabell to Eaker, May 27, 1943; Box I.20, Eaker to Portal, June 1, 1943.

44 Ibid., Box I.16, Kuter to Eaker, July 6, 1943; Eaker to Kuter, July 22, 1943; TNA, AIR 8/1103, CCS meeting, June 4, 1943; minute, Bottomley to Portal, June 10, 1943; Webster and Frankland, *Strategic Air Offensive,* 4:160, Bottomley to Harris, September 3, 1943.

45 LC, Eaker papers, Box I.19, Lovett to Eaker, July 28, 1943.

46 CCO, Portal papers, Folder 3/File 4, Portal to Churchill, November 9, 1942.

47 TNA, AIR 20/2025, Air Ministry statistics, RAF personnel, establishment and casualties, 1939–45.

48 RAFM, Harris papers, H67, "Establishment and Strength of Ancillary Staff, 31 July 1943."

49 UEA, Zuckerman archive, SZ/BBSU/3, Exercise Thunderbolt, précis no. 10, "Administrative Aspects of the Bomber Offensive"; SZ/BBSU/2, minute for Zuckerman from Claude Pelly, June 21, 1946; LC, Eaker papers, Box I.20, Harris to Balfour, January 12, 1943, on the transition from grass to concrete runways.

50 LC, Eaker papers, Box I.20, Eaker to Harris, January 4, 1943; Box I.21, Eighth Air Force memorandum, "Supply and Maintenance" [n.d.]; "Report of Lt. General Ira Eaker on USAAF Activities in the United Kingdom," December 31, 1943, 3; Brereton Greenhous, Stephen Harris, William Johnston, and William Rawling, *The Crucible of War, 1939–1945: The Official History of the Royal Canadian Air Force,* vol. 3 (Toronto: Toronto University Press/Department of National Defence, 1994), 616, 631, 636.

51 PArch, Balfour papers, BAL/4, RCAF Station, Trenton, "The British Commonwealth Air Training Plan, 1939–1945" (Ottawa, 1949), 3–8.

52 Gilbert Guinn, *The Arnold Scheme: British Pilots, the American South and the Allies' Daring Plan* (Charleston, SC: History Press, 2007), 484, 541.

53 John Herington, *Air War Against Germany and Italy, 1939–1945* (Canberra: Australian War Memorial, 1954), 450–51, 452, 454, 547–51.

54 Greenhous et al., *Crucible of War,* 616, 627–29, 634–35.

55 LC, Eaker papers, Box I.21, "Report of Lt. General Ira Eaker," 1; Donald Miller, *Eighth Air Force: The American Bomber Crews in Britain* (London: Aurum Press, 2007), 71–72.

56 AFHRA, CD A5835, "Eighth Air Force: Growth, Development and Operations 1 December 1942–31 December 1943," Air Force Supply and Maintenance, chart of Serviceability B-17s, B-24s.

57 LC, Eaker papers, Box I.20, Eighth Air Force, "Supply and Maintenance" [n.d]; "Report of Lt. General Ira Eaker," 7.

58 LC, Arnold papers, Reel 89, Spaatz to Arnold, May 28, 1943, encl. "Organization of the Eighth Air Force" by Follett Bradley; "The Bradley Plan for the United Kingdom" [n.d.], charts i, iv; Summary of Personnel Requirements for the VIII Air Force Service Command; Gen. Barney Giles to Eaker, August 26, 1943; Parton, *"Air Force Spoken Here,"* 289.

59 LC, Eaker papers, Box I.19, Lovett to Arnold, June 19, 1943.

60 Ibid., Box I.17, Arnold to Eaker, June 10, 1943; Eaker to Arnold, June 12, 1943.

61 Ibid., Arnold to Gen. Devers, June 29, 1943.

62 Ibid., Box I.16, Eaker to Col. Edgar Sorensen, Washington, DC, January 11, 1943.

63 LC, Spaatz papers, Box 143, Hansell to Eaker and Longfellow, February 26, 1943, 4–5.

64 AFHRA, 520.056-188, Eighth Air Force Statistical Summary, Aircraft Loss Rate. In January the figure was 7.5 percent, in February 8.1 percent, in March 3.2 percent, and in April 7.8 percent.

65 LC, Eaker papers, Box I.16, Brig. Gen. J. Bevans (Assistant Chief of Staff, Personnel) to Eaker, May 1, 1943; Eaker to Arnold, June 22, 1943.

66 Miller, *Eighth Air Force,* 221.

67 LC, Spaatz papers, Box 70, Brig. Gen. C. Chauncey to all Eighth Air Force commanders, December 18, 1942.

68 Ibid., HQ Eighth Air Force, Provost Marshal's "Report on Conduct of Troops with Regard to the British," 1, 3–4.

69 Ibid., Eighth Air Force, "Anglo-American Relations," September 20, 1943.

70 NC, Cherwell papers, G195, letter from MAP to War Cabinet, December 12, 1942; R. Ewell (Office of Scientific Research and Development) to Cherwell, December 12, 1942.

71 LC, Eaker papers, Box I.19, Lovett to Arnold, June 19, 1943: "The B-17 and B-24 are still useful types but their effectiveness will be reduced sharply by the end of the year."

72 Ibid., Box I.17, telegram from Arnold to Eaker, June 10, 1943.

73 Ibid., telegram from Eaker to Arnold, June 12, 1943.

74 LC, Spaatz papers, Box 316, Gen. Anderson's Diary, 1943–45, entries for February 22, March 15, May 1, May 29.

75 LC, Eaker papers, Box I.17, Eaker to Arnold, June 29, 1943. See Parton, *"Air Force Spoken Here,"* 271–78, for a full account of the acrimonious exchange.

76 LC, Eaker papers, Box I.17, Arnold to Eaker, June 29, 1943.

77 TNA, AIR 20/283, Bomber Command Operations, February–November 1943, January 2, 1944.

78 Greenhous et al., *Crucible of War,* 658–60; Randall Wakelam, *The Science of Bombing: Operational Research in RAF Bomber Command* (Toronto: Toronto University Press, 2009), 119–21, 139.

79 RAFM, Saundby papers, AC 72/12, Box 7, Signals Branch, HQ Bomber Command, "War in the Ether: Europe 1939–1945," October 1945, 14–16. "Boozer" was unable to detect enemy Airborne Interception radar at more than 1,500 yards, while "Monica" and "Boozer" interfered with each other when used together.

80 RAFM, Harris papers, H55, speech to the 21st Army Group HQ, May 14, 1945; TNA, AIR 20/283, Bomber Command Operations; CCO, Portal papers, Folder 5, "Comparison of Bombing Effort During the Year 1943," February 10, 1944.

81 See Greenhous et al., *Crucible of War,* 657–67, for a lucid account of the Ruhr operations.

82 Ralf Blank, "The Battle of the Ruhr, 1943: Aerial Warfare Against an Industrial Region," *Labour History Review* 77 (2012): 35–48.

83 Nicolaus von Below, *At Hitler's Side: The Memoirs of Hitler's Luftwaffe Adjutant, 1937–1945* (London: Greenhill, 2001), 169–70.

84 Willi A. Boelcke, ed., *The Secret Conferences of Dr. Goebbels, 1939–1943* (London: Weidenfeld & Nicolson, 1967), 388–89.

85 Heinz Boberach, ed., *Meldungen aus dem Reich: Die geheimen Lageberichte des Sicherheitsdienstes der SS, 1938–1945* (Herrsching: Pawlak Verlag, 1984), 13:4983, 5021, reports for March 22, March 29, 1943.

86 Edward Westermann, *Flak: German Anti-Aircraft Defenses, 1914–1945* (Lawrence: University Press of Kansas, 2001), 200–202.

87 Ibid., 201–2; Greenhous et al., *Crucible of War,* 662–63.

88 John A. MacBean and Arthur S. Hogben, *Bombs Gone: The Development and Use of British Air-Dropped Weapons from 1912 to the Present Day* (Wellingborough: Patrick Stephens, 1990), 158–61.

89 TNA, AIR 14/840, minute for the C-in-C by Saundby, February 14, 1943.

90 Ibid., Harris minute, April 15, 1943.

91 MacBean and Hogben, *Bombs Gone,* 164–69; Martin Middlebrook and Chris Everitt, *The Bomber Command War Diaries* (Leicester: Midland Publishing, 2000), 386–88; Olaf Groehler, *Bombenkrieg gegen Deutschland* (Berlin: Akademie Verlag, 1990), 154–56.

92	UEA, Zuckerman archive, SZ/AEAF/14, Bomber Command, ORS, "The Operational Use of Oboe Mark 1A, December 1942–June 1943," 3–4.

93	TNA, AIR 20/283, HQ Bomber Command, ORS Report, May 27, 1943; original evasion instructions in AIR 14/206, Tactical Committee paper 31, revised February 1943.

94	TNA, AIR 48/29, USSBS Civilian Defense Division: Final Report, October 26, 1945, 3; Hitler's comment in Below, *At Hitler's Side,* 172.

95	TNA, AIR 8/1109, JIC, "Effects of Bombing Offensive on German War Effort," July 22, 1943.

96	TNA, AIR 20/476, Air Ministry DoI, "Effects of Air Raids on Labour and Production," August 16, 1943, 1–2; O. Lawrence (MEW) to Morley (BOps 1), September 6, 1943; note from Lawrence to Bufton, October 24, 1943.

97	CCAC, Bufton papers, 3/42, Gen. Frank Andrews (U.S. supreme commander in United Kingdom) to Gen. Marshall and Gen. Arnold, April 3, 1943.

98	Roger A. Freeman, *The Mighty Eighth War Diary* (London: Jane's, 1981), 42–73.

99	TNA, AIR 8/1109, JIC, "Effects of Bombing Offensive," 1; AIR 9/423, director of plans minute, March 15, 1943.

100	CCAC, Bufton papers, 3/24, BOps 1 to Group Captain Barnett, November 1, 1941; Draft App. B [n.d. but late October 1941].

101	TNA, AIR 20/4768, BOps memorandum, February 25, 1942.

102	UEA, Zuckerman archive, SZ/OEMU/50/7, "Note for Advisers' Meeting," August 12, 1942.

103	Ibid., 9th Meeting of RE8 Advisory Group, September 16, 1942; 10th Meeting of RE8 Advisory Group, September 24, 1942; 15th Meeting of RE8 Advisory Group, October 29, 1942.

104	Ibid., SZ/OEMU/50/8, RE8 report, "German Domestic Architecture," April 7, 1943, 1–2.

105	CCAC, Bufton papers, 3/26, minutes of meeting at the Ministry of Works, October 9, 1941; R. Ewell (Petroleum Warfare Section) to D. A. C. Dewdney, December 22, 1942.

106	CCAC, Bufton papers, 3/24, BOps 1, draft report, "Incendiary Attack," November 8, 1941; BOps 1 to Peirse [n.d. but November 1941]; Report for DD-BOps, "Types and Weights of German Incendiary Bombs," October 11, 1941.

107	CCAC, Bufton papers, 3/26, DBOps, note on an article in *Die Sirene,* October 2, 1942. The article in the German civil defense journal explained how to fight fires even with the threat of antipersonnel bombs.

108	Ibid., Bufton papers, 3/26 DBOps to Director of Research, Air Ministry [n.d. but late October 1942]. Some 40 percent of explosive incendiaries had a three-minute delay, 5 percent from six to ten minutes.

109	CCAC, Bufton papers, 3/27, BOPs 1, "Present and Future Incendiary Technique as Applied to Area Attack," October 13, 1942, 1, 2–4.

110	LC, Spaatz papers, Box 80, Bufton memorandum, "Incendiary Attack of German Cities," January 1943, 3.

111	Armaments Design Establishment, *The Development of British Incendiary Bombs During the Period of the 1939–1945 World War,* Ministry of Supply, December 1946, 34–37.

112 CCAC, Bufton papers, 3/28, NFPA, "Conflagrations in America since 1914," Boston, 1942; NFPA, "National Defense Fires," March 1942.

113 CCAC, Bufton papers, 3/26, R. Ewell to Wing Commander A. Morley (BOPs 1), December 3, 1942, encl. Laiming to R. Russell (Standard Oil Development Co.), October 29, 1942, 3.

114 UEA, Zuckerman archive, SZ/OEMU/50/8, RE8 report, "German Domestic Architecture," 1; LC, Arnold papers, Reel 199, Maj. Gen. O. Echols to Arnold, April 28, 1943.

115 James McElroy, "The Work of the Fire Protection Engineers in Planning Fire Attacks," in Horatio Bond, ed., *Fire and the Air War: A Symposium of Expert Observations* (Boston: National Fire Protection Association, 1946), 122–30.

116 LC, Arnold papers, Reel 199, Arnold to Maj. Gen. Echols, April 26, 1943.

117 NARA, RG 107, Lovett papers, Box 9, Joint Magnesium Committee Report, June 1, 1942, 2, 12.

118 LC, Spaatz papers, Box 76, HQ Eighth Air Force, A-5 Division memorandum, "Theory and Tactics of Incendiary Bombing," including Table 2, "Incendiary Bombing Data for German Cities."

119 AFHRA, 520.805, Eighth Air Force Chemical Section History, 1–4; Report for May 1945, 2.

120 TNA, AIR 40/1271, Target Committee, Report of 87th Meeting, April 9, 1943.

121 TNA, AIR 48/33, USSBS, Hamburg Field Report no. 1, 2. There were seventy-eight in 1940, thirty-eight in 1941, ten in 1942. On 1943 see BA-B, R 3102/10046, "Zerstörung von Wohnraum in deutschen Städten, 1942–43."

122 TNA, FO 837/1315, "Bomber's Baedeker," January 1943, 131–37.

123 TNA, AIR 14/1779, report for Dickens and Tizard from RE8, "Apparent Relative Effectiveness of I.B. and H.E. Attack against German Towns," January 7, 1943.

124 RAFM, Saundby papers, AC 72/12, Box 7, "War in the Ether: Europe, 1939–1945," October 1945, 33–36.

125 Details in Alfred Price, *Instruments of Darkness: The History of Electronic Warfare, 1939–1945* (London: Greenhill, 2005), 124–33, 153–54.

126 TNA, PREM 3/11/8, Tizard memorandum for Churchill, July 22, 1943; Churchill to Ismay, July 23, 1943; Portal to Sinclair, July 24, 1943; Churchill, note for Ismay, July 30, 1943.

127 For an excellent account of the operations see Keith Lowe, *Inferno: The Devastation of Hamburg, 1943* (London: Viking, 2007), pt. 2.

128 Westermann, *Flak*, 213–14.

129 Groehler, *Bombenkrieg*, 112.

130 Ibid., 112–13; Westermann, *Flak*, 214–15; Freeman, *Mighty Eighth*, 78–79.

131 Horatio Bond, "The Fire Attacks on German Cities," in *Fire and the Air War*, 95–97; Hans Brunswig, *Feuersturm über Hamburg: Die Luftangriffe auf Hamburg im 2. Weltkrieg und ihre Folgen* (Stuttgart: Motorbuch Verlag, 1985), 269–71.

132 TNA, AIR 20/7287, Home Office, January 1946, "Secret Report by the Police President of Hamburg on the Heavy Raids on Hamburg, 1 Dec 1943," 21–22; Groehler, *Bombenkrieg*, 113–14. Even escape into Hamburg's waterways proved fatal as people plunged into near-boiling water.

133 Civil Defense Liaison Office, *Fire Effects of Bombing Attacks*, prepared for the National Security Resources Board, November 1950, 8–9; Horatio Bond, "Fire Casualties of the German Attacks," in *Fire and the Air War*, 113–18.

134 Groehler, *Bombenkrieg*, 119; TNA, AIR 20/7287, "Secret Report by the Police President of Hamburg," 17; Brunswig, *Feuersturm über Hamburg*, 278–79; Ursula Büttner, "'Gomorrha' und die Folgen der Bombenkrieg," in Hamburg Forschungsstelle für Zeitgeschichte, *Hamburg im "Dritten Reich"* (Göttingen: Wallstein Verlag, 2005), 618, 764.

135 TNA, AIR 40/425, Immediate Interpretation Report, July 27, 1943.

136 IWM, MD, vol. 63, "Besprechung beim Reichsmarschall," July 13, 1943.

137 BA-MA, RL 3/213, Flugzeug-Programme, Studie 1013, December 16, 1942.

138 IWM, MD, vol. 63, "Niederschrift der Besprechung des Reichsmarschall mit Industrierat," October 14, 1943.

139 Ibid., vol. 52, minute on radar, May 7, 1945; Göring decree, "Verantwortlichkeit und Durchführung des Funkmess-und Funknavigationsprogramms," May 2, 1943; Price, *Instruments of Darkness*, 136–39, 150.

140 BA-MA, RL 2 IV/101, Vorstudien zur Luftkriegsgeschichte, Heft 8: Reichsluftverteidigung: Teil B, Flakabwehr [n.d. 1944], 28–30; Westermann, *Flak*, 216–19. See also Ludger Tewes, *Jugend im Krieg: Von Luftwaffenhelfern und Soldaten, 1939–1945* (Essen: Reimar Hobbing, 1989), 37–50.

141 TNA, AIR 20/4761, DoI to Bufton, August 21, 1943.

142 LC, Eaker papers, Box I.19, Lovett to Eaker, July 28, 1943; Eaker to Lovett, August 9, 1943.

143 TNA, AIR 8/1109, Harris to Portal, August 12, 1943.

144 TNA, AIR 14/1779, Bomber Command, ORS, Survey of Damage to Cities, November 29, 1943.

145 TNA, AIR 14/739A, HQ Bomber Command, Intelligence Staff, "Progress of RAF Bomber Offensive against Germany," November 30, 1943, 1–2.

146 TNA, AIR 20/4761, O. Lawrence (MEW) to Morley, September 6, 1943; Lawrence to Bufton, October 24, 1943.

147 TNA, FO 837/26, "Note from Economic Intelligence," September 17, 1943; "Notes on Economic Intelligence," MEW meeting, October 1, 1943.

148 LC, Spaatz papers, Box 203, J. K. Galbraith, "Preliminary Appraisal of Achievement of Strategic Bombing of Germany" [n.d.], 6.

149 Friends House archive, Foley papers, MSS 448 3/2, *Daily Telegraph* article, August 6, 1943.

150 Ibid., Thomas Foley to Kingsley Martin (editor, *New Statesman*), November 3, 1943; "What Happened in Hamburg," leaflet reprint of article in *Basler Nachrichten*; MS 448 2/2, Corder Catchpool (Bombing Restriction Committee) to Foley, January 8, 1943; Bombing Restriction Committee leaflet, "Bomb, Burn and Ruthlessly Destroy" [n.d. but late 1943], 2.

151 LC, Eaker papers, Box I.19, Lovett to Eaker, July 1, 1943.

152 LC, Spaatz papers, Box 67, "Status of Combined Bomber Offensive from U.K.," August 8, 1943, 4.

153 TNA, AIR 8/1109, telegram Harris to Portal, August 12, 1943.

154 TNA, AIR 8/435, telegram Portal to VCAS, August 19, 1943; VCAS to Portal, August 21, 1943.

155 LC, Spaatz papers, Box 67, USSTAF DoI, "An Evaluation of the Effects of the Bomber Offensive on 'Overlord' and 'Dragoon,'" September 5, 1944, 1.

156 TNA, AIR 14/783, Portal to Harris, October 7, 1943, encl. "Effort (Planned and Effected) USAF 8th Bomber Command."

157 TNA, AIR 14/739A, "Conduct of the Strategic Bomber Offensive before Preparatory Stage of 'Overlord,'" January 17, 1944; LC, Spaatz papers, Box 143, Arnold to Spaatz, April 24, 1944.

158 TNA, AIR 8/1167, "Report by Chief of Air Staff and Commanding General US Eighth Air Force," November 7, 1943, 3–4.

159 LC, Eaker papers, Box I.20, HQ Bomber Command, "Outline of Future Intentions for the Continuation and Intensification of the Bomber Offensive," November 4, 1943.

160 TNA, AIR 8/425, Harris to Portal and Sinclair, December 7, 1943.

161 Details in Groehler, *Bombenkrieg*, 131–33; Freeman, *Mighty Eighth*, 89–91.

162 Groehler, *Bombenkrieg*, 133–34; Ferdinanrd Golücke, *Schweinfurt und der strategische Luftkrieg, 1943* (Paderborn: Ferdinand Schöningh, 1980), 356–57.

163 Groehler, *Bombenkrieg*, 134; Richard G. Davis, *Bombing the European Axis Powers: A Historical Digest of the Combined Bomber Offensive, 1939–1945* (Maxwell AFB, AL: Air University Press, 2006), 158–61; Parton, *"Air Force Spoken Here,"* 300–302.

164 Parton, *"Air Force Spoken Here,"* 316.

165 Freeman, *Mighty Eighth*, 119; Davis, *Bombing the European Axis Powers*, 176, 1 82–84.

166 AFHRA, 520.056-188, Eighth Air Force, Statistical Summary, Eighth Air Force Operations, "Aircraft Loss Rate on Combat Missions."

167 TNA, AIR 20/283, Bomber Command operational statistics, February–November 1943, January 1, 1944; AIR 20/2025, Strength of Air Force Personnel, Operational Squadrons, 1940–1945.

168 Details from Middlebrook and Everitt, *Bomber Command War Diaries*, 422–28.

169 TNA, AIR 40/345, AI 3c, Raid Assessment Summary, October 31, 1943.

170 Groehler, *Bombenkrieg*, 144–47.

171 TNA, AIR 20/4761, RE8 report, "The Economic Effects of Attacks in Force on German Targets, March–December 1943," Table 2.

172 TNA, AIR 22/203, Bomber Command War Room, Total Wastage 1939–1945.

173 LC, Eaker papers, Box I.19, Lovett to Eaker, September 19, 1943.

174 TNA, AIR 8/1103, paper prepared for CAS, October 11, 1943, 4.

175 TNA, AIR 14/783, Portal to Harris, October 7, 1943, encl. air staff memorandum, "Extent to Which the Eighth U.S.A.A.F. and Bomber Command Have Been Able to Implement the G.A.F. Plan," 1.

176 RAFM, Harris papers, H47, Bottomley to Harris, "Special Brief for Schweinfurt Operation," July 25, 1943; Harris to Bottomley, December 20, 1943, 3.

177 TNA, AIR 14/739A, Harris to Bottomley, December 28, 1943.

178 TNA, AIR 8/425, Bottomley to Harris, December 23, 1943; AIR 20/4761, "Bomber Command's Comments on R.E.8's Paper," March 13, 1944.

179 TNA, AIR 48/65, USSBS, Military Analysis Division, Report no. 2, "Weather Factors in Combat Bombardment Operations in the European Theater," November 3, 1945, 1–3, 15, 23.

180 LC, Spaatz papers, Box 143, Col. D. Zimmerman (Director of Weather) to Hansell, September 7, 1942, 2.

181 Ibid., Box 173, Report by AAF Scientific Advisory Group, "War and Weather," May 1946, 4–6.

182 LC, LeMay papers, Box 8, 305th Bomb Group: Summary of Events, November 1, 1942, to December 31, 1943.

183 CCAC, Bufton papers, 3/50, "Area Attack Employing 'Gee'" [n.d. but early 1942], 1.

184 CCAC, Bufton papers, 3/51, Harris to Portal, December 12, 1944.

185 Transcript of interview with Maurice Chick, November 1995, 49–50 (in author's possession).

186 LC, Spaatz papers, Box 76, Col. William Garland to Anderson, February 28, 1943; Anderson to all Wing Commanders, September 11, 1943, encl. ORS Report, "Effect of Spacing Between Combat Wings on Bombing Accuracy," September 11, 1943, 2.

187 Ibid., Anderson to LeMay, September 8, 1943.

188 LC, Eaker papers, Box I.20, Eaker to Portal, March 15, 1943; Eaker to Gen. Larry Kuter, September 20, 1943.

189 Davis, *Bombing the European Axis Powers*, 176–78; Freeman, *Mighty Eighth*, 118–19; W. Hays Park, "'Precision' and 'Area' Bombing: Who Did Which, and When?," *Journal of Strategic Studies* 18 (1995): 149–57.

190 LC, Spaatz papers, Box 80, Hugh Odishaw (MIT), "Radar Bombing in the Eighth Air Force," July 1946, 88–89.

191 Ibid., Eighth Air Force ORS to Doolittle, June 13, 1944, encl. "Bombing Accuracy"; Hays Park, "'Precision' and 'Area' Bombing," 154–56.

192 LC, Spaatz papers, Box 80, Odishaw, "Radar Bombing in the Eighth Air Force," 106.

193 TNA, AIR 20/283, Bomber Command Operations, February 1943 to November 1943.

194 UEA, Zuckerman archive, SZ/AEAF/14, Bomber Command ORS, "The Operational Use of Oboe Mark IA: December 1942–June 1943"; "The H2S Blind-Bombing Attack on Ludwigshafen, 17/18 November 1943," December 18, 1943; ORS, "Accuracy of H2S as a Blind-Bombing Device," December 16, 1943. See too Wakelam, *Science of Bombing*, 119–21, 158.

195 TNA, AIR 48/67, USSBS Military Analysis Division Report no. 4, November 3, 1945, 3–4 and Exhibit B, "Sample Field Order from Bomber Command."

196 LC, Eaker papers, Box I.21, "Target Selection Principles Developed by the Eighth Air Force" [n.d. but late 1943?], 1–5.

197 Mark Guglielmo, "The Contribution of Economists to Military Intelligence during World War II," *Journal of Economic History* 68 (2008): 132–34; Barry Katz, *Foreign Intelligence: Research and Analysis in the Office of Strategic Services, 1942–1945* (Cambridge, MA: Harvard University Press, 1989), 114–18; Walter W. Rostow, *Pre-Invasion Bombing Strategy: General Eisenhower's Decision of March 25, 1944* (Aldershot: Gower, 1981), 16–21.

198 LC, Spaatz papers, Box 143, Col. R. Garrison (Adjutant General's office), "Procedure Followed in Planning an Operation," July 9, 1943, 1–8, and

Annex I, "Procedure in Planning an Operation: Duties and Responsibilities," 1–5.

199 LC, LeMay papers, Box 4, HQ 1st Bombardment Wing, "Operational Procedure," October 12, 1942; HQ 1st Bombardment Wing, "Tactics and Techniques of Bombardment" [n.d.].

200 Freeman, *Mighty Eighth*, 93–94, report by Lt. Col. Beirne Lay; other quotations from interviews with Harold Nash, November 3, 1995, 20; Peter Hinchcliffe, October 24, 1995, 15; Barney D'Ath-Weston, November 1995, 22.

201 AFHRA, CD A5385, "Growth, Development and Operations": Motion Picture Attendance, December 1, 1942–November 30, 1943; Stage Show Attendance.

202 Ibid., Eighth Air Force: Combat Crew Casualties; Mark Wells, *Courage and Air Warfare: The Allied Aircrew Experience in the Second World War* (London: Frank Cass, 1995), 31–32.

203 NARA, RG 107, Lovett papers, Box 9, Office of the Air Surgeon, Psychological Branch, "Report on Survey of Aircrew Personnel in the Eighth, Ninth, and Fifteenth Air Forces," April 1944, 35.

204 FDRL, President's Secretary's Files, Box 82, memorandum from Roosevelt to Gen. Watson, encl. report from Lt. Col. John Murray on psychiatry in the Army Air Force, January 4, 1944, 3–4. See too Miller, *Eighth Air Force*, 128–34.

205 Wells, *Courage and Air Warfare*, 51.

206 LC, Eaker papers, Box I.16, Col. C. Cabell (HQ AAF) to Eaker, May 27, 1943.

207 NARA, RG 107, Box 9, "Report on Survey of Aircrew Personnel," 82–85, 88; Wells, *Courage and Air Warfare*, 174.

208 Edgar Jones, "'LMF': The Use of Psychiatric Stigma in the Royal Air Force During the Second World War," *Journal of Military History* 70 (2006): 440–41, 443–44.

209 TNA, AIR 49/357, E. C. Jewesbury, "Work and Problems of an RAF Neuropsychiatric Centre," July 1943, 10–11.

210 Ibid., 16–17.

211 Wells, *Courage and Air Warfare*, 204–5; Jones, "'LMF,'" 452.

212 LC, Eaker papers, Box I.19, Eaker to Col. George Brownwell (War Dept., Washington, DC), November 28, 1943.

213 NARA, RG 107, Box 9, "Report on Survey of Aircrew Personnel," 58, 86.

214 CCO, Portal papers, Folder 5, "Comparison of Bombing Effort during the Year 1943," February 10, 1944.

215 TNA, AIR/739, A. F. Inglis (AI) to Harris, December 13, 1943; Harris to Bottomley, December 28, 1943.

216 TNA, PREM 3/193/6A, JIC Report, "Probabilities of a German Collapse," September 9, 1943, encl. "Annex: Similarities Between Germany's Situation in August 1918 and August 1943," 6.

217 TNA, AIR 8/1167, JIC Report, "Effects of Bombing Offensive on German War Effort," November 12, 1943, Annex by PWE and AI, "Allied Air Attacks and German Morale," 1, 3, 6–8; PREM 3/193/6A, Desmond Morton to Churchill, January 21, 1944.

218 LC, Spaatz papers, Box 67, "Plan for the Completion of the Combined Bomber Offensive," March 5, 1944, Annex, "Prospect for Ending War by Air Attack Against German Morale," 1.

219 LC, Arnold papers, Reel 193, "Germany's War Potential: An Appraisal by the Committee of Historians for the Commanding General of the Army Air Forces," December 1943, 1, 2, 20–23.

220 FDRL, Map Room Files, Box 73, OSS Bulletin, March 11, 1944, 1. For a general discussion of American opinion see Richard Overy, "'The Weak Link'?: The Perception of the German Working Class by RAF Bomber Command, 1940–1945," *Labour History Review* 77 (2012): 20–21; Katz, *Foreign Intelligence*, 63–70.

221 RAFM, Bottomley papers, AC 71/2/53, Lecture on Bombing, Spring 1944, 7.

222 USAFA, McDonald papers, Box 8, Folder 8, "Extracts from News Digest, 30 March 1944," Internal Conditions, "The Air Offensive," 1.

223 LC, Arnold papers, Reel 193, "Germany's War Potential," 2.

224 LC, Doolittle papers, Box 19, Doolittle to all Eighth Air Force commanders, January 19, 1944, 1.

Chapter 3. The "Battle of Germany," 1944–45

1 LC, Eaker papers, Box I.19, Lovett to Arnold, June 19, 1943, 2.

2 LC, Spaatz papers, Box 67, script of teletype conference, Anderson for Arnold, Item Number II, February 25, 1944, 9.

3 USAFA, Hansell papers, Ser. III, Box 1, Folder 2, "Salient Features of Various Plans: AWPD-1," 3.

4 Stephen McFarland and Wesley Newton, *To Command the Sky: The Battle for Air Superiority over Germany, 1942–1944* (Washington, DC: Smithsonian Institution, 1991), 103–4.

5 Details from John F. Guilmartin, "The Aircraft That Decided World War II: Aeronautical Engineering and Grand Strategy, 1933–1945," 44th Harmon Memorial Lecture, USAFA, Colorado Springs, CO, 2001, 16–18, 20–23; Richard G. Davis, *Carl A. Spaatz and the Air War in Europe* (Washington, DC: Center for Air Force History, 1993), 361–64.

6 FDRL, President's Secretary's Files, Box 82, Roosevelt to Arnold, November 10, 1942; Arnold to Roosevelt, November 12, 1942.

7 McFarland and Newton, *To Command the Sky*, 138–40.

8 Roger A. Freeman, *The Mighty Eighth War Diary* (London: Jane's 1981), 148, 183–84, 202–3, 206–7.

9 AFHRA, CD A5835, Eighth Air Force Tactical Development, 1942–1945, 1; McFarland and Newton, *To Command the Sky*, 106, 112.

10 McFarland and Newton, *To Command the Sky*, 114–15, 145; Davis, *Carl A. Spaatz*, 302; James Parton, *"Air Force Spoken Here": General Ira Eaker and the Command of the Air* (Bethesda, MD: Adler & Adler, 1986), 273–76, 288.

11 David R. Mets, *Master of Airpower: General Carl A. Spaatz* (Novato, CA: Presidio, 1998), 179–80.

12 Parton, *"Air Force Spoken Here,"* 336–39; Mets, *Master of Airpower*, 180–81.

13 LC, Spaatz papers, Box 84, Spaatz to Doolittle, January 26, 1944; Box 143, Spaatz to Doolittle, January 28, 1944.

14 LC, Doolittle papers, Box 19, Doolittle to Spaatz, March 11, 1944; Davis, *Carl A. Spaatz*, 299–300.

15 AFHRA, CD A1722, Army Air Forces Evaluation Board, Eighth Air Force, "Tactical Development, August 1942–May 1945," 50.

16 Ibid., 50–55; Davis, *Carl A. Spaatz,* 358–63; McFarland and Newton, *To Command the Sky,* 141, 164–66.

17 LC, Spaatz papers, Box 67, script of teletype conference, Anderson for Arnold, February 27, 1944, 4.

18 IWM, MD 61/5139, minutes of GL meeting, August 28, 1943.

19 Nicolaus von Below, *At Hitler's Side: The Memoirs of Hitler's Luftwaffe Adjutant, 1937–1945* (London: Greenhill, 2001), 176–77.

20 McFarland and Newton, *To Command the Sky,* 118–20; British Air Ministry, *The Rise and Fall of the German Air Force, 1933–1945* (London: Arms & Armour Press, 1983), 239, 297–98.

21 Lt. Gen. Josef Schmid, "German Dayfighting in the Defense of the Reich 15 Sept 1943 to the End of the War," in David Isby, ed., *Fighting the Bombers: The Luftwaffe's Struggle against the Allied Bomber Offensive* (London: Greenhill, 2003), 133–40; Josef Schmid, "German Nightfighting from June 1943 to May 1945," in ibid., 88–89, 95–97; Edward Westermann, *Flak: German Anti-Aircraft Defenses, 1914–1945* (Lawrence: University Press of Kansas, 2001), 235–36.

22 On German intelligence appreciation of Allied operations see TsAMO, f.500, o.957971, d.450, Führungsstab 1c, "Einzelnachrichten des 1c Dienstes West der Luftwaffe," April 29, 1944; f.500, o.957971, d.448, "Einzelnachrichten des 1c Dienstes West: Britische Nachteinsatz," May 6, 1944; f.500, o.957971, d.433, "Einzelnachrichten des 1c Dienstes West," June 16, 1944.

23 Alfred Price, *Instruments of Darkness: The History of Electronic Warfare, 1939–1945* (London: Greenhill, 2005), 175–78, 184–86, 195–96, 205–6. On "Carpet" and countermeasures see RAFM, Saundby papers, AC 72/12, Box 7, "War in the Ether," 45–46.

24 Westermann, *Flak,* 234–35.

25 Ibid., 238–41.

26 BA-MA, RL 2 IV/101, Vorstudien zur Luftkriegsgeschichte, Heft 8, 32–33; British Air Ministry, *Rise and Fall of the German Air Force,* 283–85.

27 Westermann, *Flak,* 247–49.

28 BA-B, RL 3/237, GL C-Amt, Studie 1036; Lutz Budrass, *Flugzeugindustrie und Luftrüstung in Deutschland, 1918–1945* (Düsseldorf: Droste Verlag, 1998), 868–69; Horst Boog, "Strategischer Luftkrieg in Europa, 1943–1944," in Horst Boog ed., *Das Deutsche Reich und der Zweite Weltkrieg. Band 7: Das Deutsche Reich in der Defensive* (Stuttgart: DVA, 2001), 309–11.

29 IWM, EDS AL/1746, Karl-Otto Saur interrogation, August 10, 1945, 6.

30 IWM, MD, vol. 56, 2701–13, memorandum by Milch, "Der Jägerstab."

31 Calculated from Budrass, *Flugzeugindustrie und Luftrüstung,* 836. Serviceability rates in Charles Webster and Noble Frankland, *The Strategic Air Offensive Against Germany* (London: HMSO), 4:501.

32 McFarland and Newton, *To Command the Sky,* 135; Schmid, "German Dayfighting," 147.

33 AFHRA, CD A5835, Tactical Development, 99. Elementary training declined from 100 hours in 1942 to 70 in 1943 and 52 in 1944; Fighter School hours declined from 60 to 40; OTU hours were 50 in 1942, 16 to 18 in 1943, 20 in 1944.

34 Schmid, "German Dayfighting," 140–42.

35 Adolf Galland, *The First and the Last* (London: Methuen, 1955), 189, 200–201.

36 LC, Spaatz papers, Box 143, Anderson to Spaatz, February 28, 1944, 2.

37 LC, Spaatz papers, Box 94, statistics on total tonnage dropped by USAAF and RAF, January 1944 to May 1944.

38 TNA, AIR 14/739A, "Conduct of Strategic Bomber Offensive Before Preparatory Stage of 'Overlord,'" January 17, 1944, 4–5.

39 Ibid., HQ Bomber Command, AI, "Progress of RAF Bomber Offensive Against German Industry," February 19, 1944; Harris to Balfour, March 2, 1944.

40 CCO, Richards archive, File IV/Folder B, Portal to Sinclair, January 29, 1944.

41 W. A. Jacobs, "The British Strategic Air Offensive Against Germany in World War II," in R. Cargill Hall, ed., *Case Studies in Strategic Bombardment* (Washington, DC: Office of Air Force History, 1998), 139–40.

42 TNA, FO 935/126, REDept, "Preliminary Attack Assessment, Berlin," March 23, 1944, 1, 3.

43 Webster and Frankland, *Strategic Air Offensive*, 2:193.

44 Williamson Murray, *Luftwaffe: Strategy for Defeat, 1933–1945* (London: George Allen & Unwin, 1985), 198–99.

45 Stephen McFarland and Wesley Newton, "The American Strategic Air Offensive Against Germany in World War II," in R. Cargill Hall, ed., *Case Studies in Strategic Bombardment* (Washington, DC: Center for Air Force History, 1998), 214–16; Davis, *Carl A. Spaatz*, 322–26.

46 UEA, Zuckerman archive, SZ/BBSU/101, "Analysis of M.E.W. Estimates of German War Production" [n.d.], 10.

47 LC, Spaatz papers, Box 68, HQ USSTAF, "The Allied Air Offensive Against Germany and Principal Criticisms by the Enemy Leaders," June 1945, Table C, Interrogation of Hermann Göring, June 1, 1945.

48 TNA, AIR 10/3873, BBSU, "German Experience in the Underground Transfer of War Industries," 12.

49 Budrass, *Flugzeugindustrie und Luftrüstung*, 868; Horst Boog, "Strategischer Luftkrieg," 101–3.

50 LC, Spaatz papers, Box 67, Committee of Experts, "Plan for the Completion of the Combined Bomber Offensive," March 5, 1944, 2–4; Barry Katz, *Foreign Intelligence: Research and Analysis in the Office of Strategic Services, 1942–1945* (Cambridge, MA: Harvard University Press, 1989), 19–20; F. Harry Hinsley et al., *British Intelligence in the Second World War*, vol. 3 (London: HMSO, 1988), pt. 2, 497–99.

51 Walter W. Rostow, *Pre-Invasion Bombing Strategy: General Eisenhower's Decision of March 25, 1944* (Aldershot: Gower, 1981), 53–55.

52 Davis, *Carl A. Spaatz*, 398–400; Rostow, *Pre-Invasion Bombing Strategy*, 68.

53 Davis, *Carl A. Spaatz*, 370–79; Murray, *Luftwaffe*, 215.

54 LC, Spaatz papers, Box 67, script of teletype conference, Anderson for Arnold, Item Number II, February 25, 1944, 12.

55 LC, Eaker papers, Box I.35, "Decline of the GAF: Report from Captured Personnel," forwarded to Military Intelligence Division, March 15, 1945, 6.

56 Heinz Knocke, *I Flew for the Führer* (London: Evans Brothers, 1953), 148–49.

57 Davis, *Carl A. Spaatz*, 379–81.

58 TsAMO, f.500, o.957971, d.448, "Einzelnachrichten des 1c Dienstes West der Luftwaffe," May 6, 1944, 12.

59 Ian McLachlan and Russell Zorn, *Eighth Air Force Bomber Stories: Eyewitness Accounts from American Airmen and British Civilians in the Second World War* (Yeovil: Haynes Publishing, 1991), 110–11.

60 AFHRA, CD A1722, Eighth Air Force, "Tactical Development August 1942–May 1945," 99.

61 Boog, "Strategischer Luftkrieg," 110; Webster and Frankland, *Strategic Air Offensive*, 4:495; "Nightfighter Direction: Interrogation of Major G. S. Sandmann," in Isby, *Fighting the Bombers*, 211.

62 Hans-Detlef von Rohden, "Reich Air Defense," in Isby, *Fighting the Bombers*, 38.

63 USAFA, McDonald papers, Ser. V, Box 12, Folder 1, JIC Report, "German Strategy and Capacity to Resist," August 14, 1944, 1.

64 AHB, Translations, VII/7, 8th Abteilung report, September 22, 1944, "A Forecast of Air Developments in 1945," 1.

65 IWM, MD, vol. 53, 706–11, report by chief of German Air Force operations staff (Karl Koller), "Erforderlich Mindeststärke der fliegenden Verbände der deutschen Luftwaffe zur Behauptung des mitteleuropäischen Raumes," May 19, 1944.

66 Calculated from Webster and Frankland, *Strategic Air Offensive*, 4:497.

67 LC, Eaker papers, Box I.35, "Decline of the G.A.F.," 6: "Neither in the East nor South did 50, 80, or 100 of our aircraft ever fly in a body and carry out any major operation. In Russia they flew in 'Rotten' of two or 'Schwärme' of four . . . our fighter arm had to conduct the fight in a strength to which it was never accustomed."

68 Sönke Neitzel, *Tapping Hitler's Generals: Transcripts of Secret Conversations, 1942–1945* (Barnsley, UK: Frontline Books, 2007), 114–15, recording of Gen. Bernhard Ramcke, October 16, 1944.

69 LC, Spaatz papers, Box 134, U.S. Military Intelligence Service, HQ Air P/W, interrogation of Hermann Göring, June 1, 1945, 2.

70 Dik Daso, *Hap Arnold and the Evolution of American Airpower* (Washington, DC: Smithsonian Institution, 2000), esp. 152–68; on the problems of adjusting to defensive warfare see Boog, "Strategischer Luftkrieg," 249–58.

71 AHB, Translations, VII/7, "A Forecast of Air Developments in 1945," 2–3.

72 LC, Spaatz papers, Box 143, Spaatz to Arnold, September 30, 1944.

73 TNA, AIR 14/739A, Harris to Coryton (Air Ministry), July 19, 1944; CCO, Portal papers, Folder 5, Portal to Churchill, August 5, 1944.

74 Mark Connelly, "The British People, the Press and the Strategic Air Campaign Against Germany, 1939–1945," *Contemporary British History* 16 (2002): 54–55.

75 Hugh Thomas, *John Strachey* (London: Eyre Methuen, 1973), 219.

76 TNA, PREM 3/193/6A, JIC Report, "German Strategy and Capacity to Resist," October 16, 1944.

77 AHB, Translations, VII/7, "A Forecast of Air Developments"; VII/IX, "War Appreciation No. 17," January 15, 1945, 8.

78 LC, Spaatz papers, Box 143, Spaatz to Arnold, July 22, 1944; Spaatz to Arnold, September 3, 1944. See too JIC warnings in Hinsley et al., *British Intelligence in the Second World War*, vol. 3, pt. 2, 595–99.

79 LC, Doolittle papers, Box 18, Doolittle to Arnold, August 2, 1944; Box 19, Doo-
    little to Spaatz, October 18, 1944.

80 NARA, RG 107, Lovett papers, Box 139, memorandum for Lovett from HQ
    Army Service Forces, encl. "Periodic Report of Readiness for Chemical War-
    fare, 1 January 1945," 2.

81 Robert Harris and Jeremy Paxman, *A Higher Form of Killing: The Secret Story of Gas
    and Germ Warfare* (London: Chatto & Windus, 1982), 110–16.

82 TNA, PREM 3/193/6A, HQ AF, Algiers to the War Office, October 30, 1943
    (initialed by Churchill, November 1, 1943).

83 NARA, RG 218, Box 3, "Analysis of Foreign Weapons Division," report for the
    commanding general, Army Service Forces, October 26, 1943, forwarded to
    Arnold. On German plans the best account is Rolf-Dieter Müller, "Albert Speer
    und die Rüstungspolitik im totalen Krieg, 1942–1945," in Bernhard Kroener,
    Rolf-Dieter Müller, and Hans Umbreit, *Das Deutsche Reich und der Zweite Welt-
    krieg, Band 5/2: Organisation und Mobilisierung des deutschen Machtbereichs, 1942–
    1944/45* (Stuttgart: DVA, 1999), 713–16.

84 NARA, RG 218, Box 19, memorandum for the Gas Warfare Subcommittee, HQ
    USAAF, January 21, 1944, 3; Maj. Gen. William Porter (chief, Chemical Warfare
    Service) to JCS, "Present Status of Development of Toxic Gases," December 6, 1943.

85 RAFM, Bottomley papers, AC 71/2/29, War Cabinet Inter-Service Committee
    on Chemical Warfare, note by the air staff, January 23, 1944, 2–3, and Annex
    1, "Appreciation on Strategic Gas Effort," 5.

86 RAFM, Bottomley papers, AC 71/2/75, memorandum by Norman Bottomley,
    "Possibility of the Use of Gas by the Germans to Counter 'Overlord,'" 1–3.

87 CCAC, Churchill papers, CHAR D.217/4, Churchill to Ismay for the CoS, July
    6, 1944; Hinsley et al., *British Intelligence in the Second World War*, vol. 3, pt. 2,
    576–80.

88 Müller, "Albert Speer und die Rüstungspolitik," 714–15.

89 CCAC, Bufton papers, 3/51, "Plan for Retaliatory Gas Attack on Germany";
    NARA, RG 107, Box 139, HQ Army Service Forces memorandum, "Co-Ordi-
    nated Anglo-American Chemical Warfare Procurement and Supply Program,"
    March 10, 1945, 2–3.

90 NARA, RG 218, Box 1, report for the JCS, January 6, 1944, 1.

91 Details in RAFM, Bottomley papers, B2320, Inter-Service Sub-Committee on
    Biological Warfare, December 22, 1945, App. A, "Biological Warfare: Report
    to the Secretary of War," 1–5; NARA, RG 218, Box 1, JCS paper, December
    20, 1943, "Implications of Recent Intelligence Regarding Alleged German Se-
    cret Weapons."

92 NARA, RG 218, Box 1, "Defensive Measures Against Bacteriological War-
    fare," May 25, 1944; memorandum for Col. Newsome from General Staff, Op-
    erations Division, April 10, 1944 (shown to Gen. Marshall and forwarded to
    Field Marshal John Dill).

93 Müller, "Albert Speer und die Rüstungspolitik," 720–26.

94 See, e.g., USAFA, Hansell papers, Ser. III, Box 1, Folder 1, "Fairchild Lecture,"
    December 1, 1964, 18–24.

95 Figures from Davis, *Carl A. Spaatz*, App. 8; Mets, *Master of Airpower*, 251; Henry
    Probert, *Bomber Harris: His Life and Times* (London: Greenhill, 2006), 305–6.

96 LC, Spaatz papers, Box 143, Spaatz to Arnold, September 30, 1944.

97 Mets, *Master of Airpower*, 258–59; Davis, *Carl A. Spaatz*, 488–90.

98 CCAC, Bufton papers, 3/43, memorandum by Sq. Ldr. John Strachey (BOps), August 13, 1944; Draft operation, "Thunderclap," August 15, 1944; Bufton memorandum, August 2, 1944, "Operation Thunderclap."

99 Directives in Webster and Frankland, *Strategic Air Offensive*, 4:174–76, directive from Bottomley to Harris, October 13, 1944. See too Davis, *Carl A. Spaatz*, 494–95.

100 Solly Zuckerman, *From Apes to Warlords, 1904–46: An Autobiography* (London: Hamish Hamilton, 1978), 301–4; Hugh Melinsky, *Forming the Pathfinders: The Career of Air Vice-Marshal Sydney Bufton* (Stroud: The History Press, 2010), 130–33.

101 Webster and Frankland, *Strategic Air Offensive*, 4:177–79, "1st November 1944: Directive No. 2 for the Strategic Air Forces in Europe."

102 "Expert" in CCAC, Bufton papers, 3/51, Harris to Portal, December 12, 1944; Melinsky, *Forming the Pathfinders*, 135. See too CamUL, Andrew Boyle papers, Add 9429/1B, Harris to Boyle, June 13, 1979: "[Bufton] was a prime example in my view of a Junior Officer in the Air Ministry imagining he could run the Command."

103 CCAC, Bufton papers, 3/51, Harris to Portal, December 12, 1944. See the full discussion of the correspondence in Melinsky, *Forming the Pathfinders*, 133–35; Probert, *Bomber Harris*, 309–11.

104 USSBS, "Oil Division: Final Report," Washington, DC, August 25, 1945, fig. 7.

105 LC, Spaatz papers, Box 76, "Conference on Bombing Accuracy," HQ USSTAF, March 22–23, 1945; Box 80, Hugh Odishaw, "Radar Bombing in the Eighth Air Force," 94. See too Davis, *Carl A. Spaatz*, 503–8.

106 Davis, *Carl A. Spaatz*, 508.

107 AHB, Translations, VII/23, GAF Air Historical Branch, "Some Effects of the Allied Air Offensive on German Economic Life," December 7, 1944, 1–2; Davis, *Carl A. Spaatz*, 510–12. The best account is Alfred Mierzejewski, *The Collapse of the German War Economy: Allied Air Power and the German National Railway* (Chapel Hill: University of North Carolina Press, 1988), 191, Table A3.

108 Mierzejewski, *Collapse of the German War Economy*, 193, Table A5.

109 AHB, Translations, VII/38, Speer to Field Marshal Keitel, "Report on the Effects of Allied Air Activity Against the Ruhr," November 7, 1944.

110 AFHRA, 520.056-188, Statistical Summary Eighth Air Force Operations: Aircraft Loss Rates on Combat Operations.

111 Fighter losses in Murray, *Luftwaffe*, 364; jet production in Boog, "Strategischer Luftkrieg," 307–8.

112 CCAC, Bufton papers, 3/51, Bufton to Bottomley, June 9, 1945; RAFM, Saundby papers, AC 72/12, Box 7, "War in the Ether," App. B, "Bomber Command Loss Rate on German Targets."

113 Schmid, "German Nightfighting," 105–6.

114 Details in RAFM, Saundby papers, AC 72/12, Box 7, "War in the Ether," October 1945, 53–58 and App. F; Saundby (HQ Bomber Command) to all group commanders, October 13, 1944, on keeping radar silence. See also Bill Gunston, *Night Fighters: A Development and Combat History* (Cambridge: Patrick Stephens, 1976), 125–27; Werner Held and Holger Nauroth, *Die deutsche Nachtjagd* (Stuttgart: Motorbuch Verlag, 1992), 222–30.

115 Below, *At Hitler's Side,* 220–21.

116 LC, Eaker papers, Box I.35, "Decline of the G.A.F.," 12.

117 Galland, *First and Last,* 246–49, 251–52, 283–85; LC, Spaatz papers, Box 68, memorandum by George McDonald (G-2, HQ USSTAF), "The Allied Air Offensive Against Germany and Principal Criticisms by Enemy Leaders," Table F, interrogation of Gen. Galland, May 16, 1945.

118 CCAC, Bufton papers, 3/51, Morley (BOps 2) to SHAEF A-3, January 21, 1945.

119 USAFA, McDonald papers, Ser. V, Box 12, Folder 1, JIC SHAEF, "Bombing Policy in Germany," October 6, 1944.

120 NARA, RG 107, Box 28, Lovett to Arnold, January 9, 1945, 2–3.

121 RAFM, Harris papers, Misc. Box A, Folder 4, "One Hundred Towns of Leading Economic Importance."

122 AFHRA, Disc MAAF/233, Air Ministry to HQ 15th Air Force, October 14, 1944, additions to target list. (As well as Dresden, the additions were Eberswalde, Plauen, Jenbach, and Obergrafendorf.)

123 CCAC, Bufton papers, 3/51, Combined Strategic Targets Committee, "Target Priorities for Attack of Industrial Areas," November 27, 1944.

124 CCO, Portal papers, Folder 5, Portal to Churchill, October 4, 1944.

125 Ibid., Folder 6, report by A. H. Birse (Churchill's interpreter), "Notes on Air Chief Marshal Sir A. Tedder's Meeting with Marshal Stalin," January 15, 1945.

126 Probert, *Bomber Harris,* 318; UEA, Zuckerman archive, SZ/BBSU/58, note by the air staff, "Strategic Bombing in Relation to the Present Russian Offensive," January 25, 1945; Hinsley et al., *British Intelligence in the Second World War,* vol. 3, pt. 2, 611.

127 Ian Hunter, ed., *Winston and Archie: The Collected Correspondence of Winston Churchill and Archibald Sinclair, 1915–1960* (London: Politico's, 2005), 410–11: Sinclair to Churchill, January 26, 1945; Churchill to Sinclair, January 26, 1945; Sinclair to Churchill, January 27, 1945.

128 CCO, Portal papers, Folder 6, Portal to Churchill, January 28, 1945.

129 Webster and Frankland, *Strategic Air Offensive,* 4:301: Bottomley to Harris, January 27, 1945; Sebastian Cox, "The Dresden Raids: Why and How," in Paul Addison and Jeremy Crang, eds., *Firestorm: The Bombing of Dresden, 1945* (London: Pimlico, 2006), 22–25; Hinsley et al., *British Intelligence in the Second World War,* vol. 3, pt. 2, 611.

130 CCAC, Bufton papers, 3/51, "Strategic Bombing in Reaction to the Present Russian Offensive," note by the air staff for CoS Meeting, January 31, 1945, 1.

131 Davis, *Carl A. Spaatz,* 546–48.

132 S. M. Plokhy, *Yalta: The Price of Peace* (New York: Penguin, 2010), 213–14; AFHRA, K239.046-38, Joseph Angell, "Historical Analysis of the 14–15 February Bombings of Dresden" [n.d. but 1953], 12.

133 RAFM, Harris papers, H136, "Notes on Bomber Command" [n.d. but 1961 or 1962], 7.

134 Freeman, *Mighty Eighth,* 432; Davis, *Carl A. Spaatz,* 551–53; Olaf Groehler, *Bombenkrieg gegen Deutschland* (Berlin: Akademie Verlag, 1990), 388–89, 398–400; Richard Overy, "The Post-War Debate," in Addison and Crang, *Firestorm,* 129–30.

135 Götz Bergander, *Dresden im Luftkrieg: Vorgeschichte—Zerstörung—Folgen* (Munich: Heyne Verlag, 1985), 256–57; Groehler, *Bombenkrieg,* 412; Matthias Gretzschel,

"Dresden im Dritten Reich," in *Hamburg und Dresden im Dritten Reich: Bombenkrieg und Kriegsende; sieben Beiträge* (Hamburg: Landeszentrale für politische Bildung, 2000), 97.

136 Tami Davis Biddle, "Wartime Reactions," in Addison and Crang, *Firestorm*, 107–10.

137 Ibid., 113.

138 CamUL, Boyle papers, Add 9429/1B, Harris to Boyle, June 13, 1979.

139 CCAC, Bufton papers, 3/51, HQ Bomber Command, "Bomber Command's 'Battle of the Ruhr,'" March 24, 1945.

140 Brereton Greenhous, Stephen Harris, William Johnston, and William Rawling, *The Crucible of War, 1939–1945: The Official History of the Canadian Air Force*, vol. 3 (Toronto: Toronto University Press/Department of National Defence, 1994), 862.

141 CCO, Portal papers, Folder 6, Portal to Churchill, April 20, 1945; Hunter, *Winston and Archie*, 414, Churchill to Sinclair, April 19, 1945.

142 Webster and Frankland, *Strategic Air Offensive*, 4:183–84, Strategic Directive no. 4, April 16, 1945.

143 Davis, *Carl A. Spaatz*, 582–84.

144 Mets, *Master of Airpower*, 283–84.

145 TNA, HO 196/30, RE8 report, May 25, 1945.

146 LC, Spaatz papers, Box 143, Spaatz to commanding generals, 8th, 9th, and 15th air forces, August 24, 1944.

147 Henry H. Arnold, *Global Mission* (New York: Harper&Row, 1949), 490–91; USSBS, "Over-all Report (European War)," Washington, DC, September 30, 1945, vol. 2, ix; Gordon Daniels, ed., *A Guide to the Reports of the United States Strategic Bombing Survey* (London: Royal Historical Society, 1981), xix–xxii; Gian Gentile, *How Effective Is Strategic Bombing? Lessons Learned from World War II to Kosovo* (New York: New York University Press, 2000), 33–54.

148 NC, Cherwell papers, F247, Churchill to Sinclair, January 3, 1945; on the problems surrounding the survey see Sebastian Cox, ed., *The Strategic Air War Against Germany, 1939–1945: The Official Report of the British Bombing Survey Unit* (London: Frank Cass, 1998), xvii–xix.

149 UEA, Zuckerman archive, SZ/BBSU/1, BBSU Advisory Committee, minutes of 1st meeting, June 6, 1945; note for Air Ministry and SHAEF, June 13, 1945; Cox, *Strategic Air War Against Germany*, xx–xxi.

150 TNA, AIR 14/1779, minutes of meeting, February 27, 1945, on the future of the RE8 Department. The personnel were absorbed into the Air Ministry establishment on March 1, 1945.

151 CCAC, Bufton papers, 3/51, "Proposals for the Establishment of a British Strategic Bombing Unit," May 30, 1945, 1–3.

152 CCAC, Bufton papers, 3/65, ADI (K) Report, "Factors in Germany's Defeat," May 17, 1945.

153 LC, Spaatz papers, Box 68, HQ USSTAF, "The Allied Air Offensive Against Germany and Principal Criticisms by the Enemy Leaders," 4–5, 6.

154 Ibid., Table D, Ninth Air Force interrogation of Hermann Göring, June 1, 1945; interrogation of Milch, May 23, 1945; Table E, SHAEF interrogation of Speer, June 3, 1945; Gentile, *How Effective Is Strategic Bombing?*, 69.

155 Gentile, *How Effective Is Strategic Bombing?*, 7; LC, Spaatz papers, Box 134, "Interrogation of Reich Marshal Hermann Goering," May 10, 1945, 5.

156 LC, Spaatz papers, Box 134, USSBS Interrogation no. 8, Lt. Gen. Karl Koller, May 23–24, 1945, 6–7.

157 USSBS, Over-all Report (European Theatre), 25–26, 37–38, 73–74; Gentile, *How Effective Is Strategic Bombing?*, 55–56. For a convincing case on the diminishing returns from bombing, see the recent economic analysis by Jurgen Brauer and Hubert van Tuyll, *Castles, Battles, and Bombs: How Economics Explains Military History* (Chicago: University of Chicago Press, 2008), 211–13, 217–19, 235–36.

158 Cox, *Strategic Air War Against Germany*, 129–34.

159 Ibid., 154.

160 Ibid., 94–97.

161 CCAC, Bufton papers, 3/51, Bufton to Portal, January 3, 1945. The report was passed on to Harris by Portal, but with the reference to Hamburg deleted.

162 UEA, Zuckerman archive, SZ/BBSU/3, Exercise Thunderbolt, précis no. 8, "The Course of the Combined Bomber Offensive from January 1943 to April 1944," 2; précis no. 18, "The Course of the Combined Strategic Bomber Offensive from 14 April 1944 to the End of the European War," 3–4.

163 UEA, Zuckerman archive, SZ/BBSU/2, précis of lecture by Wing Commander G. A. Carey Foster, "On the Effects of Strategic Bombing on Germany's Capacity to Make War."

164 UEA, Zuckerman archive, SZ/BBSU/3, Zuckerman, rough notes on Exercise Thunderbolt, August 13–16, 1947.

165 UEA, Zuckerman archive, SZ/BBSU/103, Nicholas Kaldor typescript, "The Nature of Strategic Bombing," 4–6; Kaldor typescript, "Capacity of German Industry," 2–5.

166 Nicholas Kaldor, "The German War Economy," *Review of Economic Statistics* 13 (1946): 20ff.; see Richard Overy, "Mobilisation for Total War in Germany, 1939–1941," *English Historical Review* 103 (1988): 613–39, and more recently Adam Tooze, "No Room for Miracles: German Industrial Output in World War II Reassessed," *Geschichte und Gesellschaft* 31 (2005): 439–64.

167 Webster and Frankland, *Strategic Air Offensive*, 4:469–70, 494, App. 49 (iii), 49 (xxii).

168 Richard Overy, "The Economy of the German 'New Order,'" in Johannes ten Cate, Gerhard Otto, and Richard Overy, eds., *Die "Neuordnung" Europas: NS-Wirtschaftspolitik in den besetzten Gebieten* (Berlin: Metropol Verlag, 1997), 14–26; on financial contributions, Willi Boelcke, *Die Kosten von Hitlers Krieg* (Paderborn: Ferdinand Schöningh, 1985), 98, 110. On labor, Ulrich Herbert, ed., *Europa und der "Reichseinsatz: Ausländische Zivilarbeiter, Kriegsgefangene und KZ-Häftlinge in Deutschland, 1938–1945* (Essen: Klartext, 1991), 7–8. The totals were: POWs 1,930,087; forced laborers, 5,976,673. On booty policy and its results, Götz Aly, *Hitlers Volksstaat: Raub, Rassenkrieg und Nationaler Sozialismus* (Frankfurt am Main: S. Fischer Verlag, 2005), 59ff.

169 UEA, Zuckerman archive, SZ/BBSU/103, "Nature of Strategic Bombing," 6–7.

170 LC, Spaatz papers, J. K. Galbraith, "Preliminary Appraisal of Achievement of Strategic Bombing of Germany," 2.

171 TNA, AIR 48/33, USSBS, Civilian Defense Report no. 4, Hamburg Field Report, vol. 1, 83.

172 Details from BA-B, R 3102/10031, Reichsministerium für Rüstung-und Kriegs-wirtschaft, "Vorläufige Zusammenstellung des Arbeiterstunden ausfalls durch Feindeinwirkung," Tables 1 and 4, January 4, 1945.

173 Albert Speer, *Spandau: The Secret Diaries* (London: Collins, 1976), 360, entry for April 12, 1959: "No-one has yet seen that this was the greatest lost battle on the German side."

174 CCAC, Bufton papers, 3/51, note by Bufton, "Part Played by the RAF in the Crossing of the Rhine—24 March 1945."

175 UEA, Zuckerman archive, SZ/BBSU/3, Portal to Tedder, September 10, 1947.

176 British Air Ministry, *Rise and Fall of the German Air Force*, 274, 302; Boog, "Strategischer Luftkrieg," 287.

177 Cox, *Strategic Air War Against Germany*, 97; British Air Ministry, *Rise and Fall of the German Air Force*, 274, 298; Friedhelm Golücke, *Schweinfurt und der strategische Luftkrieg, 1943* (Paderborn: Ferdinand Schöningh, 1980), 153–59; IWM, MD, vol. 53, 877, German Flak Office to Milch, August 12, 1943.

178 John K. Galbraith, *A Life in Our Times: Memoirs* (London: Andre Deutsch, 1981), 240.

179 UEA, Zuckerman archive, SZ/BBSU/2, Carey Lecture, 8; TNA, AIR 10/3866, Report of the British Bombing Survey Unit, 38; NARA, RG 107, Box 138, Statistical Control Division, "An Estimate of Costs of AAF Strategic Air Forces Fighting Germany," April 12, 1945. Since this last figure covered the period up to December 31, 1944, it is likely that the final figure was between 12 and 13 percent.

180 TNA, AIR 20/2025, Casualties of RAF, Dominion and Allied Personnel at RAF Posting Disposal, May 31, 1947.

181 Greenhous et al., *Crucible of War*, 864.

182 TNA, AIR 22/203, War Room Manual of Bomber Command Operations 1939–1945, 9.

183 Davis, *Carl A. Spaatz*, App. 4, App. 9.

Chapter 4. The Logic of Total War:
German Society Under the Bombs

1 LC, Spaatz papers, Box 134, "Interrogation of Hermann Goering, Augsburg, 10 May 1945"; Hopper to Spaatz, May 12, 1945.

2 Ibid., Box 203, "Jeeping the Targets in a Country That Was," April 17–22, 1945, 1, 19.

3 CCAC, Bufton papers, 3/51, Bufton to Brig. Gen. F. Maxwell, May 17, 1945.

4 UEA, Zuckerman archive, SZ/BBSU/1, "Notes on the 'pocket,'" April 28, 1945, 4–5, 7, 10.

5 Bernd Lemke, *Luftschutz in Grossbritannien und Deutschland, 1923 bis 1939* (Munich: Oldenbourg Verlag, 2005), 255.

6 BA-B, R 1501/1513, RLM, "Grundsätze für die Führung des Luftschutzes," February 1942, 5.

7 BA-B, NS 18/1333, Göring, Goebbels, and Wilhelm Frick (interior minister) to all RVK, May 7, 1942, "Aufgabenverteilung bei Luftschutzmassnahmen."

8 Lemke, *Luftschutz*, 258–61.

9 Jörn Brinkhus, "Ziviler Luftschutz im 'Dritten Reich'—Wandel seiner Spitzen-organisation," in Dietmar Süss, ed., *Deutschland im Luftkrieg: Geschichte und Erinnerung* (Munich: Oldenbourg Verlag, 2007), 27–30.

10 Andreas Linhardt, *Feuerwehr im Luftschutz, 1926–1945: Die Umstruktierung des öffentlichen Feuerlöschwesens in Deutschland unter Gesichtspunkten des zivilen Luftschutzes* (Brunswick: VFDB, 2002), 37–38, 85–87, 114–20, 134–39, 204–5.

11 British Intelligence Objectives Sub-Committee Report no. 18, "Fire Fighting Equipment and Methods in Germany during the Period 1939–1945" (London, 1949), 7–9.

12 Lemke, *Luftschutz*, 254–56.

13 BA-B, R 1501/823, Luftschutzgesetz, 7 Durchführungsverordnung, August 31, 1943, 519–20.

14 TNA, AIR 48/29, USSBS, "Civilian Defense Division: Final Report, 26 Oct 1945," 117–26.

15 BA-MA, RL 41/3, RLB, Luftschutz-Berichte, May 21, 1941, 1. Leitsätze für Luftschutz-Warte.

16 BA-B, R 1501/1513, RLM, "Grundsätze für die Führung des Luftschutzes," February 1942, 6.

17 BA-MA, RL 41/7, RLB, Rundschreiben, October 2, 1942, "Führungsaufgaben"; October 16, 1942, "Besonderer Einsatz von Amtsträgerinnen bei Terrorangriffen."

18 Linhardt, *Feuerwehr im Luftschutz*, 108–9.

19 BA-B, R 1501/1516, Deutsche Gemeindetag to Göring, November 3, 1938; Interior Ministry to all Reich provinces, April 21, 1939.

20 Ibid., Air Ministry to all Regional Air Commands, November 1941.

21 BA-MA, RL 41/2, RLB, Luftschutz-Berichte, May 8, 1940, July 2 and 10, 1940, 1.

22 Lemke, *Luftschutz*, 328–29.

23 BA-B, R 1510/1515, Interior Ministry to Landesregierungen, Oberpräsidenten, January 6, 1940, May 17, 1940, September 26, 1940.

24 TNA, AIR 20/7287, Home Office, "Secret Report by the Police President of Hamburg on the Heavy Raids on Hamburg July/August 1943," December 1, 1943, 3–4.

25 Wilfried Beer, *Kriegsalltag an der Heimatfront: Alliierten Luftkrieg und deutsche Gegenmassnahmen zur Abwehr und Schadensbegrenzung dargestellt für den Raum Münster* (Bremen: H. M. Hauschild, 1990), 108–10.

26 BA-MA, RL 41/2, RLB, Luftschutz-Berichte, July 10, 1940; BA-B, R 1501/823, Luftschutzgesetz: Zehnte Durchführungsverordnung: Luftschutzmässiges Verhalten.

27 Ibid., 523; BA-MA, RL 41/6, RLB-Präsidium, material for the press, August 10, 1943, 1. On shelter rules see Dietmar Süss, "Wartime Societies and Shelter Politics in National Socialist Germany and Britain," in Claudia Baldoli, Andrew Knapp, and Richard Overy, eds., *Bombing, States and Peoples in Western Europe, 1940–1945* (London: Continuum, 2011), 29–31.

28 TNA, AIR 48/29, USSBS, "Civilian Defense Division: Final Report," 141–47; Marc Wiggam, "The Blackout and the Idea of Community in Britain and Germany," in Baldoli, Knapp, and Overy, *Bombing, States and Peoples*, 50–51.

29 BA-MA, RL 41/2, RLB, Luftschutz-Berichte, February 6 and 14, 1940, March 12, 1940; January 8 and 9, 1943.

30 BA-B, R 1501/1515, Interior Ministry to all RVK, October 27, 1939.

31 Wilbur Zelinsky and Leszek A. Kosinski, *The Emergency Evacuation of Cities* (Savage, MD: Rowman & Littlefield, 1991), 160–64; on Hitler see BA-B, R 1501/1515, Interior Ministry minute, October 8, 1940. On the program of child evacuation see Gerhard Kock, *"Der Führer sorgt für unsere Kinder . . .": Die Kinderlandverschickung im Zweiten Weltkrieg* (Paderborn: Ferdinand Schöningh, 1997), 69, 122, 351; Julia Torrie, *"For Their Own Good": Civilian Evacuations in Germany and France, 1939–1945* (New York: Berghahn, 2010), 52–53. On the experience of Cologne see Martin Rüther, "Die Erweiterte Kinderlandverschickung in Köln, Bonn und Umgebung," in Martin Rüther, ed., *"Zu Hause könnten sie es nicht schöner haben!": Kinderlandverschickung aus Köln und Umgebung, 1941–1945* (Cologne: Emons Verlag, 2000), 69–71, 75.

32 Anton Hoch, "Der Luftangriff auf Freiburg 1940," *Vierteljahreshefte für Zeitgeschichte* 4 (1956): 115–44.

33 Beer, *Kriegsalltag an der Heimatfront,* 107.

34 William Shirer, *Berlin Diary: The Journal of a Foreign Correspondent, 1934–1941* (London: Hamish Hamilton, 1941), 273–74, 364; Harry Flannery, *Assignment to Berlin* (London: Michael Joseph, 1942), 40–41.

35 Heinz Boberach, ed., *Meldungen aus dem Reich: Die geheimen Lageberichte des Sicherheitsdienstes der SS, 1938–1945* (Herrsching: Pawlak Verlag, 1984), 4:1140–41, Special Report, May 16, 1940; 1152, Special Report, May 20, 1940.

36 BA-MA, RL 41/2, RLB, Luftschutz-Berichte, May 6 and 22, 1940, July 10, 1940.

37 Ibid., September 11, 1940, November 6, 1940.

38 BA-B, R 1501/823, Interior Ministry to all Statthalter, RVK, Oberpräsidenten, May 16, 1940.

39 TNA, AIR 48/29, USSBS, "Civilian Defense Division: Final Report," 33–36.

40 Wolfgang Werner, *"Bleib übrig": Deutsche Arbeiter in der nationalsozialistischen Kriegswirtschaft* (Düsseldorf: Schwann, 1983), 34–41.

41 BA-B, R 1501/1071, Labor Ministry, "Änderung über Erstattung von Lohnausfällen," October 22, 1940; Ministry of Labor to all Provincial Labor Offices, February 8, 1941; Ministry of Labor Decree, November 19, 1941.

42 BA-B, NS 18/1060, Propaganda Ministry to Party Chancellery, October 9, 1941; "Bericht wegen Lohnausfall bei Luftalarm und Fliegerschäden," October 23, 1941, 1–3.

43 BA-B, R 1501/1071, General Plenipotentiary for Labor to all Gau Labor Offices, November 15, 1943; Reichsministerialblatt, vol. 72, February 18, 1944, "Erlass über Massnahmen des Arbeitsrechts und Arbeitseinsatzes bei Fliegeralarm und Fliegerschäden."

44 BA-MA, RL 41/3, RLB, Luftschutz-Berichte, March 7 and 26, 1941, 1–2.

45 Ibid., August 27, 1941, 3–4.

46 BA-B, R 1501/823, Interior Ministry to the Gemeindetag, October 2, 1940.

47 BA-B, NS 18/1333, Party Chancellery to Tiessler (Propaganda Ministry), April 27, 1942.

48 Martin Dean, *Robbing the Jews: The Confiscation of Jewish Property in the Holocaust, 1933–1945* (Cambridge: Cambridge University Press, 2008), 223–24, 239.

49 BA-MA, RL 41/2, RLB, Luftschutz-Berichte, July 6 and 31, 1940, 2.

50 Jill Stephenson, "Bombing and Rural Society in Württemberg," *Labour History Review* 77 (2012): 98–100; Edward Westermann, "Hitting the Mark but Missing the Target: Luftwaffe Deception Operations, 1939–1945," *War in History* 10 (2003): 208–13; BA-MA, RL 41/7, RLB, Rundschreiben, January 11, 1943.

51 BA-B, R 1501/823, "7th Durchführungsverordnung (Beschaffung von Selbstschutzgerät)," August 31, 1943.

52 BA-MA, RL 41/2, RLB, Luftschutz-Berichte, September 6 and 25, 1940, December 4, 1940.

53 TNA, AIR 20/7287, "Secret Report by the Police President of Hamburg," 2; Ursula Büttner, "'Gomorrha' und die Folgen der Bombenkrieg," in Hamburg Forschungsstelle für Zeitgeschichte, *Hamburg im "Dritten Reich"* (Göttingen: Wallstein Verlag, 2005), 616.

54 Beer, *Kriegsalltag an der Heimatfront*, 123–25.

55 TsAMO, f.500, o.12452, d.139, minutes of meeting in the Air Ministry, October 17, 1940, 2–3.

56 Michael Foedrowitz, *Bunkerwelten: Luftschutzanlagen in Norddeutschland* (Berlin: Links Verlag, 1998), 9–12; Ralf Blank, "Kriegsalltag und Luftkrieg an der Heimatfront," in Jörg Echternkamp, ed., *Das Deutsche Reich und der Zweite Weltkrieg, Band 9, erster Halbband: Die Deutsche Kriegsgesellschaft* (Stuttgart: DVA, 2004)," 395–96.

57 BA-MA, RL 41/3, Luftschutz-Berichte, November 7 and 19, 1941, 2.

58 Hans Hesse and Elke Purpus, "Vom Luftschutzraum zum Denkmalschutz— Bunker in Köln," in Inge Marszolek and Marc Buggeln, eds., *Bunker: Kriegsort, Zuflucht, Erinnerungsraum* (Frankfurt am Main: Campus Verlag, 2008), 66–68.

59 Blank, "Kriegsalltag und Luftkrieg," 396–97; Olaf Groehler, *Bombenkrieg gegen Deutschland* (Berlin: Akademie Verlag, 1990), 245–47.

60 Groehler, *Bombenkrieg*, 245–46; Richard Evans, *The Third Reich at War* (London: Allen Lane, 2008), 454–55.

61 Howard K. Smith, *Last Train from Berlin* (London: Cresset, 1942), 116; Süss, "Wartime Societies," 25–26; Blank, "Kriegsalltag und Luftkrieg," 403–5. See too Roger Moorhouse, *Berlin at War: Life and Death in Hitler's Capital, 1939–1945* (London: Bodley Head, 2010), 310–11.

62 Details in Michael Foedrowitz, *Flak-Towers* (Berlin: Berlin Underworlds Association, 2008), 3–4, 11–13, 17–18.

63 Ursula Büttner, "'Gomorrha,'" 614–15; Beer, *Kriegsalltag an der Heimatfront*, 19–21.

64 Figures calculated from BA-B, NS 18/1063, Partei-Kanzlei, "Angaben über die Verluste nach Fliegerangriffen," October 2, 1942.

65 BA-MA, RL 41/7, RLB, Landesgruppe Hesse-Rheinland, Rundschreiben, October 2, 1942; Merkblatt über Aussehen, Wirkung und Bekämpfung Brandabwurfmitteln.

66 BA-MA, RL 41/3, Luftschutz-Berichte, April 7 and 23, 1941, 2–3.

67 TsAMO, f.500, 393761c/34, RLM, Luftschutz-Arbeitsstab, "Anordnung auf Grund der letzten Erfahrungen aus Luftangriffen," February 19, 1941, 1–3, 4–5; 12452/139, minutes of meeting in the Air Ministry, October 10, 1940, 7.

68 TsAMO, f.500, 12452/139, OKW, "Weisungen für den Einsatz der Luftschutzkräfte und die Verwendung der Wehrmacht," March 7, 1941.

69 BA-B, R 1501/823, Interior Ministry to all RVK, Statthalter, May 2, 1941; Torrie, *For Their Own Good,* 129–30.

70 Groehler, *Bombenkrieg,* 264–66. On the NSV see Armin Nolzen, "'Sozialismus der Tat?' Die Nationalsozialistische Volkswohlfahrt (NSV) und der allierte Luftkrieg gegen das Deutsche Reich," in Süss, *Deutschland im Luftkrieg,* 58–59.

71 BA-MA, RL 41/3, Luftschutz-Berichte, July 16, 1941.

72 BA-B, NS 18/1058, action report to NSDAP Reichsleitung, "Angriff auf Lübeck," April 6, 1942.

73 Ibid., Gauleiter Hildebrandt to Party Reichsleitung, April 26, 1942; Gauleitung Mecklenburg to Goebbels, Bormann, April 27, 1942 (1).

74 Ibid., Gauleitung Mecklenburg to Goebbels, Bormann, April 27, 1942 (2); April 28, 1942; April 29, 1942.

75 Ibid., Gauleiter Hildebrandt to Führer HQ, May 2, 1942.

76 BA-B, NS 18/1333, Goebbels to all Gauleiter, Reichsstatthalter, RVK, April 28, 1942; see too Dietmar Süss, "Steuerung durch Information? Joseph Goebbels als 'Kommissar der Heimatfront' und die Reichsinspektion für den zivilen Luftschutz," in Rüdiger Hachtmann and Winfried Süss, eds., *Hitlers Kommissare: Sondergewalten in der nationalsozialistischen Diktatur* (Göttingen: Wallstein Verlag, 2006), 185–87; Brinkhus, "Ziviler Luftschutz," 34–35.

77 Nolzen, "'Sozialismus der Tat?,'" 60–62.

78 Cited in Eleanor Hancock, *The National Socialist Leadership and Total War, 1941–45* (New York: St. Martin's, 1991), 103.

79 BA-B, NS 18/1333, Circular to all Reich defense commissars, "Aufgabenverteilung bei Luftschutzmassnahmen," May 7, 1942; note for Goebbels, May 7, 1942.

80 BA-B, R 1501/3791, Arbeitsstab L5 (Air Ministry), "Abgrenzung von Befehlsbefugnissen," December 17, 1942; Göring Directive, December 17, 1942, 3.

81 Süss, "Steuerung durch Information?," 188–91; Brinkhus, "Ziviler Luftschutz," 34–36.

82 BA-B, R 1501/823, RVK Hamburg, "Richtlinien für die Tätigkeit eines Einsatzstabes bei katastrophen Luftangriffen," April 9, 1942; Interior Ministry to all Reich authorities, May 6, 1942.

83 BA-B, R 3101/31135, "Polizeiliche Anordnung über die Luftschutzdienstpflicht," August 27, 1943; BA-MA, RL 41/7, RLB, Rundschreiben, October 2, 1942, based on a Göring Decree, August 12, 1942.

84 Dieter Busch, *Der Luftkrieg im Raum Mainz während des Zweiten Weltkrieges, 1939–1945* (Mainz: Hase & Koehler, 1988), 67.

85 BA-B, R 13/XVII/21, draft Führer Decree, August 1943; Armaments Ministry, "Durchführungsanordnung zum Führererlass," August 23, 1943.

86 BA-B, R 1501/938, Verwaltungsbezirk Schöneberg, "Übersicht über die Sammelunterkünfte für Obdachlose," August 1942.

87 Ibid., Interior Ministry memorandum, "Besprechung im Rathaus Schöneberg," April 9, 1943, 1–3.

88 BA-B, R 1501/823, Interior Ministry, May 6, 1942, "Planmässige Vorbereitung der Hilfsmassnahmen," 2–4.

89 BA-B, R 1501/904, Interior Ministry, "Richtlinien für die Durchführung von Bauarbeiten zur Beseitigung von Fliegerschäden," April 12, 1943.

90 BA-B, R 1501/938, memorandum on activity of Baugruppe Pfeil, March 9, 1943.

91 BA-B, R 1501/949, Stadt der Reichsparteistadt Nürnberg, "Übersicht über die Fliegerschäden aus dem Luftangriffen vom 28/29.8.1942 bis 8/9.3 1943," May 3, 1943.

92 Ibid., Finance Ministry, Justice Ministry, minutes of meeting, "Ausgaben für Kriegssachschäden," February 17, 1944, 1.

93 Stephan Glienke, "The Allied Air War and German Society," in Baldoli, Knapp, and Overy, *Bombing, States and Peoples*, 186–88.

94 BA-B, NS 18/1062, Party Chancellery, "Vorlage: Material und Arbeitskräfte für die Beseitigung von Fliegerschäden" [n.d.].

95 BA-B, R 1501/938, ration cards for bomb victims, Berlin, March 1943; report from Wirtschaftsamt Schöneberg, April 9, 1943, 1–6.

96 RAFM, Harris papers, H51, Summary of the Foreign Press, August 29, 1942, *Die Weltwoche*, June 12, 1942.

97 BA-B, R 1501/938, memorandum from Bezirksamt Schöneberg on the work of the Quartieramt (accommodation office), April 9, 1943, 1–2, 3–4.

98 BA-B, R 1501/949, Stadt der Reichsparteitage Nürnberg, May 3, 1943.

99 Ibid., minutes of meeting, "Ausgaben für Kriegssachschäden," February 17, 1944, 2.

100 TNA, AIR 48/33, USSBS, Civilian Defense Report no. 4: Hamburg Field Report, vol. 1, 2, 30.

101 TNA, AIR 20/7287, "Secret Report of the Police President of Hamburg," 2–12; AIR 48/33, USSBS, Hamburg Field Report, vol. 1, 45.

102 BA-B, NS 18/573, Luftkriegsmeldedienst, Luftangriffe, May 14–17, 1943, June 22–23, 1943; NS 18/1060, Luftangriffe auf deutsche Reichsgebiet, May 27–28, 1943.

103 *Hamburg und Dresden im Dritten Reich: Bombenkrieg und Kriegsende; Sieben Beiträge* (Hamburg: Landeszentrale für politische Bildung, 2000), 31–33; BA-B, NS 18/1060, Luftkriegsmeldedienst, Luftangriffe auf deutsche Reichsgebiet, July 29–30, 1943.

104 Ursula Büttner, "'Gomorrha,'" 47, 69.

105 TNA, AIR 20/7287, "Secret Report by the Police President of Hamburg," 22; BA-B, R 1501/3791, report from Reich Health Leader (Leonardo Conti), "Ärztliche Erfahrungen im Luftschutz," March 27, 1944.

106 BA-B, R 1501/949, memorandum by Goebbels, "Reichsinspektion zur Durchführung ziviler Luftkriegsmassnahmen," January 28, 1944, 3.

107 TNA, AIR 20/7287, "Secret Report by the Police President of Hamburg," 23.

108 TNA, AIR 48/33, Hamburg Field Report, vol. 1, 36. The fire service also calculated injury to a further 46,252; AIR 20/7287, "Secret Report by the Police President of Hamburg," 17, 75.

109 Hans Nossack, *The End: Hamburg, 1943* (Chicago: University of Chicago Press, 2004), 17–18, 44 (originally published in Germany in 1948 as *Der Untergang*).

110 Gretl Büttner, "Zwischen Leben und Tod," in Volker Hage, ed., *Hamburg 1943: Literarische Zeugnisse zum Feuersturm* (Frankfurt am Main: Fischer Verlag, 2003), 30–31.

111 BA-B, R 1501/3791, Conti to the ILA, August 5, 1943; Dr. Illig (Hamburg) to Conti, August 5, 1943; City Medical Council (Hannover) to Conti, August 13, 1943.

112 BA-B, R 1501/37723, Luftschutz-Chemiker, Hamburg to Interior Ministry, November 5, 1943, encl. report "Trinkwasser-Notversorgung."

113 BA-B, R 1501/3791, RVK, Hamburg to Conti, August 17, 1943, 2–3; minute by Dr. Cropp, Interior Ministry, August 3, 1943.

114 TNA, AIR 48/29, USSBS, Civilian Defense Division: Final Report, 72.

115 Hans Brunswig, *Feuersturm über Hamburg: Die Luftangriffe auf Hamburg im 2. Weltkrieg und ihre Folgen* (Stuttgart: Motorbuch Verlag, 1985), 300–301.

116 Boberach, *Meldungen aus dem Reich*, 14:5562–63, report for August 2, 1943. Göring visit in Brunswig, *Feuersturm*, 296.

117 Albert Speer, *Inside the Third Reich* (London: Weidenfeld & Nicolson, 1970), 284.

118 BA-B, R 13/XVII/21, Armaments Ministry, "Durchführungsanordnung zum Führererlass," August 23, 1943.

119 BA-B, R 1501/949, "Bericht über die Dienstreise des Reichsrichter Dr. Danckelmann nach Hamburg, 20 bis 22 Juni 1944," 3–5.

120 Fred Iklé, *The Social Impact of Bomb Destruction* (Norman: University of Oklahoma Press, 1958), 67–68.

121 BA-MA, RL 41/7, RLB, Rundschreiben, July 1943.

122 TsAMO, f.500, o.393761c, d.34, LS-Arbeitsstab, Erfahrungsbericht, October 6, 1943, 4; no. 22, January 20, 1944, 1; no. 23, March 5, 1944, 4.

123 Ibid., no. 20, December 4, 1943, 1.

124 TNA, AIR 20/7287, "Secret Report by the Police President of Hamburg," 87–90.

125 BA-MA, RL 41/6, RLB, Presse-Material, November 2, 1943; TsAMO, f.500, o.393761c, d.34, LS-Arbeitsstab, Erfahrungsbericht no. 18, 7.

126 TsAMO, f.500, o.393761c, d.34, Erfahrungsbericht no. 17, September 23, 1943, 9; BA-MA, RL 41/6, RLB, Presse-Material, August 10, 1943, 1; November 2, 1943, 1.

127 Heinz Pettenberg, *Starke Verbände im Anflug auf Köln*, ed. Hella Reuter-Pettenberg (Cologne: J. P. Bachem Verlag, 1981), 90–91, entry for May 31, 1942.

128 Details from Linhardt, *Feuerwehr im Luftschutz*, 171–72, 173, 178, 180–82; Hans Rumpf, *The Bombing of Germany* (London: White Lion, 1957).

129 Kock, *"Der Führer sorgt für unsere Kinder,"* 139–43; Katja Klee, *Im "Luftschutzkeller des Reiches": Evakuierte in Bayern, 1939–1953* (Munich: Oldenbourg Verlag, 1999), 165–67.

130 BA-B, R 1501/823, Interior Ministry to all local authorities, July 27, 1942.

131 BA-B, R 1501/1515, Interior Ministry to provincial governments, February 2, 1943; Kock, *"Der Führer sorgt für unsere Kinder,"* 141.

132 Groehler, *Bombenkrieg*, 266–67.

133 BA-B, R 1501/3791, State Secretary Ganzenmüller, Transport Ministry, "Transport Questions in Evacuation of Air War Regions," June 1943, 1; Groehler, *Bombenkrieg*, 282; Klee, *Im "Luftschutzkeller des Reiches,"* 171.

134 BA-B, R 3102/10044, Statistical Office, "Stand der Umquartierung aus luftgefährdeten Gebieten," September 15, 1943.

135 BA-B, NS 18/1062, minute for Tiessler, Party Chancellery, "Attitude of the Evacuees in the Reception Areas," May 11, 1943.

136 BA-B, NS 18/1333, Propaganda Ministry, Inter-Ministerial Committee to all Gauleiter, August 19, 1943, 1, 4.

137 Jill Stephenson, *Hitler's Home Front: Württemberg Under the Nazis* (London: Continuum, 2006), 299–301, 306–11; Glienke, "Allied Air War," 196–98; Torrie, *"For Their Own Good,"* 100–106. On tensions between evacuees and local populations see Nicholas Stargardt, *Witnesses of War: Children's Lives Under the Nazis* (London: Jonathan Cape, 2005), 256–59.

138 BA-B, R 1501/3791, Mayor of Berlin to Reichsgesundheitsführer, Conti, August 21, 1943; RVK, Hamburg to Conti, August 17, 1943, "Verteilung von Ärzten."

139 Ibid., NS DAP, Hauptamt für Volkswohlfahrt to Conti, July 13, 1943.

140 BA-B, R 1501/3809, Conti papers, "Gedanken zur ärtzlichen Planwirtschaft," October 12, 1943; R 1501/3791, Meeting of the Inter-Ministerial Committee, July 21, 1943; Reich Health Leader to Oberpräsident Münster, July 30, 1943.

141 BA-B, R 1501/3791, memorandum to Reich Health Leader, June 29, 1943; Generalreferent für Luftkriegsschäden to Speer, June 29, 1943; RVK, Westfalen-Nord to Conti, July 22, 1943.

142 Ibid., President, German Red Cross, to all provincial offices, July 2, 1943; Conti to all RVK, "Gesundheitliche Versorgung der Zivilbevölkerung bei Luftgrossangriffen," July 5, 1943.

143 BA-B, NS 18/1062, Karl Brandt, Führer HQ, circular report, October 8, 1941. Hitler's decision was taken on August 24.

144 BA-B, R 1501/3809, Brandt to the Interior Ministry (Conti), Bormann, and Hans Lammers, June 24, 1943; Brandt to Lammers, June 30, 1943; Brandt memorandum, "Aufstellung der im Rahmen des Führerauftrages durch zuführenden Massnahmen."

145 Süss, "Wartime Societies and Shelter Politics," 36–38; Dietmar Süss, *Tod aus der Luft: Kriegsgesellschaft und Luftkrieg in Deutschland und England* (Munich: Siedler Verlag, 2011), 368–72. See too Peter Heinl, "Invisible Psychological Ruins: Unconscious Long-Term War Trauma," workshop paper, Reading University, March 13, 2009. Heinl was able to explain serious psychiatric and psychosomatic conditions among a cohort of elderly Germans by exposing their childhood experiences under bombing.

146 BA-B, NS 18/1063, Notice for Tiessler, March 17, 1943.

147 Boberach, *Meldungen aus dem Reich*, 13:4983, March 22, 1943.

148 BA-MA, RL 41/7, RLB, measures to be taken as a result of recent air raids, September 1943.

149 BA-B, NS 18/1333, Propaganda Ministry, Vorlage für den Herrn Minister, September 28, 1942. See too Stargardt, *Witnesses of War*, 253–54.

150 BA-B, NS 18/1333, Vorlage für den Herrn Minister, July 3, 1943, "Vermeidung von Gerüchten über die Bombardierung von Vulkanen."

151 Waltraud Süssmilch, *Im Bunker: Eine Überlebende berichtet vom Bombenkrieg in Berlin* (Berlin: Ullstein, 2004), 7.

152 Friedrich Reck-Malleczewen, *Diary of a Man in Despair* (London: Audiogrove, 1995), 188–89.

153 BA-B, NS 18/1058, conference with Goebbels, May 20, 1943, report by Mayor Ellgering; Michael Balfour, *Propaganda in War, 1939–1945* (London: Routledge, 1979), 341.

154 Elke Fröhlich, ed., *Die Tagebücher von Joseph Goebbels. Teil II, Band 7: Januar–März 1943* (Munich: K. G. Saur, 1993), 540.

155 Ralf Reuth, *Goebbels: The Life of Joseph Goebbels, the Mephistophelean Genius of Nazi Propaganda* (London: Constable, 1993), 315–16; Hancock, *National Socialist Leadership*, 69–73; Daniel Uziel, *The Propaganda Warriors: The Wehrmacht and the Consolidation of the German Home Front* (Bern: Peter Lang, 2008), 303–4.

156 Boberach, *Meldungen aus dem Reich*, 13:5217, May 6, 1943.

157 Uziel, *Propaganda Warriors*, 318–19; BA-B, NS 18/1333, Propaganda Ministry, Vorlage für den Herrn Minister, September 28, 1942; Bormann, Party Chancellery, "Führungshinweis Nr. 7," November 4, 1943.

158 BA-B, NS 18/1063, NSDAP, Propagandaleitung, notice, March 17, 1943.

159 Ralf Blank, "The Battle of the Ruhr, 1943: Aerial Warfare Against an Industrial Region," *Labour History Review* 77 (2012): 45.

160 Uziel, *Propaganda Warriors*, 316–17; Balfour, *Propaganda in War*, 343–44.

161 Boberach, *Meldungen aus dem Reich*, 13:5187, April 29, 1943; 14:5699, September 2, 1943.

162 Uziel, *Propaganda Warriors*, 319–21; Blank, "Aerial Warfare Against an Industrial Region," 45–46.

163 Cited in Jeffrey Herf, *The Jewish Enemy: Nazi Propaganda During World War II and the Holocaust* (Cambridge, MA: Harvard University Press, 2006), 215–16, 230; see too Balfour, *Propaganda in War*, 343–44.

164 BA-B, NS 18/1063, Propaganda-Kompanie Rundspruch, March 13, 1942, "Todesanzeigen für Opfer bei Fliegerangriffen"; Reichspropagandamt Weser-Ems to Hans Fritzsche, Propaganda Ministry, February 23, 1942.

165 Ibid., OKW to Reichspropagandaleitung, May 18, 1942; Goebbels notice, May 7, 1943. See also Nicole Kramer, " 'Kämpfende Mutter' und 'gefallene Heldinnen'—Frauen im Luftschutz," in Süss, *Deutschland im Luftkrieg*, 94–96.

166 Boberach, *Meldungen aus dem Reich*, 14:5698, September 2, 1943. For a full account of the Witten incident see Torrie, *"For Their Own Good,"* 97–105.

167 Süssmilch, *Im Bunker*, 41–42.

168 Nossack, *The End*, 33; Rumpf, *Bombing of Germany*, 202.

169 Boberach, *Meldungen aus dem Reich*, 14:5620, August 16, 1943.

170 Ibid., 14:5716, September 6, 1943; see also Glienke, "Allied Air War," 191–92.

171 Hester Vaizey, *Surviving Hitler's War: Family Life in Germany, 1939–48* (Basingstoke: Palgrave, 2010), 65.

172 Nossack, *The End*, 31–32.

173 Ibid., 32.

174 Adam Tooze, "No Room for Miracles: German Industrial Output in World War II Reassessed," *Geschichte und Gesellschaft* 31 (2005): 439–64; Lutz Budrass, Jonas Scherner, and Jochen Streb, "Fixed-Price Contracts, Learning, and Outsourcing: Explaining the Continuous Growth of Output and Labour Productivity in the German Aircraft Industry During the Second World War," *Economic History Review*, 2nd ser., 63 (2010): 107–36.

175 IWM, S363, Saur papers, Kartei des Technischen Amtes, 17, speech by the Führer, September 23, 1944.

176 BA-B, R 7/2249, Bezirksgruppe Nordwest, Wirtschaftsgruppe Eisenschaffende Industrie, "Zusammenhänge und Lage der nordwestlichen Eisenindustrie," August 17, 1945.

177 IWM, MD, vol. 13, minutes of GL meeting, April 27, 1942.

178 Ibid., vol. 56, letter from Technical Office to Milch, October 22, 1942, "Verlegung luftgefährdeter Betriebe."

179 Westermann, "Hitting the Mark," 213–14; Werner Wolf, *Luftangriffe auf die deutsche Industrie, 1942–1945* (Munich: Universitas, 1985), 129–30.

180 Smith, *Last Train from Berlin*, 117–18.

181 Westermann, "Hitting the Mark," 214–16.

182 Richard Overy, "Guns or Butter? Living Standards, Finance and Labour in Germany, 1939–1942," in *War and Economy in the Third Reich* (Oxford: Oxford University Press, 1994), 278, 293–95.

183 Rolf-Dieter Müller, "Das Scheitern der wirtschaftlichen 'Blitzkriegsstrategie,'" in Horst Boog et al., *Das Deutsche Reich und der Zweite Weltkrieg. Band 4: Der Angriff auf die Sowjetunion* (Stuttgart: DVA, 1983), 936–49, 1022–29; Rolf-Dieter Müller, "Albert Speer und die Rüstungspolitik im totalen Krieg, 1942–1945," in Bernhard Kroener, Rolf-Dieter Müller, and Hans Umbreit, *Das Deutsche Reich und der Zweite Weltkrieg. Band 5/2: Organisation und Mobilisierung des deutschen Machtbereichs, 1942–1944/45* (Stuttgart: DVA, 1999), 275–317.

184 CIOS Report, Item 21, Metallurgy, "German Iron and Steel Industry: Ruhr and Salzgitter Areas," June 1945, 11, 17; USSBS Report 69, *Fr. Krupp AG: Friedrich Alfred Hütte. Heavy Industry Plant Report No. 2* (Washington, DC, September 12, 1945), 1.

185 USSBS, Special Paper 3, *The Effects of Strategic Bombing upon the Operations of the Hermann Göring Works During World War II* (Washington, DC, 1946), 60; Control Office for Germany and Austria, "German Industrial Complexes: The Hermann Göring Complex," June 1946, 42.

186 Müller, "Albert Speer und die Rüstungspolitik," 620, 630–31, 632, 642. The argument developed by Adam Tooze, *Wages of Destruction: The Making and Breaking of the Nazi Economy* (London: Allen Lane, 2006), 598–600, that bombing brought arms production to a halt, remains unconvincing given the substantial increases in military output throughout the period from March 1943 to summer 1944.

187 IWM, Box S368, Report 54, interrogation of Albert Speer, July 13, 1945, 3–4, 7–8. Air supply figures calculated from BA-MA, RL 3/38, GL-Office, "Überblick über den Rüstungsstand der Luftwaffe: 1 Januar 1945"; RL 3/36, GL-Technical Office Report, "Über die Gründe der erhöhten Lieferungen im Rahmen des Luftwaffenprogrammes von März bis Juni 1944." On the overall effect of losses see Müller, "Albert Speer und die Rüstungspolitik," 648–58.

188 BA-B, R 13/XVII/21, draft Führer Decree, August 1943, on the repair of "damage regions"; Ministry of Armaments and Munitions, "Durchführungsanordnung zum Führererlass," August 23, 1943.

189 TsAMO, f.500, o.393761c, d.34, LS-Arbeitsstab, Erfahrungsbericht, November 15, 1943, 12.

190 BA-B, R 3101/31135, Economics Ministry to all Reich authorities, October 1, 1943.

191 Wolf, *Luftangriffe auf die deutsche Industrie*, 69–74.

192 BA-B, R 1501/1071, Four Year Plan, Price Commissar Decree, September 4, 1942.

193 Ibid., Plenipotentiary for Labor Supply (Fritz Sauckel) to Reich Trustees of Labor, July 9, 1943.

194 IWM, Box S368, Report 85, interrogation of Dr. Theodor Hupfauer (Ministry of War Production, chief of labor supply), September 10, 1945, 3; Hans Pohl and Wilhelm Treue, *Die Daimler-Benz AG in den Jahren 1933 bis 1945* (Wiesbaden: Franz Steiner Verlag, 1986), 173–74, 179.

195 IWM, Box S368, Report 85, Hupfauer interrogation, 8, 14.

196 TsAMO, f.500, o.393761c, d.34, LS-Arbeitsstab, Erfahrungsbericht, July 1, 1944, 1–2.

197 See the intelligence report from interrogation of the former Italian consul general in Frankfurt, TNA, PREM 3/193/6A, HQ Algiers to War Office, October 30, 1943: "Workers particularly were depressed for they now had a reasonable standard of living which they knew would disappear if war lost." Also LC, Spaatz papers, Box 203, Propaganda Research Section, "Morale in Hamburg," January 29, 1942, based on conversations with Hamburg workers from a Belgian source who identified three principal fears: fear of unemployment and starvation; fear of retribution by the Allies; and fear of the dismemberment of Germany.

198 Martin Moll, ed., *"Führer-Erlasse," 1939–1945* (Stuttgart: Franz Steiner Verlag, 1997), 345, decree of June 28, 1943.

199 BA-B, R 3101/31170, Führer Decree, "Über Sicherstellung vom Raumen zur Aufnahme von Rüstungsfertigungen aus luftgefährdeten Gebieten"; Armaments Ministry order, "Betriebsverlagerung und Verlagerung von Lager," July 14, 1943.

200 IWM, MD, vol. 56, Air Ministry Technical Office to Milch, October 22, 1942; report from Planning Office for Milch, October 14, 1942.

201 Ibid., Planning Office to Milch on dispersal policy, November 17, 1942; BA-MA, RL 36/52, report on conferences of July 22, 23, 26, 28, 29, and 30, 1943, "Über die Massnahmen zur Verstärkung der Luftverteidigung."

202 Details from Friedhelm Golücke, *Schweinfurt und der strategische Luftkrieg, 1943* (Paderborn: Ferdinand Schöningh, 1980), 351–53, 357–58, 363–64, 368–70, 372, 378–80.

203 BA-B, RL 3/36, Air Ministry Technical Office Report, "Über die Gründe."

204 Details in USSBS, Report 7, "Erla Maschinenwerke GmbH, Leipzig," 1–2, 6; Report 9, "Gothaer Waggonfabrik AG, Gotha," 1–2, 13; Report 14, "Wiener-Neustädter Flugzeugwerke," 1–2, 9–12.

205 IWM, MD, vol. 51, Main Committee Iron Production (Dr. Helmut Rohland) to all industry heads, March 27, 1944, 2.

206 IWM, EDS MI 14/133, Army High Command, "Studie über Rüstung," January 25, 1944.

207 IWM, EDS AL/1746, interrogation of Karl-Otto Saur, August 10, 1945; Box S368, Report 90, "Rationalisation in the Components Industry," 34; Dietrich Eichholtz, *Geschichte der deutschen Kriegswirtschaft. Band 2: 1941–1943* (Munich: K. G. Saur, 1999), 316–17.

208 BA-B, R 3101/11921, Economics Ministry, Weekly Reports on Economic Conditions, February 7, 1944, 1; May 27, 1944, 1; September 28, 1944, 1; October 21, 1944, 7. See too Bernhard Kroener, "'Menschenbewirtschaftung,' Bevölkerungsverteilung und personelle Rüstung in der zweiten Kriegshälfte (1942–1944)," in Kroener, Müller, and Umbreit, *Das Deutsche Reich und der Zweite Weltkriege,* Band 5/2, 931–34.

209 BA-B, R 3101/11921, Economics Ministry Weekly Report, February 14, 1944, 1; IWM, Box S366, FIAT Report, "Statistical Material on the German Manpower Position During the War Period," July 31, 1945. On Daimler-Benz, see Pohl and Treue, *Die Daimler-Benz AG,* 145.

210 BA-B, R 3101/11921, Economics Ministry Weekly Report, December 18, 1944, 7. See too Cornelia Rauh-Kühne, "Hitlers Hehler? Unternehmerprofite und Zwangsarbeiterlöhne," *Historische Zeitschrift* 275 (2002): 40–41.

211 BA-B, R 3101/11921, Economics Ministry Weekly Report, December 18, 1944, 7. The proportion of hours lost for each category was as follows: air raids 2.5 percent, illness 5.7 percent, leave 3.0 percent, truancy 1.3 percent, workplace problems 3.5 percent.

212 BA-B, R 3102/10031, Statistical Office, "Vermerk über die Auswirkung der feindlichen Luftangriffe auf die Arbeiterstundenleistung der Industrie," January 27, 1945, 2.

213 IWM, Box S126, BBSU, "MS notes on Ford Cologne."

214 TNA, AIR 10/3873, BBSU, "German Experience in the Underground Transfer of War Industries," App. 1, "Survey of Natural Underground Facilities in Greater Germany," July 1, 1943; BA-B, R 3101/31170, Mining Office, Bavaria to Mines Department, Economics Ministry, July 29, 1943; Dortmund Mining Office to Mines Department, August 7, 1943. For an excellent overview of the underground program see Paul Clemence, "German Underground Factories of the Second World War: An Essential Folly" (unpublished PhD thesis, University of Exeter, 2008), chaps. 2–3.

215 TNA, AIR 10/3873, BBSU, "German Experience," 5.

216 CIOS Report XXX-80, "Bavarian Motor Works: A Production Survey" (1946), 44–45, 50–51; Hans Mommsen and Manfried Grieger, *Das Volkswagenwerk und seine Arbeiter im Dritten Reich* (Düsseldorf: Econ, 1997), 844–45, 879, 1027; Rauh-Kühne, "Hitlers Hehler?," 44–45.

217 TNA, AIR 10/3873, BBSU, "German Experience," 10, 14–15.

218 BA-B, R 3101/11921, Economic Ministry weekly reports, February 12, 1944, 1; March 11, 1944, 1; July 28, 1944, 1; September 23, 1944, 1.

219 IWM, S368, FIAT Report 67, "Causes in the Decline of German Industrial Production," December 13, 1945, 5, interrogation of Wilhelm Schaaf, 13, interrogation of Karl-Otto Saur, 13.

220 Ibid., Report 52, interrogation of S. Stieler von Heydekampf, October 6, 1945, 10.

221 LC, Spaatz papers, Box 203, J. K. Galbraith, "Preliminary Appraisal of Achievement of Strategic Bombing of Germany," 2.

222 BA-B, R 3102/10031, Statistical Office, "Statistik der Luftkriegsschädenbetroffene Industriebetriebe: November 1944"; Reich Statistical Office, "Die Tätigkeit der feindlichen Luftwaffe über den Reichsgebiete im September 1944."

223 IWM, Box S368, FIAT Report 67, interrogation of Karl-Otto Saur, 12.

224 IWM, EDS MI 14/133, OKH, General-Quartermaster Planning Office, "Sturm-Programm," January 9, 1945, 1–6.

225 IWM, Box S369, SHAEF-G2, interrogation of Albert Speer, June 7, 1945, 3; Box S368, FIAT Report 83, April 5, 1946, App. 1, "Speer's Outside Organization"; on the autarkic zones, BA-B, R 12 I/9, Reichsgruppe Industrie to all Economic Groups,

March 5, 1945, "Verkehrsnot: Bildung eines Verkehrsstabes"; Reichsgruppe Industrie to Economic Groups, March 8, 1945, "Einsatz von Rüstungsbevollmächtigten."

226 Rumpf, *Bombing of Germany*, 130–31.

227 BA-B, R 1501/949, Himmler to all Reich authorities, February 21, 1944.

228 Irmtraud Permooser, *Der Luftkrieg über München, 1942–1945: Bomben auf die Hauptstadt der Bewegung* (Oberhachung: Aviatic Verlag, 1996), 359; Busch, *Der Luftkrieg im Raum Mainz*, 367.

229 Süssmilch, *Im Bunker*, 55.

230 Linhardt, *Feuerwehr im Luftschutz*, 172–74; Brinkhus, "Ziviler Luftschutz," 38–39. On the "Air Protection Regiments" (*Luftschutz-Regimenten*) see, e.g., RL 13/4, Einsatz LS-Regiment 7, Luftgau VII, February 26–March 25, 1945.

231 BA-MA, RL 41/7, RLB, Hesse-Rheinland, Rundschreiben, June 9, 1944.

232 BA-B, R 1501/1513, Interior Ministry to RVK, Gauleiter, Reichsstatthalter, January 6, 1944, encl. "Erlass des Führers über die Errichtung einer Reichsinspektion der zivilen Luftkriegsmassnahmen," December 21, 1943.

233 BA-B, R 1501/949, Himmler to all RVK, September 10, 1944, "Vorbereitungen für die Verteidigung des Reiches." On Goebbels's new office, see Süss, "Steuerung durch Information?, 202–4; Reuth, *Goebbels*, 324–27.

234 BA-B, R 1501/1513, Gauleitung Sudetenland to NSDAP-Leitung, February 3, 1944; Report from Reich Defense Commissar Hannover-Ost, August 1944.

235 BA-B, R 3101/31135, Polizeiliche Anordnung über die Luftschutzdienstpflicht im Selbstschutz, August 27, 1943.

236 BA-B, R 1501/949, Propaganda Ministry (Berndt) to the Inter-Ministerial Committee, January 29, 1944, encl. memorandum from Goebbels, 2.

237 Süssmilch, *Im Bunker*, 54–55.

238 BA-MA, RL 41/7, RLB, Hesse-Rheinland, Rundschreiben, May 6, 1944.

239 BA-B, R 1501/906, Speer to all OT-Einsatzgruppenleiter and RVK Baubeauftragten, September 28, 1944, 2.

240 BA-B, R 3101/11922, Reichsgruppe Handwerk memorandum, June 9, 1943; Reichsgruppe Handwerk to Transport Ministry, August 23, 1943; Reichsgruppe Handwerk to Economics Ministry, May 22, 1944; Finance Ministry to Economics Ministry, July 15, 1944.

241 BA-B, R 3102/10031, Otto Ohlendorf (Economics Ministry) to Reich Statistical Office, March 9, 1944.

242 Ibid., Economics Ministry note, "Fliegerschäden in Monat Oktober 1944"; "Fliegerschäden Januar/Dezember 1943."

243 Ibid., Air Ministry, LS-Arbeitsstab, "Übersicht über Luftangriffe und Bombenabwürfe im Heimatkriegsgebiet," November 1944.

244 BA-B, R 1501/3723, Interior Ministry to all Reich authorities, June 24, 1944.

245 Ibid., Interior Ministry (Murray), "Für die Trinkwasserversorgung bereitgestellte Tankfahrzeuge," June 1944; Generalinspektor für Wasser und Energie, memorandum for Wirtschaftsgruppe Wasser, "Luftschutz an Wasserversorgungsanlagen," August 7, 1944.

246 Ibid., Eastern German Brewing Association to Interior Ministry, September 13, 1943; "Brunnenvorhaben in Gross-Berlin," June 30, 1944; Interior Ministry memorandum, June 30, 1944.

247 BA-B, R 13/XVII/21, Wirtschaftsgruppe Gas-und Wasserversorgung, Angriff auf Leipzig, December 6, 1943; Luftangriffsmeldung, September 4, 1943; on gas capacity see "Durchschnittliche Tagesleistung der 950 Erzeugerwerke von Stadtgas, Juli bis November 1943," which shows spare capacity on each date approximately double the capacity damaged by bombing.

248 BA-B, R 13/XVII/49, "Fliegergeschädigte Werke, Stand 1.6.1944"; General-inspektor für Wasser und Energie to Wirtschaftsgruppe, November 22, 1944; Generalinspektor to Niederrheinische Licht-und Kraftwerke AG, November 1, 1944, approving the permanent closure of the Mönchengladbach gasholder.

249 Anon., *A Woman in Berlin* (London: Virago, 2005), 19.

250 BA-B, R 3102/10031, list of damaged cultural and artistic treasures, May 15, 1944; Stadtsynodalverband, Berlin, "Fliegerschäden an kirchlichen Gebäude 28 April bis 1 Juni 1944."

251 Permooser, *Der Luftkrieg über München*, 372–75.

252 Busch, *Der Luftkrieg im Raum Mainz*, 361.

253 BA-B, R 1501/949, Goebbels memorandum, January 28, 1944, 3.

254 Ibid., Himmler to all Reich authorities, February 21, 1944.

255 BA-B, R 3102/10044, NSDAP, Reichsleitung, Hauptamt für Volkswohlfahrt, Stand der Umquartierung, January 11, 1945. See too Groehler, *Bombenkrieg*, 281–82; Zelinsky and Kosinski, *Emergency Evacuation*, 167–68, 171–73; Klee, *Im "Luftschutzkeller des Reiches*," 150–51, 172–73.

256 Iklé, *Social Impact of Bomb Destruction*, 66–67.

257 Boberach, *Meldungen aus dem Reich*, 14:5645, August 19, 1943.

258 Groehler, *Bombenkrieg*, 447.

259 BA-B, R 3102/10031, Economics Ministry, "Fliegerschäden in Monat August 1944"; "Fliegerschäden in Monat Oktober 1944"; Reich Statistical Office, "Die Tätigkeit der feindlichen Luftwaffe über dem Reichsgebiet, Oktober 1944," January 10, 1945, 9.

260 TNA, AIR 48/29, USSBS, Civilian Defense Division: Final Report, 3 (using LS-Arbeitsstab figures for Greater Germany).

261 BA-B, NS 18/1063, Partei-Kanzlei, Abt. PG, "Angaben über die Verluste nach Fliegerangriffen," October 2, 1942; Groehler, *Bombenkrieg*, 316–20.

262 Hans Sperling, "Deutsche Bevölkerungsbilanz des 2. Weltkrieges," *Wirtschaft und Statistik* 8 (1956): 498–99.

263 Groehler, *Bombenkrieg*, 320; Blank, "Kriegsalltag und Luftkrieg," 459–60.

264 Calculated from Martin Middlebrook and Chris Everitt, *The Bomber Command War Diaries* (Leicester: Midland Publishing, 2000), 657–701.

265 Anon., *Woman in Berlin*, 22–23.

266 Boberach, *Meldungen aus dem Reich*, 16:6466, April 6, 1944.

267 Ibid., 17:6618, June 29, 1944; 6646, July 14, 1944; 6697–98, August 8, 1944.

268 Ibid., 16:6298, February 3, 1944; 6414, March 1944; 17:6509–10, May 4, 1944; 6565, June 1, 1944; Neil Gregor, "A *Schicksalsgemeinschaft*? Allied Bombing, Ci-vilian Morale, and Social Dissolution in Nuremberg, 1942–1945," *Historical Journal* 43 (2000): 1051–70.

269 USSBS, Report 64b, "Effects of Bombing on German Morale," 19–20.

270 Ibid., 16. The percentages were: military reverses, 48 percent; Allied superiority, 24 percent; air raids, 15 percent; war shortages, 2 percent; miscellaneous, 11 percent.

271 Dietmar Süss, "Nationalsozialistische Deutungen des Luftkrieges," in *Deutschland im Luftkrieg*, 104–8. On living standards see Gernot Wiese, "Die Versorgungslage in Deutschland," in Michael Salewski and Guntram Schulze-Wegener, eds., *Kriegsjahr 1944: Im Grossen und im Kleinen* (Stuttgart: Franz Steiner Verlag, 1995), 340–46.

272 Hans Schlange-Schoeningen, *The Morning After* (London: Gollancz, 1948), 229, entry for January 1, 1945.

273 Boberach, *Meldungen aus dem Reich*, 16:6302–4, February 7, 1944, "Gefühlsmässige Einstellung der Bevölkerung gegenüber den Feinden."

274 Barbara Grimm, "Lynchmorde an alliierten Fliegern im Zweiten Weltkrieg," in Süss, *Deutschland im Luftkrieg*, 75–76; Neville Wylie, "Muted Applause? British Prisoners of War as Observers and Victims of the Allied Bombing Campaign over Germany," in Baldoli, Knapp, and Overy, *Bombing, States and Peoples*, 266–67; Blank, "Kriegsalltag und Luftkrieg," 449–50.

275 Boberach, *Meldungen aus dem Reich*, 17:6566, June 1, 1944; Hugh Trevor-Roper, ed., *Hitler's Table Talk, 1941–1944* (London: Weidenfeld & Nicolson, 1973), 696, entry for September 6, 1942; Grimm, "Lynchmorde," 79–80.

276 Nossack, *The End*, 34; criticism of Goebbels in Boberach, *Meldungen aus dem Reich*, 17:6566.

277 Marlene Hiller, "Stuttgarter erzählen vom Luftkrieg," in Marlene Hiller, ed., *Stuttgart im Zweiten Weltkrieg* (Gerlingen: Bleicher Verlag, 1989), 425.

278 Süssmilch, *Im Bunker*, 10, 14–15.

279 BA-MA, RL 13/2, Luftschutz-Regiment 3 to Luftgaukommando III, Einsatzbericht, August 9, 1944.

280 BA-MA, RL 13/4, LS-Regiment 7, Luftgau VII, Erfahrungsbericht, February 26–March 25, 1945; LS-Regiment, Abteilung 22 to LS-Regimentstab, February 25, 1945, "Einsatzbericht: Nürnberg von 20 bis 23 Februar 1945."

281 Matthias Gretzschel, *Als Dresden im Feuersturm versank* (Hamburg: Eller & Richter, 2004), 148–49; Victor Klemperer, *To the Bitter End: The Diaries of Victor Klemperer, 1942–45* (London: Weidenfeld & Nicolson, 1999), 387. The fullest account of the raid is Frederick Taylor, *Dresden: Tuesday 13 February 1945* (London: Bloomsbury, 2004).

282 Klemperer, *To the Bitter End*, 393, entry for February 22–24, 1945.

283 Erich Hampe, . . . *als alles in Scherben fiel* (Osnabrück: Biblio Verlag, 1979), 119–21.

284 Oliver Reinhard, Matthias Neutzner, and Wolfgang Hesse, *Das rote Leuchten: Dresden und der Bombenkrieg* (Dresden: Sächsische Zeitung, 2005), 101–2.

285 Gretzschel, *Als Dresden im Feuersturm versank*, 149; Gretzschel, "Dresden im Dritten Reich," in *Hamburg und Dresden im Dritten Reich*, 97–98.

286 Klemperer, *To the Bitter End*, 398, entry for February 19, 1945; Matthias Neutzner, "Wozu leben wir nun noch?" Die Dresdner Bevölkerung vom 13/14 Februar bis zum 17 April 1945," in *Hamburg und Dresden im Dritten Reich*, 100.

287 Schlange-Schoeningen, *Morning After*, 232–33.

288 Süssmilch, *Im Bunker*, 21–22.

289 Anon., *Woman in Berlin*, 48.

290 Irmgard Hunt, *On Hitler's Mountain: My Nazi Childhood* (London: Atlantic Books, 2005), 220, 222–23, 225.

291 Süssmilch, *Im Bunker*, 221–22.

Chapter 5. Italy: The War of Bombs and Words

1 British Committee on the Preservation and Restitution of Works of Art, *Works of Art in Italy: Losses and Survival in the War: Part I—South of Bologna* (London: HMSO, 1945); *Part II—North of Bologna* (London: HMSO, 1946).

2 IWM, Duxford, Italian Series (Air Force), Box 22, E2566, Italian air staff study, "Contributo italiano allo sforzo bellico: Attività della RA dall' 8 settembre 1943 all' 8 maggio 1945," 15–16.

3 Gregory Alegi, "Qualità del materiale bellico e dottrina d'impiego italiana nella seconda guerra mondiale: Il caso della Regia Aeronautica," *Storia Contemporanea* 18 (1987): 1213.

4 TNA, AIR 2/7197, HQ British Air Force in France to the Air Ministry, April 26, 1940. See too Claudia Baldoli and Andrew Knapp, *Forgotten Blitzes: France and Italy under Allied Air Attack, 1940–1945* (London: Continuum, 2012), 19–20.

5 TNA, AIR 75/8, Slessor papers, "Operation Haddock: Plan for Attack of Italian War Industry," June 2, 1940.

6 TNA, AIR 35/325, report for the Air Ministry, "Haddock Force—Historical Diary," June 20, 1940, 2–9; Denis Richards, *Royal Air Force, 1939–1945*, vol. 1, *The Fight at Odds* (London: HMSO, 1974), 145–47.

7 Stephen Harvey, "The Italian War Effort and the Strategic Bombing of Italy," *History* 70 (1985): 38.

8 TNA, AIR 20/283, Air Ministry, notes on bomb attacks, August 20, 1940.

9 CCO, Portal papers, Folder 9, Walter Monckton (MoI) to Portal, November 8, 1940.

10 TNA, FO 898/457, PWE, "Annual Dissemination of Leaflets by Aircraft and Balloon, 1939–1945."

11 TNA, AIR 23/7325, Air Ministry propaganda department to RAF commander, Malta, December 4, 1940.

12 TNA, AIR 23/7375, AI, HQ RAF, Malta, to Malta Information Office, November 28, 1940.

13 Ibid., Air Ministry to C-in-C, Malta, January 18, 1941; HQ RAF Med to Luqa airbase, February 13, 1941; War Office, Deputy Director Military Intelligence to C-in-C, Malta, April 21, 1941.

14 TNA, AIR 2/7397, Air Ministry to HQ Middle East, September 5, 1941.

15 TNA, AIR 23/5752, Wellington Operations from Malta; Marco Gioannini and Giulio Massobrio, *Bombardate l'Italia: Storia della guerra di distruzione aerea, 1940–45* (Milan: Rizzoli, 2007), online appendix.

16 TNA, AIR 2/7397, HQ RAF Med to Bomber Command HQ, November 1, 1940; HQ Malta to HQ Middle East, November 14, 1940; HQ Malta to HQ Middle East, November 23, 1940.

17 TNA, AIR 8/436, Cadogan (Permanent Secretary, Foreign Office) to Portal, October 21, 1941; Portal to Cadogan, October 26, 1941.

18 TNA, AIR 2/7397, Cadogan to Freeman (DCAS), January 8, 1942; Freeman to Cadogan, January 9, 1942.

19 Ibid., reports on raids in October and November 1941 classified nine of the sixteen raids as nuisance raids, using fewer than seven aircraft. On British policy see Baldoli and Knapp, *Forgotten Blitzes*, 20–21, 25.

20 TNA, AIR 2/7397, RAF HQ Malta to Air Ministry, November 9, 1940; Portal to Deputy Chief of Staff (Harris), November 10, 1940.

21 TNA, AIR 8/435, minute by Churchill for Portal and Sinclair, December 3, 1942.

22 TNA, AIR 19/215, Portal to Churchill, November 29, 1942; Portal to Churchill, December 1, 1942.

23 UEA, Zuckerman archive, SZ/OEMU/50, Ministry of Home Security, RE8, "Note on Italian Construction and Its Vulnerability to I.B. and H.E. Bombs," December 30, 1942; RE8, "Note on Italian Domestic Architecture," November 4, 1943, 1. On the Milan raid, CCAC, Bufton papers, 3/26, Memorandum BOps, November 15, 1942, "Milan: Daylight Raid 24 October 1942."

24 CCAC, Bufton papers, 3/26, BOps to director of tactics, May 31, 1943.

25 Macgregor Knox, *Hitler's Italian Allies: Royal Armed Forces, Fascist Regime and the War of 1940–1943* (Cambridge: Cambridge University Press, 2000), 101.

26 IWM, Italian Series, Box 25, "Relazione statistica sull'attività operativa," 8.

27 Paolo Formiconi, "La protezione e la difesa contraerea del regime fascista: Evoluzione istituzionale," in Nicola Labanca, ed., *I bombardamenti aerei sull'Italia* (Bologna: Il Mulino, 2012), 123–25.

28 IWM, Italian Series, Box 1, E2476, Ufficio operazioni aeronautica, memorandum for the commanding general, March 5, 1943, 1–2.

29 IWM, Italian Series, Box 2, E2485, Relazioni critiche mensili dei reparti intercettori, December 1942, January and May 1943. On radios see Box 3, E2489, Superaereo to department of air armament, "Riunione del 28 novembre 1942; tipo di onda per la caccia notturna," December 1, 1942.

30 IWM, Italian Series, Box 3, E2489, liaison officer of XII Fliegerkorps, "Protocollo della riunione, 9 June 1943"; Box 1, E2476, Comando Supremo to Superaereo, Supereserciti, Supermarina, March 13, 1943, "Difesa contro-aerea"; Comando Supremo, memorandum for Gen. Addetto, March 10, 1943.

31 IWM, Italian Series, Box 2, E2485, Relazioni critiche mensili dei reparti intercettori, May 1943, 1–2.

32 IWM, Italian Series, Box 3, E2489, maps of "Nuovo progetto di schieramento di caccia notturna," June 9, 1943, July 1943, August 15, 1943; Luigi Castioni, "I radar industriali italiani: Ricerche, ricordi, considerazioni per una loro storia," *Storia Contemporanea* (1987): 1250–51, 1254.

33 IWM, Italian Series, Box 1, E2470, Antiaircraft CoS to Gen. Presso, February 20, 1943; Gen. von Pohl to Italian Army Staff (Air Defense), March 15, 1943.

34 Andrea Natalini, *I rapporti tra aeronautica italiana e tedesca durante la seconda guerra mondiale* (Cosenza: Edizioni Lionello Giordano, 2004), 157–61. Night fighters in IWM, Italian Series, Box 3, E2489, MdAe, "Appunto per il Duce," May 1943, 4.

35 Natalini, *I rapporti tra aeronautica italiana e tedesca*, 162–64; IWM, Italian Series, Box 3, E2489, MdAe, "Appunto per il Duce," May 1943.

36 IWM, Italian Series, Box 10, E2528, Italian embassy, Berlin, to the minister for air, July 25, 1941; Italian embassy to minister for air, July 23, 1941, encl. "Collaborazione industriale aeronautica fra Italia e Germania."

37 Nicola della Volpe, *Difesa del territorio e protezione antiaerea, 1915–1943: Storia,*

documenti, immagini (Rome: Ufficio storico SME, 1986), 194–203, doc. 17, "Istruzione sulla protezione antiaerea."

38   ACS, MdAe, Busta 82, Ministry of War to all ministries, February 18, 1939; Volpe, *Difesa del territorio*, 36. Active air defense was allocated 252 million lire in 1938–39 but civil defense only 20.8 million.

39   ACS, MdAe, Busta 82, Gen. Valle to Mussolini, April 23, 1939, encl. air staff memorandum, April 18, 1939.

40   Volpe, *Difesa del territorio*, 209–10, doc. 18, Army Council meeting, May 8, 1939.

41   ACS, MdAe, Busta 82, Ministry of War to all prefects and regional military authorities, June 10, 1940.

42   Baldoli and Knapp, *Forgotten Blitzes*, 54; Volpe, *Difesa del territorio*, 46–48.

43   Baldoli and Knapp, *Forgotten Blitzes*, 71–73.

44   ACS, MdAe, Busta 82, War Ministry to all ministries and prefects, May 29, 1940; Interior Ministry to Air Ministry, October 2, 1940; Comando della 3 Zona Aerea to Air Ministry, November 11, 1940; note from secretary to the Duce to the Air Ministry, November 16, 1940.

45   TNA, AIR 20/5384, Genoa prefect to Interior Ministry, June 18, 1940.

46   ACS, MdAe, Busta 82, Commissariat for War Production to the War Ministry, June 24, 1940.

47   Franco Manaresi, "La protezione antiaerea," in Cristina Bersani and Valeria Monaco, eds., *Delenda Bononia: Immagini dei bombardamenti, 1943–1945* (Bologna: Patron Editori, 1995), 29–30.

48   Carlotta Coccoli, "I 'fortilizi inespugnabili della civiltà italiana': La protezione antiaerea del patrimonio monumentale italiano durante la seconda guerra mondiale," *Scienza e Beni Culturali* 26 (2010): 410–12.

49   Marta Nezzo, "The Defence of Works of Art in Italy During the Second World War," in Claudia Baldoli, Andrew Knapp, and Richard Overy, eds., *Bombing, States and Peoples in Western Europe, 1940–1945* (London: Continuum, 2011), 104–6.

50   ACS, MdAe, Busta 56, telecommunications inspectorate report for Air Ministry, "Danni di guerra a stabilimenti ausiliari," February 9, 1943; director general of construction, Air Ministry, January 15, 1943; TNA, AIR 20/5387, Italian Ministry of Public Works, "Damage Caused by Air Raids on Piemonte—October and November 1942"; report from prefect in Genoa on air raids of November 13–14, 15–16, and 18, 1942 (both translations from Italian originals).

51   ACS, MdAe, Busta 46, Ministry of War to all ministries, November 15, 1942; memorandum for the Comando Supremo, November 19, 1942, 1–2.

52   Ibid., MdAE memorandum for Mussolini, December 10, 1942, "Dislocamento dell'industrie aeronautiche"; Air Ministry, "Appunti per il Duce," December 15, 1942; Office of MdAE Inspectorate, minutes of meeting with Ministry of Corporations, December 14, 1942.

53   ACS, MdAe, Busta 56, memorandum, "Ripresa produzione officine Alfa Romeo, Pomigliano," June 14, 1943.

54   Cited in Leonardo Paggi, *Il "popolo dei morti": La repubblica italiana nata della guerra (1940–1946)* (Bologna: Il Mulino, 2009), 108–9.

55   Iris Origo, *War in Val d'Orcia: An Italian War Diary, 1943–1944* (London: Allison & Busby, 2003), 28–29, entry for January 30, 1943.

56 ACS, MdAe, Busta 55, Air Ministry minute, July 18, 1943; Busta 46, memorandum by Col. Galante, November 30, 1942.

57 ACS, Ministero dell'Interno, Busta 21, Police HQ Genoa to Ministry, November 14, 1942; prefect of Turin to ministry, December 19, 1942; sticker samples, "Merda!"

58 Elena Cortesi, "Evacuation in Italy during the Second World War: Evolution and Management," in Baldoli, Knapp, and Overy, *Bombing, States and Peoples*, 60–62.

59 Paggi, *Il "popolo dei morti,"* 107, 110–11; Cortesi, "Evacuation in Italy," 62–63.

60 Paggi, *Il "popolo dei morti,"* 110–12; Manuela Lanari and Stefano Musso, "Un dramma mal calcolato: Sfollamento e istituzioni nella provincia di Torino," in Bruno Maida, ed., *Guerra e società nella provincia di Torino* (Turin: Blu Edizioni, 2007), 14, 24–26, 28–29.

61 TNA, AIR 19/215, Sinclair to Churchill, December 4, 1942.

62 FDRL, Map Room Files, Box 72, OSS Bulletin, April 7, 1943; OSS Report, April 19, 1943 (from Bern).

63 TNA, FO 898/175, "Report on Colonel Thornhill's Mission on Political Warfare in General Eisenhower's Command," November 16, 1943, App. 10 and App. 14.

64 ACS, Ministero dell'Interno, Busta 21, Office of Caribinieri, Genoa, to Ministry of Interior, November 16, 1942.

65 TNA, FO 898/175, Allied Force HQ, Algiers, PWB memorandum, "Combat Propaganda—Leaflet Distribution," June 15, 1943.

66 Cesare de Simone, *Venti angeli sopra Roma: I bombardamenti aerei sulla Città Eterna* (Milan: Mursia, 1993), 266. On Fascist propaganda see Claudia Baldoli and Marco Fincardi, "Italian Society Under Anglo-American Bombs: Propaganda, Experience and Legend, 1940–1945," *Historical Journal* 52 (2009): 1032–34, 1037.

67 ACS, Ministero dell'Interno, Busta 21, "Appunto per il Duce," July 7, 1943.

68 TNA, AIR 2/7397, Air Ministry to C-in-C Bomber Command, October 28, 1940; Air Ministry to C-in-C Bomber Command, October 29, 1940; Sinclair to Churchill, February 24, 1941; Churchill to Sinclair, February 28, 1941.

69 TNA, AIR 8/436, HQ RAF Middle East to Air Ministry, September 4, 1941; Sir Miles Lampson (ambassador in Cairo) to the Foreign Office, September 17, 1941; AIR 2/7397, Air Ministry to HQ RAF Middle East, March 27, 1941; Air Ministry to HQ RAF Middle East, September 5, 1941.

70 TNA, AIR 8/436, Portal to Cadogan (Permanent Secretary, Foreign Office), October 26, 1941.

71 TNA, AIR 19/215, note for Sinclair, "Bombing of Targets in Rome," December 1942; Sinclair to Churchill, December 4, 1942, 1–2.

72 Ibid., marginalia on "Bombing of Targets in Rome," December 1942; Sinclair to Churchill, December 4, 1942; Sinclair to Portal, December 11, 1942; Foreign Office to British embassy, Bern, December 17, 1942.

73 CCO, Portal papers, Folder 4/File 2, Eden to Churchill, July 14, 1943; TNA, AIR 19/215, Portal to Sinclair, December 3, 1942; Portal to Churchill, July 13, 1943.

74 Warren Kimball, ed., *Churchill and Roosevelt: The Complete Correspondence* (London: Collins, 1984), 2:234–35, Churchill to Roosevelt, June 10, 1943; 250–51, Roosevelt to Churchill, June 14, 1943.

75 TNA, AIR 19/215, RAF Delegation, Washington, DC, to Air Ministry, June 26, 1943.

76 Ibid., Archbishop Temple to Sinclair, July 9, 1943; note by the ACAS (Information), "Air Attacks on Objectives in Rome," July 4, 1943; minute by ACAS, July 15, 1943; Sinclair to Temple, July 17, 1943.

77 LC, Eaker papers, Box I.36, North-West African Strategic Air Forces (NWASAF), Report and Evaluation, Rome, July 19, 1943: Rome Railroad Yards, Mission Report.

78 Claudia Baldoli, "Bombing the Eternal City," *History Today*, May 2012, 11; Simone, *Venti angeli sopra Roma*, 262–64.

79 Marco Fincardi, "Gli italiani e l'attesa di un bombardamento della capitale (1940–1943)," in Labanca, *I bombardamenti aerei*, 239.

80 FDRL, Map Room Files, Box 33, CCS to Eisenhower, June 25, 1943; Eisenhower to War Dept., Washington, DC, July 18, 1943.

81 FDRL, Map Room Files, Box 72, OSS Bulletin, July 30, 1943; Fincardi, "Gli italiani e l'attesa di un bombardamento della capitale," 233–34, 242–43.

82 Raymond Klibansky, ed., *Mussolini's Memoirs, 1942–1943* (London: Phoenix Press, 2000), 51–55.

83 TNA, FO 898/175, Report of Col. Thornhill's Mission, November 16, 1943, App. 14.

84 LC, Spaatz papers, Box 94, Total tonnage dropped, August 1942–May 1944.

85 TNA, AIR 20/5387, Ministry of Public Works, Statistics on Bomb Damage, June 10, 1940–March 31, 1943. The list did not include buildings lost in Milan, Genoa, and Palermo.

86 Paggi, *Il "popolo dei morti,"* 114–17.

87 Cited in Gloria Chianese, *"Quando uscimmo dai rifugi": Il Mezzogiorno tra guerra e dopoguerra (1943–46)* (Rome: Carocci editore, 2004), 35–36. On Naples see Gabriella Gribaudi, Guerra totale: Tra bombe alleate e violenza naziste; Napoli e il fronte meridionale, 1940–44 (Turin: Bollati Boringhieri, 2005), chap. 3.

88 See Gabriella Gribaudi, "Tra discorsi pubblici e memorie private: Alcune riflessioni sui bombardamenti e sulla loro legittimazione," in Labanca, *I bombardamenti aerei*, 315–18; Marco Gioannini, "Bombardate l'Italia: Le strategie alleate e le vittime civili," in Gioannini and Massobrio, *Bombardate l'Italia*, 92–93.

89 Claudia Baldoli, "Spring 1943: The Fiat Strikes and the Collapse of the Italian Home Front," *History Workshop Journal* 72 (2011): 183–86.

90 TNA, AIR 20/5383, report from the Commune of Rome, May 1943; province of Genoa, "Situation During the Month of May 1943"; province of Turin, "Situation during the Month of May 1943"; province of Palermo, "Report for the Month May 1943."

91 Origo, *War in Val d'Orcia*, 35, 39–40, entry for April 1, 1943.

92 Paggi, *Il "popolo dei morti,"* 119; the prayer in Origo, *War in Val d'Orcia*, 36. The best account of the role of religion in Italian efforts to cope with bombing is Claudia Baldoli, "Religion and Bombing in Italy," in Baldoli, Knapp, and Overy, *Bombing, States and Peoples*, 136–53.

93 TNA, AIR 19/215, VCAS (Air Marshal Evill) to Sinclair, July 31, 1943; CCO, Portal papers, Folder 3/File 3, Portal to Tedder, July 30, 1943.

94 TNA, FO 898/496, leaflet, "Fuori i tedeschi—oppure ferro e fuoco," July 29, 1943; leaflet, "Il governo," August 14, 1943.

95 FDRL, Map Room Files, Box 33, CCS to Eisenhower (n.d.); message for the president from Gen. Marshall, August 2, 1943; Churchill to Roosevelt, August 3, 1943; memorandum for the president from Admiral Leahy, August 16, 1943; CCS to Eisenhower, August 15, 1943; Simone, *Venti angeli sopra Roma*, 301.

96 FDRL, Map Room Files, Box 72, OSS Bulletin, August 3, 1943; report, August 17, 1943, "Italy: Badoglio's Position vis-à-vis the Germans." Details of raids in Chianese, *"Quando uscimmo dai rifugi,"* 31; Gioannini and Massobrio, *Bombardate l'Italia*, 360–61, 365–66.

97 The best guide to the complex web of command and the thicket of acronyms is Wesley F. Craven and James L. Cate, *The Army Air Forces in World War II*, vol. 3, *Europe: Argument to V-E Day* (Chicago: University of Chicago Press, 1951), 326–35.

98 AFHRA, Disc MAAF 233, American embassy (Economic Warfare Division) to NAAF, December 16, 1943, 2, 4–5.

99 Ibid., HQ NAAF (Norstad) to commanding general NAAF, November 14, 1943.

100 Ibid., Cabell to Eaker, Bombing Directive, March 1, 1945.

101 LC, Spaatz papers, Box 94, Total tonnage AAF-RAF, January–May 1944.

102 Richard G. Davis, *Carl A. Spaatz and the Air War in Europe* (Washington, DC: Center for Air Force History, 1993), App. 10 and App. 18.

103 TNA, AIR 8/777, Harris to Portal, November 13, 1942.

104 Harvey, "Italian War Effort," 41.

105 TNA, AIR 20/283, Statistics on Bombing, February–November 1943.

106 British Air Ministry, *The Rise and Fall of the German Air Force, 1933–1945* (London: Arms & Armour Press, 1983), 219, 258–60, 265–66.

107 Davis, *Carl A. Spaatz*, App. 24.

108 Joseph Heller, *Catch-22* (London: Vintage, 1994), 55.

109 Ronald Schaffer, *Wings of Judgment: American Bombing in World War II* (New York: Oxford University Press, 1985), 47–48; Solly Zuckerman, *From Apes to Warlords, 1904–19: An Autobiography* (London: Hamish Hamilton, 1978), 211.

110 TNA, AIR 19/215, HQ MAAF (Eaker) to Air Ministry, April 7, 1944.

111 Schaffer, *Wings of Judgment*, 49–50.

112 TNA, AIR 19/215, Slessor to Air Ministry, February 29, 1944; Ismay to Churchill, March 1, 1944; conclusions of CoS meeting, March 2, 1944.

113 AFHRA, Disc MAAF 233, Norstad to Allied Tactical Air Forces, Bombing Directive: Florence Marshaling Yards, March 2, 1944.

114 TNA, AIR 19/215, Slessor to Sinclair, May 7, 1944.

115 FDRL, Map Room Files, Box 33, Marshall to Eisenhower, September 27, 1943; JCS to Eisenhower, November 2, 1943; TNA, AIR 8/438, Foreign Office to JSM, Washington, DC, September 23, 1943; CCS memorandum, "Rome Open City," September 24, 1943; Osborne (ambassador to Holy See) to Foreign Office, October 14, 1943.

116 TNA, AIR 19/215, Osborne to Foreign Office (War Cabinet distribution), November 6, 1943; resident minister Algiers (Harold Macmillan) to Foreign Office, November 8, 1943.

117 FDRL, Map Room Files, Box 33, JCS memorandum for the president, December 4, 1943; memorandum for the president from Admiral Leahy, December 5, 1943; Roosevelt to Cordell Hull, December 7, 1943.

118 TNA, WO 204/12508, Maj. F. Jones, "Report on the Events Leading to the Bombing of the Abbey of Monte Cassino on 15 February 1944," October 14, 1949, 7–13.

119 Ibid., 20–23.

120 James Parton, *"Air Force Spoken Here": General Ira Eaker and the Command of the Air* (Bethesda, MD: Adler & Adler, 1986), 363–64.

121 Peter Caddick-Adams, *Monte Cassino: Ten Armies in Hell* (London: Preface Publishing, 2012), 145–46.

122 TNA, AIR 8/777, Wilson to the CoS, March 9, 1944.

123 John Slessor, *The Central Blue: Recollections and Reflections* (London: Cassell, 1956), 576–77.

124 TNA, WO 204/12508, "Report on the Events," 31–33; App. 3, Doc. 26A, HQ Fifth Army memorandum, "Monte Cassino Abbey," February 28, 1944.

125 Slessor, *Central Blue*, 574, reproducing his memorandum for Portal, April 16, 1944.

126 Zuckerman, *Apes to Warlords*, 198, 210–11.

127 Slessor, *Central Blue*, 566–68.

128 AFHRA, Disc MAAF 233, MAAF Bombing Directive, February 18, 1944.

129 TNA, AIR 20/2050, Summary of MAAF Effort, Operation "Strangle," March 15–May 11, 1944.

130 Ibid., Summary of MAAF Effort: Operation "Diadem," May 12–June 22; Parton, *"Air Force Spoken Here,"* 383–84.

131 AFHRA, Disc MAAF 230, memorandum by Lt. Col. W. Ballard, Analysis Section, MAAF, September 28, 1944, 2.

132 UEA, Zuckerman archive, SZ/BBSU/1/49, interview with Kesselring, August 23, 1945, 3.

133 Paolo Ferrari, "Un arma versatile: I bombardamenti strategici anglo-americani e l'industria italiana," in Paolo Ferrari, ed., *L'aeronautica italiana: Una storia del Novecento* (Milan: Franco Angeli, 2004), 401–2; Alessandro Massignani, "L'industria bellica italiana e la Germania nella seconda guerra mondiale," *Italia Contemporanea* 190 (1993), 195; Natalini, *I rapporti tra aeronautica italiana e tedesca,* 165–66.

134 Lutz Klinkhammer, *L'occupazione tedesca in Italia, 1943–1945* (Turin: Bollati Boringhieri, 1996), 78–84; Natalini, *I rapporti tra aeronautica italiana e tedesca,* 166–67.

135 Andrea Villa, *Guerra aerea sull'Italia (1943–1945)* (Milan: Angelo Guerini, 2010), 217–18.

136 Achille Rastelli, *Bombe sulla città: Gli attacchi aerei alleati; Le vittime civili a Milano* (Milan: Mursia, 2000), 145–47, 184. The figure of 197 dead recorded from the other seventeen raids is clearly an incomplete figure, but an indication that casualties in most raids on Italy at this stage of the war in a city with wide experience of bombing were relatively low.

137 Villa, *Guerra aerea*, 219–20; Natalini, *I rapporti tra aeronautica italiana e tedesca*, 167.

138 AFHRA, Disc MAAF 230, MAAF, Target Committee, minutes of meeting, February 23, 1945, 4.

139 Villa, *Guerra aerea*, 226–27. For other estimates see vera Zamagni, "Italy: How to Lose the War and Win the Peace," in Mark Harrison, ed., *The Economics of World War II* (Cambridge: Cambridge University Press, 1998), C207–12.

140 Ferrari, "Un arma versatile," 397–99. Housing loss in Zamagni, "Italy: How to Lose the War," 212, who shows that because of additional housing built between 1938 and 1941, the stock of housing was almost the same in 1945 as in 1938.

141 FDRL, Map Room Files, Box 72, OSS Bulletin, "The Situation in Italy," Bern station, September 27, 1943.

142 TNA, AIR 8/777, D'Arcy Osborne to the Foreign Office, March 22, 1944.

143 TNA, AIR 19/215, Eden to Sinclair, May 15, 1944.

144 Ibid., Sinclair to Eden, May 17, 1944; CCO, Portal papers, Folder 5, Evill to Churchill, May 6, 1944.

145 Origo, *War in Val d'Orcia*, 71–72, entry for August 1, 1944.

146 Corrado Di Pompeo, *Più della fame e più dei bombardamenti: Diario dell'occupazione di Roma* (Bologna: Il Mulino, 2009), 107, 112, entries for February 25 and March 25, 1944.

147 For a full account see Klinkhammer, *L'occupazione tedesca*, 318–66.

148 Baldoli, "Religion and Bombing in Italy," 146–47.

149 Simone, *Venti angeli sopra Roma*, 301.

150 Anna Scattigno, "Il clero in Toscana durante il passaggio del fronte: Diari e cronache parrocchiali," in Labanca, *I bombardamenti aerei*, 253–58.

151 Franco Manaresi, "I bombardamenti aerei di Bologna," in Bersani and Monaco, *Delenda Bononia*, 47–48; Manaresi, "La protezione antiaerea," in ibid., 40.

152 Manaresi, "La protezione antiaerea," in Bersani and Monaco, *Delenda Bononia*, 34–35.

153 ACS, Ministero dell'Interno, Busta 106, memorandum for the Milan prefect, March 4, 1943, "Ricoveri pubblici."

154 Baldoli and Knapp, *Forgotten Blitzes*, 188–89.

155 TNA, AIR 20/5387, Province of Palermo, report for the month, May 1943; inspector of Air Raid Protection, Rome, "Report Concerning Air Attack on Rome 13 August 1943," 13–14.

156 Cortesi, "Evacuation in Italy," 65–66.

157 Lanari and Musso, "Un dramma mal calcolato," 28–29.

158 Calculated from Mauro Maggiorani, "Uscire dalla città: Lo sfollamento," in Brunella Dalla Casa and Alberto Preti, eds., *Bologna in Guerra, 1940–1945* (Milan: Franco Angeli, 1995), 376.

159 Cortesi, "Evacuation in Italy," 70–71.

160 Baldoli and Knapp, *Forgotten Blitzes*, 144–49.

161 The only full account is George Southern, *Poisonous Inferno: World War II Tragedy at Bari Harbour* (Shrewsbury: Airlife, 2002).

162 NARA, RG 107, Box 139, HQ Army Service Forces for Lovett, "United States Chemical Warfare Committee: Periodic Report of Readiness for Chemical Warfare as of January 1 1945," 114–15.

163 AFHRA, Disc MAAF 230, Brig. Gen. Cabell (Operations) to Eaker, "Employment of Chemical Weapons by the Allied Air Forces," August 12, 1944; Operational Memorandum, "Chemical Warfare—Policy for Offensive Action," August 11, 1944.

164 Coccoli, "I 'fortilizi inespugnabili della civiltà italiana,'" 414; Marta Nezzo, "La protezione delle città d'arte," in Labanca, *I bombardamenti aerei*, 202.
165 Nezzo, "La protezione delle città d'arte," 205–6; Nezzo, "Defence of Works of Art," 112–13.
166 Coccoli, "I 'fortilizi inespugnabili della civiltà italiana,'" 415; Nezzo, "La protezione delle città d'arte," 202–3.
167 Lynn Nicholas, *The Rape of Europa: The Fate of Europe's Treasures in the Third Reich and the Second World War* (London: Macmillan, 1994), 260.
168 Baldoli and Knapp, *Forgotten Blitzes*, 228–29.
169 Ibid., 236–38.
170 TNA, AIR 8/777, Osborne to the Foreign Office, March 22, 1944; Baldoli and Knapp, *Forgotten Blitzes*, 238–39.
171 Chianese, *"Quando uscimmo dai rifugi,"* 41, for figure on Sicily.
172 Istituto Nazionale di Statistica, *Morti e dispersi per cause belliche negli anni, 1940–45* (Rome, 1957), Table 2.8. For a discussion of the problems of assessing wartime casualties see Baldoli and Knapp, *Forgotten Blitzes*, App., 260–62.
173 ACS, Ministero dell'Interno, Busta 22, Railway Commissariat, Palermo to Interior Ministry, April 1, 1943; TNA, FO 898/496, PWE, "Foglio volante," July 5, 1943.

Chapter 6. Bombing Friends, Bombing Enemies: Germany's New Order

1 *Target: Germany; The U.S Army Air Forces' Official Story of the VIII Bomber Command's First Year over Europe* (London: HMSO, 1944).
2 USSBS, "Over-All Report (European Theater)," Washington, DC, September 30, 1945, 2. The figures are France 21.8 percent, Other 7.5 percent, Austria, Hungary, Balkans 6.7 percent.
3 TNA, FO 898/313, memorandum by Ritchie Calder, PWE, "Bombing (military, economic and morale objectives)," 1–5.
4 TNA, AIR 19/217, War Cabinet, July 24, 1940, memorandum by the air minister, "Bombardment Policy in France."
5 TNA, AIR 20/5831, AI to Air Ministry (Plans), August 17, 1940, encl. "Fringe Targets: Norway, Denmark, Holland, Belgium and France."
6 Ibid., AI to Air Ministry (Plans), August 20, 1940, "France: Targets Within 30 Miles of Coast Dunkirk—Bordeaux"; February 13, 1941, "France: Fringe Targets Within 30 miles of the Coast of Occupied France"; February 6, 1941, "Belgium: Fringe Targets from North to South" (included three rated three-star); "Norway: Industrial Fringe Targets from North to South" (seven marked three-star).
7 Ibid., Air Marshal Leigh-Mallory to AI (AI9), July 1, 1941.
8 Ibid., "Information received from Lt. Commander Molenburg," August 7, 1940.
9 TNA, FO 371/28541, British embassy (Bern) to French department (Foreign Office), July 31, 1941.
10 TNA, FO 898/312, Mr. Harman (Foreign Office) to Air Commodore Groves (PWE), February 14, 1942; Mr. Harman to Brigadier Brookes (PWE), February 18, 1942; PWE, "Extrait du journal clandestin belge 'Le Peuple' du mois d'avril 1942."

11 Joris van Esch, "Restrained Policy and Careless Execution: Allied Strategic Bombing on the Netherlands in the Second World War" (Fort Leavenworth, KS: School of Advanced Military Studies, 2011), 18–19.

12 TNA, AIR 40/1720, Report from Military Intelligence Division, G2, MAAF, May 30, 1944, on "Centre de documentation des services spéciaux," Annex 1, "Comparative Table of Bombing in France since 1940" (based on Bulletin de Sécurité Militaire, Direction Technique des Services Spéciaux, May 21, 1944).

13 TNA, FO 371/28541, French department, Foreign Office, to W. Mackenzie (Air Ministry), May 15, 1941; Foreign Office to Mackenzie, May 31, 1941; W. Law (MoI) to Foreign Office, May 7, 1941.

14 TNA, AIR 2/7503, Samuel Hoare (British ambassador to Spain) to the Foreign Office, September 27, 1941, encl. "Note verbale" from Le Havre Municipal Council; Foreign Office 371/28541, Hoare to Foreign Office, August 19, 1941, encl. "Note verbale" from the French embassy in Madrid. See also Claudia Baldoli and Andrew Knapp, *Forgotten Blitzes: France and Italy Under Allied Air Attack, 1940–1945* (London: Continuum, 2012), 35.

15 FO 371/28541, Air Vice Marshal Medhurst to Mack (Foreign Office), October 17, 1941; AIR 2/7503, minute by DBOps for Foreign Office, October 25, 1941.

16 For a full account of German exploitation in 1940–41 see Hein Klemann and Sergei Kudryashov, *Occupied Economies: An Economic History of Nazi-Occupied Europe, 1939–1945* (London: Berg, 2012), 75–88.

17 TNA, FO 371/28541, War Cabinet paper, "Air Policy—Attack on Factories in Occupied France," November 6, 1941; AIR 19/217, War Cabinet conclusions, October 20, 1941. On RAF restrictions on bombing Paris, CCO, Portal papers, Folder 2/File 1, Portal to Churchill, September 7, 1941.

18 Michael Stenton, *Radio London and Resistance in Occupied Europe: British Political Warfare, 1939–1943* (Oxford: Oxford University Press, 2000), 13, 88; Ben Pimlott, *Hugh Dalton* (London: Macmillan, 1985), 331–35, 343.

19 Stenton, *Radio London and Resistance*, 100.

20 CCO, Portal papers, Folder 9/File 3, AI, "Air Activity over Norway," April 24, 1942.

21 TNA, FO 898/313, Ritchie Calder, "Notes for Morale Bombing," August 18, 1941; Calder to Reginald Leeper, "RAF and Morale-Making in Occupied Countries," August 25, 1941, 1–2; Calder memorandum, "Bombing (military, economic and morale objectives)," March 1942, 1, 4–5.

22 TNA, FO 898/437, PWE memorandum, "Why Drop Nickels?," September 1943, 1.

23 Ibid., 4.

24 TNA, FO 898/319, PWE Report, April 14, 1942.

25 TNA, FO 898/319, directive for BBC European Service, "Plan for Propaganda (Occupied Countries) to Accompany RAF Attacks," March 1942.

26 TNA, FO 898/234, T. G. Harman to Leeper (PWE), "Plan for Propaganda to Belgium," February 26, 1941; Report on an interview with Mademoiselle Depuich [October 1941], 2; "Plan of Propaganda to Holland," 6.

27 TNA, AIR 19/217, paper from the Air Ministry (Plans) for the War Cabinet, November 11, 1941; director of plans (Air Ministry) to Churchill, January 8,

1942; Norman Bottomley to acting C-in-C, Bomber Command, February 5, 1942; FO 371/28541, War Cabinet, November 6, 1941; FO 371/31999, Attlee to Churchill, January 8, 1942.

28 TNA, AIR 20/4768, Directorate of Bombing, "Incendiary Attacks in Occupied Countries," November 13, 1941.

29 RAFM, Harris papers, H47, Bottomley to Harris, "Psychological Aspects of Bombing Policy," April 14, 1942.

30 TNA, FO 898/313, PWE, "Progress Report No. 1," March 1942.

31 TNA, AIR 19/217, Baker to Bottomley, March 4, 1942; casualty figures from Matt Perry, "Bombing Billancourt: Labour Agency and the Limitations of the Public Opinion Model of Wartime France," *Labour History Review* 77 (2012): 49, and SHAA, Vincennes, Paris, 3D/48/Dossier 2, Direction de Défense Passive, Bulletin de Renseignements, March 30, 1942.

32 SHAA, 3D/112/Dossier 3, propagande anglo-saxonne, "Aux populations de la France occupée"; TNA, FO 898/319, P. C. Groves (PWE) to the BBC, February 6, 1942.

33 TNA, FO 898/319, memorandum by I. Black (PWE), "The Bombardment of Paris Factories," March 5, 1942.

34 Ibid., U.S. embassy London to Sinclair, encl. message from Admiral Leahy, March 13, 1942; Eden to Sinclair, March 16, 1942.

35 Perry, "Bombing Billancourt," 61–62.

36 TNA, FO 898/319, PWE Report, "The Bombing of French Factories," April 10, 1942; PWE Report, "Evidence of Effect of RAF Bombing on Morale in Enemy-Occupied Territories," April 14, 1942, 3.

37 TNA, AIR 19/217, Sir Samuel Hoare (Madrid) to Foreign Office, June 9, 1942; U.S. embassy (Bern) to secretary of state, June 22, 1942.

38 Lindsey Dodd and Andew Knapp, "'How Many Frenchmen Did You Kill?': British Bombing Policy towards France (1940–1945)," *French History* 22 (2008): 474–80.

39 Simon Kitson, "Criminals or Liberators? French Public Opinion and the Allied Bombings of France, 1940–1945," in Claudia Baldoli, Andrew Knapp, and Richard Overy, eds., *Bombings, States and Peoples in Western Europe, 1940–1945* (London: Continuum, 2011), 279–84.

40 TNA, AIR 8/428, Harris to Portal, April 7, 1942: "Real Blitzes as Opposed to Dock Bombing."

41 TNA, AIR 9/187, Slessor to all air commands, "Bombardment Policy," October 29, 1942.

42 TNA, AIR 19/217, Bottomley to Harris, January 14, 1943; Baldoli and Knapp, *Forgotten Blitzes*, 25–26; Dodd and Knapp, "'How Many Frenchmen Did You Kill?,'" 479–80.

43 Arthur T. Harris, *Bomber Offensive* (London: Collins, 1947), 136–37.

44 TNA, ADM 199/2467, NID to assistant chief of naval staff, "U/Boat Bases— West Coast of France," January 13, 1943; HQ Eighth Bomber Command to NID, February 18, 1943.

45 TNA, FO 898/319, PWE minute, "Campaign to the French Coastal Populations," June 1, 1942; Peck to Baker, enclosing leaflet "Aux ouvriers français des ports de l'ouest," June 1942.

Notes   503

46 TNA, ADM 199/2467, NID Report, "The Bombing of the U-Boat Bases,"
March 11, 1943; NID, "Factual Statement on the Lorient Base and on Bombing
Attacks."

47 SHAA, 3D/322/Dossier 1, Air Force Report, "Bombardement de l'Arsenal et
de la ville de Lorient, Janvier–Mars 1943," 6–7, 9.

48 TNA, FO 898/319, PWE, draft statement on the bombing of Lorient; Air Ministry (VCAS) to PWE, February 23, 1943.

49 TNA, ADM 199/2467, NID note, "Lorient"; AIR 19/218, Bottomley to Harris,
April 6, 1943. See too Charles Webster and Noble Frankland, *The Strategic Air
Offensive against Germany* (London: HMSO, 1961), 2:96–97.

50 Stephen Flower, *Barnes Wallis' Bombs: Tallboy, Dambuster and Grand Slam* (Stroud:
Tempus, 2002), 124–25, 189–90, 192–95, 412.

51 TNA, ADM 199/2467, NID, French division, "France: Reaction to the Paris
and Anvers Raids," April 18, 1943.

52 TNA, FO 371/36038, Air Ministry to Foreign Office, December 30, 1942; Political Intelligence Dept, Foreign Office, "Avis no. 7," BBC French Service, December 29, 1942.

53 Eddy Florentin, *Quand les Alliés bombardaient la France, 1940–1945* (Paris: Perrin,
2008), 159–61.

54 SHAA, 3D/322/Dossier 1, "Bombardement du centre industriel de Boulogne-
Billancourt, 4 Avril 1943"; BN, Défense Passive, Bulletin de Renseignements,
March–May 1943, Table V.

55 TNA, FO 371/36038, minute by William Strang (Foreign Office), April 16,
1943; AIR 19/218, Massigli to Eden, April 16, 1943.

56 TNA, AIR 19/218, telegram JSM, Washington, DC, to Air Ministry, April 28,
1943; Sinclair to Eden, May 9, 1943; Air Vice Marshal Evill to Eaker, May 10,
1943; Sinclair to Eden, June 5, 1943.

57 Richard Overy, "The Luftwaffe and the European Economy, 1939–1945," *Militärgeschichtliche Mitteilungen* 55 (1979): 58–60.

58 Florentin, *Quand les Alliés bombardaient la France*, 238–43.

59 Roger Freeman, *The Mighty Eighth War Diary* (London: Jane's, 1981), 112, 115.

60 BN, Bulletin de Renseignements, October 1943, 8–11.

61 TNA, AIR 40/1720, MAAF Military Intelligence Division Report from Centre
de Documentation des Services Spéciaux, 7, 18.

62 SHAA, 3D/322/Dossier 1, "Bombardement de l'usine Dunlop, 16 septembre,
1943," 1.

63 Ibid., Armée de l'Air, "Bombardements aériens en territoire français: Avant
propos: 1944" [May 1944], 1–3.

64 Ibid., "Bombardement de St. Étienne, 26 Mai 1944," 7–8.

65 BN, Bulletin d'Information de la Défense Passive, May 1944, 7–8; SHAA,
3D/322/Dossier 1, "Bombardement de la gare d'Avignon, 27 Mai, 25 Juin
1944," 4.

66 Baldoli and Knapp, *Forgotten Blitzes*, 51–53, 55.

67 Ibid., 92–93, 99.

68 BA-MA, RL 13/21, Luftschutz-Abteilung 15, Allgemeiner Erfahrungsbericht,
April 30, 1942.

69 SHAA, 3D/44/Dossier 2, Admiral Duplat to General Pintor (president of IAC), November 17, 1940; IAC to French delegation, April 1, 1941; IAC to French delegation, September 23, 1941.

70 Ibid., German Armistice Commission (Air Force) to French delegation, November 27, 1941.

71 Ibid., note for the French delegation at Wiesbaden, February 3, 1942; note from Direction des Services de l'Armistice to French delegation, June 3, 1942; Sécrétariat à l'Aviation, "Obscurissement de la zone non occupée," August 6, 1942.

72 Ibid., memorandum of the German Armistice Commission to the French delegation, November 27, 1941, 1.

73 BA-MA, RL 7/141, Intelligence Report, Air Fleet 3, "Aufbau der französischen Heimatluftverteidigung," May 1, 1943; Intelligence Report, Air Fleet 3, August 1, 1943.

74 SHAA, 3D/44/Dossier 1, SGDA, CoS to the Interior Ministry, June 5, 1943, encl. memorandum from Air Fleet 3, February 16, 1943; Direction de la Défense Aérienne to SGDA, Bureau C, June 24, 1943.

75 BA-MA, RL 7/141, Air Fleet 3, Intelligence Report, May 1, 1943; SGDA to Secrétariat Général à la Défense Terrestre, April 27, 1943.

76 SHAA, 3D/279/Dossier 2, Commandant de Groupe de SAP, Lyon, February 20, 1943; Dossier 1, Defense Secretary to Minister of Industrial Production, "Service d'alerte," October 1, 1943; SGDA, Bureau A, "Recapitulation des effectifs des formations de SAP," September 13, 1943; SGDA to Director of Air Services, Northern Zone, September 20, 1943. The main centers in the south were at Lyon, Montpellier, Marseille, Limoges, and Toulouse; in the north at Paris, Tours, Dijon, Bordeaux, and Reims.

77 SHAA, 3D/43/Dossier 1, Plenipotentiary Air Fleet 3 to SGDA, August 20, 1943; 3D/44/Dossier 1, Plenipotentiary Air Fleet 3 to SGDA, July 4, 1943.

78 Baldoli and Knapp, *Forgotten Blitzes*, 92–93.

79 SHAA, 3D/44/Dossier 1, SGDA to Air Fleet 3, March 20, 1944; "Formations et effectifs réels, Défense Passive," January 15, 1944; Ministry of Interior, "Instruction: Service de protection," April 26, 1944.

80 BA-MA, RL 7/141, Plenipotentiary Air Fleet 3, "Tätigkeitsbericht 1.2–15.3. 1944," March 19, 1944; SHAA, 3D/44/Dossier 1, SGDA to Plenipotentiary Air Fleet 3, March 20, 1944.

81 BA-MA, RL 13/24, *Kriegstagebuch* [War Diary] of LS-Abt. 34, entries for January 15, 16, and 29–30, 1943; SHAA, 3D/322/Dossier 1, "Bombardement de l'Arsenal et de la ville de Lorient," May 1944, 4–5, 8.

82 Michael Schmiedel, "Les Allemands et la défense passive en France: Le cas de Nantes," in Michèle Battesti and Patrick Facon, eds., *Les bombardements alliés sur la France durant la Seconde Guerre Mondiale: Stratégies, bilans matériaux et humains* (Paris: Ministère de la Défense, 2009), 53–55.

83 BN, Bulletin de Renseignements, October 1943, "L'Oeuvre accomplice par le Service Municipal de la ville de Nantes."

84 Julia Torrie, *"For Their Own Good": Civilian Evacuations in Germany and France, 1939–1945* (New York: Berghahn, 2010), 115–17.

85 Ibid., 125–27.

86 SHAA, 3D/44/Dossier 1, SIPEG to Directorate of Passive Defense, January 26, 1944; Pierre Laval to all ministries, February 4, 1944, 1.

87 Michael Schmiedel, "Orchestrated Solidarity: The Allied Air War in France and the Development of Local and State-Organised Solidarity Movements," in Baldoli, Knapp, and Overy, *Bombing, States and Peoples,* 207–11.

88 Ibid., 211–13; Torrie, *"For Their Own Good,"* 153–54; Baldoli and Knapp, *Forgotten Blitzes,* 150–51.

89 SHAA, 3D/44/Dossier 1, Laval to all ministers, February 4, 1944, 1–2, 5; SIPEG to Directorate of Passive Defense, January 26, 1944.

90 Ibid., Laval to all ministers, 2–3; Torrie, *"For Their Own Good,"* 159; Baldoli and Knapp, *Forgotten Blitzes,* 153–54.

91 Olivier Dumoulin, "A Comparative Approach to Newsreels and Bombing in the Second World War: Britain, France and Germany," in Baldoli, Knapp, and Overy, *Bombing, States and Peoples,* 302–3; Baldoli and Knapp, *Forgotten Blitzes,* 118–19.

92 Lindsey Dodd, "'Relieving Sorrow and Misfortune'? State, Charity, Ideology and Aid in Bombed-Out France, 1940–1944," in Baldoli, Knapp, and Overy, *Bombing, States and Peoples,* 83–85.

93 Ibid., 80–81, 86–87.

94 Torrie, *"For Their Own Good,"* 135–37.

95 Stenton, *Radio London and Resistance,* 110.

96 TNA, FO 898/457, PWE, "Annual Dissemination of Leaflets by Aircraft and Balloon, 1939–1945."

97 LC, Spaatz papers, Box 157, memorandum, CoS of Eighth Air Force, August 11, 1942; USAAF Adjutant-General to commander of Eighth Air Force, September 25, 1943.

98 Ibid., Box 157, Frank Kaufman, Chief (Leaflet Section) PWB, to Robert Bruce Lockhart (PWE), April 22, 1944, "Leaflet Production and Dissemination Program Between Now and D-Day"; Political Warfare Division (SHAEF), "The Leaflet Propaganda Front," June 19, 1944, 3.

99 Philippe Boiry, *Paris sous les bombes: Auteuil, septembre 1943* (Paris: L'Harmattan, 2000), 37–38.

100 TNA, AIR 40/1720, MAAF Military Intelligence Division Report, May 30, 1944, 1, 8. See too Kitson, "Criminals or Liberators?," 285–88.

101 TNA, AIR 40/1720, MAAF Military Intelligence Division Report, May 30, 1944, 13–15.

102 TNA, FO 371/41984, minute for Churchill from Desmond Morton, May 9, 1944; Direction Technique des Services Spéciaux, "Les bombardements alliés et leurs repercussions sur le moral français," April 25, 1944.

103 Ibid., "France: Cardinals' Message to British and U.S. Episcopates," May 14, 1944; archbishop of Westminster to French cardinals, May 20, 1944.

104 Patrick Facon, "Les bombardements alliés sur la France durant la Seconde Guerre Mondiale: Enjeux, thématiques et problématiques," in Battesti and Facon, *Les bombardements alliés,* 13–14.

105 Baldoli and Knapp, *Forgotten Blitzes,* 211–13.

106 TNA, AIR 40/1720, MAAF, Military Intelligence Division Report, May 30, 1944, 17–18.

107 Baldoli and Knapp, *Forgotten Blitzes,* 210–11; Torrie, *"For Their Own Good,"* 113.

108 Jean-Marie Pontaut and Éric Pelletier, eds., *Chronique d'une France occupée: Les rapports confidentiels de la gendarmerie, 1940–1945* (Neuilly-sur-Seine: Michel Lafon, 2008), 444, "Rapport du commandant de gendarmerie de la Charente," July 1943.

109 BA-MA, RL 7/141, Intelligence Report, Air Fleet 3, August 1, 1943, 2; minute, July 14, 1943, "Überwachung der einzustehenden französischen Eisenbahnflakbatterien"; Intelligence Report, Air Fleet 3, September 2, 1943.

110 Ibid., Intelligence Report, Air Fleet 3, October 1, 1943; SHAA, 3D/43/Dossier 1, Sec. Gen. of Air Defense to Col. von Merhart, September 18, 1943; plenipotentiary of the German Air Force, Paris, to Col. Cornillon (Liaison Service), November 18, 1943.

111 BA-MA, RL 7/141, Intelligence Report, Air Fleet 3, August 1, 1943, 2.

112 UEA, Zuckerman archive, SZ/AEAF/7, War Cabinet Defence Committee, April 5, 1944, 1.

113 TNA, AIR 40/1882, Bottomley to Portal, January 18, 1944; Bufton to Harris, January 14, 1944.

114 TNA, AIR 37/752, Harris memorandum for Leigh-Mallory, "The Employment of the Night Bomber Force in Connection with the Invasion of the Continent," January 13, 1944.

115 LC, Spaatz papers, Box 143, Spaatz to Eisenhower [n.d. but April 1944].

116 Ibid., Arnold to Spaatz, April 24, 1944; see too Anderson to Spaatz, February 28, 1944, 3, "there be complete accord . . . as to the continuation of POINT-BLANK."

117 Walter W. Rostow, *Pre-Invasion Bombing Strategy: General Eisenhower's Decision of March 25, 1944* (Aldershot: Gower, 1981), 13–14, 88–98; Solly Zuckerman, *From Apes to Warlords, 1904–19: An Autobiography* (London: Hamish Hamilton, 1978), 220–24, 231–45.

118 Lord Arthur Tedder, *With Prejudice: The War Memoirs of Marshal of the Royal Air Force Lord Tedder* (London: Cassell, 1966), 520–25.

119 CCO, Portal papers, Folder 5, Portal to Churchill, March 29, 1944; UEA, Zuckerman archive, SZ/AEAF/7, Defence Committee minutes, April 5, 1944; Defence Committee minutes, April 13, 1944.

120 CCO, Portal papers, Folder 5, Portal to Churchill, April 13, 1944; UEA, Zuckerman archive, SZ/AEAF/7, Defence Committee, note by the secretary, "Bombing Policy"; Zuckerman memorandum, "Estimates of Civilian Casualties," April 6, 1944.

121 Ibid., "Number of Fatal Casualties" [n.d. but April 1944]; "Casualties Among French Civilians Resulting from Rail Centre Attacks."

122 Warren Kimball, ed., *Churchill and Roosevelt: The Complete Correspondence,* vol. 3, *Alliance Declining* (London: Collins, 1984), 122–23, Churchill to Roosevelt, May 7, 1944, and 127, Roosevelt to Churchill, May 11, 1944; Tedder, *With Prejudice,* 531–32.

123 BN, Bulletin de Renseignements, April 1944, 16; Bulletin d'Information de la Défense Passive, August 1944, 18.

124 SHAA, 3D/322/Dossier 1, "Tableau des projectiles explosifs lancés de janvier 1942 à août 1944."

125 BN, Bulletin d'Information de la Défense Passive, May 1944, 7–8.

126 Details from ibid., June 1944, 1–3, 6–7, 10–11, 13.

127 SHAA, 3D/322/Dossier 1, "Bombardement de St. Étienne, 26 mai 1944," 4, 7–8; "Bombardement de Marseille, 27 mai 1944," 1, 4–6; BN, Bulletin d'Information de la Défense Passive, "Bombardement de Saint-Étienne, 26 mai 1944," 2–4; "Bombardement de Marseille, 27 mai 1944," 2–5; statistics on human losses from Georges Ribeill and Yves Machefert-Tassin, *Une saison en Enfer: Les bombardements des Alliés sur les rails français (1942–1945)* (Migennes: 2004), 142–43.

128 TNA, FO 371/41984, memorandum from the French Commissariat for Foreign Affairs, "Allied Bombardment of Metropolitan France," May 5, 1944; AIR 19/218, telegram for the War Cabinet from the British chargé d'affaires in Algiers, June 8, 1944. See too Baldoli and Knapp, *Forgotten Blitzes*, 233–35, for a fuller discussion of the views of the French Resistance.

129 FDRL, Map Room Files, Box 73, deputy director OSS to the White House, May 17, 1944, encl. OSS Bulletin from Madrid.

130 Baldoli and Knapp, *Forgotten Blitzes*, 29.

131 FDRL, Map Room Files, Box 72, OSS Bulletin, February 8, 1944.

132 CCAC, Bufton papers, Bufton papers, 3/51, SHAEF Report, "The Effect of the Overlord Plan to Disrupt Enemy Rail Communications," 1–2.

133 Georges Ribeill, "Aux prises avec les voies ferrées: Bombarder ou saboter? Un dilemme revisité," in Battesti and Facon, *Les bombardements alliés*, 162.

134 TNA, AIR 37/719, Solly Zuckerman, "Times for Re-Establishment of Traffic through Bombed Rail Centres and Junctions and Across Bridges," August 11, 1944, 2, and App. 9, 11; Ribeill and Machefert-Tassin, *Une saison en Enfer*, 138–39.

135 Ribeill and Machefert-Tassin, *Une saison en Enfer*, 153–55, 204; TNA, AIR 37/719, Railway Research Service, London, "German Military Movements in France and Belgium August 1944," October 13, 1944, App. B.

136 Steve Darlow, *Sledgehammers for Tintacks: Bomber Command Combats the V-1 Menace, 1943–1944* (London: Grub Street, 2002), 195–97.

137 Joachim Ludewig, *Rückzug: The German Retreat from France, 1944* (Lexington: University Press of Kentucky, 2012), 23–24.

138 Maud Jarry, "Les bombardements des sites V en France," in Battesti and Facon, *Les bombardements alliés*, 39–43.

139 TNA, AIR 40/1882, Report from Dewdney (RE8) to Bufton, April 15, 1944, "Crossbow—Large Sites."

140 TNA, AIR 19/218, Sinclair to Portal, July 9, 1944.

141 TNA, AIR 40/1882, Air Marshal Colyer to director of intelligence, July 2, 1944; AI Report, "Examination of 'Crossbow' Sites in the Cherbourg Peninsula," July 6, 1944.

142 Jean Quellien, "Les bombardements pendant la campagne de Normandie," in Battesti and Facon, *Les bombardements alliés*, 61–68.

143 BN, Bulletin de Renseignements, June, July, and August 1944; Quellien, "Les bombardements," 70–71.

144 TNA, AIR 37/761, AEAF HQ, "Observations of RAF Bomber Command's Attack on Caen July 7 1944," July 14, 1944, 3–5.

145   William Hitchcock, *The Bitter Road to Freedom: A New History of the Liberation of Europe* (New York: Free Press, 2008), 32–33, 34, 44.

146   USMA, Bradley papers, War Diary, vol. 3, entry for July 24, 1944; LC, Spaatz papers, Box 84, USSTAF HQ, "Report of Investigation of Tactical Bombing, 25 July 1944," August 14, 1944, 3–4.

147   USMA, Bradley papers, War Diary, vol. 3, entry for July 25, 1944. Eisenhower was reported as saying, "I don't believe they [strategic bombers] can be used in support of ground troops."

148   Ibid., memorandum by Bradley, "Combined Air and Ground Operations West of St. Lô on Tuesday 25 July 1944"; Bradley memorandum for the record, November 19, 1944.

149   Andrew Knapp, "The Destruction and Liberation of Le Havre in Modern Memory," *War in History* 14 (2007): 477–82.

150   TNA, AIR 8/842, minute by Portal, January 7, 1945; Bottomley to Portal, January 9, 1945; Bottomley to Portal, January 25, 1945; Florentin, *Quand les Alliés bombardaient la France*, 596–97.

151   Ibid., 597–98.

152   TNA, AIR 40/1720, MAAF Intelligence Division Report, May 30, 1944, 14.

153   Baldoli and Knapp, *Forgotten Blitzes*, gives a figure of 54,631 for overall deaths; Florentin, *Quand les Alliés bombardaient la France*, 600–601, gives both the official figure (53,601) and the postwar estimate of 67,078, which seems to have been derived from the assertion that of the 133,000 civilian dead in France, half came from bombing. Danièle Voldman suggests a figure of at least 70,000, but does not explore how this figure is arrived at. See Voldman, "Les populations civiles, enjeux du bombardement des villes (1914–1945)," in Stéphane Audoin-Rouzeau, Annette Becker, Christian Ingrao, and Henry Rousso, eds., *La violence de guerre, 1914–1945* (Paris: Éditions complexes, 2002), 161–62.

154   LC, Spaatz papers, Box 143, notes by Spaatz for Eisenhower, April 1944.

155   LC, Doolittle papers, Doolittle to Spaatz, August 10, 1944; Doolittle to Eisenhower, August 5, 1944.

156   TNA, AIR 19/218, Portal to Eaker, June 3, 1943.

157   CCO, Portal papers, Folder 9/File 2, Stefan Zamoyski to Peirse, January 4, 1941, encl. letter from Polish Army HQ, December 30, 1940; Peirse to Sikorski, January 15, 1941; Tami Davis Biddle, *Rhetoric and Reality in Air Warfare: The Evolution of British and American Ideas About Strategic Bombing, 1914–1945* (Princeton, NJ: Princeton University Press, 2002), 191–92.

158   TNA, AIR 19/218, Eden to Sinclair, July 7, 1944; Sinclair to Eden, July 15, 1944; Sinclair to Vice CoS (RAF), July 26, 1944; Richard H. Levy, "The Bombing of Auschwitz Revisited: A Critical Analysis," *Holocaust and Genocide Studies* 10 (1996): 268–69, 272–73. See too Michael Neufeld and Michael Berenbaum, eds., *The Bombing of Auschwitz: Should the Allies Have Attempted It?* (New York: St. Martin's/United States Holocaust Memorial Museum, 2000), 263–64, 266–67, for the full correspondence.

159   TNA, AIR 19/218, Bottomley to ACAS (Intelligence), August 2, 1944; V. Cavendish-Bentinck (JIC) to Bottomley, August 13, 1944. See too Stuart Erdheim, "Could the Allies Have Bombed Auschwitz-Birkenau?," *Holocaust and Genocide Studies* 11 (1997): 131–37.

160 David Wyman, *The Abandonment of the Jews: America and the Holocaust, 1941–1945* (New York: Pantheon, 1984), 290–91, 295; Levy, "Bombing of Auschwitz," 277–78. The McCloy letters of August 14 and November 18, 1944, are reproduced in Neufeld and Berenbaum, *Bombing of Auschwitz*, 274, 279–80.

161 TNA, AIR 19/218, Richard Law (Foreign Office) to Sinclair, September 1, 1944; Air Ministry to Spaatz, September 1, 1944.

162 Neufeld and Berenbaum, *Bombing of Auschwitz*, has fifteen papers arguing the case for or against.

163 AFHRA, Disc MAAF 233, Economic Warfare Division to Maj. Ballard, NAAF, "Strategic Target Priority List," December 16, 1943. Oświęcim was number fourteen out of fifteen priority targets.

164 Joseph White, "Target Auschwitz: Historical and Hypothetical German Responses to Allied Attack," *Holocaust and Genocide Studies* 16 (2002): 58–59; Randall Rice, "Bombing Auschwitz: US 15th Air Force and the Military Aspects of a Possible Attack," *War in History* 6 (1999): 205–30.

165 Norman Davies, *Rising '44: The Battle for Warsaw* (London: Macmillan, 2003), 310–11.

166 TNA, AIR 8/1169, Portal to Slessor, August 5, 1944; Slessor to Portal, August 6, 1944; Slessor to Portal, August 9, 1944.

167 Ibid., AMSSO to British Mission, Moscow, August 8, 1944; Slessor to Portal, August 16, 1944. See too Halik Kochanski, *The Eagle Unbowed: Poland and the Poles in the Second World War* (London: Allen Lane, 2012), 419.

168 TNA, AIR 8/1169, Despatches from MAAF on Dropping Operations to Warsaw [n.d.]; Davies, *Rising '44*, 311; Kochanski, *Eagle Unbowed*, 408–11. The successful drops included 4.5 million rounds of ammunition, 14,000 hand grenades, 250 antitank guns, and 1,000 Sten guns.

169 TNA, FO 898/151, PWE, "Rumanian Policy," December 2, 1943; PWE minute, "Air Attack on Bucharest," March 20, 1944.

170 C. O. Richardson, "French Plans for Allied Attacks on the Caucasus Oil Fields, January–April 1940," *French Historical Studies* 8 (1973): 136–42; Ronald Cooke and Roy Nesbit, *Target: Hitler's Oil; Allied Attacks on German Oil Supplies, 1939–45* (London: William Kimber, 1985), 25–28, 37–38.

171 TNA, AIR 9/138, Air Ministry (Plans) for the CAS, "Appreciation on the Attack of the Russian Oil Industry," April 2, 1940, 1–2; memorandum by Air Ministry (Plans), "Russian Oil Industry in the Caucasus," May 30, 1940.

172 Ibid., "Memorandum on the Russian Petroleum Industry in the Caucasus," App. E, "Calculation of Effort"; Cooke and Nesbit, *Target: Hitler's Oil*, 49–51.

173 TNA, AIR 9/138, letter from E. A. Berthoud (British embassy, Cairo) to HQ RAF Middle East, June 13, 1941; Air Ministry (Plans) to HQ RAF Middle East, June 13, 1941; Air Ministry to British C-in-C (India) [n.d. but June 1941].

174 TNA, PREM 3/374/6, HQ RAF Middle East to Air Marshal Evill, June 14, 1942.

175 TNA, FO 898/176, PWB, Allied Forces HQ, "Psychological Warfare in the Mediterranean Theater," August 31, 1945, 4–5, 15.

176 LC, Spaatz papers, Box 157, Col. Earl Thomson to director of intelligence, USSTAF Europe, February 1, 1944.

177 Ibid., Carl Spaatz article for *Air Force Star*, "Leaflets: An Important Weapon of Total War," 5.

178 Ibid., Lt. Col. Lindsey Braxton to Spaatz [n.d. but February 1944]; Thomson to director of intelligence, USSTAF, February 1, 1944. For an example of whole bundles falling see TNA, FO 898/437, H. Knatchbull-Hugesson (British embassy, Ankara) to MoI, January 18, 1944, on Bulgarian leaflets.
179 TNA, FO 898/176, "Psychological Warfare in the Mediterranean Theater," August 31, 1945, 14; FO 898/318, Dr. Vojacek to PWE, February 19, 1943; Dr. Vojacek to PWE, January 11, 1943.
180 TNA, FO 898/318, memorandum by Elizabeth Barker (PWE), "Probable Effects of Intensified Large-Scale Bombing of Densely Populated Areas in South-Eastern Europe," January 26, 1944; PWE memorandum, "The Bombing of Romania, Austria, Czechoslovakia and Jugoslavia" [n.d.].
181 Ibid., PWE regional director (Czechoslovakia) to Calder, January 25, 1944.
182 TNA, FO 898/437, Wing Commander Burt-Andrews to Elizabeth Barker, December 10, 1943; FO 898/318, Barker memorandum, January 26, 1944, 2.
183 Webster and Frankland, *Strategic Air Offensive*, 4:508–9, 518.
184 TNA, AIR 20/3238, HQ RAF Middle East to Air Ministry, April 26, 1942; Air Ministry memorandum, "Tactical Appreciation on the Interruption of Axis Supplies of Oil from Romania," December 21, 1942; Churchill to Portal, February 28, 1943; Portal to Churchill, March 9, 1943.
185 TNA, PREM 3/374/6, Churchill to Eden, March 10, 1943; Ismay to Churchill, May 18, 1943; Eisenhower to the CCS, May 25, 1943.
186 TNA, AIR 20/3238, Air Ministry to Mediterranean Air Command, May 31, 1943; Portal to Tedder, June 2, 1943.
187 Ibid., Eisenhower to CCS, May 25, 1943; PREM 3/374/6, minute by Ismay, June 19, 1943; Ismay to Churchill, June 23, 1943.
188 TNA, AIR 20/3238, Lt. Col. W. Forster to E. Berthoud (Cairo embassy), August 3, 1943.
189 Cooke and Nesbit, *Target: Hitler's Oil*, 86–87.
190 TNA, AIR 20/3238, HQ RAF Middle East to Air Ministry, August 3, 1943; Report, "Bombing of Roumanian Oilfields," August 9, 1943. For details of both raids see Wesley F. Craven and James L. Cate, *The Army Air Forces in World War II*, vol. 2, *Europe: Torch to Pointblank* (Chicago: University of Chicago Press, 1949), 481–84; Cooke and Nesbit, *Target: Hitler's Oil*, 89–96.
191 TNA, AIR 20/3238, H. Knatchbull-Hugesson to the Foreign Office, August 8, 1943.
192 AFHRA, Disc MAAF 233, HQ MAAF, "Notes on Strategic Bombardment Conference, Gibraltar, 8–10 November 1943," November 11, 1943, 2; Richard G. Davis, *Bombing the European Axis Powers: A Historical Digest of the Combined Bomber Offensive, 1939–1945* (Maxwell AFB, AL: Air University Press, 2006), 322–24.
193 FDRL, Map Room Files, Box 136, Arnold to Spaatz, March 17, 1944; CoS to Wilson and Spaatz, March 22, 1944; AFHRA, Disc MAAF 233, Air Ministry to Eaker, April 11, 1944.
194 *Akten zur deutschen auswärtigen Politik. Serie E, Band VIII: 1 Mai 1944 bis 8 Mai 1945* (Göttingen: Vandenhoeck & Ruprecht, 1979), 99–100, Joachim von Ribbentrop to Bucharest embassy, June 6, 1944.
195 Ibid., 114, OKW to Ambassador Ritter, June 7, 1944 (appointment from June 4, 1944).

196 TNA, AIR 23/7776, Fifteenth Air Force, "The Air Battle of Ploesti," March 1945, 2, 6, 61–68, 81.

197 Cooke and Nesbit, *Target: Hitler's Oil,* 105–6; AFHRA, Disc MAAF 233, HQ MAAF, Operation Order for Mining the Danube, April 25, 1944.

198 *Akten zur deutschen auswärtigen Politik. Serie E, Band VIII,* 383–84, Budapest embassy to the German Foreign Office, August 30, 1944; Karl-Heinz Frieser, ed., *Das Deutsche Reich und der Zweite Weltkrieg,* Band 8, *Die Ostfront 1943/44* (Stuttgart: DVA, 2007), 782–800.

199 NARA, RG 107, Lovett papers, Box 28, Eaker to Robert Lovett, September 18, 1944; FDRL, President's Secretary's Files, Box 82, Arnold to Roosevelt, September 22, 1944.

200 TNA, WO 204/1068, Air Ministry to Air Force HQ, Algiers, April 4, 1944.

201 AFHRA, Disc MAAF 233, HQ MAAF, Intelligence Section, "The Balkan Situation—Possibilities of Air Attack," April 24, 1944, 13.

202 Ibid., Portal to Spaatz and Wilson, May 30, 1944.

203 NARA, RG 107, Box 28, Eaker to Lovett, September 18, 1944, 2–3; Davis, *Bombing the European Axis Powers,* 323.

204 AFHRA, Disc MAAF 233, HQ MAAF, Intelligence Section, "Priority List of Strategic Targets in MAAF Area," July 31, 1944.

205 Ibid., Operational Instruction 111, March 21, 1945, 1–2.

206 Ibid., cipher message to all air staff, April 24, 1944. See too John Deane, *The Strange Alliance: The Story of American Efforts at Wartime Co-operation with Russia* (London: John Murray, 1947), 128–29.

207 TNA, AIR 20/3229, HQ MAAF to Air Ministry, November 9, 1944; JSM Washington to AMSSO (Moscow), November 19, 1944; Deane, *Strange Alliance,* 132–34.

208 Ibid., Spaatz to Arnold, November 29, 1944; U.S. Joint Chiefs to John Deane, Military Mission, Moscow; JPS memorandum, "Co-ordination of Allied Operations," January 23, 1945.

209 FDRL, President's Secretary's Files, Box 82, Arnold to Roosevelt, September 17, 1944, 2.

210 Gordon Daniels, ed., *A Guide to the Reports of the United States Strategic Bombing Survey* (London: Royal Historical Society, 1981), xxii; Wagenführ story in John K. Galbraith, *A Life in Our Times: Memoirs* (London: Andre Deutsch, 1981), 235–36.

211 See, e.g., Maria Bucur, *Heroes and Victims: Remembering War in Twentieth-Century Romania* (Bloomington: Indiana University Press, 2009), 198–99, 212–13.

212 A. Korthals Altes, *Luchtgevaar: Luchtaanvallen op Nederland, 1940–1945* (Amsterdam: Sijthoff, 1984), 332.

213 Groninger Archieven, http://www.groningerarchieven.nl, "Groningers gedood door Engelse bommen."

214 Altes, *Luchtgevaar,* 332.

215 TNA, FO 898/312, Foreign Office to Brigadier Brooks (PWE), February 14, 1942.

216 TNA, AIR 9/187, Slessor (ACAS) to all air commands, October 29, 1942, "Bombardment Policy," 3.

217 Pieter Serrien, *Tranen over Mortsel: De laatste getuigen over het zwaarste bombardement ooit in België* (Antwerp: Standaard Uitgeverij, 2008), 12–19. See too the report in TNA, ADM 199/2467, NID, minute on bombing of Antwerp, April 20, 1943.

218 TNA, AIR 40/399, HQ VIII Bomber Command, ORS Report on April 5, 1943, operations, May 18, 1943.

219 Serrien, *Tranen over Mortsel*, 41, from an anonymous letter on the bombing.

220 TNA, FO 898/312, Foreign Office to director of political warfare (Operations), April 9, 1943.

221 TNA, AIR 19/218, Sinclair to Portal, April 30, 1943; Sinclair to Portal, May 3, 1943; Air Marshal Evill to Eaker, May 10, 1943, encl. App. A, "Targets in Occupied Countries Recommended for Attack by the Eighth Air Force"; Air Ministry to Harris, May 21, 1943.

222 Ibid., Portal to Eaker, June 3, 1943; Sinclair to Eden, June 5, 1943; Eden to Sinclair, June 11, 1943.

223 Ibid., draft leaflet, "An Urgent Warning to the Belgian People," June 16, 1943; Bottomley to Harris and Eaker, June 25 and July 15, 1943; E. Michiels van Verduynen (Netherlands Foreign Office) to Sir Nevile Bland (British ambassador), June 23, 1943.

224 Esch, "Restrained Policy and Careless Execution," 35–36.

225 Altes, *Luchtgevaar*, 167–69.

226 LC, Eaker papers, Box I.20, Eaker to Portal, July 28, 1943; TNA, AIR 19/218, Portal to Eaker, July 25, 1943.

227 Pieter Serrien, "Bombardementen in België tijdens WOII," http://pieterserrien.wordpress.com/2010/10/11.

228 Esch, "Restrained Policy and Careless Execution," 37–38.

229 B. A. Sijes, *De Razzia van Rotterdam, 10–11 November 1944* (Gravenhage: Martinus Nijhoff, 1951), 27–29.

230 On aircraft see Overy, "The Luftwaffe and the European Economy," 58–60.

231 NARA, Film T901, Roll 2018, Reichsgruppe Industrie, "Anlagen zu den Ergebnissen der Industrieberichterstattung: Belgien, Oktober 1943"; ibid., "Niederlande, November 1943."

232 Altes, *Luchtgevaar*, 334–36.

233 Netherlands Institute, Amsterdam, File 222, *Haagsche Courant*, May 30, 1944; *Het Nieuws van den Dag*, January 30, 1942.

234 TNA, FO 898/234, Stockholm Despatch to PWE, November 25, 1943 (based on information from a Dutch visitor to Sweden).

235 AFHRA, 519.12535, U.S. Strategic Air Forces in Europe, "Heavy Bombers: Targets in Low Countries."

236 Serrien, "Bombardementen in België," 2–3.

237 Esch, "Restrained Policy and Careless Execution," 39–44; Altes, *Luchtgevaar*, 189–98, 202–3. The figure of 800 dead includes those classified as missing, those who died of wounds, and a number of German personnel.

238 LC, Spaatz papers, Box 157, PWB chief, Leaflet Section, to Bruce Lockhart (PWE), April 22, 1944; Esch, "Restrained Policy and Careless Execution," 43–44.

239 Henrik Kristensen, Claus Kofoed, and Frank Weber, *Vestallierede luftangreb: I Danmark under 2. Verdenskrig* (Aarhus: Aarhus Universitetsforlag, 1988), 2:731–32.

240 Ibid., 2:742–43, 745–47, 748.

241 LC, Spaatz papers, Box 67, "Status of Combined Bomber Offensive: First Phase, April 1–August 31 [1943]."

242 TNA, AIR 2/8002, memorandum by the Norwegian minister of foreign affairs, December 1, 1943; Laurence Collier (Foreign Office) to Eden, November 26, 1943.

243 Ibid., Air Ministry, "Priority Targets in Norway" [n.d. but April 1944]; Norwegian high command, "Comments on Priority Targets in Norway," May 31, 1944.

244 Ibid., Norwegian embassy to Air Ministry, November 2, 1944; Norwegian embassy to Collier, December 13, 1944; Maurice Dean (Air Ministry) to Foreign Office, January 11, 1945; on the raid, Martin Middlebrook and Chris Everitt, *The Bomber Command War Diaries* (Leicester: Midland Publishing, 2000), 609.

245 AFHRA, Disc MAAF 233, HQ MAAF, Intelligence Section, "V-Weapons," March 27, 1945; Altes, *Luchtgevaar*, 302–3; TNA, AIR 37/999, SHAEF Air Defense Division, "An Account of the Continental Crossbow Operation 1944–1945," 1, 13.

246 Serrien, "Bombardementen in België," 3.

247 CCAC, Hodsoll papers, HDSL 5/4, Sir John Hodsoll, "Review of Civil Defence 1944," 1, 13; TNA, AIR 37/999, SHAEF, "Continental Crossbow," 24.

248 TNA, AIR 37/999, SHAEF, "Continental Crossbow," 7–9, 19–20, 23.

249 Serrien, "Bombardementen in België," 1, 3–4.

250 Altes, *Luchtgevaar*, 293; Esch, "Restrained Policy and Careless Execution," 45–47.

251 Altes, *Luchtgevaar*, 324; Esch, "Restrained Policy and Careless Execution," 5. The figure of 8,000 was calculated by the Netherlands Institute of War Documentation, Amsterdam. Uncertainty over the exact figure derives partly from the difficulty in distinguishing between deaths from aerial bombing and deaths from artillery bombardment or ground strafing.

252 TNA, AIR 2/7894, Arthur Street (Air Ministry) to Orme Sargent (Foreign Office), "Draft Broadcast to the Dutch People," March 21, 1945; E. Michiels van Verduynen (Dutch ambassador) to Eden, June 15, 1945.

253 Ibid., Street to Alexander Cadogan (Foreign Office), June 30, 1945.

254 Ibid., Mary C. van Pesch-Wittop Koning to King George VI, December 20, 1945.

255 Ibid., A. Rumbold (Foreign Office) to M. Low (Air Ministry), March 4, 1946; Low to Rumbold, March 18, 1946.

256 TNA, AIR 19/218, Sinclair to Eden, June 5, 1943; Eden to Sinclair, June 11, 1943.

Epilogue. Lessons Learned and Not Learned: Bombing into the Postwar World

1 Lord Tedder, "Air Power in War: The Lees Knowles Lectures," Air Ministry pamphlet 235, September 1947, 13.

2 USMA, Lincoln papers, Box 5, File 5/2, presentation to the president by Maj. Gen. Lauris Norstad, October 29, 1946, "Postwar Military Establishment," 11. Also 5, "future war" will be "truly total," and 6, "We must prepare for total war."

3 Ibid., File 5/2, "Industrial Mobilization," lecture to the General Session of the National Industrial Conference Board, May 28, 1947.

4 Tedder, "Air Power in War," 12–13; USMA, Lincoln papers, Box 5, File 5/2, address by Lauris Norstad, National War College, "U.S. Vital Strategic Interests," November 22, 1946, 2 (emphasis in both originals).

5 RAFM, Bottomley papers, AC 71/2/97, director of command and staff training to Bottomley, April 23, 1947; TNA, AIR 20/6361, Air Ministry Exercise Thunderbolt, vol. 1, August 1947, foreword by Lord Tedder; UEA, Zuckerman archive, SZ/BBSU/3/75, Exercise Thunderbolt, Joining Instructions, pt. 2.

6 UEA, Zuckerman archive, SZ/BBSU/3/75, Exercise Thunderbolt: Précis Folder, August 10–17, 1947; on the economy, TNA, AIR 20/6361, Air Ministry Exercise Thunderbolt, Presentation and Report, vol. 2, item 20: "Neither the day nor the night offensive succeeded in their strategic task of destroying the enemy's economy."

7 Tedder, "Air Power in War," 13. See also TNA, AIR 20/6361, Exercise Thunderbolt, vol. 2, item 20, 130.

8 RAFM, Bottomley papers, B2318, "Thunderbolt Exercise: Note on the Potentialities of Biological Warfare," August 13, 1947; note by Bottomley [n.d. but August 1947].

9 USMA, Lincoln papers, Box 5, File 5/2, Somervell address, "Industrial Mobilization," 7.

10 Ibid., draft address by Gen. Wedemeyer to the National War College on "Strategy," January 15, 1947, 4, 16, 21.

11 Ibid., Norstad, "Presentation Given to the President," October 27, 1946, 1, 6.

12 Ibid., File 5/3, Maj. Gen. O. Weyland, Air Force–Civilian Seminar, Maxwell AFB, May 20, 1947.

13 Warren Kozak, *LeMay: The Life and Wars of General Curtis LeMay* (Washington, DC: Regnery, 2009), 277–81.

14 TNA, AIR 8/799, Air Ministry (Plans), memorandum for the Defence Committee, October 16, 1946, 1.

15 D. A. Rosenberg, "American Atomic Strategy and the Hydrogen Bomb Decision," *Journal of American History* 66 (1979): 68.

16 TNA, DEFE 10/390, Joint Inter-Service Group for Study of All-Out Warfare (JIGSAW) papers, minutes of meeting February 23, 1960, 1–2; meeting June 2, 1960, 1; meeting August 4, 1960, 2.

17 Kenneth Hewitt, "Place Annihilation: Area Bombing and the Fate of Urban Places," *Annals of the Association of American Geographers* 73 (1983): 278–81.

18 On Britain see Nick Tiratsoo, "The Reconstruction of Blitzed British Cities, 1945–55: Myths and Reality," *Contemporary British History* 14 (2000): 27–44; Stephen Essex and Mark Brayshay, "Boldness Diminished? The Post-War Battle to Replan a Bomb-Damaged Provincial City," *Urban History* 35 (2008): 437–61.

19 Jeffry Diefendorf, *In the Wake of War: The Reconstruction of German Cities after World War II* (New York: Oxford University Press, 1993), 14–15.

20 LSE archive, WILPF/2009/52/3, Mary Phillips (Women's International League), "Germany Today: Report on Visit to British Zone May 9 to 27 1947," 2–3, 5.

21 Leo Grebler, "Continuity in the Rebuilding of Bombed Cities in Western Europe," *American Journal of Sociology* 61 (1956): 465–66.

22 LC, Eaker papers, Box I.30, Intelligence Section MAAF, "What Is the German Saying?," recording "G."

23 Fred Iklé, *The Social Impact of Bomb Destruction* (Norman: University of Oklahoma Press, 1958), 213–15, 218–20.

24 Cited in Tiratsoo, "Reconstruction of Blitzed British Cities," 28.

25 Grebler, "Continuity in Rebuilding," 467–68.

26 Steven Brakman, Harry Garretsen, and Marc Schramm, "The Strategic Bombing of German Cities during World War II and Its Impact on City Growth," *Journal of Economic Geography* 4 (2004): 205, 212.

27 Grebler, "Continuity in Rebuilding," 467.

28 Nicola Lambourne, "The Reconstruction of the City's Historic Monuments," in Paul Addison and Jeremy Crang, eds., *Firestorm: The Bombing of Dresden, 1945* (London: Pimlico, 2006), 151–52, 156–60.

29 Andreas Huyssen, "Air War Legacies: From Dresden to Baghdad," in Bill Niven, ed., *Germans as Victims* (Basingstoke: Palgrave, 2006), 184–89; Peter Schneider, "Deutsche als Opfer? Über ein Tabu der Nachkriegsgeneration," in Lothar Kettenacker, ed., *Ein Volk von Opfern? Die neue Debatte um den Bombenkrieg, 1940–1945* (Berlin: Rohwolt, 2003), 158–65.

30 Mark Connelly and Stefan Goebel, "Zwischen Erinnerungspolitik und Erinnerungskonsum: Der Luftkrieg in Grossbritannien," in Jörg Arnold, Dietmar Süss, and Malte Thiessen, eds., *Luftkrieg: Erinnerungen in Deutschland und Europa* (Göttingen: Wallstein Verlag, 2009), 55–60, 65.

31 I am grateful to Professor Dobrinka Parusheva for supplying me with information on the Bulgarian protests.

BIBLIOGRAPHY AND SOURCES

1. Archive sources
2. Published documents and reports
3. Official histories
4. Contemporary publications and memoirs
5. Publications since 1950

1. Archive Sources

United Kingdom

Air Historical Branch, Northolt, Middlesex
AHB narratives
German document translations, vols. 1–12

Bodleian Library, Oxford
Arthur Ponsonby papers
Richard Stokes papers

Cambridge University Library
Stanley Baldwin papers
Andrew Boyle papers, interviews with Arthur Harris
Templewood Papers

Christ Church, Oxford
Charles Portal papers
Denis Richards archive

Churchill College Archive Centre, Cambridge
Sydney Bufton papers
Chartwell archive

Friends House archive, London
Thomas Foley papers

Imperial War Museum, London
Enemy Document Section papers

Italian Series (Air Force), Boxes 1–25
Erhard Milch documents
Speer Collection, German private firms
Speer Collection, Hamburg and Flensburg series

London School of Economics
Hugh Dalton papers
Fellowship of Reconciliation papers
National Peace Council
Peace Pledge Union papers
Women's International League of Peace and Freedom

National Archives, Kew, London
Admiralty
Air Ministry
Defence Ministry
Foreign Office (Ministry of Economic Warfare, Political Warfare Executive)
Home Office
Ministry of Aircraft Production
Ministry of Home Security
Ministry of Information
Ministry of Supply
Prime Minister's papers
John Slessor papers
War Office

National Library of Wales, Aberystwyth
H. Stanley Jevons papers

Nuffield College, Oxford
Lord Cherwell papers

Parliamentary Archives, Westminster, London
Harold Balfour papers
Beaverbrook papers

RAF Museum, Hendon, London
Norman Bottomley papers
Sholto Douglas papers
Arthur Travers Harris papers
Trafford Leigh-Mallory papers
Richard Peirse papers
Robert Saundby papers
Arthur Tedder papers

Royal Society, London
Patrick Blackett papers

University of East Anglia, Special Collections
Solly Zuckerman archive

France

Château de Vincennes, Archives de la Défense
Archives du secrétariat d'état à l'aviation
Archives du secrétariat général à la défense aérienne, 1940–1944

Germany

Bundesarchiv-Berlin
NS-Partei-Kanzlei
Organisation Todt
Reichsarbeitsministerium
Reichskanzlei
Reichsministerium des Innern
Reichsministerium für Bewaffnung und Munition
Reichspropagandaleitung-NSDAP
Reichswirtschaftsministerium
Statistisches Reichsamt
Wirtschaftsgruppe Gas-und Wasserversorgung

Bundesarchiv-Militärarchiv, Freiburg im Breisgau
Dienststellen für technische Erprobungen der Luftwaffe
Generalluftzeugmeister
Göring-Akten
Kriegswissenschaftliche Abteilung
Luftflotte 3
Luftschutztruppe
Reichsluftschutzbund
Reichsminister der Luftfahrt
Wehrwirtschaft-und Rüstungsstab papers

Italy

Archivio Centrale dello Stato, Rome
Ministero dell'Aeronautica
Ministero dell'Interno

Malta

National Archives of Malta
ARP papers, 1934–1945

Russia

Central Archive of the Ministry of Defense of the Russian Federation (TsAMO), Podolsk
Generalstab der Luftwaffe, Luftwaffe Führungsstab papers
Luftflotte 4 papers
II Fliegerkorps

United States of America

Air Force Historical Research Agency, Maxwell AFB, Alabama
Eighth Air Force archive
Mediterranean Allied Air Forces

Franklin D. Roosevelt Library, Hyde Park, New York
Morgenthau papers
Franklin D. Roosevelt archive

Library of Congress, Washington, D.C.
Frank Maxwell Andrews papers
Henry H. Arnold papers
James Doolittle papers
Ira C. Eaker papers
Curtis LeMay papers
Carl Spaatz papers

National Archives II, College Park, Maryland
RG 18 Army Air Forces
RG 94 Office of the Adjutant-General
RG 107 Robert Lovett papers
RG 165 War Department General Staff
RG 208 Office of War Information
RG 218 Joint Chiefs of Staff
RG 243 USSBS documents

United States Air Force Academy, Colorado Springs
Haywood Hansell papers
Larry Kuter papers
George McDonald papers

United States Military Academy, West Point
Omar Bradley papers
Benjamin A. Dickson papers
George A. Lincoln papers

2. Published Documents and Reports

Akten zur deutschen auswärtigen Politik, 1918–1945. 70 vols. (Göttingen: Vandenhoeck &
    Ruprecht, 1950–95).

Boberach, Heinz, ed. *Meldungen aus dem Reich: Die geheimen Lageberichte des Sicherheitsdienstes der SS, 1938–1945.* 17 vols. Herrsching: Pawlak Verlag, 1984.

Boelcke, Willi, A., ed. *The Secret Conferences of Dr. Goebbels, 1939–1943.* Translated by Ewald Osers. London: Weidenfeld & Nicolson, 1967.

Colville, John. *The Fringes of Power: Downing Street Diaries, 1939–1945.* London: Weidenfeld & Nicolson, 2004.

Committee of the Red Cross. *Protocols Additional to the Geneva Convention of 12 August 1949.* Geneva: ICRC, 1977.

Cox, Sebastian, ed. *The Strategic Air War Against Germany, 1939–1945: The Official Report of the British Bombing Survey Unit.* London: Frank Cass, 1998.

Daniels, Gordon, ed. *A Guide to the Reports of the United States Strategic Bombing Survey.* London: Royal Historical Society, 1981.

Di Pompeo, Corrado. *Più della fame e più dei bombardamenti: Diario dell'occupazione di Roma.* Bologna: Il Mulino, 2009.

Domarus, Max, ed. *Hitler: Reden und Proklomationen.* 3 vols. Munich: Süddeutscher Verlag, 1965.

Eberle, Henrik, and Matthias Uhl, eds. *The Hitler Book: The Secret Dossier Prepared for Stalin.* London: John Murray, 2005.

Foreign and Commonwealth Office. *Churchill and Stalin: Documents from the British Archives.* London: F&CO, 2002.

Fröhlich, Elke, ed. *Die Tagebücher von Joseph Goebbels: Sämtliche Fragmente.* 4 vols. Munich: K. G. Saur, 1987.

Fuehrer Conferences on Naval Affairs, 1939–1945. London: Greenhill, 1990.

Gallup, George, ed. *The Gallup International Public Opinion Polls: Great Britain, 1937–1975.* 2 vols. New York: Random House, 1976.

Gilbert, Martin, ed. *The Churchill War Papers.* Vol. 2, *Never Surrender: May 1940–December 1940.* London: Heinemann, 1994.

Hubatsch, Walter, ed. *Hitlers Weisungen für die Kriegführung.* Munich: Deutscher Taschenbuch Verlag, 1965.

Hunter, Ian, ed. *Winston and Archie: The Collected Correspondence of Winston Churchill and Archibald Sinclair, 1915–1960.* London: Politico's, 2005.

Huston, John, ed. *American Airpower Comes of Age: General Henry H. "Hap" Arnold's World War II Diaries.* 2 vols. Maxwell, AL: Air University Press, 2002.

Isby, David, ed. *Fighting the Bombers: The Luftwaffe's Struggle against the Allied Bomber Offensive.* London: Greenhill, 2003.

Kimball, Warren, ed. *Churchill and Roosevelt: The Complete Correspondence.* 4 vols. London: Collins, 1984.

Klemperer, Victor. *To the Bitter End: The Diaries of Victor Klemperer, 1942–45.* London: Weidenfeld & Nicolson, 1999.

Maurer, M., ed. *The U.S. Air Service in World War I.* 4 vols. Washington, DC: Office of Air Force History, 1978.

Moll, Martin, ed. *"Führer-Erlasse," 1939–1945.* Stuttgart: Franz Steiner Verlag, 1997.

Neitzel, Sönke. *Tapping Hitler's Generals: Transcripts of Secret Conversations, 1942–1945.* Barnsley, UK: Frontline Books, 2007.

Nicolson, Nigel, ed. *Harold Nicolson: Diaries and Letters, 1939–1945.* London: Collins, 1967.

Origo, Iris. *War in Val d'Orcia: An Italian War Diary, 1943–1944.* London: Allison & Busby, 2003.

Pontaut, Jean-Marie, and Éric Pelletier, eds. *Chronique d'une France occupée: Les rapports confidentiels de la gendarmerie, 1940–1945.* Neuilly-sur-Seine: Michel Lafon, 2008.

Roberts, Adam, and R. Guelff, eds. *Documents on the Laws of War.* 3rd ed. Oxford: Oxford University Press, 2000.

Savelli, Alfredo. *Offesa aerea: Mezzi di difesa e protezione.* Milan: Gontrano Martucci, 1936.

Schlange-Schoeningen, Hans. *The Morning After.* London: Gollancz, 1948.

Schramm, Percy, ed. *Kriegstagebuch des OKW: Eine Dokumentation.* 7 vols. Augsburg: Weltbild, 2007.

Speer, Albert. *Spandau: The Secret Diaries.* London: Collins, 1976.

Target: Germany; The U.S. Army Air Forces' Official Story of the VIII Bomber Command's First Year over Europe. London: HMSO, 1944.

Trevor-Roper, Hugh, ed. *Hitler's Table Talk, 1941–1944.* London: Weidenfeld & Nicolson, 1973.

Völker, Karl-Heinz. *Dokumente und Dokumentarfotos zur Geschichte der deutschen Luftwaffe.* Stuttgart: DVA, 1968.

3. Official Histories

British Air Ministry. *The Rise and Fall of the German Air Force, 1933–1945.* London: Arms & Armour Press, 1983.

British Committee on the Preservation and Restitution of Works of Art. *Works of Art in Italy: Losses and Survival in the War; Part I—South of Bologna.* London: HMSO, 1945; *Part II—North of Bologna.* London: HMSO, 1946.

Collier, Basil. *The Defence of the United Kingdom.* London: HMSO, 1957.

Craven, Wesley F., and James L. Cate. *The Army Air Forces in World War II.* 7 vols. Chicago: University of Chicago Press, 1948–58.

Della Volpe, Nicola. *Difesa del territorio e protezione antiaerea, 1915–1943: Storia, documenti, immagini.* Rome: Ufficio storico SME, 1986.

Greenhous, Brereton, Stephen Harris, William Johnston, and William Rawling. *The Crucible of War, 1939–1945: The Official History of the Royal Canadian Air Force.* Vol. 3. Toronto: Toronto University Press/Department of National Defence, 1994.

Herington, John. *Air War against Germany and Italy, 1939–1945.* Canberra: Australian War Memorial, 1954.

———. *Air Power over Europe, 1944–1945.* Canberra: Australian War Memorial, 1963.

Hinsley, F. Harry, et al. *British Intelligence in the Second World War.* 4 vols. London: HMSO, 1979–90.

Hornby, W. *Factories and Plant.* London: HMSO, 1958.

Istituto Nazionale di Stastica. *Morti e dispersi per cause belliche negli anni, 1940–45.* Rome, 1957.

Maurer, M. *Aviation in the U.S. Army, 1919–1939.* 4 vols. Washington, DC: Office of Air Force History, 1987.

Postan, Michael. *British War Production.* London: HMSO, 1957.

Richards, Denis. *Royal Air Force, 1939–1945.* 3 vols. London: HMSO, 1974.

Ritchie, Sebastian. *The RAF, Small Wars and Insurgencies in the Middle East, 1919–1939.* Northolt: Air Historical Branch, 2011.

Statistical Digest of the War. London: HMSO, 1951.

Webster, Charles, and Noble Frankland. *The Strategic Air Offensive Against Germany.* 4 vols. London: HMSO, 1961.

4. Contemporary Publications and Memoirs

Anon. *A Woman in Berlin.* London: Virago, 2005.

Arnold, Henry H. *Global Mission.* New York: Harper & Row, 1949.

Balfour, Harold. *Wings over Westminster.* London: Hutchinson, 1973.

Below, Nicolaus von. *At Hitler's Side: The Memoirs of Hitler's Luftwaffe Adjutant, 1937– 1945.* London: Greenhill, 2001.

Birse, A. H. *Memoirs of an Interpreter.* London: Michael Joseph, 1967.

Bond, Horatio, ed. *Fire and the Air War: A Compilation of Expent Observations.* Boston: National Fire Protection Association, 1946.

Churchill, Winston S. *The Second World War.* 6 vols. London: Cassell, 1948–54.

Ciano, Galeazzo. *Diario, 1937–1943.* Edited by Renzo De Felice. Milan: RCS, 1990.

Davy, M. Bernard. *Air Power and Civilisation.* London: George Allen & Unwin, 1941.

Deane, John. *The Strange Alliance: The Story of American Efforts at Wartime Co-operation with Russia.* London: John Murray, 1947.

Douglas, Sholto. *Years of Command.* London: Collins, 1966.

Douhet, Giulio. *The Command of the Air.* Translated by Dino Ferrari. Washington, DC: Office of Air Force History, 1983.

Flannery, Harry. *Assignment to Berlin.* London: Michael Joseph, 1942.

Gafencu, Grigore. *The Last Days of Europe: A Diplomatic Journey in 1939.* London: Frederick Muller, 1947.

Galbraith, John K. *A Life in Our Times: Memoirs.* London: Andre Deutsch, 1981.

Galland, Adolf. *The First and the Last.* London: Methuen, 1955.

Hampe, Erich. . . . *als alles in Scherben fiel.* Osnabrück: Biblio Verlag, 1979.

Hansell, Haywood. *The Air Plan That Defeated Hitler.* Atlanta: Higgins McArthur, 1972.

Harris, Arthur T. *Bomber Offensive.* London: Collins, 1947.

Harrison, Tom. *Living Through the Blitz.* London: Collins, 1976.

Heinkel, Ernst. *He 1000.* London: Hutchinson, 1956.

Heller, Joseph. *Catch-22.* London: Vintage, 1994.

Hunt, Irmgard. *On Hitler's Mountain: My Nazi Childhood.* London: Atlantic Books, 2005.

Iklé, Fred. "The Effect of War Destruction upon the Ecology of Cities." *Social Forces* 29 (1950–51): 383–91.

Jones, R. V. *Most Secret War: British Scientific Intelligence, 1939–1945.* London: Hamish Hamilton, 1978.

Kesselring, Albert. *The Memoirs of Field-Marshal Kesselring.* London: Greenhill, 2007.

Klibansky, Raymond, ed. *Mussolini's Memoirs, 1942–1943.* London: Phoenix Press, 2000.

Knocke, Heinz. *I Flew for the Führer.* London: Evans Brothers, 1953.

Ley, Willy. *Bombs and Bombing.* New York: Modern Age Books, 1941.

Lloyd, Hugh. *Briefed to Attack: Malta's Part in the African Victory.* London: Hodder & Stoughton, 1949.

Lucas, Laddie. *Malta: The Thorn in Rommel's Side.* London: Penguin, 1993.

Maisky, Ivan. *Memoirs of a Soviet Ambassador.* London: Hutchinson, 1967.

Mitchell, William. *Winged Defense.* New York: G. P. Putnam & Sons, 1925.

Nossack, Hans. *The End: Hamburg, 1943.* Chicago: University of Chicago Press, 2004.

Pile, Frederick. *Ack-Ack: Britain's Defence Against Air Attack During the Second World War.* London: George Harrap, 1949.

Portal, Charles. "Air Force Co-operation in Policing the Empire." *Journal of the Royal United Services Institution* 82 (1937): 343–57.

Reck-Malleczewen, Friedrich. *Diary of a Man in Despair.* London: Audiogrove, 1995.

Rostow, Walter W. *Pre-Invasion Bombing Strategy: General Eisenhower's Decision of March 25, 1944.* Aldershot: Gower, 1981.

Rumpf, Hans. *The Bombing of Germany.* London: White Lion, 1957.

Schneider, Helga. *The Bonfire of Berlin: A Lost Childhood in Wartime Germany.* London: Vintage, 2005.

Shirer, William. *Berlin Diary: The Journal of a Foreign Correspondent, 1934–1941.* London: Hamish Hamilton, 1941.

Slessor, John. *The Central Blue: Recollections and Reflections.* London: Cassell, 1956.

Smith, Howard. *Last Train from Berlin.* London: Cresset, 1942.

Southern, George. *Poisonous Inferno: World War II Tragedy at Bari Harbour.* Shrewsbury: Airlife, 2002.

Speer, Albert. *Inside the Third Reich.* London: Weidenfeld & Nicolson, 1970.

Sperling, Hans. "Deutsche Bevölkerungsbilanz des 2. Weltkrieges." *Wirtschaft und Statistik* 8 (1956): 493–500.

Stein, Anja vom. *Unser Köln: Erinnerungen, 1910–1960.* Erfurt: Sutton Verlag, 1999.

Stengel, E. "Air-Raid Phobia." *British Journal of Medical Psychology* 20 (1944–46): 135–43.

Stewart, Oliver. "The Doctrine of Strategical Bombing." *Journal of the Royal United Services Institution* 81 (1936): 97–101.

Süssmilch, Waltraud. *Im Bunker: Eine Überlebende berichtet vom Bombenkrieg in Berlin.* Berlin: Ullstein, 2004.

Tedder, Lord Arthur. *With Prejudice: The War Memoirs of Marshal of the Royal Air Force Lord Tedder.* London: Cassell, 1966.

Warlimont, Walter. *Inside Hitler's Headquarters, 1939–1945.* London: Weidenfeld & Nicolson, 1964.

Wells, H. G. *The War in the Air.* London: George Bell, 1908.

Wilmott, H. G. "Air Control in Ovamboland." *Journal of the Royal United Services Institution* 83 (1938): 823–29.

Wintringham, Tom. *The Coming World War.* London: Lawrence Wishart, 1935.

Zuckerman, Solly. *From Apes to Warlords, 1904–46: An Autobiography.* London: Hamish Hamilton, 1978.

5. Publications Since 1950

Addison, Paul, and Jeremy Crang, eds. *Firestorm: The Bombing of Dresden, 1945.* London: Pimlico, 2006.

Alegi, Gregory. "Qualità del materiale bellico e dottrina d'impiego italiana nella seconda guerra mondiale: Il caso della Regia Aeronautica." *Storia Contemporanea* 18 (1987): 1197–219.

Altes, A. Korthals. *Luchtgevaar: Luchtaanvallen op Nederland, 1940–1945.* Amsterdam: Sijthoff, 1984.

Aly, Götz. *Hitlers Volksstaat: Raub, Rassenkrieg und Nationaler Sozialismus.* Frankfurt am Main: S. Fischer Verlag, 2005.

Austin, Douglas. *Malta and British Strategic Policy, 1925–1943.* London: Frank Cass, 2004.

Baker, Nicholson. *Human Smoke: The Beginnings of World War II and the End of Civilization.* New York: Simon & Schuster, 2008.

Baldoli, Claudia. "Bombing the Eternal City." *History Today*, May 2012, 11–15.

———. "The 'Northern Dominator' and the Mare Nostrum: Fascist Italy's 'Cultural War' in Malta." *Modern Italy* 13 (2008): 5–20.

——— "Spring 1943: The Fiat Strikes and the Collapse of the Italian Home Front." *History Workshop Journal* 72 (2011): 181–89.

Baldoli, Claudia, and Marco Fincardi. "Italian Society Under Anglo-American Bombs: Propaganda, Experience and Legend, 1940–1945." *Historical Journal* 52 (2009): 1017–38.

Baldoli, Claudia, and Andrew Knapp. *Forgotten Blitzes: France and Italy Under Allied Air Attack, 1940–1945.* London: Continuum, 2012.

Baldoli, Claudia, Andrew Knapp, and Richard Overy, eds. *Bombing, States and Peoples in Western Europe, 1940–1945.* London: Continuum, 2011.

Balfour, Michael, *Propaganda in War, 1939–1945.* London: Routledge, 1979.

Beck, Earl. *Under the Bombs: The German Home Front, 1942–1945.* Lexington: University Press of Kentucky, 1986.

Beer, Wilfried. *Kriegsalltag an der Heimatfront: Alliierten Luftkrieg und deutsche Gegenmassnahmen zur Abwehr und Schadensbegrenzung dargestellt für den Raum Münster.* Bremen: H. M. Hauschild, 1990.

Bergander, Götz. *Dresden im Luftkrieg: Vorgeschichte—Zerstörung—Folgen.* Munich: Heyne Verlag, 1985.

Berrington, Hugh. "When Does Personality Make a Difference? Lord Cherwell and the Area Bombing of Germany." *International Political Science Review* 10 (1989): 9–34.

Best, Geoffrey. *Humanity in Warfare: The Modern History of International Law of Armed Conflict.* London: Routledge, 1980.

Bialer, Uri. "Humanization of Air Warfare in British Foreign Policy on the Eve of the Second World War." *Journal of Contemporary History* 13 (1978): 79–96.

Biddle, Tami Davis. "British and American Approaches to Strategic Bombing: Their Origins and Implementation in the World War II Bomber Offensive." In *Airpower: Theory and Practice*, edited by John Gooch, 91–120. London: Frank Cass, 1995.

———. *Rhetoric and Reality in Air Warfare: The Evolution of British and American Ideas About Strategic Bombing, 1914–1945.* Princeton, NJ: Princeton University Press, 2002.

———. "Wartime Reactions." In *Firestorm: The Bombing of Dresden, 1945,* edited by Paul Addison and Jeremy Crang, 96–122. London: Pimlico, 2006.

Blank, Ralf. "The Battle of the Ruhr, 1943: Aerial Warfare Against an Industrial Region." *Labour History Review* 77 (2012): 35–48.

———. "Kriegsalltag und Luftkrieg an der Heimatfront." In *Das Deutsche Reich und der Zweite Weltkrieg. Band 9, erster Halbband, Die deutsche Kriegsgesellschaft,* edited by Jörg Echternkamp, 357–464. Stuttgart: DVA, 2004.

Boelcke, Willi. *Die Kosten von Hitlers Krieg.* Paderborn: Ferdinand Schöningh, 1985.

Boiry, Philippe. *Paris sous les bombes: Auteuil, septembre 1943.* Paris: L'Harmattan, 2000.

Boll, Michael M., ed. *The American Military Mission in the Allied Control Commission for Bulgaria, 1944–1947: History and Transcripts.* New York: Columbia University Press, 1985.

Boog, Horst. "Strategischer Luftkrieg in Europa, 1943–1944." In Horst Boog et al., *Das Deutsche Reich und der Zweite Weltkrieg. Band 7: Das Deutsche Reich in der Defensive,* 309–11. Stuttgart: DVA, 2001.

————, ed. *The Conduct of the Air War in the Second World War: An International Comparison.* Oxford: Berg, 1992.

Boog, Horst, et al. *Das Deutsche Reich und der Zweite Weltkrieg. Band 4: Der Angriff auf die Sowjetunion.* Stuttgart: DVA, 1983.

Bothe, M., K. J. Partsch, and W. A. Solf, eds. *New Rules for Victims of Armed Conflicts: Commentary on the Two 1977 Protocols Additional to the Geneva Convention of 1949.* The Hague: Martinus Nijhoff, 1982.

Botti, Ferruccio. "Amedeo Mecozzi." In *Actes du colloque international "Précurseurs et prophètes de l'aviation militaire,"* 134–39. Paris: Service historique de l'armée de l'air, 1992.

Bourke, Joanna. *Fear: A Cultural History.* London: Virago, 2005.

Brakman, Steven, Harry Garretsen, and Marc Schramm. "The Strategic Bombing of German Cities During World War II and Its Impact on City Growth." *Journal of Economic Geography* 4 (2004): 201–18.

Brauer, Jurgen, and Hubert van Tuyll. *Castles, Battles, and Bombs: How Economics Explains Military History.* Chicago: University of Chicago Press, 2008.

Brinkhus, Jörn. "Ziviler Luftschutz im 'Dritten Reich'—Wandel seiner Spitzenorganisation." In *Deutschland im Luftkrieg: Geschichte und Erinnerung,* edited by Dietmar Süss, 27–40. Munich: Oldenbourg Verlag, 2007.

Brooks, Geoffrey. *Hitler's Nuclear Weapons.* London: Leo Cooper, 1992.

Brunswig, Hans. *Feuersturm über Hamburg: Die Luftangriffe auf Hamburg im 2. Weltkrieg und ihre Folgen.* Stuttgart: Motorbuch Verlag, 1985.

Buckley, John. *Air Power in the Age of Total War.* London: UCL Press, 1999.

Bucur, Maria. *Heroes and Victims: Remembering War in Twentieth-Century Romania.* Bloomington: Indiana University Press, 2009.

Budden, Michael. "Defending the Indefensible? The Air Defence of Malta, 1936–40." *War in History* 6 (1999): 447–67.

Budiansky, Stephen. *Air Power.* New York: Viking, 2004.

Budrass, Lutz. *Flugzeugindustrie und Luftrüstung in Deutschland, 1918–1945.* Düsseldorf: Droste Verlag, 1998.

Budrass, Lutz, Jonas Scherner, and Jochen Streb. "Fixed-Price Contracts, Learning, and Outsourcing: Explaining the Continuous Growth of Output and Labour Productivity in the German Aircraft Industry During the Second World War." *Economic History Review,* 2nd ser., 63 (2010): 107–36.

Burleigh, Michael. *Moral Combat: A History of World War II.* London: HarperCollins, 2010.

Busch, Dieter. *Der Luftkrieg im Raum Mainz während des Zweiten Weltkrieges, 1939–1945.* Mainz: Hase & Koehler, 1988.

Büttner, Gretl. "Zwischen Leben und Tod." In *Hamburg 1943: Literarische Zeugnisse zum Feuersturm,* edited by Volker Hage, 21–35. Frankfurt am Main: Fischer Verlag, 2003.

Büttner, Ursula. "'Gomorrha' und die Folgen der Bombenkrieg." In Hamburg Forschungsstelle für Zeitgeschichte, *Hamburg im "Dritten Reich,"* 613–32. Göttingen: Wallstein Verlag, 2005.

Caddick-Adams, Peter. *Monte Cassino: Ten Armies in Hell*. London: Preface Publishing, 2012.

Calder, Angus. *The Myth of the Blitz*. London: Jonathan Cape, 1991.

Castioni, Luigi. "I radar industriali italiani: Ricerche, ricordi, considerazioni per una loro storia." *Storia Contemporanea* 18 (1987): 1221–65.

Cate, Johannes ten, Gerhard Otto, and Richard Overy, eds. *Die "Neuordnung" Europas: NS-Wirtschaftspolitik in den besetzten Gebieten*. Berlin: Metropol Verlag, 1997.

Chary, Frederick B. *The Bulgarian Jews and the Final Solution, 1940–1944*. Pittsburgh: University of Pittsburgh Press, 1972.

Chianese, Gloria. *"Quando uscimmo dai rifugi": Il Mezzogiorno tra guerra e dopoguerra (1943–46)*. Rome: Carocci editore, 2004.

Clodfelter, Mark. *Beneficial Bombing: The Progressive Foundations of American Air Power, 1917–1945*. Lincoln: University of Nebraska Press, 2010.

Cluet, M. *L'Architecture du IIIe Reich: Origines intellectuelles et visées idéologiques*. Bern: Peter Lang, 1987.

Coccoli, Carlotta. "I 'fortilizi inespugnabili della civiltà italiana': La protezione antiaerea del patrimonio monumentale italiano durante la seconda guerra mondiale." *Scienza e Beni Culturali* 26 (2010): 409–18.

Connelly, Mark. "The British People, the Press and the Strategic Air Campaign Against Germany, 1939–1945." *Contemporary British History* 16 (2002): 39–58.

———. *Reaching for the Stars: A New History of Bomber Command in World War II*. London: I. B. Tauris, 2001.

———. *We Can Take It! Britain and the Memory of the Second World War*. Harlow: Longman, 2004.

Connelly, Mark, and Stefan Goebel. "Zwischen Erinnerungspolitik und Erinnerungskonsum: Der Luftkrieg in Grossbritannien." In *Luftkrieg: Erinnerungen in Deutschland und Europa*, edited by Jörg Arnold, Dietmar Süss, and Malte Thiessen, 50–65. Göttingen: Wallstein Verlag, 2009.

Conversino, Mark. *Fighting with the Soviets: The Failure of Operation Frantic, 1944–1945*. Lawrence: University Press of Kansas, 1997.

Cooke, Ronald, and Roy Nesbit. *Target: Hitler's Oil; Allied Attacks on German Oil Supplies, 1939–45*. London: William Kimber, 1985.

Cortesi, Elena. "Evacuation in Italy During the Second World War: Evolution and Management." In *Bombing, States and Peoples in Western Europe, 1940–1945*, edited by Claudia Baldoli, Andrew Knapp, and Richard Overy, 59–74. London: Continuum, 2011.

———. "Il 'primo sfollamento' (maggio 1940–ottobre 1942)." In *I bombardamenti aerei sull'Italia*, edited by Nicola Labanca, 177–94. Bologna: Il Mulino, 2012.

Corum, James. "Airpower Thought in Continental Europe Between the Wars." In *The Paths to Heaven: The Evolution of Airpower Theory*, edited by Philip Meilinger, 151–81. Maxwell AFB, AL: Air University Press, 1997.

———. "From Biplanes to Blitzkrieg: The Development of German Air Force Doctrine between the Wars." *War in History* 3 (1996): 85–101.

———. *The Luftwaffe: Creating the Operational Air War, 1918–1940*. Lawrence: University Press of Kansas, 1997.

———. *Wolfram von Richthofen: Master of the German Air War.* Lawrence: University Press of Kansas, 2008.

Cox, Sebastian. "A Comparative Analysis of RAF and Luftwaffe Intelligence in the Battle of Britain." *Intelligence and National Security* 5 (1990): 425–43.

———. "The Dresden Raids: Why and How." In *Firestorm: The Bombing of Dresden, 1945,* edited by Paul Addison and Jeremy Crang, 18–61. London: Pimlico, 2006.

Crampton, Richard J. *Bulgaria.* Oxford: Oxford University Press, 2007.

Crane, Conrad C. *Bombs, Cities and Civilians: American Airpower Strategy in World War II.* Lawrence: University Press of Kansas, 1993.

———. "Evolution of U.S. Strategic Bombing of Urban Areas." *Historian* 50 (1987): 14–39.

Creveld, Martin van. *The Age of Airpower.* New York: Public Affairs, 2011.

———. *Hitler's Strategy, 1940–1941: The Balkan Clue.* Cambridge: Cambridge University Press, 1973.

Curami, Andrea, Paolo Ferrari, and Achille Rastelli. *Alle origini della Breda Meccanica Bresciana.* Brescia: Fondazione Negri, 2009.

Darlow, Steve. *Sledgehammers for Tintacks: Bomber Command Combats the V-1 Menace, 1943–1944.* London: Grub Street, 2002.

Daso, Dik. *Hap Arnold and the Evolution of American Airpower.* Washington, DC: Smithsonian Institution, 2000.

Davies, Norman. *Rising '44: The Battle for Warsaw.* London: Macmillan, 2003.

Davis, Richard G. *Bombing the European Axis Powers: A Historical Digest of the Combined Bomber Offensive, 1939–1945.* Maxwell AFB, AL: Air University Press, 2006.

———. *Carl A. Spaatz and the Air War in Europe.* Washington, DC: Center for Air Force History, 1993.

Dean, Martin. *Robbing the Jews: The Confiscation of Jewish Property in the Holocaust, 1933–1945.* Cambridge: Cambridge University Press, 2008.

Del Boca, Angelo. *I gas di Mussolini.* Rome: Editori Riuniti, 1996.

De Simone, Cesare. *Venti angeli sopra Roma: I bombardamenti aerei sulla Città Eterna.* Milan: Mursia, 1993.

Diefendorf, Jeffry. *In the Wake of War: The Reconstruction of German Cities After World War II.* New York: Oxford University Press, 1993.

Dobinson, Colin. *AA Command: Britain's Anti-Aircraft Defences in World War II.* London: Methuen, 2001.

———. *Building Radar: Forging Britain's Early-Warning Chain, 1935–45.* London: Methuen, 2010.

Dodd, Lindsey. "'Relieving Sorrow and Misfortune'? State, Charity, Ideology and Aid in Bombed-Out France, 1940–1944." In *Bombing, States and Peoples in Western Europe, 1940–1945,* edited by Claudia Baldoli, Andrew Knapp, and Richard Overy, 75–98. London: Continuum, 2011.

Dodd, Lindsey, and Andrew Knapp. "'How Many Frenchmen Did You Kill?': British Bombing Policy Towards France (1940–1945)." *French History* 22 (2008): 469–92.

Donnelly, Peter, ed. *Mrs. Milburn's Diaries: An Englishwoman's Day-to-Day Reflections, 1939–1945.* London: Harrap, 1979.

Donoughue, Bernard, and G. W. Jones. *Herbert Morrison: Portrait of a Politician.* London: Phoenix Press, 2001.

Duffy, James. *Target America: Hitler's Plan to Attack the United States*. Guilford, CT: Lyons Press, 2006.

Dumoulin, Olivier. "A Comparative Approach to Newsreels and Bombing in the Second World War: Britain, France and Germany." In *Bombing, States and Peoples in Western Europe, 1940–1945*, edited by Claudia Baldoli, Andrew Knapp, and Richard Overy, 298–314. London: Continuum, 2011.

Dunning, Christopher. *Courage Alone: The Italian Air Force, 1940–1943*. Manchester: Hikoki Publications, 2010.

———. *Regia Aeronautica: The Italian Air Force, 1923–1945*. Hersham: Ian Allan, 2009.

Edgerton, David. *Britain's War Machine: Weapons, Resources and Experts in the Second World War*. London: Allen Lane, 2011.

Ehlers, Robert S. Jr. "Bombers, 'Butchers,' and Britain's Bête Noire: Reappraising RAF Bomber Command's Role in World War II." *Air Power Review* 14 (2011): 5–18.

———. *Targeting the Third Reich: Air Intelligence and the Allied Bombing Campaigns*. Lawrence: University Press of Kansas, 2009.

Eichholtz, Dietrich. *Geschichte der deutschen Kriegswirtschaft*. 4 vols. Munich: K. G. Saur, 1999.

Emme, E. M. "Technical Change and Western Military Thought." *Military Affairs* 24 (1960): 6–19.

Erdheim, Stuart "Could the Allies Have Bombed Auschwitz-Birkenau?" *Holocaust and Genocide Studies* 11 (1997): 129–70.

Esch, Joris van. "Restrained Policy and Careless Execution: Allied Strategic Bombing on the Netherlands in the Second World War." Fort Leavenworth, KS: School of Advanced Military Studies, 2011.

Essex, Stephen, and Mark Brayshay. "Boldness Diminished? The Post-War Battle to Replan a Bomb-Damaged Provincial City." *Urban History* 35 (2008): 437–61.

Evans, Richard. *The Third Reich at War*. London: Allen Lane, 2008.

Facon, Patrick. "Les Bombardements alliés sur la France durant la Seconde Guerre Mondiale: Enjeux, thématiques et problématiques." In *Les bombardements alliés sur la France durant la Seconde Guerre Mondiale: Stratégies, bilans materiaux et humains*, edited by Michèle Battesti and Patrick Facon, 13–14. Paris: Ministére de la Défense, 2009 (Cahiers du Centre d'Études d'Histoire de la Défense, no. 37).

Farr, Martin. "The Labour Party and Strategic Bombing in the Second World War." *Labour History Review* 77 (2012): 133–54.

Fedorowich, Kent. "Axis Prisoners of War as Sources for British Military Intelligence, 1939–42." *Intelligence and National Security* 14 (1999): 156–78.

Feigel, Lara. *The Love-Charm of Bombs*. London: Bloomsbury, 2013.

Ferrari, Paolo. "Un arma versatile: I bombardamenti strategici anglo-americani e l'industria italiana." In *L'aeronautica italiana: Una storia del Novecento*, edited by Paolo Ferrari, 391–432. Milan: Franco Angeli, 2004.

Fincardi, Marco. "Gli italiani e l'attesa di un bombardamento della capitae (1940–1943)." In *I bombardamenti aerei sull'Italia*, edited by Nicola Labanca, 213–46. Bologna: Il Mulino, 2012.

Florentin, Eddy. *Quand les Alliés bombardaient la France, 1940–1945*. Paris: Perrin, 2008.

Flower, Stephen. *Barnes Wallis' Bombs: Tallboy, Dambusters and Grand Slam*. Stroud: Tempus, 2002.

Foedrowitz, Michael. *Bunkerwelten: Luftschutzanlagen in Norddeutschland.* Berlin: Links Verlag, 1998.

———. *Flak-Towers.* Berlin: Berlin Underworlds Association, 2008.

Formiconi, Paolo. "La protezione e la difesa contraerea del regime fascista: Evoluzione istituzionale." In *I bombardamenti aerei sull'Italia,* edited by Nicola Labanca, 117–30. Bologna: Il Mulino, 2012.

Förster, Gerhard. *Totaler Krieg und Blitzkrieg.* Berlin: Deutscher Militärverlag, 1967.

Förster, Jürgen. "Hitler Turns East: German War Policy in 1940 and 1941." In *From Peace to War: Germany, Soviet Russia and the World, 1939–1941,* edited by Bernd Wegner. Oxford: Berg, 1997.

Freeman, Roger A. *The Mighty Eighth War Diary.* London: Jane's, 1981.

Friedrich, Jörg. *Der Brand: Deutschland im Bombenkrieg, 1940–1945.* Munich: Propyläen Verlag, 2002. Translated by Allison Brown as *The Fire: The Bombing of Germany, 1940–1945.* New York: Columbia University Press, 2006.

Frieser, Karl-Heinz, ed. *Das Deutsche Reich und der Zweite Weltkrieg.* Band 8, *Die Ostfront, 1943/44.* Stuttgart: DVA, 2007.

Fritzsche, Peter. *A Nation of Flyers: German Aviation and the Popular Imagination.* Cambridge, MA: Harvard University Press, 1992.

Furse, Anthony. *Wilfrid Freeman: The Genius Behind Allied Survival and Air Supremacy, 1939 to 1945.* Staplehurst, Kent: Spellmount, 2000.

Futrell, Robert F. *Ideas, Concepts, Doctrine: A History of Basic Thinking in the United States Air Force.* Maxwell AFB, AL: Air University Press, 1971.

Gabriele, Mariano. "L'offensiva su Malta (1941)." In *Italia in guerra: Il secondo anno, 1941,* edited by R. Rainero and A. Biagini, 435–50. Rome: Commissione Italiana di Storia Militare, 1992.

Gardiner, Juliet. *The Blitz: The British Under Attack.* London: HarperCollins, 2010.

Garrett, Stephen A. *Ethics and Airpower in World War II: The British Bombing of German Cities.* New York: St. Martin's, 1993.

Gentile, Gian. *How Effective Is Strategic Bombing? Lessons Learned from World War II to Kosovo.* New York: New York University Press, 2000.

Gilbert, Martin. *Finest Hour: Winston S. Churchill, 1939–1941.* London: Heinemann, 1983.

Gioannini, Marco, and Giulio Massobrio. *Bombardate l'Italia: Storia della guerra di distruzione aerea, 1940–1945.* Milan: Rizzoli, 2007.

Glienke, Stephan. "The Allied Air War and German Society." In *Bombing, States and Peoples in Western Europe, 1940–1945,* edited by Claudia Baldoli, Andrew Knapp, and Richard Overy, 184–205. London: Continuum, 2011.

Goldberg, Alfred, ed. *A History of the United States Air Force, 1907–1957.* Princeton, NJ: Princeton University Press, 1957.

Golücke, Friedhelm. *Schweinfurt und der strategische Luftkrieg, 1943.* Paderborn: Ferdinand Schöningh, 1980.

Gray, Peter. "The Gloves Will Have to Come Off: A Reappraisal of the Legitimacy of the RAF Bomber Offensive Against Germany." *Air Power Review* 13 (2010): 9–40.

Grayling, Anthony. *Among the Dead Cities: Was the Allied Bombing of Civilians in World War II a Necessity or a Crime?* London: Bloomsbury, 2005.

Grayzel, Susan. *At Home and Under Fire: Air Raids and Culture in Britain from the Great War to the Blitz*. Cambridge: Cambridge University Press, 2012.

Grebler, Leo. "Continuity in the Rebuilding of Bombed Cities in Western Europe." *American Journal of Sociology* 61 (1956): 463–69.

Green, William. *Warplanes of the Third Reich*. London: Macdonald, 1970.

Gregor, Neil. "A *Schicksalsgemeinschaft*? Allied Bombing, Civilian Morale, and Social Dissolution in Nuremberg, 1942–1945." *Historical Journal* 43 (2000): 1051–70.

Gretzschel, Matthias. *Als Dresden im Feuersturm versank*. Hamburg: Eller & Richter, 2004.

———. "Dresdan im Dritten Reich." In *Hamburg und Dresden im Dritten Reich: Bombenkrieg und Kriegsende; sieben Beiträge*, 97. Hamburg: Landeszentrale für politische Bildung, 2000.

Gribaudi, Gabriella. *Guerra totale: Tra bombe alleate e violenza naziste; Napoli e il fronte meridionale, 1940–44*. Turin: Bollati Boringhieri, 2005.

———. "Tra discorsi pubblici e memorie private: Alcune riflessioni sui bombardamenti e sulla loro legittimazione." In *I bombardamenti aerei sull'Italia*, edited by Nicola Labanca, 305–24. Bologna: Il Mulino, 2012.

Griehl, Manfred. *Junkers Ju88: Star of the Luftwaffe*. London: Arms & Armour, 1990.

Grimm, Barbara. "Lynchmorde an alliierten Fliegern im Zweiten Weltkrieg." In *Deutschland im Luftkrieg: Geschichte und Erinnerung*, edited by Dietmar Süss, 71–84. Munich: Oldenbourg Verlag, 2007.

Groehler, Olaf. *Bombenkrieg gegen Deutschland*. Berlin: Akademie Verlag, 1990.

———. *Geschichte des Luftkriegs*. Berlin: Militärverlag der DDR, 1981.

Grosscup, Beau. *Strategic Terror: The Politics and Ethics of Aerial Bombardment*. London: Zed Books, 2006.

Guglielmo, Mark. "The Contribution of Economists to Military Intelligence During World War II." *Journal of Economic History* 68 (2008): 109–50.

Guinn, Gilbert. *The Arnold Scheme: British Pilots, the American South and the Allies' Daring Plan*. Charleston, SC: History Press, 2007.

Gunston, Bill. *Night Fighters: A Development and Combat History*. Cambridge: Patrick Stephens, 1976.

Haining, Peter. *The Chianti Raiders: The Extraordinary Story of the Italian Air Force in the Battle of Britain*. London: Robson Books, 2005.

Hall, R. Cargill, ed. *Case Studies in Strategic Bombardment*. Washington, DC: Office of Air Force History, 1998.

Hamburg und Dresden im Dritten Reich: Bombenkrieg und Kriegsende; sieben Beiträge. Hamburg: Landeszentrale für politische Bildung, 2000.

Hancock, Eleanor. *The National Socialist Leadership and Total War, 1941–45*. New York: St. Martin's, 1991.

Hanke, Heinz M. *Luftkrieg und Zivilbevölkerung*. Frankfurt am Main: Peter Lang, 1991.

Hansen, Randall. *Fire and Fury: The Allied Bombing of Germany, 1942–1945*. New York: NAL Caliber, 2009.

Harmon, Christopher C. *"Are We Beasts?": Churchill and the Moral Question of World War II "Area Bombing."* Newport, RI: Naval War College, 1991 (Newport Papers, no. 1).

Harris, Robert, and Jeremy Paxman. *A Higher Form of Killing: The Secret Story of Gas and Germ Warfare*. London: Chatto & Windus, 1982.

Harvey, Stephen. "The Italian War Effort and the Strategic Bombing of Italy." *History* 70 (1985): 32–45.

Hayward, Joel. "Air Power, Ethics, and Civilian Immunity During the First World War and Its Aftermath." *Global War Studies* 7 (2010): 102–30.

Held, Werner, and Holger Nauroth. *Die deutsche Nachtjagd*. Stuttgart: Motorbuch Verlag, 1992.

Herbert, Ulrich, ed. *Europa und der "Reichseinsatz": Ausländische Zivilarbeiter, Kriegsgefangene und KZ-Häftlinge in Deutschland, 1938–1945*. Essen: Klartext, 1991.

Herf, Jeffrey. *The Jewish Enemy: Nazi Propaganda During World War II and the Holocaust*. Cambridge, MA: Harvard University Press, 2006.

Hesse, Hans, and Elke Purpus. "Vom Luftschutzraum zum Denkmalschutz—Bunker in Köln." In *Bunker: Kriegsort, Zuflucht, Erinnerungsraum*, edited by Inge Marszolek and Marc Buggeln, 61–74. Frankfurt am Main: Campus Verlag, 2008.

Hewitt, Kenneth. "Place Annihilation: Area Bombing and the Fate of Urban Places." *Annals of the Association of American Geographers* 73 (1983): 257–84.

Higham, Robin. *Two Roads to War: The French and British Air Arms from Versailles to Dunkirk*. Annapolis, MD: Naval Institute Press, 2012.

Hiller, Marlene. "Stuttgarter erzählen vom Luftkrieg." In *Stuttgart im Zweiten Weltkrieg*, edited by Marlene Hiller, 417–40. Gerlingen: Bleicher Verlag, 1989.

Hirschleifer, Jack. "Some Thoughts on the Social Structure After a Bombing Disaster." *World Politics* 8 (1955–56): 206–27.

Hitchcock, William. *The Bitter Road to Freedom: A New History of the Liberation of Europe*. New York: Free Press, 2008.

Hoch, Anton. "Der Luftangriff auf Freiburg 1940." Vierteljahreshefte für Zeitgeschichte 4 (1956): 115–44.

Holland, James. *Fortress Malta: An Island Under Siege, 1940–1943*. London: Orion, 2003.

Holman, Brett. "The Air Panic of 1935: British Press Opinion between Disarmament and Rearmament." *Journal of Contemporary History* 46 (2011): 288–307.

———. "'Bomb Back and Bomb Hard': Debating Reprisals During the Blitz." *Australian Journal of Politics and History* 58 (2012): 394–407.

Hopkins, G. E. "Bombing and the American Conscience During World War II." *Historian* 28 (1966): 451–73.

Hugh-Jones, Martin. "Wickham Steed and German Biological Warfare Research." *Intelligence and National Security* 7 (1992): 379–402.

Huyssen, Andreas. "Air War Legacies: From Dresden to Baghdad." In *Germans as Victims*, edited by Bill Niven, 181–93. Basingstoke: Palgrave, 2006.

Iklé, Fred. *The Social Impact of Bomb Destruction*. Norman: University of Oklahoma Press, 1958.

Irons, Roy. *The Relentless Offensive: War and Bomber Command, 1939–1945*. Barnsley: Pen & Sword, 2009.

Jackson, Ashley. *The British Empire and the Second World War*. London: Hambledon, 2000.

Jacobs, W. A. "The British Strategic Air Offensive Against Germany in World War II." In *Case Studies in Strategic Bombardment*, edited by R. Cargill Hall, 91–182. Washington, DC: Office of Air Force History, 1998.

Jarry, Maud. "Le bombardements des sites V en France." In *Les bombardements alliés sur la France durant la Seconde Guerre Mondiale: Stratégies, bilans matériaux et humains,* edited by Michèle Battesti and Patrick Facon, 39–48. Paris: Ministère de la Défense, 2009 (Cahiers du Centre d'Études d'Histoire de la Défense, no. 37).

Johnson, David E. *Fast Tanks and Heavy Bombers: Innovation in the U.S. Army, 1917–1945.* Ithaca, NY: Cornell University Press, 1998.

Jones, Edgar "'LMF': The Use of Psychiatric Stigma in the Royal Air Force During the Second World War." *Journal of Military History* 70 (2006): 439–58.

Jones, Edgar, Robin Woolven, and Simon Wessely. "Civilian Morale During the Second World War: Responses to Air-Raids Re-examined." *Social History of Medicine* 17 (2004): 463–79.

Jones, Helen. *British Civilians in the Front Line: Air Raids, Productivity and Wartime Culture, 1939–1945.* Manchester: Manchester University Press, 2006.

Jones, Kevin. "From the Horse's Mouth: *Luftwaffe* POWs as Sources for Air Ministry Intelligence During the Battle of Britain." *Intelligence and National Security* 15 (2000): 60–80.

Jones, Neville. *The Beginnings of Strategic Air Power: A History of the British Bomber Force, 1923–1929.* London: Frank Cass, 1987.

Kaldor, Nicholas. "The German War Economy." *Review of Economic Statistics* 13 (1946).

Karlsch, Rainer. *Hitlers Bombe: Die geheime Geschichte der deutschen Kernwaffenversuche.* Munich: DVA, 2005.

Katz, Barry. *Foreign Intelligence: Research and Analysis in the Office of Strategic Services, 1942–1945.* Cambridge, MA: Harvard University Press, 1989.

Kettenacker, Lothar, ed. *Ein Volk von Opfern? Die neue Debatte um den Bombenkrieg, 1940–1945.* Berlin: Rohwolt, 2003.

Kirwin, G. "Allied Bombing and Nazi Domestic Propaganda." *European History Quarterly* 15 (1985): 341–62.

Kitson, Simon. "Criminals or Liberators? French Public Opinion and the Allied Bombings of France, 1940–1945." In *Bombing, States and Peoples in Western Europe, 1940–1945,* edited by Claudia Baldoli, Andrew Knapp, and Richard Overy, 279–97. London: Continuum, 2011.

Klee, Katja. *Im "Luftschutzkeller des Reiches": Evakuierte in Bayern, 1939–1953.* Munich: Oldenbourg Verlag, 1999.

Klemann, Hein, and Sergei Kudryashov. *Occupied Economies: An Economic History of Nazi-Occupied Europe, 1939–1945.* London: Berg, 2012.

Klinkhammer, Lutz. *L'occupazione tedesca in Italia, 1943–1945.* Turin: Bollati Boringhieri, 1996.

Knapp, Andrew. "The Destruction and Liberation of Le Havre in Modern Memory." *War in History* 14 (2007): 477–98.

Knell, Hermann. *To Destroy a City: Strategic Bombing and Its Human Consequences in World War II.* Cambridge, MA: Da Capo, 2003.

Knox, Macgregor. *Hitler's Italian Allies: Royal Armed Forces, Fascist Regime and the War of 1940–1943.* Cambridge: Cambridge University Press, 2000.

Kochanski, Halik. *The Eagle Unbowed: Poland and the Poles in the Second World War.* London: Allen Lane, 2012.

Kock, Gerhard. *"Der Führer sorgt für unsere Kinder . . .": Die Kinderlandverschickung im Zweiten Weltkrieg.* Paderborn: Ferdinand Schöningh, 1997.

Konvitz, Josef. "Représentations urbaines et bombardements stratégiques, 1914–1945." *Annales* (1989): 823–47.

Kozak, Warren. *LeMay: The Life and Wars of General Curtis LeMay.* Washington, DC: Regnery, 2009.

Kramer, Nicole. "'Kämpfende Mutter' und 'gefallene Heldinnen'—Frauen in Luftschutz." In *Deutschlandim Luftkrieg: Geschichte und Erinnerung,* edited by Dietmar Süss, 94–96. Munich: Oldenburg Verlag, 2007.

Krauskopf, R. W. "The Army and the Strategic Bomber, 1930–1939." Parts I and II. *Military Affairs* 22 (1958–59): 84–94, 209–15.

Kreis, John F., ed. *Piercing the Fog: Intelligence and Army Air Forces Operations in World War II.* Washington, DC: Air Force History Program, 1996.

Kristensen, Henrik, Claus Kofoed, and Frank Weber. *Vestallierede luftangreb: I Danmark under 2. Verdenskrig.* 2 vols. Aarhus: Aarhus Universitetsforlag, 1988.

Kroener, Bernhard. "'Menschenbewirtschaftung,' Bevölkerungsverteilung und personelle Rüstung in der zweiten Kriegshälfte (1942–1944)." In Bernhard Kroener, Rolf-Dieter Müller, and Hans Umbreit, *Das Deutsche Reich und die Zweite Weltkrieg. Band 5/2. Organisation und Mobilisierung des deutschen Machtbereichs 1942–1944/45,* 777–995. Stuttgart: DVA, 1999.

Kube, Alfred. *Pour le Mérite und Hakenzreuz: Hermann Göring im Dritten Reich.* Munich: Oldenbourg Verlag, 1986.

Labanca, Nicola, ed. *I bombardamenti aerei sull'Italia.* Bologna: Il Mulino, 2012.

Lackey, Douglas. "The Bombing Campaign of the USAAF." In *Terror from the Sky: The Bombing of German Cities in World War II,* edited by Igor Primoratz, 41–45. Oxford: Berghahn, 2010.

———. "Four Types of Mass Murderer: Stalin, Hitler, Churchill, Truman." In *Terror from the Sky: The Bombing of German Cities in World War II,* edited by Igor Primoratz, 134–54. Oxford: Berghahn, 2010.

Lambourne, Nicola. "The Reconstruction of the City's Historic Monuments." In *Firestorm: The Bombing of Dresden, 1945,* edited by Paul Addison and Jeremy Crang, 143–60. London: Pimlico, 2006.

———. *War Damage in Western Europe: The Destruction of Historic Monuments During the Second World War.* Edinburgh: Edinburgh University Press, 2001.

Lanari, Manuela, and Stefano Musso. "Un dramma mal calcolato: Sfollamento e istituzioni nella provincia di Torino." In *Guerra e società nella provincia di Torino,* edited by Bruno Maida, 1–68. Turin: Blu Edizioni, 2007.

Lee, Gerald. "'I See Dead People': Air-Raid Phobia and Britain's Behaviour in the Munich Crisis." *Security Studies* 13 (2003–4): 230–72.

Lehman, Eric. *Le ali del potere: La propaganda aeronautica nell'Italia fascista.* Turin: Utet, 2010.

Lemke, Bernd. *Luftschutz in Grossbritannien und Deutschland, 1923 bis 1939.* Munich: Oldenbourg Verlag, 2005.

Levy, Richard H. "The Bombing of Auschwitz Revisited: A Critical Analysis." *Holocaust and Genocide Studies* 10 (1996): 267–98.

Linhardt, Andreas. *Feuerwehr im Luftschutz, 1926–1945: Die Umstrukturierung des öffentlichen Feuerlöschwesens in Deutschland unter Gesichtspunkten des zivilen Luftschutzes.* Brunswick: VFDB, 2002.

Lowe, Keith. *Inferno: The Devastation of Hamburg, 1943*. London: Viking, 2007.

Ludewig, Joachim. *Rückzug: The German Retreat from France, 1944*. Translated and edited by Major General David T. Zabecki. Lexington: University Press of Kentucky, 2012.

MacBean, John A., and Arthur S. Hogben. *Bombs Gone: The Development and Use of British Air-Dropped Weapons from 1912 to the Present Day*. Wellingborough: Patrick Stephens, 1990.

McCormack, Timothy, and Helen Durham. "Aerial Bombardment of Civilians: The Current International Legal Framework." In *Bombing Civilians: A Twentieth-Century History*, edited by Yuki Tanaka and Marilyn Young, 215–39. New York: New Press, 2009.

McFarland, Stephen, and Wesley Newton. "The American Strategic Air Offensive Against Germany in World War II." In *Case Studies in Strategic Bombardment*, edited by R. Cargill Hall, 183–252. Washington, DC: Office of Air Force History, 1998.

———. *To Command the Sky: The Battle for Air Superiority over Germany, 1942–1944*. Washington, DC: Smithsonian Institution, 1991.

McLachlan, Ian, and Russell Zorn. *Eighth Air Force Bomber Stories: Eyewitness Accounts from American Airmen and British Civilians in the Second World War*. Yeovil: Haynes Publishing, 1991.

Maggiorani, Mauro, "Uscire dalla città: lo sfollamento." In *Bologna in Guerra 1940–1945*, edited by Brunella Dalla Casa and Alberto Preti, 361–93. Milan: Franco Angeli, 1995.

Maier, Klaus. "Total War and German Air Doctrine Before the Second World War." In *The German Military in the Age of Total War*, edited by Wilhelm Deist, 210–19. Oxford: Berg, 1985.

Maiolo, Joseph. *Cry Havoc: How the Arms Race Drove the World to War, 1931–1941*. New York: Basic Books, 2006.

Manaresi, Franco. "I bombardamenti aerei di Bologna." In *Delenda Bononia: Immagini dei bombardamenti, 1943–1945*, edited by Cristina Bersani and Valeria Monaco, 47–55. Bologna: Patron Editori, 1995.

———. "La protezione antiaerea." *Delenda Bononia: Immagini dei bombardamenti, 1943–1945*, edited by Cristina Bersani and Valeria Monaco, 29–45. Bologna: Patron Editori, 1995.

Markusen, Eric, and David Kopf. "Was It Genocidal?" In *Terror from the Sky: The Bombing of German Cities in World War II*, edited by Igor Primoratz, 160–71. Oxford: Berghahn, 2010.

Martens, Stefan. *Hermann Göring: Erster Paladin des Führers und Zweiter Mann im Reich*. Paderborn: Schöningh, 1985.

Massignani, Alessandro. "L'industria bellica italiana e la Germania nella seconda guerra mondiale." *Italia Contemporanea* 190 (1993): 192–95.

Melinsky, Hugh. *Forming the Pathfinders: The Career of Air Vice-Marshal Sydney Bufton*. Stroud: The History Press, 2010.

Mets, David R. *Master of Airpower: General Carl A. Spaatz*. Novato, CA: Presidio, 1998.

Middlebrook, Martin, and Chris Everitt. *The Bomber Command War Diaries*. Leicester: Midland Publishing, 2000.

Mierzejewski, Alfred. *The Collapse of the German War Economy: Allied Air Power and the German National Railway*. Chapel Hill: University of North Carolina Press, 1988.

Miller, Donald. *Eighth Air Force: The American Bomber Crews in Britain.* London: Aurum Press, 2007.

Miller, Marshall L. *Bulgaria During the Second World War.* Stanford, CA: Stanford University Press, 1975.

Mommsen, Hans, and Manfried Grieger. *Das Volkswagenwerk und seine Arbeiter im Dritten Reich.* Düsseldorf: Econ, 1997.

Moorhouse, Roger. *Berlin at War: Life and Death in Hitler's Capital, 1939–1945.* London: Bodley Head, 2010.

Müller, Rolf-Dieter. "Albert Speer und die Rüstungspolitik im totalen Krieg, 1942–1945." In Bernhard Kroener, Rolf-Dieter Müller, and Hans Umbreit, *Das Deutsche Reich und der Zweite Weltkrieg. Band 5/2: Organisation und Mobilisierung des deutschen Machtbereichs 1942–1944/45,* 713–16. Stuttgart: DVA, 1999.

———. *Der Bombenkrieg, 1939–1945.* Berlin: Ch. Links Verlag, 2004.

———. "Das Scheitern der wirtschaftlichen 'Blitzkriegsstrategie.'" In Horst Boog et al., *Das Deutsche Reich und der Zweite Weltkrieg. Band 4: Der Angriff auf die Sowjetunion,* 936–1029. Stuttgart: DVA, 1983.

Murray, Williamson. *Luftwaffe: Strategy for Defeat, 1933–1945.* London: George Allen & Unwin, 1985.

Natalini, Andrea. *I rapporti tra aeronautica italiana e tedesca durante la seconda guerra mondiale.* Cosenza: Edizioni Lionello Giordano, 2004.

Nath, Peter. *Luftkriegsoperationen gegen die Stadt Offenburg im Ersten und Zweiten Weltkrieg.* Offenburg: Historisches Verein für Mittelbaden, 1990.

Neitzel, Sönke. *Der Einsatz der deutschen Luftwaffe über dem Atlantik und der Nordsee, 1939–1945.* Bonn: Bernard & Graefe, 1995.

Neufeld, Michael. "The Guided Missile and the Reich: Pennemünde and the Forging of a Technological Revolution." In *Science, Technology and National Socialism,* edited by Monika Renneberg and Mark Walker, 51–71. Cambridge: Cambridge University Press, 1994.

Neufeld, Michael, and Michael Berenbaum, eds. *The Bombing of Auschwitz: Should the Allies Have Attempted It?* New York: St. Martin's/United States Holocaust Memorial Museum, 2000.

Neutzer, Matthias. "Wozu leben wir nun noch?" In *Hamburg und Dresden im Dritten Reich: Bombenkrieg und Kriegsende; sieben Beiträge,* 100. Hamburg: Landeszentrale für politische Bildung, 2000.

Nezzo, Marta. "The Defence of Works of Art in Italy During the Second World War." In *Bombing, States and Peoples in Western Europe, 1940–1945,* edited by Claudia Baldoli, Andrew Knapp, and Richard Overy, 101–20. London: Continuum, 2011.

———. "La protezione delle città d'arte." In *I bombardamenti aerei sull'Italia,* edited by Nicola Labanca, 195–212. Bologna: Il Mulino, 2012.

Nicholas, Lynn. *The Rape of Europa: The Fate of Europe's Treasures in the Third Reich and the Second World War.* London: Macmillan, 1994.

Nielsen, Andreas. *The German Air Force General Staff.* New York: Arno Press, 1959.

Nolzen, Armin. "'Sozialismus der Tat?' Die Nationalsozialistische Volkswohlfahrt (NSV) und der alliierte Luftkrieg gegen das Deutsche Reich." In *Deutschland im Luftkrieg: Geschichte und Erinnerung,* edited by Dietmar Süss, 58–59. Munich: Oldenburg Verlag, 2007.

Overy, Richard. "Allied Bombing and the Destruction of German Cities." In *A World at Total War: Global Conflict and the Politics of Destruction, 1937–1945*, edited by Roger Chickering, Stig Förster, and Bernd Greiner, 277–95. Cambridge: Cambridge University Press, 2005.

———. "Apocalyptic Fears: Bombing and Popular Anxiety in Inter-War Britain." *S-NODI: Pubblici e Private Nella Storia Contemporanea* 2 (spring 2008): 7–30.

———. *The Battle of Britain: The Myth and the Reality.* London: Penguin, 2010.

———. *Bomber Command, 1939–1945.* London: HarperCollins, 1997.

———. "From 'Uralbomber' to 'Amerikabomber': The Luftwaffe and Strategic Bombing." *Journal of Strategic Studies* 1 (1978): 154–78.

———. *Goering: Hitler's Iron Knight.* 3rd ed. London: I. B. Tauris, 2012.

———. *Interrogations: The Nazi Elite in Allied Hands, 1945.* London: Allen Lane, 2001.

———. "The Luftwaffe and the European Economy, 1939–1945." *Militärgeshichtliche Mitteilungen* 55 (1979): 55–78.

———. "Mobilisation for Total War in Germany, 1939–1941." *English Historical Review* 103 (1988): 613–39.

———. *The Morbid Age: Britain and the Crisis of Civilisation Between the Wars.* London: Allen Lane, 2009.

———. *War and Economy in the Third Reich.* Oxford: Oxford University Press, 1994.

———. "The 'Weak Link'?: The Perception of the German Working Class by RAF Bomber Command, 1940–1945." *Labour History Review* 77 (2012): 11–34.

Paggi, Leonardo. *Il "popolo dei morti": La repubblica italiana nata della guerra (1940–1946).* Bologna: Il Mulino, 2009.

Pape, Robert A. *Bombing to Win: Air Power and Coercion in War.* Ithaca, NY: Cornell University Press, 1996.

Park, W. Hays. "'Precision' and 'Area' Bombing: Who Did Which, and When?" *Journal of Strategic Studies* 18 (1995): 145–74.

Parton, James. *"Air Force Spoken Here": General Ira Eaker and the Command of the Air.* Bethesda, MD: Adler & Adler, 1986.

Patterson, Ian. *Guernica and Total War.* London: Profile Books, 2007.

Pauw, Hans van der. *Rotterdam in de Tweede Wereloorlog.* Rotterdam: Uitgevereij Boom, 2006.

Peden, George. *Arms, Economics and British Strategy: From Dreadnoughts to Hydrogen Bombs.* Cambridge: Cambridge University Press, 2007.

Permooser, Irmtraud. *Der Luftkrieg über München, 1942–1945: Bomben auf die Hauptstadt der Bewegung.* Oberhachung: Aviatic Verlag, 1996.

Perry, Matt. "Bombing Billancourt: Labour Agency and the Limitations of the Public Opinion Model of Wartime France." *Labour History Review* 77 (2012): 49–74.

Pettenberg, Heinz. *Starke Verbände im Anflug auf Köln.* Edited by Hella Reuter-Pettenberg. Cologne: J. P. Bachem Verlag, 1981.

Pimlott, Ben. *Hugh Dalton.* London: Macmillan, 1985.

Plokhy, S. M. *Yalta: The Price of Peace.* New York: Penguin, 2010.

Pohl, Hans, and Wilhelm Treue. *Die Daimler-Benz AG in den Jahren 1933 bis 1945.* Wiesbaden: Franz Steiner Verlag, 1986.

Poolman, K. *Focke-Wulf Condor: Scourge of the Atlantic.* London: Macdonald & Jane's, 1978.

Price, Alfred. *Instruments of Darkness: The History of Electronic Warfare, 1939–1945.* London: Greenhill, 2005.

———. *The Luftwaffe Data Book.* London: Greenhill, 1997.

Primoratz, Igor, ed. *Terror from the Sky: The Bombing of German Cities in World War II.* Oxford: Berghahn, 2010.

Probert, Henry. *Bomber Harris: His Life and Times.* London: Greenhill, 2006.

Pugh, Michael. "An International Police Force: Lord Davies and the British Debate in the 1930s." *International Relations* 9 (1988): 335–51.

Quellien, Jean. "Les bombardements pendant la campagne de Normandie." In *Les bombardements alliés sur la France durant la Seconde Guerre Mondiale: Stratégies, bilans matériaux et humains,* edited by Michèle Battesti and Patrick Facon, 59–76. Paris: Ministère de la Défense, 2009 (Cahiers du Centre d'Études d'Histoire de la Défense, no. 37).

Rastelli, Achille. *Bombe sulla città: Gli attacchi aerei alleati; Le vittime civili a Milano.* Milan: Mursia, 2000.

Rauh-Kühne, Cornelia. "Hitlers Hehler? Unternehmerprofite und Zwangsarbeiterlöhne." *Historische Zeitschrift* 275 (2002): 1–55.

Ray, John. *The Night Blitz, 1940–1941.* London: Arms & Armour, 1996.

Reinhard, Oliver, Matthias Neutzner, and Wolfgang Hesse. *Das rote Leuchten: Dresden und der Bombenkrieg.* Dresden: Sächsische Zeitung, 2005.

Reuth, Ralf. *Goebbels: The Life of Joseph Goebbels, the Mephistophelean Genius of Nazi Propaganda.* London: Constable, 1993.

Reynolds, David. *In Command of History: Churchill Fighting and Writing the Second World War.* London: Allen Lane, 2004.

Ribeill, Georges. "Aux prises avec les voies ferrées: Bombarder ou saboter? Un dilemme revisité." In *Les bombardements alliés sur la France durant la Seconde Guerre Mondiale: Stratégies, bilans matériaux et humains,* edited by Michèle Battesti and Patrick Facon, 135–62. Paris: Ministère de la Défense, 2009 (Cahiers du Centre d'Études d'Histoire de la Défense, no. 37).

Ribeill, Georges, and Yves Machefert-Tassin. *Une saison en Enfer: Les bombardements des Alliés sur les rails français (1942–1945).* Migennes, 2004.

Rice, Randall. "Bombing Auschwitz: US 15th Air Force and the Military Aspects of a Possible Attack." *War in History* 6 (1999): 205–30.

Richards, Denis. *Portal of Hungerford.* London: Heinemann, 1978.

Richardson, C. O. "French Plans for Allied Attacks on the Caucasus Oil Fields, January–April 1940." *French Historical Studies* 8 (1973): 130–53.

Ritchie, Sebastian. *Industry and Air Power: The Expansion of British Aircraft Production, 1935–1941.* London: Frank Cass, 1997.

———. "A Political Intrigue Against the Chief of the Air Staff: The Downfall of Air Chief Marshal Sir Cyril Newall." *War and Society* 16 (1998): 83–104.

Rochat, Giorgio. *Le guerre italiane, 1935–1943: Dall'impero d'Etiopia alla disfatta.* Turin: Einaudi, 2005.

———. *Guerre italiane in Libia e in Etiopia: Studi militari, 1921–1939.* Paese: Pagus Edizioni, 1991.

Rose, Sonya. *Which People's War? National Identity and Citizenship in Wartime Britain, 1939–1945.* Oxford: Oxford University Press, 2003.

Rosenberg, D. A. "American Atomic Strategy and the Hydrogen Bomb Decision." *Journal of American History* 66 (1979): 68.

Rumenin, Rumen. *Letyashti Kreposti Nad Bulgariya.* Kyustendil: Ivan Sapunjiev, 2009.

Rüther, Martin. *Köln 31. Mai 1942: Der 1000-Bomber-Angriff.* Cologne: Janus, 1992.

————, ed. *"Zu Hause könnten sie es nicht schöner haben!": Kinderlandverschickung aus Köln und Umgebung, 1941–1945.* Cologne: Emons Verlag, 2000.

Saint-Amour, Paul. "Air War Prophecy and Interwar Modernism." *Comparative Literature Studies* 42 (2005): 130–61.

Sallagar, Frederick. *The Road to Total War.* New York: Van Nostrand Reinhold, 1969.

Satia, Priya. "The Defense of Inhumanity: Air Control and the British Idea of Arabia," *American Historical Review* 111 (2006): 25–38.

Saward, Dudley. *"Bomber Harris": The Authorised Biography.* London: Cassell, 1984.

Scattigno, Anna. "Il clero in Toscana durante il passaggio del fronte: Diari e cronache parrocchiali." In *I bombardamenti aerei sull'Italia,* edited by Nicola Labanca, 247–80. Bologna: Il Mulino, 2012.

Schaffer, Ronald. "American Military Ethics in World War II: The Bombing of German Civilians." *Journal of American History* 67 (1980): 318–34.

————. *Wings of Judgment: American Bombing in World War II.* New York: Oxford University Press, 1985.

Schmidt, Ulf. "Justifying Chemical Warfare: The Origins and Ethics of Britain's Chemical Warfare Programme, 1915–1939." In *Justifying War: Propaganda, Politics and the Modern Age,* edited by Jo Fox and David Welch, 129–58. Basingstoke: Palgrave, 2012.

Schmiedel, Michael. "Les Allemands et la défense passive en France: Le cas de Nantes." In *Les bombardements alliés sur la France durant la Seconde Guerre Mondiale: Stratégies, bilans matériaux et humains,* edited by Michèle Battesti and Patrick Facon, 49–56. Paris: Ministère de la Défense, 2009 (Cahiers du Centre d'Études d'Histoire de la Défense, no. 37).

————. "Orchestrated Solidarity: The Allied Air War in France and the Development of Local and State-Organised Solidarity Movements." In *Bombing, States and Peoples in Western Europe, 1940–1945,* edited by Claudia Baldoli, Andrew Knapp, and Richard Overy, 206–18. London: Continuum, 2011.

Schneider, Peter. "Deutsche als Opfer? Über ein Tabu der Nachkriegsgeneration." In *Ein Volk von Opfern? Die neue Debatte um den Bombenkrieg, 1940–1945,* edited by Lothar Kettenacker, 158–65. Berlin: Rohwolt, 2003.

Segrè, Claudio. "Giulio Douhet: Strategist, Theorist, Prophet?" *Journal of Strategic Studies* 15 (1992): 351–66.

Serrien, Pieter. *Tranen over Mortsel: De laatste getuigen over het zwaarste bombardement ooit in België.* Antwerp: Standaard Uitgeverij, 2008.

Sherry, Michael. *The Rise of American Air Power: The Creation of Armageddon.* New Haven, CT: Yale University Press, 1987.

Sijes, B. A. *De Razzia van Rotterdam, 10–11 November 1944.* Gravenhage: Martinus Nijhoff, 1951.

Silveri, Umberto, and Maddalena Carli. *Bombardare Roma: Gli Alleati e la "città aperta" (1940–1944).* Bologna: Il Mulino, 2007.

Smith, Bradley. *Sharing Secrets with Stalin: How the Allies Traded Intelligence, 1941–1945.* Lawrence: University Press of Kansas, 1996.

Spooner, Tony. *Supreme Gallantry: Malta's Role in the Allied Victory, 1939–1945.* London: John Murray, 1996.

Stargardt, Nicholas. *Witnesses of War: Children's Lives Under the Nazis*. London: Jonathan Cape, 2005.

Stegemann, Bernd. "The Italo-German Conduct of the War in the Mediterranean and North Africa." In Gerhard Schreiber, Bernd Stegemann, and Detlef Vogel, *Germany and the Second World War*, vol. 3, *The Mediterranean, South-East Europe and North Africa, 1939–1941*, 641–754. Oxford: Oxford University Press, 1995.

Stenton, Michael. *Radio London and Resistance in Occupied Europe: British Political Warfare, 1939–1943*. Oxford: Oxford University Press, 2000.

Stephenson, Jill. "Bombing and Rural Society in Württemberg." *Labour History Review* 77 (2012): 93–112.

———. *Hitler's Home Front: Württemberg Under the Nazis*. London: Continuum, 2006.

Suchenwirth, Richard. *Command and Leadership in the German Air Force: USAF Historical Studies, No. 174*. New York: Arno Press/Air University, 1969.

Süss, Dietmar. "Steuerung durch Information? Joseph Goebbels als 'Kommissar der Heimatfront' und die Reichsinspektion für den zivilen Luftschutz." In *Hitlers Kommissare: Sondergewalten in der nationalsozialistischen Diktatur*, edited by Rüdiger Hachtmann and Winfried Süss, 183–206. Göttingen: Wallstein Verlag, 2006.

———. *Tod aus der Luft: Kriegsgesellschaft und Luftkrieg in Deutschland und England*. Munich: Siedler Verlag, 2011.

———. "Wartime Societies and Shelter Politics in National Socialist Germany and Britain." In *Bombing, States and Peoples in Western Europe, 1940–1945*, edited by Claudia Baldoli, Andrew Knapp, and Richard Overy, 23–42. London: Continuum, 2011.

Sweetman, John. "The Smuts Report of 1917: Merely Political Window Dressing?" *Journal of Strategic Studies* 4 (1981): 152–74.

Tanaka, Yuki, and Marilyn Young, eds. *Bombing Civilians: A Twentieth-Century History*. New York: New Press, 2009.

Taylor, Frederick. *Dresden: Tuesday 13 February 1945*. London: Bloomsbury, 2004.

Tewes, Ludger. *Jugend im Krieg: Von Luftwaffenhelfern und Soldaten, 1939–1945*. Essen: Reimar Hobbing, 1989.

Thetford, Owen. *Aircraft of the Royal Air Force since 1918*. London: Guild Publishing, 1988.

Thomas, Hugh. *John Strachey*. London: Eyre Methuen, 1973.

Thorpe, Andrew. *Parties at War: Political Organization in Second World War Britain*. Oxford: Oxford University Press, 2009.

Tiratsoo, Nick. "The Reconstruction of Blitzed British Cities, 1945–55: Myths and Reality." *Contemporary British History* 14 (2000): 27–44.

Tooze, Adam. "No Room for Miracles: German Industrial Output in World War II Reassessed." *Geschichte und Gesellschaft* 31 (2005): 439–64.

———. *Wages of Destruction: The Making and Breaking of the Nazi Economy*. London: Allen Lane, 2006.

Torrie, Julia. *"For Their Own Good": Civilian Evacuations in Germany and France, 1939–1945*. New York: Berghahn, 2010.

Underwood, Jeffery. *The Wings of Democracy: The Influence of Air Power on the Roosevelt Administration, 1933–1941*. College Station: Texas A&M University Press, 1991.

Uziel, Daniel. *The Propaganda Warriors: The Wehrmacht and the Consolidation of the German Home Front*. Bern: Peter Lang, 2008.

Vaizey, Hester. *Surviving Hitler's War: Family Life in Germany, 1939–48*. Basingstoke: Palgrave, 2010.

Verhoeyen, Etienne. *La Belgique occupée: De l'an 40 à la libération*. Brussels: De Boeck, 1994.

Villa, Andrea. *Guerra aerea sull'Italia (1943–1945)*. Milan: Angelo Guerini, 2010.

Voldman, Danièle. "Les populations civiles, enjeux du bombardement des villes (1914–1945)." In *La violence de guerre, 1914–1945*, edited by Stéphane Audoin-Rouzeau, Annette Becker, Christian Ingrao, and Henri Rousso, 151–74. Paris: Éditions complexes, 2002.

Wakefield, Kenneth. *The First Pathfinders: The Operational History of Kampfgruppe 100*. London: William Kimber, 1981.

Wakelam, Randall. *The Science of Bombing: Operational Research in RAF Bomber Command*. Toronto: Toronto University Press, 2009.

Wells, Mark. *Courage and Air Warfare: The Allied Aircrew Experience in the Second World War*. London: Frank Cass, 1995.

Werner, Wolfgang. *"Bleib übrig": Deutsche Arbeiter in der nationalsozialistischen Kriegswirtschaft*. Düsseldorf: Schwann, 1983.

Westermann, Edward. *Flak: German Anti-Aircraft Defenses, 1914–1945*. Lawrence: University Press of Kansas, 2001.

———. "Hitting the Mark but Missing the Target: Luftwaffe Deception Operations, 1939–1945." *War in History* 10 (2003): 206–21.

White, Joseph. "Target Auschwitz: Historical and Hypothetical German Responses to Allied Attack." *Holocaust and Genocide Studies* 16 (2002): 54–76.

Wiese, Gernot. "Die Versorgungslage in Deutschland." In *Kriegsjahr 1944: Im Grossen und im Kleinen*, edited by Michael Salewski and Guntram Schulze-Wegener, 340–46. Stuttgart: Franz Steiner Verlag, 1995.

Wiggam, Marc. "The Blackout and the Idea of Community in Britain and Germany." In *Bombing, States and Peoples in Western Europe, 1940–1945*, edited by Claudia Baldoli, Andrew Knapp, and Richard Overy, 43–58. London: Continuum, 2011.

Willis, Kirk. "The Origins of British Nuclear Culture, 1895–1939." *Journal of British Studies* 34 (1995): 59–89.

Wolf, Werner. *Luftangriffe auf die deutsche Industrie, 1942–1945*. Munich: Universitas, 1985.

Wylie, Neville. "Muted Applause? British Prisoners of War as Observers and Victims of the Allied Bombing Campaign over Germany." In *Bombing, States and Peoples in Western Europe, 1940–1945*, edited by Claudia Baldoli, Andrew Knapp, and Richard Overy, 256–78. London: Continuum, 2011.

Wyman, David. *The Abandonment of the Jews: America and the Holocaust, 1941–1945*. New York: Pantheon, 1984.

Zamagni, Vera. "Italy: How to Lose the War and Win the Peace." In *The Economics of World War II*, edited by Mark Harrison, 177–223. Cambridge: Cambridge University Press, 1998.

Zelinsky, Wilbur, and Leszek A. Kosinski. *The Emergency Evacuation of Cities*. Savage, MD: Rowman & Littlefield, 1991.

INDEX

Page numbers in *italics* refer to tables.